The New Catalog of Maya Hieroglyphs

VOLUME TWO

The Civilization of the American Indian Series

The New Catalog of Maya Hieroglyphs

VOLUME TWO

The Codical Texts

Martha J. Macri

Gabrielle Vail

Grapheme drawings by Martha J. Macri

UNIVERSITY OF OKLAHOMA PRESS : NORMAN

Cataloging-in-Publication Data available from Library of Congress

ISBN 0-8061-3497-6

The New Catalog of Maya Hieroglyphs, Volume Two: The Codical Texts is Volume 264
in The Civilization of the American Indian Series.

The paper in this book meets the guidelines for permanence and durability of the
Committee on Production Guidelines for Book Longevity of the Council on Library Resources, Inc. ∞

1 2 3 4 5 6 7 8 9 10

To Austin,

Bailey,

Chelsea,

Destinee,

Hannah,

and Joshua,

and

To Hans and Sammi,

who love to excavate

Contents

Figures and Tables

FIGURES

TABLES

Acknowledgments

The authors would like first of all to acknowledge the contributions of Matthew Looper, coauthor of volume 1. All aspects of volume 2 have benefited from his analytical skills and bibliographic research. His drawings of graphemes from the Classic period are included in the index of graphemes in this volume.

We would also like to thank the Dumbarton Oaks Research Library and Collection, Washington, D.C., especially Jeffrey Quilter, Director of Pre-Columbian Studies and Curator, Pre-Columbian Collection from 1995 to 2005; Joanne Pillsbury, current Director of Pre-Columbian Studies; Loa Traxler, Assistant Curator from 1998 to 2001; and Bridget Gazzo, Librarian, Pre-Columbian Studies. In recent years both authors have held fellowships at the library. In addition, Dumbarton Oaks has hosted us several times so that we could work there together.

We would also like to express our thanks to Merle Greene Robertson for the generous use of her library at the Pre-Columbian Art Research Institute and for her continued encouragement, and to George and Melinda Stuart for sharing the resources and facilities at Boundary End Archaeology Research Center in Barnardsville, North Carolina, with us and allowing us to scan and photograph their collection of facsimiles of the Maya codices. We are also grateful to Victoria and Harvey Bricker for sharing their knowledge and expertise of the codices with us through many discussions over the years; to Christine Hernández for her collaboration on the Maya Codices Database and Website, which contributed significantly to the development of the catalog; and to Barbara MacLeod for correspondence that has spanned many years and provided invaluable insights into the current project. For the ongoing statistical analysis of the Maya corpus, we are grateful for the assistance of Monique Aw, and we thank Cynthia Vail for her editorial expertise.

Over the years a number of research assistants both in California and in Florida have helped with this volume. In particular we would like to thank James Brooks, Michael Evans, José Godínez Samperio, Michael Grofe, Sidney Lippman, Catherine Macri, Jason Richardson, Lynn Robinson, Sarah Robinson, Janferie Stone, Carrie Todd, William Werner, Jessica Wheeler, and Eostra Yarrow for their help in scanning and preparing images, entering data, and checking references. We would also like to thank Jeri Kemp for her encouragement and assistance with the initiation of the project and the members of the New College glyph group for providing a monthly forum for discussing a number of the ideas described here.

The research for this volume has been funded in part by the National Endowment for the Humanities, grants RT21365-92, RT21608-94, and PA22844-96; the National Science Foundation, grants SBR-9710961 and BCS-9905357; and the Native American Language Center, Department of Native American Studies, University of California, Davis.

Both of the authors would like to thank their families, especially Judy and Ty, for their continued support and encouragement, and Emmy Ezzell, Sarah Nestor, Julie Shilling, and the other members of the editorial staff for their dedication and professionalism.

Editorial Note on Orthography and Transcription

As in volume 1, words in Mayan languages are spelled in the orthography of the Academia de las Lenguas Mayas de Guatemala, with two additions. First, the Academia's spelling system does not distinguish between a soft *h* (a glottal fricative), spelled in this volume with *h,* and a hard *h* (a velar fricative), spelled here with *j.* Second, the short *a* reconstructed for proto-Ch'olan and proto-Yucatecan is represented by *ä.* We retain the original orthography of any sources we have cited, with the following exceptions: backward *c* is spelled *tz, č* is *ch,* and š is *x.* Early authors cited in the catalog references, in accordance with colonial Yucatec orthography, used the letter *c* for the sound *k* and the letter *k* for the glottalized *k'.* Beginning in the 1970s, some epigraphers began to follow linguists in using *k* and *k',* a source of some confusion. Likewise, *b* has now been replaced by *b',* though unlike *k,* this variation is not ambiguous. Additionally, the sound *w* is spelled with *u* in the colonial alphabet.

Mayan language names are spelled in the orthography of the Academia de las Lenguas Mayas, except when they are quoted from other published sources. However, within the introduction, the language names Lacandón, Yucatec, and Yucatecan are spelled with *c* instead of *k,* in conformity with the spelling of Mexican geographic names.

Readings of Maya signs are shown in bold lowercase letters, whether the reading is logographic (a word) or syllabic (a consonant plus a vowel [CV]). This differs from the popular convention of writing logographs (word signs) with bold uppercase letters and syllabic signs with bold lowercase letters. That system ignores the fact that some CV syllabic signs can represent words composed of only a consonant and a vowel (sometimes followed by *'* or *h*). For example, 32A can represent the syllable **ma** or the morpheme **ma** *ma'* 'no', and 3M2 can represent the sound **ti** or the preposition **ti(')**, *ti* 'in, at, on', and so forth. Lowercase letters also facilitate the use of diacritics necessary for writing *ä* and for representing tone on vowels in Yucatecan glosses, as in *ká'an* 'sky' and *kàan* 'snake'. In this volume, unlike volume 1, proposed logographic readings for Yucatecan words do not indicate the contrast between *j* and *h* or between *a* and *ä* due to inconclusive evidence that these sounds were contrasted by codical scribes. The contrast between *h* and *j* is documented in the Classic period script but appears to have been lost in Ch'olan languages following the Terminal Classic period (Grube 2004). Although widespread evidence shows the distinction was maintained in Yucatec until the nineteenth century (V. Bricker, personal communication, 2008), whether it is represented consistently in the codices has not yet been satisfactorily addressed. The texts in the extant codices consist of a compilation of texts originally written in both Yucatecan and Ch'olan languages over a period of many centuries (see discussion below). Because of this, we feel that it is not advisable to make a priori assumptions about the presence or absence of particular sound contrasts in the codices in the absence of rigorous testing of the complete hieroglyphic corpus. These contrasts are shown, however, when they occur in Yucatecan and Ch'olan dictionary entries.

When the logographic readings of Yucatecan and Ch'olan cognates differ, they are separated by a slash mark, with the Yucatecan form given first, as in *b'áalam/b'ahläm* 'jaguar'. For Yucatecan glosses, we have followed the vowel length and tone in V. Bricker, Po'ot Yah, and Dzul de Po'ot (1998). We have only indicated long vowels when they occur in Yucatecan languages. We have not indicated any long or otherwise complex vowels (VV, Vh, V') that have been inferred from proto-Mayan reconstructions, nor from proposed synharmonic spellings; that is, we do not assume that words spelled with a final syllabic sign whose vowel differs from that of the preceding syllable have long root vowels, as proposed by some epigraphers (see, e.g., Houston, Robertson, and Stuart 1998, 2000; Houston, Stuart, and Robertson 2004). In other words, 'bone' spelled syllabically **b'a-ki** or logographically **b'ak-ki** is not assumed to have had a long vowel merely because the vowel of the second sign is *i* rather than *a.* Some disharmonic spellings seem to have been motivated morphologically; that is, they appear to indicate *-i* or *-ih* or *-il* suffixes and thus do not necessarily suggest complex root vowels.

Both the body and the appendices of the catalog are printed directly from a database program that does not allow multiple-font formatting on a word-by-word basis within fields. Since italics and boldface can be applied only to an entire field, we have made use of the following conventions. In the primary citation, logographic and syllabic values are printed from individual fields and appear in boldface type, with the logographic values italicized. Within the five reference fields, CV readings appear between slash marks (e.g., /ta/), logographic readings inside double quotation marks (e.g., "ahaw"), and glosses in English, Spanish, German, or French inside single quotation marks (e.g., 'calebasse'). In both the reference citations and the lexical entries, species names, normally italicized, are shown within double quotation marks. Words or phrases that describe a sign but are not intended as a reading are often set off by parentheses. Nicknames, such as "toothache" or "water group," that were originally created to name certain signs but are neither readings nor graphic descriptions appear within double quotation marks. Orthography of calendrical periods (day names, month names, etc.) usually follows that of the source.

In lexical entries, the Mayan words are unmarked, with glosses (brief definitions) indicated by single quotation marks. In the Motul dictionary of Yucatec (Martínez Hernández 1929), the velar fricative and the glottal fricative (hard and soft *j*) are both spelled with *h* but are alphabetized separately as *h rezia* and *h simple* ("rough *h*" and "plain *h*"). In these cases we have indicated an initial velar fricative, *j,* by *h[rezia].* The sound t^{y} is spelled *ty*; the velar nasal *ŋ* is spelled with a capital *N.*

We use the word *hieroglyph,* literally 'sacred, holy, or priestly writing', following its usage by Eric Thompson in *A Catalog of Maya Hieroglyphs* (1962). Some researchers have begun to eschew this term, recognizing that the bulk of the Classic period texts record the secular political history of the Classic Maya. The literal meaning of *hieroglyph* does, however, seem completely appropriate to the extant Maya codices, which contain prognostications and astronomical almanacs that give evidence of the Maya's achievements in what some researchers term sacred science.

The New Catalog of Maya Hieroglyphs

VOLUME TWO

Introduction

> *Speculation on this glyph could run wild. It occurs with numerals, only one or two prefixes, back to back with itself, and then almost wholly with month or celestial signs. Three times it is drawn upside down.*
>
> —William Gates (1931:122)

Since the 1930s, when William Gates offered his observations on what are now considered to be three distinct signs: HT2, a seated, headless human body; HT3, two headless bodies back to back; and HT4, an inverted body (see the index for illustration of signs mentioned by the three-letter grapheme code in the introduction), speculation about the nature of the Maya script has been steadily replaced by reasoned arguments. Yet, even today, of these three signs, a fairly secure reading is known only for HT4, *éem* in Yucatec and *ehm* in the Ch'olan languages, meaning 'to descend'.

The process of decipherment is multilayered. At the level of the individual distinctive sign (grapheme), decipherment is considered accomplished when the phonetic value (the sound it represents) or the logographic reading (the word it represents) is known. For example, contextual evidence indicates that a certain animal with an upturned nose (a peccary?), ACD, represents the planet Mars, but we do not know the Mayan word for Mars that the sign might represent. Likewise, we suspect, based on its occurrence in the first position of statements, that a rather complex sign apparently showing a sun above a mountain, YGD, is a verb. Further supporting this inference, in 11 of 13 occurrences YGD carries affixes characteristic of verbs. In this case, although we know certain syntactic features associated with the sign (for example, that it is probably an intransitive verb), we have no specific semantic information. We do not know what word it represented.

Many of the Maya signs are abstract, making it impossible to imagine what real-world object they might represent. Most, however, are representational; that is, the object depicted can be identified as a head, hand, animal, or physical object. Contrary to what one might expect, this has been as much a hindrance as an advantage in decipherment. The relationship of the represented image (visual form) to the value (linguistic form) of the sign is typically obscure. For purposes of decipherment, many early researchers relied on visually motivated readings, but more recently, epigraphers have argued for new readings with more success when they base them on contextual clues and substitution patterns rather than on the graphic form of the sign.

With what level of certainty can phonetic and logographic values for the Maya graphemes be offered? What is the standard, and what are the criteria for accepting a suggested reading as established? For a phonetic reading to be considered reliable, it must be supported by some combination of textual, visual, and linguistic data; for example, it must be used with other syllabic signs to spell various words or used as a phonetic complement to logographic signs of known value. The presence of **ki** 1B2 as a phonetic complement to the graphemes *ixik,* 'woman', *pik,* 'skirt', and the name Chaak supports its syllabic reading of **k(i)**. Likewise, **na** 1G1 is suffixed to *ká'an/chan* 'sky', the name Itzamna, and *í'inah/hinaj* 'seed', all ending in *an, na,* or *nah.* However, many syllabic and logographic values, rather than being considered *proven,* are better thought of as *hypotheses* or *assertions* offered with varying degrees of confidence.

The decipherment of sentences or of longer text segments involves not just knowing the values of individual graphemes, but understanding how they are combined to represent words and phrases. A still more complex level of decipherment requires an interpretation of the meaning of a given text within the culture of its readers.

The two volumes of the *New Catalog* do not examine questions of decipherment beyond the level of the smallest graphic unit of the Maya script, the grapheme. Volume 2 lists all graphemes found in the Maya codices. The index shows signs from both the codices and the Classic period texts.

MAYA SCREENFOLD MANUSCRIPTS

Three or four screenfold manuscripts painted with images and hieroglyphic texts can be attributed to the prehispanic Maya area—the Dresden, Madrid, Paris, and Grolier codices. The first three are named after the European cities where they are presently housed. Their early histories, before they were "discovered" in European collections in the eighteenth and nineteenth centuries, remain undocumented, although researchers have attempted to learn more about their origin by piecing together certain clues.

In 1519 Hernán Cortés sent a consignment of materials collected during his military campaign in Mexico to Charles V in Spain, who had just been elected Holy Roman Emperor. This material, known as the Royal Fifth (because the king of Spain was entitled to one-fifth of all spoils of war), included several books that, based on their descriptions, were almost certainly Maya codices (Coe 1989b, 1992:78). Michael Coe suggests that they were collected during a visit to Cozumel made by Cortés in February 1519, at which time the Spanish invaders came across "innumerable" books in the houses of the Maya who had fled at their arrival. These, according to Coe (1992:79), must have been the books included in the shipment to Spain and mentioned by Peter Martyr D'Anghera, who examined them in Valladolid (Martyr D'Anghera 1912). It is possible, as Coe suggests, that the Dresden Codex, purchased by the director of the Royal Library of Dresden in 1739 from a private collector in Vienna, was one of the codices that reached Europe as part of the Royal Fifth.

A series of recent discoveries raises the possibility that the Madrid Codex may have been confiscated in the Chancenote region of northwestern Yucatán by Pedro Sánchez de Aguilar between 1603 and 1608 in his position as ecclesiastical judge (Chuchiak 2004a). An original provenience in the Mayapán region is a possibility, based on similarities to murals at the site, especially the Temple of the Fisherman mural, which depicts a serpent very similar to those on pages 12b–18b of the Madrid Codex (Milbrath and Peraza Lope 2003:38). Since Mayapán was no longer occupied at the time of the Spanish conquest, the codex would not have remained there (if that is, indeed, where it was painted) but would have been taken to a new home by religious specialists after the site was abandoned.

A Mayapán provenience has also been suggested for the Paris Codex, based on what are perceived to be close similarities in terms of both iconography and content with monuments discovered at Mayapán (Love 1994:10, 12; Morley 1920:574–76). The codex also has thematic ties with murals from the site of Santa Rita Corozal on the east coast of the Yucatán Peninsula, in addition to certain iconographic and calendrical similarities. Additionally, a grapheme not known from any other site (HTA) occurs both at Santa Rita and in the Paris Codex (Love 1994:35–37).

The Grolier Codex, named after the Grolier Club in New York where it was first exhibited, does not contain writing in the strictest sense, its glyphic texts being limited to calendrical signs. Consequently, we frequently refer to "the three codices," meaning the three codices with written texts, in our discussion. The Grolier Codex was purportedly found in a wooden box in a cave in Chiapas, Mexico, in the 1960s, along with several other artifacts (including sheets of blank bark paper). It was first published in 1973 by Coe, who believed the codex was genuine. Coe (1973:150) submitted a fragment of the bark paper for radiocarbon testing, which yielded a date of 1230 ± 130 years. Eric Thompson (1975) suggested that while this date could refer to the paper, the manuscript was likely painted in more recent times by forgers familiar with Mesoamerican iconography. John Carlson (1983) convinced many Mayanists of the authenticity of the manuscript, which contains a fragmentary almanac referring to the 584-day synodic period of Venus (the time required for the planet to return to the same position in the sky as seen from earth). Nevertheless, two recent articles have again proposed that the codex is a forgery (Baudez 2002; Milbrath 2002). Ongoing studies of the manuscript at the Universidad Nacional Autónoma de México in Mexico City, reported by Susan Milbrath (2002:60), should help to resolve this issue.

DATING AND PROVENIENCE OF THE CODICES

The extant codices date from the very end of the tradition of Maya hieroglyphic writing, which itself can be traced back to the Preclassic period. The earliest datable examples of the Maya script occur at the site of San Bartolo (300–200 B.C.E.), in association with images in both Olmec and Maya traditions (Saturno 2006; Saturno, Stuart, and Beltrán 2006; Saturno, Taube, and Stuart 2005; see figure 1 for the location of sites mentioned in the introduction). These and other early indications of Maya texts, from sites such as El Portón in the Guatemalan highlands (c. 400 B.C.E.) and El Mirador in the lowland region (c. 300 B.C.E.–50 C.E.), are roughly coeval with the Zapotec hieroglyphic tradition from Oaxaca (Urcid Serrano 2001) and the later Epi-Olmec script from the Gulf Coast (Winfield Capitaine 1988). Although the relationships among early Mesoamerican scripts are currently under investigation, it appears certain that writing developed against the backdrop of a multiethnic milieu, probably at about the middle of the first millennium B.C.E. (Houston 2006).

On the basis of stylistic evidence, the Dresden, Madrid, and Paris codices have been attributed to the Late Postclassic period (c. 1250–1520 C.E.); their iconography can be compared to images in murals from Postclassic contexts at the sites of Tulum, Tancah, Santa Rita, and Mayapán in the northern lowlands (Milbrath and Peraza Lope 2003; Paxton 1986; Taube 1992:4). Their hieroglyphic texts are generally considered to represent a much later stage in the Maya written tradition than those recorded on stone monuments or from other media such as ceramics. According to recent analyses, the Madrid Codex was most likely painted in the late fifteenth century (Vail and Aveni 2004), just prior to Spanish contact. Although the codices postdate by several centuries the latest texts known from the southern Maya lowlands in the tenth century C.E. or even somewhat later texts from some northern sites such as Mayapán, they contain almanacs and astronomical tables developed for use at various times, including some that are coeval with the Classic period inscriptions. The almanacs in the Dresden, Madrid, and Paris codices seem to have been written over a period of many years and compiled from a number of original sources. Some of these almanacs likely represent copies of copies. Thus, certain codical texts can be seen as archaic in that they reflect a much earlier period than the date of the manuscripts that contain them. For example, analysis of the calendrical component of the Venus table on pages 24 and 46–50 of the Dresden Codex demonstrates that it was originally intended to be used as early as 934 C.E. (H. Bricker and V. Bricker 2007; V. Bricker and H. Bricker 1992:83; Lounsbury 1983a).

Hieroglyphic writing did not end with the arrival of the Spaniards but was practiced for several centuries after

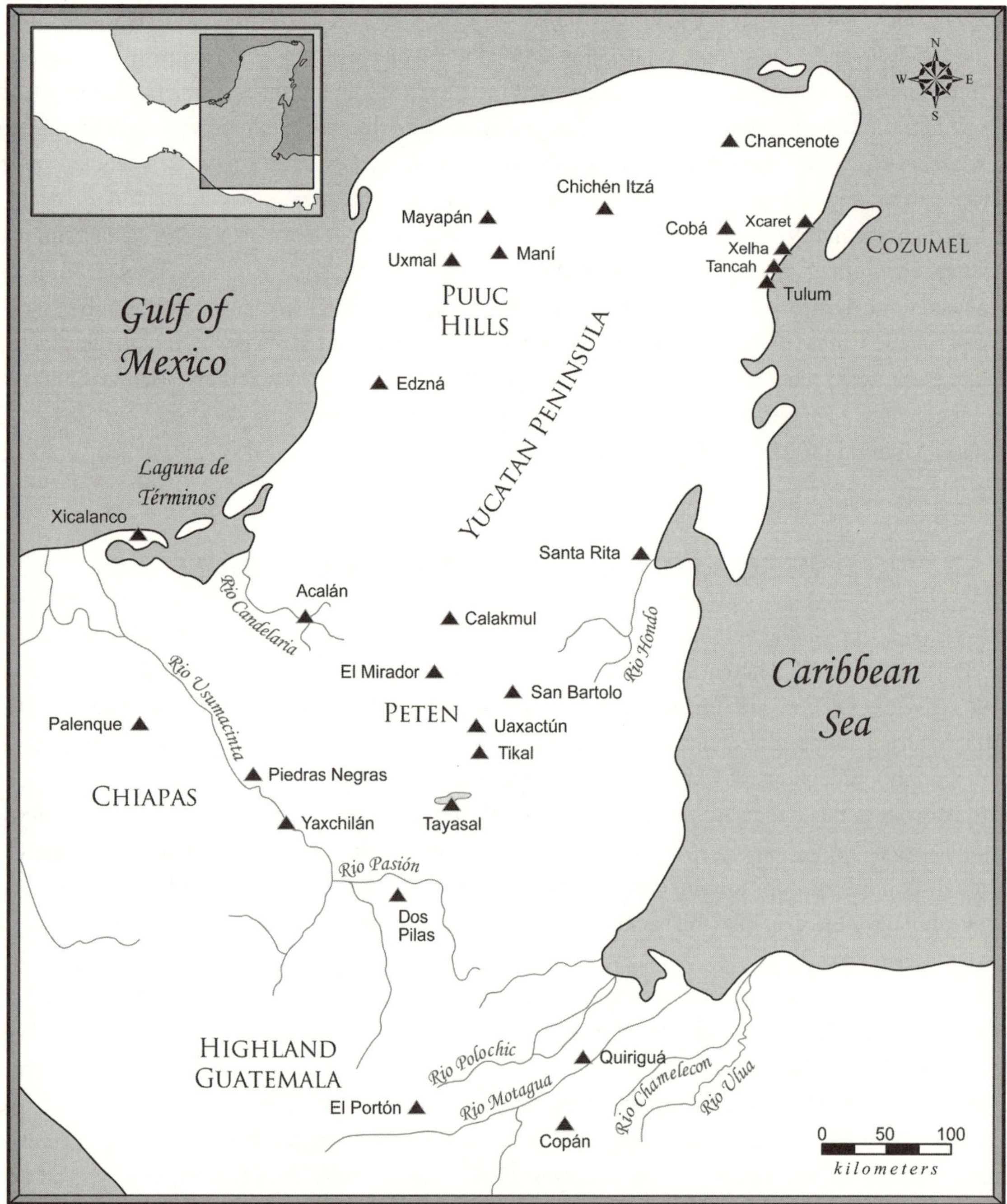

Figure 1. The Maya region. *Map by David R. Hixson.*

contact—often in secret, since Spanish priests and civil authorities forbade the use of the Maya script, which was considered evidence of idolatry (Chuchiak 2004b). The colonial period *Books of Chilam Balam,* written in the Latin alphabet, represent a continuation of the indigenous scribal tradition, although they show evidence of substantial European influence (V. Bricker 2000; V. Bricker and Miram 2002). Dennis Tedlock (1992, 1996) has demonstrated that the Popol Vuh, the creation story recorded by the highland K'iche' Maya in the early colonial period, has features that suggest it, too, was handed down from an earlier codical tradition, and Barbara Tedlock (1999a) discusses an alphabetic version of a K'iche' "codex" from the early eighteenth century.

LANGUAGES OF THE CODICES

At the time of Spanish contact, the area where hieroglyphic inscriptions were recorded during the prehispanic period was inhabited by speakers of Ch'olan and Yucatecan languages. Both of these subgroups are part of the Mayan language family. In addition to similarities resulting from their common origin some thousands of years ago, the two groups share a number of loan words and some grammatical features as a result of more recent periods of contact.

According to historical reconstructions of the sixteenth-century Maya area, Yucatecan languages (Yucatec, Lacandón, Itzaj, and Mopán) were spoken throughout the Yucatán Peninsula, including Belize and some parts of the Petén region of Guatemala. Ch'olan languages were found along the Usumacinta and Pasión rivers (the Western Ch'olan languages) and along the Motagua River and in the area of Copán (the Eastern Ch'olan languages). From an early date, researchers have attributed the Dresden, Paris, and Madrid codices to the northern Maya lowlands on the basis of stylistic and iconographic correspondences to murals found throughout the Yucatán Peninsula. Even more significantly, ceremonies recorded in the manuscripts correlate closely with sixteenth-century ethnohistoric accounts by Spanish priests and explorers living in what is now the state of Yucatán (see, e.g., Taube 1992; Thomas 1882; Vail 2005).

On the basis of this evidence, it had long been asserted that the hieroglyphic texts written in the codices record a Yucatecan language similar to that spoken at the time of the conquest. This is largely based on findings of phonetic spellings of words that differ between the two groups. One example of such a difference is a set of words that have the sound *k* in Yucatec but have *ch* in Ch'olan languages. Yuri Knorozov and later scholars found evidence of Yucatec vocabulary in the codices, including, for example, **bu-lu-ku** *b'uluk* 'eleven', and **nu-chu** in *nuch hol* 'confer' (literally 'to put heads together') (Kelley 1976:173; Knorozov 1952; Lounsbury 1984; Schele and Grube 1997). In Ch'olan languages, 'eleven' is *b'uluch,* not *b'uluk,* and 'to put together,' as in 'confer', is *nut* rather than *nuch.* Another example is the direction *xaman* 'north', written with the logographic sign for 'north' plus the syllabic signs for **ma** and **na:** NORTH-**ma-na**. *Xaman* is not attested in the available documentation of colonial or contemporary Ch'olan languages.

In the 1980s researchers found increasing evidence of Ch'olan vocabulary and morphological patterns in the Classic period script (Josserand, Schele, and Hopkins 1985; Justeson 1984; Justeson et al. 1985; Mathews and Schele 1974:65), leading to more recent proposals concerning the existence of an Eastern Ch'olan so-called *prestige* or common literary language used by scribes throughout the Maya area (Houston, Robertson, and Stuart 1998). As a result of these studies, researchers returned to the codices and reexamined the hieroglyphic texts to look for Ch'olan (as opposed to Yucatec) features. Robert Wald (2004 [1994 ms.]), for example, found evidence of both Yucatec and Ch'olan vocabulary and morphology in the texts recorded in the Dresden Codex, and Alfonso Lacadena (1997a) reported a similar situation in the Madrid Codex.

Later studies (V. Bricker 2000; Vail 2000a) consider the mixed nature of the codical texts within a cultural context. Gabrielle Vail proposes that the Madrid Codex is a Yucatecan manuscript that contains intrusive Ch'olan features. These, she suggests, are comparable to the Spanish loan words, and occasionally entire passages, found in the *Books of Chilam Balam,* in which texts were copied from a variety of European and Maya sources. In the *Chilam Balam of Kaua,* some Spanish texts were copied verbatim (although with numerous spelling errors); others were translated directly from Spanish into Yucatec; and still others were only partially translated (V. Bricker 2000:111). V. Bricker notes that the codices show a similar mixed history. These texts derived from multiple sources, primarily of Yucatecan and Ch'olan origin, and even contain some evidence suggesting influence from the Nahua languages of Central Mexico and the Gulf Coast (V. Bricker 2000; Macri 2006; Macri and Looper 2003b; Taube and Bade 1991; Whittaker 1986).

HISTORY OF DECIPHERMENT AND RESEARCH ON THE MAYA CODICES

Decipherments of individual graphemes in the Maya codices have most commonly resulted from efforts to understand and interpret their overall content and structure. The catalog lists contributions made by researchers during five somewhat arbitrarily divided periods in epigraphic studies: 1860–1915, rediscovery and early research, including an assertion and rejection of phoneticism; 1916–1950, an era dominated by calendrical and astronomical studies and the early research of Thompson; 1951–1980, the reassertion of phoneticism by Knorozov and the production of valuable catalogs by Günter Zimmermann and Thompson, resulting in a dramatic increase in decipherment; 1981–1990, a period marked by continued decipherment and new research directions focused on linguistic and textual analysis; and 1991 to the present, which has been characterized by a resurgence of interest in codical studies. References from each of these periods are provided, as relevant, for each catalog entry. Although not every possible source has been included, the reader can easily review earlier work and get a sense of the history of glyphic research.

Rediscovery and Early Research, 1860–1915

The Dresden Codex was the first of the Maya manuscripts to come to light in European collections. It was acquired by the Royal Library in Dresden in 1739 from a private collector in Vienna but remained unpublished for over seventy years. Five pages of the manuscript were included in Alexander von Humboldt's *Vues des Cordillères, et monumens des peuples indigènes de l'Amérique* in 1810. A complete facsimile was published by Edward Kingsborough in 1831; it consists of watercolors of each of the pages painted by the artist Agostino Aglio. Following this publication, early researchers recognized that the glyphic texts in the codex were very similar to—and represented the same tradition as—those being recorded by European and American explorers on monuments from the Maya area (e.g., the drawings by Frederick Catherwood in Stephens 1841, 1843).

The discovery of two other codices—the Paris Codex in 1859 by León de Rosny in the Bibliothèque Nationale (Rosny 1875, 1876) and the Madrid Codex, which was found in two parts (the Troano and Cortesianus) and reunited by Rosny in 1880 (Rosny 1882)—provided the impetus for further research and study. The first real breakthrough in deciphering the glyphic texts can be attributed to Charles Brasseur de Bourbourg's recovery of an edition of Bishop Diego de Landa's *Relación de las cosas de Yucatán.* Originally composed in c. 1566 during the time that he spent in Spain defending himself against charges of cruelty to the natives, Landa's *Relación* includes a wealth of information on Maya culture, religion, hieroglyphic writing, and the calendar.[1] Using Landa's *Relación,* Brasseur was able to identify day and month glyphs in the Dresden and Paris codices. He also deciphered the Maya system of bar-and-dot numbers, something that had been worked out independently several decades earlier by the Turkish-born scholar Constantine Rafinesque (see Coe 1992:91 for a discussion of Rafinesque's contributions).

Because of their earlier discovery, the hieroglyphic texts in the codices were the subject of intense research well before monumental texts became available for study. Important efforts at cataloging and classifying the hieroglyphs recorded in the codical texts were undertaken by a number of early scholars, including Brasseur de Bourbourg (1869–1870), Rosny (1883), Daniel Brinton (1895), and Paul Schellhas (1904 [1892]) (see discussion below). In addition to the days and months, early decipherments included the collocations referring to the world directions, made by Rosny (1876), and for the colors, attributed to Eduard Seler (Coe 1992:121; Kelley 1976:4).

The most significant research during this period involved advances in our understanding of the Maya calendrical system and the structure of codical almanacs, on the one hand, and the iconography of Maya almanacs, on the other. The two areas of study were largely kept separate by their investigators. Ernst Förstemann's interest in the Maya codices, for example, focused primarily on the calendrical component, while researchers such as Schellhas, Seler, and Cyrus Thomas were looking to the iconography for clues about the glyphic texts.[2] Although several early researchers discovered important principles about the nature of Maya hieroglyphic writing, presaging later work on the phonetic component of the Maya script (Rosny 1876, 1878; Thomas 1882, 1892a, b, 1893), their proposals were not widely accepted.

Förstemann, a librarian at the Royal Library in Dresden in the late nineteenth century, published the first chromophotographic facsimile of the Dresden Codex in 1880, with a later edition in 1892. Through his work with this manuscript and later the Madrid and Paris codices, he made several significant discoveries about the Maya Long Count calendar, which he determined was structured according to a base-20 system. He also demonstrated that 4 Ahaw 8 Kumk'u forms the base date of the Long Count; determined how the *tzolk'in* almanacs in the Dresden and Madrid codices, based on the 260-day ritual calendar, operated; identified the Venus table in the Dresden Codex; and proposed that the same codex also contained a lunar table (now recognized as an eclipse table) (Förstemann 1880, 1886, 1893, 1906). On the basis of Förstemann's discoveries, Joseph Goodman (1905) proposed a correlation between the Long Count and Gregorian calendar, which, with slight modifications by Juan Martínez Hernández (1926) and Thompson (see below), is still widely accepted by Mayanists today.

Other scholars who made important contributions at the turn of the century include Paul Schellhas, Eduard Seler, and Cyrus Thomas. Schellhas was the first person to systematically relate the images of the different gods appearing in the codices to their corresponding name glyphs. He gave each deity a distinct letter designation (God A, God B, God C, etc.) in order to distinguish them from each other. Although we now know the glyphic names of the majority of codical deities, Schellhas's lettering system, as modified by later scholars (e.g., Kelley 1976; Taube 1992; Zimmermann 1956), is still in use.

---

1. Landa's original text has never been found. The edition that Brasseur discovered dates to 1661 and consists of a copy written in several hands. As Restall and Chuchiak (2002) note, the *Relación* manuscript was compiled by three or four separate copyists, using excerpts from Landa's writings and possibly also those of his informants and contemporaries that were found with his papers.

2. Only recently, influenced by Victoria and Harvey Bricker and their "conjunctive approach" to the codices (V. Bricker and H. Bricker 1988, 1992), have glyphic and iconographic studies been fully integrated with a calendrical analysis of codical almanacs. Prior to this time, the pictures and texts were often considered together, but they were divorced contextually from the calendrical information contained in almanacs.

Seler is considered the founder of Mesoamerican iconographic research (Coe 1992:120). He had an encyclopedic knowledge of both the Maya and Central Mexican codices and published a series of essays that have since been republished in six volumes (Seler 1990–1998). His most important contributions include his discussions of astronomical content in the "Mexican" Borgia group codices, as well as his astute comparisons of Maya and Central Mexican deities and ideology. His pan-Mesoamerican approach to understanding pre-Columbian art and material culture, although highly productive, was dismissed by subsequent generations of scholars and has only resurfaced within recent decades as the focus of studies of Maya and Central Mexican connections during the Late Postclassic period (see Taube 1988, 1992; Vail and Aveni 2004; Vail and Hernández 2009).

Thomas made several contributions to our understanding of the Maya codices and the hieroglyphic script. His groundbreaking studies of the Wayeb' and New Year's pages in the Madrid and Dresden codices (Thomas 1882) provided the basis for future research on these important ceremonies, and he was the first to relate them to descriptions in Landa's *Relación.* Another seminal publication involved the first systematic study of the animals pictured in the codices in relation to the glyphs that identify them (Tozzer and Allen 1910). Additionally, Seler's study of "The Animal Pictures of the Mexican and Maya Manuscripts," although often overlooked by researchers, provides an encyclopedic coverage of this topic and is especially valuable for its comparison of Maya and highland Mexican forms (Seler [1909–1910] 1990–1998, vol. 5).

Several early scholars were pioneers in decipherment in that they were proponents of the idea that the Maya script had a phonetic component. Rosny (1876), for example, recognized phonetic elements occurring in the day and month glyphs illustrated by Landa and found in the Maya codices. He believed that the Maya script was composed of a mixture of what are today referred to as phonetic or syllabic glyphs and logographs. Thomas (1892a, 1892b, 1893), following in the footsteps of Rosny, identified several important phonetic elements, including **ka** (AA1), **e** (AA7), and **chi** (MR7). He believed not only that the Maya script had a phonetic component, but that some graphemes could represent both logographs and syllabic signs. However, his methodology was vigorously attacked by Seler (1892a, b, 1893), the preeminent Mesoamericanist of the time. Although Thomas had correctly understood the principles underlying the script, he offered a number of faulty identifications of specific graphemes that formed the basis for Seler's criticisms of his methodology. As a result of Seler's critiques, Thomas recanted his views that the Maya script had an underlying phonetic component in 1903. The debate concerning phoneticism was only beginning, however, and continued well into the first half of the twentieth century, with Benjamin Whorf (1933, 1942) as a major proponent and Thompson as a staunch and intractable opponent.

Research, 1916–1950

During the first half of the twentieth century, codical research lagged behind studies of the Maya monuments. Thompson was the preeminent figure during this era; he, along with Sylvanus Morley (1915), contributed substantially to our understanding of the calendrical component of the inscriptions. Thompson can be credited with solving the correlation between the Maya Long Count and Gregorian calendars (with contributions by Goodman and Martínez; see above), correctly interpreting distance numbers, and with identifying another calendrical system recorded in monumental inscriptions—the 819-day count (Thompson 1937, 1943, 1950). During the same period, several important contributions were made to the understanding of Maya astronomy (Teeple 1931; Willson 1924).

Thompson's contributions to codical research include detailed studies of several deities found in the codices (including the goddesses and the Bacabs) and his discussions of Maya religion, in which he employed ethnographic and ethnohistoric sources in his interpretations, a significant innovation in methodology (Thompson 1939, 1950,

1970a, 1970b). He also made several correct identifications of graphemes, including T1 as the possessive pronoun *u*; T87 as *te* 'tree, wood' and as a numeral classifier; T59 as the preposition *ti* 'on, at'; and T90 as *tu,* which includes the preposition *ti* plus the third person possessive pronoun *u* (Thompson 1950:54); significantly, all four have syllabic as well as logographic values.

Research into the phonetic component of the script was carried out by the linguist Benjamin Whorf, who, working exclusively with the codices, proposed that the glyphic captions mirrored the structure of Yucatec Maya sentences, consisting of a verb, followed by an object, and then a subject phrase (Whorf 1933). In this Whorf showed considerable acumen, anticipating the work of Knorozov by several decades. Although he made several correct identifications (including the verb 'to drill' and the phonetic spelling of the month Mak), Whorf's numerous erroneous phonetic interpretations provided Thompson (1950) with ample fodder for an attack on his methodology, as well as on his ideas regarding phoneticism in the Maya script. It was not until the 1950s that irrefutable evidence of phoneticism was demonstrated by Knorozov, a Russian scholar who showed that the "alphabet" recorded by Landa (Tozzer 1941:170) in fact represented part of a syllabary.

Research, 1951–1980

The story of Knorozov's (1952, 1955, 1958, 1963, 1967) breakthrough in deciphering the Maya script is well known to Maya scholars. Using Landa's "alphabet" as a guide, he showed that the prehispanic Maya signs were not "letters" representing single sounds, but syllables—that is, each represents a vowel or a vowel preceded by a consonant (*'a, b'e, tze, te, 'e,* etc.). Knorozov was then able to propose syllabic readings for each of the signs from Landa's chart. Thus, he demonstrated that the syllable **k'u**, when doubled, represents the Yucatec word *k'uk'* 'quetzal'—and that it does indeed occur with an image of a crested bird in the codices; and the same syllable, when paired with the "*chi* hand" (as in the spelling of *chik'in* 'west'), forms the Yucatec word *k'uch* 'vulture'—and occurs with an image of a vulture (Coe 1992:149–51; Knorozov 1955).

Because of a very direct relationship between text and image in the codices, Knorozov made substantial progress in his efforts to decipher the Maya codical texts. In his enthusiasm, however, he at times went beyond the data available and proposed readings that could not be substantiated. This provided the opening that Thompson needed for his critique—and dismissal—of the methodology.

Thompson's major achievements during this period include the publication of his *Catalog of Maya Hieroglyphs* (1962), the earliest comprehensive catalog of Maya graphemes (discussed below), and his *Commentary on the Dresden Codex* (1972). The latter is invaluable for its exposition of the calendrical structure of Maya almanacs and astronomical tables, but Thompson's analysis of the glyphic texts is substantially outdated.[3]

In spite of Thompson's censure, several epigraphers supported Knorozov's ideas, including David Kelley (1962a, 1962b, 1976), Floyd Lounsbury (1984), and Michael Coe (1973). Knorozov's work eventually gained widespread acceptance. A series of conferences in the 1970s, beginning with the Primera Mesa Redonda de Palenque and continuing with several small meetings at the Dumbarton Oaks Research Library in Washington, D.C., culminated in a conference on phoneticism at the State University of New York in Albany in 1979. The conference proceedings,

---

3. Ironically, Knorozov's commentary on the Dresden Codex (as well as the Madrid and Paris codices), published in English in 1982, is just as unreliable. His interpretations of the glyphic texts extend far beyond what can be substantiated by the data, and there is little of value in his translations.

published in 1984, include chapters by both linguists and epigraphers: Lyle Campbell, James Fox, John Justeson, Terrence Kaufman, Floyd Lounsbury, Barbara MacLeod, Peter Mathews, William Norman, Berthold Riese, Linda Schele, and David Stuart (Justeson and Campbell 1984).

The workshop participants demonstrated conclusively that the script has a phonetic component, and they prepared a chart listing proposed syllabic values for 108 graphemes (Mathews 1984), many of which were initially proposed by Knorozov (1967) and Kelley (1962a, 1962b, 1976). Nearly all of them are still accepted by epigraphers today. Justeson (1984), in an appendix to the volume, summarized the findings of the conference participants regarding the logographic, syllabic, and calendrical values and provided an identification of the object pictured of several hundred graphemes arranged by T number. This appendix demonstrates the consensus among researchers regarding the values of some signs and their disagreements about others. An ever-growing consensus was to be the product of research in the following decades.

Research, 1981–1990 and 1991–2008

The last two periods, separated in the catalog, are discussed together here as a reflection of the continuity of ongoing research on the Maya script. The Albany conference marked the start of a new era in glyphic decipherment, which proceeded at an unprecedented rate during the 1980s and 1990s. Decipherment during this period was driven primarily by researchers working with the monumental inscriptions rather than the codices, by scholars such as Victoria Bricker, Nikolai Grube, Stephen Houston, John Justeson, Barbara MacLeod, Peter Mathews, Linda Schele, and David Stuart. Of note for their emphasis on graphemes that occur in the codical texts as well as the monumental inscriptions are Bricker's *Grammar of Mayan Hieroglyphs* (1986) and Stuart's "Ten Phonetic Syllables" (1987).

Research focused more exclusively on the Maya codices can be grouped into several categories, including studies of deities (Taube 1992; Vail 1996, 2000b); investigations of the astronomical content of the Maya codices (e.g., Aveni 1992, 2001; H. Bricker and V. Bricker 1983, 2007, n.d.; V. Bricker and H. Bricker 1986, 1988, 2005; Closs 1979, 1989, 1992; Grofe 2007; Lounsbury 1983a; Milbrath 1999); studies of the calendrical structure of Maya almanacs (V. Bricker and H. Bricker 1992; V. Bricker and Vail 1997; Vail and Aveni 2004); and interpretations of the ritual content of the Maya codices (V. Bricker and Vail 1997; Love 1991, 1994; Vail 2000b, 2002a). A methodological approach allowing almanacs to be dated in real time, pioneered by the Brickers (V. Bricker 1988; V. Bricker and H. Bricker 1992), has opened up new avenues for exploring the structure and function of Maya almanacs. Additionally, Vail (2002a) has proposed a model for interpreting certain Maya almanacs as 52-year instruments, which allows the possibility of explicating the content of the Maya codices within the context of ceremonies described in the ethnohistoric and ethnographic literature.

Commentaries on all four of the Maya codices have been published during the past two decades (Carlson 1983 for the Grolier Codex; Love 1994 for the Paris Codex; V. Bricker and Vail 1997 for the Madrid Codex; and Davoust 1997 and Schele and Grube 1997 for the Dresden Codex). They offer new interpretations of both the pictorial and the glyphic content of these manuscripts. Vail has recently completed an analysis of the Madrid Codex (Vail 2002b; Vail and Hernández 2005–2008), which is available to researchers online. Analyses of the other three codices are expected to be available in online format by July 2010 at mayacodices.org.

Other recent trends include an emphasis on a linguistic analysis of texts, an approach that was pioneered by researchers in the 1980s. In 1989, for example, "The Language of Maya Hieroglyphs: An Interdisciplinary Conference," was held at the University of California at Santa Barbara. Ten papers from this meeting were later published by the Pre-Columbian Art Research Institute (Macri and Ford 1997), including a paper by V. Bricker (1997b) on discourse in the Maya codices. Other seminal studies that focus on an understanding of the linguistic structure of prehispanic Maya texts include those by Macri (1988; Macri and Ford 1997), Kathryn Josserand (1991, 1997), V. Bricker (1989, 2000), and Charles Hofling (1989, 2000).

Recently there has been renewed interest in cross-cultural comparisons of the Maya and Central Mexican prehispanic codices, in the tradition of Seler (see Taube 1988 and discussion in Vail 2006). At two workshops held at Tulane University on the Madrid Codex, researchers brought to light a number of correspondences among the Maya and Borgia group codices that offer tantalizing clues about the nature of elite interaction in Late Postclassic Mesoamerica (Vail and V. Bricker 2003; Vail and Aveni 2004; see also Boone 2003). These correspondences were explored in more detail at a symposium sponsored by Dumbarton Oaks in October 2006 at the Library of Congress (Vail and Hernández 2009).

NATURE OF THE MAYA SCRIPT

The Maya script can be described as a mixed logo-syllabic system in which some signs represent words in Mayan languages, while others represent various consonant plus vowel (CV) combinations. Individual graphemes are usually combined into *glyph blocks,* which are the graphic units of glyphic texts. The rectangular shape of glyph blocks results from the arrangement of texts into rows and columns, read from left to right and top to bottom. Occasionally, glyph blocks are shown in a single column, read from top to bottom. Signs on the top and to the left side of a block are read first, central signs next, and signs on the bottom and to the right are read last. Usually, but not always, when there are signs both on the top and to the left or on the bottom and to the right, the one occupying an entire edge is read first for prefixes and last for suffixes. Exceptions to these principles occur several times in the Madrid Codex. Hernández and V. Bricker (2004:312–14) see such variant orderings as reflective of the Mexican tradition, which followed less rigid patterns for arrangement of individual signs.[4] A few signs, notably **nal** (2S1) and **ahaw** (2M1), although usually positioned above a central sign, were probably pronounced last. A single glyph block may include a noun phrase or verb phrase or even a complete sentence, though such complexity within glyph blocks is more common in the large-format Classic monumental texts than in the codices.

Syllabic signs composed of a consonant plus a vowel (CV) are used to spell words, without reference to the object these signs depict. That is, they are abstract phonetic signs. Logographs represent free morphemes (words) and bound morphemes (meaningful elements that can only occur as parts of words). Examples of free morphemes are *b'áalam/b'ahläm* 'jaguar' and *tí'/ti,* a locative preposition. An example of a bound morpheme is *u-* 'he/she/it' or 'his/her/its'. The term "phonetic" is not the opposite of "logographic." All logographs have a phonetic value in that they were pronounced. For example, a picture of a deer (AV1) probably represented the Yucatecan or Ch'olan word 'deer' (*kéeh/chij*). A hypothetical phonetic value of a logograph is supported when the sign occurs with syllabic complements or when there are substitutions in equivalent contexts in which the word is spelled with syllabic signs. In some instances syllabic spellings or syllabic complements were used to cue an atypical pronunciation—a synonym or a loanword. For instance, in the codices the word 'dog' is written **tzu-lu** six times, despite the fact that the word commonly used for 'dog' at the time appears to have been *tz'i* in the Ch'olan languages and *peek'* in Yucatec. Logographic value is often related to, but generally not precisely equivalent to, the visual referent of the sign.

4. As they and other authors discuss (see Vail and Aveni 2004, pt. 3), the Madrid Codex has a number of similarities to codices from the highland Mexican tradition. We find their explanation of the variant reading order of some of the Madrid's glyph blocks more convincing than Kelley's (1976:15–16) suggestion that the Madrid scribe was dyslexic or earlier suggestions that the variation reflects a tradition of "cultural decline" characterizing the Postclassic period (Thompson 1950:26).

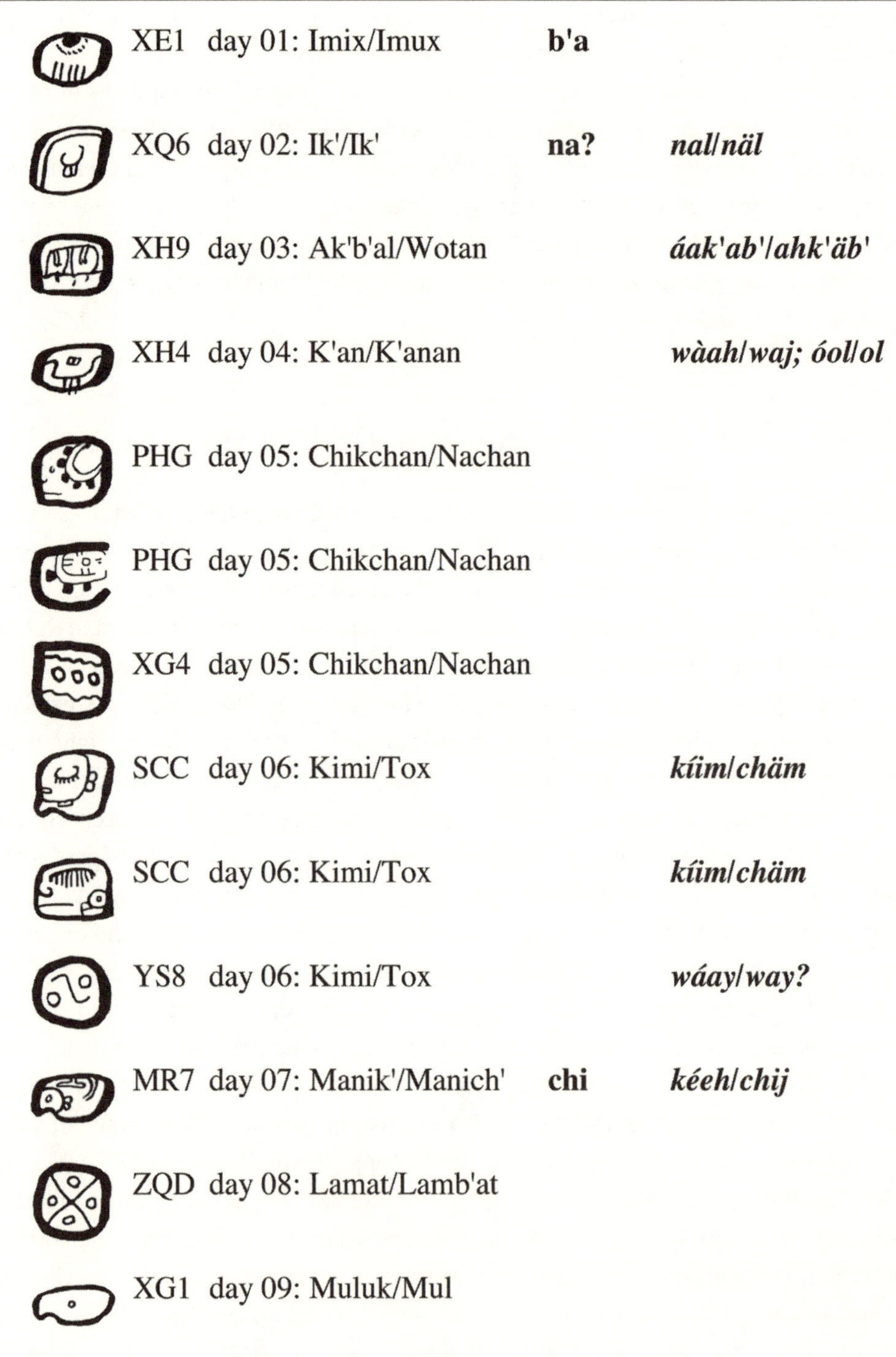

Code	Day	Syllabic	Logographic
XE1	day 01: Imix/Imux	**b'a**	
XQ6	day 02: Ik'/Ik'	**na?**	***nal/näl***
XH9	day 03: Ak'b'al/Wotan		***áak'ab'/ahk'äb'***
XH4	day 04: K'an/K'anan		***wàah/waj; óol/ol***
PHG	day 05: Chikchan/Nachan		
PHG	day 05: Chikchan/Nachan		
XG4	day 05: Chikchan/Nachan		
SCC	day 06: Kimi/Tox		***kíim/chäm***
SCC	day 06: Kimi/Tox		***kíim/chäm***
YS8	day 06: Kimi/Tox		***wáay/way?***
MR7	day 07: Manik'/Manich'	**chi**	***kéeh/chij***
ZQD	day 08: Lamat/Lamb'at		
XG1	day 09: Muluk/Mul		

Figure 2. Day signs with syllabic and logographic values.

AP5	day 10: Ok/Ok		***ok/och; òok/ok***
AP5	day 10: Ok/Ok		
XS1	day 11: Chuwen/B'atz'		***wűnik/winik; winal***
SC4	day 12: Eb'/Eb'		
XH1	day 13: B'en/B'in		***ah/aj***
AT1	day 14: Ix/Ix		***hix?***
AT7	day 14: Ix/Ix		***hix?***
1SD	day 15: Men	**le; me?**	***mèen?***
XH6	day 16: Kib'/Chib'in		
YS1	day 17: Kab'an/Tzanab'		***kàab'/kab'; kàab'/chab', chäb'***
XQ8	day 18: Etz'nab'/Chab'		
ZC1	day 19: Kawak/Chak	**ku**	***tùun/tun***
AM1	day 20: Ahaw/Ajwal		***nik/nich***

A footprint in a cartouche, for example, represents the syllable **b'e**, from the Yucatec word for road (*b'eeh*), but also the syllable **b'i**, from the Ch'olan word for road (*b'ih*). 'Hand' is not a logographic reading for all of the many hand signs, even though the objects depicted are obviously hands.

Calendrical signs constitute a distinct category of logographs. Day signs are ubiquitous in the almanacs of the codices (figure 2). Some of these graphemes have seemingly unrelated logographic and/or syllabic values when they occur in noncalendrical contexts. ZC1, for example, is the day Kawak (the nineteenth day of the twenty named days); when used in noncalendrical contexts, however, it has a logographic value of *tùun/tun* 'stone' and a syllabic value **ku**. Month signs and period glyphs also occur, although much less frequently than in the historical texts from the Classic period. Many of these are formed by collocations composed of several graphemes and hence are not included in the *New Catalog.*

Subgraphemic features are not listed as individual signs. These iconographic elements are important in formal recognition, but they have no logographic or syllabic value. Examples include the closed eye that occurs with PE6, PX4, and MZ3 and the circle containing a dot shown frequently on hands and wrists. Graphemes sometimes can be used as subgraphemic features, such as the *k'an* cross (XQ1) in AP9, the "ak'b'al" sign that occurs in several glyphs (e.g., AP9, APB, and PE7), or the "mirror" sign that occurs as part of several deity names.

JUSTIFICATION FOR SEPARATE CLASSIC AND CODICAL SIGN LISTS

In Maya studies there exists the anomalous situation of two distinct varieties of the script from two completely different corpuses. The inscriptions from the Classic period, although exhibiting considerable variation depending upon location and time period, contrast with the texts in the Maya codices in several obvious ways, particularly in terms of the media used and the time period in which they were written. Likewise the Maya codices, in spite of variations among the three as well as variations within segments of single codices, constitute a set that contrasts with Classic period texts.

How have scholars dealt with these differences in cataloging Maya graphemes? One approach has been to develop catalogs limited to (or primarily featuring) the signs in the three codices known at that time (the Dresden, Paris, and Madrid). The best known of these include the early efforts of Gates (1931), which we have found to contain a number of important insights, and the later sign lists produced by Zimmermann (1956) and Knorozov (1967). A different approach was followed by Thompson, who included both Classic and codical glyphs in his 1962 catalog. The authors of the two volumes of *The New Catalog of Maya Hieroglyphs* (Macri, Looper, and Vail) have chosen a different system of organization in producing separate sign lists for the Classic and codical graphemes. What this has clarified is that the two systems, albeit related, represent two distinct traditions, probably resulting from a combination of geographic, temporal, and linguistic differences. The earliest researchers were certainly correct in recognizing that the hieroglyphic texts on the monuments of the Maya region were written in the same script as that of the screenfold books that had recently been found in European collections. And it is likewise true that the decipherment of the codices has aided our understanding of the monumental texts and vice versa.

However, a number of differences suggest that the two sets of texts were produced by separate scribal traditions. For example, research for the *New Catalog* indicates that some logographic and/or syllabic values can be supported only for one set or the other. Moreover, in several cases visually similar graphemes seem to have distinct values in the codical and Classic traditions. Many graphemes and variants of graphemes are particular to one corpus or the other. The writings of the Classic period and the codices differ in their physical form, in the volume of extant texts, and in the kinds of information that they record. The subject matter, the formulaic patterns, and consequently the vocabulary, vary dramatically. Treating the two systems as if they were identical has resulted in a lack of precision in describing them.

Just as it was once believed that the archaeological sites in the north were settled as the result of the migration of peoples from the Petén to the northern Yucatán Peninsula (earlier called the New Kingdom) following the Classic period, it was also supposed that writing was brought to the north from centers such as Tikal, Copán, and Palenque (the Old Kingdom). The assumption was that the codices contained many syllabic spellings, resulting from an ongoing progression from a logographic to a phonetic script. The inscriptions of Chichén Itzá were viewed as an intermediate phase between the Classic texts and the codices. The codices were believed to reflect the final evolutionary phase of the script. Even after the idea that northern sites had been peopled by refugees from the southern collapse had been abandoned, a vague notion that somehow the codical scribes in the north had inherited the southern script persisted. A careful comparison of the graphemes of the codices and the Classic inscriptions challenges these earlier assumptions.

The most obvious difference between the codices and the Classic texts is their media. Few legible carved or sculpted texts are contemporaneous with the codices, and no codices are known to have survived from the Classic period (even though they are pictured on painted ceramics from the Classic period and disintegrated examples have been recovered from several Classic period tombs). Therefore, in comparing sign forms, we have to consider whether script variation results from styles common to painting as opposed to carving or whether they reflect a more essential difference. Clearly, variant forms for a single grapheme can be found within the Classic period that seem to depend on whether a sign was being painted, incised as a very small text, or carved or sculpted on a large monument. In the codices, sets of four to six glyph blocks are typically associated with a single image of one or two anthropomorphic figures in a variety of postures and locations, often holding objects in their hands. These contrast with a wider variety of images associated with Classic texts, ranging from the posed figures of rulers on carved monuments to less formal treatments of ceremonies, battles, and court scenes depicted on murals and polychrome vases.

Macri and Looper (2003a) identify nearly 680 (677) graphemes in the Classic set. This compares with nearly 400 graphemes in the codices. Again, these totals are approximations, subject to expansion as more texts become available or as variants are separated into two or more graphemes, or to reduction when two or more graphemes are recognized as variants of a single sign.

Of the 677 Classic signs, one-third are shared with the codices and two-thirds are unique to the Classic texts. This contrasts with the 57 percent of codical graphemes that are also found in the Classic script and 43 percent that are unique to the codices. While a third of the Classic signs are found in the codices, over half of the signs in the codices are shared with the Classic system. Signs with a proposed logographic reading offer an even greater contrast. In the Classic texts approximately half of the logographic signs are unique to the Classic script and half are shared with the codices. But in the codical texts, a large majority, 82 percent, of graphemes with logographic readings are shared with the Classic texts.

A comparison of signs with proposed syllabic values is even more dramatic and perhaps a bit surprising. Of Classic syllabic graphemes, a little more than half are shared (56 percent) with the codices and slightly less than half are unique (44 percent). Of the 101 syllabic signs in the codices, however, nearly all, 91 percent, are shared with the Classic graphemes. Of the 9 signs that are unique, 4 have values that are questioned and 4 others are near equivalents to Classic syllabic signs. Thus, almost all syllabic signs in the codices are also found in Classic period texts. If the script of the codices represents an evolution from the Classic script, we would expect to find new syllabic signs in the codices. Rather than seeing an expansion of the number of syllabic signs, the codical script exhibits a subset of the Classic syllabic signs, suggesting that the two script varieties share a common origin in which the syllabic component was maintained in the codical tradition and elaborated by Classic period scribes.

Since most of the Classic period monumental texts include contemporaneous dates, we have a close approximation of the time of carving, which, for the most part, associates them with a specific time and place. Thus, it is possible to find the earliest known examples of each of the Classic graphemes (with the understanding that the extant texts represent a small and probably unrepresentative portion of the original corpus). Most of the shared syllabic signs were in use by the Early Classic period. Only 11 appear for the first time after 600 C.E., and only 20 occur for the first time after 500 C.E. An examination of the dates of the first appearance of logographic signs also shows that most of the signs that occur in both the codices and the Classic texts appeared early on. The codices contain few logographic signs that appear for the first time in the Late Classic period; instead, most pre-date 600 C.E.

What emerges from these data is a model in which the two script traditions probably shared a common origin but, beginning early in the Classic period, appear to have developed with minimal influence on one another. The Classic script can be characterized by innovation, while the codical tradition remained closer to the original shared script. Although we are not the first to suggest that the codical texts exhibit conservative elements (e.g., Grube 1994b), this is the first time that quantifiable data are available to support this observation. We (Macri, Looper, and Vail) are currently preparing a more detailed statistical comparison of the Classic and codical script varieties.

Many questions remain. Are the extant codices part of a northern tradition that remained separate from the Classic period tradition? Did the script of Classic period codices differ from the script used on the monuments? What insights can be gained from comparing painted texts on ceramics and murals? Without having codical texts from Classic period contexts or carved monumental texts from the Late Postclassic period, we can only speculate on the relationship between the two extant scribal traditions. But a simple evolutionary development of the codical script from the Classic period script can no longer be supported. The traits shared by the two traditions are the oldest. The unique signs tend to appear later. Given the differences between the sign inventories of the Classic and codical scripts, the enumeration of two separate grapheme lists becomes even more imperative.

LISTS AND CATALOGS OF CODICAL GRAPHEMES

New signs described in volume 1 of the *New Catalog* have resulted from a significant increase in the number of known signs from the Classic period (partially due to new discoveries and partially to improved images of the texts), as well as from the dramatic progress in decipherment since the publication of Thompson's catalog (1962), resulting in the division of some of his signs into two or more separate graphemes and the recognition of several of them as a single item. But while a new sign list was required by the continued discovery of Classic texts, the same cannot be said for the codices. Nearly all codical graphemes were recognized by Zimmermann (1956) and Thompson (1962) and were included in their catalogs. However, even these catalogs were limited in several respects. Nearly all previous catalogs employed stylized images of the signs. The authors of this volume have worked with all available reproductions of the codices, in addition to examining the original manuscripts in Madrid and Paris, and realize the importance of precision in studying the small size of the painted signs. For that reason, the image for each grapheme in the *New Catalog* is a drawing of an actual example of that grapheme. Sources consulted for the codical images include early photographs: the Paris Codex photographed in 1864 (Rosny 1888, Gates 1909), the Dresden Codex photographed by Förstemann (1880, 1892), and the Madrid Codex photographed by Rosny (1883) and Gates (1911, 1933), as well as the more recent Graz editions (Anders 1967, 1968; Deckert and Anders 1975). Each image was chosen based on its being representative of the set of images of that grapheme. Each has been enlarged so that its larger dimension (either height or width) measures approximately 1.5 inches (though it is not printed at that size in the catalog). The original size of the graphemes and the width of the lines vary considerably, because of the relatively different drawing styles and glyph block sizes of the three codices and because some graphemes only occur combined with one or more other signs in a single glyph block, making them very small. Consequently, when the size of the graphemes is standardized, the line widths of the images vary greatly. When the outline of a grapheme has been excessively distorted by an overlapping grapheme, the outline has been omitted. Some obviously broken lines have been reconstructed, and graphemes from the Paris Codex pages that were written from right to left have been flipped along the horizontal axis so that they conform to the usual orientation of signs (with the exception of ZC6, the triple "Kawak" image, which the scribe neglected to reverse). Images have not been otherwise modified.

We know, from working for some years on revising and refining this sign list, that it is an ongoing process. It is not our intention to fossilize this list, but instead, to provide organizing principles that will foster ongoing sign identification. The descriptions of what the glyphs picture, our categorization of the signs, our inclusion or exclusion of examples under the umbrella of a single grapheme, our choice of illustration for each sign—each of these decisions is subject to refinement and is secondary to the primary focus of creating a list that is as complete as possible.

The earliest researchers referred to individual glyphs by picturing them. Later it became common to refer to them by precise location. Identifying the discrete graphemes of a script requires a way to refer to each grapheme individually. This can be a largely random system of numbering or lettering or an ordering of signs into related groups or sequences based on a variety of criteria. Except for separating graphemes into affixes, main signs, and portrait glyphs, Thompson (1962) arbitrarily numbered the signs. After Thompson's catalog was published, scholars began referring to signs using his numbers, commonly called Thompson numbers or T numbers.

The *New Catalog* employs a three-digit coding system that is not arbitrary but is based on the visual form of the graphemes. The first two digits provide information about the graphic characteristics of the sign. The letter and number combinations are designed so that, except for the bar/dot numerals one through nineteen (001–019), all codes have at least one letter, insuring that there can be no confusion with the three- or four-digit Thompson numbers. This three-digit system was developed to facilitate transcription, cross-referencing, and computer searches, but it was not created with the intention that the codes be used as *names* for the graphemes in the same way that Thompson's numbers have been used. In fact, within our notes and references we continue to employ T numbers to differentiate certain stylistic variants.

The authors are well aware that the Maya graphemes can potentially be grouped in many ways other than those we have chosen. Trying to group signs according to function—for example, putting all of the numeral head variants together—presents difficulties in that many of them have additional syllabic, logographic, and functional values. Each year brings the discovery of additional Classic period texts and subsequent advances in decipherment, many of which are equally relevant to an understanding of the codices. Even grouping signs according to their visual characteristics, as we have attempted to do, requires arbitrary choices between two or more categories. As the visual referents of signs are better understood, some of these may need to be further refined.

A comparison of our sign list with those developed by earlier scholars such as Knorozov, Thompson, and Zimmermann underscores the importance of volume 2 of the *New Catalog.* Its advantage lies in the reclassification of signs that were not fully understood when they were initially classified by these scholars and in its emphasis on a detailed exploration of relationships between Classic period and codical graphemes. Although Thompson's catalog is more adequate for the codices than for the larger and ever-expanding corpus of Classic period texts, his sign list is deficient for current epigraphic analysis in that it omits some signs, groups together others that are now recognized as distinct, and fails to recognize the equivalency of other signs. In several cases he gave different numbers to the Classic and codical variants of the same sign.

The classification of graphemes in the *New Catalog* has several additional advantages over previous catalogs:

1. Grouping signs by form allows the reader to locate signs more easily.
2. Grouping similar signs together allows the reader to see the distinctions between similar signs.
3. Using letters and numbers in the codes prevents confusion between these designations and Thompson numbers or other three- and four-digit numbers proposed as additions to Thompson's system, for example, Ringle and Smith-Stark (1996).
4. The categories are expandable. Newly recognized graphemes can easily be integrated into the system by adding them at the end of each two-digit category. Pending the discovery of additional codices or other contemporary texts, the need for expandability is relevant primarily to the Classic corpus.
5. Signs that are only partially legible can be coded to account for the information that is available. Partial information can be represented by using the appropriate first digit followed by two zeros or the first and second digits followed by one zero.
6. Glyphs that cannot be read at all can be represented by three zeros instead of question marks or blanks.
7. Using arabic numbers instead of roman numerals for numbers is easier to read and allows for more efficient sorting.

This classification was developed to accommodate the transcription of both Classic and codical texts. Since the number of Classic signs is significantly greater than those found in the codices, some subcategories of signs do not occur in the codices (see index).

The Maya script exhibits an unusual degree of graphic variation of individual signs, sometimes even within a single passage, so the task of deciding which signs are distinct graphemes and which are *allographs* (graphic variations) is difficult. These allographs depict the same object or part of the same object and in most cases have equivalent syllabic and logographic values. Scribes created allographs in several ways: by reducing graphemes to the minimal component(s) necessary for identification; by elaborating graphemes, often adding features of a human or animal face to an otherwise abstract sign—again, a practice more common in Classic texts than in the codices; or by simply distorting the shape of one sign relative to another. Some variants do not substitute for each other in all contexts. For example, in the codices the first subsort of XH4 is used for the day K'an/K'anan and for 'tortilla, food', but the second subsort appears only once, where it would seem to represent 'tortilla; food'. Presumably, if a large enough corpus were available, we might expect to find examples of the second allograph used as a day sign as well. We have chosen the more commonly occurring allograph or the simplest form as the basis for categorization.

Ordinarily, allographic variation is irrelevant to the reading of a text. Although it amounts to no more than differences in lettering style or font, it can provide insight into the period, scribal traditions, or place of origin of a given text. If referring to a particular variant is necessary, it can be indicated by using the number preceding the picture descriptions—for example, XH3.2—or a particular example can be located by page, register, and coordinate, as in Dresden 72c I1.

To repeat, the categories in the *New Catalog* are based on visual form, not on function. Thus, grouping all day signs together would violate this convention. Clearly, any attempt to create a system to group hundreds of graphemes will never meet universal agreement. One reason for this is that any given sign might fit well into more than one category. For example, the head SB6 from the Paris Codex might be grouped with either birds or supernaturals. Also, even though it is possible to identify the referent of many signs, most are open to interpretation; for example, is the original referent of the day sign Imix, XE1, a fist, as Goodman (1897) thought, or a waterlily, as Thompson (1950) suggested? A scribe in the fourth century might have believed the original referent to be different from what a scribe in the fourteenth century believed it to be. Finally, as the process of decipherment continues, the consensus on what the referent of a grapheme is may well change; for example, AA3 **tz'u** was originally identified as a fish by Brinton (1895), later by Beyer (1937) as possibly a mollusk, and by Barthel (1955) as a penis. Its correct identification as a fish is confirmed in two ways: by comparing it with images of fish from the codices and the Tulum murals that show the bifurcated tail as well as a double line around the tail, and by the fact that it has the same syllabic value as the "sucking" fish known from Classic period texts.

The First Digit

Macri began the development of the major categories of graphemes used in volumes 1 and 2 of the catalog in the 1980s, based on the formal characteristics of the primary variant (see table 1). She first divided seemingly abstract signs from those with recognizable referents. Of those with recognizable referents, faces were divided from animals. Because there were so many birds, they were separated from the other animals. Likewise, the number of hand signs suggested that a separate category be made for them, distinct from torsos and other body parts. The faces

TABLE 1. Major Categories of Sign Forms

A	Animals (fauna except birds and humans)
B	Birds
H	Body parts (body parts, except heads and hands)
M	Hands (human and capuchin monkey)
P	Human faces (faces that have human characteristics)
S	Supernatural faces (faces with square eyes and other exaggerated or mixed human and animal characteristics)
X	Square symmetrical signs
Y	Square asymmetrical signs
Z	Signs with irregular shapes
0	(followed by two numbers) bar/dot numerals
0	(followed by 00) unreadable glyph
1	Elongated signs, single element
2	Elongated signs, two elements
3	Elongated signs, three or more elements

were divided into supernatural and human faces based on several criteria, although this division is more relevant to the Classic graphemes than to those from the codices. Early on, square signs were separated from elongated signs. Square signs were further subdivided into groups that are symmetrical, asymmetrical, or have irregular cartouches. Elongated signs are not defined in this system as affixes, as they are in Thompson's system, but rather as signs that almost never occur as square or squarish signs. Likewise, the other signs are not functionally main signs, but signs that almost never occur in an elongated form. It was only after the system had been designed that Macri realized the total number of categories was 13—a sacred number throughout Mesoamerica.

The six letters *A, B, H, M, P,* and *S* were chosen from English and Spanish mnemonics to order semantically or formally similar categories consecutively. Animals and birds occur first, then human body parts and hands (*manos*), then human and nonhuman faces (persons and supernaturals). *X, Y,* and *Z* are three categories of square signs; signs for numbers begin with *0*; and the numbers *1, 2,* and *3* categorize the elongated signs roughly according to the number of segments they have.

The categories beginning with *X, Y,* and *Z* designate any square signs not included in previous sets: *X* is for square symmetrical signs in smooth cartouches; *Y* is for square asymmetrical signs inside smooth cartouches; and *Z* is for square signs with irregular cartouches, including those composed of multiple elements. Some of these signs depict recognizable objects, often plants or fruit, but for most of them the original referent is either completely unknown or highly debatable.

Elongated signs of one, two, or three or more elements not included in any of the above categories are introduced by the numbers *1, 2,* and *3.* These categories are not equivalent to Thompson's "affix" category. He noted, among other characteristics, that when an affix is joined to a square sign, some affixes keep the same side toward a main sign. In other words, true affixes can be rotated without resulting in a change in their meaning. The same is not usually true for signs in his main sign category. This characteristic does argue for a conceptual category of affixes that contrasts with "main signs." Nevertheless, in this catalog the signs beginning with *1, 2,* or *3* signify only that these graphemes tend to be elongated in shape.

Signs composed of two identical elements begin with *22*; those composed of three identical elements begin with *33.* Signs with three or more elements begin with *3.* Labels beginning with two numbers always have a letter for the third digit in order to avoid any confusion with Thompson numbers. *Zero* followed by two numbers indicates a bar/dot numeral of *01* through *19* (e.g., *001, 002*). This contrasts with earlier uses of roman numerals for Maya numbers. Note that any code beginning with *1*, *2*, or *3* is only followed by a letter, thus avoiding any confusion between the graphemes and the numbers. Head variants for the numbers have individual codes based on graphic characteristics. This system was originally developed for the Classic monumental corpus. However, because the codices provide a much more limited data set, only a few of these head variants have been identified in the codices. The letters *I* and *O,* easily confused with the numbers *1* and *0* respectively, are not used in any coding capacity.

All of the categories in this coding system are hierarchical. Signs with hands are normally assigned to the *M* (*manos*) category regardless of any other features they may include. The *A–S* categories have precedence over *X, Y, Z* and *1, 2, 3.* Thus, a jawbone in a square cartouche is given the letter *H* (human) rather than *Y* (asymmetrical square signs). Square and elongated categories include only those signs that do not fit into the *A–S* categories. Again, categorization is based on the primary variant of the sign. Other less common variants may fit less harmoniously into the category of what we have designated as the primary variant. For example, AMB, the inverted ahaw "face," represents the syllable **la**. Subsort 2, an elongated variant composed of circles and dots, would not otherwise fit into the *animal* category. The equivalency is based on the frequent substitution of one variant for the other, as well as intermediate variants not included in the catalog, such as one showing the inverted ahaw face doubled.

The proportions of signs across all the primary categories are not equal in the Classic and codical texts. For example, the codices have far fewer hand signs and human faces than are found in those grapheme categories for the Classic period corpus.

The Second Digit

Categories are further subdivided according to more specific characteristics. Again, bilingual English and Spanish mnemonics are employed to cue the subcategories (table 2). Zero in the second digit following a letter or number signifies an unreadable sign that can be identified as belonging to one of the twelve major categories. For example, A00 would designate an unidentifiable animal. Because this coding scheme was designed to accommodate the graphemes in both the Classic and codical texts, several of the two-digit categories have no examples in the codices (HB, HJ, HM, 34), and another, 1X, has no examples in the Classic texts.

The Third Digit

The third digit is not based on the form of the sign. It simply differentiates the graphemes in the category, sometimes sequencing them roughly in order of frequency or according to similarity of form. Signs are ordered by a number, 1–9, continuing with letters when there are more than 9 signs in a particular category. For those signs in the categories beginning with 1, 2, or 3, the third digit is always a letter, so that these codes cannot be confused with Thompson numbers. Zero in the third digit signifies a sign that can only be partially identified as belonging to a two-digit category; for example, SC0 designates an image of a skull that lacks any identifying detail. Sequences of signs with discontinuous numbering reflect the fact that some three-digit codes have been assigned to graphemes that occur only in the Classic texts or only in the codices.

Notable Items in this Volume

In the process of compiling this catalog, we had the opportunity to look very closely at the glyphic texts and to identify features of certain graphemes that have not previously been widely recognized. We call the reader's attention to a few of these items.

AL3 ***áak/ahk*** *'turtle' and AL5* ***mak/mäk*** *'turtle carapace; cover'*

Following Marc Zender's (2006) recent proposal that the Classic grapheme AL3 is actually two distinct signs, we have likewise found a distinction between the turtle grapheme AL3 and the turtle carapace AL5 in the codices. The form of AL3 in the Paris Codex with the infixed **k'an** cross, XQ1, is the same as the main signs of the Cancuen emblem glyph and the name of Piedras Negras Ruler 2.

AT1 ***b'áalam/b'ahläm?*** *'jaguar'*

The image of the head of a jaguar is used once as the day Ix (on Madrid 45c) in place of the more standard AT7. This example provides support for a relationship proposed by previous researchers between the day Ix and the value 'jaguar'.

TABLE 2. Subcategories of Sign Forms

CODE	SUBCATEGORY WITH MNEMONIC	DESCRIPTION
animals		
AA	aquatic	animals and animal parts associated with water: fish, shells, amphibians
AC	snake (*culebra*)	snake heads, bodies, body parts
AL	lizard	all reptiles except snakes
AM	monkey/Ajaw	complete monkeys, heads, faces, and Ajaw faces
AP	dog/rodent (*perro*)	various mammals not included in more specific categories
AT	jaguar (*tigre*)	jaguar heads, bodies, and parts
AV	deer (*venado*)	deer heads, bodies, and body parts
birds		
BM	mixed	generic and miscellaneous birds and body parts
BP	parrot	parrots
BT	owl (*tecolote*)	owls and other raptors
BV	vulture	vultures
human body		
HB	bun	hair bun
HE	eye	human eyes
HH	bone (*hueso*)	bones
HJ	jaw	mandibles
HM	male genitals	male genitals
HT	torso	other body parts: torsos, legs, feet
hands		
MB	both	two hands or single digit
MR	right	right hands
MZ	left (*izquierdo*)	left hands
persons		
PC	face (*cara*)	human faces with plain eyes
PE	hidden eye	human faces with covered or decorated eye
PM	mouth	human faces with object in or on mouth
PT	top	human faces with forehead adornment or object on head
PX	mixed	right-facing or frontal faces
supernaturals		
SB	bird	birds with exaggerated or mixed animal characteristics
SC	skull (*calavera*)	human and animal skulls
SN	human nose	supernatural beings with human nose
SS	supernatural nose	supernatural beings with nonhuman nose
ST	jaguar (*tigre*)	supernatural beings with jaguar features
square shape, symmetrical		
XD	design	patterned or plain
XE	imix type	similar to the day sign for Imix

TABLE 2. Subcategories of Sign Forms *(continued)*

CODE	SUBCATEGORY WITH MNEMONIC	DESCRIPTION
XG	drops (*gotas*)	having one or more circlets
XH	horizontal	divided by a horizontal line
XQ	quadripartite	divided into four parts
XS	spiral	having spirals or curved lines
XV	vertical	divided by a vertical line
square shape, asymmetrical		
YG	drops (*gotas*)	having one or more circlets
YM	mirror	having mirror markings
YS	spiral	having spirals or curved lines
irregular square shape or complex		
ZB	bundle	ties or binding
ZC	*kawak*	having a *kawak* "stone" infix
ZD	design	patterned or plain
ZE	elbow	occupying adjoining vertical and horizontal sides
ZH	horizontal	divided by a horizontal line
ZQ	quadripartite	divided into four parts
ZS	spiral	having spirals or curved lines
ZU	U-shaped	catouche open on one side
ZV	vessel	pottery vessels or baskets
ZX	mixed	composed of two or more cartouches
ZZ	knobbed	having a notch or point on one side
numerals		
00	numeral	numerals depicted by bars and circles (lines and dots)
elongated shape, one element		
1B	bundle	appearing to be tied or bound
1C	*kawak*	having a *kawak* "stone" infix
1G	drops (*gotas*)	having one or more circlets
1M	mirror	having curved "mirror" signs
1S	spiral	having spirals or curved lines
elongated shape, two elements		
22	2	two identical components
2G	drops (*gotas*)	one or more circlets
2M	mixed	miscellaneous signs of two parts
2S	spiral	having spirals or curved lines
elongated shape, three elements		
32	2	three components, two identical
33	3	three identical components
34	4	four or more components
3M	mixed	miscellaneous signs of three components

*MRB **tzúutz/tzutz** 'finish, complete'*

Thompson coded the glyph block on Dresden 60bA2 as T85:17:165. He noted that it was "apparently a completion compound to be read with the adjacent *katun* glyph; it appears to correspond to the 218–575 compound of the stelae" (1962:40f. note 1). That is, he recognized that the glyph in the Dresden was the same as the completion sign we now read as **tzúutz/tzutz**. The grapheme, consisting of a right hand with an object (flower? bead? baton?) hanging from an extended first finger, occurs frequently in texts from the Classic period. Early on it was recognized as signifying completion (Morley 1915:78, and others summarized in Kelley 1962b:40). Stuart (2001) has identified it as *tzutz* 'finish'. The suffix **-yi** is one of three affixes commonly occurring with **tzúutz/tzutz** in Classic period texts. The Dresden form is significant in that it provides an example of this grapheme that may be identified explicitly as **yi** ZUH. In most cases in the codices, ZUH **yi** and ZUJ **yax/yäx** are not graphically differentiated.

*MZB **kelem** 'young man'*

In the Classic texts, particularly those found on ceramic vessels, the sign **kelem** consists of a hand with the thumb in the mouth of a monkey, or occasionally in the mouth of a human face. In the six examples found in the codices, however, the faces are those of various supernaturals, including Itzamna and the maize god.

*PE8 **nal/näl** 'maize'*

Images of personified maize or of the maize god, PE8, occur frequently throughout the codices. However, we have identified an additional example on Madrid 28 that is visually distinct from the typical head variant (PE8, subsorts 1 and 2). Here an elongated head of the maize god facing upward has been drawn above two glyphs representing tortillas, XH4, **wàah/waj**. Gates (1931:133) grouped this glyph block with "animal figures." Other researchers, including Thompson (1962) and Zimmermann (1956), do not seem to have commented on it.

PHG day Chikchan

A unique example of the day glyph Chikchan appears on Madrid 30b with an XQ3 **k'in** 'sun, day' infix. We have yet to determine the significance of the **k'in** infix in connection with a day linked to the serpent.

*PT3 **nik ahaw/nich ajaw?** 'wind and flower god, God H'*

Karl Taube (1992:59) notes that an *ik'* sign typically occurs on the cheek or ear ornament of examples of PT3 from the Classic period. A careful examination of glyphs referring to God H in photographs of the codices has resulted in the identification of an example with the *ik'* sign on the cheek on Dresden 11a. The cheek decoration was drawn by Gates (1932:120), who very astutely recognized that PT3 and PT9 (a jaguar deity) were distinct graphemes. However, neither he nor other scholars have, to our knowledge, commented specifically on this particular example.

*XD1 **pa***

A codical variant of T1023, first identified as **pa** by Kelley (1976:334), occurs on page 67b of the Madrid Codex. Vail (2003) has recently identified it as part of a collocation reading *pa'alk'in* 'broken sun' in reference to a solar eclipse. Although not correct in all of the details, more than a century earlier Thomas (1893:266) likewise interpreted this collocation as referring to a solar eclipse.

*ZQH and 32H **i'inah/hinaj** 'seed'*

By noting a series of related variations, Vail was able to identify previously unrecognized variants of the grapheme for 'seed', 32H, in the Madrid Codex. All occur suffixed by the syllabic sign **na**, 1G1.

*1S3 **ne** and 1S4 **hu***

Two scroll-like graphemes not consistently distinguished are **ne** 1S3 and **hu** 1S4. The two signs contrast consistently in the direction of their scroll and in their positions relative to the other graphemes in the glyph block. **ne** occurs as a suffix, while **hu** is a prefix.

*2G4 **pat?/pät?** 'make, form'*

2G4 has two variants—one is a compound grapheme and the other, an abbreviated sign, consists of the upper element only. The reading of **pat/pät** for 2G4, as suggested originally by Stuart (1995:355) for Classic period contexts, receives support from Paris 7d, where the second variant is followed by two phonetic elements: XD1 **pa** and 1B1 **ta**.

COMPARISON OF THE THREE CODICES

Figure 3 compares a single page from the Dresden, Madrid, and Paris codices. Of the three Maya codices, impressionistically the Madrid Codex is the most dissimilar, based solely on the relative size of the line width, size of the glyphs, and style of painting of the glyphic signs. All three codices share a focus on recording astronomical events, although this information is organized differently in the three manuscripts. Tables for calculating recurring astronomical cycles are found in the Dresden and Paris codices, whereas in the Madrid, in the absence of astronomical tables, references to celestial events occur in almanacs. The Madrid and Dresden are more similar from the perspective of containing similarly organized almanacs (i.e., beginning with a column of day glyphs and having frames with hieroglyphic captions, dates, and pictures), while the Paris has a number of almanacs that are unique in both format and content (such as the *tun* and *k'atun* series; see Love 1994). The Dresden is unique in being the only one that provides information for calculating Long Count dates.

Table 3 compares the three codices by total area (document height and width), by page size, by the number of extant pages, by the approximate number of glyph blocks (not including the day signs that occur as part of the almanacs' calendrical structures), and by the percentage of the total number of texts within each codex counted by legible, or nearly legible, glyph blocks. The Madrid accounts for nearly half of all codical texts, while the Dresden has slightly more than a third. The Paris, the smallest, represents less than 20 percent of the codical corpus.

Examining the distribution of graphemes across the three codices provides another dimension for comparison. Over a third of all graphemes are present in all three codices.

In addition to illustrating their relative sizes, figure 3 also shows the relative sizes and line widths of painted glyphs from each codex. Although the Paris has the largest page size, the glyphs from the Madrid are much larger, with the widest lines, while the Paris and the Dresden are more similar in form. Coe and Kerr (1997:178, 180, 181), commenting on the calligraphy of the three manuscripts, note that the fine lines in the Dresden must have been the result of a quill pen, whereas the thicker lines in the Paris and Madrid can be explained by the use of a brush. Macri's work with high-quality photographic scans of the Dresden in preparing the images for the catalog bears this out. On several pages, lines have been created by a row of consecutive circles, suggesting the use of a hollow writing

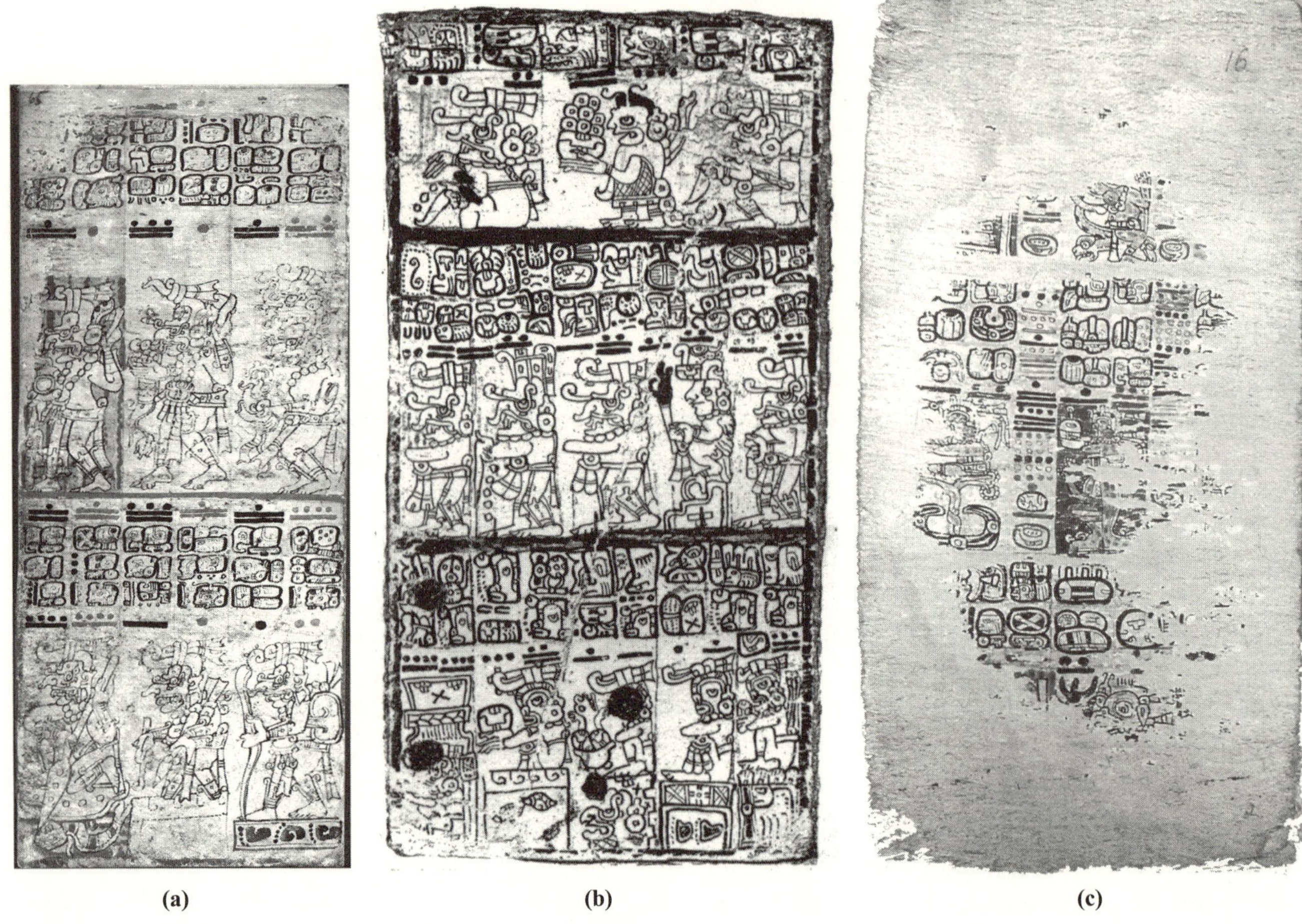

(a) (b) (c)

Figure 3. Comparison pages from the Dresden, Madrid, and Paris codices: (a) Dresden page 65, after Förstemann 1880; (b) Madrid page 11, after Rosny 1883; (c) Paris page 16, courtesy of George Stuart, Boundary End Archaeology Research Center.

TABLE 3. Codices Compared by Size and by Number of Text Glyph Blocks

CODEX	HEIGHT	LENGTH	AREA (2•H•W)	PAGE W	PAGES	GL BLOCKS	% OF TOTAL
Dresden	20.5cm	1.8m	7,380cm^2	9.1cm	74	3,000+	37%
Madrid	23.5cm	6.8m	32,054cm^2	12.2cm	112	3,700+	46%
Paris	24.5cm	4.1m	2,009cm^2	12.5cm	24	1,400+	17%
TOTALS					210	8,100+	100%

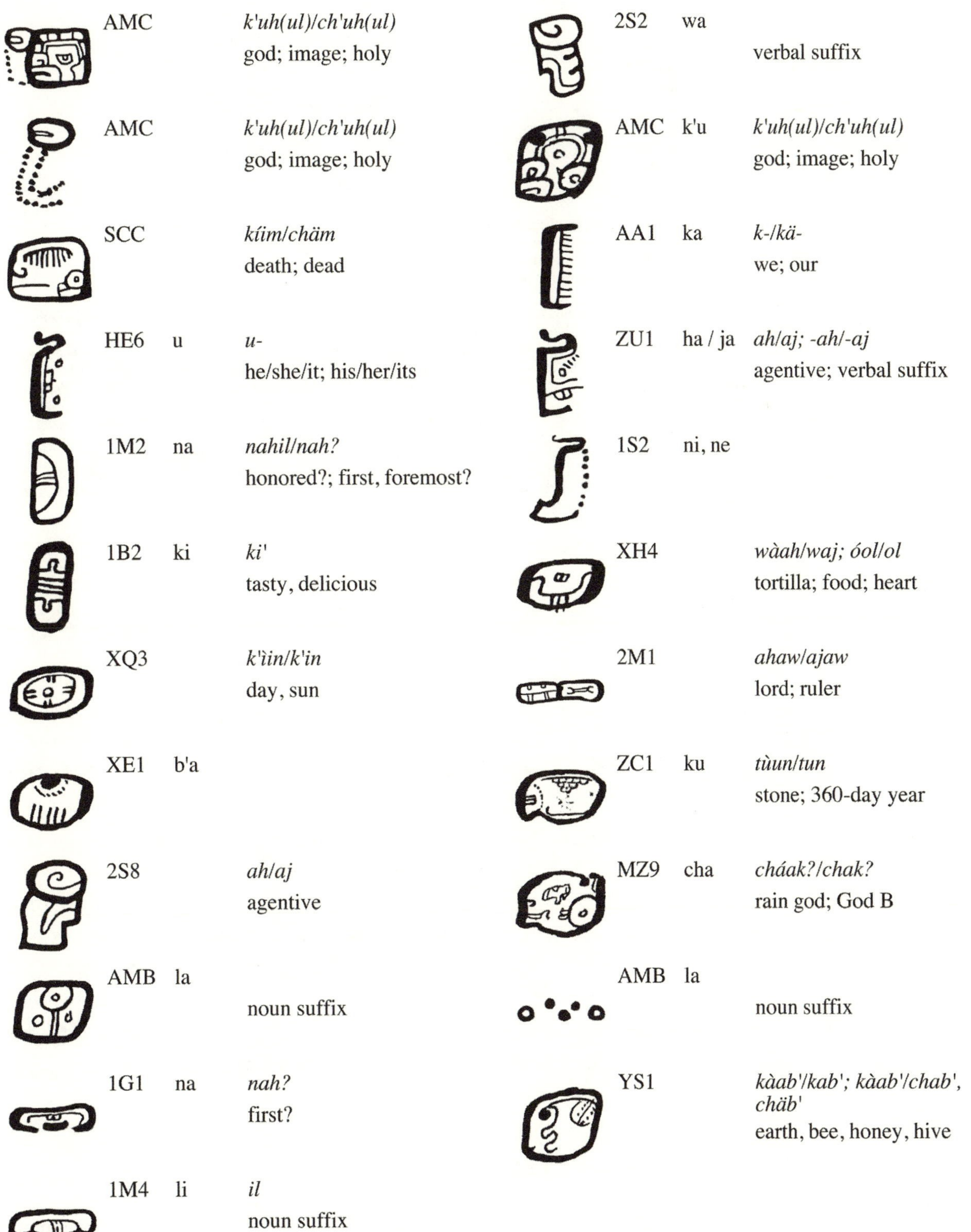

Figure 4. Graphemes occurring over two hundred times.

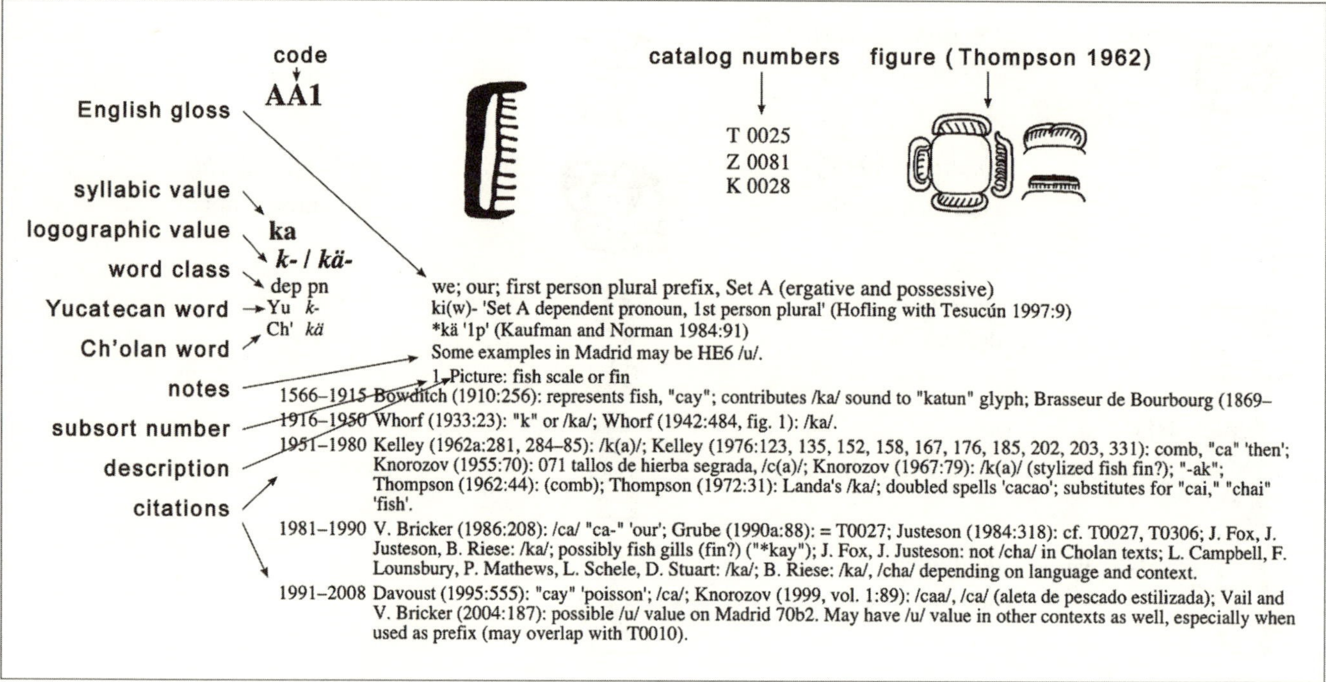

Figure 5. Sample catalog entry.

implement—a quill, or perhaps a small bone spine, or another reedlike object. On some pages the very fine lines show evidence of skips, which would more likely have been produced by a rigid implement rather than a brush. The wider lines vary in width, as would be expected from a brush stroke, while the finer lines tend to have a consistent width.

Having closely examined the codical texts, we have been able to calculate the number of occurrences of individual graphemes (due to the number of day signs in almanacs and tables, they are not included in this tally). Of the approximately 500 distinctive signs in the codices, 314 occur fewer than 10 times, some of these only once. About 100 graphemes occur 11–50 times. This means that more than three-quarters of all the signs occur fewer than 50 times. Another 55 signs occur 51–200 times. Figure 4 illustrates the 23 most frequent graphemes in the codices, all occurring over 200 times. All of these have known syllabic and/or logographic values. The most frequently occurring grapheme is HE6, signifying the third person subject and possessive prefix *u-* 'he/she/it' and 'his/her/its'. For most graphemes, the fewer times they occur, the less likely they are to have an established reading.

GUIDE TO THE CATALOG AND APPENDICES

Entries in the body of the *New Catalog,* as shown in figure 5, begin with the three-digit code, followed by an image of the grapheme redrawn by Macri from the photographic facsimilies mentioned above. Next are the Thompson number, if there is one, and images of the grapheme from Thompson (1962). When Thompson offers multiple illustrations for a single number, we have often not pictured all of them. Sometimes two or more of Thompson's signs constitute a single grapheme. We have matched our entries with only one of these, usually the most commonly occurring form. We have also listed the catalog numbers from Zimmermann (1956) and Knorozov (1967). Their numbers are preceded by Z and K, respectively.

In bold letters directly beneath the three-digit code are the proposed syllabic and logographic values. Values are listed for a grapheme only when general agreement exists among epigraphers or when the values are supported by substitutions, context, or graphic appearance. Proposed values that are widely accepted, despite a lack of conclusive evidence to substantiate a particular reading, are also sometimes included, followed by a question mark to indicate their uncertain status. Yucatecan and Ch'olan logographic values are italicized. A slash divides the Yucatecan form from the Ch'olan form when the two are different. For logographic signs, the word class (part of speech) is shown beneath the word, followed by an English gloss. The English gloss is to the right of the logographic reading. Selected definitions for logographs are listed only in the first subsort of each grapheme.

The calendrical significance, if any, of a sign follows the lexical entries. Notes containing additional information about the sign occur below the calendrical data (none occur in the sample entry). Beneath that is the number for each grapheme variant (unique or first variants have *1,* other subsorts are ordered consecutively) and a phrase describing the grapheme's appearance. These phrases are intended only as a means of verbally distinguishing the images.

Bibliographical citations make up the last part of the entry. They have been divided into five chronological periods that represent various stages in the "recovery" of the Maya script: the earliest dates from the colonial period to the early twentieth century; the second includes most of the first half of the twentieth century; the third incorporates Knorozov's assertion of phoneticism and the subsequent decades of debate about the nature of the script; the fourth includes the dramatic strides in decipherment in the 1980s; and the fifth summarizes work from 1991 to the present.

1566–1915 includes Landa's "alphabet," material from the Codex Pérez, and readings by Brasseur de Bourbourg, Brinton, Goodman, Rosny, Seler, Schellhas, Thomas, Tozzer and Allen, and other early scholars.

1916–1950 includes readings by Morley, Gates, and Thompson's summary of the field to 1950, as summarized in *Maya Hieroglyphic Writing: Introduction.*

1951–1980 contains material by Berlin, Kelley, Knorozov, Proskouriakoff, Thompson's *Catalog* (1962), and early material by Lounsbury, Mathews, and Schele.

1981–1990 contains the summary of readings in Justeson (1984), material from V. Bricker's grammar (1986), the sign list from Grube (1990a, b), and readings by Fox, Houston, Justeson, MacLeod, Schele, Stuart, and many other contributors.

1991–2008 includes summary readings by Davoust, revisions to the Thompson (1962) classification by Ringle and Smith-Stark (1996), the recent summary of Knorozov (1999), and recent decipherments by various epigraphers. Note that the numbers assigned to graphemes by Knorozov are not consistent across his various publications (Knorozov 1955, 1967, 1999). All four-digit numbers in Ringle and Smith-Stark (1996) refer to T numbers.

Citations are listed alphabetically by author. The list is not comprehensive, but it does allow the reader to trace the progression of decipherment. Sometimes a correct reading was given early on, dismissed, and not taken up again for many decades. In others instances, early scholars surmised a correct reading, but only much later was substitution evidence presented to confirm the reading. These references underscore the nature of the decipherment process as cumulative and inclusive of the work of many scholars. The arguments for syllabic and logographic values are often difficult to summarize in a cursory fashion. Generally, we have not presented supporting evidence nor summarized arguments for readings, except to give syllabic substitutions for logographic signs when noted in the literature. For specific details of an argument, the reader should refer to the original publications.

Citations of primary sources in which authors develop their own arguments for decipherment are the most valuable. In some cases, however, an author merely refers to a reading, suggesting only acceptance of someone else's proposal. Much of the early work by Förstemann, Schellhas, and Seler that is cited is from the English translations of their work, which appeared several years later than the original publications. For example, Schellhas's article on deity names was first published in 1892, whereas the English version did not appear until 1904. Most of Seler's work was republished several times. The later versions sometimes contain Seler's own revisions. We have generally cited early material from later English language editions (e.g., Seler 1976, 1990–1998), providing the dates of the original publication in brackets. For details on the publication of these items, the readers should see the editorial notes in the later editions.

We have cited only a sampling of early readings, a large number of which have proven insupportable, sometimes including unidentifiable graphemes or elements that are now recognized as subgraphemic particles. We have made an effort to include references to those readings that have later been demonstrated to be correct. Many early decipherments consist merely of a passing remark or observation embedded within long discussions of a variety of topics. Students of the history of decipherment can be assured that many gems of insight await rediscovery in the works of these early writers. Seminal discussions are included in Houston, Mazariegos, and Stuart's (2001) recent publication of primary source materials, which contains selections from over forty articles.

Some citations represent secondary sources; that is, another researcher is quoted or credited with a particular reading. Two summaries, Kelley (1962a) and Justeson (1984), were especially complete for their periods. In both publications, the authors refer to scholars by their initials. In the *New Catalog,* we have indicated the first initials and written out the last names. This distinguishes these references from citations to published sources for which only the last name and date are given. The reader can consult the original summaries for the full names and for additional information about sources. Angled brackets within the bibliographic citations indicate letter equivalents offered by Bishop Landa (Tozzer 1941). We follow some sources, such as Knorozov, in distinguishing logographic readings from identification of visual referents by placing the latter within parentheses.

In a few cases, we have relied on personal communications for unpublished glyph readings. In the last three decades, progress has proceeded at a rapid pace. Many decipherments are presented at professional meetings or workshops, or circulated in unpublished papers, long before they appear in print. The author of the earliest cited publication is therefore not necessarily the one credited with decipherment. We have made every attempt to credit appropriately those responsible for recognizing or explicating new readings. However, the purpose of this study is not to assign credit to specific researchers, but to document the cooperative nature of glyphic scholarship.

A series of appendices follows the body of the *New Catalog*: appendix 1 lists signs arranged alphabetically by proposed syllabic values; appendix 2 lists signs with proposed logographic values arranged alphabetically by Mayan words; appendix 3 lists signs with logographic values ordered by their English glosses; and appendix 4 is a correspondence between T numbers and the catalog codes.

At the end of the volume is the *Index to the New Catalog, Volumes 1 and 2.* It contains images of all of the graphemes and grapheme variants ordered by the three-digit grapheme code. Each Classic grapheme and its variants follow the examples of the same grapheme from the codices. Not all graphemes are found in both corpuses.

The printed version of this catalog does not include a concordance to the codical texts; however, this information is available in the online Maya Codices Database developed by Vail and Hernández (2005–2008). It can be searched in a variety of ways: by syllabic spellings, Mayan and English words, sequences of three-digit codes, and sequences of Thompson numbers.

The New Catalog of Maya Hieroglyphs

VOLUME TWO

Abbreviations

ABBREVIATIONS FOR WORD CLASSES

adj	adjective
adv	adverb
aff v	affect verb
conj	conjunction
dep pn	dependent pronoun
intr v	intransitive verb
loc	locative
n	noun
nm cl	numeral classifier
num	number
pos	positional root
prep	preposition
refl pn	reflexive pronoun
rel n	relational noun
suf	suffix
trans v	transitive verb

OTHER ABBREVIATIONS

ant possibly antonyme (in references from Brasseur de Bourbourg 1869-1870)

C consonant

D Dresden Codex, followed by page number and section

G Gates catalog number

K followed by a number refers to entries in Knorozov (1967)

lit literalmente (in references from Barrera Vásquez et al. 1980)

M Madrid Codex, followed by page number and section

n note

P Paris Codex, followed by page number and section

pCT proto Ch'olan

prép loc préposition locatif (in references from Davoust 1995)

T Thompson catalog number

V vowel

Z Zimmermann catalog number

< from

ABBREVIATIONS USED ONLY IN ENTRIES FROM RINGLE AND SMITH-STARK (1996)

a–t specific element variants

A affixed

H head profile of an element

M main sign

v unspecified variant, usually referring to T numbers

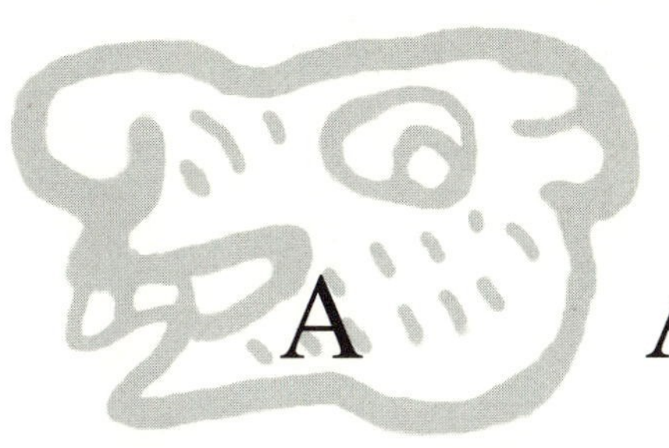

A Animals

AA1

T 0025
Z 0081
K 0028

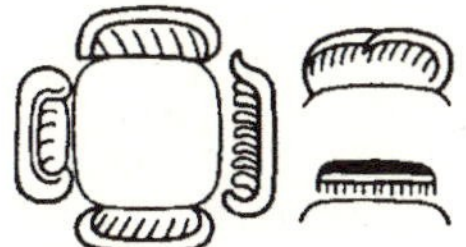

ka
k- / kä-

dep pn — we; our; first person plural prefix, Set A (ergative and possessive)

Yu *k-* — k- 'Set A 1st person plural' (Bricker et al. 1998:329); k- 'our' (Bricker et al. 1998:358); ki(w)- 'Set A dependent pronoun, 1st person plural' (Hofling with Tesucún 1997:9)

Ch' *kä-* — *kä '1st person plural' (Kaufman and Norman 1984:91)

Some examples in Madrid may be HE6 /u/.

1. Picture: fish scale or fin

1566–1915 Bowditch (1910:256): represents fish, "cay"; contributes /ka/ sound to "katun" glyph; Brasseur de Bourbourg (1869–1870, vol. 1:202): "ca" 'mâchoire'; "cáa" 'pierre à moudre le grain; une sorte de citrouille'; Landa [1566] (Tozzer 1941:170): <ca>; Thomas (1888:355, 369): /ca/; Thomas (1892b:44): /ca/; Thomas (1893:248): Landa's "ca" 'two, twice'.

1916–1950 Whorf (1933:23): "k" or /ka/; Whorf (1942:484, fig. 1): /ka/.

1951–1980 Kelley (1962a:281, 284–85): /c(a)/; Kelley (1976:123, 135, 152, 158, 167, 176, 185, 202, 203, 331): comb, "ca" 'then'; Knorozov (1955:70): 071 (tallos de hierba segrada) /c(a)/; Knorozov (1967:79): /k(a)/ (fish fin?); "-ak"; Thompson (1962:44): (comb); Thompson (1972:31): Landa's /ka/; doubled spells 'cacao'; substitutes for "cai," "chai" 'fish'.

1981–1990 V. Bricker (1986:208): /ca/ "ca-" 'our'; Grube (1990a:88): = T0027; Justeson (1984:318): cf. T0027, T0306; J. Fox, J. Justeson, B. Riese: /ka/; possibly fish gills (fin?) ("*kay"); J. Fox, J. Justeson: not /cha/ in Cholan texts; L. Campbell, F. Lounsbury, P. Mathews, L. Schele, D. Stuart: /ka/; B. Riese: /ka/, /cha/ depending on language and context.

1991–2008 Davoust (1995:555): "cay" 'poisson'; /ca/; Knorozov (1999, vol. 1:89): /caa/, /ca/ (aleta de pescado estilizada); Vail and V. Bricker (2004:187): possible /u/ value on Madrid 70b2. May have /u/ value in other contexts as well, especially when used as prefix (may overlap with T0010).

AA3

T 0608
Z 0756
K 0374

tz'u

1. Picture: fish?

1566–1915 Brinton (1895:89): representation of a fish.

1916–1950 Beyer (1937:53): animal associated with bivalve [T0608.0149].

1951–1980 Barthel (1955): penis and testicles; Kelley (1962a:303f.): /me/; Kelley (1976:123, 333): (fish, penis, mollusk?); /me/?; Knorozov (1967:103): /tz'(u)/ (fish); Thompson (1962:231f.): [23 examples] (Beyer's mollusk); Thompson (1972:38): [with T0149] representation of shellfish, or fish and shell; cites Barthel's (1955) identification as a penis.

1981–1990 Grube (1990a:110): = T0761; Justeson (1984:347): L. Campbell, J. Justeson: /consonant + u/; not /me/; J. Fox: "to:n/ tu:n" 'penis'; F. Lounsbury: /b'u/; B. Riese: possibly /tz'u/; probably depicts penis; also "tun" 'drum' in Codex Madrid.

1991–2008 Davoust (1995:590): "ton" 'pénis'; /tz'u/; Knorozov (1999, vol. 1:161): "tz'uu" (pescado sin cabeza); Ringle and Smith-Stark (1996:335–38): 0608 = 0761v?; Ringle and Smith-Stark (1996:348): Thompson and Beyer's "mollusk," confined to the codices and Chichén Itzá, fairly clearly a penis, at least at the latter site. T0149 affixed to codical examples probably represents testicles; Schele and Grube (1997:103): /tz'u/ in T0608:0149 "tz'un"; Winters (1991:244f.): T0608 as penis correlates with fish representations of T0714.

AA4

T 0010
Z 0001a
K 0032

u

u-

dep pn he/she/it; his/her/its; third person prefix, Set A (ergative and possessive)

1. Picture: jaw with teeth

1951–1980 Knorozov (1967:79): (= K031) /u/, "u-."

1981–1990 V. Bricker (1986:208): /u/ "u" 'he, she, it; his, her, its' (Cholan, Yucatecan); Grube (1990a:87): = T0011; Justeson (1984:316): J. Fox: equivalent to T0001 logographically, but no evidence for purely phonetic use; J. Justeson, F. Lounsbury, D. Stuart: codex form of T0204; P. Mathews, L. Schele: semantic equivalent of T0001; B. Riese: in codices, equivalent to T0001 logograph; not used in monumental inscriptions.

1991–2008 Davoust (1995:553): "huh" 'iguane' or "cay" 'poisson'; /u/ or /ca/; Knorozov (1999, vol. 1:89): /u/.

AA6

T 0210
Z 0757
K 0321, 0322?

Used in name of Pawahtun on Dresden 41b, frame 1.

1. Picture: univalve shell

1566–1915 Tozzer and Allen (1910:pl. 1): glyph of mollusk, "Fasciolaria Gigantea."

1951–1980 Kelley (1976:72, 332): (conch shell); Knorozov (1967:100): (= K318) "xot" 'equal; exact'; 'zero'; Thompson (1962:59): (univalve shell); Thompson (1972:101): (turtle shell).

1981–1990 Justeson (1984:331): J. Justeson: probably grammatical suffix to numerals in counts of days; = T0574; MacLeod (1990b:337): *hVC roots in Yucatecan and Cholan languages.

1991–2008 Davoust (1995:568): "hub, huuch" 'coquillage'; /hu/?; Knorozov (1999, vol. 1:162f.): (K0748) "ul, hul" (voluta de caracol); (K0757) "xot" (concha).

AA7

T 0542a
Z 1342b
K 0116–17, 0138

e

1. Picture: reptile ear

1566–1915 Brasseur de Bourbourg (1869–1870, vol. 1: 202): "e" 'fil, tranchant d'une arme; petites pierres ensemble, oeufs d'oiseaux, en compos'; Landa [1566] (Tozzer 1941:170): /e/; Thomas (1892b:44): /e/, /ee/; Thomas (1893:251): Landa's <e>.

1916–1950 Whorf (1942:484, fig. 1): /e/.

1951–1980 Kelley (1962a:290, 295): /'e/; Kelley (1962b:41): /'e/; Kelley (1976:155, 179, 333): /'e/; Knorozov (1955:69): 053 (huevos de ave?) /e/; Knorozov (1967:88–90): /e/; (bird's eggs); Thompson (1962:154f.): [43 examples] (Ahau semblant). With T0087 almost certainly wooden mask or idol; on Madrid 102, with variable affixes, a spindle whorl and loom or weaving stick.

1981–1990 V. Bricker (1986:211): (Landa's "e") /e/; Justeson (1984:341): J. Fox, J. Justeson, F. Lounsbury, P. Mathews, B. Riese: /e/; = Landa's <e>; B. Riese: also /'e/ and /'/.

1991–2008 Davoust (1995:585): "ahwal/ahau" '20e jour'; /e/.

AA9

T 0738b
Z 0758
K 0411–14, 0540

kay / chäy

n fish
Yu *kay* kay 'fish' (V. Bricker et al. 1998:125)
Ch' *chäy* *chäy 'fish' (Kaufman and Norman 1984:118)

1. Picture: fish

1566–1915 Brinton (1895:90): fish as sacred food offering; Rosny (1883:22): "cay" 'poisson'; Thomas (1888:357): "cay" 'fish'; Tozzer and Allen (1910:pl. 6): fish as offering.

1916–1950 Whorf (1933:23): /k/.

1951–1980 Kelley (1962b:27): (with T0506): fish offering; Kelley (1976:110): "cai" 'fish'; Knorozov (1967:104): [K411, 412, 413, 414] "kay" 'fish'; Thompson (1962:316–19): [75 examples] (fish).

1981–1990 V. Bricker (1986:89, 213): /ca/ "ca-" 'our'; Grube (1990a:88): = T0203; Justeson (1984:353): J. Fox, J. Justeson: possibly = T0203; if not, then not necessarily /ka/; F. Lounsbury, P. Mathews, B. Riese: /ka/; L. Schele, D. Stuart: /ka/, not "xok."

1991–2008 V. Bricker (1991:291): "cay" 'fish'; V. Bricker and H. Bricker (1992:fig. 2.8): "cay" 'fish'; Davoust (1995:599): "cay" 'poisson'; /ca/; Knorozov (1999, vol. 1:160): /caa, ca/ (pescado con aletas).

AC3

T 0327a
Z 0085a
K 0348

luk' / lok'?

intr v? leave, emerge?
Yu *luk'* lok' 'andar paso a paso' (Barrera Vásquez et al. 1980:458); luk' 'leave' (V. Bricker et al. 1998:174)
Ch' *lok'* lok' 'outward movement' (Attinasi 1973:289); loq'uel 'salir' (Aulie and Aulie 1998:66); *lok' 'go out' (Kaufman and Norman 1984:125)

1. Picture: snake? emerging from "yi" sign

1951–1980 Cordan (1964:49): "tzikix"? 'muy caliente'; Kelley (1976:122, 155, 332): glyger for mythical or cyclical snake; Knorozov (1967:102): "xit" (flower on a stalk).

1981–1990 Justeson (1984:336): two signs: J. Fox, J. Justeson: possibly two signs; a) depicts sprout, "sih" 'to sprout, be born'; F. Lounsbury: a) depicts sprout, "sih" 'to be born'; b) zoomorphized version of a) but not necessarily restricted to "sih"; P. Mathews: "emerging serpent"; with "split yax" in codices as 'birth'; L. Schele: part of Madrid birth glyph ("sih"); may = T0324 snake.

1991–2008 Davoust (1995:577): "lok" 'émerger'; Knorozov (1999, vol. 1:87): "xit' " (una flor?); Schele and Grube (1994:21f.): in association with "star war"; when emerging from T0017, reads "lok' " 'to abandon or escape' in time of war (credit also given to A. Lacadena); "lok' " 'to come out', 'to free' (Yucatec), 'to emerge', 'to come out' (Tzotzil and Chol), 'to free from danger'; Schele and Grube (1997:195): "lok' " 'his forcing out'; Schele et al. (1991): split-open object, perhaps a squash, with a /si/ sign emerging from it; "u sih" 'he was born' reading attributed to Lounsbury; Vail and Hernández (2005–2008): Ch'olan "lok'," Yucatec "luk'."

AC6

T 0764
Z 0743a
K 0295

kàan / chan

n snake
Yu *kàan* kan 'culebra' (Barrera Vásquez et al. 1980:291); kàan 'snake, worm' (V. Bricker et al. 1998:122)
Ch' *chan* *chan 'snake' (Kaufman and Norman 1984:117)

1. Picture: snake

1916–1950 Gates (1931:132): groups with T0790.

1951–1980 Knorozov (1967:99): (= K294) morphemic; Thompson (1962:376): Z743a = T0790 [29 examples] (bird head) perhaps should be treated as three glyphs (Z743, Z744, Z1363b).

1981–1990 Grube (1990a:119): = T0790.

1991–2008 Davoust (1995:605): classifies as T0790b; "och can" 'boa'; Schele and Grube (1997:194): "snake"; see also Wanyerka (1997:160f.).

AC6

T 0737
Z 0759
K 0410

kàan / chan

n snake

Used as a rebus for 'sky' in the Dresden Codex.

2. Picture: snake

1951–1980 Kelley (1976:121–23, 334): T0737 is at least three glyphs (naturalistic snake, headless snake, and larva); example illustrated is insect larva; Knorozov (1955:68): 047 (serpiente con signo complementario, cascabel). "cuc-chan" (sinónomo de "tzab-can"), 'serpiente de cascabel'; Knorozov (1967:104): "chan" 'snake'; Thompson (1962:316): [7 examples] (snakes and larvae).

1981–1990 Grube (1990a:116): einige = T0834; Justeson (1984:353): J. Justeson: possibly "luk"; depicts worm ("*luku:m") in hook ("luk") shape.

1991–2008 Davoust (1995:599): "can" 'serpent'; Knorozov (1999, vol. 1:157): "chan, can" (serpiente enroscada).

AC8

T —
Z —
K —

1. Picture: snake with "kab'an" sign markings

1991–2008 Vail and Hernández (n.d.): unique glyphic reference to serpent with "kab' " markings on Madrid 20a, frame 1. Similar serpent pictured on Madrid 66b has been identified as Sagittarius (V. Bricker 1997a:172); Vail (2009): may reference 'snake [stone] throne' set up at 4 Ahaw 8 Kumk'u era date mentioned on Quirigua Stela C.

ACD

T 0794
Z 0719
K 0384

n Mars

1. Picture: peccary? with upturned nose

1566–1915 Tozzer and Allen (1910:pl. 33): glyph representing a peccary's head.

1916–1950 Willson (1924:33): Mars.

1951–1980 Kelley (1976:120, 334): Mars beast; Knorozov (1967:103): morphemic; tapir?; Thompson (1962:378f.): [8 examples] almost certainly a symbol of meteorological conditions; Thompson (1972:109): lightning beast.

1981–1990 V. Bricker (1986:214): 'Mars Beast'; Justeson (1984:358): J. Fox: Mars monster, caiman with curled snout.

1991–2008 V. Bricker et al. (2006:663): Mars; Davoust (1995:605): "ayin" 'crocodile'; Knorozov (1999, vol. 1:154): "tz'ay" (cabeza de animal con trompa larga); Ringle and Smith-Stark (1996:350): so-called Mars beast in the codices. May be identical with T1021, the patron of Zip; Schele and Grube (1997:245): Mars?

ACN

T 0207
Z 0026
K 0057

ok / och; ó'och

intr v; n — enter; food

Yu *ok; ó'och* — 'ok 'enter, interfere, intrude' (V. Bricker et al. 1998:15); 'ó'och 'tortilla, food [noun specifier]; woof in weaving [cross-threads]' (V. Bricker et al. 1998:15)

Ch' *och* — ochel 'entrar' (Aulie and Aulie 1998:85); *och 'go/come in' (Kaufman and Norman 1984:127)

1. Picture: rattlesnake rattle

1566–1915 Brasseur de Bourbourg (1869–1870, vol. 1:219): "th'ilib" 'chaîne ou enchaînement'; Tozzer (1907:41) "tzab"; Tozzer and Allen (1910:pl. 9): rattles.

1951–1980 Cordan (1964:27): "tzap" cascabeles de cola del crótalo, 'malo; pernicioso'; Kelley (1962b:23): rattles of rattlesnake (D. Brinton, J. E. S. Thompson, Y. Knorozov, D. Kelley); "tzab" rattle of snake (D. Kelley); "cuc" (Y. Knorozov); Kelley (1976:122, 155, 332): rattles of rattlesnake; "tzab"?; Knorozov (1955:69): 051 (cascabel de la serpiente de cascabel) "cuc"; Knorozov (1967:82): "tzub" 'addition'.

1981–1990 V. Bricker and H. Bricker (1988:S7f.): rattles of a rattlensnake; "tzab" 'to gain, recover'; Justeson (1984:331): J. Fox: locative preposition, alternates with T0059; depicts snake's rattle; J. Justeson: possibly locative preposition; depicts snake's rattle; B. Riese: depicts snake's rattles.

1991–2008 Davoust (1995:568): "och" 'opossum, nourriture, entrée'; Grofe (2007:129f.): on Dresden 61 and 69 may represent subtraction; note "hoch" 'to remove; to untie; to empty; to pour' in Yucatec (Martínez Hernández 1929:392); Knorozov (1999, vol. 1:92, 233): "tzub; tzab" 'cascabel de serpiente; aumentar, sumar; más; sufijo clasificador de objectos sumados'; Milbrath (1999:259): 'Pleiades'; depicts rattlesnake's rattles; Ringle and Smith-Stark (1996:335–38): 0207 = 0207a; Schele (1991b:56): credits Stuart with "och" 'enter'; Schele and Grube (1997:195): "och" reading confirmed by /chi/ phonetic complement to several examples; Ch'olan "enter," may also be Yucatec "hoch" 'to paint, to copy writing'. In the glyphs the weak "h" is often not written so that "hoch" would be realized as "och." On some Dresden examples it appears between the number and the cycle sign, suggesting that they may be numeral classifiers; Stuart (1998:387f.): cites own correspondence, 1990: substitution spelling "o-chi" for "och" 'enter'; Vail (1996:221): logographic preposition with meaning similar to T0059 "ti"; Vail (2002b): Yucatecan "ok" in addition to Ch'olan "och" 'enter'; Vail and Hernández (2005–2008): 'enter', also used for Yucatecan "ó'och" 'tortilla, food'; von Nagy (1997:46f.): substitutes for T0059 and T0096 on M. 40a, 41a; perhaps "ti" 'in', 'at'.

ACP

T —
Z 0729
K 0391

Unique occurrence refers to snake or other reptile pictured on Madrid 28c, frame 3.

1. Picture: head of reptile

1566–1915 Thomas (1888:350): worm; Tozzer and Allen (1910:pl. 3): animal pictured in association with glyph is larva of "Acentrocneme kollari."

1951–1980 Kelley (1976:121): larva glyph; Knorozov (1967:103): "kan" 'snake' (snake head); Thompson (1962:316, 401): Z729 = T0737 [7 examples] (snakes and larvae).

1991–2008 Davoust (1995:610): = T0858b.

AL1

T –
Z 0725
K 0273

áak? / ahk?

n turtle
Yu *áak* ak 'tortuga' (Barrera Vásquez et al. 1980:4); 'áak 'turtle' (V. Bricker et al. 1998:2)
Ch' *ahk* *ahk 'turtle' (Kaufman and Norman 1984:115)

1. Picture: turtle

1566–1915 Bowditch (1910:255): "ac" 'turtle', representing the syllable /ka/ in the month name Kayab; Brinton (1895:120, 126): turtle or tortoise; /a/ of Landa's alphabet; Schellhas [1892] (1904:44): tortoise; Thomas (1888:348): "aac" or "ac" 'turtle'; Tozzer and Allen (1910:pl. 14): turtle.

1951–1980 Kelley (1962a:302): /a/; Kelley (1962b:23): turtle head (E. Seler, J. E. S. Thompson, G. Zimmermann, D. Kelley); early confused with macaw; /a/ (D. Kelley); "aac" 'turtle' (Y. Knorozov); Kelley (1976:121f.): (turtle head); 'turtle' on M. 17a; as /a/ in Landa's alphabet; Knorozov (1955:68): 045 (cabeza de tortuga) "aak"; Knorozov (1967:98): (turtle head); Old Yucatec "aak" 'turtle'; Thompson (1962:324–26; 401): Z725 = T0743 [85 examples] (turtle).

1981–1990 Grube (1990a:116): = T0743 = T0745.

1991–2008 Davoust (1995:600): "ahc" 'tortue'.

AL3

T 0626
Z –
K 0519

áak / ahk

n turtle
Yu *áak* ak 'tortuga' (Barrera Vásquez et al. 1980:4); 'áak 'turtle' (V. Bricker et al. 1998:2)
Ch' *ahk* *ahk 'turtle' (Kaufman and Norman 1984:115)

Not differentiated from AL5 by previous researchers (see Zender 2006 below). Many of the same references are listed for both graphemes. Paris example illustrated here has XQ1 "k'an" infixed.

1. Picture: turtle carapace

1951–1980 Kelley (1976:121f., 176, 333): (turtle shell); "coc," "mac"?; Thompson (1962:244): [31 examples] (turtle carapace) first identified by Beyer.

1981–1990 Justeson (1984:349): J. Fox: month name Mac; depicts turtle shell; not the name of Pauahtun; J. Justeson: "mak," including as month Mac and [J. Justeson, J. Fox] puberty rite, in forms lacking T0281 infix; possibly also "patan" 'tribute'; P. Mathews, B. Riese, L. Schele, D. Stuart: "mak" as month name Mac; also Pauahtun, usually written with T0064, "pawah," as phonetic complement; B. Riese: also /ak/.

1991–2008 Davoust (1995:591): "mac, ac" 'tortue'; "ahcul"; /ma/; Knorozov (1999, vol. 1:156): "aac" (caparazón de tortuga); Zender (2006): "ahk" 'turtle'; distinct from glyph in Mak, which represents "mahk" 'carapace, shell'.

AL5

T –
Z 0726
K 0070

mak / mäk

n — turtle carapace; cover

Yu *mak* — mak 'galápago o concha' (Barrera Vásquez et al. 1980:479); mak 'cover' (V. Bricker et al. 1998:177)

Ch' *mäk* — *mäk 'cover, close' (Kaufman and Norman 1984:125)

Not differentiated from AL3 (T0626) by previous researchers (see Zender 2006 below). Many of the same references are listed for both graphemes.

há'ab' period: Mak

1. Picture: turtle carapace

1566–1915 Landa [1566] (Tozzer 1941:162): in month glyph Mac.

1951–1980 Kelley (1962b:23): turtle shell (E. Seler, H. Beyer, G. Zimmermann, D. Kelley); "aac" 'turtle' (D. Kelley); "ac" 'bracelet'? (Y. Knorozov); Kelley (1976:72, 122, 176, 333): (turtle shell); "coc," "mac"?; Knorozov (1955:73): 103 (brazalete?) /ac/; Knorozov (1967:84): /ak/; Thompson (1962:244, 401): Z0726 = T0626 [31 examples] (turtle carapace) some examples may represent the month Mac; Thompson (1972:79): turtle carapace, refers to the Bacabs (with T0064).

1981–1990 V. Bricker (1986:212): (T0626) "mäc" 'cover' (Cholan); "mac" 'cover' (Yucatecan); Justeson (1984:349): (T0626) J. Fox: month name Mac; depicts turtle shell; not the name of Pauahtun; J. Justeson: "mak," including as month Mac and [J. Justeson, J. Fox] puberty rite, in forms lacking T0281 infix; possibly also "patan" 'tribute'; P. Mathews, B. Riese, L. Schele, D. Stuart: "mak" as month name Mac; also Pauahtun, usually written with T0064, "pawah," as phonetic complement; B. Riese: also /ak/.

1991–2008 Davoust (1995:591): (= T0626c) "mac, ac" 'tortue'; "ahcul"; /ma/; Ringle and Smith-Stark (1996:335–38): 0626 = variants without 0281 infix classified as 0933; Schele and Grube (1997:239): with T0063, "Pawahtun"; Zender (2006): "mahk" 'carapace'; distinct from Thompson's other variant of T0626, which is "ahk" 'turtle'.

AL6

T 0792v
Z 0721
K 0382

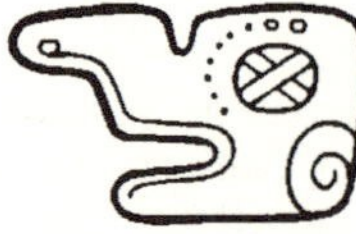

áayin / ahin?

n — alligator (caiman)?; crocodile?

Yu *áayin* — ain, ayin 'cocodrilo, caimán, lagarto' (Barrera Vásquez et al. 1980:4); 'áayin 'alligator' (V. Bricker et al. 1998:6)

Ch' *ahin* — *ahin 'alligator' (Kaufman and Norman 1984:115)

AL6 and AL7 may be variant forms of same grapheme.

1. Picture: crocodile?; alligator?

1566–1915 Rosny (1883:14): month Tzoz.

1951–1980 Kelley (1962b:31): god shown on D. 46a, Venus table (T. Barthel, D. Kelley); also on M. 71 (J. E. S. Thompson, D. Kelley); Knorozov (1967:103): morphemic (animal head); Thompson (1962:377): [5 examples].

1991–2008 Davoust (1997:175): "pawah ahin"; Schele and Grube (1997:142): "ain" 'crocodile'; Stuart (2005:64, n. 16): "ahin" value strongly indicated by syllabic substitution, /a-hi/, for Classic period variant of logograph.

AL7

T 0792a
Z 0720
K –

AL6 and AL7 may be variant forms of same grapheme.

1. Picture: animal with crossed bands in eye

1951–1980 Kelley (1962b:31): with T0064, god shown on Dresden 46a, Venus table (T. Barthel, D. Kelley), also on Madrid 71 (D. Kelley, J. E. S. Thompson); Thompson (1962:377): [5 examples].

1991–2008 Davoust (1995:605): "ayin" 'crocodile'; Knorozov (1999, vol. 1:153): "kax" (cabeza de animal); tiene el signo "kax" inscrito en el ojo.

AL7

T 0792b
Z 0720a
K 0383

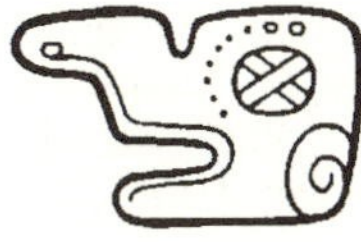

May be a distinct grapheme from subsort 1.

2. Picture: animal with crossed bands in eye

1951–1980 Knorozov (1967:103): "nich' " (animal head); Thompson (1962:377): [5 examples].

1991–2008 Davoust (1995:605): "ayin" 'crocodile'; Davoust (1997:203): "ahin" 'crocodile'; Knorozov (1999, vol. 1:153): "kax" (cabeza de animal); tiene el signo "kax" inscrito en el ojo.

AL9

T 0799
Z 0760
K 0407

hùuh / *huj*

n — iguana
Yu *hùuh* — huh 'iguana' (Barrera Vásquez et al. 1980:240); hùuh 'iguana' (V. Bricker et al. 1998:114)
Ch' *huj* — *huj 'iguana' (Kaufman and Norman 1984:120)

1. Picture: iguana offering

1566–1915 Brinton (1895:90, 122): iguana; Thomas (1888:357): "huh" 'food reptiles; iguana'; Tozzer and Allen (1910:12): iguana as offering.

1916–1950 Whorf (1942:487, fig. 2): "hu" 'iguana'.

1951–1980 Kelley (1962b:27): (with T0506) iguana offering; Kelley (1976:110): "hu" 'iguana'; Thompson (1962:380): [12 examples] (iguana); Knorozov (1967:104): "huh" 'iguana'.

1981–1990 Justeson (1984:358): L. Campbell, J. Fox, J. Justeson, P. Matthews, B. Riese: iguana; L. Schele: iguana offering.

1991–2008 V. Bricker and H. Bricker (1992:fig. 2.8): (with T0506) "huh-wah" 'iguana bread'; Davoust (1995:606): "huh" 'iguane'; Knorozov (1999, vol. 1:156): "huh"? (iguana); tiene el grafema 463 "h'a" inscrito.

ALA

T 0652
Z 0760v
K 0352

hùuh wàah / huj waj

n iguana bread

Yu *hùuh wàah* huh 'iguana' (Barrera Vásquez et al. 1980:240); hùuh 'iguana' (V. Bricker et al. 1998:114); wàah 'tortilla, bread' (V. Bricker et al. 1998:298)

Ch' *huj waj* *huj 'iguana' (Kaufman and Norman 1984:120); *waj 'tortilla; food' (Kaufman and Norman 1984:135)

Conflation of AL9 (T0799) and XH4 (T0506).

1. Picture: iguana tamale

1566–1915 Brasseur de Bourbourg (1869–1870, vol. 1:211): "ah-káan" 'le maître ou l'auteur de la terre, de l'argile soulevée, ou celui des sédiments poussés en haut, agrandis ou étendus'; Tozzer and Allen (1910:pl. 12): possibly iguana offering.

1916–1950 Gates (1931:14): "kan" 'corn'.

1951–1980 Kelley (1962b:27): iguana offering; Knorozov (1967:102, 104): (= K407) "huh" 'iguana'; Thompson (1962:256f.): [11 examples] offering; Thompson (1972:105): maize and copal offering?; Zimmermann (1956:Tafel 8): 'eidechse'.

1981–1990 Justeson (1984:349): L. Campbell: "hu/ho" based on "huh" 'iguana'; J. Fox, J. Justeson, P. Mathews: maize cakes with iguana; an offering; F. Lounsbury, B. Riese: iguana and maize offering; L. Schele: 'offering' from codices (maize).

1991–2008 V. Bricker (1991:290f.): "huh wah" 'iguana bread'; Davoust (1995:593): "ixim" 'maïs'; "huh wah" 'iguane et tortilla'; Knorozov (1999, vol. 1:156): "huh"? (iguana estilazada?).

ALB

T –
Z 0758v
K 0408

mak wàah / mäk waj

n turtle bread

Yu *mak wàah* mak 'galápago o concha' (Barrera Vásquez et al. 1980:479); mak 'cover' (V. Bricker et al. 1998:177); wàah 'tortilla, bread' (V. Bricker et al. 1998:298)

Ch' *mäk waj* *mäk 'cover, close' (Kaufman and Norman 1984:125); *waj 'tortilla; food' (Kaufman and Norman 1984:135)

1. Picture: tortoise tamale

1566–1915 Brinton (1895:90, 122): forequarter and head of a food-animal, tied up; Tozzer and Allen (1910:pl. 12): offering, possibly representing a lizard.

1916–1950 Gates (1931:17f.): one of several kinds of animal food, as distinct from 'bread'.

1951–1980 Knorozov (1967:104): morphemic (animal head); Thompson (1972:98): turtle? and maize dish; Zimmermann (1956:Tafel 8): 'fisch'.

1991–2008 V. Bricker (1991:291): "mac-wah" 'tortoise bread'; V. Bricker and H. Bricker (1992:fig. 2.8): "mac-wah" 'tortoise bread'; Schele and Grube (1997:220): "kay wah" 'fish tamale'.

ALC

T 0790
Z 0743
K 0294

tóolok / *t'olok?*

n basilisk lizard?
Yu *tóolok* tolok 'basilisco' (Barrera Vásquez et al. 1980:805); tóolok 'small lizard' (V. Bricker et al. 1998:280)
Ch' *t'olok* ah t'ólok 'crested lizard' (Knowles 1984:396)

1. Picture: lizard?, snake?

1566–1915 Tozzer and Allen (1910:pl. 18): head of black vulture.

1951–1980 Knorozov (1955:67): 028 (hocico con signo complementario) 101, "vay, vaay" 'familiar' (atributo pronóstico); Knorozov (1967:99): morphemic; Thompson (1962:376): [29 examples] (bird head) perhaps should be treated as three glyphs (Z743, Z744, Z1363b).

1991–2008 H. Bricker and V. Bricker (n.d.): "tolok" 'basilisk lizard'; constellation Cancer; V. Bricker et al. (2006:663): constellation Cancer; Davoust (1995:605): "och" 'opossum'; Davoust (1997:207): "ochcan" 'boa'; Knorozov (1999, vol. 1:158): "mo-zon"; combinación de 356.707; Schele and Grube (1997:173): "kan" 'snake'.

AM1

T 0533
Z 1320
K 0156

nik / *nich?*

n flower?
Yu *nik* nik 'flor' (Barrera Vásquez et al. 1980:569); nik 'flower' (V. Bricker et al. 1998:197)
Ch' *nich* *nich-im 'flower' (Kaufman and Norman 1984:127)

day 20: Ahaw/Ajwal

1. Picture: "ajaw" sign, monkey face?

1566–1915 Bollaert (1865–1866:52): "ahau" 'king; period of 24 years'; Brasseur de Bourbourg (1869–1870, vol. 1:208): day Ahau; "ah-au" 'canne du vase d'eau, le mâle dans le vase de la femelle'; Goodman (1897:16): day Ahau; Landa [1566] (Tozzer 1941:134): day Ajaw; Rosny (1878:52): "ahau" 'roi, chef'; Rosny (1883:10, 19): day Ahau; "ahau" 'roi, chef'; Schellhas [1892] (1904:22f.): in sign T0024.0533.0024 designating God D; Thomas (1893:262f.): "ahau" or /l/.

1916–1950 Gates (1931:52): "ahau" 'lord'; Whorf (1942:484, fig. 1): "haw; hw."

1951–1980 Kelley (1962a:296): "ahau" nominal, nombre de día; Kelley (1976:192, 333): "ahau" 'lord'; Knorozov (1955:72): 091 (cerbatana y dos bodoques) /la/; Knorozov (1967:92): /l(a)/; Thompson (1962:145–48): [254 examples] Ahau.

1981–1990 Justeson (1984:341): L. Campbell, J. Fox, J. Justeson, P. Mathews: "*a:ja:w" day Ahau; 'lord', day Ahau; 'owner'; F. Lounsbury, B. Riese, L. Schele, D. Stuart: "ahaw"; MacLeod (1987:455–58): /xa/ or /xV/ [one of her examples, on D. 9b, is actually AM6].

1991–2008 Davoust (1995:584): "ahau" '20e jour'; "nic" 'fleur'; Knorozov (1999, vol. 1:132, 236): /la/ 'cara; señor' (cara humana); MacLeod (personal communication, July 2008): some codical examples "mook" 'idol, effigy'; more generally "mook" 'maize', from Mixe-Zoque, based on the work of B. MacLeod and L. Lopes; Ringle and Smith-Stark (1996:335–38): 0533 = 0533a; Schele (1992b:217–20): correspondence from Grube n.d.: "nik" 'flower; child', substitution spelling "ni-chi" for "nich" on Tortuguero Monument 6; Schele and Grube (1997:84): "nik" 'flower'; with T0024 suffix, Itzamna's attributive "nikil" 'flowers'; Stuart (2005:25, n. 2): questions "nik" reading proposed by Grube (in Schele 1992b:217–20), since "nik/nich" 'flower' is already attested in script as T0646.

AM1

T 0533v
Z 1320
K 0157

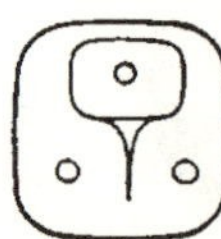

nik / nich?

n flower?

Graphically identical to AMB (T0534) /la/, but can be distinguished based on context.
day 20: Ahaw/Ajwal
2. Picture: inverted "ajaw" sign, monkey face?

AM6

T 0536
Z —
K 0310

xo

1. Picture: "ajaw" sign with decoration

1916–1950 Gates (1931:163): G399 [in part].

1951–1980 Knorozov (1967:100): /x(o)/; Thompson (1962:151): [7 examples] (decorated Ahau).

1981–1990 Stuart (1987:47): /xo/.

1991–2008 Davoust (1995:585): "xoh" 'vêtu, habillé'; /xo/; Knorozov (1999, vol. 1:133): /xo/?; Macri (2000b): /xo/ value may derive from corresponding Nahuatl day "xochitl" 'flower'.

AM7

T 0539
Z —
K 0467

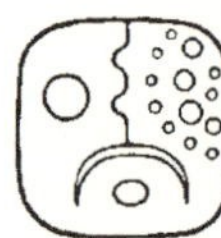

wáay / way

n spirit companion; co-essence

Yu *wáay* way 'ver visiones como entre sueños; tranfigurar por encantamiento; hechizar'; (ah) way 'brujo, nigromántico, encantador' (Barrera Vásquez et al. 1980:916); wáayt 'hex, cast a spell', h wáay 'ghost, spirit [male]' (V. Bricker et al. 1998:301)

Ch' *way* *way 'sleep' (Kaufman and Norman 1984:135)

Unique example of this sign on Dresden 47 may be an eroded AM1.
1. Picture: "ajaw" sign with jaguar pelt?

1916–1950 Spinden (1924:152): 'equinox'.

1951–1980 Thompson (1962:152f.): [27 examples] (half-spotted Ahau).

1981–1990 Houston and Stuart (1989): /wa/ and /ya/ complements suggest "way" 'co-essence; spirit companion'; = T0572; Justeson (1984:341): J. Justeson: compound of T0533 with T0609b jaguar pelt; possibly 'hidden lord'; F. Lounsbury, P. Mathews: "b'alam ahaw" 'hidden lord; jaguar lord'; L. Schele, D. Stuart: "b'alan, b'alam ahaw" 'hidden lord; jaguar lord'; MacLeod (1987): conflation of T0533 (/xa/ or /xV/) and the head of a jaguar (read "bal" by Grube in the Primary Standard Sequence), "xibal/xabal"; related to word "Xibalba" 'underworld'; Schele (1985a): "balam/balan-ahau" 'jaguar/hidden lord' in name glyph at Palenque.

1991–2008 Davoust (1995:585): "way" 'esprit compagnon'; Freidel et al. (1993:442f.): credit Grube and Houston and Stuart with "way"; Grube and Nahm (1994:686): "way" 'shaman, sorcerer, transformation, nagual, animal companion spirit'; Knorozov (1999, vol. 1:115, 236): "lam" 'sumergir, hundir; clavar; constelación'; Ringle and Smith-Stark (1996:348): 0539 = 0539a. 0539b has infixed T0585 in mouth and may represent "uaybi(l)" (Houston and Stuart 1989:11); Stuart (1998:399): "way" 'animal companion spirit; coessence' but also verbs 'sleep' and 'dream'. With the instrumental suffix "-ib," "way-ib" 'bed' or 'dormitory'.

AM7

T 0572
Z 1307
K 0171

wáay / way

n spirit companion; co-essence

2. Picture: jaguar pelt

1951–1980 Kelley (1962a:286): "uch" 'zarigueya'?; Kelley (1976:119, 333): in opossum glyger; Knorozov (1967:93): phonetic (spotted animal skin?); Thompson (1962:198): [5 examples]; Thompson (1972:92): "balam"?

1981–1990 V. Bricker (1986:212): "way" (Yucatecan); Houston and Stuart (1989): T0539 is 'co-essence', 'spirit companion', "way"; the equivalent codical form is T0572; cites Schele (1985a; 1988:298) "balan-ahau/balam ahau" 'hidden lord'; Justeson (1984:344): J. Fox: depicts Bacab opossum actor in codices; P. Mathews: possibly opossum; B. Riese: main sign of name of Mam animal (raccoon?) impersonator in New Year ceremonies.

1991–2008 Davoust (1995:587): "way" 'esprit compagnon'; Knorozov (1999, vol. 1:113): /yuu/ (manchas de piel de un animal); Love (1991:294f.): "wayeyab" 'Uayeb idol or statue', following Fox (personal communication to Love, 1985); Schele and Grube (1997:202): "way."

AMB

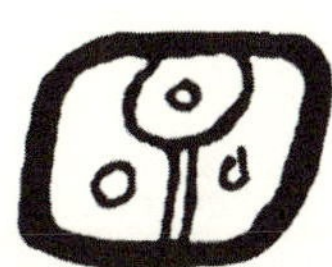

T 0534
Z 1320
K 0157

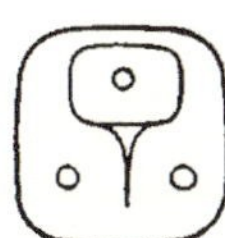

la

Graphically identical to subsort 2 of AM1.

1. Picture: inverted "ajaw" sign

1916–1950 Gates (1931:52): "ahau" 'lord'.

1951–1980 Kelley (1962a:290, 296): /la/; Kelley (1976:139, 181, 333): (= T0178; inverted "ahau"; possibly a tooth); /la/; Knorozov (1955:72): 091 (cerbatana y dos bodoques) /l(a)/; Knorozov (1967:92): (= K156) /l(a)/; Thompson (1962:149–50): [39 examples] (inverted Ahau) = T0178.

1981–1990 V. Bricker (1986:211): /la(h)/ "lah" 'end, die' (Yucatecan); Grube (1990a:106): = T0139; Justeson (1984:341): cf. T0178; L. Campbell, F. Lounsbury, P. Mathews, B. Riese, L. Schele, D. Stuart: /la/; J. Fox, J. Justeson: /la/; < "-al."

1991–2008 Davoust (1995:584): "lah" 'achèvement'; /la/; Knorozov (1999, vol. 1:132): /la/ (cara humana invertida); Ringle and Smith-Stark (1996:335–38): 0534 (retired) = 0178aM.

AMB

T 0140
Z 0063
K 0015

la

2. Picture: circles and dots

1566–1915 Schellhas [1892] (1904:10f.): suffix to name of God A, the death god; probably intended to represent blood.

1951–1980 Kelley (1976:201, 211): "-l(a)," "-lal(a)"; Knorozov (1955:76): 146 /?l/; Knorozov (1967:78): /el/.

1981–1990 V. Bricker (1986:210): /la/ "-al"?; Grube (1990a:93): = T0139; Justeson (1984:326): J. Fox, J. Justeson: "-Vl; -el"?; possibly distinct from T0178; F. Lounsbury: possibly = T0178; P. Mathews, B. Riese, L. Schele, D. Stuart: = T0178 /la/.

1991–2008 Davoust (1995:563): "lah" 'achevé'; /la/; Knorozov (1999, vol. 1:79): /el/; inscripción fonética /la-e-la/ > el; combinación decorativa simétrica 512.374.512; Ringle and Smith-Stark (1996:335–38): 0140 = 0178cv (left subfix); = 0142v (right subfix).

AMB

T 0534
Z 1320
K 0156

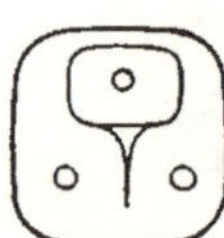

la

Variant form used occasionally in the Madrid Codex. Graphically similar to AM1 "nik/nich" 'flower'.
3. Picture: "ajaw" sign, monkey face?

AMC

T 1016c
Z 0131
K 0224

k'u

k'uh(ul) / ch'uh(ul)

n; adj — god; carved image; holy

Yu *k'uhul; k'uh* — k'uul 'cosa divina' (Barrera Vásquez et al. 1980:421); k'uh 'God; saint' (V. Bricker et al. 1998:158)

Ch' *ch'uhul; ch'uh* — ch'u:l 'sacred, holy' (Attinasi 1973:259f.); *ch'uh 'god, holy thing' (Kaufman and Norman 1984:119)

On Dresden 15a substitutes for 22B in spelling /k'u-tzu/ for "k'utz" 'tobacco'.

1. Picture: monkey? face

1566–1915 Brasseur de Bourbourg (1869–1870, vol. 1:203): "m, mo" 'l'oiseau ara; la vague sur l'eau; un mamelon soulève, montaigné'; "mu" 'la terre molle, fructifiante, génétrice'; Brinton (1895:57f., 122): god of the North Star; Förstemann [1894] (1904c:505f.): Ursa Minor; glyph symbolizes a monkey; Landa [1566] (Tozzer 1941:166): prefixed to month Cumhu; Schellhas [1892] (1904:19f.): God C; personifies a heavenly body of astronomic importance, probably the polar star; Thomas (1888:364f.): conventional representation of an idol, rather than a deity. Same head used to indicate carved idols; Thomas (1893:249, 256): /n/.

1916–1950 Gates (1931:101): god of the north; Thompson (1950:80): possibly "Ah Men" 'the wise one' or "Ah Chuen" 'the craftsman'.

1951–1980 Barthel (1952:94): /ku/, /ch'u/ based on Landa's use in glyph for Kumk'u; Knorozov (1967:96): phonetic (profile face infixed in K198).

1981–1990 Fox and Justeson (1986:14): possibly "k'oh"; Grube (1990a:130): Gott C; Justeson (1984:361): cf. T0041: J. Justeson: "k'oh"? 'scion', 'mask'; God C; not 'blood'; P. Mathews: head variant of "water group"; personification of blood; B. Riese: sometimes nominal marker for deity names; Ringle (1988): Yucatec "k'u," Cholan "ch'u" 'god; sacred, holy; idol; temple; pyramid; cedar', a supernatural marker in the codices and a specific title for deities; in codical scenes showing the carving of masks; occasionally substitutes in compounds for /k'o/ or /ch'o/; Schele (1989c:36–38): credits Stuart, Carlson, and Ringle with simultaneous reading /k'u/, "k'ul"; Stuart (1984): personified blood.

1991–2008 Davoust (1995:613): "ch'ul/kul" 'divin, âme', /ch'u/, /ku/; Knorozov (1999, vol. 1:188): "ngom" (perfil masculino); Milbrath (1999:225f.): astronomical deity; may represent male howler monkey; Stuart, Houston, and Robertson (1999:42): "kuh" 'god'; "k'uhul" 'holy'; Taube (1992:27): God C, "ku/ch'u" 'sacredness, divinity'; misidentified as 'north' based on its reputed presence in the sign for north. In the Dresden Codex, the most carefully painted of the Maya manuscripts, the God C glyph never serves as the main sign for 'north'.

AMC

T 0041
Z 0131
K –

k'uh(ul) / ch'uh(ul)

n; adj god; carved image; holy

2. Picture: monkey? face with "water group"

1566–1915 Brasseur de Bourbourg (1869–1870, vol. 1:204): "x (ch)" 'couler'; "xe" 'vomir'; "xo" 'siffler la vapeur'; Schellhas [1892] (1904:19f.): God C; personifies a heavenly body of astronomic importance, probably the polar star.

1916–1950 Gates (1931:101): god of the north; Thompson (1950:80): possibly "Ah Men" 'the wise one' or "Ah Chuen" 'the craftsman'.

1951–1980 Kelley (1962b:29): God C "Xaman Ek" 'north star' (D. Brinton, P. Schellhas, E. Förstemann, S. Morley, D. Kelley); Kelley (1976:64): God C; Pahl (1976:35–41): in relationship glyphs at Palenque, possibly "older brother, son," when used with T0041 affix.

1981–1990 Grube (1990a:88): = T1016[0032]; Justeson (1984:319): J. Fox, J. Justeson: = T1016[0032] possibly head variant of T0032, possibly comparable to T0036–T0038; J. Justeson: not 'blood'; F. Lounsbury, P. Mathews, L. Schele, D. Stuart: head variant of T0032; P. Mathews: personification of 'blood'; "water group"; P. Mathews: "yum"?; L. Schele: 'blood', possibly "ch'ich' " or "itz"; D. Stuart: 'blood'; Schele (1985b:144): God C blood glyph.

1991–2008 Davoust (1995:556): "ch'ul" 'divin'; /ch'u/; Houston and Stuart (1996:292f.): "k'u(l)" or "ch'u(l)" 'god, sacred entity; sacred'; Knorozov (1999, vol. 1:95): /xa-gnom/; combinación de 202.958; Ringle and Smith-Stark (1996:335–38): 0041 (retired) = 0036f; Stuart and Houston (1994:5, 7): "k'ul" (Yucatec) 'divine', 'holy' or "k'u" (Yucatec) 'god'; Ch'olan cognates = "ch'ul" and "ch'u"; Vail (1996:205–12): "ah ku(l)" 'priest' or "ku" 'god'; "ah ku(l)" reading based on fact that "death eye" occurs in "ah" agentive prefix T0015.

AMC

T 0014
Z 0012
K 0042

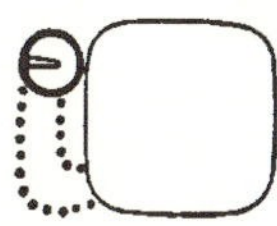

k'uh(ul) / ch'uh(ul)

n; adj god; carved image; holy

3. Picture: arc of droplets with maize kernel

1951–1980 Kelley (1976:214f., 218, 331): water-group prefix; "qiqel" 'blood, relatives'; Knorozov (1955:74): 125 (líquido que se derrama de una vasija) /x(e)/; Knorozov (1967:80): /p(u)/? (liquid pouring out of a vessel).

1981–1990 Grube (1990a:87): = T0032; Justeson (1984:317): J. Fox, J. Justeson, F. Lounsbury, P. Mathews, L. Schele, D. Stuart: codex variant of "water group" (see T0032–41); J. Fox, J. Justeson: /yo/, /yu/; Ringle (1988:11): /k'u/, /ch'u/, designating a person or place as revered, holy, or sacred; Taube (1989a:36–37): upper element (notched ball) is identified with maize; in addition to 'tamale' and 'tortilla', "wah" refers to 'sustenance' and to life itself.

1991–2008 Davoust (1995:554): "kul" 'divin'; /ku/; Davoust (1997:115): "ah" agentive; Knorozov (1999, vol. 1:94): (gotas de líquido brincando); Ringle and Smith-Stark (1996:335–38): 0014 (retired) = 0036l; Stuart and Houston (1994:5, 7): water group sign = "k'ul" (Yucatec) 'divine', 'holy' or "k'u" (Yucatec) 'god'; Ch'olan cognates = "ch'ul" and "ch'u"; Vail (1996:205, 228): may be "ah" or semantic determinative to "ku" glyph. Former interpretation suggested by fact that upper element acts as the agentive prefix "ah" in other contexts (i.e., T0015).

AME

T —
Z 0142
K 0220

màax / max

n spider monkey

Yu *màax* ma'ax 'una especie de monos, micos o simios' (Barrera Vásquez et al. 1980:511); h màax 'spider monkey' (V. Bricker et al. 1998:181); ma'ax 'spider monkey' (Hofling with Tesucún 1997:184)

Ch' *max* *max 'spider monkey' (Kaufman and Norman 1984:125)

Originally cited in literature as T0755.

1. Picture: spider monkey

1951–1980 Kelley (1976:117): "maax"? 'monkey'; Knorozov (1967:96): morphemic (face variant of K151); Thompson (1962:341, 401): Z0142 = T0755 [31 examples] 'monkey'; Thompson (1972:56): 'spider monkey', homonym for 'inflammation, particularly of the gums'.

1981–1990 Fox and Justeson (1984:31): example on Dresden 17b identified by Seler (1902-1923, 1:457–58) and Thompson (1972:55) as head of spider monkey (Yucatec "má'x"); Justeson (1984:355): (T0755) J. Fox, J. Justeson, P. Mathews, B. Riese: 'monkey'.

1991–2008 Davoust (1995:601): (= T0755c) "maax" 'singe-araignée'; /ma/; Schele and Grube (1997:122): with T0074, "max" 'monkey'.

AMK

T —
Z 0141
K 0253

k'ìin / k'in

n day, sun

Yu *k'ìin* k'in 'día, sol' (Barrera Vásquez et al. 1980:400); k'ìin 'day, sun' (V. Bricker et al. 1998:152)

Ch' *k'in* *k'in 'sun, day' (Kaufman and Norman 1984:124)

1. Picture: spider monkey with "k'in" sign

1916–1950 Gates (1931:68): "kin" 'sun, day'.

1951–1980 Knorozov (1967:93, 97): (= K172) "k'ing/k'in" 'sun'; Thompson (1962:341, 401): Z141 = T0755 [31 examples] 'monkey'.

1991–2008 Davoust (1995:601): (= T0755b) "kin" 'soleil'; Milbrath (1999:94): "As Kin substitutes, monkeys may signal a count of nights"; Schele and Grube (1997:195): substitutes for "ah mi k'in" on D. 61a; may read "ah Ma K'in."

AML

T —
Z 0117
K 0207

1. Picture: monkey? with headband

1951–1980 Knorozov (1967:92, 95): (= K156); /l(a)/; Thompson (1962:400): Z117 = T1014.

1981–1990 Grube (1990a:129): "ahau."

1991–2008 Davoust (1997:189): "ahaw" 'lord'; Schele and Grube (1997:148): "ahaw" 'king'.

AMM

T 1053b
Z 0132
K –

n death god

Conflation of AMC "k'uh/ch'uh" and SCC "kìim/chäm."

1. Picture: monkey? face with closed eye

1916–1950 Gates (1931:100): "cimi" 'death'.

1991–2008 Davoust (1995:617): "kul" 'divinité, âme'; /ku/; Knorozov (1999, vol. 1:188): "ngom" (perfil masculino); Vail (1996:210): occasionally substitutes for T1016c in contexts referring to the death god A; Vail (2002b): "kimil k'uh" 'death god'.

AP1

T 0801
Z 0709
K 0388

pèek'?; tzul?; tz'i'?

n dog

Yu *pèek', tzul* pèek' 'dog' (V. Bricker et al. 1998:213); tzul 'perro' (Barrera Vásquez et al. 1980:867)

Ch' *tz'i'* *tz'i' 'dog' (Kaufman and Norman 1984:134)

1. Picture: dog

1566–1915 Rosny (1883:20): "ekxuc" 'chat tigré'; Tozzer and Allen (1910:pl. 37): dog.

1951–1980 Kelley (1962b:23): dog (A. Tozzer and G. Allen, E. Seler, G. Zimmermann, D. Kelley); Kelley (1976:117): dog; Knorozov (1967:98, 103): (= K276) "nich' " 'toothy'; cites Zimmermann (1953:pl. 8): dog; Thompson (1962:381): [4 examples] (black-spotted dog); Zimmermann (1956:65): dog from M. 91d.

1981–1990 Justeson (1984:358): J. Fox, P. Mathews: dog.

1991–2008 Davoust (1995:606): "tzul" 'chien'; Knorozov (1999, vol. 1:154): "pek" (cabeza de perro); tiene el signo "il" inscrito.

AP5

T 0765ab
Z 0707
K 0243

òok / ok; ok / och?

intr v?; n — foot, footsteps; enter?

Yu *òok; ok* — ok 'pie del hombre o animal', 'las pisadas' (Barrera Vásquez et al. 1980:594); òok 'foot' (V. Bricker et al. 1998:16); ok 'enter, interfere, intrude' (V. Bricker et al. 1998:15); ok 'entrar' [e.g. ok ha' 'bautizar'] (Barrera Vásquez et al. 1980:595)

Ch' *ok; och* — *ok 'foot' (Kaufman and Norman 1984:127); ochel 'entrar' (Aulie and Aulie 1998:85); *och 'go/come in' (Kaufman and Norman 1984:127)

Occasionally appears where APB /ch'o/ is expected.

day 10: Ok/Ok; há'ab' period: Xul/Chichin

1. Picture: opossum

1566–1915 Goodman (1897:16): day Oc; Rosny (1883:6): day Oc; Thomas (1893:250): "xul" 'close, end'; Tozzer and Allen (1910:pl. 36): day Oc.

1916–1950 Gates (1931:31): "oc" 'dog'.

1951–1980 Knorozov (1955:67): 032 (hocico de animal, boca con vibridos, ojo redondo, orejas, pelo) "oc"; Knorozov (1967:97): phonetic (animal head); Thompson (1962:366f.): [80 examples] (black spotted dog); Thompson (1972:38, 82): 'dog'; with T0102 probably "ok" 'enter'.

1981–1990 V. Bricker (1986:214): /oc/ "oc" 'enter' (Yucatecan); Grube and Stuart (1987:4f.): /ko/ complement and substitution confirm Schele's decipherment as "ok"; Justeson (1984:357): cf. T0567; J. Fox, P. Mathews: equivalent to T0567; J. Justeson, F. Lounsbury: day Oc, and other "ok" morphemes, including 'to enter'; T0765 does not include all the functions of T0567; B. Riese: day Oc and "ok"; L. Schele, D. Stuart: "ok," "och"; day Oc; 'to enter'; Schele and J. Miller (1983:4): in "childhood rite" clause; a verb "oc" 'to enter/to become'.

1991–2008 Davoust (1995:603): "oc" '10e jour'; /ch'o/; Knorozov (1999, vol. 1:152): "och, oc" (cabeza de zarigüeya); en el nombre de la deidad Bolon Yocte; Stuart (1998:394): "ok" 'leg, foot' and not "och" 'enter'; Vail and Hernández (2005–2008): primary usage seems to be 'footsteps' in expression 'his footsteps stopped'.

AP5

T 0567
Z 1330
K 0150

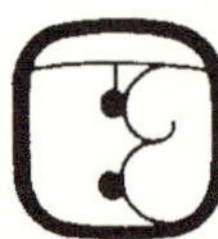

Graphically similar to upper element of YG4 "wi'il/wé'el."

day 10: Ok/Ok

2. Picture: opossum ear

1566–1915 Bollaert (1865–1866:52): "oc" 'leg'; Brasseur de Bourbourg (1869–1870, vol. 1:206): day Oc; "oc" 'pied, jambe, entrée, entrer'; Rosny (1883:6): day Oc; Thomas (1893:261): "oc"; Tozzer and Allen (1910:pl. 36): day Oc.

1916–1950 Gates (1931:58): "oc" variant; Thompson (1950:268f.): "och" 'sustenance'.

1951–1980 Knorozov (1955:68): 050 (orejas de animal) /oc/; Knorozov (1967:91): "xik" (animal ears); Thompson (1962:191): [102 examples] 'good tidings'.

1981–1990 V. Bricker (1986:212): "oc"; Justeson (1984:344): J. Fox, J. Justeson, P. Mathews, B. Riese: dog, day Oc (= Dog) and other "ok" morphemes, including "ok" (pCT "*och") 'to enter'; F. Lounsbury: day Oc; "ok" 'to enter'; L. Schele, D. Stuart: day Oc.

1991–2008 Davoust (1995:587): "oc" '10e jour; entrée'; Knorozov (1999, vol. 1:139): "xic" (oreja de animal); Love (1991:297f.): polyvalent "ok/och"; suggests "och" reading in TIII.0567:0130 "ox och wah" 'abundance of provisions'.

AP6

T —
Z 0744
K 0293

òoch / uch?

n — opossum

Yu *òoch* — och 'zorro; tacuacín' (Barrera Vásquez et al. 1980:593); òoch 'fox, weasel' (V. Bricker et al. 1998:15); och 'opossum' (Hofling with Tesucún 1997:482)

Ch' *uch* — *uch '(o)possum' (Kaufman and Norman 1984:135)

1. Picture: opossum

1951–1980 Knorozov (1955:67): 029 (hocico con dos signos complementarios "vay" and "ah") "vayah" 'hormiga'; Knorozov (1967:99): morphemic; Thompson (1962:376, 401): Z744 = T0790 [29 examples] (bird head) perhaps should be treated as three glyphs (Z743, Z744, Z1363b); Thompson (1972:76): Bacab opossum.

1981–1990 Taube (1989b:355–57): opossum wearing God N (Pawahtun) headdress, suggesting that the opossum was an aspect of God N.

1991–2008 H. Bricker and V. Bricker (n.d.): head variant of "tun"; Davoust (1995:605): (= T0790c) "pawah och."

AP7

T 0759
Z 0706
K 0242

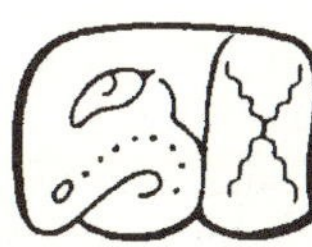

pe

Has undetermined logographic value in addition to /pe/.

1. Picture: rabbit?

1566–1915 Brasseur de Bourbourg (1869–1870, vol. 1:203): "p, pe" 'venir, marcher' ant. "pa" 'ouvrir'; Landa [1566] (Tozzer 1941:170): <p>.

1951–1980 Knorozov (1955:67): 037 (hocico de animal, boca con vibridos, ojo de fiera con signo complementario "toc") "tzie"?; Knorozov (1967:96): "tzik"; Thompson (1962:360–61): [70 examples] ("jog" with Etz'nab); Thompson (1972:97): agouti or hairless dog?

1981–1990 V. Bricker (1986:214): /pe/, "pek" 'dog'; Justeson (1984:356): L. Campbell: "t'ul" 'rabbit'; Etz'nab infix = /t'o/, /t'u/ phonetic complement (cf. Yucatec "t'oh" 'to work stone'); J. Fox, J. Justeson: "tz'ik" 'to write, (re)count' with divinatory use; depicts rabbit, value perhaps related to rabbit/scribe association; infix may indicate /t'o/, /t'u/ as complement securing "t'ul/t'uhl" identification; only sign we accept as depicting a rabbit; B. Riese: rabbit, possibly "t'ul"; L. Schele: "t'ul" rabbit; Schele and J. Miller (1983:23–60): post–600 C.E. addition as logograph 'rabbit', due to ambiguous readings of T0757/0758.

1991–2008 Davoust (1995:602): "t'uhl" 'lapin'; "loh" 'jumeau'; "lot" 'compagnon'; /lo/; Davoust (1997:102, 113, 179): /pe/, "pe' " 'apporter'; "t'ul/pek" 'lapin/chien'; Grofe (2007:124f.): with T0063 "Pawahtun" prefix on Dresden 61 and 69 may represent the full moon in the east (at sunset) on the vernal equinox; Knorozov (1999, vol. 1:152): "tzic" (cabeza de animal nocturno); tiene el signo "hetz" inscrito; Schele and Grube (1997:96): Landa's /pe/; Schele, Grube, and Martin (1998:17): /pe/; Stuart and Houston (1994:37): perhaps "t'ul" 'rabbit'; Stuart, Houston, and Robertson (1999:56): "chit."

AP8

T 0789
Z 0741
K 0292

1. Picture: animal head with "etz'nab' " sign on ear

1566–1915 Thomas (1893:264): "chaac" or "chac" 'tempest; tornado'.

1916–1950 Gates (1931:132): groups with T0766.

1951–1980 Kelley (1962b:31): Venus table god; Knorozov (1967:99): (= K291) morphemic; Thompson (1962:376): [2 examples] occurs with the Venus directional gods; Thompson (1972:67): a bird?

1991–2008 Knorozov (1999, vol. 1:153): "tzic" (cabeza de animal nocturno); Schele and Grube (1997:146): 'vulture'?

AP9

T 0757
Z 0708
K 0246

b'a

1. Picture: gopher?; kinkajou? with "ak'b'al" and "k'än" signs

1566–1915 Tozzer and Allen (1910:pl. 35): identify example from Copán Stela 4 as probably a jaguar head.

1916–1950 Gates (1931:31): "xul" 'sixth month'.

1951–1980 Dütting (1979:186): "bah" 'pocket gopher', suggests extending the reading to include the value "wah" 'bread, tortilla'; "bah" 'first one'; Kelley (1976:118, 185, 223, 224, 230, 334): allograph of T0558; = T0788; 'rodent', /ba/?; Knorozov (1955:67): 034 (hocico de animal con signos complementarios) "tzocol" ("xocol"?); Knorozov (1967:97): /b(a)/? (combination of K245-122); Proskouriakoff (1968:249): a rodent; substitutes for T0501; occurs in wide range of contexts, almost always at the beginning of a passage, and often in direct association with individual figures, must stand for widely applicable expression; Thompson (1962:350–54): [185 examples] ("jog" with T0281 infixed) may be dog, but named "jog" in deference to Tozzer and Allen's (1910:pl. 35, no. 6) jaguar identification; Thompson (1972:34): "chibal" 'affliction' (literally 'biting').

1981–1990 V. Bricker (1986:213f.): /ba(h)/ "bah" 'go' (Tzeltal); 'perforate' (Cholan, Yucatecan); /bä/, "bä" 'self' (Cholan); /ba/, "ba" 'self' (Yucatecan); Fahsen (1990): variant of T0757/0758 'to record', different from 'to write'; Grube (1990a:117): = T0788; Josserand et al. (1985): with T0001 affixed, verbal glyph in association with period endings; Justeson (1984:356): B. Riese: signs improperly divided; probably an unmarked animal head T0757 plus special infixes (T0281, T0110, T0526) differentiating them; L. Campbell, J. Fox, J. Justeson: /b'a/; morphemes approximating "b'ah"; depicts gopher ("*b'a:h"), never 'rabbit' or derived values; J. Justeson: also morphemes approximating "mul," including day Muluc; P. Mathews, D. Stuart: /b'a/; B. Riese: /b'a/ and /mul/ at least in one context in Copán; L. Schele: depicts rabbit; "umul" with T0001 or equivalent prefix; "umulih," "t'ulah"? 'to follow'; "mul, mal," /ma/, /b'a/ without T0001 or equivalent prefix; T0001.0757 also functions as a general and an auxiliary verb, probably "mal/ man"; Macri (1988): "ak'b'al maax" 'kinkajou' used for "ak' ba" 'to offer oneself'; Schele (1990a): credits Macri with reading of T0001.0757 as "u ba" 'the first' in T0606 "child of mother" relationship context; functions as "ba" 'first' in many contexts; Schele and J. Miller (1983:23–60): T0713/0757 "umul" 'rabbit'; Stuart (1987:46): /ba/.

1991–2008 V. Bricker (1991:286f.): /ba/; Davoust (1995:601): "bah" 'taupe', /ba/; Houston and Stuart (1998): "b'a(h)" 'self; head; face; person'; Knorozov (1999, vol. 1:153): "xul" (cabeza de animal con la lengua de fuera); Macri (2000a, 2001): substitutes for the day Muluk, probably acrophonically as /u/ derived from "*uyox" 'kinkajou' in proto-Tzeltalan; Stuart (1996:160, 162): in "bah" expression 'body; self'.

AP9

T 0791b
Z 0708
K –

b'a

Some evidence of conflation with APA /u/.

2. Picture: gopher?; kinkajou? with "ak'b'al" sign on head

1566–1915 Brasseur de Bourbourg (1869–1870, vol. 1:203): "p, pe" 'venir, marcher', ant. "pa" 'ouvrir'.

1916–1950 Gates (1931:31): "xul" 'sixth month'.

1951–1980 Thompson (1962:377): [7 examples] may represent a bird.

1981–1990 Justeson (1984:358): cf. T0758b; J. Fox, J. Justeson, P. Mathews: /b'a/ as codical variant of T0758a, b; B. Riese: "ikim" 'horned owl'; not /b'a/.

1991–2008 Davoust (1995:605): "ch'om" 'vautour royal'; Knorozov (1999, vol. 1:155): "zotz' " (cabeza de murciélago); Ringle and Smith-Stark (1996:350): possibly a generic word for 'animal'; Vail (1996:317): /ba/; Madrid Codex variant that substitutes for T0757 /ba/ in expression with T0234 prefix in Dresden Codex.

APA

T –
Z 0730
K 0380

u

u-

dep pn — he/she/it; his/her/its; third person prefix, Set A (ergative and possessive)

1. Picture: gopher?; kinkajou? with "ak'b'al" sign on head

1951–1980 Knorozov (1967:103): determinative (bird); Thompson (1962:377, 401): Z730 = T0791 [7 examples] may represent a bird.

1991–2008 Davoust (1995:605): = T0791b', "ch'om" 'vautour royal'; Davoust (1997:163): "u"?

APB

T 0758a
Z 0707
K 0245

ch'o

há'ab' period: Xul/Chichin
1. Picture: rodent with "ak'b'al" sign on head

1566–1915 Landa [1566] (Tozzer 1941:157): month Xul; Rosny (1883:14): month Xul.

1916–1950 Gates (1931:31): "xul" 'sixth month'.

1951–1980 Dütting (1974:50): "uay, pay" 'sorcery, call for, etc.'; T0758:0110 is "uay-tan" 'sorcerer, witch'; Knorozov (1955:67): 033 (hocico de animal con signo complementario) "tzoc" ("xoc"?); Knorozov (1967:97): /b(o)/; Thompson (1962:355–59): [201 examples] Xul; Thompson (1972:100): 'afflict'.

1981–1990 Grube (1990a:117): = T0758b (0110); Houston (1988:132, 134): /ch'o/, also cites Grube with independent decipherment of /ch'o/; Justeson (1984:356): B. Riese: signs improperly divided; probably an unmarked animal head T0757 plus special infixes (T0281, T0110, T0526); L. Campbell: never 'rabbit'; possibly /tz'u/, "tz'utz' " 'anteater'; J. Fox: T0110, often infixed to ear or suffixed, depicts agouti markings; J. Fox, J. Justeson: logographic, including month Xul; depicts agouti, never rabbit; J. Justeson: logographic, possibly for morphemes approximately "hal"; never 'rabbit'; J. Justeson: also possibly for morphemes approximately "tz(')ik" or "tz'u"; P. Mathews: month Xul; also other values; L. Schele: "chich"; T0758 became not only a phonetic sign, but a general sign for animals to which semantic determinatives were added to indicate specific species; the animal word "chikop" may relate to the "chich" rabbit; possibly "toh/tah"; month Xul; Schele (1989b:3): credits Grube with /ch'o/. Substitutes for T0093 in 'fire-drilling' glyph; Schele and J. Miller (1983:23–60): "ich, ichich, chich"?, based on substitution for T0287, "ich" 'eye'. May function as blank glyph for animal to which distinguishing features may be added; Stuart (1987:46): /ch'o/?

1991–2008 Davoust (1995:602): "bah" 'taupe'; "ch'oh" 'rat'; "xul" '6e mois'; /b'a/, /ch'o/; Dütting (1991:280): credits Grube and Houston with /ch'o/; Grube and Nahm (1994:699f.): may function as "ch'o" 'rat'; Knorozov (1999, vol. 1:152): "och-ut"; ligadura de 666-316; Ringle and Smith-Stark (1996:335–38): 0758a = 0758[0110].

APB

T —
Z 0707
K 0244

ch'o

May have second value of /hi/ (see references).
2. Picture: small rodent

1916–1950 Gates (1931:31): sixth month, Xul.

1951–1980 Knorozov (1967:97): (= K245) /b(o)/.

1991–2008 Davoust (1997:157, 159): /ch'o/, /hi/; Schele and Grube (1997:133, 136): /ch'o/, /hi/. "The animal head [on D. 22b] appears to be the same /ch'o/ head that appears in the 'drill' glyph on page 5b. However, "ch'oh" does not appear in any of the Yukatek dictionaries as a verb. We looked up the other possible phonetic values for heads like this—/hi/—and found that "hi' " means to 'pull out or harvest (estregar) maize'. Since the gods are holding maize [on D. 22b], we thought this interpretation a good possibility."

APJ

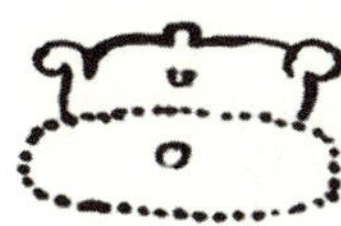

T 0159
Z 0052, 1301
K 0346–47

Upper element never occurs on its own as illustrated in Thompson's examples of T0159.

1. Picture: peccary haunch

1566–1915 Brasseur de Bourbourg (1869–1870, vol. 1:203): "o" 'cercle, vase, collier, pour "u" '; Brinton (1895:94): musical instrument.

1951–1980 Cordan (1964:40): "*tam" 'cántaro; adentro, abajo, profundo'; Kelley (1962b:31): with TVII prefix, Venus table god; peccary (Y. Knorozov, D. Kelley); macaw (E. Seler, G. Zimmermann); Pleiades (J. E. S. Thompson); Kelley (1976:120): 'peccary'; Knorozov (1955:72): 097 (brazalete con signo complementario) "keh" 'puerco montés'; Knorozov (1967:101): "k'en"; compare to Old Yucatec "ken" 'ornament'; Thompson (1972:56): The compound TVII.0159:0582 "appears twice among the deities, probable constellations, in the Venus table (p. 50) and twice in hunting scenes in Madrid (41b, 91a) in the latter case above an armadillo in a trap. I know of no constellation named after the armadillo, but can this compound possibly represent the Pleiades, whom the Maya regarded as a cluster of seven stars? The number seven is present, 582 is reminiscent of Mol which means congregrated. "Mots," the Quiche name for that constellation, signifies mass."

1981–1990 Justeson (1984:328): J. Fox, J. Justeson: this element is mistakenly disassociated from another (resembling T0582) by Thompson, the two elements forming a unitary sign rather than a sign compound; the full sign is a name of a god associated with brocket deer and having astronomical significance.

1991–2008 Ciaramella (2004:11-13): "lom" 'throw [of spear or dart and similar things]'; also used in sense of "lomtah" 'trap for catching deer' and as verb referring to trussing/wrapping (as on M. 70a and M. 102a); Davoust (1995:565): "lol" 'fleur'; Knorozov (1999, vol. 1:178): "cen, cem, chin" (brazalete, adorno); Schele and Grube (1997:128): with TVII prefix, occurs with a peccary (M. 93a), an armadillo (M. 91a), and a deer (M. 41b); Vail (1996:292f.): with T0582 may have signified 'the captured one' or 'the dead one'.

APK

T –
Z –
K 0283

ib'ach?; wèech / wech?

n armadillo

Yu *ib'ach; wèech* ibach 'armadillo' (Barrera Vásquez et al. 1980:261); h wèech 'armadillo; small pig' (V. Bricker et al. 1998:301)

Ch' *ib'ach; wech* *ib'-ach 'armadillo' (Kaufman and Norman 1984:120); wech 'armadillo' (Aulie and Aulie 1998:139)

1. Picture: armadillo

1566–1915 Rosny (1883:20): 'armadille'? (attributed to Thomas); Thomas (1882:145, 158): armadillo; Thomas (1888:348): "uech" 'armadillo'.

1951–1980 Kelley (1976:117): armadillo; Knorozov (1967:99): "vech" 'armadillo'; Taack (1973:128): "vech" 'armadillo'.

APL

T 0791a
Z 0732
K 0378

xu

1. Picture: bat with "ak'b'al" sign on head

1566–1915 Brasseur de Bourbourg (1869–1870, vol. 1:209): variant of month Sotz'; Rosny (1883:14): month Tzoz; Thomas (1888:357): "ch'om, xchom, hch'om" 'vulture'.

1951–1980 Knorozov (1955:68): (cabeza de murciélago? con el signo complementario 120, 90) "tzom; ch'om"; Knorozov (1967:103): composite grapheme K377-101; Thompson (1962:377): [7 examples] (upturned snout) may represent a bird; Thompson (1972:56): "ch'om" 'king vulture'; homonym for 'pockmarks'.

1981–1990 Justeson (1984:358): T0791a: cf. T0791b; B. Riese: "ikim" 'horned owl'; not /b'a/.

1991–2008 Davoust (1995:605): /xu/; Knorozov (1999, vol. 1:155): "zotz' " (cabeza de murciélago); contiene un grafema inscrito; Ringle and Smith-Stark (1996:350): possibly a generic word for 'animal'; Schele and Grube (1997:17): /xu/; Schele and Grube (1997:122): with T0047 prefix, "yaxun" 'cotinga'.

APL

T 0791c
Z 0733
K –

xu

yaxum, yaxun?

n? blue-green bird; cotinga?

Yu *yaxum, yaxun* ya'x 'verde' + -um 'ave, clasificador; es un sufijo de los nombres de pájaros' (Barrera Vásquez et al. 1980:900, 971)

2. Picture: bat with "ak'b'al" sign on head

1951–1980 Thompson (1962:377): [7 examples] (upturned snout) may represent a bird.

1991–2008 Knorozov (1999, vol. 1:155): "zotz' " (cabeza de murciélago); Ringle and Smith-Stark (1996:350): possibly a generic word for 'animal'; Vail (2002b): example from Madrid 94c appears to be an abbreviated spelling of "ya-xu-na" on Dresden 17b.

APM

T 0756ab
Z 0722
K 0377

há'ab' period: Sotz'/Sutz'

1. Picture: bat with "ak'b'al" sign infix

1566–1915 Brinton (1895:117): 'bat' for month Zodz; Landa [1566] (Tozzer 1941:156): month Sotz'; Tozzer and Allen (1910:pl. 38): leaf-nosed bat, "Vampyrus spectrum" or "Phyllostomus hastatus panamensis."

1916–1950 Gates (1931:29): "Sotz."

1951–1980 Dütting (1979:183): "zotz" 'bat' or "zutz" 'cloud'; Knorozov (1955:68): 042 (cabeza de murciélago con el signo complementario "itz") "tzotz, zotz' " 'murciélago'; Knorozov (1967:103): [K377] "sotz' " 'bat'; name of a month, Old Yucatec Sotz'; Thompson (1962:343–49): [264 examples] (bat) probably leaf-nosed vampire bat; in codices only as month Zotz' 'bat'.

1981–1990 Justeson (1984:355): L. Campbell: "sutz' " 'bat'; month Zotz'; J. Fox, J. Justeson, P. Mathews: 'bat'; includes month Zotz' and words whose representation as bat is unclear; F. Lounsbury, B. Riese, L. Schele, D. Stuart: "sotz'/sutz' " 'bat'; Ringle (1990:238): "yul"? 'carve'; Stuart (1987:1–11): month Zotz'; /ts'i/; substitution spelling for month Zotz' as "so/su-ts'i" at C1 on cylindrical stela in St. Louis Art Museum.

1991–2008 Davoust (1995:601): "zotz' " '4e mois'; Grube (1991:226): "sotz' " 'bat' and /tz'i/; Grube and Nahm (1994:704f.): /xu/; Knorozov (1999, vol. 1:155): "zotz' " (cabeza de murciélago).

APM

T –
Z 0722
K –

Variant pictured on Dresden 37b is only example of APM not occurring as month glyph Sotz'/Sutz'. This may be a distinct grapheme, possibly a variant of APL.

2. Picture: bat? with ear ornament

1916–1950 Zimmermann (1956:67): sehr fraglich, ob diese Form hierher gehört.

1951–1980 Thompson (1972:100): indeterminate head, perhaps a bat.

1991–2008 Schele and Grube (1997:237): /xu/.

APP

T 1036c
Z 0708
K 0379

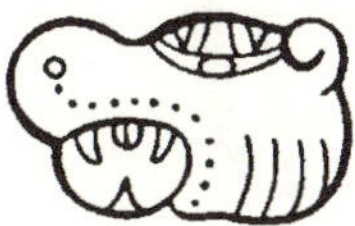

1. Picture: animal head with "ak'b'al" sign on head and "winal" sign in mouth

1951–1980 Knorozov (1967:103): composite grapheme K377-152.

1981–1990 Justeson (1984:362): J. Fox: /b'a/ in codices.

1991–2008 Knorozov (1999, vol. 1:152): /ba-k(i)/; ligadura de 668-551; Ringle and Smith-Stark (1996:335–38): 1036c = 0791d; Ringle and Smith-Stark (1996:353): occurs either before or after "mut" 'bird' on D. 17 and M. 94, 95; may be generic word for animal; von Nagy (1997:50-52): month Zodz.

APR

T —
Z 0713
K —

1. Picture: deer?, dog?

1951–1980 Thompson (1962:381, 401): Z713 = T0801 [4 examples] (black-spotted dog).
1981–1990 Grube (1990a:120): = T0801.

APS

T 0802
Z 0716
K —

1. Picture: dog?

1566–1915 Schellhas [1892] (1904:39): God P.
1951–1980 Thompson (1962:381): [5 examples].
1991–2008 Davoust (1995:606): "pek"? 'chien'; Knorozov (1999, vol. 1:153): "och"?, "ok" (cabeza de zarigüeya).

APT

T —
Z 0717
K —

1. Picture: animal head with notched ear

1951–1980 Thompson (1962:379, 401): Z0717 = T0796; [5 examples] (deer).

APU

T 0829
Z 0718
K —

1. Picture: animal head with notched ear

1566–1915 Brasseur de Bourbourg (1869–1870, vol. 1:203): "p, pe" 'venir, marcher', ant. "pa" 'ouvrir'.
1916–1950 Gates (1931:32): "xul" 'sixth month'.
1951–1980 Kelley (1976:158, 181, 334): /nu/; Thompson (1962:389): [10 examples] serves as action glyph.
1991–2008 Davoust (1995:608): /nu/; Knorozov (1999, vol. 1:153): "och"?, "ok" (cabeza de zarigüeya?).

APV

T –
Z –
K 0165

1. Picture: armadillo? in trap

1951–1980 Knorozov (1967:93): morphemic (animal in a trap, Madrid 48a); Taack (1973:128): "petzaan" 'trapped'.

1991–2008 Knorozov (1999, vol.1:137): (animal en una trampa).

APW

T –
Z –
K –

Only example occurs on Madrid 25c. May refer to animal pictured, possibly fox "wax" in Ch'olan. Followed by /xa/.

1. Picture: animal?

1916–1950 Gates (1931:130): G205 [in part].

AT1

T 0800
Z 0710
K 0276

b'áalam / b'ahläm?; b'olay?

n jaguar

Yu *b'áalam; b'olay* b'áalam, b'áalan 'jaguar' (V. Bricker et al. 1998:26); balam 'tigre, jaguar' (Barrera Vásquez et al. 1980:32) b'olay 'jaguar; gato montés' (Barrera Vásquez et al. 1980:62)

Ch' *b'ahläm;* *b'ahläm 'jaguar' (Kaufman and Norman 1984:116); bo'lay 'jaguar' (Aulie and Aulie 1998:13)

1. Picture: jaguar

1566–1915 Brasseur de Bourbourg (1869–1870, vol. 1:203): "p, pe" 'venir, marcher'; "pa" 'ouvrir'; Brinton (1895:126): jaguar; Rosny (1883:8): (T0800 variant) day Ix; Rosny (1883:20): "ekbalam" 'léopard'; Schellhas [1892] (1904:44): jaguar's head; Thomas (1888:355): "Ekbalam"; Thomas (1893:257): 'tiger'; Tozzer and Allen (1910:pl. 35): head of jaguar.

1916–1950 Gates (1931:130): "balam" or "ekel" 'tiger'.

1951–1980 Kelley (1962b:23): (with T0109 prefix) 'jaguar', 'puma'? (A. Tozzer and G. Allen, E. Seler, G. Zimmermann, D. Kelley); Kelley (1976:117): with "chac" prefixed, 'jaguar'; possibly also 'puma'; Knorozov (1955:67): 030 (hocico de fiera carnicera mostrando los dientes) "bolay" 'jaguar'; Knorozov (1967:96, 98): "nich' " 'toothy' (head of a predatory beast with protruding teeth, compare Nahuatl "ocelotl"); Thompson (1962:380–81): [10 examples] 'jaguar'; Thompson (1972:70): "bolay" 'jaguar'.

1981–1990 Justeson (1984:358): J. Fox, J. Justeson, P. Mathews: 'jaguar'; B. Riese: feline in general; color prefixes specify species, e.g., "chak b'olay" and "sak b'olay."

1991–2008 Davoust (1995:606): "balam; bolay" 'jaguar'; Knorozov (1999, vol. 1:151): "och, oc" (cabeza de zarigüeya); Ringle and Smith-Stark (1996:335–38): 0800 (retired) = 0751c; Schele and Grube (1997:98): "bolay" 'jaguar'; von Nagy (1997:46, 49): "balam" 'jaguar' or "coh" in reference to the god Cit Chac Coh, patron of month Pax. The impaled jaguar in the sixth frame on M. 40b, 41b appears to be the referent.

AT1

T 0800
Z 0710
K 0276

Unique example of AT1 on Madrid 45c used as day Ix.
day 14: Ix/Ix
2. Picture: jaguar face

1566–1915 Rosny (1883:8): day Ix; Thomas (1882:174): unusual character for Ix.

1991–2008 Vail (1997:89): probably variant of day Ix.

AT7

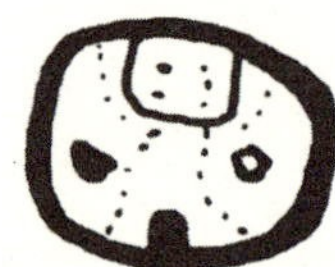

T 0524
Z 1334
K 0185

hix?

n jaguar?
Logographic value is attested only in Q'eqchi': "*hix" 'jaguar' (Campbell 1977:47).
day 14: Ix/Ix
1. Picture: jaguar eye?

1566–1915 Bollaert (1865–1866:52): "ix" 'rust; mildew'; Brasseur de Bourbourg (1869–1870, vol. 1:207): day Ix; "ix" 'trou caché, issue de l'urine chez les femmes, urine'; Landa [1566] (Tozzer 1941:134): day Ix; Rosny (1883:7): day Ix or Hiix.

1916–1950 Gates (1931:40): "Ix" 'tiger; magician'.

1951–1980 Kelley (1976:108, 109): "ix"; Knorozov (1967:94): /hix/ (vessel with water); Thompson (1962:126): [13 examples] Ix; Thompson (1972:92): "ix" jaguar' and by extension 'war'.

1981–1990 Justeson (1984:340): L. Campbell: "hix" 'jaguar'; J. Fox, J. Justeson, F. Lounsbury, B. Riese: "hi'(i)x" as day name and personal name connected with jaguars; J. Fox: depicts jaguar's ear; J. Justeson, F. Lounsbury: occurs in or as jaguar's eye; P. Mathews, L. Schele, D. Stuart: "ix/hix" 'jaguar'; jaguar's eye; Stuart (1987:19): possibly "ix."

1991–2008 Davoust (1995:583): "hix/ix" '14e jour'; "balam" 'jaguar'; Knorozov (1999, vol. 1:126): "hix" (vasija con liquido [K0457]; pelo y manchas de jaguar [K0458]); Love (1991:294, 296): "balam" 'jaguar'; Stuart and Houston (1994:20f.): "hix" 'jaguar'.

AV1

T 0796
Z –
K 0390

kéeh / chij

n deer
Yu *kéeh* keh 'venado de los grandes' (Barrera Vásquez et al. 1980:308); kéeh 'deer' (V. Bricker et al. 1998:125)
Ch' *chij* *chij 'deer' (Kaufman and Norman 1984:118)
1. Picture: deer head

1566–1915 Brasseur de Bourbourg (1869–1870, vol. 1:215, 220): "tzotz-ceh" 'tête de bête fauve avec son poil', symbole de la surface de l'eau; '1,000,000'; Rosny (1883:20): "haleu" 'lièvre' or "th'ul" 'lapin'; Tozzer and Allen (1910:pl. 31): head of doe as sacrifice.

1951–1980 Kelley (1976:117): 'deer'; Knorozov (1967:103): "keh" 'deer'; Thompson (1962:379, 401): [5 examples] (deer) = Z0711.

1981–1990 Justeson (1984:358): J. Fox, J. Justeson, P. Mathews, B. Riese: depicts deer.

1991–2008 Davoust (1995:606): "ceh/chih" 'daim'; Knorozov (1999, vol. 1:154): "ceh" (cabeza de venado).

AV1

T –
Z 0712
K 0389

kéeh / chij

n deer

2. Picture: deer

1566–1915 Rosny (1883:20): "haleu" 'lièvre' or "th'ul" 'lapin'.

1951–1980 Knorozov (1967:103): "tzul" 'dog'; Thompson (1962:379, 401): Z0712 = T0796; [5 examples] (deer).

1981–1990 Grube (1990a:119): = T0796.

AV1

T –
Z 0711
K –

kéeh / chij?

n deer?

3. Picture: deer

1566–1915 Rosny (1883:20): "haleu" 'lièvre' or "th'ul" 'lapin'; Tozzer and Allen (1910:pl. 31): head of doe as sacrifice.

1951–1980 Kelley (1962b:23): deer (A. Tozzer and G. Allen, G. Zimmermann, D. Kelley); Thompson (1962:379, 401): Z0712 = T0796; [5 examples] (deer).

1981–1990 Grube (1990a:119): = T0796.

AV6

T 0795
Z 0761
K 0344

n deer offering

1. Picture: bound deer haunch

1566–1915 Brasseur de Bourbourg (1869–1870, vol. 1:215): cuisse ou gigot de chevreuil ou de cerf; "hau" 'partie de la bête coupée', symbole de vase ou bassin d'eau; Brinton (1895:90): bound deer haunch; Rosny (1883:20): quartier de mazatl, espèce de chevreuil; peut-être aussi 'viande pour les sacrifices, sacrifice'; Thomas (1888:349): "hun" 'the quarter of a deer'; Tozzer and Allen (1910:pl. 31): haunch of vension as a sacrifice.

1951–1980 Kelley (1962b:27): haunch of deer; Kelley (1976:110): "hau" 'deer haunch'; Knorozov (1967:101): "hav" 'haunch of meat'; Thompson (1962:379): [9 examples] (deer haunch); Thompson (1972:106): haunch of venison; Zimmermann (1956:Tafel 8): 'hirsch'.

1981–1990 Justeson (1984:358): J. Fox, J. Justeson, P. Mathews, B. Riese, L. Schele: deer haunch offering.

1991–2008 V. Bricker (1991:290): "ah-ceh wah" 'deerslayer bread'; Davoust (1995:606): "ceh/chih" 'daim'; Knorozov (1999, vol. 1:171): "h'eb"?; "hav" (patas de venado atadas).

AX7

T 0803
Z 0746a
K 0297

1. Picture: snake? with "i" infix

1951–1980 Knorozov (1967:90, 99): (= K139) /i/; Thompson (1962:382): [2 examples] probably a numerical coefficient, perhaps five or thirteen, of the katun sign immediately below it.

1991–2008 Davoust (1995:606): "ho' " 'nombre 5'; Knorozov (1999, vol. 1:158): /i/.

AX7

T 0803
Z 0746
K 0297

Possibly a distinct grapheme from AX7, subsort 1.
2. Picture: snake? with "i" infix

1951–1980 Knorozov (1967:90, 99): (= K139) /i/; Thompson (1962:382): [2 examples].

1991–2008 Davoust (1995:606): "ho' " 'nombre 5'; Knorozov (1999, vol. 1:158): /i/.

AX8

T –
Z 0745
K –

1. Picture: animal head with "k'in" sign on cheek

1951–1980 Thompson (1962:323, 401): Z0745 = T0742; [7 examples] (ocelot?)
1981–1990 Grube (1990a:116): = T0742.
1991–2008 Davoust (1995:600): = T0742b.

AX9

T 0766
Z 0740
K 0291

1. Picture: eagle?

1566–1915 Förstemann [1897] (1904a:449): Bacab; Thomas (1893:264): "chaac" or "chac" 'tempest' or 'tornado'.

1951–1980 Knorozov (1967:99): morphemic; Thompson (1962:368): [11 examples]; Thompson (1972:86): "kulu," "kuleb" 'racoon'.

1991–2008 H. Bricker and V. Bricker (n.d.): represents the constellation Aquila; V. Bricker et al. (2006:663): constellation Aquila; Davoust (1995:603): "kulu/kuleb" 'raton laveur'; Knorozov (1999, vol. 1:153): "tzic" (cabeza de animal nocturno); Schele and Grube (1997:174): "kan."

AXA

T –
Z –
K –

b'(V)?

Substitutes for HTF /b'e/ in a parallel expression on Dresden 38c1.
1. Picture: ?

1916–1950 Gates (1931:161): G356.6.1 [in part].

1991–2008 Davoust (1997:307): = T0765b? "oc" 'le pied'; Schele and Grube (1997:227): /bV/ in spelling of "k'ab."

AXB

T 0763
Z 0715
K 0386

1. Picture: head of animal?

1951–1980 Knorozov (1967:103): morphemic (animal head); Thompson (1962:363): [1 example]; Thompson (1972:104): unique; unidentified animal head.

1991–2008 Knorozov (1999, vol. 1:151): "och"?, "oc" (cabeza de zarigüeya); Schele and Grube (1997:229): "witz" 'the mountain'.

B Birds

BM1

T 0236
Z 0751
K 0402, 0404–5

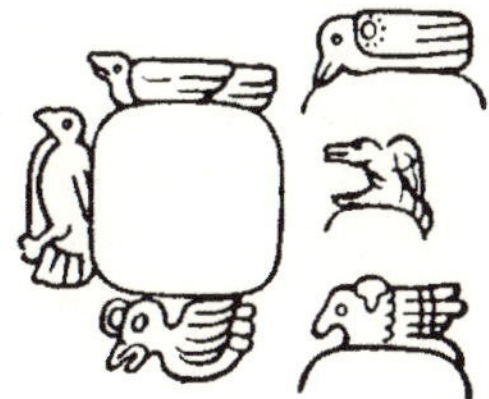

k'a?

Some examples may be BME.

1. Picture: small bird

1566–1915 Rosny (1883:21): "kox" 'l'oiseau quetzal'.

1951–1980 Knorozov (1955:68): 044 (ave en el signo "yax") "yaxum" 'quetzal'; Knorozov (1967:104, 106): [K402] "yax-um," Old Yucatec "yaxum" 'green bird'; [K404, 405] morphemic (a bird); Thompson (1962:61, 164): (various birds) "chich" 'bird'?

1981–1990 V. Bricker (1986:210): "yuhyum" 'oriole' (Ch'olan); Justeson (1984:332): P. Mathews, L. Schele, D. Stuart: a hummingbird?; reading should be homophonous with 'bat'.

1991–2008 Davoust (1995:571): three variants: (a): vautour "kuch" 'vautour'; (b): oiseau indéterminé "ch'ich" 'oiseau'; /ch'i/; (c): cotinga "yaxun" 'cotinga'; Davoust (1997:212): "mut" 'oiseau'; Grube (1991:230): substitutes for T0077 wing in Chocholá ceramics; Mora-Marín (2000): /k'i/, based on substitutions with T0077; Schele and Looper (1996:18–22): /k'a/.

BM2

T 0077v
Z —
K 0458

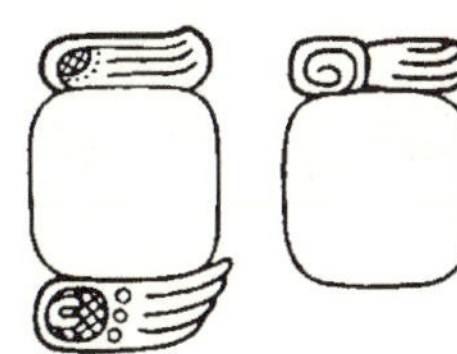

1. Picture: wing

1951–1980 Kelley (1976:221, 332): = T0076.

1981–1990 Grube (1990a:90): = T0026; Grube and MacLeod (1990:167–77): /ch'i/, /k'i/, /ch'a/, or /k'a/; Justeson (1984:321): cf. T0076; J. Fox, J. Justeson, P. Mathews: 'to end'; J. Fox, J. Justeson, P. Mathews, L. Schele: depicts wing; MacLeod and Stross (1990): /ch'i/ reading proposed by Stross; "tosh" by MacLeod. The first gives "y-uchib" 'his bowl' for the "Wing-Quincunx" collocation in the Primary Standard Sequence, and the latter "u toshib" 'water jar'; Stuart (1989b:150): credits Houston and MacLeod with /ch'i/.

1991–2008 Davoust (1995:559): "wich'," "xik," 'aile'; /ch'i/, /ch'a/; Knorozov (1999, vol. 1:110, 241): "xik" 'ala; volar'; MacLeod (1991g): likely /ch'a/; Mora-Marín (2000): /k'i/; Ringle and Smith-Stark (1996:335–38): 0077 (retired) = 0076b; Schele and Looper (1996:18–22): "k'a' " 'end' and /k'a/; substitutes for T0669 /k'a/ in 'wing-shell' death expression at Copán; Stuart (2002b): /k'i/.

BMA

T 0839
Z —
K 0406

kùutz?

n — turkey

Yu *kùutz* — kùutz 'wild turkey' (V. Bricker et al. 1998:135)

Only one (very eroded) example of a turkey without XH4.

1. Picture: turkey

1566–1915 Brasseur de Bourbourg (1869–1870, vol. 1:213): (with T0506) symbole du dieu Kin-Ich-Kak-Mó; Brinton (1895:90): wild turkey; Rosny (1883:21): "xkan-tz'ulop" 'espèce de perroquet'; Thomas (1888:357): (with T0506) "cutz" or "cax" 'game bird, wild turkey'; Tozzer and Allen (1910:pl. 16): head of turkey as offering.

1951–1980 Kelley (1962b:27): (with T0506) turkey (head) offering; Kelley (1976:110): "cutz" 'ocellated turkey'; Knorozov (1967:104): "kutz" (turkey head); Thompson (1962:391): [10 examples] (turkey) sacrificial food offering.

1981–1990 Justeson (1984:358): J. Fox, P. Mathews: depicts turkey.

1991–2008 V. Bricker (1991:288): "cutz" 'wild turkey'; V. Bricker and H. Bricker (1992:fig. 2.8): (with T0506): "cutz-wah" 'wild turkey bread'; Davoust (1995:608): "cutz" 'dindon'; Knorozov (1999, vol. 1:160): "cutz" (cabeza de pavo).

BMA

T —
Z 0762
K 0406

kùutz?

n — turkey

2. Picture: turkey

1566–1915 Brinton (1895:90): wild turkey; Rosny (1883:21): "xkan-tz'ulop" 'espèce de perroquet'; Thomas (1888:357): "cutz" or "cax" 'game bird, wild turkey'; Tozzer and Allen (1910:pl. 16): head of turkey as offering.

1951–1980 Kelley (1962b:27): turkey (head) offering; Knorozov (1967:104): "kutz" (turkey head); Thompson (1962:391, 401): Z762 = T0839 [10 examples] (turkey) sacrificial food offering; Thompson (1972:98): turkey and maize, a stew or in the form of tamales.

1981–1990 Grube (1990a:121): = T0839.

1991–2008 V. Bricker (1991:288): "cutz" 'wild turkey'; Schele and Grube (1997:137): "ulum" 'turkey'.

BMB

T —
Z 0762
K 0406

kùutz? wàah

n — turkey bread

Yu *kùutz wàah* — kùutz 'wild turkey' (V. Bricker et al. 1998:135); wàah 'tortilla, bread' (V. Bricker et al. 1998:298)

Ch' *ø waj* — *waj 'tortilla; food' (Kaufman and Norman 1984:135)

Probably a conflation of BMB and XH4.

2. Picture: turkey tamale?

1566–1915 Brinton (1895:90): wild turkey; Rosny (1883:21): "xkan-tz'ulop" 'espèce de perroquet'; Thomas (1888:357): "cutz" or "cax" 'game bird, wild turkey'; Tozzer and Allen (1910:pl. 16): head of turkey as offering.

1951–1980 Kelley (1962b:27): turkey (head) offering; Knorozov (1967:104): "kutz" (turkey head); Thompson (1962:391, 401): Z762 = T0839 [10 examples] (turkey) sacrificial food offering; Thompson (1972:98): turkey and maize, a stew or in the form of tamales.

1981–1990 Grube (1990a:121): = T0839.

1991–2008 V. Bricker (1991:288): "cutz" 'wild turkey'; Schele and Grube (1997:137): "ulum" 'turkey'.

BME

T —
Z 0752
K 0403

Possibly the same as BM1.
1. Picture: small bird

1951–1980 Knorozov (1967:104): morphemic (bird); Thompson (1962:330–34, 401): Z752 = T0747 [167 examples] (vulture).

1991–2008 Schele and Grube (1997:176): "mut."

BMF

T —
Z —
K —

Possibly the same as BP1.
1. Picture: bird?

BP1

a

T 0743
Z 0724
K —

1. Picture: turtle or parrot

1566–1915 Brasseur de Bourbourg (1869–1870, vol. 1:201): "a" 'eau, rivière, en compos.'; "ah" 'roseau', "ach' " 'phallus, aiguillon'; Landa [1566] (Tozzer 1941:170): <a>; Thomas (1888:348): Landa's /a/; Tozzer and Allen (1910:pl. 14): 'turtle'; Tozzer and Allen (1910:pl. 39): example on M. 88c possibly represents a monkey.

1951–1980 Kelley (1962a:302f.): /a/; Kelley (1976:122, 201, 218, 334): turtle head; /a/; "aac, mac" 'turtle'; interchanges with T0238, T0015; emblem glyph of Yaxhá; Kelley (1962b:23): turtle head (E. Seler, J. E. S. Thompson, G. Zimmermann, D. Kelley) (early confused with macaw); /a/ (D. Kelley); "aac" 'turtle' (Y. Knorozov); Knorozov (1955:68): 045 (cabeza de tortuga) "aak"; Knorozov (1967:98): "aak" (turtle head); Thompson (1962:324–26): [85 examples] (turtle) differentiated from T0744 by the absence of crest or markings around the eye.

1981–1990 V. Bricker (1986:213): /a(h)/; Grube (1990a:116): = T0745; Justeson (1984:354): Yaxhá emblem glyph; J. Fox, B. Riese: turtle head; J. Justeson, P. Mathews: "ak," at least with T0516 infix; depicts turtle, not parrot or macaw; B. Riese: possibly /a/; L. Schele: "ak" 'turtle'; not parrot or macaw; Stuart (1985c): T0743 that follows "yax" is /a/, which may function as "ah" and "ha" and represents a parrot (not a macaw) rather than a turtle; interchangeable with T0238.

1991–2008 Davoust (1995:600): "ac/mac" 'tortue'; /ah/, /ha/, /a/; Knorozov (1999, vol. 1:156): "aac" (cabeza de tortuga).

BP2

T —
Z 0723
K 0274

Conflation of logograph XQ1 "k'an" and syllabic BP1 /a/. Occurs rarely in non-calendrical contexts (see Dresden Venus table).

há'ab' period: K'ayab'/K'anasi

1. Picture: turtle or parrot with "k'än" sign over eye

1566–1915 Brasseur de Bourbourg (1869–1870, vol. 1:201): "a" 'eau, rivière, en compos'; "ah" 'roseau', "ach' " 'phallus, aiguillon'; Brinton (1895:126): turtle or tortoise; /a/ of Landa's alphabet; Rosny (1883:13): month Kayab; Schellhas [1892] (1904:44): tortoise head in month glyph Kayab; Thomas (1893:245): month Kayab; Tozzer and Allen (1910:pl. 25): head, probably of a turtle, in month sign Kayab.

1916–1950 Gates (1931:64): Kayab.

1951–1980 Knorozov (1955:68): (cabeza de tortuga con signo complementario 106) "aak"; Knorozov (1967:98): "ak" 'plot of land'; Thompson (1962:324–26; 401): Z723 = T0743 [85 examples] (turtle).

1991–2008 Davoust (1995:600): "ac/mac" 'tortue'; /ah/, /ha/, /a/.

BP3

T 0238
Z 0028
K 0077

a

ah / aj

agentive

Yu *ah*

Ch' *aj*

agentive

ah 'antepuesta a los apellidos de linaje denota los varones; antepuesta a los nombres de lugares' (Barrera Vásquez et al. 1980:3)

*aj 'prepound/proclitic; male; relatively large/active being (Kaufman and Norman 1984:139)

1. Picture: beak of parrot or macaw

1566–1915 Brasseur de Bourbourg (1869–1870, vol. 1:201): /a/; 'figure d'un bec d'oiseau, d'une trompe'; Landa [1566] (Tozzer 1941:170): <a>; Tozzer and Allen (1910:pl. 25): upper mandible and head of blue macaw, "Ara militaris."

1951–1980 Kelley (1962a:302f.): "a" sujeto pronominal; pronombre posesivo de la segunda persona del singular; Kelley (1976:201, 332): /a/ (interchanges with T0743 and T015); Knorozov (1955:66): 017 (miembro viril con un elemento complementario) /a/ tal vez "hach"?; Knorozov (1967:84f.): /a/ (a male sexual organ); Thompson (1962:62f.): Kakmoil 'pertaining to Kakmo'; followed in one case by the drought glyph and in the other by the death-tun compound; Thompson (1972:86): "mo' " 'macaw'.

1981–1990 V. Bricker (1986:210): /a(h)/, "ah-" (agentive) (Cholan, Yucatecan); Justeson (1984:333): J. Fox, J. Justeson: = T0228/0229; F. Lounsbury, L. Schele: /a/, "ah"; P. Mathews, B. Riese: "ah"; depicts macaw beak; L. Schele: "ah"; depicts macaw beak, more rarely turtle beak; Schele and Grube (1990): can be "mo' " 'macaw'; Stuart (1985c:2): T0229 and T0238 are abbreviated versions of T0743 /a/.

1991–2008 Davoust (1995:571): "ah" 'préf. genre masc.'; /a/; Grube (1994b:181): T0238 /a/ invented after 9.11.0.0.0; Knorozov (1999, vol. 1:170): "ach; at" (órgano masculino).

BP4

T —
Z 0734
K 0275

mo'

n macaw
Yu *mo'* mo' 'macaw' (Hofling with Tesucún 1997:451); mo(o)' 'guacamaya' (Barrera Vásquez et al. 1980:525)
Ch' *mo'* *mo' 'macaw' (Kaufman and Norman 1984:126)

1. Picture: macaw

1566–1915 Brinton (1895:126): turtle or tortoise; /a/ of Landa's alphabet; Schellhas [1892] (1904:44): tortoise; Tozzer and Allen (1910:pl. 25): blue macaw, "Ara militaris."

1951–1980 Kelley (1962a:307): identifies spelling of "mo-'o-'(o)" 'guacamaya' in Dresden 16c; Kelley (1962b:23): 'macaw' (E. Seler, A. Tozzer and G. Allen, G. Zimmermann, Y. Knorozov, D. Kelley); Kelley (1976:116): macaw; Knorozov (1955:68): 041 (cabeza de guacamayo) "moo" 'guacamayo'; Knorozov (1967:98): "moo" 'parrot'; Thompson (1962:326; 401): Z0734 = T0744 (macaw).

1981–1990 Grube (1990a:116): = T0744b; Schele and Grube (1990): "mo' " 'macaw'; Stuart and Schele (1986): "mo' " 'macaw'.

1991–2008 Davoust (1995:600): "moo' " 'ara'; Ringle and Smith-Stark (1996:324): = 0946; Stuart and Houston (1994:25f.): "mo' " 'macaw'.

BP5

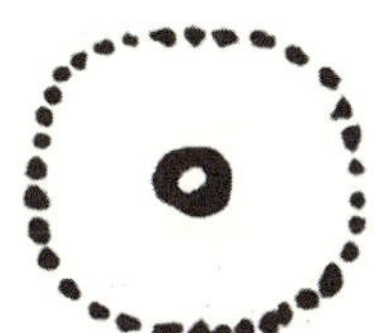

T 0582
Z 1301
K 0298

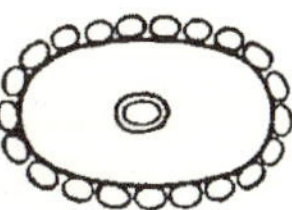

mo

1. Picture: macaw eye

1566–1915 Brasseur de Bourbourg (1869–1870, vol. 1:203, 206): "o" 'cercle, surface, vase, collier'; day Muluc; "muluc" 'amassé, fait en amas'; or "mul-uc" 'colline faite, môle soulevé par amas'; Landa [1566] (Tozzer 1941:159): in month glyph Mol; Thomas (1888:355, 370): /mo/ in "moo" 'ara, a large species of parrot'; Thomas (1893:254, 262): /m/.

1951–1980 Kelley (1962a:306f.): /mo/; Kelley (1976:180, 333): /mo/; Knorozov (1955:75): 131 /m(o)/; Knorozov (1967:99): /m(o)/; Lounsbury (1973:102–5): /mo/; Lounsbury and Coe (1968:273): /mo/; Thompson (1962:207–8): [61 examples] (Mol semblant).

1981–1990 V. Bricker (1986:212): /mo/; Justeson (1984:345): L. Campbell, J. Fox, J. Justeson, P. Mathews: /mo/; F. Lounsbury, B. Riese: /mo/; possibly "mol"; L. Schele: "mol," month Mol.

1991–2008 Davoust (1995:588): "om" 'écume, bouillir'; "yohm" 'écume'; /mo/; Knorozov (1999, vol. 1:71, 113): /mo/.

BT1

T 0099
Z 0086
K 0062

o

1. Picture: feather

1566–1915 Brasseur de Bourbourg (1869–1870, vol. 1:203): "o" 'cercle, vase, collier, pour "u" '; Thomas (1893:259): /o/.

1951–1980 Kelley (1962a:306f.): /'o/; Kelley (1976:183): /'o/; Knorozov (1955:70): 066 (mazorca de maíz? con elemento complementario) /o/; Knorozov (1967:83): /o/.

1981–1990 V. Bricker (1986:209): /o/; Grube (1990a:91): = T0075; Lounsbury (1983b:44–49): equivalence of T0099, T0279, T0280 and T0155: /'o/ or /o'/; Justeson (1984:323): cf. T0279/0280, T0345; J. Fox, J. Justeson: /o/, perhaps = T0080 (a); depicts feather; L. Campbell, F. Lounsbury: /o/, /'o/, /o'/; P. Mathews, B. Riese: /o/, /'o/, /o'/; depicts feather; L. Schele: /'o/, /'o'/; depicts feather.

1991–2008 Davoust (1995:560): /o/; Davoust (1997:319): "ol" 'le coeur'; Knorozov (1999, vol. 1:101): /o/; (pluma de ave); Ringle and Smith-Stark (1996:335–38): 0099 = 0099a.

BT1

T 0296
Z 0048
K 0063

o

2. Picture: feather

1566–1915 Brasseur de Bourbourg (1869–1870, vol. 1:203): "o" 'cercle, vase, collier, pour "u" '; Landa [1566] (Tozzer 1941:170): <o>.

1951–1980 Cordan (1964:37f.): "kakal"; "kinut"; Knorozov (1967:83): "pik'."

1981–1990 Grube (1990a:101): = T0346.

1991–2008 Davoust (1995:575): /o/; Knorozov (1999, vol. 1:100): /ti-pay/; ligadura de 254-3; Ringle and Smith-Stark (1996:335–38): 0296 is questionable: some 0099v, others 0159.

BT1

T 0155v
Z –
K 0325

o

Prefix to Kumk'u glyph.
3. Picture: curved feather

1951–1980 Knorozov (1967:100): (= K327) "kum" (pot to boil water).

1981–1990 Justeson (1984:327): L. Campbell: possibly shell, possibly "och/hoch"; J. Fox, J. Justeson: front view of T0078; alternates with T0078 as prefix in month compound for Cumku; Lounsbury (1983b:44–49): equivalence of T0099, T0279, T0280, and T0155: /'o/ or /o'/.

1991–2008 Davoust (1995:564): "cum" 'marmite', "ohl" 'coeur, formel'; /o/; Knorozov (1999, vol. 1:174): "cum; chum"; MacLeod (1991a): "ol" 'heart', /o/; Schele et al. (1991): /o/.

BT2

T 0748
Z 0735
K –

muwan

n — hawk
Yu *muwan* — muan 'gavilán' (Barrera Vásquez et al. 1980:532)
Ch' *muwan* — muhan 'milano, gabilan' (Morán 1935:46)

BT2 and BT4 recognized as separate graphemes in 1994. Some of the references below apply to both graphemes.
há'ab' period: Muwan/Muwan
1. Picture: hawk

1566–1915 Landa [1566] (Tozzer 1941:164): month Muan; Seler [1915] (1976:46): the moan bird, a mythical representation for the cloud cover of the heavens; Tozzer and Allen (1910:pl. 23): head of Moan bird, "Otus choliba thompsoni."

1916–1950 Gates (1931:64): "moan."

1951–1980 Kelley (1962b:23): muan bird (E. Seler, general consensus); owl (E. Seler; general consensus); "muan" 'crested falcon' (D. Brinton); Thompson (1962:334f.): [32 examples] (Muan bird) probably the Yucatecan screech owl.

1981–1990 V. Bricker (1986:213): "muwan"; Justeson (1984:355): several distinct signs; J. Justeson, P. Mathews, L. Schele: illustration in Thompson is early form of T0758, most examples are not; J. Justeson, P. Mathews, B. Riese: Thompson includes T0746 and main sign of Muan; B. Riese: 'screech owl'; Mathews and Justeson (1984:205): substitution spelling "mu-wa-n(i)" for "muwan."

1991–2008 Davoust (1995:600): "ch'oh" 'rat'; "muwan" '15e mois'; /ch'o/; Grube and Schele (1994): bird representing month Muwan is a hawk, not an owl; Knorozov (1999, vol. 1:159): "mu-aan"? (cabeza de lechuza); Ringle and Smith-Stark (1996:350): Thompson (1962:334) indicates that this is the Muan bird head. His illustration is actually a variant of T0758 (= 0758d).

BT4

T —
Z 0735
K 0397

ku(y) / kuh

n owl

Yu *ku(y)* ku(y) 'la lechuza agorera'; ah kuy 'especie de lechuza' (Barrera Vásquez et al. 1980:342)

Ch' *kuh* xcu 'lechuza (tipo de tecolote; ave)' (Aulie and Aulie 1998:146)

BT2 and BT4 recognized as separate graphemes in 1994. Some of the references below apply to both graphemes.

1. Picture: owl

1566–1915 Brinton (1895:73, 120): 'horned owl'; associated with gods of death and war and symbolizes clouds, darkness, and inauspicious events; often associated with number thirteen; month Muan; Schellhas [1892] (1904:41): the moan bird; Seler [1915] (1976:46): the moan bird, a mythical representation for the cloud cover of the heavens; Thomas (1888:356): "ichim"? 'horned owl'; Tozzer and Allen (1910:pl. 23): head of Yucatec screech owl or Moan bird, "Otus choliba thompsoni."

1916–1950 Gates (1931:64, 131): "moan."

1951–1980 Kelley (1962b:23): muan bird (E. Seler, general consensus); owl (E. Seler; general consensus); "muan" 'crested falcon' (D. Brinton); Kelley (1976:112): "muan" bird; Knorozov (1955:68): 039 (cabeza de buho) "muan" 'buho'; Knorozov (1967:103): morphemic 'owl'; Thompson (1962:334f., 401): Z735 = T0748 [32 examples] (Muan bird) probably the Yucatecan screech owl; Thompson (1972:55): "muan" bird, 'screech owl'.

1981–1990 Grube (1990a:116): = T0748; Justeson (1984:355): (T0748) includes several distinct signs; J. Justeson, P. Mathews, L. Schele: the example illustrated by Thompson is an early form of T0758, but most examples are not; J. Justeson, P. Mathews, B. Riese: Thompson also includes forms of T0746 and main sign of Muan here; B. Riese: 'screech owl'.

1991–2008 V. Bricker et al. (2006:663): Gemini; Davoust (1995:600): (= T0748c) "cuy" 'chouette'; /cu/; Grube and Schele (1994:10–12): "kuy" 'owl'; distinct from the bird representing the month Muwan; Knorozov (1999, vol. 1:159): "mu-aan"; Milbrath (1999:270): owl associated with Gemini; occurs in the Paris zodiacal table and in astronomical contexts in the Dresden Codex.

BT4

T —
Z 0732a
K —

ku(y) / kuh

n owl

2. Picture: head of owl

1566–1915 Tozzer and Allen (1910:pl. 23): glyph possibly representing Moan bird, "Otus choliba thompsoni."

1916–1950 Gates (1931:122): suffixed to G125.

1951–1980 Kelley (1962b:28): owl's head; Knorozov (1955:68) 039 (cabeza de buho) "muan" 'buho'; Thompson (1972:104): muan bird.

1991–2008 V. Bricker et al. (2006:663): Gemini; Davoust (1995:610): = T0858c; Davoust (1997:309): "muwan/cuy" 'l'oiseau Muwan'; Schele and Grube (1997:228): "kan" 'sky'.

BV3

T 0747b
Z 0736, 0736a
K 0392

ti

ti' / ti, ta, tä

prep — in, at, etc.; preposition

Yu *ti'* — ti' 'preposición a, con, por instrumento, adentro' (Barrera Vásquez et al. 1980:788); ti' 'to, at, in, from, for' (V. Bricker et al. 1998:274)

Ch' *ti, ta, tä* — *tä 'preposition' (Kaufman and Norman 1984:139); ta 'for, belongs to' (Knowles 1984:461); tä 'to, from, by' (Knowles 1984:463); ti 'en, a, por, de' (Warkentin and Scott 1980:98); ti 'en' (Morán 1935:26); ti' 'beside, by the side; at the edge' (Knowles 1984:465)

Used as preposition once on Dresden 39c; more commonly used for "k'uch" 'vulture' (BV4).

1. Picture: vulture with "ti" sign

1566–1915 Brasseur de Bourbourg (1869–1870, vol. 1:211): "m-ó" 'ara, montagne, vague'; Schellhas [1892] (1904:43): 'vulture'; Thomas (1888:357) "kuch" 'vulture'; Tozzer and Allen (1910:pl. 17): king vulture, "Sarcorhamphus papa."

1951–1980 Cordan (1963:110): "tiu"; Kelley (1962b:23): king vulture general; Knorozov (1955:68): 040 (cabeza de pájaro con signo complementario) "ch'om" 'buitre'; Knorozov (1967:103): "ti" 'vulture'; Thompson (1962:330–34): [167 examples] 'vulture'; "It is possible that the presence of the Ahau sign on the forehead indicates the king vulture; the 'ti' sign, the ordinary John Crow or turkey buzzard."

1981–1990 Justeson (1984:355): L. Campbell: "ta'hol" 'vulture' (< "ta hol" 'at head'); J. Fox, J. Justeson, P. Mathews: locative preposition "*ti(')/ta," with T0059 as semantic determinative; J. Fox, J. Justeson: not necessarily based on Ch'ol "ta' hol" 'vulture'; F. Lounsbury, P. Mathews: locative preposition "tä/ta/ti"? > Ch'ol "ta'hol" 'vulture'; Yucatec "k'uch" 'vulture'; B. Riese: "ta'hol" (Ch'ol) / "k'uch" (Yucatec) 'vulture'; P. Mathews: > Ch'ol "ta'-hol" 'vulture'; L. Schele, D. Stuart: "ta/ti"; Stuart (1990): replaces T0059 "ti" in directional count glyphs.

1991–2008 Davoust (1995:600): "ta'hol" 'vautour'; /ti/, /ta/; Knorozov (1999, vol. 1:159): "ti" (cabeza de zopilote); tiene los signos "ti" y "ki" inscritos; Macri (1991): at sites using only T0053, T0059, and T0747 as prepositions, possibly /ti/ or /ta/; Ringle and Smith-Stark (1996:335–38): 0747b = 0849b (0747 now has no lettered variants); Schele and Grube (1997:229): [example on D. 39c] preposition "ti."

BV4

T 0747b
Z 0736, 0736a
K 0392

k'uch?; ta'hol?

n — vulture

Yu *k'uch* — k'uch 'aura que llaman zopilote' (Barrera Vásquez et al. 1980:418)

Ch' *ta'hol* — ta'jol 'zopilote' (Aulie and Aulie 1998:113)

1. Picture: vulture with "ti" sign

1566–1915 Brasseur de Bourbourg (1869–1870, vol. 1:211): "m-ó" 'ara, montagne, vague'; Brinton (1895:73): vulture; Rosny (1883:21): "ah-cutzo" 'dindon sauvage'; Schellhas [1892] (1904:43): 'vulture'; Thomas (1888:357) "kuch" 'vulture'; Tozzer and Allen (1910:pl. 18): head of King Vulture, "Sarcorhamphus papa."

1951–1980 Cordan (1963:110): "tiu"; Kelley (1962b:23): king vulture (general consensus); Kelley (1976:112): king vulture; Knorozov (1955:68): 040 (cabeza de pájaro con signo complementario) "ch'om" 'buitre'; Knorozov (1967:103): "ti" 'vulture'; Thompson (1962:330–34): [167 examples] 'vulture'; "It is possible that the presence of the Ahau sign on the forehead indicates the king vulture; the 'ti' sign, the ordinary John Crow or turkey buzzard."; Thompson (1972:55): "zopilote" 'black vulture'; "ti/ta" sign on vulture's head may be reference to Chol term for zopilote "ta'hol" 'excrement head'; Thompson (1972:58): "kuch" 'black vulture', also homonym for "kuch" 'scabies'.

1981–1990 Justeson (1984:355): L. Campbell: "ta'hol" 'vulture' (< "ta hol" 'at head'); J. Fox, J. Justeson, P. Mathews: locative preposition "*ti(')/ta," with T0059 as semantic determinative; J. Fox, J. Justeson: not necessarily based on Ch'ol "ta' hol" 'vulture'; F. Lounsbury, P. Mathews: locative preposition "tä/ta/ti"? > Ch'ol "ta'hol" 'vulture'; Yucatec "k'uch" 'vulture'; B. Riese: "ta'hol" (Ch'ol) / "k'uch" (Yucatec) 'vulture'; P. Mathews: > Ch'ol "ta'-hol" 'vulture'; L. Schele, D. Stuart: "ta/ti"; Stuart (1990): replaces T0059 "ti" in directional count glyphs.

1991–2008 Davoust (1995:600): "ta'hol" 'vautour'; /ti/, /ta/; Davoust (1997:106): "kuch" 'le vautour zopilote'; Knorozov (1999, vol. 1:159): "ti" (cabeza de zopilote); tiene el signo "ti" inscrito; Ringle and Smith-Stark (1996:335–38): 0747b = 0849b (0747 now has no lettered variants); Schele and Grube (1997:113): "ta'hol" 'vulture'.

BV4

T —
Z —
K —

k'uch?; ta'hol?

n vulture?

2. Picture: vulture head

1566–1915 Rosny (1883:21): =205? "uxcil" 'vantour'; Tozzer and Allen (1910:pl. 18): example on M. 26c [pictured above] black vulture, "Catharista urubu."

1951–1980 Kelley (1962b:23): black vulture (A. Tozzer and G. Allen, D. Kelley).

BV4

T —
Z 0750
K 0399

k'uch?; ta'hol?

n vulture?

3. Picture: vulture

1566–1915 Rosny (1883:21): "koz" 'oiseau de proie, aigle'.

1951–1980 Kelley (1962b:23): unidentified bird; Knorozov (1967:104): morphemic (bird); Thompson (1962:330–34, 401): Z750 = T0747 [167 examples] (vulture).

1991–2008 Davoust (1995:600): pictures an eagle; "caan" 'ciel'.

BV4

T —
Z 0753
K 0401

k'uch?; ta'hol?

n vulture

4. Picture: vulture

1566–1915 Tozzer and Allen (1910:pl. 18): black vulture.

1951–1980 Knorozov (1967:104): morphemic (bird); Thompson (1962:330–34; 401): Z753 = T0747 [167 examples] (vulture); Thompson (1972:104): vulture?

BV6

T –
Z 0736
K 0394

May be equivalent to BV4.

1. Picture: vulture head?

1566–1915 Tozzer and Allen (1910:pl. 18): head of black vulture.

1951–1980 Knorozov (1967:103): morphemic (bird head); Thompson (1972:104): black-faced bird with scroll, like Chac's beneath eye; vulture?

1991–2008 Davoust (1997:310): "kuch" 'le vautour zopilote'; Schele and Grube (1997:229): "ti" 'in'.

BV7

T –
Z 0737
K 0395

1. Picture: head of vulture?; crow?

1951–1980 Kelley (1962b:23): crow-like bird on M. 28c3 (G. Zimmermann, D. Kelley); Knorozov (1967:103): morphemic (bird head); Thompson (1962:401): Z737 = T0970.

H Body Parts

HE5

T 0287
Z 0050
K 0007

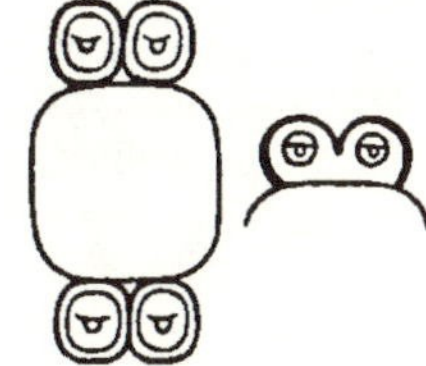

ch'o?

1. Picture: heavy lidded eyes

1951–1980 Cordan (1964:40): "tzik"; Dütting (1974:50): "tz'uh/tz'ut" 'drops (of water)'; T0287:0110 is "tzu-tan" 'sorcerer, witch'; Kelley (1976:118, 332): substitute for T0758; Knorozov (1967:78): "pak" 'sight; appear' (eyes); Schele (1979:11): "ich" locative; Thompson (1962:67): the symbolic form of T0758 (jog with infix T0007).

1981–1990 Grube (1990a:101): = T0298; Justeson (1984:335): L. Campbell: /tz'u/ < "tz'uh" 'drip'; J. Justeson: standard inscriptional form, possibly "hal" (including "ha'-al" 'rain') or "tz' "; not "chich," "(i)ch-ich" for Chuj "chich" 'rabbit'; eyes (of Tlaloc?); P. Mathews: "chich"; L. Schele: "ich/(i)chich"; (eye = "ich"); locative preposition "ich"; substitutes for animal (rabbit = "chich"/T0758) in Glyph B; Schele and J. Miller (1983:24): 'eyes' in Yucatecan "ich"; substitutes for T0758 in accession expression.

1991–2008 Davoust (1995:575): "ch'oc" 'jeune enfant'; /ch'o/; Knorozov (1999, vol. 1:76, 238): "pac" 'párpados; tempestad; presencia; rezar; sufijo clasificador para contar seres vivo' (ojos abiertos); Schele and Grube (1992): "ch'ok" 'sprout'; Schele and Grube (1997:190): "ich" 'in' on Dresden 66a; Schele and Mathews (1993:19–21): /ch'o/.

HE6

T 0001
Z 0001
K 0031

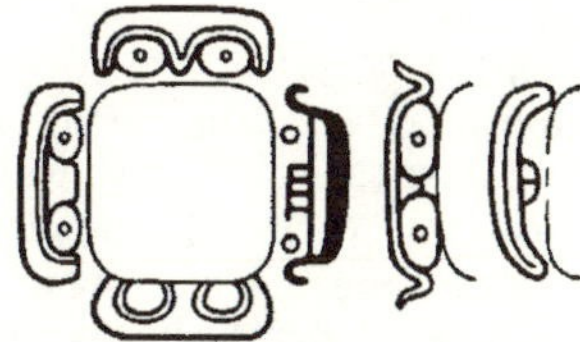

u

u-

dep pn — he/she/it; his/her/its; third person prefix, Set A (ergative and possessive)
Yu *u* — u(y)- 'Set A dependent pronoun, 3rd person' (Hofling with Tesucún 1997:9)
Ch' *u* — *u- 'ergative 3s' (Kaufman and Norman 1984:91)

1. Picture: eyeball collar

1566–1915 Brasseur de Bourbourg (1869–1870, vol. 1:204): "u" 'vase, bassin, surface circonscrite, lune'; Brinton (1895:86f.): /u/; Landa [1566] (Tozzer 1941:153, 170): <u>; Rosny (1883:17): "u" 'lune, mois'; Thomas (1888:349, 369): "u" 'vase', 'moon'; pronoun or article when joined to another symbol; /u/; Thomas (1893:246): /u/.

1916–1950 Spinden (1924:18–22): 'zero, completion'; Thompson (1950:40, 46): /u/, possessive "u"; converts cardinal numerals to ordinals; Whorf (1933:3): third person subject and third person possessive "u"; Whorf (1942:484, fig. 1): /u/; Whorf (1942:496): third-person pronominal reference "u."

1951–1980 Cordan (1964:13): "u" in codices; Kelley (1962a:290, 294): " 'u" posesivo; Kelley (1962b:41); /u/; Kelley (1976:196, 203, 331): "u" possessive; Knorozov (1955:71): 084 (cedazo?) /u/; Knorozov (1958:285): /u/; Knorozov (1967:79): /u/; "u-."

1981–1990 V. Bricker (1986:208): /u/, "u" 'he, she, it; his, her, its' (Cholan, Yucatecan); Grube (1990a:87): = T0002; Justeson (1984:316): cf. T0003, 0010, 0011, 0013, 0034, 0062, 0171, 0191, 0204, 0211, 0230, 0232; L. Campbell: "u"; J. Fox, J. Justeson, B. Riese: third singular ergative and possessive pronoun prefix, prevocalic and preconsonantal (= "u, uy, y"); limited use as /u/; F. Lounsbury, P. Mathews, L. Schele: "u" third person pronoun, used as /u/; Stross and Kerr (1990): in vision questing sequences representative of the hallucinogenic "howl," e.g., "uuuu/oooo."

1991–2008 Davoust (1995:553): "uh" 'collier'; /u/; Knorozov (1999, vol. 1:90): /u/; Ringle and Smith-Stark (1996:335–38): 0001 = 0001a.

HE6

T 0013
Z 0002
K 0049

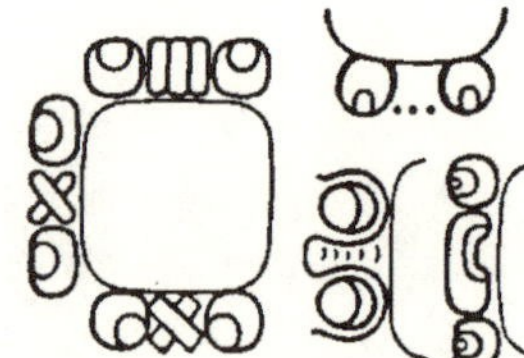

u

u-

dep pn he/she/it; his/her/its; third person prefix, Set A (ergative and possessive)

2. Picture: eyeball collar

1951–1980 Dütting (1974:50): T0013a "zat"? 'disappear; lose'; Kelley (1976:193–96, 223, 331): "ah" 'agentive'; Knorozov (1967:81): (= K048) "ah (ah')"; "ah-"; Thompson (1972:38): negative affix meaning 'there is no'.

1981–1990 V. Bricker (1986:208): /u/, "u" 'he, she, it; his, her, its' (Cholan, Yucatecan); Justeson (1984:316): J. Fox, J. Justeson, P. Mathews, D. Stuart: equivalent to T0001; /u/ documented; F. Lounsbury, L. Schele: semantic equivalent of T0001; B. Riese: equivalent to T0001; Stuart (1985c:2): T0012 and T0013 have value /a/ cf. Knorozov (1955, Sec. 2, 3–10).

1991–2008 Davoust (1995:554): "uh" 'collier'; /u/; Knorozov (1999, vol. 1:71): "ah," "ah' " (cinta o taparrabo).

HH1

T 0570
Z 1374
K 0320

b'àak / b'ak

n bone; captive

Yu *b'àak* bak 'hueso' (Barrera Vásquez et al. 1980:26f); baksah 'vencer, cautivar, esclavo, vencido, cautivo' (Barrera Vásquez et al. 1980:29); b'àak 'bone' (V. Bricker et al. 1998:24)

Ch' *b'ak* *b'ak 'bone' (Kaufman and Norman 1984:116)

1. Picture: bone

1951–1980 Barthel (1968:174–77): "baac" 'hueso'; Berlin (1958:111, 117): in Palenque emblem glyph; Kelley (1976:218, 333): Palenque emblem glyph; "baac" 'bone'; Knorozov (1967:100): phonetic; Thompson (1962:196f.): [66 examples] (wavy bone); Thompson (1972:84): with T0109 infixed might be 'turtle' glyph.

1981–1990 Justeson (1984:344): (= T0111) main sign of Palenque emblem glyph; J. Fox, J. Justeson, D. Stuart: logographic, including "*b'a:k" 'bone'; F. Lounsbury, P. Mathews: "b'ak" 'bone'; depicts bone; B. Riese: 'bone', 'captive' "b'a:k"; L. Schele: "b'ak"? 'bone'; depicts bone; Riese (1982:262): "baak" 'Knochen'; Stuart (1985a): substitution spelling "b'a-ki" for "bak" 'bone; captive'; main sign in "count of captives" glyph.

1991–2008 Davoust (1995:587): "bac" 'os'; Knorozov (1999, vol. 1:109, 130, 232): "baac" 'calabaza; hueso; débil; niño; preso, esclavo' (cráneo de recién nacido); Schele and Grube (1997:218): "bak" 'bone'.

HH2

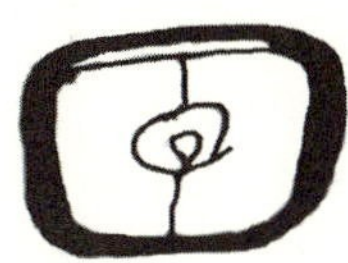

T 0663
Z 1317
K 0155

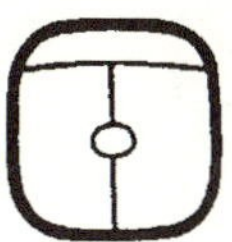

ch'é'en / ch'en?

n — cenote?, cave?; well?

Yu *ch'é'en* — ch'e'en 'pozo o cisterna o cueva de agua' (Barrera Vásquez et al. 1980:131); ch'é'en 'well' (V. Bricker et al. 1998:82)

Ch' *ch'en* — *ch'en 'cave' (Kaufman and Norman 1984:119)

Some examples appear to be 2S1. The two forms are graphically similar but appear to have different readings.

1. Picture: ?

1566–1915 Brasseur de Bourbourg (1869–1870, vol. 1:204): "p', p'a" 'sortir avec effort, rompre en sortant, ouvrir par force'.

1916–1950 Gates (1931:153f.): occurs heavily in planetary or constellation divisions of the Dresden. Paired persistently with "caban" (the earth sign); Thompson (1950:271): 'seed'.

1951–1980 Kelley (1976:333): "chumuc" 'center'; Knorozov (1955:75): 134 "tan"?; compárese "tan" 'medio, punto medio'; Knorozov (1967:92): "tang (tan)"; "tan" 'middle'; Thompson (1962:260f.): [70 examples] (seed) with T0526 'earth' indicates milpa; Thompson (1972:64): 'seed'.

1991–2008 Davoust (1995:594): "cun" 'plate-forme'; Knorozov (1999, vol. 1:132): "tang" (símbolo del centro); Knowlton (2002:10–12): "ch'een" 'cave, well', after Grube and Martin's (2000:62) interpretation of the Classic "bone" element (T0571, T0598, T0599) as "ch'een" on iconographic grounds. Occurs paired with "kab' " 'earth' to form expression "kab-ch'een" 'residence'; Schele (1992b:232–35): correspondence from MacLeod, 1991: "kun" 'seat, residence, place, origin'; Schele and Grube (1997:171): "kun" 'seat'; Stuart (2005:90): reads Classic "impinged bone" sign as "ch'een" 'cave, well, spring'.

HT2

T 0227bc
Z 0100
K 0341

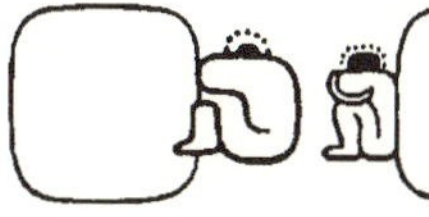

xìib' / xib'?; ná'ak?

n?; intr v? — male, man?; penis?; rise, climb?

Yu *xìib'; ná'ak* — xib 'varón; hombre; macho' (Barrera Vásquez et al. 1980:941); xiibil 'parte sexual del varón' (Barrera Vásquez et al. 1980:941); xìib' 'male, man', xìib'il 'penis' (V. Bricker et al. 1998:257); ná'ak 'rise, climb' (V. Bricker et al. 1998:194; nak'äl 'rise, ascend, go up' (Holfling with Tesucún 1997:462)

Ch' *xib'; ø* — *xib' 'male' (Kaufman and Norman 1984:136)

1. Picture: seated headless body

1566–1915 Brasseur de Bourbourg (1869–1870, vol. 1:201): /a/; 'cuisse d'homme, jambe'; Förstemann (1902:8): Mercury; Rosny (1883:17): "kinich-ahau" 'le dieu unique, oeil du soleil'.

1916–1950 Gates (1931:122): connotes an astronomical event of some sort.

1951–1980 Cordan (1963:113): "nak" 'sentado'; Dütting (1974:50): "nac" 'pain; ascend; throne'; Kelley (1976:102, 158, 332): (= T0703?); glyph for place of crossed bones; "nak" 'sit, belly, hide, smoke'?; Knorozov (1955:65): 001 (hombre sentado con signo complementario /m(o)/) "nak"; compárese con "nak" 'vientre'; Knorozov (1967:101): phonetic (corpse, swaddled in fetal position); Thompson (1962:60): [13 examples] (seated man); Thompson (1972:60): "ac" 'sit'.

1981–1990 Closs (1988:804–11): "xibah" in T0226:0501.0181; Grube (1990a:98): = T0703; Justeson (1984:332): F. Lounsbury: possibly = T0226.

1991–2008 H. Bricker and V. Bricker (n.d.): “nac” 'rise, climb' in astronomical contexts; V. Bricker (1992): "xib"; possibly "xìib(il)," 'male; penis', in substitution with T1048.0585 /xi-bi/ in Dresden Codex 22c; Davoust (1995:570): "ac" 'assis', "xib" 'male', "wa' " 'dresser'; /xi/; Davoust (1997:175): "ac" 'la tortue'; Knorozov (1999, vol. 1:164): "noc" (cadáver amortajado en posición fetal); Ringle and Smith-Stark (1996:335–38): 0227 = 0227 (antefix); 0703v (postfix only); Schele and Grube (1997:190): 'seated'.

HT2

T 0703
Z –
K –

This variant may be a distinct grapheme.

2. Picture: seated figure

1916–1950 Gates (1931:122): connotes an astronomical event of some sort.

1991–2008 Davoust (1997:214): "xib" 'effrayant'.

HT3

T –
Z –
K 0343

n equinox?

1. Picture: headless bodies back to back

1566–1915 Brinton (1895:23): represents union; Förstemann (1902:8): Mercury.

1916–1950 Gates (1931:122): connotes an astronomical event of some sort.

1951–1980 Knorozov (1967:101): "lot"? 'twins'; Thompson (1962:60): "In the doubled glyphs, the little men are seated back to back. Note that on D.68a the glyph is above a picture in two Chacs seated back to back, one in dry weather, the other in rain."

1981–1990 V. Bricker and H. Bricker (1988:S15f.): occurs in a scene referring to the vernal equinox.

1991–2008 V. Bricker (1992): "xib"; possibly "xìib(il)" 'male; penis', substitution spelling "xi-b'i" on Dresden Codex 22c; Davoust (1997:234): "wa'-aw" 'était dressé'; Knorozov (1999, vol. 1:164): "noc" (dos cadáveres amortajados en posición fetal, espalda con espalda); Schele and Grube (1997:191): 'back to back'.

HT4

T 0227a
Z 0100?
K 0342

éem / ehm

intr v descend

Yu *éem* emel 'descender o abajar de donde se había subido' (Barrera Vásquez et al. 1980:153); 'éem 'descend' (V. Bricker et al. 1998:9)

Ch' *ehm* *ehm 'go/come down' (Kaufman and Norman 1984:119)

1. Picture: body descending

1566–1915 Bowditch (1910:225): (with T0002) Mercury.

1916–1950 Gates (1931:122): connotes an astronomical event of some sort.

1951–1980 Knorozov (1967:101): morphemic (turned grapheme K341); Thompson (1972:77): "noc"? 'descend'.

1981–1990 Grube and Nahm (1990:19f.): "em"? 'descend'.

1991–2008 Davoust (1995:570): "em" 'descendre'; Knorozov (1999, vol. 1:164): "noc" (cadáver amortajado en posición fetal invertida); Mathews (in Wanyerka 1993:141): 'descending'; Ringle and Smith-Stark (1996:335–38): 0227 = 0227 (antefix); 0703v (postfix only); Schele and Grube (1997:133f.): "em" 'descended'.

HT7

T 0798
Z 0763
K 0387

Used in iconographic contexts as an offering (see Dresden 25 and 27); does not occur in a glyphic caption.
1. Picture: heart

1951–1980 Knorozov (1967:103): morphemic (fish head?); Thompson (1962:380): [3 examples] sacrificial food; Thompson (1972:91): copal?

1981–1990 Taube (1988:237): "Following a suggestion by Mary Miller (personal communication, 1983), I have recently argued that these represent human hearts."

1991–2008 Davoust (1995:606): "ohl" 'coeur'.

HT8

T 0298
Z 0018
K 0045

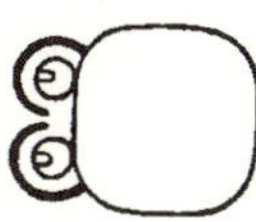

kum / chum

pos seating (of haab' period)

Yu *kum* kuma'n 'asentado'; kum 'olla' (Barrera Vásquez et al. 1980:351); kul 'sit down', kúulul 'seated' (V. Bricker et al. 1998:136)

Ch' *chum* *chum 'seated' (Kaufman and Norman 1984:118)

1. Picture: human torso?

1566–1915 Brinton (1895:21): 'twenty', identified independently by Pousee (1887) and later by Seler; according to Pousse, has the sense of 'last' or 'final', rather than of 'twenty'; Morley (1915:94): special sign for zero used exclusively as a month coefficient; Seler [1900] (1990:302–5): 'evening before'; Thomas (1893:246): "may, as Dr. Seler suggests, denote twenty or, more likely, show that the month is complete."

1916–1950 Spinden (1924:18–22): 'zero, completion'.

1951–1980 Knorozov (1967:80): /h'e/; Thompson (1972:76): 'seating'.

1981–1990 Grube (1990a:101): = T0287; Justeson (1984:335): J. Fox, J. Justeson, F. Lounsbury, P. Mathews, L. Schele: = T0644, codex form; F. Lounsbury: possibly "kum-," "kul-," or /wa/ in that order; P. Mathews: possibly 'kul."

1991–2008 Davoust (1995:575): "chum/cum" 'siège'; "ch'oc" 'jeune'; /ch'o/; Davoust (1997:195): '0'; Knorozov (1999, vol. 1:70, 235): "h'e" 'abrir'.

HTA

T 0702
Z 0103
K 0351

Unique codical example on Paris 5a; also occurs on Santa Rita murals.
1. Picture: legs with loincloth

1916–1950 Gates (1931:163): G370 [in part].

1951–1980 Kelley (1976:139, 333): lower body; Knorozov (1967:102): /x(u)/ (lower half of body with loincloth); Thompson (1962:297): [2 examples] (legs and loin cloth) at Santa Rita associated with tun 1 Ahau; in codex Paris with tuns 7 Ahau, 1 Ahau, and 8 Ahau.

1981–1990 Justeson (1984:352): J. Justeson: possibly "(w)ex"; L. Schele: body; appears to be neutral, with superfix to determine reading.

1991–2008 Davoust (1995:597): "oc" 'jambes'; Knorozov (1999, vol. 1:170): "ex" (piernas y taparrabo).

HTF

T 0301
Z 0104
K 0115

b'e

In iconographic contexts may be "b'èeh / b'ih" 'road'.

1. Picture: footprint

1566–1915 Brasseur de Bourbourg (1869–1870, vol. 1:201): "b, be" 'pas marche, chemin, voie'; Landa [1566] (Tozzer 1941:170): <b>; Thomas (1888:367f.): Landa's /b/, from "be" 'way, journey, walking'.

1951–1980 Kelley (1962a:302f.): "be" 'camino'; Kelley (1976:179, 182, 332): /be/; "be" 'road'; Knorozov (1955:66): 018 (huella de pie humano) "be"? 'camino'; Knorozov (1967:88): /b(e)/; (human footprint).

1981–1990 Hammond (1987:13): with T1010b, meaning "b'e" 'road', emphasizes progression from one god head to next; Justeson (1984:336): cf. Landa; L. Campbell, J. Fox, J. Justeson, P. Mathews, B. Riese: /b'e/, /b'i/; a footprint ("*b'e:h" 'road'); F. Lounsbury: /b'e/; D. Stuart: "b'e" footprint (for road); L. Schele: "b'e" footprint and road; Justeson et al. (1988:118f.): credit MacLeod "b'e:h" 'road', possibly numeral classifier "p'ehl"; MacLeod (1990a:509): /b'i/.

1991–2008 Davoust (1995:576): "beh" 'chemin', /be/; Knorozov (1999, vol. 1:118): /be/.

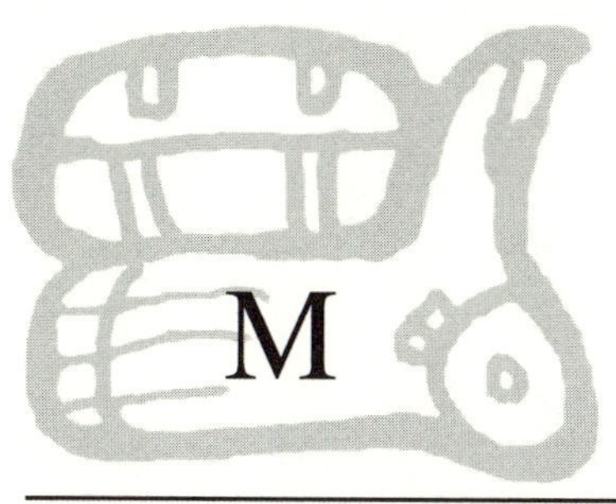

M Hands

MB1

T 0233a
Z 0047
K 0090

1. Picture: arms over head

1566–1915 Brasseur de Bourbourg (1869–1870, vol. 1:216): variante de signe "hunal-au" 'le vase d'eau entier'; Rosny (1883:18): [illustrates two variants, 179 and 180] 179: "uinic" 'homme'; 180: "xch'up" 'femme'.

1951–1980 Knorozov (1967:86): morphemic (head and uplifted arms).

1981–1990 Stuart et al. (1989:4): /a/ or "ah."

1991–2008 Davoust (1995:571): "ah" 'préf. genre masc.'; "hol" 'tête'; /a/; Davoust (1997:207): "zih" 'né'.

MB2

T 0234
Z 0005
K 0079

lòob' / lob'?

n — hurt, harm, damage?

Yu *lòob'* — lob 'cosa mala'; lobil 'maldad; pecado; ruindad' (Barrera Vásquez et al. 1980:454f.); lòob' 'wound, blow; hurt, harm, damage' (V. Bricker et al. 1998:170)

1. Picture: arm

1566–1915 Rosny (1883:19): "kab" 'bras'.

1951–1980 Dütting (1974:50): credits Barthel with "chek"? 'trample down'; Kelley (1976:139, 332): (partly an arm); Knorozov (1955:65): 010 (mano alzada abierta) /ch'(a)/; Knorozov (1967:85): /l(o)/? (raised arm with lowered hand, probably a ritual gesture); Thompson (1972:34): jaguar paw; symbol of war.

1981–1990 Justeson (1984:332): J. Fox, J. Justeson: Yucatecan "*lo:b' " 'bad'; depicts weeding stick ("indigenous hoe"), Yucatecan "*lo:b' ", cf. Huastec "lohob."

1991–2008 Davoust (1995:571): "lob" 'bâton à fouir, chose mauvaise'; /lo/; Knorozov (1999, vol. 1:99): /t'e/, /t'i/; Schele and Grube (1997:83): "lob" or "lobal" 'bad, badness'; Vail (1996:318–20): "ah" 'agentive prefix'.

MB7

T –
Z 0164?
K –

May have different value from Classic grapheme, where it represents "lahun/lajun" 'ten'; occurs on Dresden 55a as suffix to XH3 "ká'an / chan" 'sky'.

1. Picture: two hands

1951–1980 Thompson (1962:401): Z164 = T0221.

1991–2008 Schele and Grube (1997:171): /na/?

MR2

T –
Z 0163
K –

k'al?

trans v — close, fasten?

Yu *k'al* — k'al 'cerrar con cerradura y encerrar y atrancar y detener encerrado' (Barrera Vásquez et al. 1980:367); k'al 'close, cover, imprison, lock' (V. Bricker et al. 1998:143); k'älik 'close' (Hofling with Tesucún 1997:380); k'älik 'cerrar' (Ulrich and Ulrich 1976:65)

Some of the references refer to the hand without the "mirror."

1. Picture: flat hand with mirror

1566–1915 Brasseur de Bourbourg (1869–1870, vol. 1:204): "ch', ch'á" 'prendre, recevoir'; Brinton (1895:83): [hand only] 'offering'; Rosny (1883:19): [hand only] "kab" 'main'.

1951–1980 Kelley (1976:139, 160, 333): "naab" 'palm of the hand', 'measure'; Thompson (1962:303–5): [109 examples] (flat hand) may = T0217; Thompson (1972:67): may have meaning such as 'appearing' or 'is seen'.

1981–1990 Justeson (1984:353): (T0713a) J. Justeson, W. Norman: grammatical suffix deriving verb stem from noun; L. Schele: "pat/pach" 'back of hand'; verb for 'to accede' and 'to end'; Macri (1985:219): "lah" when coupled with "kab" is "u (i)lah kab" 'he saw the earth', and "lah" 'finished, ended' in period ending verbs. Note Dresden 47 "ilah" 'it was seen'.

1991–2008 Davoust (1995:Planche 165): "hol nen" 'ouvre miroir'; Davoust (1997:178): "kal" 'attache'; Fox (1997:16): (flat hand only) "kalah" 'completed' [in paper delivered in 1989]; Knorozov (1999, vol. 1:165): "naab"; MacLeod (1991d): "lik' " 'raise, rise'; Schele and Grube (1997:148): "k'alah" 'tied (to)' [in context of Dresden Venus table]; Schele and Looper (1996:19–22): /k'a/ and "k'al" 'close, fasten'; Stross (1994:192): /ye/; Stuart (1995:404–5): "k'al" 'to enclose; to tie up, fasten'; D. Tedlock and B. Tedlock (2002–2003:2): with T0181 suffix, "lik'ah" 'it is transplanted'.

MR7

T 0671
Z 0160
K 0266

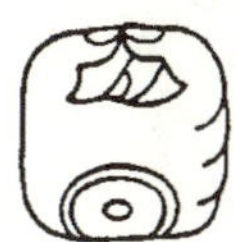

chi
kéeh / *chij*

n deer

Yu *kéeh* keh 'venado de los grandes' (Barrera Vásquez et al. 1980:308); kéeh 'deer' (V. Bricker et al. 1998:125)

Ch' *chij* *chij 'deer' (Kaufman and Norman 1984:118)

day 07: Manik'/Manich'

1. Picture: thumb to forefinger

1566–1915 Bollaert (1865–1866:52): "manik" 'feast'; Bowditch (1910:255): day Manik, /chi/; Brasseur de Bourbourg (1869–1870, vol. 1:206): day Manik; "manik, ma-nik" 'plus de force ou de vigueur' or "man-ik" for "mani-ik" 'a passe le souffle'; Brinton (1895:83): 'to grasp'; Goodman (1897:16): day Manik; Landa [1566] (Tozzer 1941:134): day Manik; Rosny (1883:5): day Manik.

1916–1950 Gates (1931:27): "Manik" 'deer; grasp'; Whorf (1933): /ma/.

1951–1980 Kelley (1962a:285, 288f.): /ce/, /chV/?; "ceh" 'deer'; Kelley (1962b:41): /ch(e)/; Kelley (1976:150, 155, 181, 333): = T0219; hand; day Manik; doubled, as "cech" 'sacrifice'; /ce/, /che/, /chi/, /ci/; Knorozov (1955:66): 014 (mano apretada) /ch(e)/; Knorozov (1967:98): /ch(i)/; Thompson (1962:271–75): [196 examples] (Manik hand); Thompson (1972:32): "chuc" 'to seize'?; Thompson (1972:45): 'deer'.

1981–1990 V. Bricker (1983:347): variant of day sign Manik (day Deer in other Mesoamerican calendars); by analogy "chih" 'deer' (Cholan); /chi/ in spelling "chikin" 'west'; V. Bricker (1983:349f.): "chi' " 'biting'; V. Bricker (1986:213): /chi/; Grube (1990a:113): = T0218b; Justeson (1984:350): L. Campbell, F. Lounsbury, B. Riese: /chi/; day Manik; J. Fox, J. Justeson, P. Mathews: /chi/; day Manik (= Deer), 'deer'; < a gesture for 'eat'; L. Schele, D. Stuart: /ti/ or /chi/; day Manik.

1991–2008 V. Bricker (1991:288, 290f.): "ceh" 'deer' in Classical Yucatec; Davoust (1995:594): "manik/manich" '7e jour'; /chi/; Davoust (1997:137): "chih" 'daim'; Knorozov (1999, vol. 1:167): /chi/ (mano en posición de asir un objeto cilíndrico); Schele and Grube (1997:118): "chih" 'deer'; Vail (2000a:52): Yucatec "keh," Ch'olan "chij" 'deer'; von Nagy (1997:46f.): "ceh" 'deer'.

MRB

T 0218abc
Z —
K 0507

tzúutz / **tzutz*

intr v finish, complete

Yu *tzúutz* tsuts 'cerrar lo que no se ha de abrir y tapar cerrando algún agujero, ventana o portillo y cerrar el camino y la llaga' (Barrera Vásquez et al. 1980:868); tzúutz 'close, fill up, obstruct, scar' (V. Bricker et al. 1998:45)

1. Picture: hand with bead

1566–1915 Morley (1915:78): ending sign, signifying completion.

1951–1980 Kelley (1962b:40): 'end, complete' (S. Morley, H. Beyer, J. E. S. Thompson, D. Kelley); "tzoc" (J. E. S. Thompson); "lah" (J. E. S. Thompson, D. Kelley); Knorozov (1967:106): "bak' " 'four hundred'.

1981–1990 Grube (1990a:97): (a) = T0713b.0165; (b) = T0219, T0221, T0671; Houston (1989:45f.): "lah" 'complete'; Justeson (1984:331): J. Justeson: completion of time periods, possibly related to T0710 'scattering'; MacLeod (1990b:339–41): "hul"? 'arrive'; Schele (1989a:3): "hom" 'end'.

1991–2008 Knorozov (1999, vol. 1:166): (mano asiendo un objeto); Ringle and Smith-Stark (1996:335–38): 0218 = 0218 = 0412 (last two examples); Schele (1991a): credits Stuart with "tzutz"; Schele and Freidel (1991:291f.): "hom" 'chasm'; Stuart (2001): substitution spellings "tzu-tza" and "tzu-tzu" for "tzutz" 'to end'.

MRF

T –
Z 0164
K –

1. Picture: right fist

1951–1980 Thompson (1962:401): Z0164 = T0221.

MRG

T 0713a
Z 0163
K 0263

May be "k'ab' / käb'" 'hand', either right or left hand.
1. Picture: flat hand

1566–1915 Brasseur de Bourbourg (1869–1870, vol. 1:204): "x (tch), chá" 'lâcher, relâcher, laisser'; Rosny (1883:19): "kab" 'main'.

1951–1980 Kelley (1976:139, 333): "naab" 'measure'; Knorozov (1955:66): 016 (mano vuelta a la derecha) "nab"?; Knorozov (1967:98): "ngab"; Thompson (1962:303–5): [109 examples] (flat hand) may be same as T0217.

1991–2008 Davoust (1995:597): "hol" 'entrée'; Knorozov (1999, vol. 1:165): "nab" (mano abierta).

MZ1

T 0217c
Z –
K –

On Madrid 34 occurs with XS1 and YS1. Collocation resembles Classic grapheme MZ2 "päs" 'dawn; open'.
1. Picture: hand

1981–1990 Justeson (1984:331): [T0217–0221] J. Justeson, F. Lounsbury, P. Mathews, B. Riese, L. Schele, D. Stuart: improperly divided and grouped; discussion needed.

1991–2008 Davoust (1995:569): "hol" 'entrée'; Knorozov (1999, vol. 1:166): "ok" (mano abierto con los dedos juntos señalando hacia arriba); Ringle and Smith-Stark (1996:335-38): 0217 = 0217 (superfix only) = 0711A (antefix) = 0713A (suffixes).

MZ1

T –
Z 0164
K 0271

Possibly equivalent to Classic grapheme MZ4 "ho' " 'five'.
2. Picture: hand

1951–1980 Knorozov (1967:98): (= K263) "ngab"; Thompson (1962:401): Z0164 = T0221.

MZ3

T 0669a
Z 0166
K 0258

k'a

1. Picture: death fist

1566–1915 Brasseur de Bourbourg (1869–1870, vol. 1:202): "k, ka" 'fiel, amertume, déjections volcaniques'; "káa" 'la pierre à broyer le grain, comme "cáa" '; Landa [1566] (Tozzer 1941:170): <k>.

1916–1950 Gates (1931:57): not a variant of day Cimi; never used as a day sign.

1951–1980 Kelley (1962a:285–87): /ka/; Kelley (1962b:41): /ka/; Kelley (1968b): /ka/; Kelley (1968c:144): /ka/; Kelley (1976:6, 139, 144, 150, 175, 177f., 200f., 333): /ka/; Knorozov (1955:65): 011 (puño con elementos complementarios) /k(a)/; Knorozov (1958:285): /k(a)/; Knorozov (1967:97): /k'(a)/; Thompson (1962:265–68): [182 examples] (death fist); when infixed with comb, an action glyph; death elements do not seem to make it a "glyph of ill omen"; Thompson (1972:30f.): "lah" in phrase "tanlahbil" 'served, taken care of' (T0074.0669.0130).

1981–1990 V. Bricker (1986:213): /ka/; Dütting (1985:110): /ka/ and "kab/kam" 'sacrificial knife/god's hand'; Furbee and Macri (1985:415): contains T0025 /ka/ as a phonetic complement; Justeson (1984:350): L. Campbell, J. Fox, J. Justeson: /k'a/; J. Fox, L. Campbell: /cha/; F. Lounsbury: /k'a/, not /cha/; P. Mathews, D. Stuart: /k'a/, /cha/; T0669a is from codices, T0669b from monuments; B. Riese: /k'a/ (cf. Landa) and /cha/ (cf. "mach" 'to grab' in codices); L. Schele: /k'a/; T0669b (Classic) and T0669a (codices) are the same sign; MacLeod (1983:50–55): /k'a/, "k'ah" 'remember'.

1991–2008 Davoust (1995:594): "kah" 'se souvenir'; /ka/; /cha/; Knorozov (1999, vol. 1:167): /ka/ (puño derecho hacia arriba); tiene 165 /ca/ inscrito.

MZ6

T 0221a
Z 0164
K –

On Dresden 66b occurs in place of the number three in "óox wí'il" expression. May not be the same as the Classic grapheme MZ6 "ok/och" 'enter'.

1. Picture: fist

1916–1950 Gates (1931:58): G024.1.5 [in part].

1981–1990 Grube (1990a:98): = T0218b; Justeson (1984:332): L. Campbell: hand form in head variant, possibly /cha/; P. Mathews: T0221 at least 4 different signs.

1991–2008 Davoust (1995:570): "ox" '3'; Ringle and Smith-Stark (1996:335–38): 0221 = 0221 (all except one with kin infix) = 0954A (with kin infix); Schele and Grube (1997:16): /k'o/; Schele and Grube (1997:192): "k'o" 'belly, stomach'.

MZ9

T 0668
Z 0169
K 0259

cha

cháak? / chahk?

n? rain god; God B

Yu *cháak* chaak 'fue un hombre así grande que enseñó la agricultura, al cual tuvieron después por Dios de los panes, del agua, de los truenos y relámpagos; Dios de la lluvia' (Barrera Vásquez et al. 1980:77); cháak 'rain' (V. Bricker et al. 1998:61)

Ch' *chahk* chajc 'rayo' (Aulie and Aulie 1998:29); *chahuk 'lightning, thunder' (Kaufman and Norman 1984:117); ah chak 'rain god' (Knowles 1984:392)

On several occasions substitutes for MZ3 /k'a/.

1. Picture: fist with "ik' " sign on eye

1566–1915 Brasseur de Bourbourg (1869–1870, vol. 1:202, 206): "k, ka" 'fiel, amertume, déjections volcaniques'; "káa" 'la pierre à broyer le grain, comme "cáa" '; day Cimi; "cimi" 'il est mort' or "ci-mi" 'non effervescence plus' or "cim-i" 'qui a pris une pointe, une pousse'; Rosny (1883:4): day Cimi; Schellhas [1892] (1904:16–19): in name of God B, who is probably Kukulcan; associated with life and creation; Thomas (1888:359): (with T0102) "Kukulcan"? long-nosed god; Maya Tlaloc.

1916–1950 Gates (1931:108): Itzamna.

1951–1980 Kelley (1962b:29): (with T0102 suffix) God B, rain; Chac (C. Brasseur de Bourbourg, E. Seler, S. Morley, J. E S. Thompson, Y. Knorozov, D. Kelley); Kukulcan (P. Schellhas, W. Fewkes, C. Thomas, E. Förstemann); Itzamna (D. Brinton); Kelley (1976:138): "chac"?; Knorozov (1955:66): 012 (puño con elementos complementarios) "chuc (chac)"; Knorozov (1967:97): "k'ax"; Thompson (1962:264f.): [207 examples] God B: sometimes denotes other deities in codices, particularly Dresden, except for three at Chichén and four at Uxmal; confirms Yucatecan origin of surviving codices; Thompson (1972:32): Chac, the rain god.

1981–1990 V. Bricker (1986:213): "chac" 'rain' (Yucatecan); Dütting (1985): /cha/; "chaac"; Fox and Justeson (1984:24–29): /cha/ and /k'a/; Justeson (1984:350): L. Campbell, J. Fox, J. Justeson: /k'a/, J. Fox: /cha/; F. Lounsbury: "k'ax," not /cha/; "ik' " 'wind' infix probably semantic determinative for Chac (suggested by B. Love); P. Mathews, D. Stuart: Chaac (God B); /k'a/, /cha/; B. Riese: /cha/; L. Schele: Chac, only with T-shaped eye; Stuart (1987:46): /cha/.

1991–2008 Davoust (1995:594): "chahc" 'divinité de la pluie'; "chah" 'se mutiler'; /ka/; /cha/; Knorozov (1999, vol. 1:168): "kax" (puño con elementos complementarios); Stuart (1997:7): /cha/; Taube (1992:17): conventional glyph of God B, Chac; usually postfixed with T0102 /ci/, probably for final consonant of Chac; Vail (1996): rain god Chac?, /cha/.

MZB

T 1028c
Z 0162 + 0110
K –

kelem

n young male

Yu *kelem* kelem 'fuerte, recio, juvenil' (Barrera Vásquez et al. 1980:310); kelem 'handsome', táan-kelem 'young man' (V. Bricker et al. 1998:126)

Ch' *kelem* *kelem 'strong' (Kaufman and Norman 1984:122)

Hand with thumb in mouth occurs with several deity heads. Prefix may signal the /ke/ of "kelem," but it does not occur in any other context.

1. Picture: supernatural face with hand

1566–1915 Schellhas [1892] (1904:40): hieroglyph of an unidentified figure in the Dresden manuscript.

1951–1980 Kelley (1962b:31): God U (G. Zimmermann, D. Kelley); Thompson (1972:56): name glyph of god pictured on D. 20b (God U).

1991–2008 Davoust (1995:614): "celem" 'jeune'; 'divinité U'; Grube (1994a:321): "kelem" 'young boy'; Knorozov (1999, vol. 1:189): "ez-cit" (combinación de 784.962); Ringle and Smith-Stark (1996:335–38): 1028c = 0220.1009; Schele and Grube (1997:88): "kelem" 'strong, young'.

MZB

T 1028v
Z 0162 + 0130?
K –

kelem

n young male

2. Picture: supernatural face with hand

1991–2008 Davoust (1997:308): "celem" 'nouvelle'; Schele and Grube (1997:228): "kelem" 'youth'.

MZD

T 0670
Z 0161
K 0268

la?

k'am / ch'äm?

trans v take; receive?

Yu *k'am* k'am 'receive' (V. Bricker et al. 1998:144); k'äm 'accept' (Hofling with Tesucún 1997:381); c'ümic 'encontrar, recibir, aceptar' (Ulrich and Ulrich 1976:65)

Ch' *ch'äm* *ch'äm 'receive; grab' (Kaufman and Norman 1984:119)

In most contexts may be /la/, but one example in Dresden is possibly "k'am / ch'äm."

1. Picture: open hand

1951–1980 Barthel (1963:172): "tz'a" 'to give', following Knorozov (1955:66); Kelley (1976:139, 333): hand; /dza/; Knorozov (1955:66): 015 (mano con el pulgar separado) /tz'a/; Knorozov (1967:98): phonetic; Thompson (1962:268–71): [92 examples].

1981–1990 V. Bricker (1986:106f.): functions as a semantic determinative or a pedestal in the 'child of mother' collocation; Dütting (1985): "pul" 'casting forth'; Justeson (1984:350): J. Fox, J. Justeson: logographic, including "b'ak' " 'to grasp'; infixed as the jaw on T1033 for the period of 400 ("*b'ahk' " '400') years of 360 days, as semantic determinative or phonetic complement; P. Mathews: refers to the holding of objects; L. Schele, D. Stuart: 'to hold or possess' (object or "term" held in hand).

1991–2008 Davoust (1995:594): "ch'am" 'recevoir'; "lah" 'achever'; /ch'a/; /la/; Knorozov (1999, vol. 1:166): "ez" (palma de la mano con el pulgar separado); Schele (1991b:42): at 1989 University of California at Santa Barbara conference suggested "ch'a" 'to take'; credits Stuart and Grube with noting examples with T0140, suggesting "ch'am" 'to receive'; Schele and Grube (1997:190): "k'am" 'receive'; Stuart (2000b:14–16): "k'a-ma" substitution spelling confirms use of Yucatecan form at Palenque; Vail (1996:350f.): may have had two functions in codices: as pedestal with no value (see V. Bricker 1986); as signal of presentation event.

MZD

T –
Z 0161
K –

k'am / ch'äm?

trans v take; receive?

Direct object of the verb may be represented by what is held in the hand.

2. Picture: open hand with object

1991–2008 Vail (2002b): "k'am" 'receive'?

MZE

T –
Z 0161
K –

àal / al; yäl

n; trans v — child of mother; throw down

Yu *àal; ø* — al, aal 'hijo o hija de la mujer' (Barrera Vásquez et al. 1980:9); 'àal 'son, daughter—woman speaking' (V. Bricker et al. 1998:4)

Ch' *al; yäl* — *al 'woman's offspring' (Kaufman and Norman 1984:115); *yäl 'throw down' (Kaufman and Norman 1984:137)

1. Picture: open hand with scroll

1566–1915 Brasseur de Bourbourg (1869–1870, vol. 1:204): "ch', ch'á" 'prendre, recevoir'.

1981–1990 Stuart (1985b): substitution spelling "ya-la" for "yal" 'child of (the woman)' on Grolier 47 in Coe (1973:103).

1991–2008 Ciaramella (1999): "al" 'child of mother'; metaphor for weaving, which is related to childbirth among the highland Maya; Hopkins (1991:255f.): "al" 'child of mother'; Schele and Grube (1997:191): "yal" 'throw' on D. 67a; Stuart (1997:2): "al" 'woman's child'; Vail (1996:351): variant form of T0019 occuring in "y-al" compound may be corn curl; /a/? value based on word "ah" 'maize' in highland languages.

MZE

T –
Z 0161
K –

àal / al

n — child of mother

2. Picture: open hand with "b'en" sign

1916–1950 Thompson (1962:209): T0584 occurs on an outstretched hand (T0670).

1981–1990 V. Bricker (1986:106f.): with T0126 prefix /ya-a-la/ "yal" 'woman's child'.

1991–2008 Hopkins (1991:255f.): "al" 'child of mother'; Schele and Grube (1997:131): "yal" 'her child'; Stuart (1997:7): "al" 'woman's child'; Vail (1996:353): "y-al" 'her child'.

MZE

T –
Z 0161
K –

àal / al

n — child of mother

3. Picture: open hand with upside-down ahaw

1981–1990 V. Bricker (1986:67, 106f.): "yal" 'woman's child'; Stuart (1985b): substitution spelling "ya-la" for "yal" 'child of (the woman)' on Grolier 47 in Coe (1973:103).

1991–2008 Hopkins (1991:255f.): "al" 'child of mother'; Stuart (1997:2): "al" 'woman's child'.

MZG

T –
Z 0164
K –

1. Picture: left hand, thumb up

1566–1915 Brinton (1895:83): 'to give'.

1951–1980 Thompson (1962:401): Z0164 = T0221.

1991–2008 Ciaramella (2002:58): "k'ab" 'punishment'.

MZJ

T 0780
Z –
K –

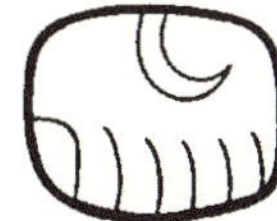

1. Picture: hand with curl

1566–1915 Brasseur de Bourbourg (1869–1870, vol. 1:208): day Imix; "im-ix" 'fond, profondeur, mamele ou canal du trou ou de l'urine, ou des sécrétions aqueuses'; "i-mix" 'de rejeton aucun, de pousse jamais'; Rosny (1883:11): day Ymix.

1951–1980 Thompson (1962:263f., 373): [11 examples]. Several examples listed as T0780 should possibly be regarded as T0667 with T0019 infixed. Gates and Zimmermann include these with T0667.

1981–1990 Grube (1990a:119): = T0667.

1991–2008 Davoust (1995:604): "ak" 'donner'; "ayan" 'être'; Knorozov (1999, vol. 1:168): "em" (puño volteado hacia abajo); Ringle and Smith-Stark (1996:350): exclusively in Madrid Codex either alone, doubled, or following T0667; resembles T0019, possibly a variant.

MZK

T 0714
Z 0164
K 0272

tzak / tzäk

trans v — conjure

Yu *tzak* — tsak 'conjurar nublados; conjurar temporales' (Barrera Vásquez et al. 1980:850)

Ch' *tzäk* — *tzäk-le 'chase after' (Kaufman and Norman 1984:133)

Fish may be an embedded phonetic complement /ka/.

1. Picture: fish in hand

1951–1980 Kelley (1976:139, 155, 334): fish-in-hand; credits de Gruyter with "tzac"; Knorozov (1967:98): phonetic (fish held in hand); Proskouriakoff (1973): associated with sacrifice; Thompson (1962:306): [30 examples] (hand grasping fish) frequently precedes glyphs for deities, particularly long-nosed god.

1981–1990 V. Bricker (1986:213): "tok" 'bleed' (Yucatecan); Justeson (1984:353): J. Fox, J. Justeson, P. Mathews: verb referring to a ritual; J. Fox, J. Justeson: possibly mutilation as in "chah" 'to maim oneself'; see Cholan "*chay" 'fish'; J. Justeson: = hand-grasping T0212, probably Thompson's last T0218 form; L. Schele, D. Stuart: bloodletting; Macri (1986): associated with bloodletting ritual, may be transitive; Ringle (1988:14-17): noting substitutions with T1016 in GI First Lord of the Night sequences, suggests possible reading of /ch'u/ or /ch'o/; related to "ch'uk" 'to take, grab, seize' or 'to lie in wait for'; a vision-related event.

1991–2008 Davoust (1995:598): "tzac" 'saisir, conjurer'; Knorozov (1999, vol. 1:161): "lut, lot" (mano con pescado asido); Schele (1991b:43, 86–89): credits Grube with identification of substitution spelling "tsa-ku" for "tsak" 'to take hold of' and 'to conjure demons' on Yaxchilán Lintel 25; Stuart (2001:15f.): "tzak, tzahk" 'to grasp, conjure'; Winters (1991): "tz'ak" 'counting/augmenting the lineage; poison/cure process', the taking of dangerous medicine to connect with one's lineage; involves conjuring/communication, rather than an explicit reference to bloodletting.

MZP

T –
Z 0164
K –

k'o?

1. Picture: closed hand

1951–1980 Thompson (1962:401): Z0164 = T0221.

1981–1990 Schele (1990b): "hob"?

1991–2008 Davoust (1995:569): "koh" 'masque'; /ko/; Davoust (1997:197): "k'o" 'l'estomac'; Schele (1992b:123): "k'oh" 'mask'; Schele and Grube (1997:202): /k'V/ in spelling of "tok' " 'flint'.

MZQ

T 0667
Z 0167
K 0260

yàan / an, ayan?

intr v — he/she/it is; there are

Yu *yàan* — an 'ser, existir, estar' (Barrera Vásquez et al. 1980:16); yan 'ser o estar en el mundo' (Barrera Vásquez et al. 1980:967); yàan 'there exists'; cf. 'an' (V. Bricker et al. 1998:312)

Ch' *an; ayan* — *ayan 'there is/are' (Kaufman and Norman 1984:116); an 'to be, exist' (Knowles 1984:397)

Graphically similar to ZYC, but the two occur in distinct contexts.

1. Picture: closed hand with mirror infix

1566–1915 Brinton (1895:83): inauspicious significance.

1916–1950 Whorf (1942:484, fig. 1): infix is "l"; /lu/; /lo/; hand is "m"; /ma/.

1951–1980 Kelley (1976:139, 144, 333): (= 0712) "et" 'to hold'; Knorozov (1955:66): 013 (puño bajado) "max (mach?)"; Knorozov (1967:97f.): "em" (fist turned down); Thompson (1962:263f.): [114 examples] (inverted fist) see T0780 for similar sign with hook infix; probably the same as T0667 with T0019 infixed; Thompson (1972:31): "dz'a" 'to give'.

1981–1990 V. Bricker (1986:213): "ak"? 'tongue' (Cholan, Yucatecan); Dütting (1985:111–12): T0667 is paleograph of T0712 epigraph, "ak/aan" 'tongue, fresh, tender, new'; Fox and Justeson (1984:56, n.34): "yàan" 'to exist; to be (in a place)'; Grube (1990a:113): = T0712, T0780, T0840; Justeson (1984:350): J. Fox, J. Justeson, B. Riese: verb 'to be (in a place), to exist'; including Yucatecan "*ya:n," Cholan "*ayan" (see also T0840); J. Fox, J. Justeson: possibly equivalent to T0712 on M. 96b, where it is not a verb 'to be' but a possessed noun; P. Mathews, L. Schele, D. Stuart: = T0712.

1991–2008 Davoust (1995:594): "ak" 'donner'; "ayan" 'être'; Knorozov (1999, vol. 1:168): "em" (puño volteado hacia abajo); MacLeod (personal communication, 1994): /ya/; Ringle and Smith-Stark (1996:335–38): 0667 (retired) = 0712v; Schele and Grube (1997:192): "an" 'to exist'; von Nagy (1997:63f.): refers to a sacrifice.

P Persons

PC3

T 1025b
Z 0115
K 0314

n moon goddess

1. Picture: moon personified

1951–1980 Kelley (1962b:30): Venus table goddess; Moon goddess (J. E. S. Thompson, D. Kelley); water goddess (T. Barthel); Knorozov (1967:105): "ha."

1981–1990 Thompson (1972:64): young moon goddess.

1991–2008 Davoust (1995:614): "na'uh" 'déesse lunaire I'; Knorozov (1999, vol. 1:184): "u-haa"; combinación de 171.446; Ringle and Smith-Stark (1996:335–38): 1025a,b (retired) = 0181H, 0683H; Schele and Grube (1997:147): "Ixik Uh" 'Moon Goddess'; Taube (1992:66): moon goddess.

PC4

T 1037
Z 0130
K 0222

nal / näl?; xìib' / xib'?

n north; maize; male, man

Yu *nal; xìib'* nal 'maíz en barra, o en caña, o en mazorca, y la mazorca antes que la desgranen' (Barrera Vásquez et al. 1980:557); nal 'ear of corn' (V. Bricker et al. 1998:194); näl 'ear of corn' (Hofling with Tesucún 1997:466); näl 'mazorca' (Ulrich and Ulrich 1976:144); xib 'varón; hombre; macho' (Barrera Vásquez et al. 1980:941); xiibil 'parte sexual del varón' (Barrera Vásquez et al. 1980:941); xìib' 'male, man', xìib'il 'penis' (V. Bricker et al. 1998:257)

Ch' *näl; xib'* *näl 'corn ear' (Kaufman and Norman 1984:126); xiba 'diablo' (Aulie and Aulie 1998:148); *xib' 'male' (Kaufman and Norman 1984:136)

1. Picture: head

1566–1915 Morley (1915:19): part of the name "Xaman Ek" 'the north star god'; Rosny (1883:18): "xaman ou xamin" 'nord'.

1916–1950 Gates (1931:99): "xaman" 'north'.

1951–1980 Barthel (1953:92) "xib"; Berlin and Kelley (1970:14): follow "xib" 'youth' reading of Barthel (1953) and Knorozov (1955); Kelley (1976:193, 194, 334): "xib" 'boy, youth'; Knorozov (1955:66): 020 (rostro con un confuso elemento complementario) "xib" 'varón'; Knorozov (1967:96): "xib"; Thompson (1972:82): 'god of the north'.

1981–1990 V. Bricker (1983:351): "caan/chan" in collocation for zenith "u chan" 'its height, above'; Grube (1990a:133): 'norden'; Schele, Mathews, and Lounsbury (1990a): /na/.

1991–2008 Davoust (1995:616): "xib" 'homme'; "nal" 'nord'; Knorozov (1999, vol. 1:188): "xib" (perfil masculino); se distingue de 973 únicamente por el elemento de la parte superior; Schele (1992b:19–22): "nal" 'north'; Schele and Grube (1997:222): "xib"; also in grapheme for "na" 'north'; Taube (1992:17): "xib" in title "chak xib chak."

PC4

T —
Z —
K —

nal?

n north

2. Picture: head with "na" sign prefix

1566–1915 Rosny (1883:18): "xaman" ou "xamin" 'nord'.

1916–1950 Gates (1931:99, 101): "xaman" 'north'.

1951–1980 Kelley (1962b:26): 'north' (L. de Rosny et al.), Yucatec "xaman"; Thompson (1972:37): 'north'.

1981–1990 V. Bricker (1983:350f.): codical variant of zenith; "u chan" 'its height, above'; Schele, Mathews, and Lounsbury (1990a): /na/.

1991–2008 V. Bricker and H. Bricker (1992:fig. 2.8): "na-caan" 'zenith'; Lamb (2005:164): "xaman"? 'north' or "na k'ul/ch'ul" 'great god' or 'great temple'; Schele and Grube (1997:21): /na/; "nal" 'north"; Stuart (1998:376f.): "nah" 'house, building, structure' in Classic texts.

PC4

T 1016v
Z 0130
K 0224

nal / näl?; xìib' / xib?

n maize (god); north; male, man?

Graphically similar to AMC. Often has 1M2 prefixed. Some examples of PC4 in the Madrid equivalent to PE8 in the Dresden. References listed below only apply to T1016 as PC4.

3. Picture: head

1566–1915 Morley (1915:19): part of the name "Xaman Ek" 'the north star god'; Rosny (1883:18): (with T0001 prefix) "xaman" ou "xamin" 'nord'; Schellhas [1892] (1904:19f.): the head of God C is contained in the sign for north; Thomas (1882:161): [with T0001 prefix] 'north'.

1916–1950 Gates (1931:101): "xaman" 'north'; 'god of the north'.

1981–1990 V. Bricker (1983:351): "caan/chan" in collocation for zenith "u chan" 'its height, above'; Ringle (1988:18f.): appears in some glyphs for north in the Madrid Codex. May be scribal carelessness; the compound T0048.1016c may represent "noh ek'," given by Morán (1935:47) for north. Support for T1016c as "ek' " 'star' comes from its appearance in skybands; Schele, Mathews, and Lounsbury (1990a): /na/.

1991–2008 Schele (1992b:19–22): "nal" 'north'; Taube (1992:27): God C, "ku/ch'u" 'sacredness, divinity'; misidentified as 'north' based on its reputed presence in the sign for north. However, in the Dresden Codex, the most carefully painted of the Maya manuscripts, the God C glyph never serves as the main sign for 'north'; Vail (2002b): substitutes for T1006c in Madrid, portrait of the maize god Nal, and occurs in Madrid in place of T1037 (possibly "nal") in Dresden; von Nagy (1997:40): "xaman" 'north'.

PCE

T 1026
Z 0109
K 0203

ix kàab' / ixik kab'

n lady earth; Goddess I

Yu *ix kàab'* x- 'feminine agent' (V. Bricker et al. 1998:363); kàab' 'land, world' (V. Bricker et al. 1998:118)

Ch' *ixik kab'* *ixik 'woman' (Kaufman and Norman 1984:121); kab' 'earth, land' (Kaufman and Norman 1984:122)

1. Picture: female head with "kab'an" sign infix

1566–1915 Schellhas [1892] (1904:31f.): Goddess I, the water goddess; a personification of water in its quality of destroyer, a goddess of floods and cloudbursts; Seler [1899] (1990:250): sign Caban contains dark bunches of hair and long locks seen in this glyph because "caban" is the earth and the earth is regarded as feminine; Thomas (1888:351): [with T0171 prefix] "chuplel" 'woman, female'.

1916–1950 Gates (1931:119): "ixchel" 'lady; woman'.

1951–1980 Kelley (1962b:30): glyphs of young (moon?) goddess (with T0058 and T0171 prefixes); identified as Ix Colel 'Our Mistress' (J. E. S. Thompson), "zac chup" (Y. Knorozov, D. Kelley), 'sterile woman' (Y. Knorozov), White Lady (W. J. de Gruyter, D. Kelley); Knorozov (1955:66): 019 (rostro con signo complementario /ti/) "ch'up" 'mujer'; Knorozov (1967:95): "ch'up" 'woman'; Thompson (1972:47): "Colel" 'our lady, the moon goddess'. "My thesis that the moon was also goddess of the earth and the maize is confirmed by Siegel (1941:66) who reports that the Mam call the moon and also the earth and maize Our Mother."

1981–1990 Grube (1990a:130): Göttin I; Justeson (1984:361): J. Fox, J. Justeson, P. Mathews, B. Riese: Moon goddess Chel, sometimes with "zac" and "chac" prefixes; Stone (1990): earth goddess, as suggested by the "kab" 'earth' infix.

1991–2008 Ciaramella (1999:46): "ch'up" 'woman'; Davoust (1995:614): "hunac" 'déesse lunaire I'; "na' " 'mere'; /na/; Davoust (1997:100): "ixic" 'la déesse I'; Grofe (2007:226): Ixik Kab'; may refer to waxing moon; Knorozov (1999, vol. 1:180): "ch'up" (perfil de mujer con un rizo de pelo); Milbrath (1999:138f.): moon goddess with T0171 'moon' infix; Schele and Grube (1997:122): "Ixik" 'goddess'; Taube (1992:64–69): young Goddess I, commonly associated with the moon; however, little direct evidence that Goddess I was the moon or was named Ix Chel; D. Tedlock and B. Tedlock (2007:124): "ixik" 'woman' with "uh" 'moon' infix; Vail (1996:278–81): youthful Goddess I, whose primary associations are with the earth, "Colel Cab" 'Mistress of the Earth'; "cab" reading suggested by infixed T0171, used in iconographic contexts with meaning of "cab" 'earth' or 'beehive'; Vail and Stone (2002): Ixik Kab' 'Lady Earth'.

PCE

T 0171
Z 0015
K 0038

ix kàab' / ixik kab'

n lady earth; Goddess I

Some of the references below refer to T0171 by itself, others to T0171 paired with T1026.

2. Picture: female head with "kab'an" sign prefix and infix

1566–1915 Brasseur de Bourbourg (1869–1870, vol. 1:204): "u"; Brinton (1895:99f.): 'woman, female' and 'earth'; Thomas (1888:351): "chuplal" 'woman, female'; scroll with heavy black dot denotes the locks of hair.

1951–1980 Cordan (1964:18f.): " 'x, *kix" prefijo de mujeres, liquido derramado (según Seler), 'mecha de pelo'; Kelley (1976:69, 332): (curl); Knorozov (1955:74): 124 (líquido que se vierte) "chup (chub?)"; Knorozov (1967:80): "ch'up" (pouring liquid?), compare Old Yucatec "chup" 'to fill'; Thompson (1972:47): "cab" 'earth' symbol; used in the name glyph of the moon goddess; also Landa's /u/, corresponding to "u" 'moon'. "Perhaps this earth symbol was assigned to the moon goddess because she was, as in other parts of Middle America, also a goddess of the soil."

1981–1990 Justeson (1984:328): L. Campbell, P. Mathews, L. Schele: possibly "u"; J. Fox, J. Justeson: sign number should be dropped; one form (D.71a) is misidentified (= T0172); others are iconic, not glyphic, attached to forehead of T1027 moon goddess; Landa's <u>, based on "*u:h" 'moon'; F. Lounsbury: /u/; Stone (1990): "kab" 'earth, honey'.

1991–2008 Davoust (1995:565): "uh" 'lune'; /u/, /hu/; Knorozov (1999, vol. 1:88): (0153) "ch'up" (rizo de cabello de mujer); aparece inscrito en la oreja del grafema 896 y delante de este mismo; (0896) "ch'up" (perfil de mujer con un rizo de pelo); Milbrath (1999:138f.): moon goddess with T0171 'moon' prefix reinforcing her lunar aspect; Ringle and Smith-Stark (1996:335–38): 0171 (retired) = (misidentified); Ringle and Smith-Stark (1996:342–43): number should be retired since Thompson's examples are either misidentified or, in the case of T1026, best viewed as attributes; Schele and Grube (1997:122): "Uh Ixik" 'Moon Goddess'; D. Tedlock and B. Tedlock (2007:124): "uh" 'moon' prefix and infix to "ixik" 'lady' main sign; Vail (1996:279): "cab" 'earth; bee, honey, beehive'; Vail and Stone (2002:210): Ixik Kab' 'Lady Earth'.

PCE

T 1028d
Z 0109
K –

ix kàab' / ixik kab'

n lady earth; Goddess I

3. Picture: female head with infixed hand

1951–1980 Thompson (1972:57): "a unique compound which from the context should denote some aspect of the moon goddess."

1991–2008 Davoust (1995:614): "hunac" 'grand, infini'?; Davoust (1997:158): "ixic" 'la déesse I'; Ringle and Smith-Stark (1996:335–38): 1028d = 0220.1026; Stone (1990): portrait substitutes for T1026 on Dresden 21; pun on "k'ab" 'hand' (this example) for "kab" 'earth' (T1026); D. Tedlock and B. Tedlock (2007:124): variant of T1026 "ixik uh" 'moon lady'; Vail (1996:281): Goddess I, earth goddess, with "kab" hand substituting for T0171 "cab" in what appears to be an example of word play.

PCF

T 1027
Z 0108
K –

ix kàab' / ixik kab'

n lady earth; Goddess I

Aged variant of PCE.

1. Picture: female head with "kab'an" sign infix and wrinkles

1566–1915 Brasseur de Bourbourg (1869–1870, vol. 1:203): "p, pe" 'venir, marcher', ant. "pa" 'ouvrir'; Schellhas [1892] (1904:38): Goddess O.

1916–1950 Gates (1931:120): old woman.

1951–1980 Kelley (1962b:30): "ix" in name glyph of Ix Chel on M. 102d; Thompson (1972:33): [T0109.1026.0145] Goddess O, old red goddess of weaving.

1981–1990 Grube (1990a:130): Göttin O; Stone (1990): earth goddess, as suggested by the "kab" 'earth' infix.

1991–2008 Davoust (1995:614): "na'cheel" 'déesse du tissage: O'; Davoust (1997:98): "chel"; Jones and Jones (1997:192): "ix"; Knorozov (1999, vol. 1:181): "ch'up" (perfil de mujer vieja); Taube (1992:64–69): aged aspect of Goddess I; associated with weaving in the codices; Vail (1996:278–81): aged Goddess I, whose primary associations are with the earth, "Colel Cab" 'Mistress of the Earth'; Vail and Stone (2002): aged variant of Ixik Kab' 'Lady Earth'.

PCG

T –
Z –
K –

1. Picture: head with wrinkles

1916–1950 Gates (1931:120): old woman.

PCH

T –
Z –
K 0202

Examples may represent more than one grapheme.

1. Picture: head

1951–1980 Knorozov (1967:95): morphemic (profile face).

1991–2008 Schele and Grube (1997:20): /na/, based on substitution for T0023 in earth + "impinged-bone" glyphs.

PCJ

T 0731
Z 0113, 0704
K 0256

u

uh?

n moon?
Yu *uh* u 'collar de cuentas o sartal' (Barrera Vásquez et al. 1980:896); 'uh 'bead; moon' (V. Bricker et al. 1998:20)
Ch' *uh* *uh 'moon' (Kaufman and Norman 1984:135)

1. Picture: head with headband

1566–1915 Brasseur de Bourbourg (1869–1870, vol. 1:204): "p', p'a"? 'sortir avec effort, rompre en sortant, ouvrir par force'.

1951–1980 Knorozov (1967:97): phonetic (animal with an additional element); Thompson (1962:312): [25 examples] two styles; the one with dots outlining the "horizontal omega" (= Z0113) may not be T0731; Thompson (1972:104): numeral classifier?; shares coefficients with "uinal" signs in passages recounting dangers at heliacal rising on the Venus pages.

1991–2008 Davoust (1995:599): "uht" 'arriver'; /u/; Davoust (1997:189): "uh" 'lune'; Knorozov (1999, vol. 1:185): "ul," "hul"; Schele and Grube (1997:152): "uh" 'moon'; Vail (1996:317f.): possibly /ba/ or "bah/bal" 'thing'; occurs with T0234 prefix, like T0558, T0757, and T0791b.

PCK

T 0735
Z 0701
K 0252

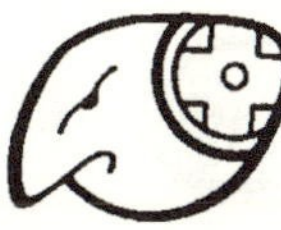

k'ìin / k'in?

n sun, day; priest?
Yu *k'ìin* k'in 'día, sol' (Barrera Vásquez et al. 1980:400); k'ìin 'day, sun' (V. Bricker et al. 1998:152); ah k'in 'sacerdote' (Barrera Vásquez et al. 1980: 401)
Ch' *k'in* *k'in 'sun, day' (Kaufman and Norman 1984:124)

1. Picture: head with "k'än" sign infix

1951–1980 Knorozov (1967:93, 97): (= K172) "k'ing/k'in" 'sun'; Thompson (1962:314): [8 examples] (head with Kan infix) may be same as T0734.

1981–1990 Grube (1990a:116): = T0734.

1991–2008 Davoust (1995:599): "kin" 'jour'; "oc kin" 'entrée du jour'; Davoust (1997:107): "on kin" 'apparenté au soleil'; Knorozov (1999, vol. 1:185): "king"; Ringle and Smith-Stark (1996:335–38): 0735 (retired) = 0734b; Schele and Grube (1997:86f.): "on"? in the expressions "onel" 'parent in direct line; distant parentage; progenitor'; "yonel" 'relative'; "ah on" 'flatterer, palliator; somebody who talks bluntly'; Vail (1996:346–47): "kan"? in expression T0115.0735:(0024/0116) "ah kan" 'precious one'; Vail (2002b): "k'in" reading in expression T0115.T0734/T0735, "y-ah? k'in" 'he is the priest'.

PCK

T 0734
Z 0700
K 0251

k'ìin / k'in?

n sun, day; priest?

2. Picture: head with "k'in" sign infix

1916–1950 Gates (1931:71): personification of "kin."

1951–1980 Knorozov (1955:67): 027 (rostro con signo complementario "kin") "kin"; Knorozov (1967:93, 97): (= K172) "k'ing/ k'in" 'sun'; Thompson (1962:313): [17 examples] (head with Kin infix) two examples are preceded by head variants of the numbers 6 and 16, suggesting that T0734 represents "kin" 'day'; Thompson (1972:84): variant of the 'sun' glyph?

1981–1990 V. Bricker and H. Bricker (1988:fig. 5): "kin"; Grube (1990a:116): = T0735, T0765c.

1991–2008 Davoust (1995:599): "kin" 'jour'; "oc kin" 'entrée du jour'; Knorozov (1999, vol. 1:185): "king"; Ringle and Smith-Stark (1996:335–38): 0734 = 0734a; Schele and Grube (1997:86f.): "on"? in the expressions "onel" 'parent in direct line; distant parentage; progenitor'; "yonel" 'relative'; "ah on" 'flatterer, palliator; somebody who talks bluntly'; Vail (1996:346f.): "kin"? in expression T0115.0734:(0024/0116) "ah kin" 'priest'; Vail (2002b): "k'in" reading in expression T0115.T0734/T0735, "y-ah? k'in" 'he is the priest'.

PCL

T 1064
Z 0135
K 0219

k'awil?

n smoking mirror?; K'awil, God K?

Yu *k'awil* k'awil 'alimento'; itsamná k'awil 'el nombre de una deidad [dadora de alimentos]' (Barrera Vásquez et al. 1980:387)

1. Picture: head with mirror infix and fire sign

1951–1980 Knorozov (1967:85, 96): (= K082) /itz/ "itz" 'dew'.

1991–2008 Davoust (1995:617): "kawil" 'divinité K'; Knorozov (1999, vol. 1:184): "itz"?; Love (1994:20): credits Taube with "God K" reading (personal communication, 1991).

PCM

T –
Z –
K –

Possibly /u/ or /a/.

1. Picture: head

PE1

T 1005
Z 0111
K 0212

kàab' ahaw / kab' ajaw?

n earth god; God R

Yu *kàab'* kab 'el mundo, pueblo o región; bajo o abajo' (Barrera Vásquez et al. 1980:277); kàab' 'land, world' (V. Bricker et al. 1998:118)

Ch' *kab'* *kab' 'earth, land; town' (Kaufman and Norman 1984:122)

1. Picture: "kab'an" sign personified

1566–1915 Brasseur de Bourbourg (1869–1870, vol. 1:202): "k, ka" 'fiel, amertume, déjections volcaniques'; "káa" 'la pierre à broyer le grain, comme "cáa" '; Brinton (1895:123): the god of war, or "a companion of the god of death"; Goodman (1897:48): 'eleven'; Schellhas [1892] (1904:25): in name of God F.

1916–1950 Gates (1931:117): not variant of God F as suggested by Schellhas. Occurs with a beneficent deity who at times resembles the corn god. May be manifestation of that deity.

1951–1980 Kelley (1962b:29): main sign of God F (P. Schellhas), a benevolent deity; relettered God R (J. E. S. Thompson); R and Q distinguished but not by these letters by E. Seler; Knorozov (1955:66): 022 (rostro con dos signos complementarios) "ch'abtan" (solamente en el nombre del dios Buluc Ch'abtan); Knorozov (1967:95): "ch'ab."

1981–1990 Grube (1990a:128): Zahl 11, Gott R; Justeson (1984:360): [T1005a] P. Mathews, L. Schele, D. Stuart: head variant of "kab' "; L. Schele, D. Stuart: 'eleven'.

1991–2008 Davoust (1995:611): "ch'abtan"?; Knorozov (1999, vol. 1:198): "ch'ab," dios R, Ch'abtan; Ringle and Smith-Stark (1996:352): Because it occurs with the coefficient 'eleven', Thompson classifies T1005b with one of the Classic period head variants for XI (1005a), which also shares "caban" markings; Taube (1992:112–15): God R, identified with the numeral eleven, may be an aspect of the spotted Headband Twin Hunahpu; Vail (1996:291): earth deity, as suggested by "cab" 'earth' infix.

PE5

T —
Z —
K —

Classic variant has suggested value /u/. Codical grapheme may have different value.

1. Picture: ?

1916–1950 Gates (1931:118): G105 [in part].

1991–2008 Davoust (1997:214): = 0188?

PE6

T 1052
Z 0154
K 0237

kíim / chäm?

n?; adj? death; dead?

Yu *kíim* kim 'morir' (Barrera Vásquez et al. 1980:317); kíim 'die' (V. Bricker et al. 1998:128)

Ch' *chäm* *chäm 'die' (Kaufman and Norman 1984:117)

1. Picture: head with closed eye

1951–1980 Knorozov (1967:96, 101): = K341; only in Paris Codex; phonetic.

1991–2008 Davoust (1995:617): "cim/cam" 'mort'; Knorozov (1999, vol. 1:192): "nup' " (cara de perfil con el ojo cerrado); Love (1994:30): T1052.0548 = 'death tun'; Paxton (1992:226f.): /k'a/ in spelling of "k'atun" in Paris Codex; Vail and Hernández (2005–2008): substitutes for T0736 "kíim/chäm" in Paris, suggesting it has this value.

PE7

T 1024
Z 0136
K 0232

kam?

n death?; God A'

1. Picture: head with "ak'b'al" sign

1951–1980 Kelley (1962b:29): with T0024 prefix, God A' (G. Zimmermann), death god; Uac Mitun Ahau (E. Seler); Knorozov (1967:96): (= K231) /b(i)/?; Thompson (1972:67): underworld god.

1981–1990 Grube (1990a:131): = T1042, Gott A.

1991–2008 Davoust (1995:614): "uh" 'lune'/divinité A'?; /u/; Grube and Nahm (1994:708f.): "akan" 'god of alchoholic beverages'; Knorozov (1999, vol. 1:191): T1024 = T1042a,b (calavera con elementos inscritos); Martin, Zender, and Grube (2002:20f.): "akan;" Ringle and Smith-Stark (1996:335–38): 1024 (retired) = 1042c; Ringle and Smith-Stark (1996:352): reclassified by Thompson (1972:67) as T1042, the name glyph of God A'; Taube (1992:14–16): God A', associated with violent sacrifice and self-decapitation; Vail (1996:251f.): main sign of God A'; other variants of his name (with T1038a and T1042) read "cam" 'death'.

PE7

T 1042
Z 0120
K 0234

kam?

n death?; God A'

2. Picture: head with death symbols

1951–1980 Kelley (1962b:29): with T0015 prefix, God A' (G. Zimmermann), death god; Uac Mitun Ahau (E. Seler); Kelley (1976:62): God A'; Knorozov (1967:96): (= K233) "tzek' " 'skull'; Thompson (1962:400): Z120 = T1047; Thompson (1972:38): death god.

1991–2008 Davoust (1997:116): "chah" 'divinité A3'; Grube and Nahm (1994:708f.): name in pottery texts has "ah" prefix and "na" suffix; suggests "akan" 'god of alchoholic beverages'; Knorozov (1999, vol. 1:191): "tzek" (calavera); tiene 383 "bang" inscrito; Martin, Zender, and Grube (2002:20f.): "akan"; Taube (1992:14–16): God A', associated with violent sacrifice and self-decapitation; Vail (1996:251f.): "cam" 'death'.

PE8

T 1006b
Z 0126
K 0214

nal / näl; waxak / waxäk

n; num — maize god; eight

Yu *nal; waxak* — nal 'maíz en barra, o en caña, o en mazorca, y la mazorca antes que la desgranen' (Barrera Vásquez et al. 1980:557); nal 'ear of corn' (V. Bricker et al. 1998:194); näl 'ear of corn' (Hofling with Tesucún 1997:466); näl 'mazorca' (Ulrich and Ulrich 1976:144); waxak 'ocho' (Barrera Vásquez et al. 1980:915); waxak 'eight' (V. Bricker et al. 1998:300)

Ch' *näl; waxäk* — *näl 'corn ear' (Kaufman and Norman 1984:126); *waxäk 'eight' (Kaufman and Norman 1984:138)

1. Picture: maize personified

1566–1915 Brasseur de Bourbourg (1869–1870, vol. 1:204): "p, pa" 'sortir avec effort, rompre en sortant, ouvrir par force'; Brinton (1895:123) Ghanan, 'a male maize god'; Goodman (1897:46): 'eight'; Schellhas [1892] (1904:24f.): God E, the maize god; Seler [1899] (1990:252): 'eight'; Tozzer and Allen (1910:pl. 24): glyph apparently representing a trogon's head (quetzal, "Pharomacrus mocinno").

1916–1950 Gates (1931:106): "yum kaax" 'corn god'.

1951–1980 Kelley (1962b:29): main sign of God E, maize; Tzeltal Ghanan (D. Brinton); Yum Kaax 'lord of harvest' (P. Schellhas, S. Morley, D. Kelley); Kelley (1976:63f., 126, 334): corn god; may be read Yum Kaax 'Lord of Harvest'; Knorozov (1955:67): 025 (rostro con signo complementario, 113, 124?); el ovalo tiene un contorno del signo mazorca; "kavil" ("chabil"); Knorozov (1967:95): "vil" 'food'; Thompson (1972:32): maize god.

1981–1990 Grube (1990a): Zahl 8, Maisgott; Justeson (1984:360): J. Fox, J. Justeson, P. Mathews: corn god in codices; F. Lounsbury: maize god "xi'im," related to T1008 "xib' " sign; P. Mathews: "xi'im"; L. Schele: maize god "ixim"?; Schele, Mathews, and Lounsbury (1990a): T1006 maize god is "nal," based on "nal" 'ear of corn'.

1991–2008 Davoust (1995:612): "ah nal" 'divinité du maïs'; Knorozov (1999, vol. 1:187): "viil"; contains sign "ngal"; Schele and Grube (1997:91): "Nal" 'maize god'; Stuart (2005:182): "ixim" 'maize' suggested by occasional presence of /i/ phonetic complement, rather than "nal" 'young maize'; Taube (1992:41f.): God E, maize god; Vail (1996:262): "na'al"? 'maize god'.

PE8

T 1006c
Z 0126
K 0214

nal / näl; waxak / waxäk

n; num — maize god; eight

2. Picture: maize personified

1566–1915 Brasseur de Bourbourg (1869–1870, vol. 1:204): "p, pa" 'sortir avec effort, rompre en sortant, ouvrir par force'; Goodman (1897:46): 'eight'; Schellhas [1892] (1904:24f.): God E, the maize god; Seler [1899] (1990:252): 'eight'; Tozzer and Allen (1910:pl. 20): head of harpy eagle, "Thrasaetos harpyia."

1916–1950 Gates (1931:106): "yum kaax" 'corn god'.

1951–1980 Kelley (1962b:29): main sign of God E, maize; Tzeltal Ghanan (D. Brinton); Yum Kaax 'lord of harvest' (P. Schellhas, S. Morley, D. Kelley); Kelley (1976:63f., 126, 334): Corn God; may be read Yum Kaax 'Lord of Harvest'; Knorozov (1955:67): 025 (rostro con signo complementario 113, 124?); el ovalo tiene un contorno del signo mazorca; "kavil" ("chabil"); Knorozov (1967:95): "vil" 'food'; Thompson (1972:32): maize god.

1981–1990 Grube (1990a): Zahl 8, Maisgott; Justeson (1984:360): J. Fox, J. Justeson, P. Mathews: corn god in codices; F. Lounsbury: maize god "xi'im," related to T1008 "xib' " sign; P. Mathews: "xi'im"; L. Schele: maize god "ixim"?; Schele, Mathews, and Lounsbury (1990a): T1006 Maize God is "nal," based on "nal" 'ear of corn'.

1991–2008 Davoust (1995:612): "ah nal" 'divinité du maïs'; Knorozov (1999, vol. 1:187): "viil"; Schele and Grube (1997:91): "Nal" 'Maize God'; Stuart (2005:182): "ixim" 'maize' suggested by occasional presence of /i/ phonetic complement, rather than "nal" 'young maize'; Taube (1992:41f.): God E, maize god; Vail (1996:262): "na'al"? 'maize god'.

PE8

T –
Z –
K –

nal / näl

n — maize god

Unique occurrence on Madrid 28c, where it is associated with T0506 "wah" 'tortilla'.

3. Picture: maize personified

PEC

T 1050a
Z 0112
K –

kisin

n — underworld god; God Q

Yu *kisin* — kisin 'devil, demon' (V. Bricker et al. 1998:129)

Ch' *kisin* — *kisin 'shame' (Kaufman and Norman 1984:123)

May not be related to Classic grapheme.

1. Picture: head with stone markings

1566–1915 Brasseur de Bourbourg (1869–1870, vol. 1:204): "p', p'a" 'sortir avec effort, rompre en sortant, ouvrir par force'; Brinton (1895:123): the god of war, or "a companion of the god of death"; Landa [1566] (Tozzer 1941:170): <pp>; Schellhas [1892] (1904:25): God F; Rosny (1883:20): "pek" 'chien'; Thomas (1888:362): symbol of the god with the banded face; seen chiefly in the Troano, not found in the Dresden Codex.

1916–1950 Gates (1931:116f.): refers to god of war and violence, God F; resembles Mexican god Xipe.

1951–1980 Kelley (1976:62): God Q, originally lumped with God R as God F; a god of war and death; Knorozov (1955:66): 024 /pp/ "ppak"?, en el nombre del dios de la guerra, compárese con Pak-oc; Thompson (1972:38): deity of sacrifice, allied to Xipe.

1981–1990 Grube (1990a:131): Gott Q.

1991–2008 Bill et al. (2000:161): “cisin”; Davoust (1995:616): "buluch p'en" 'divinité Q'; Knorozov (1999, vol. 1:187): /p'e/ (cara de perfil con una cicatriz que la atraviesa); Taube (1992:105–10): God Q, a god of violent death, may derive from Mexican god of stone and execution; Vail (1996:289; 1998): "cizin" 'devil, demon'.

PEC

T 1050b
Z 0112
K 0213

kisin

n underworld god; God Q

2. Picture: head with stone markings

1566–1915 Brasseur de Bourbourg (1869–1870, vol. 1:204): "p', p'a" 'sortir avec effort, rompre en sortant, ouvrir par force'; Brinton (1895:123): the god of war, or "a companion of the god of death"; Landa [1566] (Tozzer 1941:170): <pp>; Schellhas [1892] (1904:25): God F; Thomas (1888:362): deity pertains to underworld; closely allied to so-called god of death.

1916–1950 Gates (1931:116f.): refers to god of war and violence, God F; resembles Mexican god Xipe.

1951–1980 Kelley (1962b:29): main sign of God F (P. Schellhas), war and death god; relettered God Q (J. E. S. Thompson); Kelley (1976:62): portrait glyph of God Q; originally lumped with God R as God F. A god of war and death; Knorozov (1955:66): 024 /pp/ "ppak"?, en el nombre del dios de la guerra, compárese con Pak-oc; Knorozov (1967:95): /p'(e)/; Thompson (1972:38): deity of sacrifice, allied to Xipe.

1981–1990 Grube (1990a:131): Gott Q.

1991–2008 Bill et al. (2000:161): “cisin”; Davoust (1995:616): "buluch p'en" 'divinité Q'; Knorozov (1999, vol. 1:187): /p'e/ (cara de perfil con una cicatriz que la atraviesa); Taube (1992:105–10): God Q, a god of violent death, may derive from Mexican god of stone and execution; Vail (1996:289; 1998): "cizin" 'devil, demon'.

PEE

T 1055
Z 0123
K 0238

1. Picture: head with eye markings

1951–1980 Knorozov (1967:96): /t(u)/?

1981–1990 Thompson (1972:69f.): god of fishing?

1991–2008 Davoust (1995:617): "ah tz'ul" 'l'étranger'; Knorozov (1999, vol. 1:190): "tz'uuy"; Schele and Grube (1997:156): God Q?

PEF

T –
Z 0124
K 0240

n God P; Pawahtun

1. Picture: head with black lines behind eyes

1566–1915 Schellhas [1892] (1904:39): God P, the frog god; Tozzer and Allen (1910:pl. 8): God F, who represents a tree toad ("Hyla eximia").

1951–1980 Kelley (1962b:29): God P, frog god (P. Schellhas); tree toad, Hyla eximia (A. Tozzer and G. Allen); Kukulcan (E. Seler, D. Kelley); Thompson (1962:400): Z0124 = T0802.

1991–2008 Vail (1996:288): God P; Vail (1997:28): related to God N, Pauahtun.

PEG

T –
Z 0124?
K 0240?

Occurs once in codices on Madrid 52a, frame 2.

1. Picture: aged face with black lines behind eye

1566–1915 Schellhas [1892] (1904:35–37): God M, god of traveling merchants, Ekchuah.

1951–1980 Knorozov (1967:96): "much"? 'frog'; Thompson (1962:381, 400): Z124 = T0802 [5 examples] Madrid 52a example differs markedly from other examples.

1991–2008 Knorozov (1999, vol. 1:190): "muuch" (cara de perfil con el ojo especial).

PEH

T –
Z –
K –

1. Picture: head with bands over eye

PEJ

T 1065
Z 0119
K –

1. Picture: head with headband covering eye

1991–2008 Knorozov (1999, vol. 1:187): /p'e/.

PH6

T 1060b
Z 0122
K 0247

wáak / *wäk*

num — six; sixteen

Yu *wáak* — wak 'seis' (Barrera Vásquez et al. 1980:906); wak 'cosa enhiesta, de pie delante de otra como los palos que salen de la pared, cosa salida' (Barrera Vásquez et al. 1980:906); wáak 'six' (V. Bricker et al. 1998:298); wa'kuna'an 'stopped, stood up' (Hofling with Tesucún 1997:658)

Ch' *wäk* — *wäk 'six' (Kaufman and Norman 1984:138)

Only example is the head for 'six' with fleshless jaw representing 'ten'.

1. Picture: head with axe in eye

1916–1950 Gates (1931:111): 'sixteen'.

1951–1980 Knorozov (1967:97): face variant of 'sixteen'.

1991–2008 Davoust (1995:617): "kaba'" 'nom'; Knorozov (1999, vol. 1:181): "kax."

PHD

T –
Z 0138
K 0209

tze?

wíinik / winik?; winal?

n? person; winal

Yu *wíinik; winal* winik 'hombre'; winal 'mes antiguo de 20 días' (Barrera Vásquez et al. 1980:923); wíinik 'man' (V. Bricker et al. 1998:305)

Ch' *winik; ø* winic 'hombre' (Aulie and Aulie 1998:141)

Possibly the same as PHE.

period: 20 days, winal

1. Picture: head with "winal" sign infix on eye

1916–1950 Gates (1931:72): "vinal."

1951–1980 Knorozov (1967:91, 95): (= K152) /k'(i)/; Thompson (1962:401): Z0138 = T1022.

PHE

T 1022
Z 0137
K 0249

tze

Possibly the same as PHD.

1. Picture: head with "winal" sign infix on eye

1916–1950 Gates (1931:114): "How far this chuen-eye face is connected with the "vinal" is a matter for careful search."

1951–1980 Knorozov (1967:97): (= K248) /s(e)/.

1981–1990 V. Bricker (1985c:417): /tze/; V. Bricker (1986:214): /tze/.

1991–2008 Davoust (1995:613): "tzel" 'se déplacer'; /tze/; Knorozov (1999, vol. 1:198): /ze/; tiene inscrito el grafema 551 /ki/.

PHE

T 1022v
Z 0137
K 0248

tze?

2. Picture: head with "winal" sign on eye

1916–1950 Gates (1931:114): "How far this chuen-eye face is connected with the "vinal" is a matter for careful search."

1951–1980 Knorozov (1955:67): 035 (hocico de animal con los signos 7, 114 en lugar de ojos) /zii/; Knorozov (1967:97): /s(e)/ (animal head with K152-036 in place of eye).

1991–2008 Davoust (1997:206): /tze/.

PHF

T 1063
Z 0121
K –

1. Picture: head with blindfold across eyes

1991–2008 Davoust (1995:617): "ah chah" 'l'aveugle'.

PHG

T 0726
Z 1325
K 0142

Primarily day glyph, but used twice in Madrid in non-calendrical contexts on the yearbearer pages.
day 05: Chikchan/Nachan
1. Picture: head with serpent markings

1566–1915 Bollaert (1865–1866:52): "chicchan" 'little'?; Brasseur de Bourbourg (1869–1870, vol. 1:206): day Chic-chán; "chic-chan" 'chose manifestée, ou rendue visible, portée, élevée au-dessus, en avant'; Landa [1566] (Tozzer 1941:134): day Chicchan; Rosny (1883:3f.): day Chicchan; Thomas (1882:178): unusual character for Chicchan.

1916–1950 Gates (1931:20): "chicchan" 'serpent'.

1951–1980 Knorozov (1967:90): "kan/chan" 'serpent'; Chikchan; Thompson (1962:310): [3 examples] Chicchan, see T1022, personified form of T0726 and T1002.

1981–1990 Justeson (1984:353): cf. T0508; J. Fox, J. Justeson, F. Lounsbury, P. Mathews, B. Riese, D. Stuart: day Chicchan; L. Schele: "kan/chan"; day Chicchan.

1991–2008 Davoust (1995:598): "chicchan" '5e jour'; "can" 'serpent'; /ca/; Knorozov (1999, vol. 1:157): "chan, can" (cabeza de serpiente con la mancha característica).

PHG

T 0726v
Z –
K –

Unique variant on Madrid 30b with XQ3 "k'in" infix.
day 05: Chikchan/Nachan
2. Picture: Chikchan with "k'in" infix.

1566–1915 Thomas (1882:178): unusual character for Chicchan.

PHH

T –
Z –
K –

1. Picture: head with row of dots over eye

PM1

T 1004

sa

Thompson's first figure is a conflation.

1. Picture: head with "kab'an" sign in mouth

1951–1980 Proskouriakoff (1964): represented at Yaxchilán by abstract form T0630.0181; Thompson (1972:77): a head, probably T1038, devouring a "cab" 'earth' sign; = T1004 in the inscriptions, where almost invariably lunar affix T0181 is infixed.

1981–1990 Grube (1990a:132): "sa"; Justeson (1984:360): J. Justeson, P. Mathews: title "kah-al" (probably from "kah-al" < "kah" 'town') associated with subordinate persons and sites; possibly based on "eating earth" gesture of subordination in having T0526 'earth' in mouth; F. Lounsbury, L. Schele, D. Stuart: "*kahal" or "*ka'ahal" title; B. Riese: "kah" 'village', 'town'; "kah-al" only with suffix T0178 or equivalent; Lounsbury (1989:82): /cah/; Mathews and Justeson (1984:212): credit Lounsbury: /ka/ for T0630 and T1004, "kah" 'person bearing provincial authority'.

1991–2008 H. Bricker and V. Bricker (n.d.): /sa/; Ringle and Smith-Stark (1996:335–38): 1004a = 1004.0181a[0178a]; Schele (1991d:22f.): credits Stuart and Grube with /sa/ reading (e.g., in "sa' " 'atole') and Naranjo emblem glyph; Schele and Grube (1997:176): /sa/.

PT3

T 1059
Z 0105
K 0204

nik ahaw / nich ajaw?

n — wind and flower god, God H

Yu *nik ahaw* — nik 'flor' (Barrera Vásquez et al. 1980:569); nik 'flower' (V. Bricker et al. 1998:197); ahawlil 'regia o real cosa' (Barrera Vásquez et al. 1980:4); x 'ahaw-xíiw 'royal herb, an herbaceous plant with ornamental leaves' (V. Bricker et al. 1998:257).

Ch' *nich ajaw* — *nich-im 'flower' (Kaufman and Norman 1984:127); *ajaw 'king; lord' (Kaufman and Norman 1984:115).

1. Picture: head with bead prefix and flower infix

1566–1915 Schellhas [1892] (1904:28–31): God H, the "chicchan" god; associated with serpents.

1916–1950 Gates (1931:120): 'priestess'.

1951–1980 Kelley (1962b:29): God H, good young god (G. Zimmermann); Kukulchan (Y. Knorozov); = God P? (D. Kelley); Kelley (1976:65–67): can be distinguished from God CH, the god with serpent markings; Knorozov (1955:66): 021 (rostro con signo complementario 141) "chan" ("can") 'serpiente' (solamente en el nombre de dios Kukulcan); Knorozov (1967:95): "soot"; Thompson (1972:44): "God H's glyph can both be his name and also denote his function, some title such as the thunderer, the creator, sender of evil, etc."; may also be 'diviner', 'priest', or 'prophet'.

1981–1990 Grube (1990a:131): Gott H.

1991–2008 Davoust (1995:617): "ahaw (can)" 'seigneur serpent'; Knorozov (1999, vol. 1:183): "zoot"; Schele and Grube (1997:173): "na"? 'woman'; Stone (1995): "nik" infix suggests reading as 'flower'; Taube (1992:56–60): main sign in name of God H; associated with Chak, and head variants for 3 and 13, including the water lily serpent head; Vail (1996:225–27): 'flower god' or 'priest'; T1059 occasionally conflates with T1016c "kuh" 'god'.

PT3

T 1059
Z 0105
K 0204

nik ahaw / nich ajaw?

n wind and flower god, God H

Used as 'three' in Classic texts.

2. Picture: head with flower infix and "ik" sign on cheek

1566–1915 Schellhas [1892] (1904:28–31): God H, the "chicchan" god; associated with serpents; Thomas (1893:266): "nach (nachah)" 'to grasp, to seize with the teeth or mouth'; bears a close resemblance to symbol for Chicchan.

1916–1950 Gates (1931:120): 'priestess'.

1951–1980 Kelley (1962b:29): (with T0149 prefix) God H, good young god (G. Zimmermann); Kukulchan (Y. Knorozov); = God P? (D. Kelley); Kelley (1976:65–67): can be distinguished from God CH, the god with serpent markings; Knorozov (1955:66): 021 (rostro con signo complementario 141) "chan" ("can") 'serpiente' (solamente en el nombre de dios Kukulcan); Knorozov (1967:95): "soot"; Thompson (1972:44): "God H's glyph can both be his name and also denote his function, some title such as the thunderer, the creator, sender of evil, etc."; may also be 'diviner', 'priest', or 'prophet'.

1981–1990 Grube (1990a:131): Gott H.

1991–2008 Davoust (1995:617): "ahaw (can)" 'seigneur serpent'; Knorozov (1999, vol. 1:183): "zoot"; Stone (1995): "nik" infix suggests reading as 'flower'; Taube (1992:56–60): main sign in name of God H; associated with Chak, and head variants for 'three' and 'thirteen', including the water lily serpent head; Vail (1996:225–27): 'flower god' or 'priest'; T1059 occasionally conflates with T1016c "kuh" 'god'.

PT4

T 0064
Z 0041
K 0071

pawah

n Pawah

Yu *pawah(tun)* pawahtun 'atlantes; los dioses de los vientos' (Barrera Vásquez et al. 1980:635)

Phonetic /pa/ plus logographic "wàah/waj."

1. Picture: cloth headdress with tamale

1566–1915 Rosny (1883:23): T0063.0548 = tortilla de maïs.

1951–1980 Kelley (1962b:24): net (Y. Knorozov, D. Kelley); "bay" 'net' (Y. Knorozov); Kelley (1976:72, 133, 223, 331f.): (T0063 = T0064 = T0065); net; in Piedras Negras dynastic name; Knorozov (1955:72): 101 (red) "vay (vaay)"; Knorozov (1967:84): /vay/.

1981–1990 Grube (1990a:89): = T0063; Justeson (1984:320): cf. T0063; J. Fox: /tu/; = Z59, may be variant, depicts bag; J. Justeson: logographic, reading uncertain; depicts net bag; F. Lounsbury, B. Riese: /pa/ or /paw/; "pauah"; P. Mathews: "pauah"; L. Schele: "pauah"; Taube (1989a:36–37): conflation of /pa/ and /wa/.

1991–2008 Davoust (1995:557): "pawah"; insigne de la divinité Bacab; Knorozov (1999, vol. 1:93): "vaay" (red enrollada); Ringle and Smith-Stark (1996:335–38): 0064 = 0064a (first example); = 0060v (second example); Stuart (2005:93): "itzam"? value for hairnet commonly found with God N; Taube (1992:92): "pauah" in "pauahtun," the name of God N. The "uah" is the globular element appearing in the center.

PT4

T 0063
Z 0041
K 0072

pawah

n Pawah

Phonetic /pa/ plus logographic "wàah/waj."

2. Picture: looped element with maize tamale

1566–1915 Schellhas [1892] (1904:37f.): in the name of God N, god of Uayeb.

1951–1980 Cordan (1964:33): "chuk" 'amarrado'; Kelley (1962b:30): prefix to T0528, T0548, and shell glyphs in name of God N, god of the end of the year (D. Kelley) or Mams, earth gods of the year's end (J. E. S. Thompson, D. Kelley); Kelley (1976:72, 132, 133, 223, 331f.): (T0063 = T0064 = T0065) net; Yucatec "bay"; in Piedras Negras dynastic name; Knorozov (1967:84): (= K071) "vay"; Thompson (1972:44): with T0528, Bacab.

1981–1990 Grube (1990a:89): = T0064; Justeson (1984:320): J. Fox, J. Justeson, F. Lounsbury, B. Riese: = T0064; P. Mathews: at least some = T0064; L. Schele: = T0064; Taube (1989a:36): composed of two /pa/ elements with notched ball in center representing "wah" 'tortilla, tamale; sustenance'.

1991–2008 Davoust (1995:557): "pawah"; insigne de la divinité Bacab; Knorozov (1999, vol. 1:93): "vaay" (red enrollada); Ringle and Smith-Stark (1996:335–38): 0063 (retired) = 0064b; Stuart (2005:93): "itzam"? for hairnet commonly found with God N; Taube (1992:92): "pauah" in "pauahtun," the name of God N. The "uah" is the globular element appearing in the center.

PT4

T 1062
Z 0139
K 0210

pawahtun

n Pawahtun

3. Picture: head with "kawak" sign infix

1951–1980 Thompson (1972:77): Bacab.

1981–1990 MacLeod (1990b:337): codical God N takes 'four' or 'five' prefix; the 'five' may signal an identification with Hobnil and the 'four' with Can-Sicnal, the east Pawahtun.

1991–2008 Davoust (1995:617): "pawah tun" 'divinité N'; Knorozov (1999, vol. 1:190): /cu/; Schele and Grube (1997:175): "Pawahtun."

PT4

T –
Z 0107
K 0211

pawahtun

n Pawahtun

4. Picture: old man with net on forehead

1566–1915 Schellhas [1892] (1904:37f.): God N, god of Uayeb.

1951–1980 Knorozov (1967:84, 95): (= K071) "vay"; Thompson (1962:400): Z107 = T1014; Thompson (1972:60): "Bacab."

1981–1990 Grube (1990a:130): Gott N; MacLeod (1990b:337): the five prefixed to the name of the codical God N may signal that this Pawahtun is Hobnil; perhaps the four prefix on other examples cues Can-Sicnal, the east Pawahtun.

1991–2008 Davoust (1995:613): (= T1014e) "pawahtun" 'divinité N'; Schele and Grube (1997:130): "Pawahtun."

PT6

T –
Z 0116
K –

1. Picture: old man with net headdress

1951–1980 Thompson (1962:400): Z116 = T1014.

PT7

T 1003v
Z 0106
K 0205

ahaw / ajaw

n — ahaw; God S

Yu *ahaw* — ahawlil 'regia o real cosa' (Barrera Vásquez et al. 1980:4); x 'ahaw-xíiw 'royal herb, an herbaceous plant with ornamental leaves' (V. Bricker et al. 1998:257)

Ch' *ajaw* — *ajaw 'king; lord' (Kaufman and Norman 1984:115)

PT7 and PT9 were not distinguished as separate graphemes by early researchers.

1. Picture: head with jaguar markings

1916–1950 Gates (1931:20): "chicchan" 'serpent'.

1951–1980 Kelley (1962b:29): god from Venus table (D. 50a); god with death attributes (T. Barthel, D. Kelley); Kelley (1976:66): variant of God CH; Knorozov (1967:95): "chan," Old Yucatec "kan" 'serpent'.

1981–1990 Coe (1989a): Hunahpu's glyph in the Dresden Codex; represents a Venus regent associated with the Morning Star aspect of the planet in the Dresden Venus table.

1991–2008 Davoust (1995:Planche 87): with T0144 prefix, Hun Ahaw '1er seigneur'; Davoust (1997:175): "ahaw" 'la divinité CH'; Schele and Grube (1997:147): "ahaw"; Taube (1992:115f.): credits Schele (unpublished paper, 1985) with identifying the spotted Hero Twin Hunahpu on D. 2a, 3a, and 50a. Accompanied by portrait glyph featuring spot on cheek and cartouche at the back of the head, which is prefixed by TI. Virtually identical to the Classic name glyph of the spotted Headband Twin, Hun Ahau, or 1 Ahau.

PT9

T 1003c
Z 0106
K 0206

b'áalam / b'ahläm; b'olon

n; num jaguar god, God CH; nine

Yu *b'áalam; b'olon* balam 'tigre, jaguar' (Barrera Vásquez et al. 1980:32); b'áalam, b'áalan 'jaguar' (V. Bricker et al. 1998:26); b'olon 'nine' (V. Bricker et al. 1998:35)

Ch' *b'ahläm; b'olon* *b'ahläm 'jaguar' (Kaufman and Norman 1984:116); *b'olon 'nine' (Kaufman and Norman 1984:138)

In contrast to its frequent use as 'nine' in the Classic texts, in the codices it is used as 'nine' only once.

number (head variant) 09

1. Picture: head with jaguar markings

1566–1915 Brasseur de Bourbourg (1869–1870, vol. 1:203): "p, pe" 'venir, marcher' ant. "pa" 'ouvrir'; Schellhas [1892] (1904:28–31): God H, the "chicchan" god; associated with serpents.

1916–1950 Beyer (1933:678): head variant of 'nine' and 'nineteen'; Gates (1931:20f.): "chicchan" 'serpent'.

1951–1980 Kelley (1962b:29): God H (P. Schellhas); relettered CH (G. Zimmermann following E. Seler); Kelley (1976:66): God CH; Knorozov (1967:95): face variant of 'nineteen'; combination of K205-233.

1981–1990 Grube (1990a): Zahl 9; Schele and Freidel (1990:465–66): jaguar head and head variant for 'nine' used in spellings containing the root "tz'ib"; T0716/0778 used in the emblem glyph of Tikal can be replaced by a jaguar head (Yax Bal or Yax Balam, name of the jaguar Headband Twin).

1991–2008 Davoust (1995:611): "ahaw (can)" 'seigneur (serpent)'; Davoust (1997:117): "balam"; Knorozov (1999, vol. 1:183): "chan" (cabeza de serpiente con la mancha característica); Milbrath (1999:133, fig. 4.4a): lunar god named Yax Balam; Taube (1992:60–62): God CH in codices; head variant of 'nine' and 'nineteen' in inscriptions. Classic God CH is a Headband Twin, Classic form of the Popol Vuh Hero Twin. Jaguar-skin markings suggest identification as Xbalanque; Vail (1996:274): "balam" 'jaguar'; Xbalanque.

PTA

T —
Z —
K —

Has same infix as PT9.

1. Picture: head with jaguar markings? and object covering mouth

PTE

T 1038a
Z 0127
K 0277

kam?

n God A'

Some examples have "ak'b'al" infix similar to PE7. Originally grouped with PTF (T1038b). Some of the same references are listed for both graphemes.

1. Picture: head with open mouth

1566–1915 Brasseur de Bourbourg (1869–1870, vol. 1:203): "m, mo" 'l'oiseau ara; la vague sur l'eau; un mamelon soulève, montaigné'; "mu" 'la terre molle, fructifiante, génétrice'.

1951–1980 Kelley (1962b:29): with TIV prefix, God A' (G. Zimmermann), death god; Uac Mitun Ahau (E. Seler); Kelley (1976:62): (with TIV prefix) God A'; Uac Mitun Ahau according to Seler; Knorozov (1967:98): (= K276) "nich' " 'toothy'; Thompson (1972:35): God A'; Thompson (1972:92f.): might indicate divine devourer perhaps with the sound value "chibal" 'devour'.

1991–2008 V. Bricker (1991:289): "cam" 'death'; Davoust (1995:616): "hanal" 'nourriture'; Knorozov (1999, vol. 1:152): "nich' " (cabeza de animal con colmillos grandes—ocelote?); Taube (1992:14–16): God A', associated with violent sacrifice and self-decapitation; Vail (1996:251): "cam" 'death'.

PTF

T 1038b
Z 0128
K 0317

kan?

n offering
Yu *kan* kan 'gift, offering' (Pío Pérez 1866–1877:41)

Originally grouped with PTE (T1038a). Some of the same references are listed for both graphemes.

1. Picture: head with open mouth and antenae

1566–1915 Brasseur de Bourbourg (1869–1870, vol. 1:203): "m, mo" 'l'oiseau ara; la vague sur l'eau; un mamelon soulève, montaigné'; "mu" 'la terre molle, fructifiante, génétrice'.

1951–1980 Barthel (1953:98): "darzubringendes Opfer, Spende, Gabe"; "ziil"; Kelley (1962b:27): 'offering, gift, payment, or sacrifice' (E. Seler, T. Barthel, Y. Knorozov, D. Kelley); "ziil" 'gift' (T. Barthel); "bol" 'porción de comida' (Y. Knorozov); 'fasting' (E. Förstemann, J. Villacorta); Kelley (1968c:149): offering glyph; Kelley (1976:143f., 334): "ziil" 'offer, give, sacrifice'; Knorozov (1955:67): 031 (hocico de fiera carnicera con un confuso elemento complementario en óvalo rameado) "bol" 'porción de comida'; Knorozov (1967:100): "nich' " 'share'; Thompson (1972:91): "hanal" 'food'.

1991–2008 V. Bricker (1991:289): "can" 'offering'; Davoust (1995:616): "hanal" 'nourriture'; Davoust (1997:161): "zih" 'cadeau'; Knorozov (1999, vol. 1:152): "nich' " (cabeza de animal con colmillos grandes—ocelote?); Schele and Grube (1997:137): "sih" 'gift'.

PTG

T 1056
Z 0114
K —

1. Picture: head open at top

1991–2008 Knorozov (1999, vol. 1:190): "muuch" (cara de perfil con el contorno abierto en la parte superior).

PTH

T —
Z —
K —

1. Picture: head with "k'at" sign

PTJ

T –
Z 0118
K –

1. Picture: head with maize? headdress

1951–1980 Thompson (1962:400): Z118 = T1030[0614].

PX4

T 0537
Z 1342a
K 0119

na

1. Picture: foreward-facing head with eyes closed

1566–1915 Brasseur de Bourbourg (1869–1870, vol. 1: 202): "e" 'fil, tranchant d'une arme; petites pierres ensemble, oeufs d'oiseaux, en compos'.

1951–1980 Cordan (1963:112): "kotz"; Knorozov (1955:73): 104 (piedrecillas augurales?) /um/; Knorozov (1967:89): /m(uu)/ (a face with closed eyes?); Thompson (1962:151f.): [23 examples] Xipe.

1981–1990 Grube (1990a:106): = T0771; Justeson (1984:341): L. Campbell, J. Fox, J. Justeson, P. Mathews, B. Riese: /na/; F. Lounsbury: /na/, "nah"; L. Schele: /na/, "na" 'house'.

1991–2008 Davoust (1995:585): "nah" 'maison, premier'; /na/; Grube (1994b:181): T0537 /na/ invented after 9.11.0.0.0; Knorozov (1999, vol. 1:116, 237): /muu/ 'grupo de primos entre los cuales se realizan casamientos'; 'marchitar'.

PX4

T 0542b
Z 1342b
K –

na

2. Picture: mouth and eyes

1566–1915 Brasseur de Bourbourg (1869–1870, vol. 1: 202): "e" 'fil, tranchant d'une arme; petites pierres ensemble, oeufs d'oiseaux, en compos'; Thomas (1893:260): "thol" 'slice, cut'.

1951–1980 Knorozov (1955:75): 140 "bil"?; Thompson (1962:154f.): [43 examples] (Ahau semblant) with T0087 almost certainly a wooden mask or idol.

1981–1990 Justeson (1984:342): J. Justeson, F. Lounsbury, P. Mathews, L. Schele, D. Stuart: = T0537; Schele (1987e): /na/ substitutes for T0023.

1991–2008 Davoust (1995:585): "nah" 'maison'; /na/; Knorozov (1999, vol. 1:116, 240): "uuc" '7'?

PX4

T 1053a
Z 0129
K 0223

na?
nah

n — house; dwelling
Yu *nah* — na 'casa, no denotando cuya' (Barrera Vásquez et al. 1980:545); nah 'house' (V. Bricker et al. 1998:193)

3. Picture: head with closed eye

1916–1950 Gates (1931:100): "cimi" 'death'.

1951–1980 Knorozov (1967:96): (= K222) "xib"; Thompson (1972:43): "cim" 'death'?

1991–2008 Davoust (1995:617): "kul" 'divinité, âme'; /ku/; Davoust (1997:130): "nah" 'la maison'; Knorozov (1999, vol. 1:188): "xib" (perfil masculino con ojo cerrado); Schele and Grube (1997:16): /na/; Schele and Grube (1997:107): "nah" 'house'.

PX6

T –
Z 0101
K 0303

1. Picture: mouth and eyes in dotted cartouche

1951–1980 Knorozov (1967:99): /la/; Thompson (1962:154, 400): Z101 = T0542 (ahau semblant) possibly Ahau variant.

S Supernaturals; Skulls

SB1

T –
Z –
K 0398

pi

-pih; pih

nm cl; n — b'ak'tun; cloth

Yu *pix* — pix 'cover, wrap up' (V. Bricker et al. 1998:217); pix 'cover, lid, sheath' (Hofling with Tesucún 1997:515)

Ch' *pis(il)* — *pis-il 'clothes' (Kaufman and Norman 1984:128)

May be related to the Yucatecan numeral classifier "pis" 'cuenta para días, años y reales' (Barrera Vásquez 1980:656).

period: 144,000 days, b'ak'tun

1. Picture: supernatural bird with hand for jaw

1566–1915 Goodman (1897:25): 'twenty k'atuns' (144,000 days).

1916–1950 Thompson (1950:147): "baktun."

1951–1980 Knorozov (1967:104): morphemic (bird head with K268 as additional element).

1981–1990 V. Bricker (1986:214): (T1033) "cuc" 'cycle' (Yucatecan?); Grube (1990a:129): "baktun," /pi/; Justeson (1984:361): (T1033) J. Fox, J. Justeson, F. Lounsbury, P. Mathews, B. Riese: head variant for 'baktun', period of 400 x 360 days; L. Schele: head variant of T0528.0528; Stuart (1987:11–13): /pi/.

1991–2008 Davoust (1997:219): "pih" 'du paquet'; Schele and Grube (1993): "pih" 'bak'tun; bundle'; Stuart (2005:166, n. 52): /pi/, "pik" widespread Mayan term for counting units of 8000.

SB6

T –
Z –
K –

1. Picture: principal bird deity?

1991–2008 Stuart (2005:35, n. 7): Principal Bird Deity as avian form of Itzamnaaj, Itzamnaaj Mut.

SB7

T –
Z 0754
K 0400

Avian form of Chaak.
1. Picture: principal bird deity?

1951–1980 Knorozov (1967:104): "k'ax" (bird with head of the rain god); Thompson (1962:329-30, 402): Z754 = T0746 (eagle) "A full-figure portrait in the codices has the Imix headdress and the features of God B."

SC1

T –
Z –
K –

lajun / läjun

num	ten
Yu *lajun*	lahun 'diez' (Barrera Vásquez et al. 1980:432); lahun 'ten' (V. Bricker et al. 1998:162)
Ch' *läjun*	*läjun 'ten' (Kaufman and Norman 1984:138)
	This example is a conflation of TIX and TX (=19).
	number 10 (head variant)
	1. Picture: skull with lower jaw

1566–1915 Goodman (1897:47): 'ten'; Seler [1899] (1990:250): 'ten'.

1916–1950 Gates (1931): 'ten'.

1991–2008 Taube (1992:13): God A, 'death' as head variant of 'ten'.

SC1

T –
Z 0728
K 0284

lajun / läjun

num ten

number 10 (head variant)
2. Picture: skull with lower jaw

1951–1980 Knorozov (1967:99): morphemic (bird head); Thompson (1972:86): perhaps a bird head; paired with "tun" on D. 73a. "Clearly of ill omen."

1991–2008 Davoust (1995:610): = T0858a.

SC4

T –
Z –
K 0217

day 12: Eb'/Eb'
1. Picture: "eb' " skull

1566–1915 Bollaert (1865–1866:52): "ebs" 'ladder'; Brasseur de Bourbourg (1869–1870, vol. 1:207): day Eb; "eb" 'ce qui est monté, monter, échelle'; Goodman (1897:16): day Eb; Landa [1566] (Tozzer 1941:134): day Eb'; Rosny (1883:6): day Eb.

1916–1950 Gates (1931:38): "eb" 'broom'.

1951–1980 Knorozov (1955:66): 023 (rostro con un signo complementario) "yeeb" 'llovizna'; Knorozov (1967:96): "eeb" 'fog'; day Eb.

1991–2008 Knorozov (1999, vol. 1:184): "eeb"; Ringle and Smith-Stark (1996:351): = 1107.

SC5

T 1048
Z 0149
K 0250

xi

1. Picture: skull with dots around eye

1566–1915 Brasseur de Bourbourg (1869–1870, vol. 1:203): [variant on Madrid 99b] "p, pe" 'venir, marcher' ant. "pa" 'ouvrir'.

1916–1950 Gates (1931:114): "involved in the Venus-Lunar calculations."

1951–1980 Knorozov (1967:97): morphemic; Thompson (1972:60): main part of the name glyph of the manifestation of Venus who dominates Dresden 49e.

1981–1990 Grube (1990a:131): /xi/; Stuart (1987:31–33): /xi/.

1991–2008 Davoust (1995:616): "xih" 'taché; souillé'; /xi/; Knorozov (1999, vol. 1:192): "h'av" (calavera con elementos especiales en el ojo); Vail (1996:356): possibly "xib" 'penis, male', 'fright, death', in addition to /xi/.

SCC

T 0736ac
Z 0152
K 0235

kíim / chäm

n; adj — death; dead
Yu *kíim* — kim 'morir' (Barrera Vásquez et al. 1980:317); kíim 'die' (V. Bricker et al. 1998:128)
Ch' *chäm* — *chäm 'die' (Kaufman and Norman 1984:117)

day 06: Kimi/Tox

1. Picture: skull with vertical bands

1566–1915 Bollaert (1865–1866:52): "cimi" 'to die'?; Brasseur de Bourbourg (1869–1870, vol. 1:206): day Cimi; "cimi" 'il est mort' or "ci-mi" 'non effervescence plus' or "cim-i" 'qui a pris une pointe, une pousse'; Brinton (1895:111, 121): day Cimi, "cimil" 'death'; Landa [1566] (Tozzer 1941:134): day Cimi; Rosny (1883:4, 20): day Cimi; "cimi" 'mort'; Schellhas [1892] (1904:10f.): in name of God A, the death god; Thomas (1888:361): (with T0015 prefix) "cimi"?; supposed symbols of the god of death. "These are given chiefly on the authority of Drs. Förstemann and Schellhas, as I have some doubt in reference to this conclusion."

1916–1950 Gates (1931:22): "cimi" 'death'; Thompson (1950:268): "tzek" 'skull'.

1951–1980 Knorozov (1955:65): 005 (mandíbula con elemento complementario, "ojo muerto") "cim, cham"?; Knorozov (1967:96): "kam" 'death'; Thompson (1962:314–16): [266 examples] 'death'; Thompson (1972:35): 'death' (used in augural glyph).

1981–1990 V. Bricker (1986:213): "camal" 'death' (Yucatecan?); Justeson (1984:353): day Cimi (= Death), root 'to die'; L. Schele: death glyph.

1991–2008 Davoust (1995:599): "cim/cam" 'mort'; Knorozov (1999, vol. 1:185): [T0736a] "cim, cham" (cara de perfil con ojo cerrado y mandíbula de muerto); [0T736c] "bang"; Schele and Grube (1997:81): main sign in principal attributive glyph of the Death God A; substitutes for "God N verb" in PSS. Attributive glyph reads "hu-CV-l"; Taube (1992:11f.): occurs in appellative phrase of Postclassic God A, death god; Vail (1996:304): "cimi" or "cimil" 'death'.

SCC

T 0736b
Z 0152
K —

kíim / chäm

n; adj — death; dead

day 06: Kimi/Tox

2. Picture: head with closed eye

1566–1915 Bollaert (1865–1866:52): "cimi" 'to die'?; Brasseur de Bourbourg (1869–1870, vol. 1:206): day Cimi; "cimi" 'il est mort' or "ci-mi" 'non effervescence plus' or "cim-i" 'qui a pris une pointe, une pousse'; Brasseur de Bourbourg (1869–1870, vol. 1:211): "m-ó" 'ara, montagne, vague, etc.'; Brinton (1895:111, 121): day Cimi, "cimil" 'death'; Landa [1566] (Tozzer 1941:134): day Cimi; Rosny (1883:4, 19): day Cimi; "cimi" 'mort'; Schellhas [1892] (1904:10f.): in name of God A, the death god; Thomas (1888:361): (with T0015 prefix) "cimi"?; supposed symbols of the god of death. "These are given chiefly on the authority of Drs. Förstemann and Schellhas, as I have some doubt in reference to this conclusion."

1916–1950 Gates (1931:22): "cimi" 'death'.

1951–1980 Knorozov (1955:65): variant 005 (mandíbula con elemento complementario, "ojo muerto"); "cim, cham"?; Thompson (1962:314–16): [266 examples] 'death'.

1981–1990 V. Bricker (1986:213): "camal" 'death' (Yucatecan?); Justeson (1984:353): J. Justeson, P. Mathews, L. Schele: different sign from T0736a,c.

1991–2008 Davoust (1995:599): "kim/cam" 'mort'; Knorozov (1999, vol. 1:185): "cim, cham" (cara de perfil con ojo cerrado); Paxton (1992:242): likely that T0736b should be grouped with T1052 /k'a/; von Nagy (1997:47f.): "camal" 'God A'.

SCD

T 1047a
Z 0148
K 0233

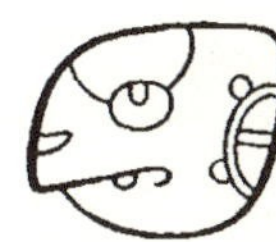

kìimil / *chämal?*

n death god

Yu *kíim; kìimil* kíim 'die'; kìimil 'dead' (V. Bricker et al. 1998:128)

Ch' *chäm; chämal* *chäm 'die' (Kaufman and Norman 1984:117)

1. Picture: skull

1566–1915 Brasseur de Bourbourg (1869–1870, vol. 1:206): day Cimi; "cimi" 'il est mort' or "ci-mi" 'non effervescence plus' or "cim-i" 'qui a pris une pointe, une pousse'; Brinton (1895:121): the god of death; Rosny (1883:4): day Cimi; Schellhas [1892] (1904:10f.): in name of God A, the death god; Thomas (1888:361): (with T0024 prefix) "cimi"?; supposed symbols of the god of death. "These are given chiefly on the authority of Drs. Förstemann and Schellhas, as I have some doubt in reference to this conclusion."

1916–1950 Gates (1931:55): 'death'.

1951–1980 Kelley (1962b:29): main sign of God A, death; Ah Puch (D. Brinton, S. Morley), Yum Cimil (D. Kelley); Kelley (1976:62) main sign of God A, the death god Yum Cimil; Knorozov (1955:65): 004 (cráneo) "tzek," 'calavera'; Knorozov (1967:96): "tzek' " 'skull'; Thompson (1972:31): death god; probably called Cizin by the users of the Dresden Codex.

1981–1990 V. Bricker (1986:116, 120): 'death'; Grube (1990a:131): "cimi."

1991–2008 Davoust (1995:616): "cizin" 'divinité de la mort: A'; "hol" 'tête'; Grofe (2007:126): occurs with T0063 "Pawahtun" prefix on Dresden 61 and 69; may represent the setting full moon in the west on the morning of the autumnal equinox; Houston (1992:529): "mas" 'goblin, dwarf'; Knorozov (1999, vol. 1:190): "tzek" (calavera); Schele and Grube (1997:99): "Kimil"; Taube (1992:11–14): Postclassic appellative of God A, death god Cizin?; Vail (1996:248; 2000b): "cimil" 'death (god)'.

SCD

T 1047b
Z 0148
K —

kìimil / *chämal?*

n death god

2. Picture: skull

1566–1915 Brasseur de Bourbourg (1869–1870, vol. 1:206): day Cimi; "cimi" 'il est mort' or "ci-mi" 'non effervescence plus' or "cim-i" 'qui a pris une pointe, une pousse'; Rosny (1883:4): day Cimi; Schellhas [1892] (1904:10f.): in name of God A, the death god; Thomas (1888:361): (with T0024 prefix) "cimi"?; supposed symbols of the god of death. "These are given chiefly on the authority of Drs. Förstemann and Schellhas, as I have some doubt in reference to this conclusion."

1916–1950 Gates (1931:55): 'death'.

1951–1980 Kelley (1962b:29): main sign of God A, death; Ah Puch (D. Brinton, S. Morley), Yum Cimil (D. Kelley); Knorozov (1955:65): 004 (cráneo) "tzek" 'calavera'.

1981–1990 Grube (1990a:131): "cimi."

1991–2008 Ciaramella (1999:38): "kimi" 'death'; Davoust (1995:616): "cizin" 'divinité de la mort: A'; "hol" 'tête'; Houston (1992:529): "mas" 'goblin, dwarf'; Schele and Grube (1997:99): Kimil; Taube (1992:11–14): Postclassic appellative of God A, death god Cizin?; Vail (1996:248; 2000b): "cimil" 'death (god)'.

SCD

T —
Z —
K —

kìimil / chämal?

n death god?

3. Picture: skull with eyeballs

1566–1915 Brasseur de Bourbourg (1869–1870, vol. 1:206): day Cimi; "cimi" 'il est mort' or "ci-mi" 'non effervescence plus' or "cim-i" 'qui a pris une pointe, une pousse'.

1916–1950 Gates (1931:55): Cimi variant.

1991–2008 Vail (2002b): 'skull'.

SCE

T 1049
Z 0150
K 0231

uh

n moon

Yu *uh* u 'collar de cuentas o sartal' (Barrera Vásquez et al. 1980:896); 'uh 'bead; moon' (V. Bricker et al. 1998:20)

Ch' *uh* *uh 'moon' (Kaufman and Norman 1984:135)

1. Picture: skull with eye band

1916–1950 Gates (1931:114): only occurs in Dresden eclipse ephemeris.

1951–1980 Knorozov (1967:96): /b(i)/?

1991–2008 H. Bricker and V. Bricker (n.d.): "uh" 'moon'; Davoust (1995:616): "uh" 'lune'; /u/; Knorozov (1999, vol. 1:192): "nip' " (calavera); ligadura de 151-524; Schele and Grube (1997:171, 175f.): "uh" 'moon'; Schele and Grube (1997:172–74): /u/.

SN4

T 1010c
Z 0140
K 0229

k'ìin / k'in

n sun, day; priest

Yu *k'ìin* k'in 'día, sol' (Barrera Vásquez et al. 1980:400); k'ìin 'day, sun' (V. Bricker et al. 1998:152)

Ch' *k'in* *k'in 'sun, day' (Kaufman and Norman 1984:124)

Used as 'four' in Classic texts.

period: 1 day, k'in

1. Picture: supernatural with "k'in" sign infixes

1566–1915 Goodman (1897:15, 44): 'day', 'four'; Seler [1899] (1990:250): 'four'.

1916–1950 Gates (1931:111): face of a solar deity; occurs only in eclipse ephemeris. May be part of G046, or the same as the tun-ending Glyph G.

1951–1980 Knorozov (1967:96): (= K225) "kit"?; determinative (god); Thompson (1972:33): 'sun god'.

1981–1990 V. Bricker (1986:214): "kin" 'day, sun' (Cholan, Yucatecan); Grube (1990a:128f.): Zahl 4; Sonnengott; "kin"; Justeson (1984:360): J. Justeson, P. Mathews, B. Riese: sun god, otherwise = T0544; F. Lounsbury, L. Schele, D. Stuart: head variant of T0544 and 'four'; includes T1010c.

1991–2008 Davoust (1995:612): "chän" '4'; "ahaw kin" 'seigneur Soleil'; Knorozov (1999, vol. 1:189, 195): "king"; Ringle and Smith-Stark (1996:352): head variant for "kin," 'ahau," and IV; Taube (1992:52): head variant of the number 'four'; "kin" 'sun'; patron of the month Yaxk'in.

SND

T 1039
Z 0134
K 0230

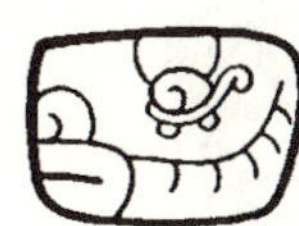

Conflation of AMC and SSD.

1. Picture: supernatural with lines on jaw

1916–1950 Gates (1931:101): (groups with G075) god of the north.

1951–1980 Knorozov (1967:96): "ch'am"? (combination of K225-198).

1991–2008 Davoust (1995:616): "am" 'angle'; H. Bricker and V. Bricker (n.d.): possible conflation of T1009d Itzamna and T1016c "kuh."

SNE

T 1057
Z 0145
K –

1. Picture: supernatural with head open at top

1991–2008 Knorozov (1999, vol. 1:189): "cit" (cara con "ojo de dios"); a veces se emplea como determinativo.

SNF

T –
Z 0108
K 0227

chéel, chak chéel

n Cheel, Chak Cheel

Yu *chak chéel* chak 'red' (V. Bricker et al. 1998:59); chel 'el arco del cielo; el arco iris'; cheel 'término, por fin' (Barrera Vásquez et al. 1980:89); chéel 'rainbow' (V. Bricker et al. 1998:68)

Codical variant of the deity known as Ix Chel during the Colonial period.

1. Picture: supernatural with age line around mouth

1566–1915 Brasseur de Bourbourg (1869–1870, vol. 1:202): "k, ka" 'fiel, amertume, déjections volcaniques'; "káa" 'la pierre à broyer le grain, comme "cáa" '.

1951–1980 Knorozov (1967:96): (= K225) "kit"?; determinative (god); Thompson (1962:400): Z108 = T1027; Thompson (1972:96): Goddess O.

1991–2008 Davoust (1997:277): = 1027 "chel"; Taube (1992:99–105): Goddess O, aged goddess, Chak Chel, associated with the rainbow, weaving, curing, and divination, possibly related to the Mexican goddess Cihuacoatl; Vail (1996:287): portrait glyph of Chac Chel.

SNK

T 1054
Z 0143
K 0228

n God L

1. Picture: supernatural with black face paint

1566–1915 Schellhas [1892] (1904:34f.): God L.

1951–1980 Closs (1979): one of a group of black gods (including L, M, Y, and Z) who are a closely related group of Venus deities; also associated with hunting and commerce; Kelley (1962b:29): God L, old black god; "Ek Chuah" (C. Thomas); Knorozov (1967:96): morphemic (K225 with additional element); Thompson (1972:35, 67): God L; manifestation of the planet Venus; may be black Bacab Hozanek.

1981–1990 Grube (1990a:131): Gott L.

1991–2008 Davoust (1995:617): "pawah" 'divinité L'; Knorozov (1999, vol. 1:189): "tox" (dios negro); Taube (1992:79–88): God L, aged black god of the underworld, a malevolent Venus god, a merchant god, associated with the moan owl and the sky sign headdress, possibly for "moan chan" 'misty sky,' the Nahuatl region Tamoanchan, possibly the southern Gulf coast.

SS1

T 1030q
Z 0125
K 0376

cháak / chahk

n Chaak, God B

Yu *cháak* chaak 'fue un hombre así grande que enseñó la agricultura, al cual tuvieron después por Dios de los panes, del agua, de los truenos y relámpagos; Dios de la lluvia' (Barrera Vásquez et al. 1980:77); cháak 'rain' (V. Bricker et al. 1998:61)

Ch' *chahk* chajc 'rayo' (Aulie and Aulie 1998:29); *chahuk 'lightning, thunder' (Kaufman and Norman 1984:117); ah chak 'rain god' (Knowles 1984:392)

1. Picture: supernatural with long nose and barbels

1566–1915 Brinton (1895:51): Itzamna.

1916–1950 Gates (1931:109): Itzamná?

1951–1980 Knorozov (1967:103): "k'ax" (head of rain god); Thompson (1972:100): Chac (personified).

1981–1990 Grube (1990a:130): K'awil, Gott K; Schele and Miller (1986:60, n. 55): credit Stuart with identification of "chac" in deity name "chac-xib-chac."

1991–2008 Davoust (1995:615): "chahc" 'divinité de la pluie: B'; Knorozov (1999, vol. 1:189): "kax"; Ringle and Smith-Stark (1996:335–38): 1030q = 1121b; Taube (1992:17–19): God B, Chac.

SSD

T 0152
Z 0013
K 0082

Itzamna

n creator god Itzamna, God D

Yu *itzamna* itzamna 'ésta es la forma más conocida de nombre de la más importante deidad maya del norte peninsular' (Barrera Vásquez et al. 1980:272)

References apply to the prefix alone.

1. Picture: supernatural with dotted "ak'b'al" sign with tassels

1566–1915 Tozzer and Allen (1910:pl. 3): apparently sign for centipede.

1916–1950 Gates (1931:10): "akbal" 'night'; Thompson (1950:283): "chapat" 'centipede'.

1951–1980 Cordan (1964:18): "tzitz"; /tz'/; Kelley (1962a:297): may represent two glyphs; Kelley (1976:63, 135f., 332): round shield; two graphemes (K082 + K019, T0166 + T0136i?); Knorozov (1967:85): "itz" 'dew'; Thompson (1972:31): creator aspect of Itzam Na.

1981–1990 Justeson (1984:327): L. Campbell: possibly shield, not "chimal"; J. Fox: shield, sometimes "pakal"; J. Justeson: shield; F. Lounsbury: "tzim" or "chim"; also 'shield', possibly "chimal"; depicts head of myriapod ("tzimes"); P. Mathews: "itz" or "itzam"; B. Riese: 'shield' "pakal"; L. Schele: 'shield', "itz" or "tzim" or "chimal"?; Riese (1982:271): Pakal.

1991–2008 Davoust (1995:564): "itz" 'rosée'; "itzam"; Knorozov (1999, vol. 1:97): "itz-am"; combinación de 233:104; Taube (1992:31–35): 'obsidian mirror', the first sign in name of God D, "itzamna," and the shield in Shield Jaguar's name, possibly /itz/ from Nahuatl "itz," a root pertaining to divination and to obsidian; Vail (1996:258): compound "itz" + /li/?; represents "itzli" 'obsidian mirror' in Nahuatl (following Taube 1992:34). Has iconic rather than phonetic function.

SSD

T 1009cd
Z 0146, 0146a
K 0225–26

Itzamna

n creator god Itzamna, God D

2. Picture: supernatural with mirror infix

1566–1915 Brasseur de Bourbourg (1869–1870, vol. 1:207): day Men; "men" 'bâti, édifié' "me-en" 'chose courbe ouverte, détruite peu à peu ou descendue au fond'; Brinton (1895:56, 122) [with T0152 prefix] Cuculcan; Schellhas [1892] (1904:22f.): in name of God D; Thomas (1888:363): (T0152.1009.0023) Zamna or Ytzamna?

1916–1950 Gates (1931:111f.): Schellhas's God D.

1951–1980 Kelley (1962a:290, 297f.): dios Itzamna; Kelley (1962b:29): (with T0152) Itzamna (E. Seler, W. Fewkes, E. Förstemann, C. Thomas, B. Whorf, S. Morley, J. E. S. Thompson, Y. Knorozov, D. Kelley); Kukulcan (D. Brinton); moon god (P. Schellhas); Kelley (1976:64): in name of God D, Itzamna?; Knorozov (1955:67): 026 (rostro con "ojo de dragón"); determinador de dios; Knorozov (1967:96): "kit"?; determinative (god); Thompson (1972:92): God D's glyph; as used on D. 25c–28c represents "acan" in expression "acante."

1981–1990 Grube (1990a:130): Itzamna; Grube and Schele (1988): main head is "am" 'squared'; Lounsbury (1984:176): Itzamna; Taube (1988:239f.): "itzam."

1991–2008 Davoust (1995:612): "am" 'angle'; Knorozov (1999, vol. 1:189): "cit" (cara con "ojo de dios"); a veces se emplea como determinativo; Ringle and Smith-Stark (1996:352): 1009c, d: part of the name of Itzam Na (God D) in the codices; Taube (1992:31f.): God D, Itzamna; Vail (1996:259): Itzamna.

SSF

T 1020
Z 0742
K 0289

k'awil

n K'awil, God K

Yu *k'awil* k'awil 'alimento'; itsamná k'awil 'el nombre de una deidad [dadora de alimentos]' (Barrera Vásquez et al. 1980:387)

1. Picture: supernatural with torch on forehead

1566–1915 Brinton (1895:54): mask of Itzamna?; Brasseur de Bourbourg (1869–1870, vol. 1:203): "p, pe" 'venir, marcher', ant. "pa" 'ouvrir'; Schellhas [1892] (1904:32–34): God K; has an astronomical significance and seems to symbolize a star; Seler [1895] (1993:331): "ah bolon tz'acab" 'lord of the nine generations'.

1916–1950 Spinden (1924:166): 'long-nosed god of rain'.

1951–1980 Kelley (1962b:29): God K (= Brinton's God B); Ah Bolon Dzacab (E. Seler, H. Beyer, J. E. S. Thompson, D. Kelley); Kukulcan (S. Morley), Itzamna (D. Brinton); Knorozov (1967:99): "moh" 'incense burner'.

1981–1990 Justeson (1984:361): J. Fox, J. Justeson, F. Lounsbury, B. Riese: God K, codex form; Schele and J. Miller (1983:3–22): T0617a always appears in forehead of God K, representing an obsidian mirror; Stuart (1987:15f.): K'awil, God K.

1991–2008 Davoust (1995:613): "kawil" 'divinité K'; Knorozov (1999, vol. 1:158): "mox, moh"; tiene 33 "tooc" inscrito; Ringle and Smith-Stark (1996:335–38): 1020 (retired) = 1030r; Taube (1992:69–79): God K "kauil," celestial lightning god; lightning axe of Chac; associated with burning torch, smoking celt, and mirror inset in forehead; identified with lightning, rain, and fertile maize.

SSL

T 0588
Z 0702
K 0315

wa'al / wa'

pos stand up

Yu *wa'al* wa'an 'cosa que está en pie o enhiesta o parada y detenida; estar en pie' (Barrera Vásquez et al. 1980:912); wá'al 'stand up, stop' (V. Bricker et al. 1998:299); wa' 'stand' (Hofling with Tesucún 1997:658)

Ch' *wa'* *wa' 'standing upright' (Kaufman and Norman 1984:135)

1. Picture: supernatural with split head and "chuwen" sign eye

1566–1915 Rosny (1883:14): T0588.0140.0181 = month Zeec.

1916–1950 Thompson (1950:265): possibly related to "uin" 'order; manner'.

1951–1980 Kelley (1962b:27): (with T0140 suffix) 'offer, give, pay, or sacrifice' (Y. Knorozov, D. Kelley); "uin" 'it is set, it moves in order' (J. E. S. Thompson); "zil" 'ofrendar' (Y. Knorozov); Kelley (1976:110, 143, 333): "zil-"? 'offer'; Knorozov (1955:67): (hocico de animal con los signos 7, 114 en lugar de ojos, en óvalo rameado) /zii/; Knorozov (1967:100): /s(e)/; Thompson (1962:216f.): [59 examples] appears on monuments with 819-day counts; Thompson (1972:103): "uinan" 'set in order'?

1981–1990 V. Bricker (1986:212): /tze/; Grube (personal communication, 1989): "wa' " 'set (the station)'; Justeson (1984:346): J. Justeson: verb root, possibly 'divination' (cf. "si" 'to divine, cast a spell'); B. Riese: 'offer'; MacLeod (1989a): "ets'-ok" 'plant the feet' [erect a stela] as 819-day count ending glyph.

1991–2008 V. Bricker (1991:285f.): /tze/; Davoust (1995:589): "wa' " 'dresser'; /he/; Grofe (2007:207f.): conflation of split sign /pa/ and /se/ for "pas" 'come, arrive, sprout' or 'dawn'; Knorozov (1999, vol. 1:153): /ze/ (cabeza de animal en contorno abierto); tiene inscritos 551 /ki/ and 22 "tooc"; Schele and Grube (1997:216): "wa' " 'to be erected, stood up, put in place'; Stuart (2005:65, n. 17): "wa' " value should be reconsidered. Compound grapheme containing "ok" and /se/; possible reading as "ok-se" or "ok-es" 'to put in something'.

SST

T —
Z —
K —

1. Picture: supernatural with deity eye, snout, and nose element

1991–2008 von Nagy (1997:40): = T0063:0790.

SSU

T —
Z —
K —

k'uk'ulkan?

n K'uk'ulkan?

Yu *k'uk'ulkan* k'uk'ulkan 'lit. serpiente-emplumada, dios introducido por los invasores mexicanos, el nombre maya es una traducción de Quetzalcóatl, el conocido dios y héroe cultural mexicano' (Barrera Vásquez et al. 1980:420).

Includes doubled 22B /k'u/.

1. Picture: supernatural with deity eye

1951–1980 Kelley (1962b:29): "kukchan," Kukulcan (Y. Knorozov, D. Kelley, T. Barthel); Kelley (1976:64): glyph apparently of Quetzal with snake infix.

ST8

T 1058b
Z 0144
K 0279

1. Picture: supernatural with scrolls in mouth, jaguar ear

1916–1950 Beyer (1931:106): head of a solar deity.

1951–1980 Kelley (1962b:31): Venus table god; pictograph for God B (J. E. S. Thompson, D. Kelley); Knorozov (1967:98): composite grapheme K225-052?

1991–2008 Davoust (1995:617): "ch'acab" 'décapité'; Knorozov (1999, vol. 1:190): "cit-aan"; ligadura de 962-230; Ringle and Smith-Stark (1996:335–38): 1058b (retired) = 1013d.

ST9

T 0680
Z 0102
K 0356

n God M

Graphically similar to the Classic period grapheme ST7, but probably not equivalent.

1. Picture: jaguar eye?

1566–1915 Brasseur de Bourbourg (1869–1870, vol. 1:216, 220): autre variante du signe "hunal-au" 'la mer des Caraïbes, avec le soulèvement de la terre engloutie ou renaissante'; '160,000,000'; Schellhas [1892] (1904:35–37): God M, god of traveling merchants, Ekchuah; Thomas (1888:358): Ekchuah, patron deity of traveling merchants.

1916–1950 Gates (1931:129): Ek-chuah.

1951–1980 Closs (1979:153): Nohoch Ich 'Great Eye,' a Yucatec name for Venus in the Motul dictionary; Kelley (1962b:29): God M, black god; Ek Chuah (C. Thomas, P. Schellhas, E. Seler, J. E. S. Thompson, D. Kelley); Ek Ahau (D. Brinton); = Aztec Mixcoatl (J. E. S. Thompson); = Aztec Yacatecuhtli (D. Kelley); Kelley (1976:139, 333): (eye), name of God M; Knorozov (1955:71): 081 (vasija con líquido y signos complementarios) Cek Chuah; Knorozov (1967:102): morphemic (vessel?); Thompson (1962:282): [21 examples] God M; Thompson (1972:47): represents a pack; glyph of merchant gods.

1981–1990 Justeson (1984:351): J. Fox, J. Justeson, L. Schele: God M; P. Mathews: God M; represents eye of God L?

1991–2008 Davoust (1995:595): "ut" 'oeil'; Knorozov (1999, vol. 1:174): "ch'uu" (vasija?); Taube (1992:88): God M, a merchant deity related to God L. Glyph represents marking around his eye. He is probably derived from the Mexican god Yacatecuhtli.

X Square; Symmetrical

XD1

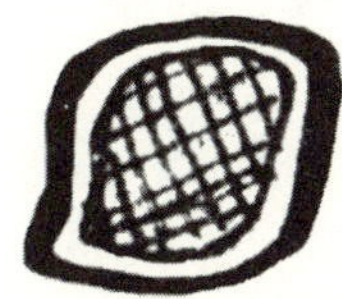

T 0586
Z 1303
K 0176

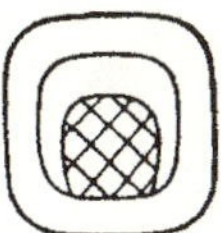

pa

1. Picture: crosshatching

1566–1915 Landa [1566] (Tozzer 1941:164): prefixed to month Pax; Thomas (1893:266): /x/ or /ch/.

1951–1980 Kelley (1962a:305f.): /pa/; Kelley (1976:15, 181f., 333): see also T0715; /pa/; Knorozov (1967:94): phonetic (textile?).

1981–1990 V. Bricker (1986:212): /pa/; Grube (1990a:110): = T0202; Justeson (1983): /pa/; Justeson (1984:346): consensus /pa/; L. Campbell, J. Fox, J. Justeson, P. Mathews: depicts section of netting (pM *pa:h 'net').

1991–2008 Davoust (1995:589): "paw" 'filet'; /pa/; Knorozov (1999, vol. 1:149): /too/ (fragmento de tela o corteza de árbol).

XD1

T 1023v
Z —
K —

pa

Unique occurrence on Madrid 67b. Only recently recognized as codical variant of T1023.

2. Picture: head with crosshatching

1566–1915 Thomas (1893:266): with T0544, refers to eclipse of the sun "chibakin."

1951–1980 Kelley (1976:334): see T0715; /pa/.

1981–1990 V. Bricker (1986:214): /pa/; Justeson (1984:361): J. Justeson, P. Mathews, B. Riese, L. Schele, D. Stuart: /pa/; Taube (1989b): Classic Maya clown.

1991–2008 Davoust (1995:614): "paw" 'filet'; /pa/; Vail (2002b, 2003): codical head variant of /pa/; Vail (2003): /pa/ in expression “pa’(al) k’in” 'broken sun' in reference to eclipse on Madrid 67b2; Vail and V. Bricker (2004:181f.): personified /pa/.

XD1

T 0586v
Z 1305
K 0338

pa

3. Picture: crosshatching

1566–1915 Brasseur de Bourbourg (1869–1870, vol. 1:208, 218): day Ezanab; "ezanab" 'silex, pierre de lance, jet de feu d'un volcan'; symbole du tremblement de terre.

1916–1950 Gates (1931:141): probably denotes the Four Quarters.

1951–1980 Knorozov (1967:101): [K338 in part] "hatz."

1981–1990 Grube (1990b): allograph of T0586 /pa/ or /pV/; MacLeod (1989a:120): with T0068, "tz'ak" 'to count'.

1991–2008 Davoust (1997:261): T0068.0592a "tz'a" 'dresser'; Schele and Grube (1997:17, 206): with T0066, /tz'a/; Vail (2002b): /pa/.

XD1

T 0715
Z 1300
K 0111

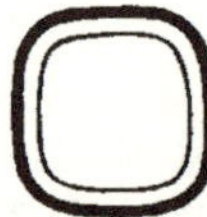

pa

Compare with similar grapheme 1X4.

4. Picture: empty cartouche

1951–1980 Kelley (1962a:285, 289): /pa/; Kelley (1976:181, 221, 334): (= T0586, T0602, T1023); /pa/; Knorozov (1955:73): 109 (estanque) /p(a)/; Knorozov (1958:285): /p(a)/; Knorozov (1967:88): /p(a)/ (a water hole); Thompson (1962:307): [36 examples].

1981–1990 V. Bricker (1986:213): /pa/; Grube (1990a:115): = T0202; Justeson (1984:353): cf T0202; J. Fox, J. Justeson, P. Mathews: = T0586; F. Lounsbury, B. Riese: equivalent to T0202, T0586, T0602; L. Schele: codex = T0602.

1991–2008 Davoust (1995:598): "paa" 'réservoir d'eau'; /pa/; Knorozov (1999, vol. 1:112): /paa/, /ap/ (laguna o muralla).

XD7

T –
Z 1304
K 0177

pìik / pik

n — skirt
Yu *pìik* — pìik 'petticoat; eaves (house)' (V. Bricker et al. 1998:215)
Ch' *pik* — *pik 'skirt' (Kaufman and Norman 1984:128)

Thompson (1962:243) grouped with T0625, Classic grapheme XD6.

1. Picture: woven cloth?

1951–1980 Knorozov (1967:94): "box" (turtle shell); Thompson (1962:243, 402): Z1304 = T0625 [9 examples] (turtle shell); Thompson (1972:33): = T0625 'tortoise shell'.

1981–1990 Justeson (1984:348): (T0625) J. Fox, J. Justeson: those on Dresden 2d are "*pik" 'skirt'; P. Mathews: indication of texture as rough, undulating, as in water lily pad, turtle shell, worked flint; B. Riese: depicts turtle shell; L. Schele, D. Stuart: texture or pattern of water lily pad or turtle shell.

1991–2008 Davoust (1995:591): (= T0625b) "pic" 'jupe'; Knorozov (1999, vol. 1:150): "box" (caparazón de tortuga).

XD8

T –
Z 1306
K –

Used in Dresden eclipse and water tables.
1. Picture: plaited object

1916–1950 Gates (1931:165): web.

XD9

T 0192
Z 1306a
K –

1. Picture: plaited or woven object

1566–1915 Brasseur de Bourbourg (1869–1870, vol. 1:212): "pop" ou "poop" 'natte, terre marécageuse crevassée par la chaleur'; Thomas (1893:264f.): symbol of a dwelling.

1951–1980 Kelley (1976:133f., 332): "pop" 'mat'?, 'thatch'?; Knorozov (1955:70): 076. techo de hojas, /h(a)/; Knorozov (1967:94): /x(a)/ (mat or roof of leaves of the "xaan" palm); Thompson (1962:59): [3 examples]; Thompson (1972:77): "pop" 'mat'.

1981–1990 Justeson (1984:330): L. Campbell, J. Fox, J. Justeson, B. Riese: logographic 'house'; depicts thatch; F. Lounsbury: "otoch" or cognate, 'house, temple' (denoting whose); abridged form of T0614; P. Mathews, L. Schele: thatch; logographic 'house'; some examples perhaps to be read "otoch" (or cognate form); Schele (1989c:39): /to/ or /ta/.

1991–2008 Davoust (1995:567): "otoch/otot" 'maison', "pop" 'natte'; /o/; Davoust (1997:206): /po/, "pop" 'natte'; Knorozov (1999, vol. 1:150): "ax" (techo de hojas de palmo o tejido de petate); Ringle and Smith-Stark (1996:335–38): 0192 (retired) = 0614A.

XE1

T 0501
Z 1321
K 0179

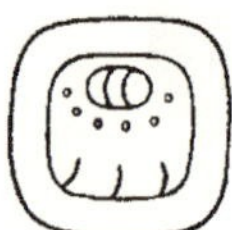

b'a

XE1 and XE2 are graphically similar; have same Thompson number (T0501). Most references listed below are for both XE1 and XE2.
day 01: Imix/Imux
1. Picture: water lily; hand?

1566–1915 Bollaert (1865–1866:52): "ymix"; Brasseur de Bourbourg (1869–1870, vol. 1:208): day Imix; "im-ix" 'fond, profondeur, mamele ou canal du trou ou de l'urine, ou des sécrétions aqueuses'; "i-mix" 'de rejeton aucun, de pousse jamais'; Goodman (1897:16, 58): day 'five', Ymix, closed hand; Landa [1566] (Tozzer 1941:134): day Imix; Rosny (1883:11): day Ymix; Thomas (1888:350): day Ymix; Thomas (1893:249, 252): day Imix; /m/, /ma/.

1916–1950 Gates (1931:1): "imix" 'sea-dragon; water; wine'; Thompson (1950:72): represents a water lily.

1951–1980 Barthel (1967:232): in addition to Imix, "nab" 'to besmear oneself with, to daub with'; Dütting (1979:185f.): "nab" 'lake, sea'; secondary value "ha" 'water' (especially terrestrial water); Kelley (1962b:25): "imix, imox" (J. E. S. Thompson, T. Barthel); "naab" 'water lily' (T. Barthel, D. Kelley); Kelley (1976:123, 182, 185, 208, 211, 332): "naab" 'water lily'; "imix, nab" 'ocean'; confused with T0556; see also T0502, T0556, T0557, T0558, Z1321, Z1360, Z1361; /ba/?; Knorozov (1955:74): 121 "in"; Knorozov (1958:285): /b(u)/; Knorozov (1967:94): "in" (female breast?); Thompson (1962:87–96): [611 examples] Imix.

1981–1990 V. Bricker (1986:211): /ba/, "ba" 'self' (Yucatecan), /bä/, "bä" 'self' (Cholan); Dütting (1985:106) possibly "naab" and /ba/; "ba" 'self' (Yucatecan); Fox and Justeson (1984:54f.): "ha' " 'water'; Grube (1990a:104): = T0556, T0558, T0655, T0690, T0771, T0811, T1300, T1323; Justeson (1984:338): J. Fox, J. Justeson: (a) with crosshatched oval: 'water', including "*nahb' " and "ha' "; day Imix; rarely used as (b), probably in error; L. Campbell, J. Fox, J. Justeson: (b) with curving lines in oval: /b'a/; never /ma/, except perhaps as sporadic error based on graphic similarity to T0502 /ma/; F. Lounsbury, B. Riese: day Imix; /b'a/; P. Mathews, D. Stuart: /b'a/; also day Imix; sometimes /ma/; Thompson included other signs under T0501; cf. T0502, T0556, T0557, T0558; B. Riese: some 'water'; never /ma/; L. Schele: day Imix, /b'a/, /ma/, possibly "mal"; MacLeod (1988b): "nab."

1991–2008 Davoust (1995:581): "ha' " 'eau'; Imix '1er jour'; Knorozov (1999, vol. 1:140): "in" (nubarrones bajando); Ringle and Smith-Stark (1996:347) darkened Imix = 0501b. Although identified as a logograph for some type of body of water (see summary in Stuart and Houston 1994:19), a and b variants both appear as Imix; Schele and Grube (1997:226): "ha" 'water'; Stuart (1997:3): "ba" 'first' on Toniná Monument 69; Stuart and Houston (1994:19f.): probably "ha' " 'water'; credit Schele with "nab" 'lake, pool, general body of water'.

XE1

T 0558
Z 1360
K 0180–81

b'a

2. Picture: water lily; hand?

1566–1915 Brasseur de Bourbourg (1869–1870, vol. 1:208): day Imix; "im-ix" 'fond, profondeur, mamele ou canal du trou ou de l'urine, ou des sécrétions aqueuses'; "i-mix" 'de rejeton aucun, de pousse jamais'; Thomas (1882:156): "ixim" 'maize'; Thomas (1888:349, 370): [with T0283.0558] "xamach; chimix" 'a vessel'; Thomas (1893:249): /m/, /ma/.

1916–1950 Gates (1931:152): must be distinguished from Imix, Mac, and Ix, each of which it resembles in part.

1951–1980 Kelley (1962a:297, 305–7): /ba/; Kelley (1962b:41): /ba/; Kelley (1976:118, 157, 194, 203, 223, 333): (= T0556, Z1360); allograph of T0757; /ba/?; "bal"?; "ba"? reflexive; Knorozov (1955:71): (vasija con líquido) "bal"; Knorozov (1958:285): /b(u)/; Knorozov (1967:94): /b(u)/ (vessel with boiling water); Thompson (1962:171f.): [72 examples] almost exclusively at Chichén Itzá and in Madrid and Dresden codices; Thompson (1972:43): "bak" 'meat', 'terror'.

1981–1990 V. Bricker (1986:212): /ba/; Dütting (1985:103–16): T0558:0103 "ba-ac" 'shed water; bone, child'; Grube (1990a:108): = T0501; Justeson (1984:343): J. Fox, J. Justeson, B. Riese: /b'a/; never /ma/; P. Mathews, D. Stuart: /b'a/; L. Schele: /b'a/, /ma/; = T0501; in codices more likely to be exclusively /b'a/; Schele (1990a): used as "ba" 'first' in Classic period titles.

1991–2008 V. Bricker (1991:286f.): /ba/; Davoust (1995:586): /ba/; Knorozov (1999, vol. 1:141): /bu/ (vasija con agua hirviendo); Love (1991:299): "ixim"? 'maize' in T0162:0506.0558 compound 'bread of maize'; Ringle and Smith-Stark (1996:335–38): 0558 (retired) = 0501c.

XE2

T 0501
Z 1321
K 0179

ha'

n water

Yu *ha'* ha(a)' 'agua' (Barrera Vásquez et al. 1980:165); ha' 'water' (V. Bricker et al. 1998:91)

Ch' *ha'* *ha' 'water' (Kaufman and Norman 1984:120)

XE1 and XE2 are graphically similar; have same Thompson number (T0501). Most references listed below are for both XE1 and XE2.

1. Picture: water lily with darkened patch

1566–1915 Bollaert (1865–1866:52): "ymix"; Brasseur de Bourbourg (1869–1870, vol. 1:208): day Imix; "im-ix" 'fond, profondeur, mamele ou canal du trou ou de l'urine, ou des sécrétions aqueuses'; "i-mix" 'de rejeton aucun, de pousse jamais'; Goodman (1897:16, 58): day five, Ymix, closed hand; Landa [1566] (Tozzer 1941:134): day Imix; Rosny (1883:11): day Ymix; Rosny (1883:19): "tzem" 'mamelle, sexe féminin'; Thomas (1888:350): day Ymix; Thomas (1893:249): /m/, /ma/.

1916–1950 Gates (1931:1): "imix" 'sea-dragon; water; wine'; Thompson (1950:72): represents a water lily.

1951–1980 Barthel (1967:232): in addition to Imix, "nab" 'to besmear oneself with, to daub with'; Dütting (1979:185f.): "nab" 'lake, sea'; secondary value "ha" 'water' (especially terrestrial water); Kelley (1962b:25): "imix, imox" (J. E. S. Thompson, T. Barthel); "naab" 'water lily' (T. Barthel, D. Kelley); Kelley (1976:123, 182, 185, 208, 211, 332): "naab" 'water lily'; "imix, nab" 'ocean'; confused with T0556; see also T0502, T0556, T0557, T0558, Z1321, Z1360, Z1361; /ba/?; Knorozov (1955:74): 121 "in"; Knorozov (1958:285): /b(u)/; Knorozov (1967:94): "in" (female breast?); Thompson (1962:87–96): [611 examples] Imix.

1981–1990 V. Bricker (1986:211): /ba/, "ba" 'self' (Yucatecan), /bä/, "bä" 'self' (Cholan); Dütting (1985:106) possibly "naab" and /ba/; "ba" 'self' (Yucatecan); Fox and Justeson (1984:54f.): "ha' " 'water'; Grube (1990a:104): = T0556, T0558, T0655, T0690, T0771, T0811, T1300, T1323; Justeson (1984:338): J. Fox, J. Justeson: (a) with crosshatched oval: 'water', including "*nahb' " and "ha' "; day Imix; rarely used as (b), probably in error; L. Campbell, J. Fox, J. Justeson: (b) with curving lines in oval: /b'a/; never /ma/, except perhaps as error based on similarity to T0502 /ma/; F. Lounsbury, B. Riese: day Imix; /b'a/; P. Mathews, D. Stuart: /b'a/; also day Imix; sometimes /ma/; Thompson included other signs under T0501; cf. T0502, T0556, T0557, T0558; B. Riese: some 'water'; never /ma/; L. Schele: day Imix, /b'a/, /ma/, possibly "mal"; MacLeod (1988b): "nab."

1991–2008 Davoust (1995:581): "ha' " 'eau'; Imix '1er jour'; Knorozov (1999, vol. 1:140): "in" (nubarrones bajando); Ringle and Smith-Stark (1996:347) darkened Imix = 0501b. Although identified as a logograph for some type of body of water (see summary in Stuart and Houston 1994:19), a and b variants both appear as Imix; Schele and Grube (1997:226): "ha" 'water'; Stuart (1997:3): "ba" 'first' on Toniná Monument 69; Stuart and Houston (1994:19ff.): probably "ha' " 'water'; credit Schele with "nab" 'lake, pool, general body of water'.

XE2

T 0164
Z 0016
K 0094

ha'

n water

Prefix to God L's portrait SNK.

2. Picture: water lily with darkened patch and drops of water

1566–1915 Thomas (1893:254): "maax" 'monkey'; "maach" 'crow'.

1951–1980 Knorozov (1967:86): "toh"?; compare to Old Yucatec "tox" 'to pour'.

1991–2008 H. Bricker and V. Bricker (n.d.): “ha” 'water'; Davoust (1995:565): "ha' " 'eau'; Knorozov (1999, vol. 1:141): /in-tox/; ligadura de 574-78; Lacadena (2004:92): possibly full form of T0143 "ha'al" 'rain' but more likely conflation of T0501 and T0143 spelling "ha'ha'al" 'rainy' or 'rainy season'; Taube (1992:84): Imix glyph symbol of water; black dots probably represent falling water or rain.

XE3

T 0557
Z 1361
K 0182

ma

1. Picture: water lily with infix

1916–1950 Gates (1931:63): "mac."

1951–1980 Kelley (1962a:285): /ma/; Kelley (1976:176, 185, 252, 333): (= T0502) replaces T0074 /ma/; Knorozov (1955:71): 080 (vasija cerrada con líquido) "mac"; Knorozov (1967:94): (= K187) phonetic; Thompson (1962:170): [11 examples].

1981–1990 V. Bricker (1986:212): /ma/; Grube (1990a:108): = T0502; Justeson (1984:343): J. Fox, J. Justeson, B. Riese, L. Schele, D. Stuart: /ma/; probably codex form of T0502; L. Campbell, F. Lounsbury, P. Mathews: /ma/.

1991–2008 Davoust (1995:586): /ma/; Grube (1994b:181): T0557 /ma/ invented after 9.11.0.0.0; Knorozov (1999, vol. 1:141): "maac"; Ringle and Smith-Stark (1996:335–38): 0557 (retired) = 0502b.

XE6

T 0610
Z —
K 0335

May not be the same as XE6 in Classic inscriptions.

1. Picture: ?

1916–1950 Gates (1931:155): 'meat; flesh'?

1951–1980 Knorozov (1967:101): /s(u)/ (vessel with liquid); Thompson (1962:233): [17 examples] occasionally prefixed to heads of animals and gods; probably same as T0283, listed separately to recognize ragged edge of T0283; thatch of house for some examples.

1981–1990 Justeson (1984:348): J. Justeson: logographic; at least with T0069 prefixed, a locative noun; = T0613; P. Mathews: equivalent of T0192; L. Schele: equivalent of T0192 and T0614?; depicts thatch.

1991–2008 Davoust (1995:590): /me/; Grube (1994b:183): /me/; Knorozov (1999, vol. 1:140): /zuu/ (vasija con agua para hervir).

XE7

T 0283
Z 1359
K 0335

ch'a?

Clearly has a phonetic value, possibly /ch'a/. Other possibilities include /ka/ or /sa/.

1. Picture: ?

1566–1915 Thomas (1888:349, 370): [with T0283.0558] "xamach; chimix" 'a vessel'; Thomas (1893:263): "cham."

1916–1950 Gates (1931:155): 'meat; flesh'?

1951–1980 Kelley (1962a:306, 308): /dza/; "dza" 'dar'; Kelley (1976:155–57, 332): (T0283:0558) 'snaring'; Knorozov (1955:71): (vasija con líquido) /z(uu)/; Knorozov (1967:101): /s(u)/ (vessel with liquid); Thompson (1962:67): [6 examples] may belong with T0610, as suggested by Gates and Zimmermann; Thompson (1972:76): "balche."

1981–1990 Justeson (1984:335): J. Fox: /k'a/; probably /si/; iconic origin in halved T0563a; J. Justeson: /tz'/ + unknown vowel (e.g., in "su-tz'(V)" for month name Zotz'); possibly /tz'i/, for which see T0563c, the probable main sign form of T0283; probably not /si/ (but cf. "*tz'a:h" 'to give', "si'h" 'to give'); TIX.0283:0526 not Bolon Dzacab; probably sometimes /k'a/; F. Lounsbury: /si/; P. Mathews: "si(h)"; L. Schele: "sih"; Justeson (1989:126, n. 41): /tz'V/, probably /tz'u/; occurs in spelling of month name Sotz'/Sutz' in two Classic period spellings; on M. 77, 78, paired with T0526 "kab' " 'earth' in series of directional compounds; may represent "tz'uh kab' ," the Classical Yucatec term for 'nadir'.

1991–2008 V. Bricker (1991:286f.): /ca/ or "cah"; Davoust (1995:574): /za/; Knorozov (1999, vol. 1:175): "zuu" (vasija con agua para hervir); Paxton (2001:27f.): when paired with T0526, "ts'u kab' " 'nadir' or 'center', following Justeson (1989:126 n. 41); Schele and Grube (1997:17, 221): /sa/; Vail (2002b): /ch'a/?; von Nagy (1997:59, 61): /ca/; combines with /ba/ to spell "cab" 'earth'.

XG1

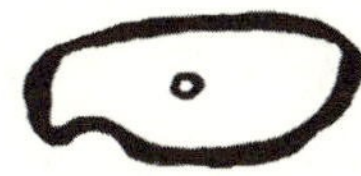

T 0511
Z 1329
K 0112

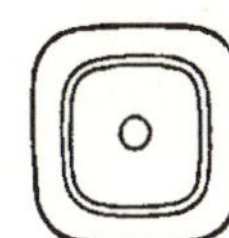

Overlaps with 2S1 "nal/näl" in Madrid Codex in non-calendrical contexts.
day 09: Muluk/Mul
1. Picture: disc, spindle whorl?

1566–1915 Bollaert (1865–1866:52): "muluv" 'to unite'; Brasseur de Bourbourg (1869–1870, vol. 1:206): day Muluc; "muluc" 'amassé, fait en amas'; or "mul-uc" 'colline faite, môle soulevé par amas'; Landa [1566] (Tozzer 1941:134): day Muluc; Rosny (1883:6): day Muluc; Thomas (1893:260): day Muluc.

1916–1950 Gates (1931:31): "muluc" 'rain'; Thompson (1950:274): "tun" 'jade'.

1951–1980 Kelley (1976:123, 200, 332): "muluc, mul"; Knorozov (1967:88): /k(o)/; "ko" 'grain'; day Muluk; Thompson (1962:110f.): [56 examples] Muluc; Thompson (1972:39): "toh" in non-calendrical contexts; an association with water and rainstorm.

1981–1990 Grube (1990a:105): = T0517, T1312; Justeson (1984:339): L. Campbell, J. Fox, J. Justeson, P. Mathews: day Muluc, root "*mul"; F. Lounsbury, P. Mathews, L. Schele, D. Stuart: "mul," "mulu," "muluk."

1991–2008 Davoust (1995:582): muluc '9e jour'; Davoust (1997:121): "pet" 'faire de rotations'; Knorozov (1999, vol. 1:112): /choo, cho, coo, co/ (grano); Schele (1992b:221f.): correspondence from Grube, n.d.: "pet" 'numeral classifier for round objects, etc.'; Schele and Grube (1997:114): in expression "petah" 'he makes it round'.

XG3

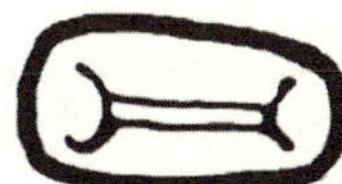

T 0687a
Z 1316
K 0113

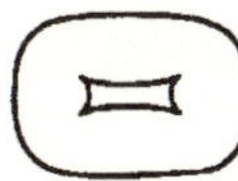

po

pòom / pom

n incense
Yu *pòom* pòom 'incense' (V. Bricker et al. 1998:220)
Ch' *pom* *pom 'incense' (Kaufman and Norman 1984:129)

1. Picture: cushion

1566–1915 Brasseur de Bourbourg (1869–1870, vol. 1:208): day Ik; "ik" 'esprit, souffle, vent'; Landa [1566] (Tozzer 1941:151): prefixed to month Pop; Rosny (1883:11): day Ik.

1916–1950 Gates (1931:155f.): not the day sign or wind sign "ik"; Thompson (1950:200): "ich."

1951–1980 Knorozov (1967:88): "tzil" (scrap of cloth); Lounsbury (1973): /po/, "pop"; Thompson (1962:291f.): [16 examples] Ich. Most often appears as part of "Ben-Ich" affix T0168.

1981–1990 V. Bricker (1986:213): /po/; Dütting (1985): /po/ (after Lounsbury 1973), 'eye, face, fruit; in front of'; Justeson (1984:352): L. Campbell, J. Fox, J. Justeson, P. Mathews, B. Riese: /po/; J. Justeson "aw," includes "ha:w" 'to end', "*a:w" 'to sow'; F. Lounsbury, L. Schele, D. Stuart: /po/, "pohp" 'throne'; Porter (1988): "its" 'resin; sorcery'.

1991–2008 Davoust (1995:596): "pom" 'copal'; /po/; /wa/; Knorozov (1999, vol. 1:114, 233): "tzil" 'trozo (de tela, papel, etc.)'.

XG3

T 0687b
Z 1316
K 0299

pòom / pom

n incense

Syllabic /po/ plus /mo/.

2. Picture: dotted circle with "po" sign infix

1916–1950 Gates (1931:164): G406 [in part].

1951–1980 Knorozov (1967:99): "tzil" 'bloodletting'; Thompson (1962:291f.): (T0687a and 0687b) [16 examples] Ich; Thompson (1972:91): "The "ich" element is drawn in the center of what is probably a ball of copal or rubber."

1981–1990 V. Bricker (1986:213): /po-mo/; "pom" 'incense'; Justeson (1984:352): L. Campbell, J. Fox, J. Justeson, P. Mathews, F. Lounsbury, L. Schele, D. Stuart: phonetic compound "po:m(o)" 'copal, incense'.

1991–2008 Davoust (1995:596): "pom" 'copal'; /po/; Knorozov (1999, vol. 1:114): "tzil" (fragmento de pliegue estirado).

XG4

T 0114
Z 0083
K 0107

xa

x-?

agentive? feminine/diminutive agentive prefix?

Yu *x-* x- 'feminine agent' (V. Bricker et al. 1998:363)

Ch' *ix-* *ix 'female; relatively small/inactive being' (Kaufman and Norman 1984:139)

May be some overlap with HE6 /u/.

1. Picture: drops?

1566–1915 Brasseur de Bourbourg (1869–1870, vol. 1:204): "u" 'vase, bassin, surface circonscrite, lune'.

1951–1980 Cordan (1964:48): "le', l' "; Knorozov (1967:88): phonetic (flute; Old Yucatec "chul").

1981–1990 V. Bricker (1983:350): "yax" 'first' in compound T0114.0566.0023 "yax caan/chan" 'first heaven'; Grube (1990a:92): = T0508; Justeson (1984:324): J. Fox, J. Justeson, P. Mathews: two signs, one = T0508, the other = Z83; J. Fox: Z83 variant possibly /kV/ (likely /ku/); possibly /ku/ in month sign Pax, Ch'ol "ahquiccu," possibly /xV/; substitutes for, or is followed by, Z87; J. Justeson, P. Mathews, L. Schele, D. Stuart: Z83 variant /xV/; F. Lounsbury, B. Riese: = T0508; "chan"; P. Mathews: "kan/chan"; also "kaan/chaan"; L. Schele: "kan," "kaan/chaan," "chan"; Stuart (1987:28–31): /xa/.

1991–2008 Davoust (1995:561): "xah" 'épine'; /xa/; Knorozov (1999, vol. 1:107): "chul, cul" (flauta?); Stross (1994:189): /xi/; Vail (2002b): "ix"? in certain contexts.

XG4

T 0508
Z —
K —

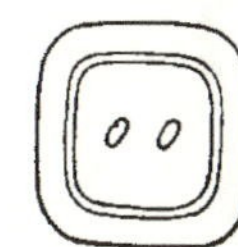

T508 variant used as day glyph only.
day 05: Chikchan/Nachan
2. Picture: drops?

1566–1915 Rosny (1883:4): day Chikchan.

1916–1950 Gates (1931:20): "chikchan" 'serpent'.

1951–1980 Thompson (1962:107): [4 examples] Chicchan.

1981–1990 Grube (1990a:105): = T0114; Justeson (1984:338): L. Campbell: "chan" 'snake'; J. Fox, J. Justeson: day Chicchan and 'snake'; F. Lounsbury, L. Schele, D. Stuart: "kan," "chan" 'serpent'; day Chicchan; P. Mathews: day Chicchan; also "kan/chan" and cognates 'serpent'; B. Riese: = T0114; day Chicchan; "chan," "cha:n"?; Riese (1982:264): "chan"; Stuart (1987:28–31): /xa/.

1991–2008 Davoust (1995:581): "chacchan" '5e jour'; "xah" 'épine'; /xa/; Knorozov (1999, vol. 1:115): "chan"; Stuart, Houston, and Robertson (1999:33): "xa-" future aspect marker? or 'again'?

XG8

T 0095
Z 0022
K 0109

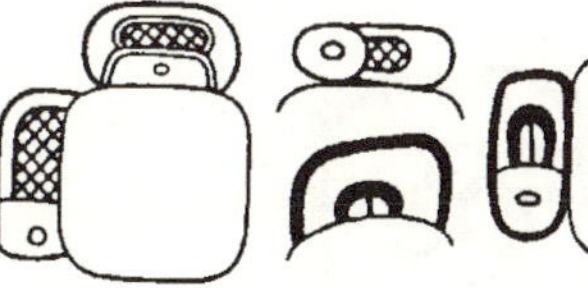

éek' / ik'

adj black
Yu *éek'* ek' 'cosa negra' (Barrera Vásquez et al. 1980:149); 'éek' 'black' (V. Bricker et al. 1998:7)
Ch' *ik'* *ik' 'black' (Kaufman and Norman 1984:121)

1. Picture: darkening

1566–1915 Brinton (1895:108): 'west'; Seler [1891] (1902–1923:31): "ek" 'black'; Thomas (1893:262): "h', oh', l'n, laan'."

1916–1950 Gates (1931:94): "ek" 'black'.

1951–1980 Knorozov (1955:70): 069 (vástago?) "cek" ("ek") 'negro'; Knorozov (1967:88): "ek' " 'black'; Thompson (1962:49f.): 'black'.

1981–1990 V. Bricker (1986:209): "ik" 'black' (Cholan); "ek" 'black' (Yucatecan); Grube (1990a:91): = T0323; Justeson (1984:322): L. Campbell, J. Fox, J. Justeson: 'black', Cholan "*ik' " and presumably the Yucatecan cognate "*e:k' "; traditional, probably not synchronically motivated in Yucatec month names Uo and Ch'en; F. Lounsbury, L. Schele: black; "ek' " and "b'ox"; P. Mathews, D. Stuart: black; possibly "ek' " or "b'ox"; B. Riese: 'black', "ek' " and cognates.

1991–2008 Davoust (1995:560): "ek/ik" 'noir'; Knorozov (1999, vol. 1:102): "hek."

XG9

T 0730
Z 1308c
K 0129

1. Picture: ?

1951–1980 Knorozov (1967:89): morphemic (= K124) "k'ak' "; Thompson (1962:311): [2 examples].

XGA

T 0580
Z 1308a
K 0130

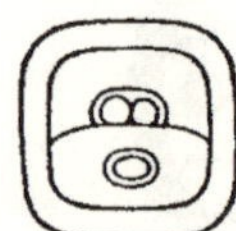

lo

1. Picture: ?

1566–1915 Landa [1566] (Tozzer 1941:159): in month glyph Mol.

1916–1950 Gates (1931:62, 161): [G033] "mol"; [G356] sprouting plant.

1951–1980 Knorozov (1955:69): 057 (vástago?) "kak"; Knorozov (1967:88): (affix K110) "h'ek' " (sprout); main sign K124; Knorozov (1967:89f.): (= K110) "h'ek' " (sprout); Mathews (1980:68): "muluc"; Thompson (1962:205f.): [61 examples] 'jade'.

1981–1990 Grube (1990a:109): (a) = T1313; (b) = T1345; Justeson (1984:345): L. Campbell: "mul/b'ul"; J. Fox, J. Justeson: probably = T0095; "*e:k" 'black'; J. Justeson: possibly rebus, Lowland Mayan "*wek' " (Cholan "*wech' ") 'to scatter' as complement or substitute to T0710; F. Lounsbury: "b'ul/mul/b'ol"; P. Mathews, L. Schele, D. Stuart: "mul" in Classic; Stuart (1987:41): /lo/.

1991–2008 Davoust (1995:588): "loh" 'jumeau'; /lo/; Houston and Stuart (1996:299): "chit"?; Knorozov (1999, vol. 1:123): "hot', hoch" (planta?); Stuart, Houston, and Robertson (1999:56): "chit."

XGA

T 0580v
Z 1308a
K –

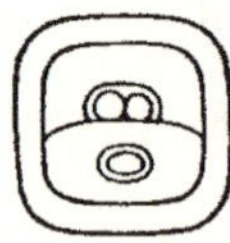

lo

2. Picture: flower?

1566–1915 Brasseur de Bourbourg (1869–1870, vol. 1:208): day Ik; "ik" 'esprit, souffle, vent'.

1916–1950 Gates (1931:161): sprouting plant.

1991–2008 Knorozov (1999, vol. 1:121): "hot', hoch"; Vail (2002b): variant of T0580 /lo/.

XGB

T 0837
Z –
K –

1. Picture: ?

1951–1980 Thompson (1962:391): [1 example].

XGC

T —
Z 1368
K —

te

che' / te'

n tree, wood, plant

Yu *che'* che' 'árbol en general, madera o palo; planta en general' (Barrera Vásquez et al. 1980:85); che' 'wood, tree, stick' (V. Bricker et al. 1998:64); te' 'tree' (V. Bricker et al. 1998:272)

Ch' *te'* *te' 'tree' (Kaufman and Norman 1984:132)

1. Picture: ?

1566–1915 Brasseur de Bourbourg (1869–1870, vol. 1:202): "t, ti" 'ici, dans, à, vers, pour, de, etc. lieu, endroit désigné'; Landa [1566] (Tozzer 1941:170): <t>; Rosny (1883:17): "ti" 'place, lieu?; soleil'.

1951–1980 Kelley (1962a:302f.): may be /th/ or /t'/; Thompson (1962:403): Z1368 = T0109.

1991–2008 Davoust (1995:593): "te' " 'arbre'; nicte' 'plumeria, fleur'; Schele (1992b:221f.): correspondence from Grube n.d.: Landa's /te/; Schele and Freidel (1991:313): credit Grube with /te/.

XGD

T —
Z —
K 0127, 0128?

1. Picture: ?

1566–1915 Brasseur de Bourbourg (1869–1870, vol. 1:207): day Ix; "ix" 'trou caché, issue de l'urine chez les femmes, urine'.

1951–1980 Knorozov (1967:89): K127 = K126; K128 = K074.

1991–2008 Davoust (1997:295): = 0163EP /mi/.

XGE

T 0585ab
Z 1343
K 0122

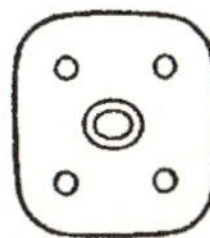

b'i, b'e

1. Picture: quincunx

1566–1915 Brasseur de Bourbourg (1869–1870, vol. 1:201): "b, ba" 'taupe, chose basse, ancêtre, personne'; root of "baab" 'ramer' and of "bat" 'batte, battre'; Brinton (1895:88): Landa's "be" 'footprints'; Landa [1566] (Tozzer 1941:170): <b>; Thomas (1888:353, 371): Landa's /b/, "be" 'journey'; also /be/?; [T0096.0585.0186] act of walking or taking steps; Thomas (1893:244–46): Landa's /b/; 'footstep, path, road'.

1916–1950 Whorf (1942:484, fig. 1): "b."

1951–1980 Kelley (1976:102, 192, 333): "bix" 'dance', numerical classifier; Knorozov (1955:73): 105 (campo sembrado; los círculos indican los hoyos donde se arroja el grano de maíz) "col"; Knorozov (1967:89): /b(a)/ (sown field?); Thompson (1962:209–13): [169 examples] (quincunx); Thompson (1972:76): possibly some evidence for "hol" 'its opening', 'its offering on high'.

1981–1990 V. Bricker (1986:212): /be/; V. Bricker and H. Bricker (1988:S37): Landa's /be/; "be" 'road'; Dütting (1985:106, 109): possibly /be/ and "bix" and "pix" 'go forward, walking'; Grube (1990a:109): = T1303, T1338; Justeson (1984:346): cf. Landa's <b>; L. Campbell: /b'e/, /b'i/; "b'ix" only in that the /b'i/ value suggests "b'ix" suffix, /x/ not explicitly represented; J. Fox, J. Justeson, B. Riese: /b'i/, /b'e/; not "b'ix"; F. Lounsbury: /b'e/, "b'ix/p'ix"; P. Mathews: /b'e/, "b'ix", "b'e"; L. Schele: /b'i/, /b'e/, possibly "b'e"; numeral classifier and possibly phonetic "b'ix"; J. Justeson, P. Mathews, L. Schele: T0585b different sign from T0585a and T0585c; Stuart (1989b): /bi/ in "wing-quincunx" of primary standard sequence.

1991–2008 Davoust (1995:588): "beh" 'chemin'; /be/; Houston, Robertson, and Stuart (2001:22–23): morphosyllable "-ib' "; can function as /b'i/, but mostly marks instrumental constructions; Knorozov (1999, vol. 1:117): "av" (campo sembrado); Schele and Grube (1997:16) /b'i/.

XGJ

T –
Z –
K –

num zero

1. Picture: ?

1566–1915 Brinton (1895:20): 'zero', following Förstemann; Förstemann (1906): 'zero'; Morley (1915:92): 'zero'; Seler [1900] (1990:279): 'zero'.

1916–1950 Thompson (1950:fig. 25, no. 59): symbol of completion.

XGJ

T –
Z –
K –

num zero

2. Picture: ?

1566–1915 Förstemann (1902:19): 'zero'.

1991–2008 Drapkin (2002:75): 'zero' on Madrid 2b, 3b.

XGK

T 0632
Z 1309
K 0300

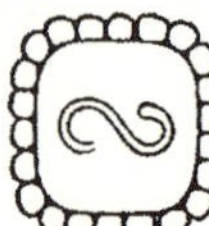

muyal

n cloud

Yu *muyal* muyal 'nube del cielo' (Barrera Vásquez et al. 1980:544); múunyal 'cloud' (V. Bricker et al. 1998:190); muyal 'cloud' (Hofling with Tesucún 1997:458)

Ch' *muyal* muyal 'nube' (Morán 1935:47)

1. Picture: dotted S-curve; cloud

1566–1915 Brasseur de Bourbourg (1869–1870, vol. 1:203): /n/; 'lettre qui est l'attribut de la grandeur, de l'excellence, de la royauté'; Brinton (1895:23): refers to alternation or change of series of years or cycles.

1916–1950 Spinden (1924:183f.): reversal of the seasons from dry to wet, based on example on Dresden 68a.

1951–1980 Knorozov (1967:99): "ni" 'elevation'?; Thompson (1962:248): [18 examples] appears as affix with T0544, T0561, T0747.

1981–1990 V. Bricker and H. Bricker (1988:S15): "reversal sign"; may refer to the solstices and equinoxes; Grube (1990a:111): = T0367; Justeson (1984:349): J. Fox: face of heavenly body; J. Justeson: apparently fusion /mo-n(e)/.

1991–2008 Davoust (1995:592): "muyal" 'nuage'; Knorozov (1999, vol. 1:87): "mo-ni"; ligadura de 356-151; Milbrath (1999:277, fig. 7.4 f): probably symbolizes Milky Way; Stone (1996): "muyal" 'cloud'; Stuart and Houston (1994:44, 47, fig. 51): "muyal" 'cloud'.

XGL

T 0808
Z –
K –

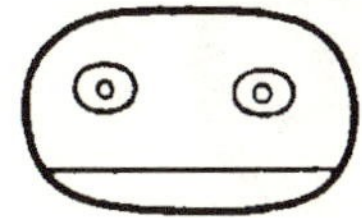

1. Picture: pair of concentric circles

1916–1950 Gates (1931:163): G371 [in part].
1951–1980 Thompson (1962:383): [1 example].

XGM

T –
Z –
K –

1. Picture: ?

XH1

T 0584
Z 1333
K 0147

ah / aj

agentive; n — agentive
Yu *ah* — ah 'antepuesta a los apellidos de linaje denota los varones; antepuesta a los nombres de lugares' (Barrera Vásquez et al. 1980:3)
Ch' *aj* — *aj 'prepound/proclitic; male; relatively large/active being (Kaufman and Norman 1984:139)

day 13: B'en/B'in
1. Picture: ?

1566–1915 Bollaert (1865–1866:52): "ben" 'go'; Brasseur de Bourbourg (1869–1870, vol. 1:207): day Been; "ben" or "be-en" 'voie, chemin, marche ouverte peu à peu, détruite ou descendue au fond'; Goodman (1897:16): day Ben; Landa [1566] (Tozzer 1941:134): day Ben; Rosny (1883:7): day Ben.

1916–1950 Gates (1931:38): "ben" 'reed'.

1951–1980 Kelley (1976:206, 214, 333): "ben" 'reed'; Knorozov (1955:70): 074 (casa, pilares, viga y entibado del techo) "ben"; Knorozov (1967:91): "ben" (hut?); Lounsbury (1976): "ah/aj" title; Thompson (1962:209): [2 examples] Ben.

1981–1990 V. Bricker (1986:212): /a(h)/; Dütting (1985:104): "ah" when compounded with other graphemes; if main sign, 'lord, first one, firstborn'; Justeson (1984:345): L. Campbell, J. Fox, J. Justeson, P. Mathews, D. Stuart: day Ben (Reed) and "*aj-" 'agentive', cf. "*a:j" 'reed'; specifically "b'e'n" at Chichén Itzá in T0584.0116 "ben-ni"; F. Lounsbury, B. Riese, D. Stuart: day Ben/Ah; "ah"; Porter (1988): masculine superlative "ah"; with T0687a, "ah-its/itsa' " 'sorcerer'.

1991–2008 Davoust (1995:588): "ben/bin" '13e jour'; "ah" 'préf. genre masc.'; Knorozov (1999, vol. 1:127, 232): "been" 'caminar' (una choza?).

XH2

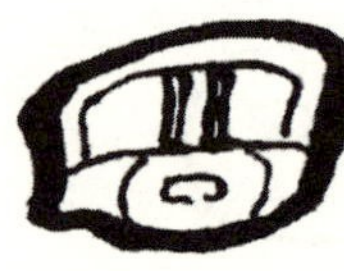

T 0548
Z 1340
K 0189

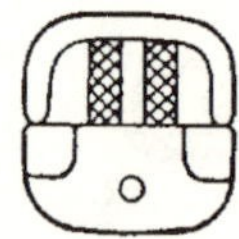

há'ab' / hab'

n; nm cl — tun; year

Yu *há'ab'* — haab 'año' (Barrera Vásquez et al. 1980:165); há'ab' 'year' (V. Bricker et al. 1998:92)

Ch' *hab'* — *hab' 'year' (Kaufman and Norman 1984:120)

period: 360 days, tun; 365 days, há'ab'

1. Picture: drum?

1566–1915 Bowditch (1910:256): "tun" 'stone; period of 360 days'; has the meaning of 'stone' on D. 25-28 and M. 34-37; Brasseur de Bourbourg (1869–1870, vol. 1:207): day Been; "ben" or "be-en" 'voie, chemin, marche ouverte peu à peu, détruite ou descendue au fond'; Brinton (1895:92): "paxan" 'it is finished'; representation of a drum; Förstemann [1897] (1904b:549): period of 360 days; Goodman (1897:23): "ahau" 'period of 360 days'; Rosny (1883:18, 19): 'pierre'? (attributed to Thomas); "ahau" 'roi, règne, époque'; Seler [1915] (1976:fig.76); "tun" 'period of 360 days'; Thomas (1882:144): denotes the "stone heap" to which the Uayeb idols were placed on M. 25–28; Thomas (1888:349, 370): "piz" 'stone; stone heap'; /p/, /p'/; Thomas (1893:249): /p/, /p'/.

1916–1950 Gates (1931:73): "tun"; Spinden (1924:211): "tun" sign used for 'zero' or 'completion'; Thompson (1950:144): "tun" or "haab."

1951–1980 Kelley (1976:33, 72, 135, 166, 192, 333): "tun" 'year'; Knorozov (1955:76): 142 "tun" 'año de 360 días'; a veces /t-/; Knorozov (1967:94): "tun" 'year'; Thompson (1962:161–64): [156 examples] "tun"; 'bedrock' in codices; on Dresden 25 and 28 dealing with new year, may be similar to piles of rock at exits of towns, important in new year ceremonies.

1981–1990 V. Bricker (1986:212): "tun" '360 day year' (Yucatecan); "hab" '365 day year' (Cholan, Yucatecan); Fox and Justeson (1984:48–53): "tun/hab"; Justeson (1984:342): J. Fox, J. Justeson, P. Mathews, B. Riese: J. Justeson: "*ha'b'," 'periods of 360 or 365 days'; "tu:n" 'end of a period of one "ha'b" '; depicts "*tu:n" 'drum'; J. Fox: possibly also "*tu:n" semantic equivalent of "*ha'b' "; J. Justeson: adverb "*tun" 'finally'; not 'end'; B. Riese: also "ha'b' " 'period of 364 days'; 'end'; L. Schele, D. Stuart: (1) 'year' (of 360 days); (2) 'drum'; (3) 'end'; MacLeod (1990b:336): outside verbal contexts, God N and the God of Five may have T0548 in their headdresses; possibly "hob/hom" 'ending' instead of, or in addition to, "hab."

1991–2008 Davoust (1995:585): "tun" 'pierre'; "hob" 'creux'; "hab" 'année de 365 jours'; /ho/; /ab/; Knorozov (1999, vol. 1:130): "tun" (tambor). Cuando se emplea como morfema (año), aparecen tres puntos (75) bajo el grafema.

XH3

T 0561c
Z 1347
K 0191

ká'an / chan

n — sky

Yu *ká'an* — ka'an 'cielo' (Barrera Vásquez et al. 1980:291); ka'anal 'cosa alta' (Barrera Vásquez et al. 1980:292); ká'an 'sky, height' (V. Bricker et al. 1998:123); ká'anhá'an 'haughty' (V. Bricker et al. 1998:123)

Ch' *chan* — chan 'alto' (Aulie and Aulie 1998:29); *chan 'sky' (Kaufman and Norman 1984:117)

1. Picture: ?

1566–1915 Schellhas [1892] (1904:41): with TXIII, hieroglyph of moan bird; Seler [1906] (1993:73): 'sky'; Thomas (1893:249f.): /tz/ or /z/; Thomas (1893:263): "tzan" 'to ruin, devastate'.

1916–1950 Gates (1931:139f.): "caan" 'sky, heavens'; Spinden (1924:147f.): part of glyph for 'observation of the sun at horizon', 'observation at sunset'; Thompson (1950:166–69): 'sky' in "sun at horizon" variant.

1951–1980 Kelley (1976:148, 150, 167, 201, 333): "caan" 'sky'; Knorozov (1955:74): 118 "chaan" ("caan")" 'cielo'; Knorozov (1967:94f.): "kaan" 'sky'; Thompson (1962:174–82): [354 examples] 'sky'; with crossed bands, "k'at," suggests sky from horizon to horizon.

1981–1990 V. Bricker (1986:212): "chan" 'sky' (Cholan); "caan" 'sky' (Yucatecan); Justeson (1984:343): L. Campbell, J. Fox, J. Justeson: 'sky' ("*ka'N") and phonetically similar forms; F. Lounsbury, P. Mathews, L. Schele, D. Stuart: T0561a–c, e–g "kaan/chan" 'sky'; P. Mathews: T0561d probably same value; B. Riese: 'sky' and "chaan"; L. Schele: T0561d possibly same value.

1991–2008 Davoust (1995:586): "ca'an/chan" 'ciel'; Knorozov (1999, vol. 1:131): "ca'an; chah' " (apoyos del cielo, árboles del universo?); Schele and Grube (1993): sky sign without /na/ complement reads /pi/; used in b'ak'tun glyph.

XH3

T 0561v
Z –
K 0192

ká'an / *chan*

n sky

2. Picture: ?

1566–1915 Thomas (1893:263): "tzan" 'to ruin, devastate'.

1916–1950 Gates (1931:140): "caan" 'sky, heavens'.

1951–1980 Kelley (1976:150): sky glyph tilted on its side; frequently associated with T0137 prefix; Knorozov (1967:94f.): (= K191 with additional element) "kaan" 'sky'; Thompson (1962:174, 177): "sky."

1991–2008 V. Bricker (personal communication, July 2008): tilted variant is not same grapheme as T0561c; Knorozov (1999, vol. 1:128): "nix" (grafema 498 girado 45°).

XH3

T 0561d
Z 1346
K 0195

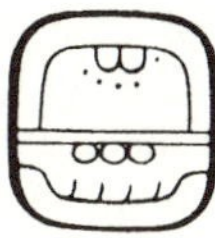

ká'an / *chan*

n sky

3. Picture: ?

1916–1950 Gates (1931:150): occurs only in eclipse chapter; Spinden (1924:146–48): part of glyph for 'observation of the sun at horizon', 'observation at sunset'; Thompson (1950:166–69): 'sky' in "sun at horizon" variant.

1951–1980 Kelley (1976:148, 150, 167, 201, 333): "caan" 'sky'; Knorozov (1967:94f.): (= K191 with additional element) "kaan" 'sky'; Thompson (1962:174–82): [354 examples] 'sky'.

1981–1990 V. Bricker (1986:212): "chan" 'sky' (Cholan); "caan" 'sky' (Yucatecan); Justeson (1984:343): L. Campbell, J. Fox, J. Justeson: 'sky' ("*ka'N") and phonetically similar forms; F. Lounsbury, P. Mathews, L. Schele, P. Mathews: T0561d probably same value; B. Riese: 'sky' and "chaan"; L. Schele: T0561d possibly same value.

1991–2008 Davoust (1995:586): "ca'an/chan" 'ciel'; Knorozov (1999, vol. 1:131): "kab-chah"; ligadura de 572-498; Schele and Grube (1993): sky sign without /na/ complement reads /pi/; used in b'ak'tun glyph.

XH3

T 0561a
Z 1345
K 0194

ká'an / *chan*

n sky

4. Picture: ?

1566–1915 Brasseur de Bourbourg (1869–1870, vol. 1:207): day Been; "ben" or "be-en" 'voie, chemin, marche ouverte peu à peu, détruite ou descendue au fond'.

1916–1950 Gates (1931:150): occurs only in eclipse chapter; Spinden (1924:146–48): part of glyph for 'observation of the sun at horizon', 'observation at sunset'; Thompson (1950:166–69): 'sky' in "sun at horizon" variant.

1951–1980 Kelley (1976:148, 150, 167, 201, 333): "caan" 'sky'; Knorozov (1967:94f.): (= K191 with additional element) "kaan" 'sky'; Thompson (1962:174–82): [354 examples] 'sky'.

1981–1990 V. Bricker (1986:212): "chan" 'sky' (Cholan); "caan" 'sky' (Yucatecan); Justeson (1984:343): L. Campbell, J. Fox, J. Justeson: 'sky' ("*ka'N") and phonetically similar forms; F. Lounsbury, P. Mathews, L. Schele, D. Stuart: T0561a–c, e–g "kaan/chan" 'sky'; B. Riese: 'sky' and "chaan."

1991–2008 Davoust (1995:586): "ca'an/chan" 'ciel'; Schele and Grube (1993): sky sign without /na/ complement reads /pi/; used in b'ak'tun glyph.

XH4

T 0506
Z 1324
K 0146

wàah / waj; óol / ol

n		tortilla; food; heart
Yu	*wàah; óol*	wàah 'tortilla, bread' (V. Bricker et al. 1998:298); ol 'corazón formal, y no el material; hoyuelo pequeño'; ol na 'puerta por donde se entra y sale; abertura o hendedura' (Barrera Vásquez et al. 1980:604); 'óol 'heart, will, energy, spirit' (V. Bricker et al. 1998:17)
Ch'	*waj; ol*	*waj 'tortilla; food' (Kaufman and Norman 1984:135); olmal 'hígado' (Aulie and Aulie 1998:86)

The "óol/ol" reading appears only rarely in the codices.

day 04: K'an/K'anan

1. Picture: ?

1566–1915 Bollaert (1865–1866:52): "kan" 'yellow'; Bowditch (1910:257): day Kan; Brasseur de Bourbourg (1869–1870, vol. 1:205): day Kan; "kán" or "káan" 'argile, terre montée, sécrétion volcanique; soulevé, agrandi, qui est élevé au-dessus d'une autre chose'; Brinton (1895:62): "kan" symbol, worn in headdress of the god of growth; associated with means and comfort; Goodman (1897:16): day Kan; Landa [1566] (Tozzer 1941:134): day Kan; Rosny (1883:3): day Kan; Thomas (1882:156): 'bread', 'tortillas', and also 'maize' when part of picture; Thomas (1888:350): cannot be milpa, but the corn grain; Thomas (1893:255f.): "kan"; /n/?

1916–1950 Gates (1931:14): "kan" 'corn'; Whorf (1942:484, fig. 1; 487, fig. 2): /hu/; "hw"; "-u."

1951–1980 Kelley (1976:158, 209, 332): "kan" 'maize'; Knorozov (1955:68): 049 (concha) "kan", determinador "alimento"; Knorozov (1967:91): /h'(a)/ (scroll?); Thompson (1962:101–4): [161 examples] Kan 'maize'.

1981–1990 V. Bricker (1985c:418): day Kan; "och" or "ooch" in month glyph Cumku (with /o/ superfix); multiple logographic readings, depending on phonetic suffixes, all with general meaning of 'food' or 'tortilla': "wah" 'tortilla' with T0130 /wa/ suffix (credits Justeson, personal communication, 1984), "tzen" 'food, sustenance' with T0116 /ne/ suffix, "nal" 'ear of corn' with T0178 /la/ suffix; Grube (1990a:105): = T0823?, T0826, T0838; Justeson (1984:338): J. Fox, J. Justeson: day Kan (Ch'ol "k'aan," Yucatec "k'a'an") and "k'an" 'corn'; J. Justeson, P. Mathews: "wah" 'tortilla' with phonetic complement T0130 "wa"; F. Lounsbury, B. Riese: day "k'a'an" (Kan) and 'maize'; P. Mathews, L. Schele, D. Stuart: "k'an" 'maize'; not 'yellow'; Love (1989): when not a day sign, it should probably be read "wah" 'bread'.

1991–2008 Davoust (1995:581): "kan" '4e jour'; "wah" 'tortilla'; /wa/; Davoust (1997:185): "ol"; Freidel et al. (1993:105, 215, 352, 450, 451): /ol/; credit Grube and Houston with independent decipherments; Grube and Nahm (1994:706): "ol" 'center, heart, entrance'; Knorozov (1999, vol. 1:126): /h'u/, /h'a/ (símbolo del cielo volteado); Love (1991:299): "wah" 'bread' when suffixed or prefixed with T0130 /wa/; MacLeod (1991a): "ol" 'sprout', 'young maize foliation', 'heart'; Schele and Grube (1997:84): "wah" 'food'.

XH4

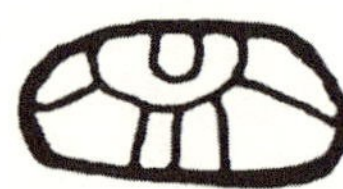

T 0774
Z —
K —

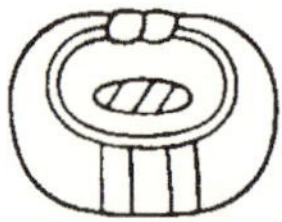

wàah / waj?

n tortilla; food?

2. Picture: ?

XH5

T 0507
Z 1362
K 0183

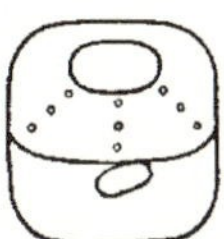
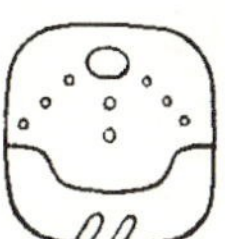

tzi

1. Picture: dotted "k'an" sign

1566–1915 Brasseur de Bourbourg (1869–1870, vol. 1:205): day Kan; "kán" or "káan" 'argile, terre montée, sécrétion volcanique; soulevé, agrandi, qui est élevé au-dessus d'une autre chose'; Rosny (1883:3): day Kan; Thomas (1893:268): /ma/.

1916–1950 Gates (1931:40): "ix" 'tiger; magician'.

1951–1980 Knorozov (1955:75): 130 "ppah (pah)"; Knorozov (1967:94): phonetic; Thompson (1962:105–7): [102 examples] (spotted Kan); Thompson (1972:98): with other affixes is an augural glyph, fortunate or unfortunate. On D. 30b is clearly a food. Its resemblance to the "kan," 'maize', sign and their frequent juxtaposition at Palenque suggest it is some form of maize.

1981–1990 Grube (1990a:105): = T0688, T0706, T0707, T0779, T1301; Justeson (1984:338): J. Fox, J. Justeson: "utz" 'good'; L. Schele: title, possibly from "k'an" 'maize'; MacLeod (1990a:395–406): "tsih" 'new, unripe, fresh'; Stuart (1987:16–25): /tsi/.

1991–2008 Davoust (1995:581): "tzih" 'cru, vert'; "itz" 'rosée'; /tzi/; Knorozov (1999, vol. 1:127, 241): "xoy" 'dar vueltos, girar' (hilos de lluvia).

XH6

T 0525
Z 1336
K 0200

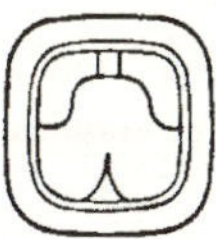

day 16: Kib'/Chib'in

1. Picture: curl

1566–1915 Bollaert (1865–1866:52): "cib" 'wax; copal'; Brasseur de Bourbourg (1869–1870, vol. 1:207): day Cib; "cib" 'lave, goutte d'un liquide épais en ébullition, cire fondue'; "ci-ib" 'embryon, chose renfermée, effervescente'; Goodman (1897:16): day Cib; Landa [1566] (Tozzer 1941:134): day Cib; Rosny (1883:9): day Cib.

1916–1950 Gates (1931:43): "cib" 'owl; vulture'.

1951–1980 Knorozov (1967:95): day Kib; Thompson (1962:127): [3 examples] Cib.

1981–1990 Justeson (1984:340): consensus: day Cib.

1991–2008 Davoust (1995:583): "cib/chabin" '16e jour'; Knorozov (1999, vol. 1:138): "cib" (cera derretida).

XH7

T 0854
Z –
K 0193

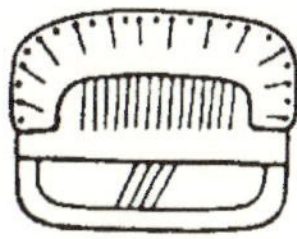

pu?

1. Picture: cattail reed?

1951–1980 Knorozov (1967:95): /h'(u)/ (upside-down sky sign); Thompson (1962:395): [1 example] lower part is inverted sky (T0561) sign.

1981–1990 Fox and Justeson (1984:39): /pV/ or /pi/; Grube (1990a:122): = T0266; Justeson (1984:359): J. Justeson = T0266b; P. Mathews, L. Schele: inverted T0561; Schele (1989c:5a): /pi/; Stuart (1987:11–13): /p-/ (with a vowel other than "i"), perhaps /pu/.

1991–2008 Davoust (1997:137): /pu/; Stuart (2000a:501–506): a cattail reed ("puh") associated by the ancient Mayas with Teotihuacan; Schele and Grube (1997:17): /pu/.

XH7

T –
Z –
K 0193

pu?

2. Picture: cattail reed?

1991–2008 Davoust (1997:189): /pu/; Schele and Grube (1997:17, 152): /pu/.

XH9

T 0504
Z 1323
K 0153

áak'ab' / ahk'äb'

n night, darkness

Yu *áak'ab'* ak'ab 'noche' (Barrera Vásquez et al. 1980:7); 'áak'ab' 'night' (V. Bricker et al. 1998:4); aak'ä' 'night; darkness' (Bruce 1979:129)

Ch' *ahk'äb', äk'b'äl* *ahk'äb'; äk'b'äl 'night' (Kaufman and Norman 1984:115)

day 03: Ak'b'al/Wotan

1. Picture: ?

1566–1915 Bollaert (1865–1866:52): "akbal" 'a plant'; Bowditch (1910:225; pl. I): day Akbal; Jupiter; Brasseur de Bourbourg (1869–1870, vol. 1:208): day Akbal; "ak-bal" "ak" or "ac" 'terre marécageuse' and "bal" "qu'elle devient telle; tourner en marais, en eau'; Goodman (1897:16): day Akbal; Landa [1566] (Tozzer 1941:134): day Akbal; Rosny (1883:11): day Akbal; Tozzer and Allen (1910:pl. 3): day Akbal, possibly representing the head of a centipede.

1916–1950 Gates (1931:10): "akbal" 'night'.

1951–1980 Kelley (1976:158, 332): "akbal" 'night'; Knorozov (1955:74): 119 (lluvia, torrentes de agua y superficie ondulada de la tierra) "ak" 'lluvia'; Knorozov (1967:92): "ak'" (streams of water and undulating land); Thompson (1962:99–101): [75 examples] Akbal.

1981–1990 V. Bricker (1986:211): "ak"? 'tongue; vine; rope' (Cholan, Yucatecan); Grube (1990a:105): = T0505inv, T0637, T0841; Hammond (1987:14): T0504 appears as infix in head variant of day Ak'b'al; Ak'b'al deity head carries general association of 'darkness, night'; Justeson (1984:338): J. Fox, J. Justeson, F. Lounsbury, P. Mathews, B. Riese: day Akbal and "ak'ab' " 'night', "ak'b'al" 'dark(ness)'; L. Campbell, L. Schele, D. Stuart: "ak'b'al" and/or cognates.

1991–2008 Davoust (1995:581): "akab" 'obscurité', "akbal" '3e jour'; Knorozov (1999, vol. 1:138): "ak" (hilos de lluvia y superficie de la tierra?); MacLeod (1991j): "ak' " used in "ak'il" 'offering'.

XHB

T 0609b
Z 1356
K 0144, 0145?

hú'un / hun

n headband; paper, book

Yu *hú'un* hu'un 'Ficus cotinifolia; libro; papel' (Barrera Vásquez et al. 1980:246); hú'un 'paper' (V. Bricker et al. 1998:116); hu'un 'paper, bark cloth' (Bruce 1979:161)

Ch' *hun* *hun 'paper, book' (Kaufman and Norman 1984:121)

1. Picture: book

1916–1950 Gates (1931:151f.): found in same position on all four Madrid New Year pages, with the "Cumhu" superfix.

1951–1980 Kelley (1962b:24): jaguar-skin bundle (J. E. S. Thompson, D. Kelley); Kelley (1976:131f.): jaguar-skin bundle; Knorozov (1955:72): 094 (tela) "zin"; Knorozov (1967:91): "sin"? (clothing, compare Old Yucatec "sin" 'skirt, textile'); Thompson (1962:232): [16 examples] (jaguar pelt); Thompson (1972:59): appears to be a title of the Bacabs; when paired with T0168, 'he of the starry night sky' or 'he of the jaguar seat'.

1981–1990 Grube (1990a:110): = T0201; Justeson (1984:347): J. Justeson: equivalent of T0060 in accession-related sense; J. Fox, P. Mathews: jaguar bundle; L. Schele: jaguar-covered throne pillow; MacLeod (1988b): credits Stuart with identification as a closed codex bound in jaguar skin. One of a substitution set with T0128 that has a proposed value of /hu/ (Schele, personal communication to MacLeod, 1988) based on the Mayan roots "huh/hun" for 'book, paper'.

1991–2008 Coe and Kerr (1997:170): "hun" 'book' representing leaves of paper between jaguar hides; Davoust (1995:590): "hu'un" 'codex'; /hu/; Davoust (1997:158): "tz'am" 'trone'; Knorozov (1999, vol. 1:130, 233): "zin" 'telaraña; tela; falda' (fragmento de tela de falda con el típico ornamento); Ringle and Smith-Stark (1996:348): variant of Glyph F of the Supplementary Series; a skin-covered codex; Schele and Grube (1997:130): "tzam" 'throne'.

XHE

T 0242
Z –
K –

1. Picture: ?

1981–1990 Grube (1990a:99): = T0614, T0620, T0621?, T0781.

1991–2008 Davoust (1995:571): "otoch" 'maison'; Knorozov (1999, vol. 1:128): "ot" (casa cubierta con un techo de hojas de palma); Ringle and Smith-Stark (1996:335–38): 0242 (retired) = 0614a or 0902.

XHF

T –
Z –
K –

1. Picture: ?

XQ1

T 0281
Z 0023
K 0170

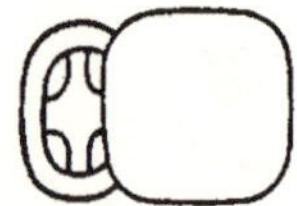

k'an / k'än

adj yellow, ripe

Yu *k'an* k'an 'cosa amarilla; fruta madura o sazonada; piedra preciosa' (Barrera Vásquez et al. 1980:374); k'an 'ripe', k'àank'an 'yellow, orange' (V. Bricker et al. 1998:144); k'än 'yellow' (Bruce 1979:174)

Ch' *k'än* *k'än 'yellow' (Kaufman and Norman 1984:123)

Previous misinterpretation as 'precious', originating with Thompson (1950:275), based on misreading of the Spanish "piedra preciosa" 'precious stone'.

1. Picture: quincunx

1566–1915 Brinton (1895:108): 'south'; Seler [1904] (1902–1923:31): "kan" 'yellow'.

1916–1950 Gates (1931:95): "kan" 'yellow'. Thompson (1950:275): 'yellow'; can substitute for "yax"; 'precious', possibly 'water'.

1951–1980 Knorozov (1955:73): 106 (campo señalado por los ángulos) "kan" 'amarillo'; Knorozov (1967:93): "k'an" 'yellow'; Thompson (1962:65–67): (kan cross) 'yellow'; possibly previously 'turquoise'; probably 'precious'; close associations with water; T0017:0281 compounds in codices may be green precious offerings or even "yax ha" 'uncontaminated water'. In Madrid Codex, "kin" sign replaces Kan cross in this compound; Thompson (1972:58): with T0017 "uil" 'food', especially maize.

1981–1990 V. Bricker (1986:211): "kan" 'yellow' (Cholan, Yucatecan); Justeson (1984:335): J. Fox, J. Justeson: "k'an" 'yellow', probably 'precious' not 'maize'; F. Lounsbury: "k'an" 'yellow' and superlative; not 'maize'; P. Mathews, L. Schele: "k'an" 'yellow, precious'; not 'maize'; Stross (1985): additional associations include 'precious' as drawn from relation to 'blood' representations; 'red' as it relates logographically to T0510 Venus/star.

1991–2008 Davoust (1995:574): "kan" 'jaune, précieux'; Knorozov (1999, vol. 1:146): "kan."

XQ2

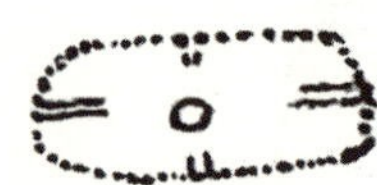

T 0646
Z 1341a
K 0305

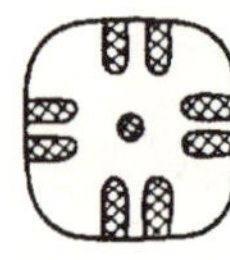

nik / nich; nikte' / nichte'

n flower; plumeria flower

Yu *nik; nikte'* nik 'flor' (Barrera Vásquez et al. 1980:569); nik 'flower' (V. Bricker et al. 1998:197); nikte' 'rosa, o flor, no denotando de qué árbol, mata o yerba; Plumeria sp' (Barrera Vásquez et al. 1980:569)

Ch' *nich; nichte'* *nich-im 'flower' (Kaufman and Norman 1984:127); nichte' 'placenta' (Wisdom 1950:541)

1. Picture: flower

1916–1950 Gates (1931:68): "kin" 'sun, day'.

1951–1980 Kelley (1962b:43): with T0087, "nicte" 'plumeria' (Y. Knorozov, T. Barthel); Kelley (1976:125): with T0087, "nicte"?; Knorozov (1955:69): 061 (flor con cuatro pétalos en óvalo punteado) "nic" 'flor'; Knorozov (1967:99): "nik" 'flower'; Thompson (1962:254): [2 examples]; Thompson (1972:44): "kin" 'day'.

1981–1990 Justeson (1984:349): J. Fox, J. Justeson: "*k'i:n" 'sun, day', etc.

1991–2008 Davoust (1995:593): "te' " 'arbre'; "nicte' " 'plumeria, fleur'; Knorozov (1999, vol. 1:146f.): Z1341 = "nic"; T0646 = "king"; Schele and Grube (1997:117): "nikte" 'flowers'.

XQ3

T 0544
Z 1341
K 0172

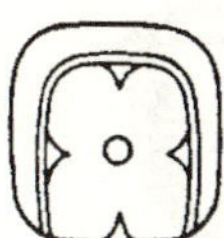

k'ìin / k'in

n day, sun
Yu *k'ìin* k'in 'día, sol' (Barrera Vásquez et al. 1980:400); k'ìin 'day, sun' (V. Bricker et al. 1998:152)
Ch' *k'in* *k'in 'sun, day' (Kaufman and Norman 1984:124)

1. Picture: flower

1566–1915 Bowditch (1910:255): "kin"; Brasseur de Bourbourg (1869–1870, vol. 1:202, 209): "t, ti"; 'ici, dans, à, vers, pour, de etc. lieu, endroit désigné'; "kin" 'soleil'; Förstemann [1897] (1904a:438): "k'in" 'sun, day'; Goodman (1897:15): 'day'; Landa [1566] (Tozzer 1941:158, 164): in month glyphs Yaxkin and Kankin; Rosny (1883:17): "kin" 'soleil, jour'; Schellhas [1892] (1904:27): sun sign "kin"; chief sign of the sun god, God G's, hieroglyph; Thomas (1888:348): "kin" 'sun' (and probably 'day'); Thomas (1893:266f.): "kin" 'sun'.

1916–1950 Gates (1931:68): "kin" 'sun, day'.

1951–1980 Kelley (1976:43, 126, 165, 192, 226–30, 333): "kin" 'day', 'sun'; 'priest'; Knorozov (1955:69): 060 (flor con cuatro pétalos) "kin" 'sol'; Knorozov (1967:93f.): "k'ing" Old Yucatec "k'in" 'sun'; Thompson (1962:155–60): [425 examples] "kin," with T0116, 'sun', 'day', 'time', and Post-Columbian 'festival'.

1981–1990 V. Bricker (1986:211): "kin" 'day, sun' (Cholan, Yucatecan); Grube (1990a:107): = T0825; Justeson (1984:342): L. Campbell: /k'in/ 'sun, day'; J. Fox, J. Justeson, P. Mathews, B. Riese: "k'i:n" 'day, sun', and possibly other meanings; F. Lounsbury, D. Stuart: "k'in"; L. Schele: "k'in."

1991–2008 Davoust (1995:585): "kin" 'soleil, jour'; "nic" 'fleur'; Knorozov (1999, vol. 1:146): "king."

XQ3

T 0281
Z 0023
K 0170

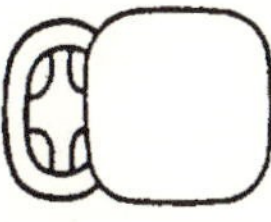

k'ìin / k'in

n day, sun

2. Picture: quincunx

1916–1950 Gates (1931:95): in places "can hardly be separated from being a mere kin-variant."

1991–2008 Vail (2002b): T0281 used for "k'in" 'sun, day' in Madrid Codex in several contexts (in both hieroglyphic texts and skybands).

XQ4

T 0727
Z 1343a
K 0304

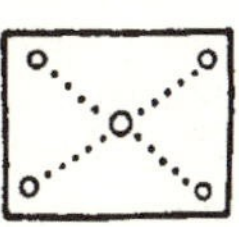

Also occurs in skybands.

1. Picture: flower?

1566–1915 Brasseur de Bourbourg (1869–1870, vol. 1:206, 218): day Lamat; "lam-at" for "lam-a-ti" 'lieu enfoncé, abîmé dans l'eau'; "lam-bat" 'enfoncée la hace, la batte'; symbole du tremblement de terre.

1916–1950 Gates (1931:167): occurs in constellation bands.

1951–1980 Knorozov (1967:99): phonetic; Thompson (1962:311): [2 examples] probably variants of T0544 "kin."

1991–2008 Davoust (1995:598): "kin" 'jour'; "nic" 'fleur'; Knorozov (1999, vol. 1:148): "ch'ah" (gotas de lluvia).

XQ6

T 0503
Z 1322
K 0114

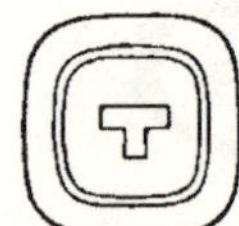

na?
nal / näl; nal

n — maize

Yu *näl; nal* — nal 'maíz en barra, o en caña, o en mazorca, y la mazorca antes que la desgranen' (Barrera Vásquez et al. 1980:557); nal 'ear of corn' (V. Bricker et al. 1998:194); näl 'ear of corn' (Hofling with Tesucún 1997:466); näl 'mazorca' (Ulrich and Ulrich 1976:144)

Ch' *näl; ø* — *näl 'corn ear' (Kaufman and Norman 1984:126)

Several examples suggest the possibility of a /na/ or "nah" reading.

day 02: Ik'/Ik'

1. Picture: ?

1566–1915 Bollaert (1865–1866:52): "ik" 'air; courage'; Brasseur de Bourbourg (1869–1870, vol. 1:208): day Ik; "ik" 'esprit, souffle, vent'; Goodman (1897:16): day Ik; Landa [1566] (Tozzer 1941:134): day Ik; Rosny (1883:11): day Ik; Thomas (1893:264): "ik" 'wind'.

1916–1950 Gates (1931:5): "ik" 'air; life'.

1951–1980 Knorozov (1955:69): 059 (fruto del pimiento, racimo?), "ik"; Knorozov (1967:88): "ik' " 'wind'; Thompson (1962:98f.): [50 examples] Ik; Thompson (1972:87): "ik" 'strong wind'.

1981–1990 V. Bricker (1986:211): "ik" 'wind'; Grube (1990a:105): = T0254; Justeson (1984:338): L. Campbell, J. Fox, J. Justeson, P. Mathews: day Ik' 'wind', also 'wind'; not Cholan "*ik' " 'black'; F. Lounsbury, P. Mathews, L. Schele, D. Stuart: "ik'."

1991–2008 Davoust (1995:581): "nal" 'maïs en tige", "ik" '2e jour'; Knorozov (1999, vol. 1:115): "ik" (nubes?); Schele (1992b:21f.): credits MacLeod with reading of "nal"; Stuart (2005:25, n. 2): "ik' " 'wind, breath' rather than "nal" as proposed by Schele (1992b:21) and Mora-Marín (2000); Vail (2002b): /na/ or "nah" in spelling of "i'inah" 'seed' on Madrid 28d.

XQ7

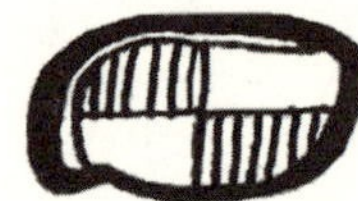

T 0593
Z 1305
K 0175

tz'a
tz'ak?

n? — heal; healer?

Yu *tz'ak* — tz'ak 'cure, heal'; tz'àak 'medicine'; h tz'àak 'doctor [male]'; x tz'àak 'doctor [female]' (V. Bricker et al. 1998:47)

1. Picture: ?

1916–1950 Gates (1931:141): probably denotes the Four Quarters, especially as used initially in division c of each of the Dresden New Year pages.

1951–1980 Knorozov (1967:94): [without dotting] "tz'ak"; Thompson (1962:220): [11 examples] may be variant of T0592; Thompson (1972:35): world directions?

1981–1990 Grube (1990a:109): = T0264.

1991–2008 Davoust (1995:589): "tz'ac" 'noeud'; /tz'a/; Knorozov (1999, vol. 1:148, 233): "tz'ac" 'nudo; generación' (estructura de la tribu); Schele and Looper (1996:155f.): /tz'a/ or possibly "tz'am" 'throne'; Schele and Grube (1997:22): /tz'a/.

XQ8

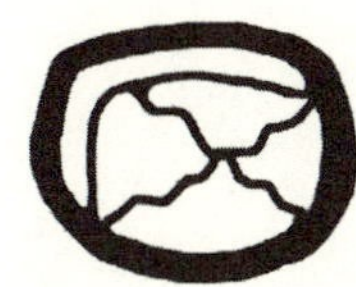

T 0527
Z 1338
K 0167

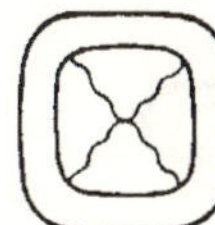

day 18: Etz'nab'/Chab'

1. Picture: flint

1566–1915 Bollaert (1865–1866:52): "etznab" 'sorcery'?; Brasseur de Bourbourg (1869–1870, vol. 1:208, 218): day Ezanab; "ezanab" 'silex, pierre de lance, jet de feu d'un volcan'; symbole du tremblement de terre; Goodman (1897:16): day Ezdnab; Landa [1566] (Tozzer 1941:134): day Ezanab; Rosny (1883:9): day Ezanab; Thomas (1882:145): placed on spearheads to indicate substance of which composed; represents "silex" or hardness.

1916–1950 Gates (1931:47): "etz'nab" 'flint knife'.

1951–1980 Knorozov (1967:93, 100): (= K319) "hetz'" (stone knife with two edges); Thompson (1962:133): [8 examples] Etz'nab.

1981–1990 Justeson (1984:340): consensus: day Etz'nab, 'flint'.

1991–2008 Davoust (1995:584): Etz'nab/Itz'nab '18e jour'; "e' " 'aiguisé'; Knorozov (1999, vol. 1:144): "hetz' " (cuchillo de pedernal con dos filos).

XQB

T 0552
Z 1350
K 0168

ta

k'at / k'ät; tan

n; prep — cross; middle, center

Yu *k'at; tan* — k'a(a)t 'pasar andando cruzando' (Barrera Vásquez et al. 1980:383); k'a(a)tal 'cosa que está atravesada' (Barrera Vásquez et al. 1980:384); k'at 'lie athwart, block, cross' (V. Bricker et al. 1998:149); k'ät 'cross' (Hofling with Tesucún 1997:385); tan 'en medio' (Swadesh et al. 1970:80); tan coch 'la mitad, en media' (Swadesh et al. 1970:80)

Ch' *k'ät; ø* — *k'ät 'crosswise' (Kaufman and Norman 1984:123)

1. Picture: crossed bands

1566–1915 Brasseur de Bourbourg (1869–1870, vol. 1:208, 218): day Ezanab; "ezanab" 'silex, pierre de lance, jet de feu d'un volcan'; symbole du tremblement de terre; Rosny (1883:10): day Ezanab; Thomas (1893:269): "etz."

1916–1950 Gates (1931:136–38): In the constellation band and in astronomical passages, it probably means conjunctions. In planting and other passages in the Madrid, it may denote seasonal changes. With the so-called "elephant-head" prefix, sex-converse is shown in the picture below; Thompson (1950:107f.): "kat"; Whorf (1942:484, fig. 1): /si/; "sin."

1951–1980 Cordan (1963:113): "kat"; Kelley (1976:152, 333): crossbands; 'conjunction'?; "kaat" 'crossed in the middle'; "kat" 'wish, desire'; Knorozov (1955:70): 075 (vigas cruzadas del techo?) /ch(a)/; Knorozov (1967:93): /ch(a)/ (crossed bindings, see fastening of beams in houses); Thompson (1962:165–68): [154 examples] (crossed bands); Thompson (1972:48f.): "kat" 'transversal'; in codices signifies 'union', 'conjunction'.

1981–1990 V. Bricker (1986:212): "tan" 'middle' (Yucatecan); "kat" 'cross' (Cholan, Yucatecan); Closs (1986:239f.): "kat," "ta"; Fox and Justeson (1986:12): "tan" in 'wife' compound; Grube (1990a:107): = T0619; Justeson (1984:342): J. Fox, J. Justeson, B. Riese: "k'at" (including "*k'a:t" 'to cross') and "tan" (including "*ta:n" 'middle, breast'); F. Lounsbury, D. Stuart: locative preposition, "ta/ti" 'at, on' or "tan" 'in the midst or presence of'; P. Mathews: "tan" locative preposition 'in the middle of'; L. Schele: "tan"; locative preposition "tan"; Lounsbury (1989:80–82): "at, ta" (in substitution for T0761) in name phrase of ruler at Copán; "tan" 'in front (of)', 'in the middle (of)', "in the presence (of)' when used as a locative preposition in the codices.

1991–2008 Closs (1992:139): "ta" 'in, on, at'; Davoust (1995:586): "kat" 'croisé, traversé'; "tan" 'milieu'; /ta/; Knorozov (1999, vol. 1:145): /cha/ (cruce de palos o de vigas); Schele and Grube (1997:128–31): /ta/; Stuart (1997:2): /ta/; von Nagy (1997:46f.): usually read "tan" 'center' but substitutes for locative pronouns on Madrid 40a, 41a; may have the value "ta" or "ti" 'in' or 'at' in this context.

XQB

T —
Z —
K —

ta?

k'at / k'ät?; tan?

n? middle, center?

2. Picture: ?

1991–2008 Vail (2002b): substitutes for T0552 "k'at," "tan," /ta/; also occurs in skybands.

XQB

T 0552v
Z 1350a
K 0359

ta

tan?

n? middle, center?

May be separate grapheme from XQB, subsort 1.

3. Picture: crossed bands

1951–1980 Thompson (1972:92): = T0552[0095].

1991–2008 Vail (2002b): /ta/?

XQB

T 0304
Z 1350
K 0311

ta?

May be separate grapheme from XQB, subsort 1.

4. Picture: crossed bands

1951–1980 Knorozov (1967:100): /ch(a)/.

1981–1990 Justeson (1984:336): J. Justeson: possibly "hax" 'to twist'.

1991–2008 Davoust (1995:576): "hol" 'percer'; Knorozov (1999, vol. 1:145): /cha/ (cruce de palos o vigas dentro de un contorno abierto; cueva?); Vail (2002b): /ta/?

XQC

T 0624a
Z 1372
K 0354

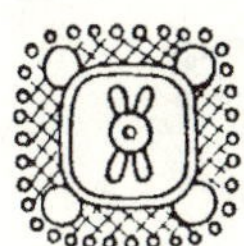

pàakal / *päkal*

n shield

Yu *pàakal* pakal 'rodela; escudo' (Barrera Vásquez et al. 1980:620); pàakal 'leaning over, folded' (V. Bricker et al. 1998:205); päk 'fold' (Hofling with Tesucún 1997:500)

Ch' *päkal* *päk 'bend, fold over' (Kaufman and Norman 1984:128); pak 'a fold, a roll of anything, a rolling up' (Wisdom 1950:556)

1. Picture: shield

1916–1950 Gates (1931:166): shield; Genet (1934): 'guerre'.

1951–1980 Kelley (1962b:24): shield (J. Genet, J. E. S. Thompson, Y. Knorozov, D. Kelley); 'war' (J. Genet, J. E. S. Thompson); "maax" cf. "maaxcinahba" 'escudarse' (Y. Knorozov); Kelley (1968b:258): "pacal" 'shield'; Kelley (1976:135f., 181, 208, 333): substitution spelling of /pa-ca-l(a)/ for "pacal" 'shield'; Knorozov (1955:72): 093 (escudo) "maax"; Knorozov (1967:102): "tlak" (a shield); Mathews and Schele (1974:63): credit Kelley with identification of substitution spelling of /pa-ca-la/ for "pacal" 'shield'; Thompson (1962:242): [58 examples] 'shield'.

1981–1990 V. Bricker (1986:212): "pacal" 'shield' (Yucatecan); Justeson (1984:348): = T0583.

1991–2008 Davoust (1995:591): "pacal"; Knorozov (1999, vol. 1:146): "maax" (escudo); Ringle and Smith-Stark (1996:335–38): 0624a, b (retired) = 0583b (0624a, b indistinguishable in practice).

XQD

T 0623
Z —
K 0368

1. Picture: crossed bones against black background

1566–1915 Brasseur de Bourbourg (1869–1870, vol. 1:218): symbole de la terre antique recouverte par la mer des Caraïbes, au moment de son immersion; Brinton (1895:65): crossed bones symbol of the god of death.

1951–1980 Knorozov (1967:102): morphemic; Thompson (1962:241): [8 examples] (cross-bones); Zimmermann (1956:Tafel 8): 'gaben'.

1991–2008 Davoust (1995:591): "bac" 'os'; Knorozov (1999, vol. 1:148): "ch'uuc"? (huesos cruzados dentro de un contorno punteado).

XS1

T 0521
Z 1331
K 0152

wíinik / winik; winal

n; nm cl — person; winal

Yu *wíinik; winal* — winik 'hombre'; winal 'mes antiguo de 20 días' (Barrera Vásquez et al. 1980:923); wíinik 'man' (V. Bricker et al. 1998:305)

Ch' *winik; ø* — winic 'hombre' (Aulie and Aulie 1998:141)

day 11: Chuwen/B'atz'; period: 20 days, winal

1. Picture: crescents on side, quatrifoil on bottom

1566–1915 Brasseur de Bourbourg (1869–1870, vol. 1:207): day Chuen; "chuen" 'nom d'une divinité changée en singe'; "chu-en" 'lac ouvert, calebasse detruite peu à peu, ou descendue au fond'; Förstemann [1897] (1904b:549): period of 20 days; Goodman (1897:22): "chuen" '20 days'; Landa [1566] (Tozzer 1941:134): day Chuen; Rosny (1883:6): day Chuen; Seler [1911] (1993:170): "uinal" '20-day period'; Thomas (1893:249): day Chuen, /ch'/.

1916–1950 Gates (1931:35): "chuen" 'monkey'.

1951–1980 Knorozov (1955:65): 007 (boca abierta incisivos superlores, colmillos, lengua y garganta); /ke/; Knorozov (1967:91): /k'(i)/ (open mouth?); Thompson (1962:123–25): [178 examples] "uinal"; in codices, indistinguishable from Chuen.

1981–1990 V. Bricker (1986:211): "winac" '20-day month'; "winal" '20-day month' (Yucatecan); Grube (1990a:106): = T1319; Justeson (1984:340): J. Fox, J. Justeson, B. Riese: '20-day period' ("winal," "*winik-Vl") and possibly 'man' ("winik" < "winaq"); F. Lounsbury, L. Schele: "winak," "winik," "winal"; '20-day month' and 'man'; P. Mathews: "winak"?, "winik"?, "winal"?; '20-day period' and 'man'.

1991–2008 Davoust (1995:583): "chuen" '11e jour'; "winic" 'homme'; '20'; Knorozov (1999, vol. 1:137): /ki/ (fauces abiertas de una fiera); Love (1994:58f.): occurs in clusters to specify number of offerings; each "uinic" glyph is '20'.

XS3

T 0523
Z —
K —

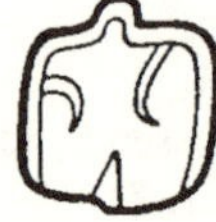

tze

Occurs in contexts where either XS1 or XS3 expected. We classify a number of examples not considered T0523 by Thompson (1962:126) as this variant.

1. Picture: ?

1566–1915 Brasseur de Bourbourg (1869–1870, vol. 1:201): "c, co" 'dent, pointe, lieu'; quelquefois pour "com" 'vase en composition'; Brinton (1895:112f.): piles of "chuen" are shown as offerings, possibly signify 'first fruits'; Rosny (1883:14): in month glyph Tzec.

1916–1950 Gates (1931:62): [Z1331a] month Tzec.

1951–1980 Thompson (1962:126): [16 examples] Uinal semblant, only on Venus pages of Dresden Codex.

1981–1990 Justeson (1984:340): J. Fox, J. Justeson, B. Riese: day Chuen and 20-day period, a conflation of T0520 and T0521 found in the codices; F. Lounsbury: codex form equivalent to both T0520 and T0521; P. Mathews, L. Schele, D. Stuart: = T0520, codex form.

1991–2008 Davoust (1995:583): /tze/; Knorozov (1999, vol. 1:137): /ki/ (fauces abiertas de una fiera); Schele and Grube (1997:146f.): /tze/.

XS3

T –
Z 1331a
K 0316

tze

2. Picture: ?

1566–1915 Brasseur de Bourbourg (1869–1870, vol. 1:201): "c, co" 'dent, pointe, lieu'; quelquefois pour "com" 'vase en composition'; Landa [1566] (Tozzer 1941:156; 170): in month glyph Tzec; <c>; Rosny (1883:14): in month glyph Tzec.

1916–1950 Gates (1931:62): month Tzec.

1951–1980 Kelley (1962a:284f.): /se/; Knorozov (1967:91f.): /k'(i)/ (open mouth?).

1981–1990 V. Bricker (1985c): /tze/.

1991–2008 Davoust (1995:583): (=T0521d) /ze/.

XS4

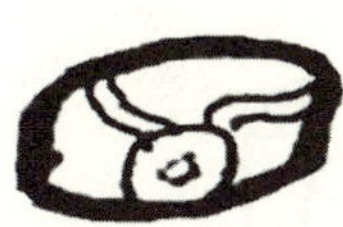

T 0804
Z –
K –

1. Picture: ?

1951–1980 Thompson (1962:382): [2 examples].

1991–2008 Davoust (1995:606): "te' " 'arbre'; /te/.

XV1

T 0563a
Z 1357
K 0162

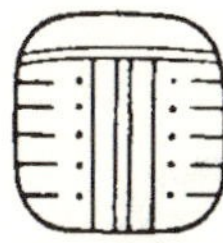

tz'i

When paired with 2S6 (T0122), represents "k'àak'/k'ahk" 'fire'.

1. Picture: ?

1566–1915 Brasseur de Bourbourg (1869–1870, vol. 1:204): "p', p'a" 'sortir avec effort, rompre en sortant, ouvrir par force'.

1916–1950 Gates (1931:146): 'wood, firewood'; Spinden (1924:202f.): part of glyph "of the sacred fires"; Whorf (1942:484, fig. 1): "kak"; /ka/.

1951–1980 Kelley (1976:148, 150, 333): in fire glyger; Knorozov (1955:73). 108 (campo de regadío?) "poc (pac)"; Knorozov (1967:93): "pok" (ditch); Thompson (1962:183–86): [90 examples] 'fire'; with T0087 becomes "kakche," Yucatec for a type of hardwood tree; Thompson (1972:52): "kak" 'fire'.

1981–1990 V. Bricker (1986:212): "kahc" 'fire' (Cholan); "kak" 'fire' (Yucatecan); Dütting (1985:110): "ch'en"; Grube (1990a:108): = T0248; Justeson (1984:343): cf. T0630, T1004a: J. Fox: 'fire' ("k'ak' "); a bundle of firewood ("si' "), and when halved (as T0283) /k'a/ and /si/; J. Justeson, F. Lounsbury, P. Mathews, B. Riese: 'fire' usually; F. Lounsbury: with T0122, semantic determinative depicting smoke or flame; = T0630; J. Justeson, P. Mathews, L. Schele, D. Stuart: in full or halved, F. Lounsbury: "*kah" 'town'; including [P. Mathews] as part of title (probably < "*kah-al") for subordinates, cf. T1004a; B. Riese: possibly /k'ak'/ 'fire'; disagrees with J. Justeson, P. Mathews, L. Schele, D. Stuart above; L. Schele, D. Stuart: = T0630; /ka/, /kah/; not 'fire' without phonetic complement or semantic determinative; Lipp (1985): compares with contemporary Mixe ritual wood bundles; Stuart (1987:1–11): /ts'i/.

1991–2008 Davoust (1995:587): "tz'ih" 'fendre'; /tzi/; Knorozov (1999, vol. 1:136): "poc" (zanja); Ringle and Smith-Stark (1996:348): 0563a = 0563.

XV2

T 0564
Z 1358
K 0163

su?

1. Picture: coiled rope?

1951–1980 Knorozov (1955:73): 107 (campo con zanjas) "thul"; Knorozov (1967:93): "t'ul" (ditch); Thompson (1962:186): [15 examples] (fire semblant) Largely confined to Chichén Itzá and the codices; supporting evidence that the codices originated in Yucatan.

1981–1990 Justeson (1984:344): J. Justeson: (T0564 = T0563c) main sign form of T0283, which appears in one or two T0216:563c spellings of the month name Zotz'; /tz'/ + unknown vowel; J. Fox notes use of T0563a in M. 23b spelling of T0563a:0585a "tz'i:b' " 'to write'; I suspect this is by a formal conflation with T0563c, suggesting that T0563c (and probably T0283) are /tz'/; possibly related to T0564.

1991–2008 Davoust (1995:587): /zu/; Davoust (1997:193): "zuy" 'tourbillon'; Knorozov (1999, vol. 1:136): "t'ul" (zanja curva); Schele and Grube (1997:154): /su/.

XV3

T 0662
Z 1318
K –

Paired with XQ3 "k'iin/k'in" 'sun, day' in picture and text on Madrid 85b.

1. Picture: ?

1566–1915 Brasseur de Bourbourg (1869–1870, vol. 1:204): "p', p'a" 'sortir avec effort, rompre en sortant, ouvrir par force'.

1951–1980 Thompson (1962:259): [10 examples].

1991–2008 Davoust (1995:594): "tz'ac" 'changement'; Knorozov (1999, vol. 1:136): "t'ul" (zanja curva); Ringle and Smith-Stark (1996:335–38): 0662 = 0662a.

XV5

T 0563b
Z 1348
K 0197

Occurs with 2S6 "k'áak'/k'ahk" 'fire' and as a doubled grapheme.

1. Picture: crossed bands

1951–1980 Kelley (1968c:153): reference to a mythological place when doubled; read by Barthel (1953:92f.) as 'Place of the two Reed Bundles'; Knorozov (1967:95): /ch'(a)/ (palm of hand with K168); Thompson (1962:183–86): [groups T0563a and T0563b together] [90 examples] 'fire'; also "kak" 'eruptive skin disease'; Thompson (1972:94): "kak" 'fire'.

1981–1990 Dütting (1985:110): "tzay" 'juntar, unir; encender fuego'; Grube (1990a:108): = T0830; Houston (1988:130): /to/; Justeson (1984:343): J. Justeson, P. Mathews, L. Schele: different sign from T0563a; Stuart (1987:47): /to/.

1991–2008 Davoust (1995:587): /za/; Knorozov (1999, vol. 1:136): /ch'a/; Ringle and Smith-Stark (1996:335–38): 0563b = 0906; Schele and Grube (1997:193): /to/.

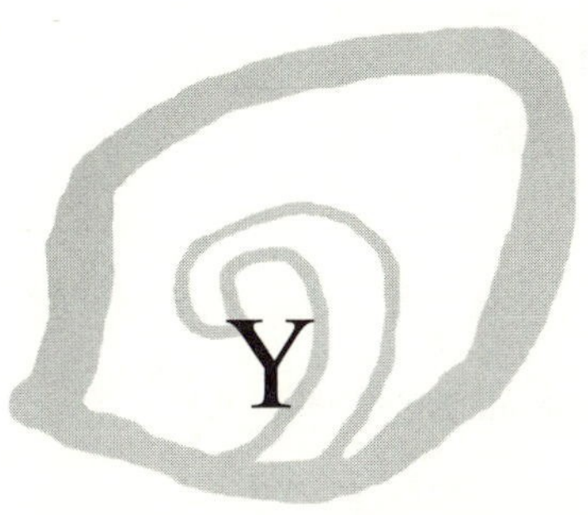

Y Square; Assymetrical

YG2

T 0516c
Z 1308b
K 0132

u
uh

n	moon
Yu *uh*	u 'collar de cuentas o sartal' (Barrera Vásquez et al. 1980:896); 'uh 'bead; moon' (V. Bricker et al. 1998:20)
Ch' *uh*	*uh 'moon' (Kaufman and Norman 1984:135)

1. Picture: ?

1916–1950 Gates (1931:127f.): appears only in the eclipse ephemeris of the Dresden, and only with the tying-up sign; Thompson (1950:162): "xoc" 'count'.

1951–1980 Knorozov (1955:69): 058 (brote?), /pp–?/; Knorozov (1967:89): /p'(i)/; Thompson (1962:118f.): [33 examples] jade variant.

1981–1990 Justeson (1984:339): J. Fox, J. Justeson: a codex variant of T0515; P. Mathews, L. Schele, D. Stuart: different from T0516a, b.

1991–2008 Davoust (1995:582): "uh" 'grain de jade'; /u/; Grube (1994b:181): T0516 /u/ invented after 9.11.0.0.0; Knorozov (1999, vol. 1:123): /p'i/; Ringle and Smith-Stark (1996:335–38): 0516c = 0513v; Schele and Grube (1997:16): /u/; Schele and Grube (1997:174): "u" 'moon' [in context of Dresden eclipse table].

YG2

T 0513
Z 1308b
K 0132

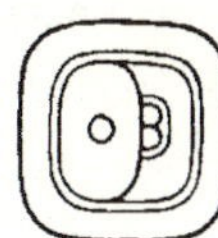

u

Day Muluk in Classic inscriptions. Does not have this value in codices.

2. Picture: ?

1916–1950 Thompson (1950:162): "xoc" 'count'.

1951–1980 Dütting (1974:50): "tzic" 'count; honor, obey'; Dütting (1979:186): "tzik" 'honorable one'; Knorozov (1967:89): /p'(i)/; Thompson (1962:112–14): [92 examples] Muluc.

1981–1990 V. Bricker (1986:211): "om" 'accumulate; want, need, lack' (Cholan); Justeson (1984:339): L. Campbell: "mul," "muluk"; J. Fox, J. Justeson, F. Lounsbury, P. Mathews: = T0511; L. Schele, D. Stuart: Muluc; sometimes = T0001; D. Stuart: possibly /u/; Stuart (1990): in posterior date indicator, /u/.

1991–2008 Davoust (1995:582): "muluc" '9e jour'; "uh" 'grain de jade'; /u/; Grube (1994b:181): T0513 /u/ invented after 9.11.0.0.0; Knorozov (1999, vol. 1:134): /p'i/.

YG4

T 0158
Z 1330
K –

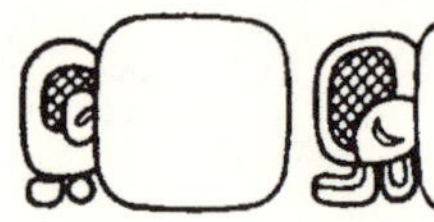

wí'il / we'el

n		food, nourishment
Yu	*wil; wí'il*	wil 'alimento' (Barrera Vásquez et al. 1980:922)
Ch'	*we'el*	*we'el 'meat' (Kaufman and Norman 1984:135); we'el 'carne, alimento' (Aulie and Aulie 1998:140)

Upper element graphically similar to AP5, subsort 2.

1. Picture: ?

1566–1915 Rosny (1883:24): "okol"? 'tristesse, plaintes, lamentations'; Thomas (1882:149): "ox okoltba" 'three prayers' [with prefix TIII].

1916–1950 Beyer (1929:46): with prefix of III, evidently a fire glyph.

1951–1980 Kelley (1962b:34): 'lacking, to go' (J. E. S. Thompson and generally); Kelley (1976:34): (Classic variant) 'lacking, to go'; Thompson (1972:35, 82): "ochbil"? 'good tidings'.

1981–1990 V. Bricker (1986:123): "oxow" 'sultry' [with TIII prefix]; Grube (1990a:94): = T0095:0130; Justeson (1984:328): J. Justeson, P. Mathews, L. Schele: a sequence of two signs; the first is a logograph not transcribed by Thompson, the second is T0130 as grammatical suffix; probably 'until' or 'lacking'.

1991–2008 Davoust (1995:565): "chum" 'siéger'; Davoust (1997:101): "wi'il" 'abondance'; Grofe (2007:130f.): "och-aw" 'subtracted' when used in expressions with period glyphs; with TIII prefix in codices may be "ox-hoch-aw" or "ox-hoch-ol" 'much harvested'; Lacadena (1994): substitution for /wi/, suggests "wi'il" 'último' or 'postrero'; Lacadena (1997b): "wi'il," functions as adverb 'again'; in codices was originally considered two graphemes (T0567 and T0130); Love (1991:297f.): with TIII prefix, "ox och wah" 'abundance of provisions'; Ringle and Smith-Stark (1996:335–38): 0158:0142/0130 (only larger sign is 0158); Schele and Grube (1997:85): "wi'il" 'food, nourishment'; Vail (1996:336f.): with TIII prefix, relates to concept of fertility; associated with deities who form part of the natural/ agricultural cycle.

YG8

T –
Z –
K –

1. Picture: ?

1916–1950 Gates (1931:164): G409 [in part].

1991–2008 Davoust (1997:212): = 0694 /o/.

YG9

T –
Z –
K 0184

1. Picture: ?

1916–1950 Gates (1931:162): G363 [in part].

1951–1980 Knorozov (1967:94): (= K183).

1991–2008 Davoust (1997:208): = T0251 /ba/.

YGC

T 0810
Z —
K —

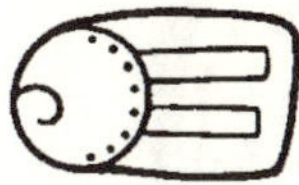

Unique occurrence on Madrid 37.
1. Picture: ?

1916–1950 Gates (1931:163): G389 [in part].

1951–1980 Thompson (1962:383): [1 example].

YGD

T 0812
Z 0730a
K 0201

1. Picture: sunrise over mountain?

1566–1915 Brasseur de Bourbourg (1869–1870, vol. 1:211): "akbal ezanab ben" 'pour tourner en eau, le jet de feu sera (ou de la voie ouverte, etc.)'.

1951–1980 Kelley (1976:63, 67, 158, 334): (= T1042 but in different position); means 'weave'; Knorozov (1967:95): "hav"; Thompson (1962:384): [11 examples].

1991–2008 Ciaramella (1999:38f.): "t'is" 'to put in rows', following Knorozov (1982:367); Davoust (1995:607): "man" 'vision'; "way" 'se transformer'; Jones and Jones (1997:197f.): "mamak" 'to weave'; form of glyph suggests it is a conflation of "man" and "-ak' " (from Ak'bal); Knorozov (1999, vol. 1:142): "t'iz" (cabeza de rana).

YM1

T 0679
Z 1333a
K 0139

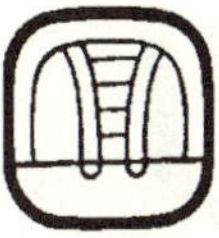

i

1. Picture: ?

1566–1915 Brasseur de Bourbourg (1869–1870, vol. 1:202): "i" 'embryon, germe, rejeton, pointe qui pousse'; Landa [1566] (Tozzer 1941:170): <i>; Thomas (1893:268): Landa's /i/.

1916–1950 Beyer (1943): 'end; ending'.

1951–1980 Kelley (1962a:290, 296f.): /'i/; Kelley (1962b:41): /i/; Kelley (1976:194, 197–200, 333): 'forward'; /i/; some evidence of interchangeability with T0074, suggesting occasional use as a negative; Knorozov (1955:73): 111 (estanque) /i/, "ich"?; Knorozov (1967:90): /i/; 'until'; Lounsbury (1974b:17): Landa's /i/ and possibly Ch'ol preposed third-person nominative and possessive pronoun "i"; Thompson (1962:280f.): [78 examples] 'forward', with forward time count or with the later of two dates; Landa's /i/; Thompson (1972:57): 'forward'.

1981–1990 V. Bricker (1985a:68): allograph for T0001 and T0204; V. Bricker (1986:213): (T0679) /i/, "y-" 'he, she it' (Cholan, Yucatecan); Dütting (1985): /i/, "ch'en"; Grube (1990a:113): = T0605; Justeson (1984:350f.): Landa's <i>; J. Fox, J. Justeson: posterior event indicator, J. Justeson, W. Norman: probably progressive aspect marker "*iwal" '(and) then'; F. Lounsbury, P. Mathews, B. Riese, L. Schele, D. Stuart: /i/; posterior date and [F. Lounsbury] event indicator. T0679b cf. Landa's <i>: J. Fox, /i/, "e:b' "? 'stairway'; probably = T0679a; J. Justeson: /i/; probably = T0679a, phonetic value < historical or folk-analyzed root "*iw" of "*iwal"; F. Lounsbury, P. Mathews, L. Schele: = T0679a. T0679c: P. Mathews: T0679c does not = T0679a, b; possibly = T0679d. T0679d: P. Mathews: does not = T0679a, b; possibly = T0679c; Schele (1987a): "iwal" 'and then'; Stuart (1990): prefix to two constants on posterior date indicator.

1991–2008 Davoust (1995:595): "iwal" 'puis, ensuite'; /i/; Josserand (1991:14): "i"; a conjunction; Justeson (personal communication to Macri, 1999): "yuwal"; Knorozov (1999, vol. 1:130): /i/; Stuart, Houston, and Robertson (1999:33): substitution spelling "i-yu-wa-la" for "iyuwal-" 'progressive aspect-marking prefix', on Copán Stela J and Jonuta panel.

YM1

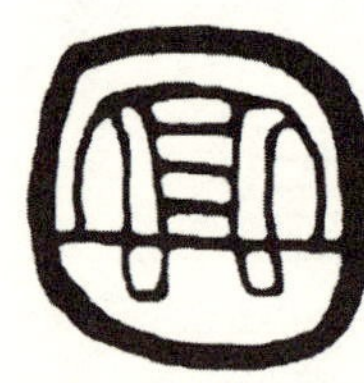

T 0679
Z 1333a
K 0139

i

1. Picture: ?

1566–1915 Brasseur de Bourbourg (1869–1870, vol. 1:202): "i" 'embryon, germe, rejeton, pointe qui pousse'; Landa [1566] (Tozzer 1941:170): <i>; Thomas (1893:268): Landa's /i/.

1916–1950 Beyer (1943): 'end; ending'.

1951–1980 Kelley (1962a:290, 296f.): /'i/; Kelley (1962b:41): /i/; Kelley (1976:194, 197–200, 333): 'forward'; /i/; some evidence of interchangeability with T0074, suggesting occasional use as a negative; Knorozov (1955:73): 111 (estanque) /i/, "ich"?; Knorozov (1967:90): /i/; 'until'; Lounsbury (1974b:17): Landa's /i/ and possibly Ch'ol preposed third-person nominative and possessive pronoun "i"; Thompson (1962:280f.): [78 examples] 'forward', with forward time count or with the later of two dates; Landa's /i/; Thompson (1972:57): 'forward'.

1981–1990 V. Bricker (1985a:68): allograph for T0001 and T0204; V. Bricker (1986:213): (T0679) /i/, "y-" 'he, she it' (Cholan, Yucatecan); Dütting (1985): /i/, "ch'en"; Grube (1990a:113): = T0605; Justeson (1984:350f.): Landa's <i>; J. Fox, J. Justeson: posterior event indicator, J. Justeson, W. Norman: probably progressive aspect marker "*iwal" '(and) then'; F. Lounsbury, P. Mathews, B. Riese, L. Schele, D. Stuart: /i/; posterior date and [F. Lounsbury] event indicator. T0679b cf. Landa's <i>: J. Fox, /i/, "e:b'"? 'stairway'; probably = T0679a; J. Justeson: /i/; probably = T0679a, phonetic value < historical or folk-analyzed root "*iw" of "*iwal"; F. Lounsbury, P. Mathews, L. Schele: = T0679a. T0679c: P. Mathews: T0679c does not = T0679a, b; possibly = T0679d. T0679d: P. Mathews: does not = T0679a, b; possibly = T0679c; Schele (1987a): "iwal" 'and then'; Stuart (1990): prefix to two constants on posterior date indicator.

1991–2008 Davoust (1995:595): "iwal" 'puis, ensuite'; /i/; Josserand (1991:14): "i"; a conjunction; Justeson (personal communication to Macri, 1999): "yuwal"; Knorozov (1999, vol. 1:130): /i/; Stuart, Houston, and Robertson (1999:33): substitution spelling "i-yu-wa-la" for "iyuwal-" 'progressive aspect-marking prefix', on Copán Stela J and Jonuta panel.

YM2

T 0565c
Z 1351
K 0199

ta

tí' / ti, ta, tä

prep — in, at, etc.; preposition

Yu *tí'* — ti' 'preposición a, con, por instrumento, adentro' (Barrera Vásquez et al. 1980:788); tí' 'to, at, in, from, for' (V. Bricker et al. 1998:274)

Ch' *ti; ta; tä* — *tä 'preposition' (Kaufman and Norman 1984:139); ta 'for, belongs to' (Knowles 1984:461); tä 'to, from, by' (Knowles 1984:463); ti 'en, a, por, de' (Warkentin and Scott 1980:98); ti 'en' (Morán 1935:26); ti' 'beside, by the side; at the edge' (Knowles 1984:465)

1. Picture: ?

1951–1980 Kelley (1976:152, 221, 240, 333): indicates relationship between individuals; Knorozov (1967:95): "ch'um"; Thompson (1962:187–90): [137 examples] (serpent segment).

1981–1990 V. Bricker (1986:212): (T0565a) /ta/, "ta" 'in, at, to' (Cholan); (T0565c) /tan/; Grube (1990a:108): = T1315; Justeson (1984:344): J. Fox, J. Justeson: = T0565a[0552], "tan"; F. Lounsbury, D. Stuart: /ta/ or "tan"; P. Mathews: locative preposition; L. Schele: locative prep; maybe "tan."

1991–2008 Davoust (1995:587): "tan" 'milieu'; /ta/; Knorozov (1999, vol. 1:142): "ch'um, ch'am" (caverna con agua subterránea y elementos cruzados); Macri (1991): /ta/, preposition "ta".

YM2

T 0565b
Z 1352
K 0198

ta

tí'? / ti?, ta, tä

prep in, at, etc.; preposition

2. Picture: ?

1951–1980 Kelley (1976:152, 221, 240, 333): indicates relationship between individuals; Knorozov (1955:73): 112 (cueva?, barranco?) "ch'am"; Knorozov (1967:95): "ch'um"; Thompson (1962:187–90): [137 examples] (serpent segment).

1981–1990 V. Bricker (1986:212): (T0565a) /ta/, "ta" 'in, at, to' (Cholan); (T0565c) /tan/; Grube (1990a:108): = T1315; Justeson (1984:344): consensus: = T0565a (= T0266); cf. T0642; /ta/ in some contexts, a locative preposition.

1991–2008 Davoust (1995:587): "tan" 'milieu'; /ta/; Knorozov (1999, vol. 1:141): "ch'um, ch'am" (caverna con estalactitas y agua subterránea); Macri (1991): /ta/, preposition "ta"; Stuart (1997:2): /ta/.

YS1

T 0526
Z 1337
K 0137

kàab' / kab'; kàab' / chab', chäb'

n earth, region; bee, honey, beehive

Yu *kàab'; kàab'* kab 'el mundo, pueblo o región; bajo o abajo' (Barrera Vásquez et al. 1980:277); kàab' 'land, world' (V. Bricker et al. 1998:118); kàab' 'honey; beehive; bee' (Barrera Vásquez et al. 1980:277)

Ch' *kab'; chab', chäb'* *kab' 'earth, land; town' (Kaufman and Norman 1984:122); *chab' 'honey', *chäb' 'beeswax, candle' (Kaufman and Norman 1984:117)

day 17: Kab'an/Tzanab'

1. Picture: ?

1566–1915 Bollaert (1865–1866:52): "caban" 'when'?; Brasseur de Bourbourg (1869–1870, vol. 1:207): day Caban; "cab-an" 'lave refroidissant en haut, lave refroidie, liquide épais refroidi'; "ca-ban" 'ce qui est amoncelé, bouleversé'; Brinton (1895:60, 99): used in reference to bee god; "caban" 'downward'; 'earth'; Förstemann [1897] (1904a:438): day Caban; also refers to the ground and the direction downward; Goodman (1897:16): day Caban; Landa [1566] (Tozzer 1941:134): day Caban; Rosny (1883:9): day Caban; "cab" 'la terre'; Thomas (1888:349, 369): "cab" 'earth; soil; honey'; lack of similarity to the things denoted suggests it is probably phonetic; Thomas (1893:246): day Caban; "cab" 'earth, soil; honey, hive'.

1916–1950 Gates (1931:43): "caban" 'force; earth'.

1951–1980 Kelley (1976:63, 67, 109, 167, 333): "cab/caban" 'earth, bee'; Knorozov (1955:74): 122 (agua que fluye) "chab (kab)"; Knorozov (1967:90): "kab"; Old Yucatec "kab an" 'earthquake', name of a day; Lounsbury (1980:112f.): day Caban, also "cab" 'earth, pueblo' and 'honey or bee'; in Classic period can combine with T0713 'hand' glyph in variant of 'birth' glyph, as "lah kab" 'to touch to earth'; Thompson (1962:127–33): [355 examples] Caban; Thompson (1972:83): 'earth', 'honey'.

1981–1990 V. Bricker (1986:211): "caban" 'earthquake'; "cab" 'earth; bee, honey, hive' (Yucatecan); Grube (1990a:106): = T1314; Justeson (1984:340): J. Fox, J. Justeson: day Caban, "*kab' " 'earth'; "*ka:b' " 'honey, bee'; J. Justeson, F. Lounsbury, P. Mathews: "kah" 'pueblo'; F. Lounsbury, P. Mathews, B. Riese: day Caban; "kab' " 'bee, honey', 'earth, region'; B. Riese: not "kah"; /ka/ and "kab' " (evidence in Copán inscriptions); L. Schele: "kab'," day Caban; 'bees, honey', 'earth, world', 'government'; Kelley (1982:11): substitution spelling /ca-ba/ for "cab"; Schele (1981:26): "cäb" in phonetic form on Palenque Tablet of the Cross, E2; Schele (1987b): "cab," name of structure in house dedication phrase.

1991–2008 Davoust (1995:584): "caban" '17e jour', "cab" 'terre, miel', /ca/; Knorozov (1999, vol. 1:121, 234): "chab, cab" 'miel; abeja' (gotas de miel chorreando?); Love (1995:360, n. 2): "cah," T0190.0528 "hats' cah" 'lightning strike'; MacLeod (1991i): "kab" 'house', 'earth'; Martin and Grube (2000:231): credit Houston with "chab' " 'supervise'; Schele and Grube (1994:18): "kah" 'make; do; begin'; /ka/.

YS6

T 0573
Z 1319
K 0158

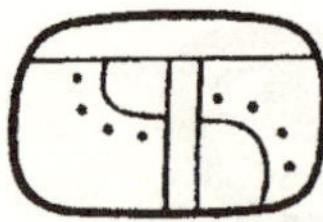

tz'áak / *tz'ak*

n; intr v? to change, stack; succession

Yu *tz'áak* -ts'ak 'cuenta de grados y escalones y otras cosas que van unas encima de otras'; ts'akab 'abolorio, casta, linaje o generación' (Barrera Vásquez et al. 1980:873); ts'a(a)k 'aumentar, añadir; contar' (Barrera Vásquez et al. 1980:872); tz'áak '[numeral classifier] 20 square meters; units of work' (V. Bricker et al. 1998:47); tz'aká'an 'exist still' (V. Bricker et al. 1998:47); -tz'aak '[numeral classifier] mecate [25 rods squared]' (Hofling with Tesucún 1997:636); tz'a'ak 'have steps' (Hofling with Tesucún 1997:634)

Ch' *tz'ak* tz'äk [numeral classifier] 'stacked' (Knowles 1984:365); tz'aki e tun 'lay stones end to end, build a stone wall' (Wisdom 1950:737)

1. Picture: twisted object?

1566–1915 Brasseur de Bourbourg (1869–1870, vol. 1:204): "p', p'a" 'sortir avec effort, rompre en sortant, ouvrir par force'; Brinton (1895:90f.): Förstemann considers that it symbolizes an astronomical event connected with the motions of the sun.

1916–1950 Gates (1931:150f.): may be "haab" 'solar year' based on contexts, including the Madrid and Dresden New Year pages; Thompson (1950:160–62): "hel" 'change; successor'.

1951–1980 Cordan (1964:10f.): "kex" 'sucesor'; Kelley (1962b:40): "hel" 'change, successor' (J. E. S. Thompson, Y. Knorozov); "bukxoc" 'sum' (J. E. S. Thompson); Kelley (1976:158, 259, 333): "hel"?; related to T0676?; Knorozov (1955:75): 132 "hel"; Knorozov (1967:92): "h'el" 'change'; Thompson (1962:198–201): [159 examples] "hel"; when T0683 moon sign precedes T0573, T0683 presumably is '20'; Thompson (1972:34): "hel" 'change, succession', 'recompense'.

1981–1990 Grube (1990a:108): = T0274; Justeson (1984:345): J. Fox, J. Justeson, D. Stuart: 'to change, follow', probably "jel, tz'ak"; F. Lounsbury, B. Riese, L. Schele: "hel"?; "k'ex"?; 'change; succession'; P. Mathews: 'succession; change'; "hel" a good candidate, but also others, e.g., "k'ex"; cf. T0676; Riese (1984): possibly "hal/hel," "tz'ak," or "k'iin"; in noncalendrical contexts 'royal succession; change of ruler'.

1991–2008 H. Bricker and V. Bricker (n.d.): "dz'a" 'gift, to give'; Davoust (1995:587): "tz'ac" 'changement'; "hal" 'changer, manifester'; Knorozov (1999, vol. 1:135, 235): "h'el" 'cambio de poder; cambio; sucesor'; Love (1994:19): possibly "helan" or "hela'an" 'a thing changed or exchanged', as suggested by the /ni/, /ne/ suffix on some examples; MacLeod (1991b): originated as "hal" = 'weaving/change' in Pocom; later Yucatec and Chol add "ts(')ak" cued by T0025 "ka" to render 'follow, succeed'.

YS7

T 0676
Z 1315
K 0166

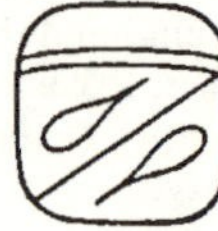

1. Picture: twisted object?

1916–1950 Gates (1931:152): astronomical sign.

1951–1980 Knorozov (1967:93): /bal/; (coiled rope); Thompson (1962:278f.): [14 examples] not day Oc; probably same as T0274.

1981–1990 Justeson (1984:350): J. Fox: probably = T0274; P. Mathews: 'succession'; some = T0573a; L. Schele, D. Stuart: 'succession'; Stuart (1989a): "tal," ordinalizer.

1991–2008 Davoust (1995:595): "tal" 'venir'; Knorozov (1999, vol. 1:144): "baal, bal" (madeja de cuerda); Schele and Grube (1997:171): "tal."

YS8

T 0509
Z 0153
K 0120

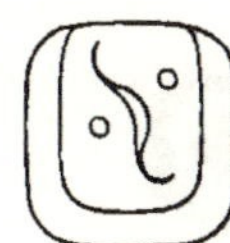

wáay / way?

n spirit companion?; sleep, dream?; transform?

Yu *wáay* way 'ver visiones como entre sueños; tranfigurar por encantamiento; hechizar'; (ah) way 'brujo, nigromántico, encantador' (Barrera Vásquez et al. 1980:916); wáayt 'hex, cast a spell', h wáay 'ghost, spirit [male]' (V. Bricker et al. 1998:301)

Ch' *way* *way 'sleep' (Kaufman and Norman 1984:135)

day 06: Kimi/Tox

1. Picture: ?

1566–1915 Brinton (1895:65): symbol of the god of death; Rosny (1883:4): day Cimi; Schellhas [1892] (1904:10f.): day Cimi; frequent symbol of God A, the death god.

1916–1950 Gates (1931:55): "cimi" variant.

1951–1980 Kelley (1976:150, 332): "cimi" 'death'; Knorozov (1967:89): phonetic; Old Yucatec day Cimi; Thompson (1962:107): [5 examples] Cimi.

1981–1990 Houston and Stuart (1989): "way" 'co-essence', 'spirit companion'; Justeson (1984:339): L. Campbell, J. Fox, J. Justeson, P. Mathews, B. Riese: day Cimi and 'death'; F. Lounsbury, L. Schele, D. Stuart: Cimi.

1991–2008 Davoust (1995:582): "cimi" '6e jour'; Knorozov (1999, vol. 1:116, 232): "bang" 'multitud'.

YSA

T 0019
Z 0091?, 1310
K 0135

mu

1. Picture: curl

1566–1915 Brasseur de Bourbourg (1869–1870, vol. 1:204): "u"; Schellhas [1892] (1904:41): [T0010.0019.0059] hieroglyph of moan bird; Thomas (1893:265): /mu'/, /mo'/.

1916–1950 Whorf (1942:484, fig. 1): "n"; "-an"; /ne/.

1951–1980 Kelley (1962a:290f.): /m(u)/; Kelley (1962b:41): /mu/; Kelley (1976:113, 181, 246, 331): /mu/, "koch"; Knorozov (1955:69): 052 (cola?) /m(u)/; Knorozov (1967:89): /m(u)/ (shell?); Thompson (1958:301): "koch" 'divinely inflicted sickness or punishment'; Thompson (1962:41f.): "koch" 'divinely sent punishment or disease' (Thompson 1958); Thompson (1972:33): "koch" 'illness or divine punishment'.

1981–1990 V. Bricker (1986:208): /mu/; Justeson (1984:317): J. Fox, J. Justeson, F. Lounsbury, P. Mathews, B. Riese, L. Schele, D. Stuart: some /mu/; J. Fox, J. Justeson: some "-Vb" (possibly by virtue of being /mu/; see T0021); Stuart (1987:46): /mu/.

1991–2008 Davoust (1995:554): /mu/; Knorozov (1999, vol. 1:119f.): /mu/ (voluta de caracol?); Ringle and Smith-Stark (1996:335–38): 0019 = 0019a (variant b has an attached frog head).

YSA

T 0648
Z 0705
K 0151

mu

mùuk / muk?

n; trans v — omen, evil omen; bury?
Yu *mùuk; muk* — muuk 'noticia, fama' (Barrera Vásquez et al. 1980:534); muk 'bury' (V. Bricker et al. 1998:188)
Ch' *ø; muk* — *muk 'hide, bury' (Kaufman and Norman 1984:126)

2. Picture: head of frog or bird?

1566–1915 Brasseur de Bourbourg (1869–1870, vol. 1:203): "l, lé" 'lacet, sorte de lac ou de fronde armée d'une pierre'; Schellhas [1892] (1904:10, 13): [T0010.0019.0059] ideogram of the owl, with T0001 representing its ears and T0025 its teeth.

1916–1950 Beyer (1929): a dog's head with an "ek" 'black' infix; has a general significance of 'death'; Gates (1931:127): determinative of the 'evil' force; Thompson (1950:268): "kaz, kazal" or "lob" 'bad'.

1951–1980 Knorozov (1955:75): 139 /m(u)/; Knorozov (1967:91): "k'as" 'evil' (howler monkey?); Thompson (1962:254f.): [123 examples] "kaz" 'misery', 'evil-tidings'; common augural glyph in the codices; Thompson (1972:34): [T0648.0025] "kaz" 'evil'.

1981–1990 V. Bricker (1986:117f., 213): "pac" 'retaliation, punishment'; Justeson (1984:349): J. Fox, J. Justeson, P. Mathews: "muk," "mut" 'omen, tidings'; J. Fox, J. Justeson retract /mu/ reading; F. Lounsbury, B. Riese, J. Fox, J. Justeson: /mu/.

1991–2008 Davoust (1995:593): "mut" 'oiseau, présage'; "muc" 'enterrer'; /mu/; Knorozov (1999, vol. 1:139): "kaz" (cabeza del mono saraguate); Schele and Grube (1997:16): /mu/.

YSB

T 0021
Z 1310a
K 0136

b'u

1. Picture: dotted curl

1951–1980 Knorozov (1967:89): "t'an" 'speech' (conventionalized speech sign); Thompson (1962:42f.): some may be T0163.

1981–1990 Grube (1990a:88): = T0022; Grube and Schele (1990): credit Grube and Nahm, /bu/; Justeson (1984:317): L. Campbell: /mu/; J. Fox: /mu/, possibly "mul," effectively "-Vb' " perhaps as a true phonetic generalization based on final /-b'/ ~ /-'m/, see T0130; J. Justeson, F. Lounsbury: "-Vb' " (including as instrumental suffix) and/or "om/um" (including as agentive suffix); perhaps equivalent to T0019; B. Riese: probably /mu/; Schele (1989c:5a): "-ab."

1991–2008 Davoust (1995:554): "ub" 'chose tachetée/caille'; /bu/; Knorozov (1999, vol. 1:120): "t'an" (símbolo del habla); Schele (1992b:155): "hub" 'shell'.

YSC

T 0551
Z 1349
K 0161

Conflation of T0664 and T0281.
há'ab': Pop/K'anjalab'
1. Picture: mat with "kän" sign infix

1566–1915 Rosny (1883:14): in month glyph Pop.

1916–1950 Gates (1931:61): Pop.

1951–1980 Knorozov (1955:72): 100 (trenzado con el signo complementario 106) "ch'ac" 'talar'; Knorozov (1967:92): "ch'ak" 'chopping' (twining); Thompson (1962:165): [3 examples] Pop.

1981–1990 Grube (1990a:107): = T0551[0281]; Justeson (1984:342): L. Campbell, J. Fox, J. Justeson, B. Riese: logographic, fusion of sign "*jal" 'to weave' with T0281 "*k'an"; main sign of month Pop (Ch'ol "k'an= hal-Vb' " 'yellow shuttle'); F. Lounsbury: month sign Pop, "k'anhalab', k'anhala'w, k'anhala'm"; P. Mathews: month sign Pop, "k'anhalab' "; B. Riese: not "k'anhalam," this being probably a misspelling; L. Schele, D. Stuart: month sign Pop, "k'anhalam."

1991–2008 Davoust (1995:586): "pop/kanhal(ab)" '1er mois'; Knorozov (1999, vol. 1:139): "ch'ac" (petate); signo del mes pop. Tiene el grafema 620 "kan" inscrito.

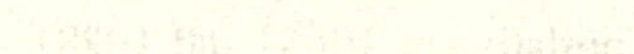

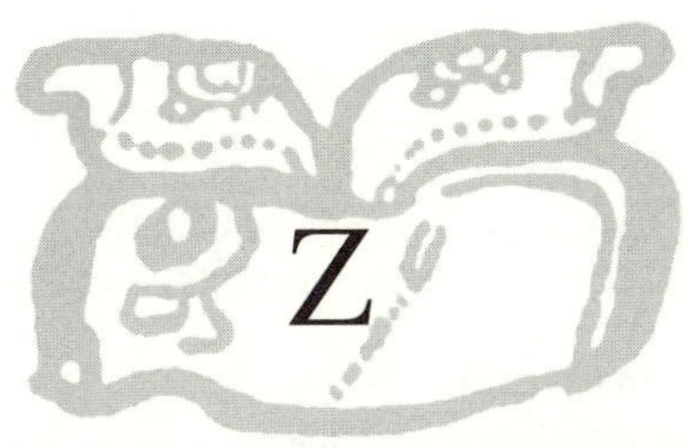

Z Irregular Shape

ZB1

T 0684
Z 0703
K 0255

hok' / jok'; hòok'?

trans v; intrans v tie up; come out?

Yu *hok'; hòok'* hok' 'ganco, garfio, garabato, lazo, nudo, anzuelo; asir, traba, pescar, atar, lazar, engarabatar, enganchar, coger' (Barrera Vásquez et al. 1980:221); hok'ol 'salir' (Barrera Vásquez et al. 1980:222); hok' 'tie loosely' (V. Bricker et al. 1998:109); h[rezia]okob 'garavato, garfio, gancho, engaravatar y assir'; h[rezia]okol 'salir fuera; manifestarse' (Martínez Hernández 1929:190v); hòok' 'come out; turn out' (V. Bricker et al. 1998:109)

Ch' *jok'* *jok' 'hanging' (Kaufman and Norman 1984:122)

1. Picture: noose; knot

1566–1915 Brasseur de Bourbourg (1869–1870, vol. 1:204): "p', p'a" 'sortir avec effort, rompre en sortant, ouvrir par force'; Seler (1902–1923, vol. 1:565f.): 'captura'.

1951–1980 Cordan (1963:45, 49): "hok" plus "kal" for "hokal" 'bound together'; Kelley (1976:152f.): "hok" 'to put in office', following Barthel (1968); 'bound together', 'hung up'; Knorozov (1967:97): "k'ax" (bound animal?); Proskouriakoff (1960:456f.): event at beginning of reign; Thompson (1962:289f.): [58 examples] ("toothache") animal glyphs are included; seem to function in same way as tied-up moon glyph; Thompson (1972:82): 'birth'?

1981–1990 V. Bricker (1986:213): (T0684a) "uh" 'moon' (Yucatecan); 'arrive'?; (T0684b) "kuch" 'arrive' (Yucatecan); Grube (1990a:114): = T060:0747; Justeson (1984:351): [knotted strap only; T0684a is compound of T0684 and T0683b, T0684b is T0684 with various animal heads including T0757 and T0758] J. Fox, J. Justeson: related verb and noun indicating succession; J. Justeson: probably "*jo:k' " 'to rise (the sun)', 'to appear'; cf. "*jok' " 'knotted cloth, noose, hang(ing)'; F. Lounsbury: 'accession'; T0684b also "xul"; P. Mathews, B. Riese, D. Stuart: 'accession'; can also take as infix T0747b, "ta" vulture; P. Mathews, D. Stuart: T0684b, with animal (peccary?) head infixed is name at Palenque; L. Schele: "pach/pat"; the sacred bundle; T0684b is "pach/pat" + T0757 with a peccary nose (name at Palenque); MacLeod (1989b): "hok' " 'come out'; as new king emerges from enclosure into public view, wearing for the first time vestments of office; Porter (1988): 'sacred bundle', associated with initiation into sorcerer rank; Ringle (1985): related to assumption of "bonds" of leadership; Schele and J. Miller (1983:61–92): glyph for inaugural events.

1991–2008 Davoust (1995:595): "hok" 'noeud, désigner'; Davoust (1997:161): "hok" 'acceder'; Knorozov (1999, vol. 1:124): "haal"; Martin and Grube (2000:231): credit Stuart with "hoy/joy"; Schele and Grube (1997:137): "hok' " 'trap, seize; take'; Vail (2002b): "hok' " fits contexts in Madrid Codex especially well 'to trap' or 'snare'.

ZB4

T —
Z —
K —

1. Picture: noose; knot

1566–1915 Förstemann [1887] (1904:401): "the circles in a way signified the minus sign (–)"; Förstemann (1906:251f.): "It is meant to denote the starting-point of the series"; Thomas (1882:42): knot denotes the tying of years or periods of years.

1916–1950 Willson (1924): refers to the Epoch placed a certain number of days before 4 Ahau [8 Cumku].

1951–1980 Thompson (1972:20f.): "Willson (1924) coined . . . the expression ring numbers since the "kin" coefficient (exceptionally the "uinal," too) is enclosed in a conspicuous red loop tied at the top. This element only occurs with ring numbers and most inexplicably around the coefficients of the suppressed day glyphs in the 54-day table on [Dresden] 71a–73a. As used with 4 Ahau 8 Cumku it serves more or less as do our letters B.C. to indicate a distance before the starting point of our current count."

1991–2008 V. Bricker and H. Bricker (2005:217): on Dresden 69–74, ring dates represent an abbreviated notation of the "tzolkin" date corresponding to each column of the table.

ZB4

T —
Z —
K —

2. Picture: noose; knot

1991–2008 Vail and Hernández (2005–2008): Madrid example (M. 33a) differs from those in Dresden in containing a distance number and coefficient pair. It appears to denote the last of those in the series to be added, suggesting that the knot is functioning here to indicate closure or termination.

ZC1

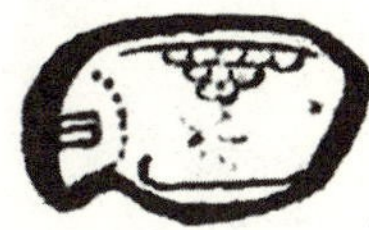

T 0528
Z 1339
K 0143

ku

tùun / tun

n — stone; 360-day year

Yu *tùun* — tun 'piedra; piedra preciosa; piedra labrada; jade' (Barrera Vásquez et al. 1980:822); tùun 'stone' (V. Bricker et al. 1998:284)

Ch' *tun* — *tun 'stone' (Kaufman and Norman 1984:133)

day 19: Kawak/Chak; period: 360 days

1. Picture: cave?, stone?

1566–1915 Bollaert (1865–1866:52): "cauac"; Brasseur de Bourbourg (1869–1870, vol. 1:202, 208): "cu," like "co," pour "cum" 'vase'; day Cauac; "ca-uac" 'qui est trop plein, qui surabone'; Landa [1566] (Tozzer 1941:134, 162, 166, 170): day Cauac; prefixed to month Cumhu; <cu>; Rosny (1883:10, 21, 25): day Cauac; "cauac"; /cu/; Thomas (1888:348): [variant used for drum on Madrid 80b–81b]: "che" 'wood'; Thomas (1888:357): [with 0559]: "cutz; cax" in place of bird symbol in Dresden almanac; Thomas (1893:248, 250f.): /che/; /c'/; /k'/; Tozzer and Allen (1910:pl. 2): day Cauac, possibly representing a honeycomb on M. 106b.

1916–1950 Gates (1931:49): "cauac" 'storm; tun'; Thompson (1950:269): "tun"; Whorf (1933:18f.): Landa's /ku/.

1951–1980 Dütting (1979:186): "haab" 'rain, celestial water'; Fought (1965:262): "haab" 'year, water'; Kelley (1962a:281–84): /c(u)/; second graphemic variant "haab" 'year'; Kelley (1962b:41): /cu/; Kelley (1976:33f., 72, 157, 167, 171, 174–76, 192, 200, 206–8, 211): Cauac; "haab" 'year' (synonym of "tun"); 'water', 'rain'; /cu/; Knorozov (1955:74): 117 (nubes? con signos complementarios), /c(u)/, 'temporada', 'período'; Knorozov (1958:285): /c(u)/; Knorozov (1967:91): /k(u)/; "ku" 'year'; determinative (season); Thompson (1962:134–43): [472 examples] Cauac; "ku, kul"; "haab"; and 'storm'; Thompson (1972:42, 52): may refer to "ku" 'god', "kul" 'divine'.

1981–1990 V. Bricker (1986:211): /cu/ "tun" '360-day year' (Yucatecan); Fahsen (1987:2): can represent "tun" or "*to:n" and probably also the male organ "to:n" or "tu:n" (after Justeson 1984:340); 'serve' (Tzotzil); Fox and Justeson (1984:48–53): /ku/; "hab/tun"; Justeson (1984:340): J. Fox, J. Justeson, P. Mathews: 'year' "haab," 'year-ending'; "*tu:n," 'stone'; "*to:nh," 'thunder, lightning'; "*kahoq"; day Cauac; /ku/; J. Fox, J. Justeson, F. Lounsbury: /ku/, cf. Mixtec day name Co for 19th day; J. Justeson, B. Riese: value /ku/ is rare in inscriptions; F. Lounsbury, B. Riese: day Cauac; "tun" 'stone'; "tun" 'year'; "haab' " 'year'; /ku/; L. Schele: /ku/, "haab'," "tun," "chahk"; 19th day; /ku/; with T0116, "tun, haab' "; D. Stuart: /ku/, "tun," "chahk"; 19th day; /ku/; with T0116 "tun"; MacLeod (1990b:335): "tun."

1991–2008 Carrasco (1994:52): "tun," "ku," on Uxmal ballcourt rings, /ku/; Davoust (1995:584): "cauac/chahac" '19e jour'; "tun" 'année; pierre'; /cu/; Knorozov (1999, vol. 1:124, 233): /cu/ 'lluvia; tormenta' (nubarrones y rocío).

ZC1

T –
Z –
K 0143

ku

2. Picture: crossed bands

1991–2008 Grube and Schele (1994:12): /ku/ in spelling of "kuy" 'owl' on Madrid 95c.

ZC5

T 0200
Z –
K –

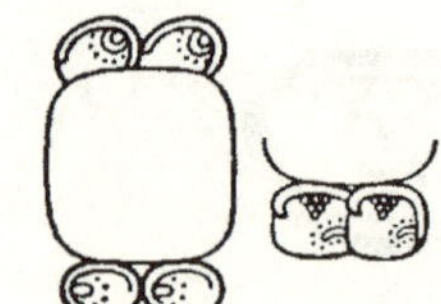

pi

-pih; pih

nm cl; n b'ak'tun; cloth

Yu *pix* pix 'cover, wrap up' (V. Bricker et al. 1998:217); pix 'cover, lid, sheath' (Hofling with Tesucún 1997:515)

Ch' *pis(il)* *pis-il 'clothes' (Kaufman and Norman 1984:128)

period: 144,000 days, b'ak'tun

1. Picture: double "kawak" sign

1566–1915 Förstemann [1897] (1904b:549): period of 144,000 days; Goodman (1897:25): 'twenty katuns, or 144,000 days'.

1916–1950 Gates (1931:75): "baktun"; Thompson (1950:147): "baktun."

1951–1980 Kelley (1962b:34): period of 400 tuns (E. Förstemann and generally); pseudo-Maya baktun (S. Morley); /cu-c(u)/ 'cycle' (D. Kelley, Y. Knorozov).

1981–1990 Grube (1990a:96): = T0177; Justeson (1984:330): J. Fox, J. Justeson: reduplicated T0528; "not necessarily both to be read," may be /ku/, /ku-k(u)/, "hab," "tun," "baktun"; "baktun" not /ku-k(u)/, but logographic/semantic 'year-year'; F. Lounsbury: "kuk"; P. Mathews, D. Stuart, L. Schele: "kuk," /ku-k(u)/; B. Riese: "baktun"; Stuart (1987:11–13): /pi/.

1991–2008 Davoust (1995:567): "pih" 'période de 400 années', /pi/; Knorozov (1999, vol. 1:76): /cu-cu/; Ringle and Smith-Stark (1996:335–38): 0200 = 0200a; Schele and Grube (1993): "pih" 'bak'tun; bundle'; Stuart (2005:166, n. 52): /pi/, "pik"; widespread Mayan term used for counting units of 8000.

ZC5

T 0177
Z –
K –

pi

2. Picture: arch with "kawak" sign

1951–1980 Dütting (1979:183): "cub" 'to gather'.

1981–1990 Grube (1990a:95): = T0200; Stuart (1987:11–13): /pi/.

1991–2008 Davoust (1995:566): /pi/; Knorozov (1999, vol. 1:77): /cu-aan/?; combinación de 442.230; Ringle and Smith-Stark (1996:335–38): 0177 (retired) = 0200b.

ZC6

T 0176b
Z 1339
K –

1. Picture: triple "kawak" sign

1951–1980 Berlin (1958:112, 118): in Seibal emblem glyph.

1991–2008 H. Bricker and V. Bricker (n.d.): constellation Orion; MacLeod (1991e): "ux tun" 'three stones'; Schele and Grube (1997:211): three stones of the Cosmic Hearth on Paris 23; B. Tedlock (1999b:51): "ox tunal" 'place with three stones'; hearthstone constellation raised at beginning of the present world; Vail and Hernández (2005–2008): "three stone [place]"; may refer to mythological place of creation—the celestial hearth represented by the stars Alnitak, Saiph, and Rigel in Orion (see Schele and Mathews 1993).

ZD2

T 0134
Z –
K –

no?

Only context in the codices is with ZUK "nohol" 'south'.

1. Picture: loops

1981–1990 V. Bricker (1983:352): semantic determinative for T0575 in directional context, "mal" 'nadir'; Justeson (1984:326): J. Fox, J. Justeson, P. Mathews, L. Schele: possibly = T0136; F. Lounsbury: = T0136; /lo/?; Schele and Grube (1988): probably /o/.

1991–2008 Davoust (1995:563): /o/; Knorozov (1999, vol. 1:89): signo diacrítico; Martin and Grube (2000:231): credit Stuart with /no/.

ZD3

T 0595
Z 1312
K 0123

1. Picture: ?

1951–1980 Knorozov (1967:89): phonetic; Thompson (1962:221f.): [14 examples] (cotton) "u" infixes resemble Nahuatl symbol for cotton; Thompson (1972:82f.): 'cotton', a metaphorical term for 'clouds'.

1981–1990 Dienhart (1986): "noc' " 'cloth, cotton'; Justeson (1984:346): J. Fox: = T0114; F. Lounsbury: pertaining to deceased person; Schele and Grube (1990): /k'o/?

1991–2008 Davoust (1995:589): "ko' " 'masque'; "kom" 'vallée, profondeur'; /ko/.

ZD7

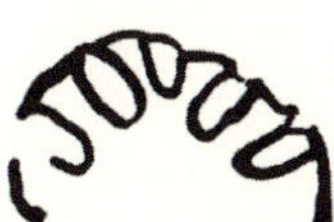

T –
Z –
K –

1. Picture: unidentified food offering

ZE1

T 0187
Z –
K –

k'àab'a' / k'ab'a'

n name

Yu *k'àab'a'* k'aba' 'nombre de cualquier cosa' (Barrera Vásquez et al. 1980:359); k'àab'a' 'name' (V. Bricker et al. 1998:142)

Ch' *k'ab'a'* *k'ab'a' 'name' (Kaufman and Norman 1984:123)

1. Picture: sky elbow

1951–1980 Dütting (1974:50): "taz"? 'layer; bed'.

1981–1990 Justeson (1984:329): J. Fox: possibly iconic origin in encircling/embracing wings; for central crossed bands cf. "ta:n" 'breast' (T0552); J. Fox, J. Justeson: possibly = , or formally derived from, T0563b; L. Schele: possibly "house"; Schele (1989c:40f.): substitution spelling "k'a-ba" for "k'ab'a" 'name' on Chichén Itzá Casa Colorada; credits D. Stuart, N. Grube, and J. Maxwell with "k'ab'a' " 'name'.

1991–2008 Davoust (1995:567): "kaba' " 'nom', "tz'at" 'savant'; /tz'a/; Knorozov (1999, vol. 1:179): "ch'a"; Stuart (1998:386): cites own correspondence to Houston, 1987: "k'aba' " 'name'.

ZE2

T –
Z –
K –

Probably a name or title. Not necessarily equivalent to ZE2 in the Classic period.

1. Picture: "chuwen" sign elbow

ZH1

T –
Z –
K –

wíinik háab' / winik hab'; k'atun

n; nm cl k'atun

Yu *wíinik háab'; k'atun* winik 'hombre'; winal 'mes antiguo de 20 días' (Barrera Vásquez et al. 1980:923); wíinik 'man' (V. Bricker et al. 1998:305); haab 'año' (Barrera Vásquez et al. 1980:165); háab' 'year' (V. Bricker et al. 1998:92); k'atun 'especie de veinte años; período de veinte años de a 360 días' (Barrera Vásquez et al. 1980:385)

Ch' *winik hab'; ø* winic 'hombre' (Aulie and Aulie 1998:141); *hab' 'year' (Kaufman and Norman 1984:120)

period: 7,200 days, k'atun

1. Picture: ?

1566–1915 Förstemann [1897] (1904b:549): period of 7,200 days; Goodman (1897:24): "katun" 'twenty years' (7,200 days).

1916–1950 Gates (1931:75): "katun" 'twenty tuns'; Thompson (1950:145–47): "katun."

1981–1990 V. Bricker (1986:208): "katun" 'score of years' (Yucatecan).

1991–2008 Davoust (1995:555): T0028: "kal" 'entourer'; /ka/; Stuart (1996:155): /wi/ complements suggest "winik" or "winak."

ZH2

T 0549
Z 1340a
K 0312

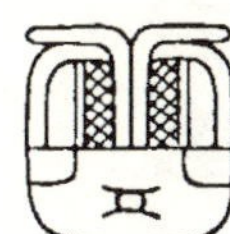

há'ab' period: Pax/Ahkiku

1. Picture: split drum?

1566–1915 Landa [1566] (Tozzer 1941:164): month Pax.

1916–1950 Gates (1931:64): "pax."

1951–1980 Kelley (1976:135, 333): "pax" 'split, divide'; Knorozov (1955:76): 143 "tun," 'sonido, ruído'; Knorozov (1967:100): "t'un"; Thompson (1962:164): [1 example] Pax.

1981–1990 Justeson (1984:342): J. Fox, J. Justeson, B. Riese: = T0299:0548, month Pax; depicts sound issuing from T0548 drum, the vertical "pax" (not the horizontal "tunkul"); F. Lounsbury, L. Schele, D. Stuart: "pax/tun" 'sounding drum'; P. Mathews: "pax/tun."

1991–2008 Davoust (1995:585): "pax" '16e mois; tambour'; Knorozov (1999, vol. 1:130): "tun" (tambor).

ZH4

T 0685
Z –
K 0329

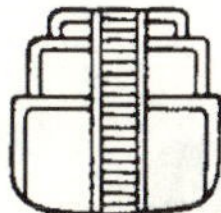

n temple, pyramid

1. Picture: temple, pyramid

1916–1950 Gates (1931:163): G402 [in part].

1951–1980 Kelley (1962b:24): pyramid (Y. Knorozov, D. Kelley); "mul" 'pyramid' (Y. Knorozov, D. Kelley); Knorozov (1955:70): 072 (pirámide) "mul" 'pirámide'; Knorozov (1967:101): morphemic (pyramid with central stairway); Thompson (1962:290f.): [7 examples] (pyramid).

1981–1990 Justeson (1984:351): J. Fox, J. Justeson, P. Mathews: 'temple, pyramid'; "*nah" 'house', at least the final part of the word, the entirety possibly "*mul-nah" 'pyramid' or "*k'uh-nah" 'temple'; F. Lounsbury, L. Schele: 'pyramid'; B. Riese: pyramid, possibly public buildings in general; Ringle (1988:10): substitutes for T1016c in the expression T0012.1016c/0685.0023. Depicts a pyramid; "ch'u/k'u na" 'god's house', 'temple'?

1991–2008 Davoust (1995:596); "ch'ul nah" 'temple'; Knorozov (1999, vol. 1:171): "vitz" (fachada de la pirámide).

ZH5

T 0193
Z –
K 0349

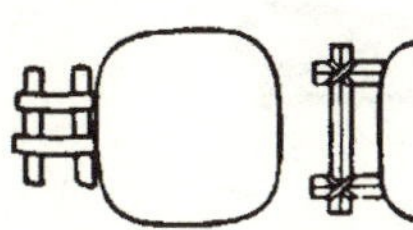

1. Picture: cage?, scaffold?

1951–1980 Kelley (1976:133, 332): wooden frame; Knorozov (1967:102): "eb" 'ladder'; Lounsbury and Coe (1968:282): "moch" 'basket made of wood; cage'.

1981–1990 Justeson (1984:330): J. Fox, J. Justeson: 'cacaxtle', 'carrying crate, cage'; no evidence for "moch"; F. Lounsbury, B. Riese: depicts cage; P. Mathews, L. Schele: "moch" 'cage' (M. 59).

1991–2008 Davoust (1995:567): "kal" 'entourer'; Grube and Martin (2000:6): substitutes for 'step' glyph "ehb' " in ruler name at Tikal; Harrison (1999:66): "ch'aktel" 'scaffold'; Knorozov (1999, vol. 1:172): "eb" (escalera de madera); Schele and Mathews (1998:63): "ch'akte'."

ZQ1

T 0326
Z 0088
K 0361–65

n?; v? eclipse

1. Picture: cartouche between "wings"

1566–1915 Brasseur de Bourbourg (1869–1870, vol. 1:216): (with T0544 and T0682) symboles de la terre brûlée et abîmée sous les eaux?

1916–1950 Gates (1931:166f.): eclipse.

1951–1980 Cordan (1964:49f.): "xak" 'nubes'; Kelley (1962b:36): clouds around sun or moon (E. Förstemann, J. E. S. Thompson); eclipse (M. Makemson); sun or moon darkened (including eclipse; J. E. S. Thompson); Kelley (1976:43, 332): 'eclipse'; Knorozov (1967:102): morphemic; Thompson (1972:100): black and white clouds?

1981–1990 V. Bricker (1986:151f., 211): T0326.0682 'lunar eclipse'; Justeson (1984:336): J. Fox, J. Justeson, F. Lounsbury, P. Mathews, B. Riese, L. Schele: 'eclipse'.

1991–2008 V. Bricker and H. Bricker (1992:73): eclipse glyph; Davoust (1995:577): "chibil" 'éclipse'; Knorozov (1999, vol. 1:179): "vaay" (contorno oscuro en el que se inscriben signos astronómicos); Love (1994:91–93): represents the sun or moon positioned in the sky; not a reference to an eclipse; Schele and Grube (1997:170): 'eclipse'; B. Tedlock (1999b:46): with T0544, "Sun is suspended between light and darkness, which is true not only during an eclipse but at sunrise and sunset."

ZQ4

T 0163
Z 0070b
K 0074

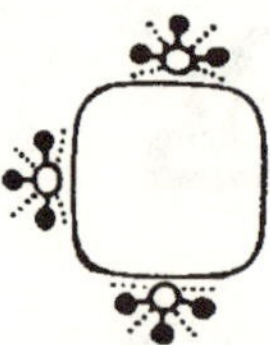

mi

1. Picture: ?

1566–1915 Brasseur de Bourbourg (1869–1870, vol. 1:219): symbole d'un cratère ouvert d'où s'élancent des pierres et du gaz.

1951–1980 Cordan (1964:44f.): "*muk-mux" 'tierra'; Knorozov (1967:84): "buk' " 'in full' (fire-making set).

1981–1990 Grube (1990a:94): = T0173; Grube and Nahm (1990): /mi/; T0163 (the codical form) is equivalent to T0173 (the Classic form); Justeson (1984:328): J. Fox, J. Justeson: "e:m" 'to descend'; possibly related to, or variant of, T0173 'completion'.

1991–2008 Davoust (1995:565): "mil" 'étrangler'; /mi/; Knorozov (1999, vol. 1:93): "ch'e" (obtención de fuego); Ringle and Smith-Stark (1996:335–38): 0163 (retired) = 0173c.

ZQ9

T 0153
Z 1353
K 0366

Occurs in codices as part of name of a deity with death attributes.

1. Picture: crossed batons, weaving sticks?

1951–1980 Knorozov (1967:102): phonetic (crossed legs?); Thompson (1962:54): T0153-0501 compound associated with the date 13.0.0.0.0 4 Ahau 8 Cumku (e.g., Cobá 1 A18).

1981–1990 Justeson (1984:327): L. Schele: era event (4 Ahau 8 Cumku).

1991–2008 Davoust (1995:564): "hal" 'tisser, exprimer'; /ha/; Davoust (1997:107): "ch'oc" 'jeune'; Knorozov (1999, vol. 1:74, 236): "kax" 'juntar; amarrar'; MacLeod (1991f): may be a different glyph than "hal" in Madrid; Schele and Grube (1997:98): in name of God A'; similar to Classic period title "ox ch'ak-kab-na." Used at Yaxchilan and Palenque in reference to a blindfolded god with avian features. Similar title occurs in name of 14th ruler of Copán; Stuart (2005:166): "jel"? 'to change over'.

ZQA

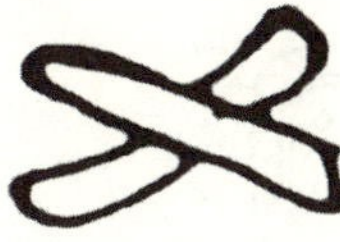

T –
Z –
K 0367

1. Picture: crossed batons, weaving sticks?

1951–1980 Knorozov (1967:102): "k'at" (the rafters of a house).

1991–2008 MacLeod (1991f.): "hal" 'weave, weaving'.

ZQD

T 0510b
Z 1328a
K 0353

èek' / ek'

n star, planet; Venus

Yu *èek'* 'èek' 'star' (V. Bricker et al. 1998:7); ek' 'estrella, nombre genérico' (Barrera Vásquez et al. 1980:150)

Ch' *ek'* *ek' 'star' (Kaufman and Norman 1984:119)

1. Picture: star

1566–1915 Bowditch (1910:226): Venus; Brasseur de Bourbourg (1869–1870, vol. 1:206): day Lamat; "lam-at" for "lam-a-ti" 'lieu enfoncé, abîmé dans l'eau'; "lam-bat" 'enfoncée la hace, la batte'; Förstemann [1897] (1904a:438): Venus; Rosny (1883:6): day Lamat; Seler [1898] (1990:212): Venus.

1916–1950 Gates (1931:149): Venus; Willson (1924:33): Venus.

1951–1980 Kelley (1962b:36): "chak ek" 'great star, Venus'; "chac kanal" 'great star'; Kelley (1976:38, 39): "ek" or "kanal"? 'star'; Knorozov (1967:102): "lem" 'star'; Thompson (1962:108–10): [117 examples] Lamat-Venus; "The presence of the "chac" affix (0109) both on the monuments and in Codex Dresden is of interest since a name for the planet Venus is "chac ek," 'great star' or 'red star'."

1981–1990 Justeson (1984:339): J. Fox, J. Justeson, P. Mathews, B. Riese: 'star' (not 'black'; cf. Lowland Mayan "*e:k' " 'star'; proto-Yucatecan "*e:k'," proto-Cholan "*ik' " 'black'); F. Lounsbury: Venus; L. Schele, D. Stuart: 'Venus' and 'star'.

1991–2008 Davoust (1995:582): "ek" 'étoile'; Knorozov (1999, vol. 1:172): "ek, ech' " (estrella con cuatro rayos).

ZQD

T 0002
Z 1328b
K 0326

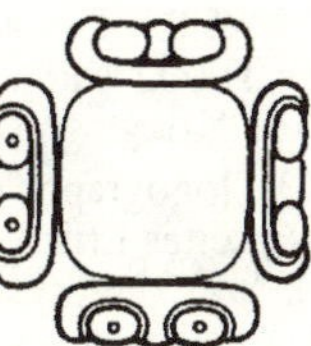

èek' / ek'

n star, planet; Venus

2. Picture: star

1566–1915 Bowditch (1910:226): Venus; Förstemann [1897] (1904a:438): Venus; Seler [1898] (1990:212): Venus.

1916–1950 Gates (1931:149): Venus; Willson (1924:33): Venus.

1951–1980 Kelley (1962b:36): variants of Venus (E. Förstemann and most others); 'star' (D. Kelley); Kelley (1976:38, 39): "ek" or "kanal"? 'star'; Knorozov (1967:100, 102): (= K353); "lem" 'star'; Thompson (1972:64): 'Venus'.

1981–1990 Grube (1990a:87): = T0001; Justeson (1984:316): J. Fox, J. Justeson: = T0024; suffix "-il," perhaps other "-Vl" suffixes; B. Riese: "I do not see the evidence for J. Justeson's proposal."

1991–2008 Davoust (1995:553): "uh" 'collier'; /u/, /li/?; Knorozov (1999, vol. 1:90): "ek, ech' " 'estrella'; Ringle and Smith-Stark (1996:335–38): 0003 (retired) = 0001b.

ZQD

T 0510a
Z 1328
K 0174

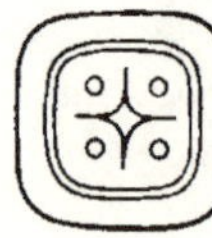

Except for one occurrence, this subsort only used as day Lamat/Lamb'at, not Venus.
day 08: Lamat/Lamb'at
3. Picture: star

1566–1915 Bollaert (1865–1866:52): "lamat"; Brasseur de Bourbourg (1869–1870, vol. 1:206): day Lamat; "lam-at" for "lam-a-ti" 'lieu enfoncé, abîmé dans l'eau'; "lam-bat" 'enfoncée la hace, la batte'; Goodman (1897:16): day Lamat; Landa [1566] (Tozzer 1941:134): day Lamat.

1916–1950 Gates (1931:30): "lamat" 'rabbit'.

1951–1980 Knorozov (1967:94, 102): = 353, "lem" 'star'; Thompson (1962:108–10): [117 examples] Lamat-Venus.

1981–1990 Grube (1990a:105): = T0638; Justeson (1984:339): L. Campbell, J. Fox, J. Justeson, P. Mathews, B. Riese: day Lamat ("lamb'at," "lamat"); F. Lounsbury: day Lamat; L. Schele, D. Stuart: day Lamat.

1991–2008 Davoust (1995:582): "lamat" '8e jour'; Knorozov (1999, vol. 1:147f.): "ek, ech' " (estrella con cuatro rayos).

ZQE

T –
Z –
K –

hub'?

intr v? fall?

Yu *hub'* hub' 'derribar paredes y desbaratar' (Barrera Vásquez et al. 1980:238); hub' 'disturb, disarrange, loosen' (V. Bricker et al. 1998:113)

Ch' *hub'* jubel 'bajar' (Aulie and Aulie 1998:58)

Only two examples, both from the Paris Codex. Example pictured shows star over ZUH /yi/, possibly a verbal suffix. Also occurs in Classic contexts with ZUH, YS1 'earth; region', and various site names.

1. Picture: star over "shell"

1951–1980 Closs (1979): earth-star and shell-star glyphs associated with Venus but in general do not relate to significant positions of the Venus cycle in any correlation.

1981–1990 Lounsbury (1982): T0002 'star' combines with T0526 'earth' to designate war event; Riese (1982:274–77): [with T0510b and T0575] 'Krieg'.

1991–2008 Aldana (2005: 313): logograph "ek' " used in rebus fashion for the first syllable in the verb "ek'emey" 'to fall'; Chinchilla (2006:6): cites Erik Velásquez García (in Grazioso 2002) "chek' " or "tek' " 'to step on, kick, humiliate'; Chinchilla (2006): "uk' " 'to cry, weep, lament'; graphic form of logograph, frequently used in context of war events, may allude to role of stars in warfare myths and beliefs, but this should be considered rhetorical rather than a specific textual meaning; Macri (2009): analogous to the Mexican "water-hill" glyph; substituted in Maya glyphic inscriptions for the intransitive verb 'to fall; to be defeated'; Stuart (1995:265, 311–13): perhaps "hub' " 'fall; collapse'.

ZQE

T —
Z —
K —

hub'?

intr v? fall?

Example pictured shows star over 2S1, a locative, "nal/näl."

2. Picture: star over 'place'

1951–1980 Closs (1979): earth-star and shell-star glyphs associated with Venus but in general do not relate to significant positions of the Venus cycle in any correlation.

1981–1990 Lounsbury (1982): T0002 'star' combines with T0526 'earth' to designate war event; Riese (1982:274–77): [with T0510b and T0575] 'Krieg'.

1991–2008 Aldana (2005: 313): logograph "ek' " used in rebus fashion for the first syllable in the verb "ek'emey" 'to fall'; Chinchilla (2006:6): cites Erik Velásquez García (in Grazioso 2002) "chek' " or "tek' " 'to step on, kick, humiliate'; Chinchilla (2006): "uk' " 'to cry, weep, lament'; graphic form of logograph, frequently used in context of war events, may allude to role of stars in warfare myths and beliefs, but this should be considered rhetorical rather than a specific textual meaning; Macri (2009): analogous to the Mexican "water-hill" glyph; substituted in Maya glyphic inscriptions for the intransitive verb 'to fall; to be defeated'; Stuart (1995:265, 311–13): perhaps "hub' " 'fall; collapse'.

ZQH

T —
Z —
K —

1. Picture: four elements around circle

1991–2008 Knorozov (1999:172): "lol" (flor de cuatro pétalos).

ZQJ

T —
Z 1301
K —

May be the same as ZQK.

1. Picture: four comb elements around dotted circle

1951–1980 Zimmermann (1956:79): Z1301, in part.

ZQK

T —
Z 1301
K 0369

May be the same as ZQJ.

1. Picture: four elements around dotted circle

1951–1980 Knorozov (1967:102): morphemic (K005 in a punctate oval); Zimmermann (1956:79): Z1301, in part.

ZS2

T 0274
Z 1373
K 0323

May be a variant of YS7.

1. Picture: twisted object

1566–1915 Brasseur de Bourbourg (1869–1870, vol. 1:216): "ex" 'ceinture de l'homme ou double miroir'.

1951–1980 Knorozov (1955:72): 099 (manojo de cuerdas) "bel, bal"?; Knorozov (1967:100): "bal" (coiled rope).

1981–1990 Grube (1990a:100): = T0573, T0768a; Justeson (1984:334): J. Fox: probably = T0676.

1991–2008 Davoust (1995:574): "tal" 'venir'; Knorozov (1999, vol. 1:144): "baal, bal" (madeja de cuerda); Ringle and Smith-Stark (1996:335–38): 0274 = doubtful; 0676A or 0098v.

ZS2

T 0098
Z 1373
K 0324

2. Picture: twisted object

1566–1915 Thomas (1893:250): /tz/.

1951–1980 Knorozov (1967:100): (= K323) "bal."

1981–1990 Schele (1987d): /ta/.

1991–2008 Davoust (1995:560): /nu/; Knorozov (1999, vol. 1:178): "baal" (madeja de cuerda); Schele and Grube (1997:175): "tal."

ZS3

T 0729
Z —
K —

1. Picture: twisted object

1566–1915 Brasseur de Bourbourg (1869–1870, vol. 1:216, 220): l'oeil double, figuré dans la ceinture commune aux hommes, "ex"; '8000'; Brinton (1895:91): 'to tie together, to join', or, as a rebus, 'rain, to rain'; Rosny (1883:16): "hun-pic" 'huit mille'? (credits Brasseur de Bourbourg).

1951–1980 Knorozov (1967:100): "bal" (coiled rope); Thompson (1962:311): [1 example].

1991–2008 Knorozov (1999, vol. 1:178): "baal" (madeja de cuerda).

ZS4

T 0559
Z 1355
K 0160

tzu

May have logographic as well as phonetic reading.
part of há'ab' period: K'ank'in/Uniw
1. Picture: gourd

1566–1915 Brasseur de Bourbourg (1869–1870, vol. 1:208): day Ahau; "ah-au" 'canne du vase d'eau, le mâle dans le vase de la femelle'; Brinton (1895:120): sign for a breastbone, a shield, or a dog; Rosny (1883:25): /tzo/; Thomas (1888:357): [with T0528] "cutz; cax" in place of bird symbol in Dresden almanac; Thomas (1893:251): /tz/; Tozzer and Allen (1910:pl. 37): glyph supposed to represent a dog's ribs.

1916–1950 Gates (1931:63, 160): "kankin"; also clearly shown as an animal backbone and ribs.

1951–1980 Closs (1979:158–65): "tzul" 'dog', 'backbone' in "ah tzul," a name associated with Venus; Fox and Justeson (1980): "uniw"; Kelley (1962a:281): /tzu/; Kelley (1962b:41): /tzu/; Kelley (1976:168, 171, 333): /tzu/; Knorozov (1955:65): 003 (esqueleto, columna vertebral, pelvis y costillas), /tz(u)/; Knorozov (1958:285): /tz(u)/; Knorozov (1967:92): /tz(u)/ (backbone and ribs of skeleton); Thompson (1962:172f.): [35 examples] Kankin; Thompson (1972:64): tentatively "ek" 'star' or "ekel" 'species of jaguar'; the compound T0012.0168.0559 may read 'he/lord of the star(s)' or 'jaguar man' (meaning 'warrior').

1981–1990 V. Bricker (1986:212): "onew"? 'avocado'; Grube (1990a:108): = T0782; Justeson (1984:343): L. Campbell, J. Fox, J. Justeson: month Kankin ("uniw"); L. Campbell: /tzu/ < "*tzuh" 'bottle gourd', which codex sign may depict; J. Fox, J. Justeson: polyvalence ("Kankin/tzu") due to loss of fruit diacritic (avocado?) in Kankin, loss of gourd construction for /tzu/ (see T0370); F. Lounsbury: month Kankin, "uniw"; possibly name of mythical 'jaguar dog'; astronomical significance related to maximum elongation of Evening Star Venus; B. Riese: in codices /tzu/, in monumental inscriptions with black dot "on/un"; also main sign for month Kankin ("uniw").

1991–2008 Closs (1992:134): "tzul" 'spine', 'dog', in the name (Ah) Tsul Ahaw 'Venus as evening star'; Closs (1994): "tzul" 'dog', 'spine', T0547, T0559, T0560, and T0753 substitute in the Quiriguá emblem glyph; Davoust (1995:586): "kankin" '14e mois'; "tzuc" 'division'; Knorozov (1999, vol. 1:139): /tzu/ (fragmento de la columna vertebral con costillas); Ringle and Smith-Stark (1996:335–38): 0559 = 0559a; Stuart (2001:17f.): /tzu/.

ZS7

T —
Z —
K —

1. Picture: number tree

1981–1990 MacLeod (1989a:114): object associated with glyph represents "acante'."

1991–2008 Houston and Stuart (1996:298): substitution spelling "a-nu" for "anul" or "anum" 'famous' on Naranjo Stela 24 D4; Ringle and Smith-Stark (1996:323): = 0924; Schele, Grube, and Fahsen (1994:6): "an" 'hew, carve'; Vail (2002b): "number tree."

ZSJ

T 0249
Z 0054
K –

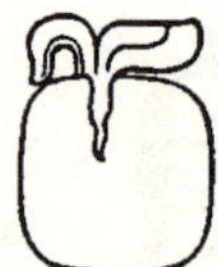

1. Picture: split earth with foliage

1951–1980 Cordan (1964:41): "nan" 'título'; Knorozov (1967:86): morphemic (two ears of corn); Thompson (1972:35): 'productive earth'?

1981–1990 Justeson (1984:333): J. Justeson: = T0563a; F. Lounsbury, L. Schele: 'emergence'.

1991–2008 Davoust (1995:572): "yol" 'germe'; Davoust (1997:104): "nal cab" 'maïs de la terre'; Knorozov (1999, vol. 1:73): (planta brotando); MacLeod (1991i): "y-ol-kab," reading the leaves as "y-ol" 'sprout', 'be born', and the earth sign as "kab"; Schele and Grube (1997:87f.): sprouting maize plants.

ZU1

T 0181
Z 0060
K 0034

ha / ja

ah / aj; -ah / -aj

agentive; suf — agentive; verbal suffix

Yu *ah* — ah 'antepuesta a los apellidos de linaje denota los varones; antepuesta a los nombres de lugares' (Barrera Vásquez et al. 1980:3)

Ch' *aj* — *aj 'prepound/proclitic; male; relatively large/active being' (Kaufman and Norman 1984:139)

1. Picture: moon

1566–1915 Brasseur de Bourbourg (1869–1870, vol. 1:202, 205): "ca" 'mâchoire'; "cáa" 'pierre à moudre le grain; une sorte de citrouille'; "ha" 'eau, rivière'; Landa [1566] (Tozzer 1941:170): <ha>; Rosny (1883:17): "háa" 'eau'; Thomas (1893:260): "ah, ha, hal."

1951–1980 Barthel (1964:237): "-ic"; forms verbal nouns; Kelley (1976:15, 75, 143, 158, 160, 176, 196f., 219, 256, 332): half moon; past-tense affix: "-ah"; Kelley (1962b:): /ha/; Knorozov (1955:74): 127 (una gota y elementos confusos) /h(-?)/, "-ah"; Knorozov (1958:285): /h(a)/; Knorozov (1967:79): (= K140); /h(a)/; Thompson (1962:56f.): 'moon'; Thompson (1972:31, 34f.): "kal" an auxiliary verb 'to do; to make'.

1981–1990 V. Bricker (1986:210): /a(h)/, "ah-" (agentive) (Cholan, Yucatecan); "-ah" (perfective) (Yucatecan); Grube (1990a:95): = T0683b; Justeson (1984:329): J. Justeson, F. Lounsbury, P. Mathews, B. Riese, D. Stuart: "-ah"; /a/, /ha/; = T0683b; L. Schele: /ah/ and "-ah" verbal suffix; Stuart (1985c:4): verbal suffix "-ah," /ha/; Stuart (1987:45): cites Knorozov (1958:285): /ha/.

1991–2008 Davoust (1995:566): "ha' " 'eau'; "uh" 'lune'; /ha/; Grube (2004:72): /ja/, not /ha/; Houston, Robertson, and Stuart (2001:23): morphosyllable "-aj"; Knorozov (1999, vol. 1:91, 124): /haa/, "ah" (charco o laguna con gotas de agua); Ringle and Smith-Stark (1996:335–38): 0181 = 0181a.

ZU1

T 0682b
Z 0147
K 0140

ha / ja

ah / aj; -ah / -aj

agentive; suf — agentive; verbal suffix

This variant is the same as T0683b in the Classic period. Not graphically distinct from ZU2. Most of the references listed below are for both variants of T0682b (ZU1 and ZU2).

2. Picture: moon

1566–1915 Bowditch (1910:226): 'moon'; Brasseur de Bourbourg (1869–1870, vol. 1:206): day Cimi; "cimi" 'il est mort' or "ci-mi" 'non effervescence plus' or "cim-i" 'qui a pris une pointe, une pousse'; Förstemann (1902:97): 'twenty'; Rosny (1883:4): day Cimi; Schellhas [1892] (1904:22): the sign of the moon; 'twenty'; Thomas (1888:348, 371): "kal" 'twenty' used also for 'imprison; compose'.

1916–1950 Gates (1931:89f.): 'twenty'; not 'moon'; Spinden (1924:18–22): 'twenty'.

1951–1980 Kelley (1976:23): Yucatec "kal," Tzeltal "tab" 'twenty'; Knorozov (1955:73): 110 (orificio de poso, cenote) "kal" 'veinte'; Knorozov (1967:90): /h(a)/ (waterhole with rainwater); Thompson (1962:282f.): [55 examples] = T0683 'moon'; 'twenty'; Thompson (1972:64): "kal" 'to do, make', 'affect'.

1981–1990 V. Bricker (1986:213): "-ah" (perfective) (Yucatecan); "winac" 'twenty'; Grube (1990a:114): (T0683b) = T0181; Justeson (1984:351): J. Fox, J. Justeson: T0682b is 'moon', 'twenty'; F. Lounsbury, L. Schele: "ah," "k'al:" codex = T0683b; P. Mathews: "ah/k'al"; = T0683a,b (in part); usually 'twenty'; B. Riese: codical form of T0683a and T0683b, 'twenty'; Stuart (1985c:4): verbal suffix "-ah," /ha/.

1991–2008 Davoust (1995:595): (T0682a) "ha' " 'eau'; "uh" 'Lune'; /ha/; Grube (2004:72): /ja/, not /ha/; Knorozov (1999, vol. 1:124): "haa," "ah" (charco o laguna con gotas de agua); Ringle and Smith-Stark (1996:335–38): 0682a,b = 0181bv.

ZU2

T 0682b
Z 0147
K 0140

wíinik / winik; k'àal / k'al?; uh

num; n — twenty; moon

Yu *wíinik; k'àal; uh* — wíinik 'man' (V. Bricker et al. 1998:305); hun-tul-winik 'twenty' (Bruce 1968:70); -k'al 'cuenta de veintes'; k'aal 'veinte' (Barrera Vásquez et al. 1980:368); k'àal [numeral classifier] 'twenty' (V. Bricker et al. 1998:144); u 'collar de cuentas o sartal' (Barrera Vásquez et al. 1980:896); 'uh 'bead; moon' (V. Bricker et al. 1998:20)

Ch' *winik; k'al; uh* — winic 'hombre' (Aulie and Aulie 1998:141); *k'al 'veintena; score' [twenty] (Kaufman and Norman 1984:138); *uh 'moon' (Kaufman and Norman 1984:135)

This variant is the same as T0683b in the Classic period. Not graphically distinct from ZU1. Most of the references listed below are for both variants of T0682b (ZU1 and ZU2).

1. Picture: moon

1566–1915 Bowditch (1910:226): 'moon'; Brasseur de Bourbourg (1869–1870, vol. 1:206): day Cimi; "cimi" 'il est mort' or "ci-mi" 'non effervescence plus' or "cim-i" 'qui a pris une pointe, une pousse'; Brinton (1895:21, 87): 'twenty'; "u" 'moon'; Förstemann (1902:97): 'twenty'; Morley (1915:152f.): month indicator; Rosny (1883:4): day Cimi; Schellhas [1892] (1904:22): the sign of the moon; 'twenty'; Thomas (1888:348, 371): "kal" 'twenty' used also for 'imprison; compose'; Thomas (1893:269): "kal" 'twenty'.

1916–1950 Gates (1931:89f.): 'twenty'; not 'moon'; Spinden (1924:18–22): 'twenty'.

1951–1980 Kelley (1976:23): Yucatec "kal," Tzeltal "tab" 'twenty'; Kelley (1976:160, 333): T0683 = "kal" 'twenty'; Knorozov (1955:73): 110 (orificio de poso, cenote) "kal" 'veinte'; Knorozov (1967:90): /h(a)/ (waterhole with rainwater); Thompson (1962:282f.): [55 examples] = T0683 'moon'; 'twenty'; Thompson (1972:64): "kal" 'to do, make', 'affect'.

1981–1990 V. Bricker (1985b): "twenty" in epithet "Hun-uinac-u-cuc" 'twenty-one in his cycle'; V. Bricker (1986:213): "winac" 'twenty'; "winal" 'twenty-day month' (Yucatecan); Grube (1990a:114): = T0683a; Justeson (1984:351): J. Fox, J. Justeson: T0682b is 'moon', 'twenty'; F. Lounsbury, L. Schele: "ah," "k'al"; codex = T0683b; P. Mathews: "ah/k'al"; = T0683a,b (in part); usually 'twenty'; B. Riese: codical form of T0683a and T0683b, 'twenty'.

1991–2008 Davoust (1995:595): "winic" 'twenty'.

ZUB

T 0591
Z 1371
K 0355

tz'onó'ot?

n — cenote
Yu *tz'onó'ot* — tz'onó'ot 'cenote, sinkhole' (V. Bricker et al. 1998:54)

1. Picture: cenote

1566–1915 Brasseur de Bourbourg (1869–1870, vol. 1:215): l'image de la mer des Caraïbes après son effondrement, probablement dans la partie entre la côte de Caracas et l'isthme de Panama.

1916–1950 Gates (1931:143): 'water'.

1951–1980 Knorozov (1967:102): "chul" 'water'; Thompson (1962:219): [3 examples] 'cenote', following José Franco; only in codices, rarely in texts, often in pictures.

1981–1990 Grube (1990a:109): = T0157; Justeson (1984:346): J. Fox, J. Justeson: "*ch'e'n" 'well'; P. Mathews: depicts jawbone of earth monster; B. Riese: "ch'en," "tz'onot," and others meaning 'hole; excavation; well'; L. Schele: possibly "ch'en" or "hol"; depicts depression in earth; Schele (1989c:42): in locations: a black hole; watery place; Schele (1990c): variants at Copán, skeletal maw of underworld (Stelae A and 29).

1991–2008 H. Bricker and V. Bricker (n.d.): "ha" 'water'; Davoust (1995:589): "way" 'esprit compagnon'; "tz'onot" 'puits naturel'; Knorozov (1999, vol. 1:177): "tuul, tul, chuul" (laguna u otro cuerpo de agua); MacLeod (personal communication, 1994): "way"; Ringle and Smith-Stark (1996:335–38): 0591 (retired) = 0769c; Schele and Grube (1997:229, 242): "ol"? 'hole'; Stross (1993): "way" 'hole'; 'maw'; von Nagy (1997:67): "dzonot" 'cenote'.

ZUC

T 0728
Z 1376
K 0360

1. Picture: skeletal jaw?

1566–1915 Schellhas [1892] (1904:40): hieroglyph of an unidentified figure in the Dresden manuscript.

1951–1980 Knorozov (1967:90, 102): (= K140) /h(a)/; Thompson (1962:311): [1 example] perhaps is T0157 used as a main sign.

1981–1990 Grube (1990a:116): = T0157; Thompson (1972:56): affix T0157 of "Uayeb" used as a main sign?; may stand for "nagual."

1991–2008 Davoust (1995:598): "way" 'transformer'; Knorozov (1999, vol. 1:180): "vaay"; Schele and Grube (1997:133): doubled /ha/ sign; "hah" 'to make something permanent, fix in place'.

ZUD

T 0157b
Z —
K —

Occurs only as a prefix to the há'ab' period Wayeb'.
1. Picture: ?

1981–1990 Grube (1990a): = T0591, 0728, 0769a, 0769b; Justeson (1984:327): cf. T0591, T0769; P. Mathews: jaws of earth monster; B. Riese: two different sign forms; one form probably depicts crustacean claws.

1991–2008 Davoust (1995:564): "way" 'esprit compagnon'; Ringle and Smith-Stark (1996:335–38): 0157 = 0769A.

ZUE

T —
Z —
K —

Possibly same as ZUC.
1. Picture: cenote?

ZUF

T 0589
Z 1369
K 0345

ho / jo

1. Picture: ?

1566–1915 Rosny (1883:17): "kak" 'feu'; Thomas (1888:351): [with T0093] the action of whirling a stick to produce fire or rolling a pestle in grinding paint.

1916–1950 Gates (1931:143): 'fire-drill'; Thompson (1950:265; 1972:38): "hax" 'drill'; Whorf (1942:484, fig. 1): /h-e-x/; /xa/.

1951–1980 Kelley (1962b:40): 'drill' (E. Seler, H. Beyer, B. Whorf, J. E. S. Thompson, T. Barthel, D. Kelley); drilled Spondylus shell (H. Beyer, T. Barthel, D. Kelley); shell (H. Spinden); "hax" 'drill' (B. Whorf, J. E. S. Thompson, T. Barthel); signo de producir fuego (J. Villacorta); "dzacatan" 'medicine drum' (D. Brinton); "buk" 'rolling a pestle or whirling a fire stick' (C. Thomas, Y. Knorozov); Kelley (1976:144–48, 333): (drilled Spondylus shell) " hax"? 'drill'; Knorozov (1955:72): 095 (ropa?) "buc" "lem"?; Knorozov (1967:101): "boh"; Thompson (1962:217): [59 examples] with T0093 symbol for drilling for fire; with T0580, probably indicates drilling jade.

1981–1990 Grube (1990a:109): = T0607; Justeson (1984:346): J. Fox, J. Justeson: "hax" 'to twist'; F. Lounsbury, P. Mathews, B. Riese, L. Schele, D. Stuart: "hax."

1991–2008 Davoust (1995:589): "hol" 'percer'; /ho/; Grube (2004:75f.): /jo/, not /ho/; Knorozov (1999, vol. 1:177): "boh"; Ringle and Smith-Stark (1996:335–38): 0589 (retired) = 0607c.

ZUG

T 0568b
Z 1354
K 0372

lu

1. Picture: ?

1566–1915 Brasseur de Bourbourg (1869–1870, vol. 1:203): "l, lé" 'lacet, sorte de lac ou de fronde armée d'une pierre'.

1916–1950 Gates (1931:156f.): occurs in the codices, associated with plants growing, the eclipse ephemeris, and the Venus pages.

1951–1980 Kelley (1962a:280f.): /l(u)/; Kelley (1962b:41): /lu/; Kelley (1976:126, 168, 171, 333): alleged 'sacrifice'; /lu/; Knorozov (1955:75): 138 /l(u)/; Knorozov (1958:285): /l(u)/; Knorozov (1967:103): /l(u)/; Thompson (1962:192–94): [136 examples] 'sacrifice'; Thompson (1972:95): 'sacrifice'.

1981–1990 V. Bricker (1986:212): /lu/; Grube (1990a:108): = T0082; Justeson (1984:344): L. Campbell, F. Lounsbury, P. Mathews, B. Riese: /lu/; J. Fox, J. Justeson: /lu/; "ol/ul" < "*ohl" 'heart'; depicts heart; see T0082/0083.

1991–2008 Davoust (1995:587): "ohl" 'coeur'; "-lu' " 'bagre'; /lu/; Knorozov (1999, vol. 1:161): /lu/ (pescado).

ZUG

T 0568a
Z 1300a
K 0372

lu

2. Picture: ?

1566–1915 Brasseur de Bourbourg (1869–1870, vol. 1:203): "l, lé" 'lacet, sorte de lac ou de fronde armée d'une pierre'; Landa [1566] (Tozzer 1941:170): <l>.

1916–1950 Gates (1931:156f.): occurs in the codices, associated with plants growing, the eclipse ephemeris, and the Venus pages.

1951–1980 Kelley (1962a:280f.): /l(u)/; Kelley (1976:126, 168, 171, 333): alleged 'sacrifice'; /lu/; Knorozov (1955:75): variant 138 /l(u)/; Knorozov (1958:285): /l(u)/; Knorozov (1967:103): /l(u)/; Thompson (1962:192–94): [136 examples] 'sacrifice'.

1981–1990 V. Bricker (1986:212): /lu/; Grube (1990a:108): = T0082; Justeson (1984:344): L. Campbell, F. Lounsbury, P. Mathews, B. Riese: /lu/; J. Fox, J. Justeson: /lu/; < "ol/ul" < "*ohl" 'heart'; depicts heart; see T0082/0083.

1991–2008 Davoust (1995:587): "ohl" 'coeur'; "-lu' " 'bagre'; /lu/; Knorozov (1999, vol. 1:161): /lu/ (pescado).

ZUH

T 0017
Z 0024, 1344
K 0164

yi

Occurs as verbal suffix with MRB "tzúutz/tzutz" 'finish; complete' on Dresden 60b. Graphically similar to ZUJ. Some of the notes below apply to both ZUH and ZUJ.

1. Picture: shell?

1566–1915 Rosny (1876): "ya" 'plaie, blessure' or "yax" 'premier, origine'; Rosny (1883:19): "yax" 'organe mâle; origine, virilité, premier'; Thomas (1893:250, 269): /y/; "yax" 'new; first'.

1916–1950 Gates (1931:96): "yax" 'green; new'.

1951–1980 Kelley (1976:122, 155, 203, 331): = T0016; in snake glyger; Knorozov (1967:93): /h(o)/; "yax" 'green; new'; Thompson (1962:40f.): "Yax."

1981–1990 V. Bricker (1986:115, 120–22): "yax" 'green/blue; first'; Grube (1990a:87): = T0018, T0575, T0814; Justeson (1984:317): consensus = T0016, T0575, only B. Riese uncertain on = T0018; Schele (1987d): /yi/; Stuart (1987:25–28): /yi/; T0017a and T0017b early and late forms, respectively, of the same sign; not variants of the "yax" logograph.

1991–2008 Davoust (1995:554): "yih" 'épi de maïs'; /yi/; Ringle and Smith-Stark (1996:335–38): 0017 = 0017a, b; Stuart (1997:5–8): /yi/.

ZUJ

T 0017
Z 0024, 1344
K 0164

yáax; yá'ax / yäx

adv; adj — first; green, blue

Yu *yáax; yá'ax* — yax 'en composición de nombres, cosa primera, la primera vez'; ya'x 'verde; azul' (Barrera Vásquez et al. 1980:971); yáax 'first, prior' (V. Bricker et al. 1998:312); yá'ax 'green; tender' (V. Bricker et al. 1998:312)

Ch' *ø; yäx* — *yäx 'green' (Kaufman and Norman 1984:137)

Some examples may be ZUH. Some of the notes below apply to both ZUH and ZUJ.

1. Picture: shell?

1566–1915 Bowditch (1910:255, 257): "yax" 'vigorous, fresh, green'; /xa/; may be masculine sign "ah"; Brasseur de Bourbourg (1869–1870, vol. 1:205): "yax" 'frais, neuf, robuste, rejeton vigoureux'; Brinton (1895:94f.): common feather decoration made of short green or blue feathers, attached to a style or staff; called "yax kukul" from which rebus value of sign derived—"yax" for 'green' and metaphorically 'new, young, fresh, strong, virile, etc.'; Landa [1566] (Tozzer 1941:158, 161): in glyph for month Yax; Rosny (1876): "ya" 'plaie, blessure' or "yax" 'premier, origine'; Rosny (1883:19): "yax" 'organe mâle; origine, virilité, premier'; Seler (1888): "yax" 'green, blue'; 'new, original'; Thomas (1893:250, 269): /y'/; "yax" 'new; first'.

1916–1950 Gates (1931:96f.): "yax" 'green; new'; with G325, "nohol" 'south'.

1951–1980 Kelley (1962a:281): "yax" in month Yax; Kelley (1976:122, 155, 203, 331): (= T0016) "yax" 'blue, green, new'; in snake glyger; Knorozov (1955:69): 055 (tallo) /hal/, "yax" 'verde'; Knorozov (1967:93): /h(o)/; "yax" 'green' (stalk with leaves); Thompson (1962:40–41): "Yax."

1981–1990 V. Bricker (1986:115, 120–22, 208): "yax" 'blue, green' (Cholan, Yucatecan); 'first' (Yucatecan); Grube (1990a:87): T0016 = T0017a, T0265; T0017 = T0018, T0575, T0814; Justeson (1984:317): T0016: J. Fox, J. Justeson, L. Schele, D. Stuart: *ya'x, 'green, new', and with derived meanings 'first', etc., apparently known only from Yucatecan; F. Lounsbury, P. Mathews, L. Schele: "yax"; B. Riese: phonetic /yax/ and semantic 'new, green, first'; L. Schele, D. Stuart: meaning 'first' is documented at Palenque; T0017: consensus = T0016, T0575, only B. Riese uncertain on = T0018; Love (1986:276f.): "noh" 'great'; Stuart (1985c:1): T0016: "yax."

1991–2008 Davoust (1995:554): T0016: "yax/yäx" 'vert, nouveau'; Knorozov (1999, vol. 1:95): /ho/, "yax"; para distinquir su uso fonético (/ho/) del morfémico ("yax") se emplea un signo diacrítico; Lacadena (1997b): adverbial function as 'for the first time'; Love (1991:299–301): "noh" 'great'; Ringle and Smith-Stark (1996:335–38): codical variant = 0017b; Vail (1996:354): appears to represent a seed in some contexts.

ZUJ

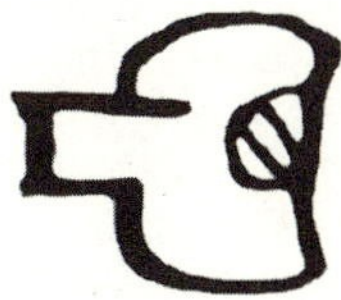

T 0275
Z —
K —

yáax; yá'ax / yäx

adv; adj — first; green, blue

2. Picture: shell?

1916–1950 Gates (1931:136): prefix to G302.14b.

1981–1990 Grube (1990a:100): = T0016.

1991–2008 Davoust (1995:574): "yax" 'vert, nouveau'; /yi/?; Knorozov (1999, vol. 1:95): /ho/, "yax" (tallo con hojas); para distinguir su uso fonético (/ho/) del morfémico ("yax"), se emplea un signo diacrítico; Ringle and Smith-Stark (1996:335–38): 0275 = 0017bv; Vail (2002b): "yax" 'first, green'.

ZUK

T –
Z –
K –

nohol?

n? south
Yu *nohol* 'nohol' south (V. Bricker et al. 1998:199)

1. Picture: "shell" with "ma" sign and loops

1566–1915 Bowditch (1910:256f.): placement on M. 75-76 suggests refers to the north ("xaman") rather than to the south; "yax" glyph gives /xa/ value and upper element is /ma/; Brasseur de Bourbourg (1869–1870, vol. 1:203): "ku, kúu" 'nid d'oiseau; gîte; saint, divin, Dieu'; Rosny (1883:18, 26): "mayam" ou "nohol" 'sud'; "maya" 'nom antique du Yucatan; le pays du midi et du centre de la terre'.

1916–1950 Gates (1931:96f.): "nohol" 'south'.

1951–1980 Kelley (1962b:26): 'south' (L. de Rosny et al.), Yucatec "nohol"; Thompson (1972:37): 'south'.

1981–1990 V. Bricker (1983:351f.): T0074 phonetic complement /ma/ to main sign "mal" 'nadir'; Fox and Justeson (1984:45): Yucatec "nohol," probably from "noh" 'great' + "-ol."

1991–2008 V. Bricker and H. Bricker (1992:fig. 2.8): "mal" 'nadir'; Davoust (1997:113): "nohol" 'sud'; Lamb (2005:164): "maj jool" 'large hole', perhaps a reference to the underworld; Love (1991:301): may be a fossilized convention with the reading "nohol" 'south'; Ringle and Smith-Stark (1996:339): the use of 0017b in the glyph for south in the codices makes it clear that it could function as other T0017 glyphs; Schele and Grube (1997:232): "nohol" 'south'; Stuart (2002a): "noh"? 'right'; von Nagy (1997:40): "nohol" 'south'.

ZUK

T –
Z –
K –

nohol?

n? south

References not differentiated from ZUK, subsort 1.

2. Picture: "shell" with "ma" sign

1566–1915 Bowditch (1910:256f.): placement on M. 75-76 suggests refers to the north ("xaman") rather than to the south; "yax" glyph gives /xa/ value and upper element is /ma/; Brasseur de Bourbourg (1869–1870, vol. 1:203): "ku, kúu" 'nid d'oiseau; gîte; saint, divin, Dieu'; Rosny (1883:18, 26): "mayam" ou "nohol" 'sud'; "maya" 'nom antique du Yucatan; le pays du midi et du centre de la terre'.

1916–1950 Gates (1931:96f.): "nohol" 'south'.

1951–1980 Kelley (1962b:26): 'south' (L. de Rosny et al.), Yucatec "nohol"; Thompson (1972:37): 'south'.

1981–1990 V. Bricker (1983:351f.): T0074 phonetic complement /ma/ to main sign "mal" 'nadir'; Fox and Justeson (1984:45): Yucatec "nohol," probably from "noh" 'great' + "-ol."

1991–2008 V. Bricker and H. Bricker (1992:fig. 2.8): "mal" 'nadir'; Davoust (1997:113): "nohol" 'sud'; Lamb (2005:164): "maj jool" 'large hole', perhaps a reference to the underworld; Love (1991:301): may be a fossilized convention with the reading "nohol" 'south'; Ringle and Smith-Stark (1996:339): the use of 0017b in the glyph for south in the codices makes it clear that it could function as other T0017 glyphs; Schele and Grube (1997:232): "nohol" 'south'; Stuart (2002a): "noh"? 'right'; von Nagy (1997:40): "nohol" 'south'.

ZUQ

T 0577
Z 1311
K 0134

n rubber

1. Picture: rubber ball offering?

1566–1915 Brasseur de Bourbourg (1869–1870, vol. 1:214): "butz' " 'fumée'; Brinton (1895:23): represents union.

1951–1980 Knorozov (1967:89): "ol"; Lounsbury (1973:113): 'rubber'; Thompson (1962:203f.): [11 examples] (spiral) associations with water and pottery vessels, including a drum; Thompson (1972:99): 'water'; may also refer to stored rain water.

1981–1990 Justeson (1984:345): F. Lounsbury, P. Mathews, B. Riese: offering of rolls of coagulated rubber; B. Riese: sometimes also "pom" 'copal'.

1991–2008 Davoust (1995:588): "kik" 'sang, balle de caoutchouc'; Eberl and V. Bricker (2004:36): coiled rubber ball; pictured framed by a stylized ballcourt on Dresden 41a; Knorozov (1999, vol. 1:162): "ul, hul" (voluta de caracol); Schele and Grube (1997:234): "k'ik' " 'rubber offerings'; Stone (2002): spiral representing rubber ball in Postclassic codices; most frequently pictured as burnt offering but on occasion represents a gaming ball.

ZUR

T 0797
Z —
K —

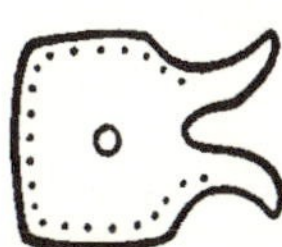

1. Picture: ?

1951–1980 Thompson (1962:379): [2 examples] probably a fish tail.

1991–2008 Davoust (1995:606): "cay" 'poisson'; /ca/.

ZUS

T —
Z —
K —

Sole example occurs with "pawah" prefix.

1. Picture: cartouche with "ka" sign infix

ZV1

T 0182
Z —
K —

1. Picture: inverted vase with "k'in" sign infix

1981–1990 Justeson (1984:329): cf. T0292; J. Justeson, P. Mathews: inverted pot with T0544 "k'in" infix; sometimes with T0552, crossed bands infix; L. Schele: inverted vase; possibly "mal" (see T1001); MacLeod (1990b:338): associated with /ho-ya/, possibly "ho(o)y" 'pour, sprinkle liquid'.

1991–2008 Davoust (1995:566): "hoy" 'verser, répandre, compagne'; Schele and Grube (1997:173): "huy" 'companion'.

ZV6

T 0686b
Z –
K 0331

1. Picture: vase

1916–1950 Gates (1931:165): jar.

1951–1980 Knorozov (1967:101): "xam"; Thompson (1962:291): [17 examples] (pottery vessel).

1981–1990 Justeson (1984:351): J. Fox, J. Justeson, P. Mathews, B. Riese: depicts various pots; use of some is equivalent to T0513, root "*mul" and/or derived forms; F. Lounsbury: Yucatec "xamach"; rim of pot is /sam/, a glyphic prefix without its own transcription number in Thompson's (1962) catalog.

1991–2008 Davoust (1995:596): "cum" 'marmite'; Davoust (1999, vol. 1:175): "xam"; Knorozov (1999, vol. 1:175): "xam" (vasija).

ZV7

T –
Z –
K 0332

1. Picture: vase with "ha' " 'water' sign infix

1951–1980 Knorozov (1967:101): composite grapheme K331-179.

1991–2008 Knorozov (1999, vol. 1:175): "xam" (vasija); tiene los grafemas 574 "in" y 169 /nga/ inscritos.

ZV8

T –
Z –
K –

The "feet" may be the affix 33F /hi/.
1. Picture: vessel with "ahaw" sign

ZVA

T –
Z –
K –

yum k'ak'?

n incensario

Yu *yum k'ak'?* yum k'ak' 'incensario' (Barrera Vásquez et al. 1980:983)

Only example includes 32D /yu/ and 1S3 /ne/ as possible phonetic complements for "yum" ("yun" in some dialects); in Yucatec "yum k'ak' " 'incensario' (Barrera Vásquez et al. 1980:983).

1. Picture: incensario

1566–1915 Brinton (1895:93): drum.

1991–2008 Vail (2002b): 'incensario'.

ZVC

T 0546
Z —
K —

1. Picture: plate with "k'in" sign infix

1916–1950 Gates (1931:68): "kin" 'sun, day'.
1951–1980 Thompson (1962:160f.): [17 examples] (kin variant); Thompson (1972:87): 'sun'.
1981–1990 V. Bricker (1983:348f.): "lak" in "lak'in" 'east'; V. Bricker (1986:211): "lak"?; Grube (1990a:107): = T0183; Justeson (1984:342): J. Fox, P. Mathews, B. Riese: in 'east' glyph; forehead of Quadripartite God; J. Justeson, P. Mathews, L. Schele: "la'," "lak," or "lak' "; shallow bowl or deep plate (proto-Mayan "*laq"); F. Lounsbury: "lak'in" 'east'.
1991–2008 Davoust (1995:585): "lac" 'plat'; Knorozov (1999, vol. 1:147): "king."

ZVD

T 0836
Z —
K —

Grapheme includes a bowl or container with a /na/ infix.
1. Picture: plate with flint and obsidian bloodletters

1951–1980 Thompson (1962:390): [1 example].

ZVH

T 0686c
Z —
K —

n drum?
1. Picture: drum?

1566–1915 Brinton (1895:93): medicine drum, played in sacred ceremonies.
1951–1980 Thompson (1962:291): [17 examples] (drum).
1981–1990 Justeson (1984:351): J. Fox, P. Mathews, B. Riese: depicts ceramic drum.
1991–2008 Davoust (1995:596): "tun" 'tambour'; Knorozov (1999, vol. 1:1175): "pax" (tambor forrado de piel).

ZX7

T 0809
Z —
K —

1. Picture: darkened cartouche with two "k'in" signs

1951–1980 Thompson (1962:383): [1 example].
1991–2008 Closs (1992:142): 'the sun is darkened'? (possible solar eclipse reference); see Treiber (1987:68); Knorozov (1999, vol. 1:180): 'king'?

ZX8

T –
Z –
K 0371

n rattle?; fan?

1. Picture: rattle?; fan?

1566–1915 Brasseur de Bourbourg (1869–1870, vol. 1:216): "nen" 'mirror'; Brinton (1895:103f.): medicine rattle; Rosny (1883:22): 'miroir'? (attributed to Brasseur de Bourbourg); 'roue du calendrier'? (attributed to Thomas).

1951–1980 Knorozov (1967:103): morphemic (rattle).

1991–2008 Knorozov (1999, vol. 1:176): "zoot" (zonaja); Vail (2002b): fan or rattle.

ZX9

T –
Z –
K –

1. Picture: ?

ZXA

T 0835
Z –
K –

1. Picture: ?

1951–1980 Thompson (1962:390): [1 example] similar elements in Mexican art suggest this may represent rain.

1991–2008 Knorozov (1999, vol. 1:90): "ngal" (elote envuelto en hojas).

ZXB

T –
Z –
K 0081

1. Picture: ?

1566–1915 Brasseur de Bourbourg (1869–1870, vol. 1:203): "l, lé" 'lacet, sorte de lac ou de fronde armée d'une pierre'.

1951–1980 Knorozov (1967:85): 'bloodletting' (ear pierced for ritual bloodletting).

1991–2008 Knorozov (1999, vol. 1:98): (oreja atravesada por una aguja).

ZY4

T 0806
Z 1363c
K 0290

1. Picture: ?

1566–1915 Brasseur de Bourbourg (1869–1870, vol. 1:208): day Ik; "ik" 'esprit, souffle, vent'.

1951–1980 Knorozov (1967:99): (= K289) "moh" 'incense burner'; Thompson (1962:382): [2 examples]; Thompson (1972:77): has eye markings of T1055, a deity associated with the Venus and lunar tables.

1991–2008 Davoust (1995:606): /chu/; Knorozov (1999, vol. 1:158): (cabeza de animal) tiene el grafema 33 "tooc" inscrito.

ZY5

T 0614
Z 1306a
K 0148

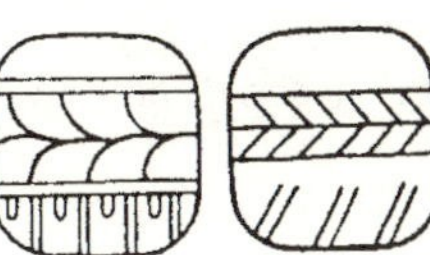

otoch / otot

n — house; dwelling

Yu *otoch* — yotoch 'casa, habitación, domicilio' (Barrera Vásquez et al. 1980:980); 'otoch 'home' (V. Bricker et al. 1998:19)

Ch' *otot* — *otot 'house' (Kaufman and Norman 1984:127)

1. Picture: house platform and roof

1566–1915 Brasseur de Bourbourg (1869–1870, vol. 1:207): day Been; "ben" or "be-en" 'voie, chemin, marche ouverte peu à peu, détruite ou descendue au fond'; Seler [1887] (1990:99): throne overshadowed by a mat roof; Thomas (1888:351): "otoch" 'house'; Thomas (1893:267): "otoch" 'house'.

1951–1980 Kelley (1962b:24): thatching; thatched canopy (D. Brinton); "otoch" 'house' (Y. Knorozov); Kelley (1976:133, 333): canopy or house? "otoch"?; Knorozov (1955:70): 073 (casa, techo de hojas, puntales) "otoch" ("ot"?) 'casa'; Knorozov (1967:91): "ot" 'house'; compare to Old Yucatec "otoch"; Thompson (1962:236f.): [79 examples] (thatch); Thompson (1972:93, 95): 'mat'; the jaguar skin trimming of T0614 rules out a thatch interpretation.

1981–1990 V. Bricker (1986:212): "otot" 'house' (Ch'olan); "otoch" 'house' (Yucatecan); Closs (1987): "otoch/otot" 'house'; Grube (1990a:110): = T0242; Justeson (1984:348): L. Campbell: 'house'; "otot" or "otoch" specified by /ta/ or /cho/ complement; J. Justeson: 'house', always "*oto:t" (Ch'ol and pre-proto-Yucatecan) in monuments; F. Lounsbury: iconographic 'house'; inscribed form with T0059, Ch'ol "otot"; P. Mathews: "otoch" (or cognate specified by complements); B. Riese: 'house'; L. Schele, D. Stuart: "otoch" 'house' (/chu/ and /ti/ are complements to indicate "otoch" or "otot"). T0614b: J. Fox, J. Justeson, P. Mathews, F. Lounsbury, L. Schele: probably = T0614a; Schele (1989c:39): /to/ or /ta/; Stuart (1987:33–41): T0115 /yo/ complement signals initial "o" of "otoch/otot" 'house'. Various syllabic spellings of "yo-to-t(i)" for "yotot" at Chichén Itzá and Palenque.

1991–2008 Davoust (1995:590): "otot/tana, otoch" 'maison'; "cab" 'terre'; /ta/; Knorozov (1999, vol. 1:128): "ot" (casa cubierta con un techo de hojas de palma); Stuart (1998:377f.): "otot" 'home, dwelling'. In previous discussions, the lower platform element has been mistaken as a separate phonetic sign.

ZY5

T 0192ab
Z –
K 0178

otoch / otot

n house; dwelling

2. Picture: thatched roof

1566–1915 Brasseur de Bourbourg (1869–1870, vol. 1:212): "pop" ou "poop" 'natte, terre marécageuse crevassée par la chaleur'; Brinton (1895:96): 'canopy'; Thomas (1893:264f.): symbol of a dwelling.

1916–1950 Gates (1931:165): web.

1951–1980 Kelley (1976:133f., 332): "pop" 'mat, thatch'?; Knorozov (1955:70): 076 (techo de hojas) /h(a)/; Knorozov (1967:94): /x(a)/ (mat or roof of the leaves of the "xaan" palm); Thompson (1962:59): [3 examples]; Thompson (1972:77): "pop" 'mat'.

1981–1990 Justeson (1984:330): L. Campbell, J. Fox, J. Justeson, B. Riese: logographic 'house'; depicts thatch; F. Lounsbury: "otoch" or cognate, 'house, temple' (denoting whose); abridged form of T0614; P. Mathews, L. Schele: thatch; logographic 'house'; some examples perhaps to be read "otoch" (or cognate form); Schele (1989c:39): /to/ or /ta/.

1991–2008 Davoust (1995:567): "otoch/otot" 'maison', "pop" 'natte'; /o/; Davoust (1997:206): /po/, "pop" 'natte'; Knorozov (1999, vol. 1:150): "ax" (techo de hojas de palmo o tejido de petate); Ringle and Smith-Stark (1996:335–38): 0192 (retired) = 0614A.

ZY9

T 0601v
Z 1363
K 0286

chu

1. Picture: ? with "te' " sign

1566–1915 Seler [1892] (1902–23, vol. 1:562): carrying a load on the back, "cuch"; Thomas (1893:267f.): "pak (pakal)" 'building; wall; fortification'; "pacac (paccah)" 'fasten, bind'; /p'c/, /p'k/.

1916–1950 Gates (1931:135f.): When attached to the "cauac" or the mat or roof element, associated with binding, or carrying away bound, or with the product of that action, of binding.

1951–1980 Kelley (1962a:281, 284): /chu/; Kelley (1962b:24): carrying device (H. Beyer, Y. Knorozov, D. Kelley); "cuch" 'burden' (J. E. S. Thompson, T. Barthel); /chu/ (Y. Knorozov, D. Kelley); Kelley (1976:131–33, 152, 176, 333): (carrying device) /chu/; in "cuch" 'burden'; same as T0512; Knorozov (1955:71): 083 (accesoria para transporte de pesos) /ch(u)/; Knorozov (1967:99): /ch(u)/ (foot in a sandal); Thompson (1962:225f.): [71 examples] "cuch" 'burden', 'office', 'charge', or 'prophecy'; Thompson (1972:39): "cuch" 'destiny' or 'burden'.

1981–1990 V. Bricker (1986:212): /chu/; Grube (1990a:110): = T0512; Justeson (1984:347): J. Justeson, J. Fox: a codex form of T0512/0515; /cho/, /chu/; with T0087, /chu/; F. Lounsbury: codex form of T0515; /cho/; with T0087, /chu/; L. Campbell, P. Mathews, B. Riese, L. Schele: /cho/, /chu/; "chu" with T0087.

1991–2008 Davoust (1995:589): "chuh" 'calebasse'; /chu/; Ringle and Smith-Stark (1996:335–38): 0601 (retired) = 0515d.

ZY9

T 0601
Z 1363
K 0281

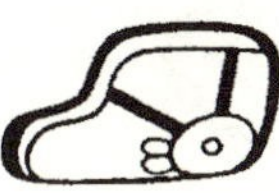

chu

2. Picture: ?

1566–1915 Brasseur de Bourbourg (1869–1870, vol. 1:203): "p, pe" 'venir, marcher' ant. "pa" 'ouvrir'; Seler [1892] (1902–23, vol. 1:562): carrying a load on the back, "cuch"; Thomas (1893:267f.): "pak (pakal)" 'building; wall; fortification'; "pacac (paccah)" 'fasten, bind'; /p'c/, /p'k/.

1916–1950 Gates (1931:135f.): When attached to the "cauac" or the mat or roof element, associated with binding, or carrying away bound, or with the product of that action, of binding.

1951–1980 Kelley (1962a:281, 284): /chu/; Kelley (1962b:24): carrying device (H. Beyer, Y. Knorozov, D. Kelley); "cuch" 'burden' (J. E. S. Thompson, T. Barthel); /chu/ (Y. Knorozov, D. Kelley); Kelley (1976:131–33, 152, 176, 333): (carrying device) /chu/; in "cuch" 'burden'; same as T0512; Knorozov (1967:99): (= K286) /ch(u)/; Thompson (1962:225f.): [71 examples] "cuch" 'burden', 'office', 'charge', or 'prophecy'; Thompson (1972:91): "cuch" 'burden'.

1981–1990 V. Bricker (1986:212): /chu/; Grube (1990a:110): = T0512; Justeson (1984:347): J. Justeson, J. Fox: a codex form of T0512/0515; /cho/, /chu/; with T0087, /chu/; F. Lounsbury: codex form of T0515; /cho/; with T0087, /chu/; L. Campbell, P. Mathews, B. Riese, L. Schele: /cho/, /chu/; "chu" with T0087.

1991–2008 Davoust (1995:589): "chuh" 'calebasse'; /chu/; Knorozov (1999, vol. 1:171): /chuu/, /chu/ (pie en sandalia); Ringle and Smith-Stark (1996:335–38): 0601 (retired) = 0515d.

ZY9

T 0857
Z 1363a
K 0282

chu

3. Picture: ? with "te' " sign

1566–1915 Thomas (1893:260): /ch'/, probably /ch'o/ or /ch'u/.

1916–1950 Gates (1931:128): weaving glyph.

1951–1980 Kelley (1962a:306–8): /po/; Kelley (1962b:40): (variant with T0087) making a mat or net with a needle (C. Thomas, T. Barthel, D. Kelley); "chuyah" 'sewing' (C. Thomas); cf. Pokomam "poh" 'sew' (D. Kelley); Kelley (1976:182): /po/?; Knorozov (1955:65): 002 (cabeza con signo complementario 058) /p(oo)/; Knorozov (1967:99): (= K287) phonetic; Thompson (1962:115–17): [88 examples] (Muluc burden) compare to T0512, T0515, and T0614; Thompson (1972:33): mistakenly included with T0515 in Thompson (1962); assigned new number, T0857.

1981–1990 Fox and Justeson (1984:64–67): /chu/ value most common but appears to read /tu/ on Madrid 80b-81b; Justeson (1984:359): new number introduced by Thompson (1972:33); J. Fox, J. Justeson: /tu/, /chu/; polyvalent in Yucatec; = T0515 with eye infixed.

1991–2008 Davoust (1995:609): "chuh" 'calebasse'; hut 'oeil'; /chu/, /tu/; Ringle and Smith-Stark (1996:335–38): 0857 (retired) = 0515f.

ZY9

T 0857v
Z 1363a
K –

chu?

Possibly a distinct grapheme.

4. Picture: ? with "te' " sign

ZYC

T 0712
Z –
K –

intr v? let blood?

Graphically similar to MZQ, but the two occur in different contexts. Some of the references below may apply to MZQ.

1. Picture: bloodletter, perforator

1566–1915 Brasseur de Bourbourg (1869–1870, vol. 1:206): day Cimi; "cimi" 'il est mort' or "ci-mi" 'non effervescence plus' or "cim-i" 'qui a pris une pointe, une pousse'.

1951–1980 Kelley (1976:144, 333): tongue piercing; "lom"? 'pierce'; Thompson (1962:302f.): [46 examples] (pseudo inverted fist).

1981–1990 V. Bricker (1986:213): "ni" 'nose, tip, point' (Ch'olan, Yucatecan); Dütting (1985:112): epigraphic counterpart of paleographic T0667; Grube (1990a:115): = T0667; Josserand et al. (1985): with T0059 "ti" 'bloodletting', from obsidian bloodletter, 'lancet'; Justeson (1984:353): J. Fox, J. Justeson: possibly "*a:k' " 'tongue' in bloodletting passages, or contextually coreferential noun; possibly bloodletter; P. Mathews, B. Riese, L. Schele, D. Stuart: probably = T0667; obsidian lancet; 'to let blood'; MacLeod (1988a): variable infixes may indicate material of T0712 bloodletter (obsidian, shell, etc.). Represents 'blood(lines)' in parentage statement, or 'he perforates his tongue/he lets blood'; Schele (1982:31): bloodletter; Stross and Kerr (1990:352–54): a male genital shaped enema (gourd) clyster or bag, rather than an obsidian bloodletter; associated with vision questing through hallucinogenic enemas, rather than bloodletting.

1991–2008 Davoust (1995:597): "ch'am" 'moissonner'; "ch'ab" 'pénitence, créateur'; Houston et al. (2006:130f.): "ch'ahb" 'fast', may also relate to "a K'iche'an expression for penitence and, ultimately, to acts of creation and renewal (Allen Christenson, personal communication, 2003)"; Knorozov (1999, vol. 1:168): "yal" (puño volteado hacia abajo); MacLeod (1991j): "ch'ab" 'fast, abstain; be chaste'; 'create'; Schele (1992b:42): "ch'am" 'harvest'; Stuart (1995:231): credits Houston and MacLeod with independent decipherment as "ch'ab."

ZYD

T 0653v
Z –
K 0373

hul / jul

trans v pierce

Yu *hul* hul kamas 'hacer camas [tejerlas]' (Barrera Vásquez et al. 1980:242); hul 'pasar una cosa delgada o puntaguida a través de otra u otras' (Barrera Vásquez et al. 1980:242); hul 'focus; light; thrust, thread/needle, plunge' (V. Bricker et al. 1998:115); h[rezia]ul 'tirar la flecha'; h[rezia]ul kuch ti yit putz' 'enhilar la aguja' (Martínez Hernández 1929:194v)

Ch' *jul* *jul 'shoot with arrow or blowgun pellet' (Kaufman and Norman 1984:122)

Conflation of T0653 and T0568 /lu/.

1. Picture: pierced "lu" sign

1916–1950 Gates (1931:156f.): [examples also include T0568 /lu/] occurs in the codices, associated with plants growing, the eclipse ephemeris, and the Venus pages.

1951–1980 Knorozov (1967:103): "h'ul" 'to pierce' (K372 with an additional element representing a needle); Thompson (1972:67): 'sacrifice' or 'victim'?

1981–1990 Justeson (1984:349): J. Justeson, P. Mathews, B. Riese: "*jul" 'to pierce'; F. Lounsbury: iconogram 'pierce'; with T0568 phonetic complement, "hul"; L. Schele: possibly "hul" 'pierce, spear'.

1991–2008 Davoust (1997:181): "hul" 'transpercer'; Knorozov (1999, vol. 1:161): "h'ul"; Schele and Grube (1997:148): "hul" 'to spear'.

ZYE

T –
Z 0755
K 0270

1. Picture: ?

1916–1950 Gates (1931:164): G407 [in part].
1951–1980 Knorozov (1967:98): (= K268) phonetic; Thompson (1962:402): Z755 = T0078.
1991–2008 Davoust (1997:253): = 0077EP "xik."

ZYF

T –
Z –
K –

1. Picture: ?

ZZD

T –
Z –
K –

1. Picture: ?

ZZE

T –
Z –
K –

1. Picture: ?

ZZF

T –
Z –
K 0385

1. Picture: fish?

1951–1980 Knorozov (1967:103): morphemic (animal); Thompson (1972:104): leg of deer or fish?
1991–2008 Davoust (1997:307): = T0608? "ach"?; 'le viril'?

00 & Numeral

001

T 0144c
Z I
K 0012

hun / jun

num — one

Yu *hun* — hun 'uno' (Barrera Vásquez et al. 1980:245); h[rezia]un 'número de uno' (Martínez Hernández 1929:195); hun 'one' (V. Bricker et al. 1998:115)

Ch' *jun* — *jun 'one' (Kaufman and Norman 1984:137)

number 01

1. Picture: dot and fillers

1566–1915 Bowditch (1910:246): 'one'; Codex Pérez [ca. 1793] (Craine and Reindorp 1979:92): 'one'.

1951–1980 Knorozov (1967:78): 'one'.

1981–1990 Justeson (1984:326): F. Lounsbury, L. Schele, D. Stuart: some may be numerical 'one' and 'two'.

1991–2008 Davoust (1995:564): "hun" 'un'; Knorozov (1999, vol. 1:69, 235): "h'un" 'uno; unico, completo; común'.

002

T 0144abd
Z –
K 0013

ká'ah / cha'

num — two

Yu *ká'ah* — ka' 'dos' (Barrera Vásquez et al. 1980:277); ká'ah 'two' (V. Bricker et al. 1998:120); kaa 'otra vez' (Barrera Vásquez et al. 1980:277); ká'ah máal 'twice', ká'ah-'á'al 'repeat' (V. Bricker et al. 1998:120f.); ka' 'again, repetitive adverb' (Hofling with Tesucún 1997:338)

Ch' *cha'* — *cha' 'two' (Kaufman and Norman 1984:137); cha' 'otra vez' (Aulie and Aulie 1998:30)

number 02

1. Picture: two dots and filler

1566–1915 Bowditch (1910:246): 'two'; Codex Perez [ca. 1793] (Craine and Reindorp 1979:92): 'two'; Thomas (1893:247): probably a determinative indicating something that may be counted.

1951–1980 Knorozov (1955:75): 136 "ca" 'dos', /ca/; Knorozov (1967:78): 'two'.

1981–1990 Justeson (1984:326): F. Lounsbury, L. Schele, D. Stuart: some may be numerical 'one' and 'two'.

1991–2008 Davoust (1995:564): "ca' " 'deux'; Knorozov (1999, vol. 1:89): "ca" 'dos'; Lacadena (1997b): "cha'/ka' " 'two'; 'again'.

003

T III
Z III
K –

óox / ux

num; adv three; abundance
Yu *óox* ox 'three; abundance' (Barrera Vásquez et al. 1980:298)
Ch' *ux* *ux 'three' (Kaufman and Norman 1984:137)
number 03
1. Picture: three circles

1951–1980 Knorozov (1955:75): 135 "ox" 'tres'; Thompson (1971:129): has "intensificatory value" that adds emphasis to a phrase.

1981–1990 V. Bricker (1986:123f.): "ox" 'three'; used in expression TIII.0567:0130 "oxow" 'sultry'.

1991–2008 Knorozov (1999, vol. 1:78): "ox" 'tres'; Schele and Grube (1997:85): numeral prefix "ox" is used in Yucatec for 'abundance'.

004

T IV
Z IV
K –

kan / chän; ká'an / chan

num; n; adj four; sky
Yu *kan; ká'an* kan 'cuatro' (Barrera Vásquez et al. 1980:291); ka'anal 'cosa alta' (Barrera Vásquez et al. 1980:292); kan 'four' (V. Bricker et al. 1998:122); ká'an 'sky, height' (V. Bricker et al. 1998:123); ká'anhá'an 'haughty' (V. Bricker et al. 1998:123); ka'an 'cielo' (Barrera Vásquez et al. 1980:291); kän- 'four' (Hofling with Tesucún 1997:342)
Ch' *chän; chan* *chän 'four' (Kaufman and Norman 1984:137); *chan 'sky' (Kaufman and Norman 1984:117), chan 'alto' (Aulie and Aulie 1998:29)
number 04
1. Picture: four circles

1566–1915 Codex Pérez [ca. 1793] (Craine and Reindorp 1979:92): 'four'.

1951–1980 Thompson (1972:69): "can" 'four' may be rebus for "can" 'fierce'; Thompson (1972:100): represents the sun god on D. 40b. As a rule, it is the other way round, the head of the sun god or the "kin" glyph standing for the number four.

1981–1990 Houston (1984): occurs in substitution sets with "ka'an" 'sky' and "kan" 'snake'; substitutes for 'snake' glyph in the captive/guardian expression; MacLeod (1990b:337): the five prefixed to the name of the codical God N may signal that this Pawahtun is Hobnil; perhaps the four prefix on other examples cues Can-Sicnal, the east Pawahtun.

1991–2008 V. Bricker (1991:289): prefixes T1038b on D. 28b; "can" 'four'; could have served as a phonetic complement for T1038a indicating the "can" allomorph of "cam" 'death'; Knorozov (1999, vol. 1:88): "cang" 'cuatro'; Vail (2003): rebus for "ká'an" 'sky' in codices; used with T0085 to form "ká'anal" 'celestial'.

009

T IX
Z IX
K –

b'olon

num nine; many
Yu *b'olon* bolon 'nueve' (Barrera Vásquez et al. 1980:63); bolonk'ak' 'muchos fuegos' (Barrera Vásquez et al. 1980:63); b'olon 'nine' (V. Bricker et al. 1998:35)
Ch' *b'olon* *b'olon 'nine' (Kaufman and Norman 1984:138)
number 09
1. Picture: bar, circles

1566–1915 Codex Pérez [ca. 1793] (Craine and Reindorp 1979:92): 'nine'.

1951–1980 Thompson (1972:106): "bolon" 'virgin'.

1991–2008 Knorozov (1999, vol. 1:91): "bolon" 'nueve'.

010

T X
Z X
K —

lahun / läjun; lah? / laj?

num; intr v? ten; terminate?

Yu *lahun; lah* lah 'acabar' (Barrera Vásquez et al. 1980:431); lahun 'diez' (Barrera Vásquez et al. 1980:432); lahun 'ten' (V. Bricker et al. 1998:162)

Ch' *läjun; laj* *läjun 'ten' (Kaufman and Norman 1984:138); *laj 'finish' (Kaufman and Norman 1984:124);

number 10

1. Picture: two bars

1566–1915 Codex Pérez [ca. 1793] (Craine and Reindorp 1979:92): 'ten'.

1991–2008 Knorozov (1999, vol. 1:70): "lah" 'diez'; Taube (1992:105): "lahun" 'ten'; "lah" 'completion'; accompanies portrait glyph of God Q; Vail (1998): occurs with 2S8 (subsort 3) as prefix to God Q's name glyph; may read "ah lahun" 'he who completes/terminates' or 'the terminator'.

1 One Segment

1B1

T 0096
Z 0071
K 0104

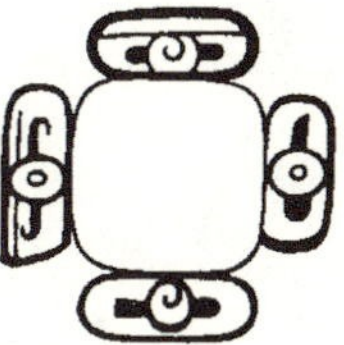

ta

tí' / ti, ta, tä

prep — in, at, etc.; preposition

Yu *tí'* — ti' 'preposición a, con, por instrumento, adentro' (Barrera Vásquez et al. 1980:788); tí' 'to, at, in, from, for' (V. Bricker et al. 1998:274)

Ch' *ti; ta; tä* — *tä 'preposition' (Kaufman and Norman 1984:139); ta 'for, belongs to' (Knowles 1984:461); tä 'to, from, by' (Knowles 1984:463); ti 'en, a, por, de' (Warkentin and Scott 1980:98); ti 'en' (Morán 1935:26); ti' 'beside, by the side; at the edge' (Knowles 1984:465)

1. Picture: torch?

1566–1915 Brasseur de Bourbourg (1869–1870, vol. 1:206): day Oc; "oc" 'pied, jambe, entrée, entrer'; Thomas (1893:296): "ah."

1951–1980 Cordan (1964:45): " 'ich," "chi" ("*sü") 'adentro'; Kelley (1976:72, 139, 191, 332): "yol," "ich"; Knorozov (1955:65): 006 (ojo) "ich"; Knorozov (1967:87): "ich" 'in' (eye); Thompson (1972:39): "ol."

1981–1990 V. Bricker (1986:6): /ta/; Grube (1990a:91): = T0103; Fox and Justeson (1984:47–48): "(w)ich" and /ta/; Justeson (1984:323): cf. T0103; L. Campbell: locative preposition; J. Fox, J. Justeson: "ich" 'in, within'; also = manuscript form of T0103 "ta"; F. Lounsbury, D. Stuart: locative preposition; /ta/; probably not "ich" or "yol;" P. Mathews: includes locative preposition, "ich" or "yol"; B. Riese: locative preposition; L. Schele: probably "yol," possibly "ich."

1991–2008 Davoust (1995:560): /ta/; Knorozov (1999, vol. 1:109): "ich" (ojo estilizado).

1B1

T 0103de
Z –
K –

ta

tí' / ti, ta, tä

prep — in, at, etc.; preposition

2. Picture: torch?

1566–1915 Thomas (1893:256): /h/.

1951–1980 Kelley (1976:69, 131, 200, 201, 202, 332): (bundle) "al"?; Schele (1979:11): "ta" locative.

1981–1990 V. Bricker (1986:6): /ta/; Fox and Justeson (1984:47–48): "(w)ich" and /ta/; Grube (1990a:91): = T0096, T0113, T0167; Justeson (1984:323): T0103b [consensus /ta/]; L. Schele, D. Stuart: locative preposition and phonetic /ta/.

1991–2008 Davoust (1995:561): "lac" 'plat'; /ta/; Grube (1994b:181): T0103 /ta/ invented after 9.11.0.0.0; Knorozov (1999, vol. 1:108): "ix" (taparrabo estilizado); Macri (1991): always /ta/; Ringle and Smith-Stark (1996:335–38): 0103 = 0102b (only Thompson's last example) = 0103 (others).

1B2

T 0102 (0103g)
Z 0061
K 0102

ki

ki'

adj tasty, delicious
Yu *ki'* ki' 'tasty, delicious'; kí'il 'meat, filling' (V. Bricker et al. 1998:127)
Ch' *chi'* *chi' 'sweet' (Kaufman and Norman 1984:118)

No specific evidence for the Ch'olan value. Equivalent to T0103g.

1. Picture: henequen bundle?

1566–1915 Brasseur de Bourbourg (1869–1870, vol. 1:202): "h, ah" 'canne, roseau; caractère du sexe masculin'; Brinton (1895:100): 'union', conjunctive conjunction "yetal" 'and'; Thomas (1893:256): Landa's /h/.

1916–1950 Gates (1932:202): "appears to mark the major gods as their distinctive? honorific"; also acts as "a sort of table for offerings in the pictures."

1951–1980 Cordan (1964:43): "tzik" 'fardo; respeto'; Dütting (1968): plural suffixes "-ob, -ab, -ib," and/or plural particle "-tak"; Fought (1965): "-al" when subfixed or postfixed to a main sign in the codices; Kelley (1962a:290, 296): "cimV"?; Kelley (1976:69, 131, 200, 201, 202, 332): (bundle; merchant's pack) "al"?; Knorozov (1955:76): 147 /n(-?)/, "h(e)"?; determinador "sacrificio," "fecundo"; Knorozov (1967:87): "-ih" (loincloth); Thompson (1972:54): "reverential postfix," associated with deity names.

1981–1990 V. Bricker (1986:209): /ci/; Fox and Justeson (1984:29–47): /ki/ and /VL/; "ki' " 'sweet, delicious' when used as base for food offerings; Justeson (1984:323): L. Campbell: possibly "ki," J. Fox, J. Justeson: "-Vl," not equivalent to T0002/0024/0082/0083, probably no specific vowel represented, probably harmonic with root; /ki/; F. Lounsbury: "al"; not "ki"; P. Mathews, L. Schele, D. Stuart: /ki/, "-al"; B. Riese: /ki/ and "al" depending on context; T0103a = Z61, codex form of T0102; Stuart (1985a): suffixed to T0501 in "count of captives" glyph, probably /ci/, in "bac," 'bone, captive'.

1991–2008 Davoust (1995:560): "ci' " 'agave', /ci/; Freidel et al. (1993:74): "ki" 'heart' on Palenque Tablet of the Cross; /ki/; Knorozov (1999, vol. 1:108): "ix" 'cinturón'; Ringle and Smith-Stark (1996:335–38): 0103 = 0102b (only Thompson's last example) = 0103 (others).

1B3

T 0724
Z 1314
K –

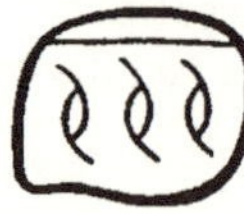

su

1. Picture: coiled rope

1951–1980 Thompson (1962:310): [1 example].

1991–2008 Davoust (1997:106): /za/; Prager (1997:37): /so/ or /su/.

1B4

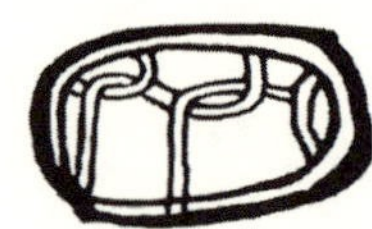

T 0725
Z 1377
K –

1. Picture: netting

1951–1980 Thompson (1962:310): [1 example].

1991–2008 Davoust (1995:598): "paw" 'filet'; Schele and Grube (1997:211): the sky umbilicus.

1B5

T 0060ae
Z 0058
K 0068

1. Picture: tied band

1566–1915 Thomas (1893:250): "tzil."

1951–1980 Cordan (1964:43): "hok" 'nudo'; Kelley (1976:118, 219, 331): knot; "tab"?; T0740 substitutes; Knorozov (1955:72): 102 (franja de tela, formando nudo) "zut"?; Knorozov (1967:83): "tul" (loincloth).

1981–1990 V. Bricker (1986:209): (T0060) /ta/, "ta"; Justeson (1984:320): J. Justeson: logographic, including "*jó:k' " 'to appear' (see T0684); L. Schele "pat," "pa"; = T0684 bundle; Schele, Mathews, and Lounsbury (1990b): substitution spellings for "hunal" 'headband'; Schele and J. Miller (1983:66): allograph for T0684 'topknot'; bundle implies "pat" 'taking possession of'.

1991–2008 Davoust (1995:557): "hok" 'noeud'; /ho/; Knorozov (1999, vol. 1:104, 239): "tul" 'rebozo; alrededor'; Ringle and Smith-Stark (1996:335–38): 0060 = 0060 (single stranded examples) = 0405 (multistranded examples); Schele (1991b:23–25): substitution spelling of "hu-na(-la)" for "hun(al)" 'headband'.

1B7

T 0145abc
Z 0046
K 0330

che

1. Picture: bundle

1566–1915 Brasseur de Bourbourg (1869–1870, vol. 1:204): "u" 'vase, bassin, surface circonscrite, lune'; Landa [1566] (Tozzer 1941:170): <h> written for Spanish "hache."

1916–1950 Thompson (1950:83f.): refers to weaving.

1951–1980 Dütting (1974:50): "hal"? 'weave; braid'; Kelley (1962a:290, 295): /che/; Kelley (1962b:30): /che/; Kelley (1976:179, 332): /che/?; Knorozov (1955:69): 056 (agave) /ch'(e)/, tal vez "ch'el"; Knorozov (1967:101): /ch(e)/ (agave); Thompson (1962:53): [6 examples] (hank of cloth) symbol of the old goddess, patroness of weaving in the codices.

1981–1990 V. Bricker (1986:210): (Landa's "h") /che/; Grube (1990a:94): = T0148; Justeson (1984:326): consensus /che/.

1991–2008 Davoust (1995:564): "che' " 'arbre'; /che/; Knorozov (1999, vol. 1:105): /te/, /che/; (agave estilizado); Ringle and Smith-Stark (1996:335–38): 0145 = 0145 (first antefix, superfix) = 0148 (postfix only) = 0017d (skein-like superfixes) = 0405 (skein-like subfix); Ringle and Smith-Stark (1996:342): Justeson et al. (in Justeson 1984) suggest that T0145 and T0148 may be equivalent. However, if Thompson's postfixed example of T0145 is reclassified as T0148v, which it more closely resembles, the two show different distribution in the codices.

1B9

T 0109
Z 0020
K 0106

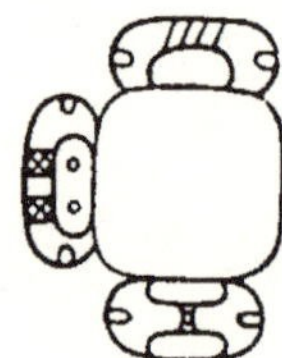

chak / chäk

adj — red; great, large

Yu *chak* — chak 'rojo, grande, fuerte, aguacero; cosa colorada; muy o mucho' (Barrera Vásquez et al. 1980:76); chak 'red, pink, orange, rust colored' (V. Bricker et al. 1998:59); chäk 'red' (Bruce 1979:137); chäk 'red' (Hofling with Tesucún 1997:194); chäk 'rojo' (Ulrich and Ulrich 1976:78)

Ch' *chäk* — *chäk 'red' (Kaufman and Norman 1984:117); chak 'great' (Wisdom 1950:690)

Some of Thompson's (1962:51) examples of the third superfix are T0570.

1. Picture: bone?

1566–1915 Brasseur de Bourbourg (1869–1870, vol. 1:202): "t, ti"; 'ici, dans, à, vers, pour, de, etc.', 'lieu, endroit désigné'; Brinton (1895:108): 'east'; Seler [1891] (1902–1923:31): "chac" 'red'; Thomas (1893:257): /k'/, /ke/, or "ek."

1916–1950 Gates (1931:93): "chac" 'red'.

1951–1980 Kelley (1962a:281, 295): in month glyph Ceh; "chac" 'rojo'; Kelley (1976:53–55, 179, 202, 203, 332): "chac" 'red', 'great'; or /ta/; Thompson readings include "yax"; Knorozov (1955:73): 115 (hoguera? /t(a)/); "chac" ("tac"?) 'rojo'; Knorozov (1967:87f.): "chak" 'red; big'; Thompson (1962:51): 'red'.

1981–1990 V. Bricker (1986:209): /chac/, "chac" 'red' (Yucatecan); Justeson (1984:324): L. Campbell: "chak" 'red'; J. Fox, J. Justeson: Yucatec, Cholan "*chak" 'red' or (Yucatec only) 'great'; F. Lounsbury: "chak"; P. Mathews, L. Schele, D. Stuart: "chak"; B. Riese: "chak" 'great', 'red'.

1991–2008 Davoust (1995:561): "chac/chäc" 'rouge, grand'; Knorozov (1999, vol. 1:109): "chac" (hoguera?).

1BA

T 0110
Z 0032
K 0105

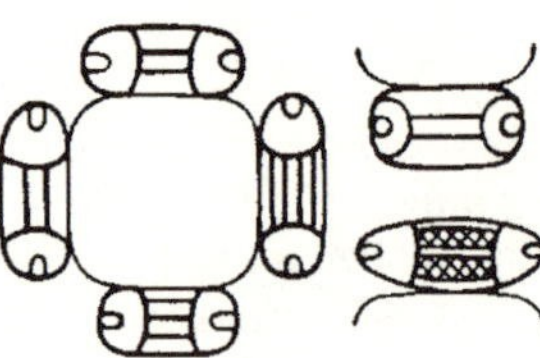

ko

1. Picture: bone?

1566–1915 Brinton (1895:88f.): flint knife.

1951–1980 Cordan (1964:29f.): "pak" 'cuchillo de pedernal'; Kelley (1976:148–50, 202, 332): long bone or flint knife?, /ta/?; with T0049, "toc"; variant of T0112; Knorozov (1955:71): 089 (lanceta de obsidiana) /t(a)/; Knorozov (1967:87): /t(u)/? (blowpipe?); Thompson (1962:51f.): (bone) "The example at Piedras Negras of 0287:0110 is an interesting link between that city and Codex Dresden."

1981–1990 Grube (1990a:92): = T0783; Grube and Stuart (1987): /ko/ (representation of teeth, not a bone); Justeson (1984:324): J. Fox, B. Riese: probably /ha/; J. Justeson: logographic, reading uncertain; F. Lounsbury: /to/; P. Mathews: "toh/tah"?

1991–2008 Davoust (1995:561): "coc" 'carapace de tortue'; /co/; Dütting (1991): "co/coh"; Knorozov (1999, vol. 1:108): /tu/ (cerbatana).

1BB

T 0270
Z –
K –

1. Picture: ?

1991–2008 Davoust (1995:573): "chac/chäc" 'rouge'; Knorozov (1999, vol. 1:108): /tu/ (cerbatana); Ringle and Smith-Stark (1996:295): 0270 (retired) = 0109v.

1BC

T —
Z —
K —

1. Picture: ?

1BD

T —
Z —
K —

1. Picture: ?

1991–2008 Davoust (1997:293): = 0111 "bac" 'captif'.

1C1

T 0112
Z 0031
K 0319

tòok' / tok'

n flint; bloodletter

Yu *tòok'* tok' 'pedernal' (Barrera Vásquez et al. 1980:805); tòok' 'flint; fang (of snake); lancet' (V. Bricker et al. 1998:279)

Ch' *tok'* *tok' 'flint' (Kaufman and Norman 1984:132)

1. Picture: flint blade

1566–1915 Brasseur de Bourbourg (1869–1870, vol. 1:208, 218): day Ezanab; "ezanab" 'silex, pierre de lance, jet de feu d'un volcan'; symbole du tremblement de terre; Brinton (1895:88f.): flint knife; Rosny (1883:10): day Ezanab.

1916–1950 Gates (1931:47): "etz'nab" 'flint knife'.

1951–1980 Kelley (1962b:24): flint knife (D. Brinton, J. Thompson, Y. Knorozov, D. Kelley); "ta" 'flint knife' (D. Brinton); "tok" 'flint' (Y. Knorozov); Kelley (1976:135, 148–50, 332): "tok" 'flint'; "ta" 'flint knife'; Knorozov (1955:71): 088 (punta de lanza con elementos complementarios) "tok"; Knorozov (1967:100): "hetz' " (stone knife with two edges); Thompson (1962:52f.): [20 examples] (flint knife) appears on Dresden 23b in a context of food offerings; Thompson (1972:36, 92): 'flint knife'; metaphor for 'war'.

1981–1990 Justeson (1984:324): J. Fox, J. Justeson: probably = T0527; depicts flaked blade; P. Mathews, B. Riese, L. Schele, D. Stuart: flint knife; "tok' "?

1991–2008 Davoust (1995:561): "tok" 'silex'; Knorozov (1999, vol. 1:109): "hetz' " (cuchillo de pedernal con dos filos); Ringle and Smith-Stark (1996:335–38): 0112 = 0112a.

1C6

T 0268
Z 1313
K 0336

Syllabic reading suggested by fact that sometimes appears doubled.

1. Picture: flint blade

1916–1950 Gates (1931:49): "cauac" 'storm; tun'.

1951–1980 Knorozov (1967:101): phonetic.

1991–2008 Davoust (1995:573): /ch'a/; Knorozov (1999, vol. 1:175): "zul" (vaso acostado).

1G1

T 0023
Z 0079
K 0029

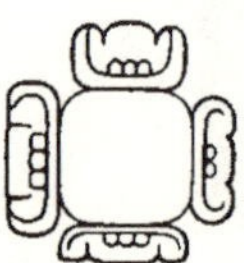

na
nah?

adj first?
Yu *ø* na 'casa, no denotando cuya' (Barrera Vásquez et al. 1980:545); nah 'house' (V. Bricker et al. 1998:193)
Ch' *nah* *nah- 'in front, forward; before; first' (Kaufman and Norman 1984:138)
In the codices 1G1 occasionally substitutes for 1M4 /li/. This variant does not appear to be used for 'house'.
1. Picture: ?

1566–1915 Brasseur de Bourbourg (1869–1870, vol. 1:204): "u" 'vase, bassin, surface circonscrite, lune'; Thomas (1893:250): determinative signifying /u/.
1916–1950 Gates (1932): used as subfix with "caan" 'sky'; Whorf (1942:484, fig. 1): /ha/; "-a"; "-ah."
1951–1980 Barthel (1954): "al"; Kelley (1962a:290, 298): /na/; Kelley (1976:63, 150, 185, 201, 202, 219, 221–23, 225, 230, 331): 'mother'?; /na/; "-na"?; Knorozov (1955:71): 085 (tapa?) /n(a)/; Knorozov (1967:79): /ng(a)/ (plate with thick edges); Lounsbury (1974b:13): /na/ or /an/; Thompson (1962:43, 1972:37): "al."
1981–1990 V. Bricker (1986:208): /na/, "na" 'first; feminine agentive' (Ch'olan); Dütting (1985:108): polyvalent "al," /na/; Grube (1990a:88): = T0343; Justeson (1984:317): consensus /na/; Lounsbury (1984): /nV/.
1991–2008 Davoust (1995:554): "nah" 'maison'; /na/; Knorozov (1999, vol. 1:89f.): /nga/, "ang" (plato con bordes gruesos).

1G1

T 0048
Z –
K 0030

na
nah

adj first
2. Picture: ?

1916–1950 Whorf (1942:484, fig. 1): /ha/; "-a"; "-ah."
1951–1980 Knorozov (1967:79): "xam" (a vessel); Schele (1976:12, n. 3): credits Lounsbury with "nabe" 'first'.
1981–1990 V. Bricker (1986:208): /na/, "na" 'first' (Ch'olan); Grube (1990a:89): = T0004; Justeson (1984:319): (a) consensus /na/; (b) J. Justeson: probably not "xam"; L. Campbell, F. Lounsbury, P. Mathews, L. Schele: "xam"; Ringle (1988:18): "noh"?; occasionally substitutes for T0023 /na/ but in general has a different distribution, suggesting they shared the same consonant but not the same vowel; von Winning and Dütting (1987): "xan" 'to go'.
1991–2008 Davoust (1995:556): "nah" 'maison, premier'; Grube (1994b:181): T0048 /na/ used syllabically after 9.11.0.0.0; Knorozov (1999, vol. 1:90): /nga/ "ang"; Ringle and Smith-Stark (1996:335–38): 0004b; Stuart (1998:376f.): "nah" 'house; building; structure'.

1G1

T –
Z –
K –

nah?

n house; dwelling?
3. Picture: ? plus "ik' " sign

1991–2008 H. Bricker and V. Bricker (n.d.): compound grapheme: "nah" 'house'; Vail and Hernández (2005–2008): /na/ plus "nal" 'maize; place'.

1G4

T 0012
Z 0025
K 0048

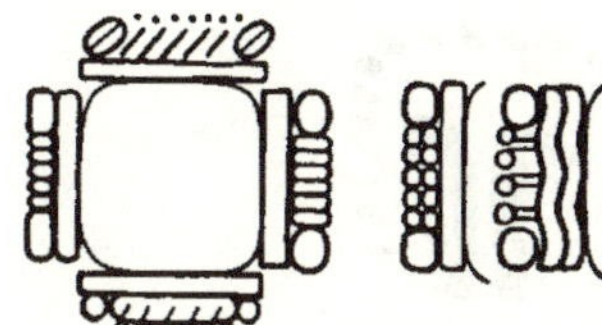

a?
ah / aj

agentive — agentive
Yu *ah* — ah 'antepuesta a los apellidos de linaje denota los varones; antepuesta a los nombres de lugares' (Barrera Vásquez et al. 1980:3)
Ch' *aj* — *aj 'prepound/proclitic; male; relatively large/active being' (Kaufman and Norman 1984:139)

1. Picture: ?

1916–1950 Thompson (1950:189): "tz'oc; xoc; hitz' " 'end; die'.

1951–1980 Kelley (1976:136, 331): possible allograph of T0013 "ah"; occurs with "mul" 'pyramid', probably to be read "ah mul" 'the pyramid builder'; Knorozov (1955:72): 096 (cinturón?) /ah/; Knorozov (1967:81): "ah (ah')"; "ah-" 'he who' [agentive]; Mathews (1980:68): "ah"; Thompson (1972:75): "hitz' " 'end of'?

1981–1990 V. Bricker (1986:208): /a(h)/, "ah-" (agentive) (Ch'olan, Yucatecan); "-ah" (perfective) (Yucatecan); Dütting (1985:112): "ah" and "xul" 'end, death'; Justeson (1984:316): L. Campbell: agent "aj-," /ah/; J. Fox, J. Justeson: various "ah" morphemes, usually proclitic "*aj-"; F. Lounsbury: "ah," includes agentive; P. Mathews: "ah" male agent; possibly also /a/; L. Schele, D. Stuart: "ah," male article and /ah/; B. Riese: /ah/ and "ah" agentive; Stuart (1985a): masculine article "ah"; 'he of x captives' in "count-of-captives" glyph; Stuart (1985c:2): /a/ attributed to Knorozov (1955, sec. 2, 3–10); = T0743 /a/, sometimes "ah."

1991–2008 Davoust (1995:553): "ah" 'préf., genre masc.'; /a/; Dütting (1991:276): "ah" and "haw" 'cease, end; lie face up'; Knorozov (1999, vol. 1:80): "ah" (cinta o taparrabo); Stuart and Houston (1994:33–39): prefix marking place of origin.

1G5

T 0166
Z 0027
K –

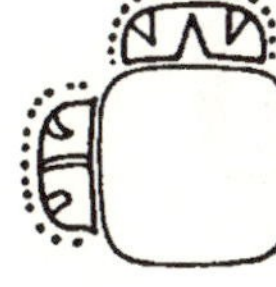

hu / ju

1. Picture: dotted "ak'b'al" sign

1916–1950 Gates (1931:10): "akbal" 'night'; Thompson (1950:283): "chapat" 'centipede'; Whorf (1942:484, fig. 1): "ts" ["tz"].

1951–1980 Fought (1965:268): "itz" 'milk, sap'; Kelley (1962a:290, 297f.): " 'itz"?; Kelley (1962b:23): head of centipede (A. Tozzer and G. Allen, D. Kelley); torrents of water, "itz" (Y. Knorozov); Kelley (1976:135f., 332): see T0152; Knorozov (1955:74): 120 (torrentes de agua en óvalo punteado) "itz"; Thompson (1972:92, 106): "ak"? prefix of God D; 'fresh'.

1981–1990 Grube (1990a:95): = T0045; Justeson (1984:328): J. Fox, J. Justeson: = one variant of T0045; F. Lounsbury, L. Schele: = T0045; P. Mathews: possibly = T0045; B. Riese: in codices /itz/; MacLeod (1990b:341): relates to Classic T0045 /hu/.

1991–2008 Davoust (1995:565): "hoy/huy"? 'cavité'; /hu/; Davoust (1997:158): "uh" 'lune' (on D. 21b, where it prefixes T1026); Grube (2004:76): /ju/, not /hu/ in Classic period contexts; /hu/ rather than /ju/ in Dresden spelling of Moon Goddess as Uh Ixik, 'Lady Moon'; Knorozov (1999, vol. 1:96): "itz"; Love (1991:294, 297): "its" reading, suggested by Riese (Justeson 1984:328), seems reasonable; Ringle and Smith-Stark (1996:342): not = T0045 as suggested by Justeson et al. (1984); retained as separate sign; Schele and Grube (1997:129): /hu/; D. Tedlock and B. Tedlock (2007:124): "uh" 'moon' when prefixed to T1026; Vail (1996:257f.): "itz" after Riese (cited in Justeson 1984:328); von Nagy (1997:44, 46): "tzim" or "chim" reading suggested by Lounsbury (1984:176).

1G8

T 0042
Z —
K 0302

period: part of piktun glyph
1. Picture: dotted scrolls

1951–1980 Knorozov (1967:99): "took."

1981–1990 Justeson (1984:319): J. Fox, J. Justeson: logographic or semantic, unknown; T0042:0528.0528 (= T0042 + "baktun") represents "pictun"; F. Lounsbury, P. Mathews, B. Riese, L. Schele, D. Stuart: "pictun" superfix.

1991–2008 Knorozov (1999, vol. 1:73): "tooc"? (volutas de humo dentro de un contorno punteado).

1G9

T —
Z —
K —

Unique occurrence on Madrid 78.
1. Picture: food offering

1GA

T —
Z 1375
K 0328

1. Picture: U-shape with curved line of dots

1916–1950 Gates (1931:163): G392 [in part].

1951–1980 Kelley (1962a:290, 294): /n(V)/; Knorozov (1967:100, 101): (= K327) "kum" (pot to boil water); Thompson (1962:403): Z1375 = T0250.

1991–2008 Davoust (1997:204): /nu/; Knorozov (1999, vol. 1:97): (una cueva?); Ringle and Smith-Stark (1996:344): "A U-shaped version of T0250, however, is a suffix to T0610 and T0059. This may be a different element, but in view of the similarity of both forms to T0155, it seems best to reclassify all as T0155v and retire 0250."

1GB

T 0161
Z 0018
K 0045

1. Picture: ?

1916–1950 Gates (1931:86): 'zero-time'.

1951–1980 Knorozov (1967:80): /h(e)/; "he" 'beginning'; Thompson (1972:76): example on D. 54b = 0298 'seating'.

1981–1990 Grube (1990a:94): = T0277.

1991–2008 Davoust (1995:565): "wi' " 'racine d'arbre'; /wi/; Davoust (1997:209): = T0298 "cum" 'assise'; Knorozov (1999, vol. 1:70): "h'e"; Ringle and Smith-Stark (1996:335–38): 0161 (retired) = (misidentified).

1M2

T 0024
Z 0080
K 0101

na

nahil / nah?

adj honored?; first, foremost?
Yu *nahil* nahil 'mérito o merecimiento' (Martínez Hernández 1929:658)
Ch' *nah* *nah- 'in front, forward; first' (Kaufman and Norman 1984:138)

Graphically similar to 1M4, but two have different values. References listed below are those attributed to T0024.

1. Picture: celt, reflective stone

1566–1915 Brasseur de Bourbourg (1869–1870, vol. 1:204): "u" 'vase, bassin, surface circonscrite, lune'; Brinton (1895:88f.): "bul" 'all, the whole of anything'; Schellhas [1892] (1904:10f.): sacrificial knife or flint found in name of God A, the death god; Thomas (1893:267): /k'/.

1916–1950 Thompson (1950:285): "il"; Whorf (1942:484, fig. 1): /ka/.

1951–1980 Kelley (1976:133–35, 152, 160, 221, 331): (shell ornament) "-il"; Knorozov (1955:72): 090 (cuchillo de pedernal?) "om (un, hun)"; Knorozov (1967:86): "um" (stone mano); Thompson (1962:43): "il."

1981–1990 V. Bricker (1983:349): /li/, nominal suffix "-il"; V. Bricker (1986:208): /li/, "-il"?; Grube (1990a:88): = T0308, T0342?, T0617, T0677, T0821; Justeson (1984:317): see T0002, T0082, T0083, T0102; J. Fox, J. Justeson: "-il"; = T0002; F. Lounsbury: /ne/; "nen" 'mirror', semantic determinative for deities; = T0617; L. Schele, D. Stuart: possibly "-il," or "-Vn"; = T0082 and "worm bird"; B. Riese: "-Vl" in monumental inscriptions; MacLeod (1983:54): "-Vl"; Schele (1987c): "Vl"; Stuart (1987:16): /li/ or "-il".

1991–2008 Davoust (1995:554): "il" 'voir, regarder'; "nen" 'miroir'; "ah" 'préf. agt. masc.'; /li/, /ne/; Grofe (2008): Classic form (T0617 "mirror/celt") is /le/, "lem" 'flash, spark, shine'; Grube (1991:224): main sign form of T0024 is also possibly /al/ or /Vl/; Houston, Robertson, and Stuart (2001:24): the "-il" glyph must be distinguished from another logographic sign that represents precious, polished objects; the two began to blur graphically in the Early Classic period; Knorozov (1999, vol. 1:106, 240): "um" 'señor, padre; círculo; alrededor' (mano de metate); MacLeod (personal communication, June 2008): "lem" or "leem" 'lightning, brilliance, shiny, brilliant'; attributed to Stuart; Schele and Grube (1997:84): looks identical to T0024 suffix, but may have different functions; prefix fulfills same function as before nominal glyphs of certain gods, such as Maize God and God A; Stuart (2005:67, n. 20): based on pattern of affixation in Classic period contexts, may be "win" (e.g., "winbah" 'mask, image') or "sat" (e.g., "sat chan," literally 'face-sky'); note Ch'olan "*wut" (in the no longer attested term "*wut chan" 'face-sky'); Stuart (2007): "celt" glyph as "lem" or "leem"; Vail (2000b): "yanil" 'esteemed'; Vail (1996:244f.): /nV/; "nen" 'mirror'; "li" demonstrative pronoun; Vail (2002b): "nah"? 'first, honored'?, /na/.

1M4

T 0024
Z 0080
K 0101

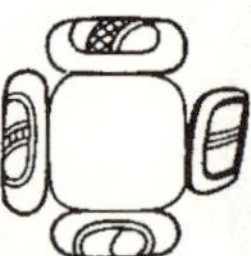

li
-il

suf noun suffix

A similar grapheme, 1M2, usually occurs as a prefix. Some references below refer to 1M2.

1. Picture: celt, reflective stone

1566–1915 Brasseur de Bourbourg (1869–1870, vol. 1:204): "u" 'vase, bassin, surface circonscrite, lune'; Brinton (1895:88f.): "bul" 'all, the whole of anything'; Schellhas [1892] (1904:10f.): sacrificial knife or flint found in name of God A, the death god; Thomas (1893:267): /c'/, /ic/, or /ci/; often used as a determinative.

1916–1950 Thompson (1950:285): "il"; Whorf (1942:484, fig. 1): /ka/.

1951–1980 Kelley (1976:133–35, 152, 160, 221, 331): (shell ornament) "-il"; Knorozov (1955:72): 090 (cuchillo de pedernal?) "om (un, hun)"; Knorozov (1967:86): "um" (stone mano); Thompson (1962:43): "il."

1981–1990 V. Bricker (1983:349): /li/, nominal suffix "-il"; V. Bricker (1986:208): /li/, "-il"?; Grube (1990a:88): = T0308, T0342?, T0617, T0677, T0821; Justeson (1984:317): see T0002, T0082, T0083, T0102; J. Fox, J. Justeson: "-il"; = T0002; F. Lounsbury: /ne/; "nen" 'mirror', semantic determinative for deities; = T0617; L. Schele, D. Stuart: possibly "-il," or "-Vn"; = T0082 and "worm bird"; B. Riese: "-Vl" in monumental inscriptions; MacLeod (1983:54): "-Vl"; Schele (1987c): "Vl"; Stuart (1987:16): /li/ or "-il."

1991–2008 Davoust (1995:554): "il" 'voir, regarder'; "nen" 'miroir'; "ah" 'préf. agt. masc.'; /li/, /ne/; Grube (1991:224): main sign form of T0024 is also possibly /al/ or /Vl/; Houston, Robertson, and Stuart (2001:24): morphosyllable "-il"; must be distinguished from another logographic sign that represents precious, polished objects; the two began to blur graphically in the Early Classic period; Knorozov (1999, vol. 1:106, 240): "um" 'señor, padre; círculo; alrededor' (mano de metate); Vail (1996:234): /li/; also /nV/ based substitution for T0023 /na/ in certain compounds.

1S1

T 0277
Z 0029
K 0067

wi

1. Picture: root?

1951–1980 Cordan (1964:28f.): "mukan" ideograma, 'culebra'; Knorozov (1967:83): "vin"?

1981–1990 Grube (1990a:100): = T0161; Justeson (1984:334): J. Fox, J. Justeson: /wi/; depicts 'root' "wi' "; Stuart (1987:13–16): /wi/; = T0117; cites Fox and Justeson (Justeson 1984:334) with T0277 /wi/; cites V. Bricker (1986:6) and Justeson (1984:324) with T0117 /na/.

1991–2008 Davoust (1995:574): "wi' " 'racine d'arbre'; /wi/; Knorozov (1999, vol. 1:107, 240): "vin" '20'; Ringle and Smith-Stark (1996:335–38): 0277 = 0117b.

1S2

T 0116
Z 0062
K 0035

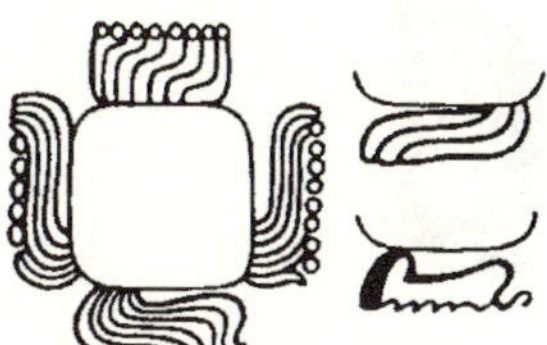

ni, ne

1. Picture: tail

1566–1915 Brasseur de Bourbourg (1869–1870, vol. 1:202): "ca" 'mâchoire'; "cáa" 'pierre à moudre le grain; une sorte de citrouille'; Förstemann [1897] (1904a:438): affixed to "k'in" glyph, "might almost be taken for a sign of the plural"; Rosny (1876:95): déterminatif des mois; Thomas (1893:255): "tal."

1951–1980 Kelley (1962a:290): "-il"; Kelley (1976:181, 193, 332): "-il," attributive affix; Knorozov (1955:73): 113 (fuego) "(i)l"; Knorozov (1967:79f.): "-il"; Thompson (1972:92): "haab" 'year' when used with T0168.0573 on D. 25–28.

1981–1990 V. Bricker (1983:347): /ne/; V. Bricker (1986:209): /ne/; Grube (1990a:92): = T0260; Justeson (1984:324): L. Campbell, J. Fox, J. Justeson, B. Riese, D. Stuart: /ne/, /ni/; F. Lounsbury: /ne/ or /-n/; P. Mathews: /n/, possibly /ne/; L. Schele: /n/ or /ne/; Lounsbury (1984): /nV/; Schele (1987f): /ne/ or /ni/ in proper name "wa-a-n(i)," Copán St. A, 'a stood-up or erected thing'; Schele (1989c:5a): /ni/.

1991–2008 Carrasco (1994:52): /il/ or /ne/; Davoust (1995:562): "ni' " 'queue, extrémité'; /ni/, /ne/; Knorozov (1999, vol. 1:91, 235): "il" 'arder; sufijo de sustantivos' (llamas altas de fuego); Schele and Grube (1997:17): /ni/; Stuart (1997:11, n. 3): /ni/ seems equally probable, if not preferable, to /ne/.

1S3

T 0120bcd
Z 0087
K 0027

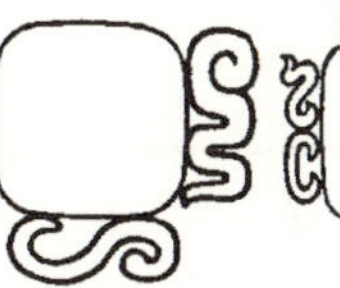

ne

A similar grapheme 1S4 is used only as a prefix. Some notes do not distinguish between 1S3 and 1S4.

1. Picture: tail

1566–1915 Brasseur de Bourbourg (1869–1870, vol. 1:203): /n/; 'lettre qui est l'attribut de la grandeur, de l'excellence, de la royauté'; Landa [1566] (Tozzer 1941:170): <n>.

1951–1980 Kelley (1962a:302f.): "ne" 'cola'; Knorozov (1955:68): 048 (gusano) "nuc"; Knorozov (1967:79): /n(i)/ (caterpillar, from which paint was extracted?).

1981–1990 Justeson (1984:325): includes Landa's <n>.

1991–2008 Davoust (1995:562): "nen" 'miroir'; /ni/; Davoust (1997:100): "ne' "; Knorozov (1999, vol. 1:87): /ni/ (gusano del que se extraía un tinte?); Schele and Grube (1997:118): /ne/.

1S4

T 0120a
Z 0087
K 0027

u, hu

A similar grapheme 1S3 is used only as a suffix. Some references below do not distinguish between 1S3 and 1S4.

1. Picture: scroll

1566–1915 Brasseur de Bourbourg (1869–1870, vol. 1:204): "u"; Landa [1566] (Tozzer 1941:170): <u>.

1951–1980 Knorozov (1955:68): 048 (gusano) "nuc"; Knorozov (1967:79): /n(i)/ (caterpillar, from which paint was extracted?); Thompson (1972:84): represents animal noises—it issues from the mouths of dogs, a monkey and other animals; may represent "pec" 'thunder' and its homonym "pec" 'round'.

1981–1990 V. Bricker (1987): /hu/.

1991–2008 Bricker (1991:290): resembles Landa's second grapheme for /u/; "huh" 'iguana'; Davoust (1995:Planche 41): /u/ (attributed to Kelley 1976); Davoust (1995:562): "pec" 'tonnerre' (E. Thompson); "huh" 'iguane', "uh" 'lune' (V. Bricker); /hu/; Grube (2004:80): /hu/ rather than /ju/ in spelling of "huj waaj" 'iguana bread' in Dresden Codex; Schele and Grube (1997:81f.): /u/, /hu/.

1S5

T 0172
Z 0004
K 0033

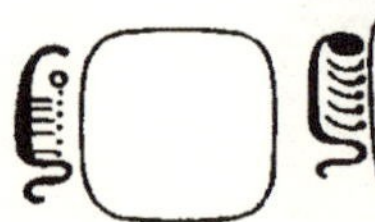

yah?

adj? wounded?; damaged?
Yu *yah* yah 'painful'; yàah 'painful; pain' (V. Bricker et al. 1998:310)
Ch' *yah* *yah 'painful'; *yaj 'sick, sickness; sore, wound' (Kaufman and Norman 1984:137)

1. Picture: ?

1951–1980 Cordan (1964:15): "tzab" 'gotear', 'dueño'; Kelley (1976:202f., 332): meaning like 'against', 'toward', 'at', or 'on'; Knorozov (1955:74): 128 (una gota y un elemento confuso) "et"; Knorozov (1967:79): "et"; Old Yucatec "yetel" 'with, and'; Thompson (1972:64): "ya" or "numya" 'woe to'.

1981–1990 Justeson (1984:328): J. Justeson: "*aj-," possibly third singular pronoun prefix; may be basis for convergence of T0001 and T0025 in Madrid (cf. T0025.0648:0025 form); frequent prefix to apparent deity names/epithets.

1991–2008 Davoust (1995:565): "yah" 'douleur'; /ya/; Knorozov (1999, vol. 1:92): "et" (una gota?); Schele and Grube (1997:143): "yah" 'to wound; to damage'; "Although we have no direct phonetic evidence in support of this verb, it is one that is known in Classic-period inscriptions and fits the context."

1S7

T 0243
Z –
K –

1. Picture: ?

1916–1950 Gates (1931:128): affix to G145.

1981–1990 Grube (1990a:99): = T0181?

1991–2008 Davoust (1995:571): "hal" 'tisser'; Knorozov (1999, vol. 1:87): "tep' " (cuerda estilizada).

1S8

T –
Z –
K –

Substitutes for 1S7 on Madrid 21c.

1. Picture: ?

1916–1950 Gates (1931:128): affix to G145.

1981–1990 Grube (1990a:99): = T0181?

1991–2008 Knorozov (1999, vol. 1:86): "tep' " (cuerda).

1SA

T 0115
Z 0006
K 0078

yo

uy-; (u)y-

dep pn — he/she/it; his/her/its; third person prefix, Set A (ergative and possessive), prevocalic
Yu *uy-* — u(y)- 'Set A dependent pronoun, 3rd person' (Hofling with Tesucún 1997:9)
Ch' *uy-* — *u- 'ergative 3s' ; *(u)y- 'ergative 3s prevocalic' (Kaufman and Norman 1984:91)

Substitutes for 2S8 "aj/ah" in some contexts, especially in the Madrid Codex.

1. Picture: leaf

1951–1980 Dütting (1974:50): "le"? 'leaf; demonstrative pronoun'; Knorozov (1967:85): "tich' " 'offering'; Thompson (1972:76): "okol" 'upon'; used as homonym for "okol" 'to weep'.

1981–1990 Justeson (1984:324): L. Campbell, J. Fox, B. Riese: "t-u"; "(y)-"; J. Justeson: sometimes undetermined locative preposition, but not always locative; possibly includes pronoun specifically when prefixed to inalienably possessed roots; possibly sometimes a prefixed aspect marker; F. Lounsbury: /tu(y)/, /tä(y)/, /to(y)/, and /t-/; P. Mathews: /tu/; possibly /tV/; L. Schele: "tu," locative preposition + pronoun; /tu/; Lounsbury (1989:87): /tiy-/; Stuart (1987:33–41): /yo/.

1991–2008 Davoust (1995:561): "yol" 'germe'; /yo/; Knorozov (1999, vol. 1:167): "tich' " (mano levantada como ofreciendo algo); Vail (1996:205, 305, 347): occasionally conflates with T0015 "ah" in the Madrid Codex.

1SC

T 0612
Z 0731a
K 0257

le

1. Picture: ?

1566–1915 Brasseur de Bourbourg (1869–1870, vol. 1:203): "l, el" 'sortir, brûler, s'élever'; Brinton (1895:91): may symbolize the waters; Landa [1566] (Tozzer 1941:170): /le/; Thomas (1893:251): /l/ and /le/.

1916–1950 Gates (1931:59): "men" variant?

1951–1980 Kelley (1962a:290, 295f.): /le/; Kelley (1962b:41): /le/; Kelley (1976:122, 155, 179, 333): /le/; like T0613?; Knorozov (1955:75): 137 /l(e)/; Knorozov (1967:97): /l(e)/ (animal?); Thompson (1962:234f.): (Men semblant); Thompson (1972:33): similar to the day Men; with T0168 prefix "ah men" 'the worker'.

1981–1990 V. Bricker (1986:212): (Landa's "le") /le/; Grube (1990a:110): = T0056; Justeson (1984:348): L. Campbell, P. Mathews, L. Schele: /le/; J. Fox, J. Justeson, F. Lounsbury, B. Riese, D. Stuart: /le/ (codex form).

1991–2008 Davoust (1995:590): "le' " 'feuille'; /le/; Knorozov (1999, vol. 1:111): /le/ (animal acuático, posiblement manatí); MacLeod (1991f.): may have logographic reading on M. 21c, "le" 'loop, tie' (verb and noun); used in the context of weaving; Ringle and Smith-Stark (1996:335–38): 0612 (retired) = 0188b; Ringle and Smith-Stark (1996:348): sometimes confused with T0613 in codices, especially with T0168 prefix.

1SD

T 0613
Z 0731
K 0254

le; me?

Occasionally substitutes for 1SC. May be equivalent to /me/ XE6. In some contexts has an undetermined logographic value.
day 15: Men
1. Picture: ?

1566–1915 Bollaert (1865–1866:52): "men" 'to build'; Brasseur de Bourbourg (1869–1870, vol. 1:207): day Men; "men" bâti, édifié' "me-en" 'chose courbe ouverte, détruite peu à peu ou descendue au fond'; Landa [1566] (Tozzer 1941:134): day Men; Rosny (1883:8): day Men; Tozzer and Allen (1910:pl. 6): (with T0069) possibly a shark.

1916–1950 Gates (1931:41): "men" 'bird; eagle; wise one'.

1951–1980 Kelley (1976:122, 333): (a bird?) day Men; Knorozov (1955:68): 038 (animal acuático, manatí?) /men/; Knorozov (1967:97): phonetic (animal); name of a day, Men; Thompson (1962:235f.): [97 examples] Men; T0612 and T0613 probably variants, in large part they take the same affixes and appear interchangeable; nevertheless, certain affixes are found with one glyph but not with the other; may indicate differences in meaning; with T0145, the name of the old goddess of weaving; T0267:0613 is a fairly common augural glyph of evil character, commonly associated with the moon goddess Ixchel.

1981–1990 V. Bricker (1986:212): /le/; Grube (1990a:110): = T0852; Grube and Schele (1988): head variant of day Men; /am/; with T0087 'te' "am-te (tun)" 'tree-stone; stela'; Justeson (1984:348): L. Campbell, F. Lounsbury, P. Mathews: day Men in codices; also possibly "men"; J. Fox, B. Riese: codex day Men; in Madrid Codex also /le/; J. Justeson, P. Mathews: two originally distinct signs, T0610 and T0852, have converged graphically in T0613 in the codices; L. Schele, D. Stuart: "men," day sign and morphemic.

1991–2008 Davoust (1995:590): Men '15e jour'; /me/; Knorozov (1999, vol. 1:110): "men" (animal acuático); este grafema se confunde fácilmente con el 337 /le/; Ringle and Smith-Stark (1996:348): sometimes confused with T0612 in codices, especially with T0168 prefix; Schele and Grube (1997:16): /me/; Schele and Grube (1997:131): "men" 'work'; Stuart (2005:180, n. 59): in combination with T0069, single grapheme with possible reading of "ak" or "akan" 'grass, grassland, bajo," not "hem" 'valley' interpretation of Schele and Grube (1997).

1SG

T 0319
Z —
K —

1. Picture: ?

1981–1990 Justeson (1984:336): F. Lounsbury, P. Mathews: possibly variant of T0589 "hax"; L. Schele: "hax."

1991–2008 Davoust (1995:577): "ch'ac" 'couper'; /ch'a/; Knorozov (1999, vol. 1:177): "boh"; MacLeod (1991f.): /ho/.

1SJ

T 0155bd
Z 0051
K 0327

o?

May be equivalent to 1GA.

1. Picture: circles connected by dots

1566–1915 Brasseur de Bourbourg (1869–1870, vol. 1:213): calebasse remplie des signes du gaz, image de la terre boursouflée par le feu et soulevant les montagnes.

1951–1980 Knorozov (1955:71): 078 (vasija de cuello estrecho con líquido hirviente) "cum (com)"; Knorozov (1967:100): "kum" (pot to boil water); Thompson (1962:55): (arched body of a snake).

1981–1990 Houston (1988:133): /'o/; Justeson (1984:327): L. Campbell: possibly shell, possibly "och/hoch"; J. Fox, J. Justeson: front view of T0078; alternates with T0078 as prefix in month compound for Cumku; J. Fox: iconic origin as decapitated bird and, metaphorically, mutilated penis ("bird"); possibly = T0250; Lounsbury (1983:44–49): equivalence of T0099, T0279, T0280, and T0155: /'o/ or /o'/.

1991–2008 Davoust (1995:564): "cum" 'marmite', "ohl" 'coeur, formel'; /o/; Knorozov (1999, vol. 1:174): "cum, chum" (vasija para hervir agua); MacLeod (1991a): /o/, "ol" 'sprout', 'young maize foliation'; Schele et al. (1991): /o/.

1SJ

T 0156
Z —
K —

o?

May have a value related to 'flowering'.

2. Picture: circles connected by dots

1981–1990 Justeson (1984:327): J. Fox, J. Justeson, F. Lounsbury, B. Riese: codex variant of T0155.

1991–2008 Davoust (1995:564): "cum" 'marmite', "ohl" 'coeur'; /o/; Knorozov (1999, vol. 1:174): "cum, chum" (vasija para hervir agua); Ringle and Smith-Stark (1996:342): distinct from T0155; does not appear as a prefix to Cumku in the codices.

1SJ

T 0250
Z —
K —

o?

3. Picture: curved line of dots

1916–1950 Gates (1931:163): G392 [in part].

1951–1980 Knorozov (1967:100, 101): (= K327) "kum" (pot to boil water).

1981–1990 Justeson (1984:333): J. Fox: possibly = T0155.

1991–2008 Davoust (1995:572): /nu/; Knorozov (1999, vol. 1:115): "cum, chum" (vasija para hervir agua); Ringle and Smith-Stark (1996:335–38): 0250 (retired) = 0155v; Ringle and Smith-Stark (1996:344): A U-shaped version of T0250 is a suffix to T0610 and T0059. This may be a different element, but in view of the similarity of both forms to T0155, it seems best to reclassify all as T0155v and retire 0250; Vail (2002b): substitutes for T0155 /o/.

1X1

T –
Z –
K –

1. Picture: ?

1566–1915 Brasseur de Bourbourg (1869–1870, vol. 1:205): day Kan; "kán" or "káan" 'argile, terre montée, sécrétion volcanique; soulevé, agrandi, qui est élevé au-dessus d'une autre chose'.

1X2

T 0307
Z –
K –

1. Picture: ?

1981–1990 Grube (1990a:102): = Zeichen nicht unter Thomspon's Beleg zu erkennen.

1991–2008 Davoust (1995:576): "il"?; /h/?; Ringle and Smith-Stark (1996:346): Thompson lists a single occurrence, as a prefix to the unidentified (and unillustrated) T1329. His provenience is in error; it actually appears on Madrid 35 in the top right passage.

1X3

T 0309
Z –
K –

1. Picture: ?

1991–2008 Knorozov (1999, vol. 1:90): "xam" (tapa estilizada de olla).

1X4

T 0357
Z –
K –

na

nahil / nah?; nah?

n honored?; first, foremost?; building, house

Yu *nahil, nah* nahil 'mérito o merecimiento' (Martínez Hernández 1929:658); na 'casa, no denotando cuya' (Barrera Vásquez et al. 1980:545); nah 'house' (V. Bricker et al. 1998:193)

Ch' *ø; nah* *nah- 'in front, forward; first' (Kaufman and Norman 1984:138)

Some apparent examples may be other partially eroded graphemes.

1. Picture: empty cartouche

1981–1990 Grube (1990a:103): = verschiedene von Thompson nicht richtig erkannte Zeichen.

1991–2008 Davoust (1995:580): "paa" 'réservoir d'eau'; /pa/; Knorozov (1999, vol. 1:105): /paa/ (laguna o muralla); Love (1992): /na/, "nah" 'house' (main sign only); not catalogued as main sign by Thompson; Ringle and Smith-Stark (1996:335–38): 0357 (retired) = (misidentified).

1X5

T —
Z —
K —

1. Picture: dotted comb

1566–1915 Brasseur de Bourbourg (1869–1870, vol. 1:202): "ca" 'mâchoire'; "cáa" 'pierre à moudre le grain; une sorte de citrouille'.

1X6

T —
Z —
K —

1. Picture: ?

1X7

T —
Z —
K —

1. Picture: ?

1X8

T —
Z —
K —

1. Picture: ?

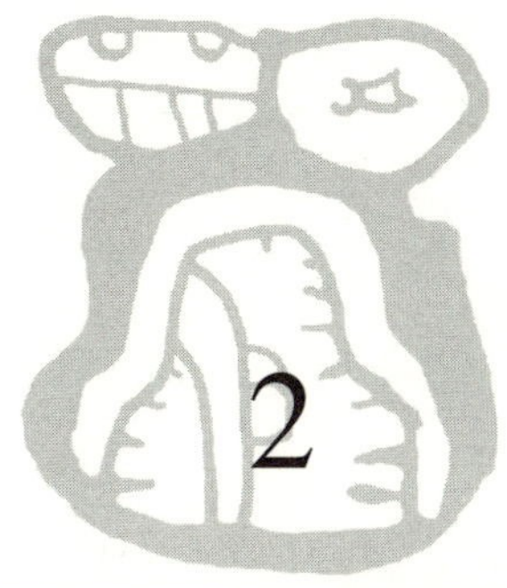

2 Two Segments

22B

T 0604
Z 1302
K 0370

k'u

1. Picture: eggs in nest

1566–1915 Brasseur de Bourbourg (1869–1870, vol. 1:203): "ku, kúu" 'nid d'oiseau; gîte; saint, divin, Dieu'; Landa [1566] (Tozzer 1941:170): <ku>; Thomas (1888:356f., 368): /ku/; when doubled "kukuitz"? 'quetzal'; Thomas (1893:258): /ku/.

1951–1980 Barthel (1964:223–44): "ku" 'dios'; Kelley (1962a:285, 287): /ku/; Kelley (1962b:41): /ku/; Kelley (1976:177f., 333): /ku/; Knorozov (1955:76): 145 /k(u)/; Knorozov (1967:102): /k'(u)/ (underground bird's nest); Thompson (1962:227f.): [57 examples] without hachure seems to be 'quetzal'; with T0219 may represent some species of vulture (as proposed sixty years ago by Cyrus Thomas).

1981–1990 V. Bricker (1986:212): (Landa's "ku") /ku/; Justeson (1984:347): L. Campbell, J. Fox, J. Justeson, B. Riese: /k'u/; depicts nest ("*k'u' "); cf. T0149b; J. Justeson: rare use "k'uk' "; F. Lounsbury, L. Schele: /k'u/, "k'uk' "; P. Mathews, D. Stuart: /k'u/; possibly also "k'uk' "; B. Riese: nest with two eggs; not for "k'uk' "; to be read "k'uk' " has to be reduplicated.

1991–2008 Davoust (1995:590): "ku' " 'nid d'oiseau'; /ku/; Knorozov (1999, vol. 1:178): /ku/ (nido de pájaros bajo la tierra).

22B

T 0149ef
Z —
K 0083

k'u

2. Picture: eggs

1916–1950 Gates (1931:155): prefix to G341.

1951–1980 Knorozov (1955:76): 144 /b(a)/; Knorozov (1967:85): (= K084) /ab/.

1981–1990 Justeson (1984:327): J. Fox: same iconically as T0149a, but functions in larger iconogram as eggs in nest ("k'u" 'nest'); J. Justeson, F. Lounsbury: upper part of T0406 /k'u/, occasionally sufficient by itself as /k'u/; L. Campbell, P. Mathews, L. Schele, D. Stuart: /k'u/, "k'uk"; B. Riese: "k'uk."

1991–2008 Davoust (1995:564): "ku' " 'nid d'oiseau'; /ku/; Knorozov (1999, vol. 1:74, 231): "ab" 'tierra, propiedad, campo dividido en parcelas; red; representar (como en teatro); romper; tributo' (campo dividido en parcelas); Ringle and Smith-Stark (1996:335–38): 0149 = 0604A (two final superfixes only, others remain 0149).

22B

T –
Z –
K –

k'u

Occurs as part of AMC on M. 77–78.
3. Picture: bird's nest?

22F

T 0149abcd
Z 0084
K 0375

nu

1. Picture: two ovals

1566–1915 Brinton (1895:89): representation of oyster.
1916–1950 Beyer (1937:53): [with T0608] bivalve with its animal.
1951–1980 Knorozov (1967:103): /n(u)/ (open bivalve shell); Thompson (1972:38): shell.
1981–1990 Justeson (1984:327): J. Fox: iconic origin in testicles; logographic "tu:n" of "to:n" ' 'testicles, penis'; consensus /nu/.
1991–2008 Davoust (1995:564): /nu/; Knorozov (1999, vol. 1:161): /nu/ (concha abierta); Ringle and Smith-Stark (1996:335–38): 0149 = 0604A (two final superfixes only, others remain 0149).

22H

T 0295
Z –
K –

1. Picture: ?

1991–2008 Davoust (1995:575): dans le glyphe Bolon Taz 'les neuf couches de tortillas'; /za/; Schele and Grube (1997:217): /tV/ in T0552:0295 "tat."

22J

T 0085a
Z –
K –

1. Picture: maize foliage

1951–1980 Kelley (1976:126, 197, 332): (= T0085, T0086?); corncob; grammatical affixes based on corn representations.
1981–1990 Grube (1990a:90): = T0084; Justeson (1984:322): J. Justeson: hand sign, possible variant of T0714, D. 73c (cf. D. 65a).
1991–2008 Davoust (1995:559): "nal" 'maïs en tige, jeune maïs'; Knorozov (1999, vol. 1:98): "ngal" (elote envuelto en hojas); Ringle and Smith-Stark (1996:335–38): 0085 (retired) = 0084b.

22K

T 0290
Z —
K —

1. Picture: foliage

1991–2008 Davoust (1995:575): "nal"? 'épi de maïs'; "yol" 'germe'; Ringle and Smith-Stark (1996:335–38): 0290 (retired) = 0267v.

22L

T 0273
Z —
K —

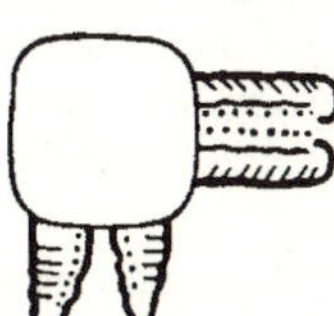

1. Picture: ?

1991–2008 Davoust (1995:574): /ba/; Knorozov (1999, vol. 1:75): "poc" (zanja).

22M

T —
Z —
K —

1. Picture: ?

22N

T 0256
Z —
K 0088

1. Picture: maize foliage

1951–1980 Knorozov (1967:86): morphemic (two ears of corn).

1991–2008 Davoust (1995:572): "nal" 'épi de maïs"; "yol" 'germe'; Knorozov (1999, vol. 1:75): "ngal" (hoja de elote).

2G1

T 0087
Z 0082
K 0065

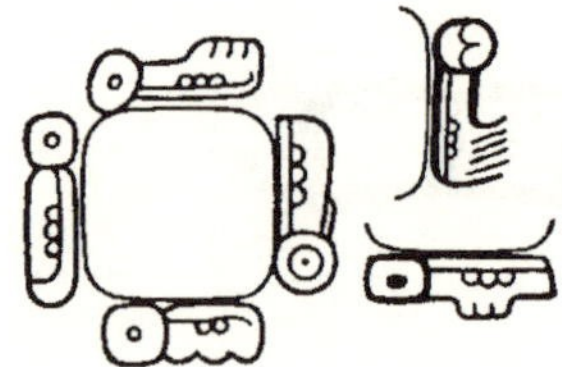

te

che'? / te'; -te

n; nm cl — tree, wood, plant; numeral classifier

Yu *te'; che'* — che' 'árbol en general, madera o palo; planta en general' (Barrera Vásquez et al. 1980:85); che' 'wood, tree, stick' (V. Bricker et al. 1998:64); te' 'tree' (V. Bricker et al. 1998:272); -te 'cuenta para años y para los días de los meses y para leguas' (Barrera Vásquez et al. 1980:782); té 'for counts of years, months, days, leagues, cocoa, eggs, and calabashes or squashes' (Tozzer 1921:292)

Ch' *te; te'* — *te' 'tree' (Kaufman and Norman 1984:132); hun-te 'contar piedras; el generico de la quenta' (Morán 1935:14)

Possible use as numeral classifier on Madrid 106b.

1. Picture: ?

1566–1915 Brinton (1895:102): usually taken to represent a chopper or machete; Rosny (1883:22): pièce de bois, massue, sorte de casse-tête, en maya "bat"; Thomas (1893:250): /t/, /th/, "thib."

1916–1950 Gates (1931:165): club; Thompson (1950:282–84): "te" classifier, 'tree, wood'.

1951–1980 Kelley (1962a:290, 295): "te" 'clasificador numérico', 'arból'; /te/; Kelley (1962b:43): "te," "che" 'tree'; Kelley (1976:15, 84, 123–26, 155, 157, 179f., 191, 192, 246, 332): "te," numerical classifier; 'tree'; Knorozov (1955:72): 092 (lanzadera de dardos?, rama?) /te/, "te" " 'árbol'; Knorozov (1967:83): /t(e)/; "te" 'there' (tree branch); Miller (1974:155): /te/; Thompson (1972:100): "che" 'wood'; read as 'club, chastisement' on Dresden 37b.

1981–1990 V. Bricker (1986:209): /te/, "te" 'tree, wood' (Ch'olan, Yucatecan); Grube (1990a:90): = T0350, T0513b; Justeson (1984:322): cf. T0350, T1071; L. Campbell, J. Fox, J. Justeson, P. Mathews: "te" (Yucatec and Cholan) and "che" (Yucatec only); as infix, semantic determinative for tree/wood (proto-Mayan "*tye:' "); F. Lounsbury: /te/, "te', che' "; B. Riese: /te/, /che/; 'tree', 'wood', 'pole'; L. Schele: "te," Yucatec "che" sometimes; 'tree'; /che/; D. Stuart: /te/ = T1070; Love (1989:346f.): used as a generic numeral classifier; "te" reading in some contexts, "tas" in others.

1991–2008 Davoust (1995:559): "che'/te' " 'arbre'; /che/, /te/; Knorozov (1999, vol. 1:98): /te/, /che/ (rama de árbol); Love (1991:301): "te/che" 'tree or wood product', /te/, /che/; Vail (2000a): Yucatec "che' " in addition to Ch'olan "te'."

2G2

T 0093a–d
Z 0085
K 0350

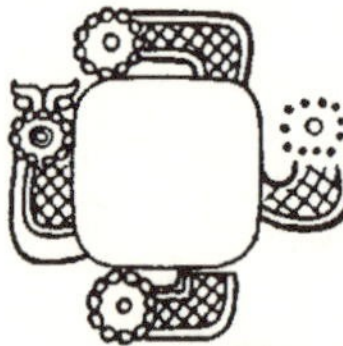

ch'a

ch'áah / ch'äj

n — droplet

Yu *ch'áah* — ch'ah 'gota de cualquier licor o resina de árbol' (Barrera Vásquez et al. 1980:121); ch'áah 'drip; drop' (V. Bricker et al. 1998:78)

Ch' *ch'äj* — *ch'äj 'ground parched corn' (Kaufman and Norman 1984:119)

1. Picture: incense

1916–1950 Thompson (1950:265): perhaps depicts smoke or fire; Whorf (1942:484, fig. 1): "s"; /sa/.

1951–1980 Barthel (1965:147f.): "butz" 'humo, ahumar'; Cordan (1964:48f.): "kichin" (signo de fuego); Kelley (1976:192, 332): /ka/ or "chac"; locative; Knorozov (1967:102): "chuh" (offering being burnt on altar); Thompson (1972:92): 'sparks and smoke'.

1981–1990 V. Bricker (1986:209): "pom" 'incense' (Ch'olan, Yucatecan); Grube (1990a:91): = T0603; Justeson (1984:322): J. Fox: suffixed to "hax", probably /xa/, otherwise /b'a/; possibly iconically related to Landa's second <x> sign; J. Justeson: possibly suffix deriving intransitive verb from transitive verb, or antipassive inflection; F. Lounsbury: /ha/; B. Riese: possibly /ha/, "ah"; iconically related to Landa's second <x> sign; P. Mathews: two different signs, /ha/? possibly the same; L. Schele: some may be Classic = codical "hax" and "b'e," /ha/; Love (1987:7): /ch'a/; "ch'ah" 'drop of any liquid'; Schele (1989b): /ch'a/; appears with T0673 in "shell-fist" glyph.

1991–2008 Davoust (1995:560): "ch'ah" 'goutte de résine d'arbre', /ch'a/; Knorozov (1999, vol. 1:103, 234): "chuh" 'quemar, encender; tostar, curtir, chamuscar, secar; ofrendar; incienso' (ofrenda quemada en el altar); Love (1991:294, 297): /ch'a/, "ch'ah" 'drops of liquid or tree resin'.

2G2

T 0634
Z –
K –

ch'a?

Sole example occurs in an eroded context. Appears to be used with syllabic value of /ch'a/ in a verbal expression.

2. Picture: incense

1951–1980 Thompson (1962:249): [6 examples] composite glyph, main element of which is T0023.

1981–1990 Grube (1990a:111): = T0093.0093.0093.

1991–2008 Davoust (1995:592): "ch'ah" 'gouttes de résine d'arbre'.

2G4

T –
Z 1306a
K –

pat / pät?

trans v — make, form?

Yu *pat* — pat 'form with hands, shape, knead, mold; invent' (V. Bricker et al. 1998:209); pat 'formar, dar forma a alguna cosa, hacer ollas, cántaros y otras vasijas y cosas de barro, de cera o masa; inventar; fingir' (Barrera Vásquez et al. 1980:632); pät 'to make pots' (Hofling with Tesucún 1997:502); pätic 'formar, tallar, moldear, esculpir' (Ulrich and Ulrich 1976:166)

Ch' *pät* — *pät 'construct, build' (Kaufman and Norman 1984:128)

1. Picture: dotted circle, comb, and thatch

1981–1990 V. Bricker and H. Bricker (1988:S7f.): "(o)toch" 'house'; functions as minus sign on Dresden 61.

1991–2008 H. Bricker and V. Bricker (n.d.): "pat" 'atras de, detras de' in Chontal, suggesting it is being used to indicate subtraction on Dresden 61 and 69; Davoust (1995:559): T0079: "pat" 'créer'; Davoust (1997:207): "pat" 'mainfester'; Grofe (2007:129): "pät" 'to create'; on Dresden 61 and 69 may indicate the creation of a positive integer (i.e., addition); MacLeod (1991i): positional compound "ok-kab" 'to seat (or base) firmly'; Ringle and Smith-Stark (1996:341): T0079 (= 0079a) in inscriptions and T0080 (= 0079b) in codices both prefix an event whose main sign is 0614; Schele and Grube (1997:195): Schele: "k'at" 'to want, to ask for, and to cross something'; Stuart (1998:381f.): "pat" 'to make, do; to build a house'.

2G4

T 0079
Z –
K –

pat / pät?

trans v — make, form?

Unique example on Paris 7d with /pa/ plus /ta/ suffixes.

2. Picture: dotted disk and comb

1951–1980 Lounsbury and Coe (1968): "moch" 'cage'.

1981–1990 V. Bricker (1986:209): /o/.

1991–2008 Davoust (1995:559): "pat" 'créer'; MacLeod (1991i): "ok" 'foot, base, post'; MacLeod (1993b): credits D. Stuart with "pat" 'build houses'; credits Schele (personal communication, 1992) with T0079:0628 "patil" 'and then'; Ringle and Smith-Stark (1996:335–38): 0079 = 0079a; Schele and Looper (1996:22f.): "k'al," /k'a/?; Stuart (1995:355): substitution spelling of /pa-ta/ for "pat" 'to make, build'.

2G5

T 0346
Z –
K –

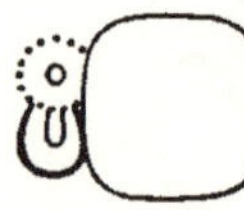

Occurs between numeral and "winik;" may function as a numeral classifier.

1. Picture: ?

1981–1990 Grube (1990a:103): = T0296.

1991–2008 Davoust (1995:579): "p'iz" 'mesure'; Ringle and Smith-Stark (1996:335–38): 0346 (retired) = 0099/0159.

2G6

T 0097
Z –
K –

1. Picture: ?

1991–2008 Knorozov (1999, vol. 1:91, 124): "hek"; Ringle and Smith-Stark (1996:335–38): 0097 (retired) = 0095d (upright), 0147v (inverted).

2M1

T 0168
Z 0042
K 0100

ahaw / ajaw

n lord

Yu *ahaw* ahawlil 'regia o real cosa' (Barrera Vásquez et al. 1980:4); x 'ahaw-xíiw 'royal herb, an herbaceous plant with ornamental leaves' (V. Bricker et al. 1998:257)

Ch' *ajaw* *ajaw 'king; lord' (Kaufman and Norman 1984:115)

Order of the two components is variable.

1. Picture: ?

1566–1915 Bowditch (1910:244): may be 'thirteen'; Brinton (1895:91): in a general sense signifies strength and deific power; Förstemann [1897] (1904a:471): lunar month; Seler [1915] (1976:45): "been-ix" or "been-kak" 'a sign of victory or conquest'.

1916–1950 Gates (1931:38f.): composite sign with "ben" 'reed'; Thompson (1950:294): "ben-ich."

1951–1980 Barthel (1964:231): 'encima; delante'; Barthel (1965:148f.): terminología de parentesco; Barthel (1968:161f.): 'el primero de adelante' or 'el que está encima'; Cordan (1964:33f.): "ah kich" superfijo, en titulos de dioses y ciudades; Kelley (1976:6, 83, 206, 214, 218, 259, 278, 332): = T0584 + T0687a; "ahpo"; Knorozov (1967:86): composite grapheme K147-113; "ben-tzil"; Lounsbury (1973): "Ahpo, Ah Pop, Aj po, Ahau" 'lord, ruler, king'; Mathews (1980:60): "ahpo"; Thompson (1972:34): "ah"?

1981–1990 V. Bricker (1986:210): "ahaw" 'lord, ruler' (Ch'olan, Yucatecan); Justeson (1984:328): J. Fox, B. Riese: possibly "*a:ja:w"; earlier "ajpo"; L. Campbell, J. Justeson, P. Mathews: logographic compound T0584.0687a or T0678a.0584 "*a:ja:w" 'lord'; not "ajpo" or "ajpohp" (T0687a polyvalent "po/aw"); usually T0168 reads after the sign to which it is prefixed; F. Lounsbury, L. Schele, D. Stuart: "ahpo/ahpoh," "ahaw" when accompanied by T0130; Macri (1988:86f.): title "*ajaw" < "aj" agentive + "uh" or "po" 'moon,' 'he of the moon'; Porter (1988): "itza" 'sorcerer'; Schele and Freidel (1990:54): substitution spelling "ah-ha-wa" for "ahau."

1991–2008 Davoust (1995:565): "ahaw" 'seigneur'; Knorozov (1999, vol. 1:127f.): "been-tzil" or "tzil-been" depending on order.

2M1

T 0300
Z –
K –

ahaw / ajaw

n lord; ruler

2. Picture: ?

1981–1990 Justeson (1984:335): cf. T0168; L. Campbell, J. Justeson, P. Mathews: compound T0533[0687a] "ahaw:(aw)" "*a:ja:w" 'lord'; J. Fox: "a:ja:w"; F. Lounsbury: variant of T0168, probably "ahaw"; L. Schele: "ahaw."

1991–2008 Davoust (1995:576): "ahaw" 'seigneur'; Knorozov (1999, vol. 1:132): /la-tzil/; combinación de 509.363; Ringle and Smith-Stark (1996:335–38): 0300 = 0168v; Ringle and Smith-Stark (1996:346): probably reads "ahau."

2M1

T 0518ab
Z –
K –

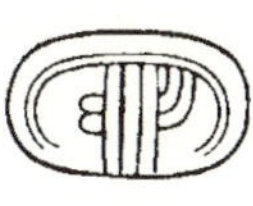

ahaw / ajaw

n lord; ruler

3. Picture: ?

1951–1980 Thompson (1962:119–21): [82 examples] Muluc variant = T0513.

1981–1990 Closs (1985): on Stela 22 at Naranjo, accession verb of rulership; Justeson (1984:339): J. Justeson: title; is infixed above in earliest Classic Lowland Mayan forms of day Ben; related to (possibly main form of) T0102.

1991–2008 Davoust (1995:583): "ahaw" 'seigneur'; Ringle and Smith-Stark (1996:335–38): 0518a,b = 0518a (indistiguishable); Schele (1992a:140): "ahauyan" accession event.

2M5

T 0194
Z 0009
K 0058

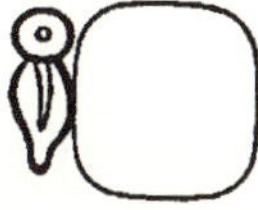

1. Picture: ?

1951–1980 Knorozov (1967:82): (= K057) "tzub" 'addition'.

1991–2008 Davoust (1995:567): "pi'z" 'mesure'; Knorozov (1999, vol. 1:99): "tzub," "tzab" (cascabel de serpiente estilizada).

2M7

T 0190
Z 0033
K 0076

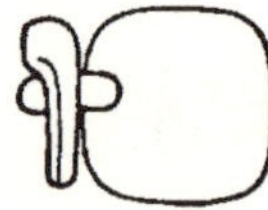

ch'ak / ch'äk

trans v; intrans v? cut, chop, injure; traverse?

Yu *ch'ak* ch'ak 'cortar con golpe, con hacha u otro instrumento' (Barrera Vásquez et al. 1980:122); ch'ak 'cut [with a blow], axe' (V. Bricker et al. 1998:78); ch'äk 'cut' (Hofling with Tesucún 1997:222); ch'äquic 'cortar, talar' (Ulrich and Ulrich 1976:87); ch'ak 'atravesar a la otra parte' (Barrera Vásquez et al. 1980:122)

Ch' *ch'äk* *ch'äk 'injure' (Kaufman and Norman 1984:119)

1. Picture: axe

1566–1915 Brasseur de Bourbourg (1869–1870, vol. 1:206): day Cimi; "cimi" 'il est mort' or "ci-mi" 'non effervescence plus' or "cim-i" 'qui a pris une pointe, une pousse'; Brinton (1895:104): "bat" 'tomahawk' possibly symbol or rebus for "batul" 'to fight', "batab" 'chief'; Rosny (1883:22): "nemazcab" 'hache, instrument tranchant'; Thomas (1888:371): machete or hatchet.

1916–1950 Gates (1931:166): hatchet.

1951–1980 Kelley (1962b:24): "bat" 'axe, hail' (D. Brinton, N. Cordy, D. Kelley); Kelley (1976:63, 135, 158, 332): "bat" 'axe'; Knorozov (1955:71): 087 (hacha) "bat, baat"; Knorozov (1967:84): "baat" 'axe'; Thompson (1962:59): [4 examples]; Thompson (1972:32): "bateel" affliction'; Thompson (1972:109): 'lightning storm'.

1981–1990 V. Bricker (1986:158–60, 210): "wac" 'to extrude, pop out'; V. Bricker and H. Bricker (1986:56): "wac" 'to extrude, pop out'; Grube (1990a:96): = T0320; Justeson (1984:330): L. Campbell: "b'at" 'axe'; J. Fox: depicts axe, "b'a:t," /b'a/; J. Justeson: depicts axe; F. Lounsbury: "b'aat"; P. Mathews: axe; B. Riese: 'axe'; no good evidence for morphemic/ phonetic use; L. Schele, D. Stuart: axe, possibly "b'aat," but there are other possibilities; Orejel (1990): /ch'a/ in expression "ch'ak" 'to chop' (war events) or 'to cross' (astronomical contexts).

1991–2008 Davoust (1995:567): "ch'ac" 'couper', "ch'ac-ab" 'hache'; /ch'a/; Knorozov (1999, vol. 1:178): "t'ac, ch'ac" (hacha); Schele and Grube (1997:91, 245): "ch'ak" 'to axe'; "ch'ak" 'to cross over' [in context of the Mars table]; Stuart (2005:69, n. 21): "ch'ak" 'cut, chop'; may also be "ch'ak" 'conquer, defeat' as in K'iche (Edmonson 1965).

2M9

T 0104
Z 0057
K –

Thompson (1962:400) incorrectly relates Z57 to T285.

1. Picture: maize and "ka" sign

1951–1980 Thompson (1972:84): evil affix.

1991–2008 Davoust (1995:561): "muc" 'enterrer'?; Ringle and Smith-Stark (1996:335–38): 0104 (retired) = most are misidentified; Dresden 68b is 0078v.

2MA

T 0080b
Z 0056
K 0096

1. Picture: dotted circle and "ka" sign

1951–1980 Knorozov (1967:86): composite grapheme K005-028.

1981–1990 V. Bricker (1986:209): (Landa's "o") /o/; Justeson (1984:321): probably two different signs; (b) J. Fox, J. Justeson: possibly phonetic compound /mo-k(a)/.

1991–2008 Davoust (1995:559): "pat" 'créer'; Knorozov (1999, vol. 1:77): /mo-ca/?; combinación de 356.165; Ringle and Smith-Stark (1996:335–38): 0080 (retired) = 0079b.

2MB

T —
Z —
K —

1. Picture: circle and empty cartouche

2S1

T 0084
Z 0077
K 0066

nal / näl; -nal

n; loc — maize; locative suffix

Yu *nal; nal* — nal 'maíz en barra, o en caña, o en mazorca, y la mazorca antes que la desgranen' (Barrera Vásquez et al. 1980:557); nal 'ear of corn' (V. Bricker et al. 1998:194); näl 'ear of corn' (Hofling with Tesucún 1997:466); näl 'mazorca' (Ulrich and Ulrich 1976:144); na 'casa, no denotando cuya' (Barrera Vásquez et al. 1980:545); nah 'house' (V. Bricker et al. 1998:193)

Ch' *näl; ø* — *näl 'corn ear' (Kaufman and Norman 1984:126)

For locative function of "-nal" suffix, see Stuart (1998:380, n. 3).

1. Picture: maize foliage

1566–1915 Thomas (1893:248): Landa's /l/.

1951–1980 Dütting (1974:50): "han"? 'food; flor de milpa'; Dütting (1979:183f.): "och" 'tender, grainless ear of corn'; Kelley (1976:126, 197, 332): (= T0085, T0086?) corncob; grammatical affixes based on corn representations; Knorozov (1955:69): 062 (mazorca de maíz en su envoltura) "nal" ("mal, mol"); Knorozov (1967:83): "nal, -nal" 'corn' (ear of corn in husk); Thompson (1972:36): "taz" 'layer'? when paired with T0561 'sky'; in other contexts hardly bears that interpretation; Thompson (1972:45): numeral classifier.

1981–1990 Grube (1990a:90): = T0085; Justeson (1984:322): F. Lounsbury, P. Mathews, L. Schele: possibly "ah"; J. Fox: T0084, T0085, T0086 probably all the same sign, possibly numeral classifier; Schele, Mathews, and Lounsbury (1990a): in "impinged bone" expressions of Dresden Codex, reads "nal."

1991–2008 Davoust (1995:559): "nal" 'maïs en tige, jeune maïs'; Knorozov (1999, vol. 1:98): "ngal" (elote envuelto en hojas); Ringle and Smith-Stark (1996:335–38): 0084 = 0084a; Stuart and Houston (1994:23, fig. 22): "nal"; Vail and Hernández (2005–2008): "nal" serves as complement to T0521 "winal" on Madrid 65–72.

2S1

T 0085bc
Z 0077
K 0066

nal / näl; nal

n; loc — maize; locative suffix

2. Picture: maize foliage

1566–1915 Thomas (1893:248): /l/.

1916–1950 Thompson (1950:285): "te."

1951–1980 Kelley (1976:126, 197, 332): (= T0085, T0086?) corncob; grammatical affixes based on corn representations; Knorozov (1967:83): "nal, -nal" 'corn' (ear of corn in husk); Thompson (1972:76): (with T0663) 'seed corn'.

1981–1990 Grube (1990a:90): = T0084; Justeson (1984:322): J. Justeson: two signs; J. Fox: T0084, T0085, T0086 probably all the same sign, possibly numeral classifier.

1991–2008 Davoust (1995:559): "nal" 'maïs en tige, jeune maïs'; Knorozov (1999, vol. 1:98): "ngal" (elote envuelto en hojas); Ringle and Smith-Stark (1996:335–38): 0085 (retired) = 0084b; Schele and Grube (1997:243): "nal."

2S1

T –
Z –
K 0357

nal / näl?; nal?

n; loc — maize; locative suffix

Central element possibly HH2 "ch'éen."

3. Picture: maize ear with foliage

1916–1950 Thompson (1950:fig. 43, nos. 41–42): maize seed.

1951–1980 Knorozov (1967:92, 102): (= K155) "tang (tan)"; "tan" 'middle'.

1991–2008 Davoust (1997:197): "cu nal" 'les plates-formes de maïs'; Knorozov (1999, vol. 1:179): "vaay-tang" (ligadura de 194-508); 'casa del centro'?; Schele and Grube (1997:239): "kunal" 'seat'; Stuart and Houston (1994:23, fig. 22): "nal."

2S1

T –
Z –
K –

nal / näl?; nal?

n; loc — maize; village, town

Variant form of 2S1, subsort 3

4. Picture: ?

1916–1950 Thompson (1950:271): seed.

1991–2008 Vail and Hernández (2005–2008): "nal" 'maize'; also used as a locative suffix indicating 'place'.

2S1

T 0723
Z 1317
K –

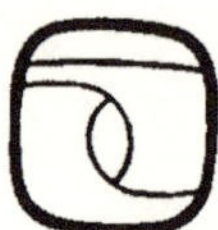

nal / näl?; nal?

n; loc — maize?; locative suffix?

This variant is grouped with 2S1 because it sometimes has the T0084 "nal" suffix. Some examples may be HH2 "ch'é'en/ch'en"? 'centote, cave, well'.

5. Picture: ?

1566–1915 Brasseur de Bourbourg (1869–1870, vol. 1:204): "p', p'a" 'sortir avec effort, rompre en sortant, ouvrir par force'.

1951–1980 Thompson (1962:309): [1 example] Perhaps a misdrawn T0663, but appears with affix T0047, unlike T0663.

1991–2008 Davoust (1995:598): "tz'ac" 'changement'; Knorozov (1999, vol. 1:135): "h'el"?; Ringle and Smith-Stark (1996:335–38): 0723 (retired) = 0662b; Vail (2002b): "nal"? 'place'.

2S1

T 0611
Z –
K 0121, 0358

nal / näl; nal

n; loc maize; locative suffix

6. Picture: maize foliage with number 8

1916–1950 Thompson (1950:fig. 43, nos. 44–45): 'eight' as maize symbol.

1951–1980 Kelley (1976:22): "uaxac" 'eight'; Knorozov (1967:89): "bix" 'eight'; Thompson (1972:82): Uaxac Yol Kauil? 'maize god'.

1991–2008 Davoust (1995:590): "waxac" '8'; Davoust (1997:233): "waxac nal" '8 épis de maïs'; Knorozov (1999, vol. 1:117): "vix, bix, vax"; cifra '8' Schele and Grube (1997:191): "nal" 'place'; Vail and Hernández (2005–2008): TVIII infix suggests association with maize god Nal.

2S2

T 0130
Z 0076
K 0052

wa

1. Picture: maize with foliage

1566–1915 Brasseur de Bourbourg (1869–1870, vol. 1:202): "ca" 'mâchoire'; "cáa" 'pierre à moudre le grain; une sorte de citrouille'; Brinton (1895:84): (bird's wing) 'superior' or 'supremacy'; Thomas (1893:245, 261): /u/; may be used as a month sign or determinative.

1916–1950 Thompson (1950:268–69, 281f.): "ak."

1951–1980 Barthel (1968:162–65): most likely "tac" or "aan"; Kelley (1962a:291): "-an, -'an"; Kelley (1976:176, 181, 214, 332): "aan"; an immature ear of corn; Knorozov (1955:70): 068 (una hoja?) "an, aan"; Knorozov (1967:81): "an, -an"; Lounsbury (1973:138): possibly /wa/; Thompson (1972:30): "bil" 'to sprout'; "-bil" 'suffix used to convert active verbs into participles'.

1981–1990 V. Bricker (1986:210): /wa/, "-aw" (imperfective); Dütting (1985:106): "aan/an"; probably functions as the past participle "-aan" (Yucatec); Fox and Justeson (1984:66–68): /wa/; "ab"; Grube (1990a:93): = T0131, T0289?; Justeson (1984:326): consensus /wa/; J. Justeson: "-Vb'," instrumental suffix; J. Fox, F. Lounsbury: final /'w/ as reflex of earlier /b'/; B. Riese: sometimes used with unknown referent; Stuart (1987:15): /wa/.

1991–2008 Davoust (1995:563): "wah" 'tortilla'; /wa/; Knorozov (1999, vol. 1:97, 231): "aan" 'ser; sufijo de participios del pasado' (bejuco o cordel).

2S2

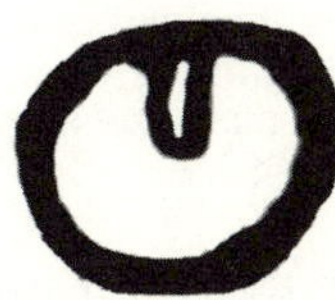

T –
Z –
K 0003

wa

Also occurs as element of PT4 and 2S2, subsort 1.

2. Picture: maize tamale

1951–1980 Knorozov (1967:78): (= K157) /la/.

1981–1990 Taube (1989a:36): notched ball of T0014; represents maize tamale "wah."

1991–2008 Knorozov (1999, vol. 1:69): /la/.

2S2

T 0019v
Z 0091
K 0004?

wa

Graphically similar to YSA /mu/ but seems to have a distinct value.
3. Picture: maize curl

1951–1980 Knorozov (1967:78): (= K135) /mu/; Thompson (1972:103): "koch" 'punishment, divinely sent disease'.
1981–1990 Taube (1985:178): corn curl; Taube (1989a:35): /wa/.
1991–2008 Davoust (1997:304): "-aw."

2S6

T –
Z –
K –

k'áak' / k'ahk

n fire
Yu *k'áak'* k'ak' 'fuego' (Barrera Vásquez et al. 1980:364); k'áak' 'flame, fire' (V. Bricker et al. 1998:143); k'aak' 'fire' (Hofling with Tesucún 1997:386)
Ch' *k'ahk* *k'ahk 'fire' (Kaufman and Norman 1984:123); k'ak' 'fuego, lumbre' (Keller and Luciano G. 1997:64)
1. Picture: fire

1916–1950 Gates (1931:146): 'wood; firewood'.
1951–1980 Kelley (1962b:35): 'fire, torch' (E. Seler, H Spinden, B. Whorf , J. E. S. Thompson, Y. Knorozov, D. Kelley); burning wood bundle (H. Beyer); "tooc kak" 'burning fire' (B. Whorf); "kak" 'fire' (J. E. S. Thompson); "poc (poc)" cf. "pocob" 'hearth' (Y. Knorozov); lightning dog (J. Villacorta); Kelley (1968c): 'fire'.
1981–1990 Stuart (1987:10f.): "buts' " 'smoke' or possibly "k'ak' " 'fire'.
1991–2008 Davoust (1995:562): "kak" 'flamme'; "butz" 'fumée'; Schele and Grube (1997:127): "k'ak' " 'fire'.

2S6

T 0122
Z 0038, 0040
K 0036

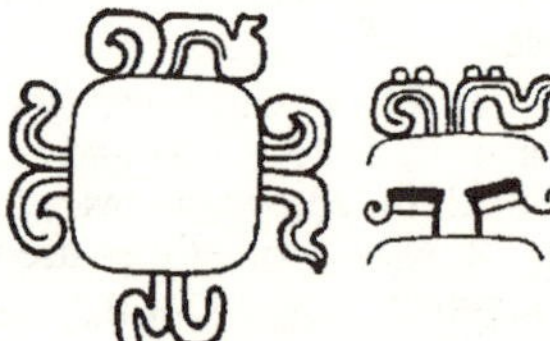

k'´áak' / k'ahk

n fire

2. Picture: fire

1566–1915 Brasseur de Bourbourg (1869–1870, vol. 1:219): signe qui paraît avoir été adopté pour signifier l'enchaînement d'une période avec une autre; Brinton (1895:98): various explanations, as typifying fire, lightning, or wind (Seler, Schellhas); instead seems to represent magical or divine power exerted by blowing; may also signify the idea of speech or sound.
1916–1950 Gates (1931:146): 'wood; firewood'; Whorf (1942:484, fig. 1): /to/, /tu/.
1951–1980 Kelley (1976:177, 332): "kak"; Knorozov (1955:73): 114 (lenguas de fuego) "pok" ("kak"?) 'fuego'; Knorozov (1967:80): "took" 'fire'; Thompson (1972:59): flames; when used with T0563a may signify pustules and eruptions.
1981–1990 V. Bricker (1986:209): smoke (semantic determinative); Justeson (1984:325): cf. T0150; J. Fox, P. Mathews, L. Schele: smoke and/or flame; J. Justeson, P. Mathews: semantic determinative to T0150 for "*taj" 'torch'; J. Justeson: smoke/flame and speech scrolls; as speech scroll is phonetic determinative for morpheme with approximate shape "al" based on "*a'l" 'to speak'; F. Lounsbury: flame or smoke; "tah"; MacLeod (1988b): may be phonetic /k'a/ unless otherwise specified as "butz' " 'smoke'; Schele and Stuart (1986): "butz' " 'smoke'; Stuart (1987:10f.): "buts' " 'smoke' and "k'ak' " 'fire'.
1991–2008 Davoust (1995:562): "kak" 'flamme', "butz" 'fumée'; Knorozov (1999, vol. 1:72, 239): "tooc" 'fuego; quemar, devastar, abandonar, dejar, brillante' (volutas de humo que suben sobre el fuego); Stuart and Houston (1994:23, fig. 22): "k'ak'."

2S7

T 0299
Z –
K –

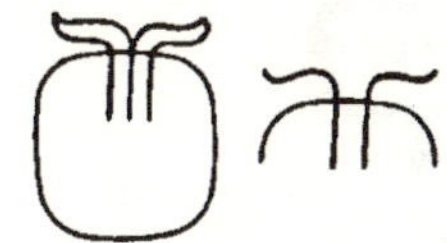

1. Picture: top cleft

1981–1990 V. Bricker and H. Bricker (1988:S12, S14): (with T0561.0023.0181) "caan-ah" inchoative verb 'to rise'; Justeson (1984:335): J. Justeson, P. Mathews: semantic determinative for sound issuing from object; F. Lounsbury: sound coming from the "tunk'ul"; distinguishes Pax from T0548 "tun"; L. Schele: morphemic for sound of an object.

1991–2008 Davoust (1995:575): "zih" 'naître'; /zi/; Knorozov (1999, vol. 1:73, 239): "tooc" 'fuego; quemar, devastar, abandonar, dejar, brillante' (volutas de humo que suben sobre el fuego); Schele and Grube (1994:17): /si/; Schele and Grube (1997:191): "si(h)" 'born'.

2S8

T 0015a
Z 0010
K 0051

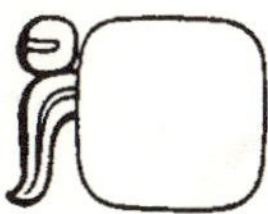

ah / aj

agentive — agentive

Yu *ah* — ah 'antepuesta a los apellidos de linaje denota los varones; antepuesta a los nombres de lugares' (Barrera Vásquez et al. 1980:3)

Ch' *aj* — *aj 'prepound/proclitic; male; relatively large/active being' (Kaufman and Norman 1984:139)

1. Picture: maize kernel with foliation?

1566–1915 Brasseur de Bourbourg (1869–1870, vol. 1:201): /a/; 'figure d'un bec d'oiseau, d'une trompe'; "a" 'cuisse d'homme, jambe'; Brinton (1895:84): sign for stars.

1951–1980 Kelley (1962a:302f.): /a/; Kelley (1976:201, 331): /a/ (interchanges with T0743 and T0238); Knorozov (1955:70): 067 (una hoja? con elemento complementario) /a/; Knorozov (1967:80f.): = K040 /ye/; Thompson (1972:38): prefix to glyphs of death or evil.

1981–1990 V. Bricker (1986:208): (Landa's "a") /a(h)/, "ah-" (agentive) (Cholan, Yucatecan); Justeson (1984:317): J. Justeson: some (= codex form of T0228) /a/; B. Riese: possibly /a/.

1991–2008 Davoust (1995:554): "ah" 'préf. genre masc.'; /a/; Knorozov (1999, vol. 1:88): /ye/ (gota de agua cayendo?); Schele and Grube (1997:81): /u/ or /hu/.

2S8

T 0015b
Z 0010a
K 0040–41

ah / aj
agentive

agentive

2. Picture: maize kernel or death eye

1566–1915 Brasseur de Bourbourg (1869–1870, vol. 1:203): /n/; 'lettre qui est l'attribut de la grandeur, de l'excellence, de la royauté'.

1951–1980 Kelley (1962a:302): /a/; Kelley (1976:201, 331): /a/ (interchanges with T0743 and T0238); Knorozov (1955:74): 123 (líquido que se vierte) "vatz, vah?"; Knorozov (1967:80): /ye/ (falling drop?); Thompson (1972:38): prefix to glyphs of death or evil.

1981–1990 V. Bricker (1986:208): (Landa's "a") /a(h)/, "ah-" (agentive) (Ch'olan, Yucatecan); Grube (1990a:87): = T0228, T0229; Justeson (1984:317): J. Justeson: some (= codex form of T0228) /a/; B. Riese: possibly /a/.

1991–2008 Davoust (1995:554): "ah" 'préf. genre masc.'; /a/; Knorozov (1999, vol. 1:88): /ye/ (gota de agua cayendo?); Schele and Grube (1997:81): /u/ or /hu/.

2S8

T 0015v
Z —
K 0002

ah / aj
agentive

agentive

Sometimes may be variant form of AMC.

3. Picture: maize tamale

1916–1950 Thompson (1950:189): death eye.

1951–1980 Knorozov (1967:78): 'one'.

1991–2008 Knorozov (1999, vol. 1:69, 235): "h'un" 'one'; Vail (1996:226): substitutes for T0015 in Madrid Codex; may have same value, agentive "ah."

2S8

T —
Z —
K —

ah / aj
agentive

agentive

4. Picture: curved line of dots

1991–2008 Vail (1996:251): "ah" agentive prefix.

3 Three Segments

32A

T 0074
Z 0075
K 0069

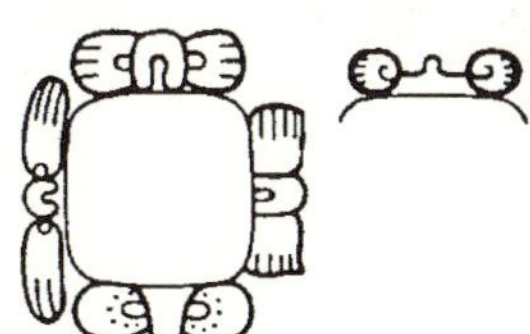

ma

ma(')

adv	no, negative
Yu *má'*	ma' 'no' (Barrera Vásquez et al. 1980:469); má' 'no, not' (V. Bricker et al. 1998:176)
Ch' *ma(')*	*ma(') 'negative' (Kaufman and Norman 1984:139)

1. Picture: hands?

1566–1915 Bowditch (1910:257): Landa's /ma/; Brasseur de Bourbourg (1869–1870, vol. 1:205): "ma" 'bras, main, anciennement; négation et signe du passé; optatif, anciennement'; Landa [1566] (Tozzer 1941:162, 170): in month glyph Mac; <ma>; Rosny (1883:23): "ma" 'non, pas, négation'; Thomas (1893:249): Landa's /ma/.

1916–1950 Whorf (1933:23): /ma/.

1951–1980 Kelley (1962a:285–87): /ma/; Kelley (1962b:40): /ma/; Kelley (1976:152, 176–78, 185, 200, 252, 332): "ma" 'until'; Knorozov (1955:65): 008 (manos separadas, gesto de negación) /m(a)/; Knorozov (1958:285): /m(a)/; Knorozov (1967:84): /m(a)/; "ma" 'big; not'; Lounsbury (1974a): "mah" 'great'; Thompson (1962:47): (down balls); Thompson (1972:30f.): "tan" in phrase "tanlahbil" 'served, taken care of' (T0074.0669.0130); Thompson (1972:96): "tan"; may refer to down or cotton, of which, myths tell us, clouds were made.

1981–1990 V. Bricker (1986:209): /ma/; Grube (1990a:90): = T0071?, T0072; Justeson (1984:321): cf. Landa's "ma" in "ma' in-k'at-i"; L. Campbell, J. Fox, J. Justeson, F. Lounsbury, P. Mathews, L. Schele, D. Stuart: /ma/; J. Fox: possibly originally 'great'; J. Justeson: 'great', includes "*noj"; probably based on Greater Izapan logogram, Mixe-Zoquean "*mäh" 'great'; F. Lounsbury, P. Mathews: "noh" or "mah" 'great'.

1991–2008 Davoust (1995:558): "mah" 'grand, très'; /ma/; Knorozov (1999, vol. 1:92): /ma/ (manos abiertas como señal de algo grande); Love (1991:301): Landa's /ma/ in <ma in ka ti>; apparently derived from Mixe-Zoquean "mah" 'big' (Justeson et al. 1985:44, 60); Maya borrowed the /ma/ value for the sign, but may also have borrowed the 'great' value and read it "noh."

32A

T 0070
Z 0017
K 0039

ma

2. Picture: hand?

1951–1980 Cordan (1964:20): "maax" 'mico de noche'; Knorozov (1967:80, 84): (= K069?) /m(a)/; "ma" 'big; not'.

1981–1990 Justeson (1984:321): L. Campbell: /ma/; J. Fox, J. Justeson, F. Lounsbury, P. Mathews, B. Riese: more than one sign; /ma/, origin as truncated version of T0074.

1991–2008 Davoust (1995:558): "mah" 'grand, très'; /ma/; Knorozov (1999, vol. 1:88, 140): /ma/; Ringle and Smith-Stark (1996:335–38): 0070 = 0070 (superfix and left subfix); = 0074v (antefix and right subfix).

32A

T 0073
Z 0044a
K 0044

ma?

Resembles BM2 but probably not equivalent.

3. Picture: hands?

1951–1980 Knorozov (1967:80): /h'e/.

1991–2008 Davoust (1995:558): "he' " 'ouvrir'; /he/; Knorozov (1999, vol. 1:71, 235): "h'e" 'abrir'; Ringle and Smith-Stark (1996:335–38): 0073 (retired) = codical examples probably 0074; others may be 0076v; Schele and Grube (1997:98): /he/ on Dresden 8a in spelling of T0073:0612 "hel" 'recompense'.

32D

T 0062
Z 0059, 0073
K 0103

yu

uy-; (u)y-

dep pn he/she/it; his/her/its; third person prefix, Set A (ergative and possessive), prevocalic
Yu *uy-* u(y)- 'Set A dependent pronoun, 3rd person' (Hofling with Tesucún 1997:9)
Ch' *uy-* *u- 'ergative 3rd person' ; *(u)y- 'ergative 3rd person prevocalic' (Kaufman and Norman 1984:91)

1. Picture: ear flare?

1566–1915 Brasseur de Bourbourg (1869–1870, vol. 1:206): day Oc; "oc" 'pied, jambe, entrée, entrer'.

1951–1980 Cordan (1964:43): "kax"; Kelley (1962b:24): knot; Kelley (1976:157, 197, 331): misidentified as T0219; present-tense suffix?; Knorozov (1955:72): 098 (pendiente?) /n(–?)/; Knorozov (1967:87): "lak" (earplug).

1981–1990 V. Bricker (1986:209): /ti/?; Grube (1990a:89): = T0061; Justeson (1984:320): J. Fox: Thompson includes two distinct signs here; one is Z59, the others are /u/, /hu/, and /yu/; see T0064; J. Justeson: /u/, /hu/, /yu/; D. Stuart: possibly /yu/; Stuart (1985b:7–8): T0061/0062/0065 may be possessive pronominal, perhaps "u," as initial sign in relationship glyph; Stuart (1987:16): cites Lounsbury (personal communication, 1983): /yu/ or /u/.

1991–2008 Ciaramella (2004:14): "hok' " 'to tie up' on Madrid 60b and 61b; credits Dütting (1965) with initially proposing this reading; Davoust (1995:557): "uh" 'collier'?, "yul" 'polir'; /yu/; Knorozov (1999, vol. 1:109): "lich" (orejera); Ringle and Smith-Stark (1996:335–38): 0062 (retired) = 0061b.

32G

T 0135acd
Z –
K 0008

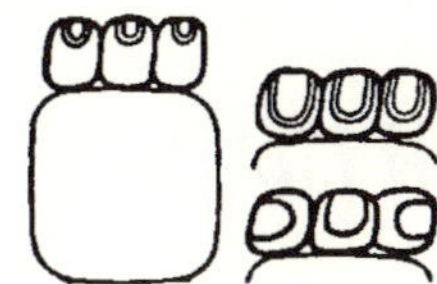

1. Picture: maize tamales?

1951–1980 Knorozov (1967:78): (= K330)?

1991–2008 Davoust (1995:563): "chah" 'obscur'; /cha/; Knorozov (1999, vol. 1:82, 231): "am" 'sufijo formativo de sustantivos'; MacLeod (1991h): /ka/ or /cha/.

32H

T 0066
Z 0053
K 0086

i'inah / hinaj

n — seed; seed maize
Yu *i'inah* — i'inah 'seed corn' (V. Bricker et al. 1998:13)
Ch' *hinaj* — *(h)inaj 'seed' (Kaufman and Norman 1984:120)

1. Picture: grains of maize

1951–1980 Cordan (1964:40f.): "kuk-yal" 'Señora de las flores'; Knorozov (1967:86): "pom" 'copal'; Thompson (1972:39): reminiscent of the 'jade' sign (T0580).

1981–1990 Justeson (1984:321): J. Fox, J. Justeson, F. Lounsbury: "*hinäj" 'seed'; Lounsbury (1984:177): "hinah" 'seed'.

1991–2008 Davoust (1995:558): "inah" 'grain de maïs'; Knorozov (1999, vol. 1:85): "pom" (bolas de copal colocadas en un plato?).

32H

T –
Z 1370
K 0087

i'inah / hinaj

n — seed; seed maize

Thompson (1962:53) catalogs the grapheme illustrated as an example of T0136.

2. Picture: grains of maize

1566–1915 Brasseur de Bourbourg (1869–1870, vol. 1:218): symbole de la glace.

1951–1980 Knorozov (1967:86): = K086 "pom" 'copal'; Thompson (1962:53, 403): Z1370 = T0136 [8 examples].

1991–2008 Vail (2002b): variant of T0066, "i'inah" 'seed'?

32J

T 0124
Z 0045
K 0023

1. Picture: triple scroll

1951–1980 Cordan (1964:34): "tzik (*tik)"; Knorozov (1967:78): (= K019) "am" 'interval'.

1991–2008 Davoust (1995:562): "tzol" 'ordre'; "ci' " 'agave'; /tzo/; Knorozov (1999, vol. 1:82): "am" (olas como señal de intervalos o sucesos periódicos); aparece en el periodo olmeca; Schele (1991a): credits Stuart and MacLeod with /tzo/; but may also be /kV/; /ki/ or /ko/ is the value when used as a subfix; for example, Tikal Temple 4 Lintel 3 and Tikal St. 31, and the Dresden Codex "k'u-ok" phrases; Schele and Grube (1994:83): /tzi/; Schele and Grube (1997:17): /tzi/; Schele, Grube, and Fahsen (1994): /tzi/.

32K

T –
Z –
K 0073

Classic 32K is /hi/; no evidence for this reading in codices.
há'ab' period: Ch'en/Sihora
1. Picture: "kawak" sign with knot

1916–1950 Gates (1931:63): "Ch'en."

1951–1980 Knorozov (1967:84): phonetic (rope tied in knot?); ". . . -ku" name of a month, Old Yucatec Ch'en; Thompson (1950:fig. 17, no. 32): month Ch'en.

1991–2008 Schele (1991b:5a): /hi/; Schele (1992b:228f.): correspondence from Stuart 1989: /hi/.

32L

hi

T 0186
Z 0070a
K 0075

1. Picture: noose?

1566–1915 Brasseur de Bourbourg (1869–1870, vol. 1:215): paraît être une variante de la précédente [T0591].

1951–1980 Dütting (1974:50): "lok"? 'come out; beloved'; Kelley (1976:102, 332): (knot); locative suffix, 'place of'; Knorozov (1955:70): 070 (manojo de ramas) "tah"; Knorozov (1967:84): phonetic (bundle of stalks).

1981–1990 Justeson (1984:329): J. Fox, J. Justeson: "-el," "-il."

1991–2008 Davoust (1995:566): /li/; Grube (2004:80): a late variant of the T0060 /hi/ knot; used in spelling of 'road' (b'ih) on D. 41c and 65b and in the word for 'house' ("naah") on D. 8c and 33c; Knorozov (1999, vol. 1:93): "tah" (haz de tallos); Schele and Grube (1997: 83): /hi/; Vail (1996:316, 385f.): /lV/ or /hV/; Vail (1999): /le/ or /hV/.

32M

T 0126
Z 0074
K 0037

ya
uy-; (u)y-

dep pn — he/she/it; his/her/its; third person prefix, Set A (ergative and possessive), prevocalic
Yu *uy-* — u(y) 'Set A dependent pronoun, 3rd person' (Hofling with Tesucún 1997:9)
Ch' *uy-* — *u- 'ergative 3rd person' ; *(u)y- 'ergative 3rd person prevocalic' (Kaufman and Norman 1984:91)

1. Picture: ?

1916–1950 Thompson (1950:163): indicates anteriority in time.

1951–1980 Dütting (1974:50): credits Barthel and Dütting with "ah/ih"; Kelley (1976:196, 197, 332): affix, 'back'; "-ah" (past tense), "-hi" (past tense); Knorozov (1955:75): 129 (una gota y un elemento confuso) /hi/; Knorozov (1967:80): "ngi, -ngi."

1981–1990 V. Bricker (1986:210): /ya/, "-ya" 'then, there' (Ch'olan); Dütting (1985:108): "ah" and "ih/hi"; Fox and Justeson (1984:54–62): /a/; "y-"; "-ih"; "ix"; Grube (1990a:93): = T0047; Justeson (1984:325): cf. T0125(b); L. Campbell: "i(h)," /hi/ < "hi' " 'sand'; J. Fox, J. Justeson, B. Riese, L. Schele, D. Stuart: "iy," "ih"; /a/; J. Fox, J. Justeson: /i/, possibly /hi/; "*aj-" prefix; J. Fox, J. Justeson, B. Riese: "-Vh" (B. Riese: especially "ah"); J. Fox, J. Justeson, L. Schele, D. Stuart: completive aspect suffix, and proto-Mayan "*e:j" 'time hence' and proto-Mayan "*e:r" 'time ago' as distance number suffix; /a/ possibly by generalization from use of "-ah" and "-ih" as completive aspect suffixes; J. Fox, J. Justeson: also "y-"; iconic origin in vegetal sprout ("*yi'h" 'maize tassel', "*yi'j" 'ripe'); J. Fox, J. Justeson: derived from T0125 (with dots for "hi' " 'sand'); P. Mathews, L. Schele, D. Stuart: anterior event and date indicator; verbal suffix; sometimes "ah," male article; P. Mathews: /a/, /i/; possibly "ih"; W. Norman: possibly enclitic "-ix" 'already', at least with verbs and distance numbers; MacLeod (1983:50–55): /i(h)/, /a(h)/; Schele (1987d): generally /ya/ prefix; Stuart (1985c): /-i/; Stuart (1987:47): /ya/; Stuart (1990): suffix to two constants of anterior date indicator.

1991–2008 Davoust (1995:562): "y-at" 'son pénis'; /ya/; Grube (1991:223) "i/ih"; Knorozov (1999, vol. 1:71, 237): "ngi" 'ave; pasado de "ngal"; sufijo de verbos del pasado'; Ringle and Smith-Stark (1996:335–38): 0126 (retired) = 0125b; Stuart (1997:1f.): /ya/; Stuart (2005:62): as verbal suffix "-iiy," referring to time ago.

32M

T 0047
Z 0074
K –

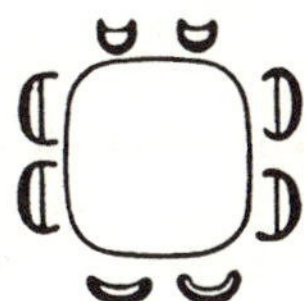

ya
uy-; (u)y-

dep pn — he/she/it; his/her/its; third person prefix, Set A (ergative and possessive), prevocalic

2. Picture: ?

1951–1980 Kelley (1976:152, 331): "buhul."

1981–1990 V. Bricker (1986:208): /ya/; Fox and Justeson (1984:54–62): /a/; "y-"; "-ih"; "ix"; Grube (1990a:89): = T0125, T0126, T0133; Justeson (1984:319): J. Fox, J. Justeson, B. Riese: = T0125 and T0126; P. Mathews: codex equivalent of T0126; codex equivalent of only a very few T0125; L. Schele, D. Stuart: codex equivalent of T0126.

1991–2008 Davoust (1995:556): "y-at" 'son pénis'; /ya/; Knorozov (1999, vol. 1:71, 237): "ngi" 'ave; pasado de "ngal"; sufijo de verbos del pasado'; Ringle and Smith-Stark (1996:335–38): 0047 (retired) = 00125c; Stuart (2005:62): as verbal suffix "-iiy," referring to time ago; Vail (1996:224f.): may have had a function similar to the discourse particle "-e" in Classical Yucatec in certain contexts.

32N

T 0241
Z –
K –

Used in contexts where appears to be substituting for 33F /hi/.

1. Picture: ?

32P

T 0162
Z 0055
K 0085

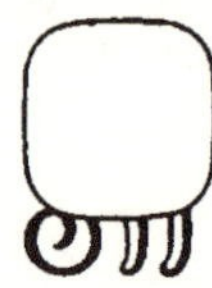

adj?; n? abundance of?

1. Picture: ?

1951–1980 Cordan (1964:41f.): "tik(le)pekil" asociado al dios del maíz; Knorozov (1955:71): 086 (vasijas con líquido?) "ooch" 'comida, alimento'; Knorozov (1967:85): "och" 'food'.

1991–2008 Davoust (1995:565): "ch'a" 'saisir, porter'; Davoust (1997:99): "ka' " 'beaucoup de'; Knorozov (1999, vol. 1:72): "ooch" (granos de maíz); MacLeod (1991c): Classic variant (T0128) as /k'a/ and "k'al" 'close'; Schele and Grube (1997:84): codical variant of T0128; "k'aa" 'what remains; abundance'; Vail and Hernández (2005–2008): read by V. Bricker (personal communication, 2003) as "o'och" 'food, sustenance'.

32S

T 0285
Z 0057
K 0097?

1. Picture: ?

1951–1980 Knorozov (1967:86): composite grapheme K135?-028-028.

1991–2008 Davoust (1995:574): "za' " 'boisson de maïs'; /za/; Knorozov (1999, vol. 1:84): /mu-ca-ca/; combinación de 8.165.165; Ringle and Smith-Stark (1996:335–38): 0285 (retired) = 0278v?

32V

T 0020
Z 0090
K 0089

1. Picture: ?

1951–1980 Knorozov (1967:86): = K090 morphemic; Thompson (1972:86): includes the hooked element with the value "koch" 'punishment, disease'.

1991–2008 Davoust (1995:554): "yol/hol" 'germe'; /yo-ho/?; Davoust (1997:248): "hol."

32W

T —
Z —
K —

1. Picture: ?

33A

T 0049
Z 0049
K 0024

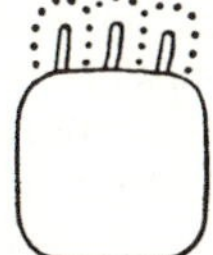

to

1. Picture: dotted scrolls

1951–1980 Cordan (1964:38–40): "pi' " 'chispa'; Kelley (1976:148–50, 208, 331): (determinative for 'fire'?) T0049:0110, 'fire, torch', "tooc"?; Knorozov (1955:74): 116 (fuego, determinor) 'fuego'; Knorozov (1967:77f.): "k'aak' " 'fire'.

1981–1990 Grube (1990a:89): = T0044; Grube and Stuart (1987:8f.): /to/; Justeson (1984:319): J. Fox: "tah" 'torch' when suffixed by T0110 (/ha/); possibly obsidian or flint blade when suffixed by T0112; F. Lounsbury, B. Riese, L. Schele, D. Stuart: = T044, if so possibly /to/.

1991–2008 Davoust (1995:556): "to' " 'enveloppe'; /to/; Knorozov (1999, vol. 1:81): "kaak" (llamas chispeantes); Ringle and Smith-Stark (1996:335–38): 0049 (retired) = 0044c.

33B

T 0069
Z 0044
K 0009

he / je?

1. Picture: eggs?

1951–1980 Knorozov (1967:78): morphemic (feathers?); Thompson (1972:96): "tan"; may refer to down or cotton, of which, myths tell us, clouds were made.

1981–1990 Justeson (1984:321): J. Fox, J. Justeson: probably logographic; pronunciation approximates "ma"; F. Lounsbury, P. Mathews: "mam"?; Schele (1989c:5a): /hi/.

1991–2008 Davoust (1995:Planche 45): /he/ (attributes to Grube, paper presented at 1989 Palenque Mesa Redonda); Davoust (1995:558): /he/; Grube (2004:73): /je/, not /he/; Knorozov (1999, vol. 1:81): (K0098) "tok" (plumón de ave que se usaba en los dardos?); Schele (1991b:20): cites Stuart (correspondence, 1988): substitution for /hi/ at Chichén Itzá; credits Grube with /he/ based on appearance in possible "hem" 'valley'; Schele confirms /hV/ value with example from Palenque, Tableritos; Schele and Grube (1997:16): /he/; Stuart (2005:180, n. 59): in combination with T0613, single grapheme with possible reading of "ak" or "akan" 'grass, grassland, bajo," not "hem" 'valley' interpretation of Schele and Grube (1997).

33C

T 0123
Z —
K —

1. Picture: sprouts

1991–2008 Davoust (1995:562): "tal" 'aller'?

33F

T 0136
Z 0065, 0078
K 0018

hi / ji

1. Picture: curls

1566–1915 Thomas (1893:253, 264): /h/ aspiration; "ha" 'water'.

1916–1950 Whorf (1942:484, fig. 1): /i/.

1951–1980 Barthel (1968): "may" 'offering, gift'; Kelley (1976:209, 332): determinant of meaning; Knorozov (1955:76): 150 determinador del 'sentido'; Knorozov (1967:78): diacritical sign, showing that a morphemic sign, especially calendrical, is used as a phonetic sign.

1981–1990 Justeson (1984:326): see T0134; J. Fox: two signs, Z1370 and other = T0134; L. Schele, D. Stuart: = T0018, T0088, T0758b; Schele and Grube (1988): probably /o/; Stuart (1987:42–45): /hi/.

1991–2008 Davoust (1995:563): "hi' " 'sable'?; "huh" 'iguane'; /hi/; Grube (2004:74f): /ji/, not /hi/; Knorozov (1999, vol. 1:89): signo diacrítico, generalmente indica que el signo morfémico está empleado en el calidad de fonético; Vail (1996:224f.): may have functioned as a deictic particle, rather than /hi/, in certain contexts in the Madrid Codex.

33G

T 0143
Z –
K 0010

1. Picture: ?

1951–1980 Knorozov (1967:78): (= K017)?

1991–2008 Lacadena (2004:88–93): “ha'al” ‘rain’; Taube (1992:19): 'water lily flower' equivalent to T0501, "ha."

33H

T 0251
Z 0064
K 0084

b'a

1. Picture: ?

1566–1915 Brasseur de Bourbourg (1869–1870, vol. 1:201): "b, be" 'pas marche, chemin, voie'.

1951–1980 Knorozov (1967:85): "ab" (a field divided into plots).

1981–1990 Grube (1990a:99): = T0252; Justeson (1984:333): two signs: J. Fox, J. Justeson, P. Mathews: (a) /b'a/; (b) = T0149a; F. Lounsbury, B. Riese, D. Stuart: (a) "b'a," "-(a)b' "; L. Schele: /b'/.

1991–2008 V. Bricker (1991:286f.): /ba/; Davoust (1995:572): /ba/; Grube (1994b:181): T0501 /ba/ invented after 9.11.0.0.0; Knorozov (1999, vol. 1:82): /ab/ (campo dividido en parcelas).

33H

T 0252
Z 0064
K –

b'a

Thompson (1962:400) incorrectly relates Z64 to T0138, instead of T0252.
2. Picture: ?

1981–1990 Grube (1990a:99): = T0251; Justeson (1984:333): P. Mathews: = T0251; L. Schele: = T0251 in codex style; Stuart (1987:46): /ba/.

1991–2008 Davoust (1995:572): /ba/; Grube (1994b:181): T0252 /ba/ invented after 9.11.0.0.0; Ringle and Smith-Stark (1996:335–38): 0252 (retired) = 0251v.

33K

T 0142bc
Z –
K –

1. Picture: circles

1981–1990 Grube (1990a:93): T0255; Grube and Stuart (1987): T0255 may be a precursor; sometimes replaced by T0074 /ma/ in final position; may read "-Vm" or /-mV/, to stress a final /-m/ or /-n/, as in the case of the "k'atun" glyph; Justeson (1984:326): T0142a and T0142b, c two different signs; Schele (1989c:5a): /ma/.

1991–2008 Davoust (1995:563): /mV/; Knorozov (1999, vol. 1:78): "ox"; Ringle and Smith-Stark (1996:335–38): 0142 = 0135 (superfix only, others remain 0142); Stuart, Houston, and Robertson (1999:26): "-oob' "? 'plural ending'.

33L

T 0137
Z 0007
K 0017

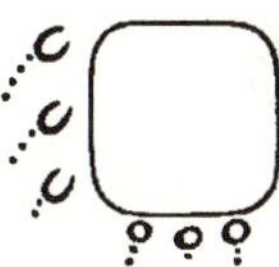

1. Picture: loops or circles with rows of dots

1566–1915 Thomas (1893:263): "ha, haa" 'water; rain; shower'.

1916–1950 Thompson (1950:260): rain.

1951–1980 Kelley (1962b:24): rain, rainy (C. Thomas, J. E. S. Thompson, Y. Knorozov, D. Kelley); "toz" (Y. Knorozov); Kelley (1976:150): 'rain' seems entirely plausible; Knorozov (1955:74): 126 (gotas de agua) "toz, taz"; Knorozov (1967:78): "ch'ah" (drops); Thompson (1972:75): 'raining'?

1981–1990 Justeson (1984:326): J. Fox: possibly either a locative preposition or a pronoun (but not both).

1991–2008 Davoust (1995:563): "ha' " 'eau'; /ha/; Knorozov (1999, vol. 1:78): "tox" (gotas de agua cayendo); Lacadena (2004:90, 96, n. 6): = T0143, "ha'al" 'rain'.

3M1

T 0058
Z 0021
K 0061

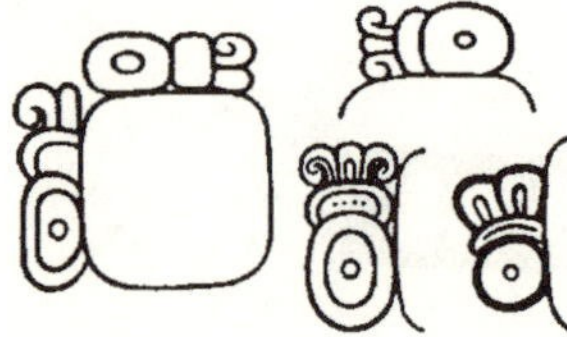

sak / säk

adj white, bright

Yu *sak* sak 'cosa blanca; en composición denota cosa artificial o cosa hecha por la mano o industria humana' (Barrera Vásquez et al. 1980:709); sak 'white; false' (V. Bricker et al. 1998:238); säk 'white' (Hofling with Tesucún 1997:551)

Ch' *säk* *säk 'white' (Kaufman and Norman 1984:130)

1. Picture: ear flare? with scrolls

1566–1915 Brasseur de Bourbourg (1869–1870, vol. 1:203): "o" 'surface, vase, collier'; Brinton (1895:108): 'north'; Seler (1888): "zak" 'white'; Thomas (1893:256): "zac."

1916–1950 Gates (1931:89): "sac" 'white'.

1951–1980 Cordan (1964:21f.): "sak" 'blanco; arte; artificio'; Dütting (1979:185): "zac"; sometimes replaced by T0050; Kelley (1962a:281): "zac" in month glyph Zac; Kelley (1976:69, 331): "zac" 'white'; Knorozov (1955:69): 063 (tallo seco de maíz?) "zac" 'blanco'; Knorozov (1967:82): "sak" 'white' (knotted rope); Mathews (1980:68): "zac"; Thompson (1972:55): "zac" 'white', also root of terms for 'weaving'; Thompson (1972:92): "zac"; in addition to its meaning of 'white' may also mean 'fear' (as on D. 26a).

1981–1990 V. Bricker (1986:209): "zäc" 'white' (Cholan), "zac" 'white' (Yucatecan); Grube (1990a:89): = T0050; Justeson (1984:320): consensus "sak" 'white'; J. Justeson, F. Lounsbury, B. Riese: also "*sas" 'light (of color)' in "saskab' "; F. Lounsbury: as "sak," connotation of 'resplendent'; Stross (1989): iconographic representation of crayfish; Mixe-Zoquean root is translated into Mayan languages as T0058 (as well as T0051, T0053, and T0059).

1991–2008 Davoust (1995:557): "zac/zäc" 'blanc, brillant'; Knorozov (1999, vol. 1:102, 233): "zac" 'blanco; cosa artificial, falsedad; falso'.

3M2

T 0059
Z 0072
K 0059

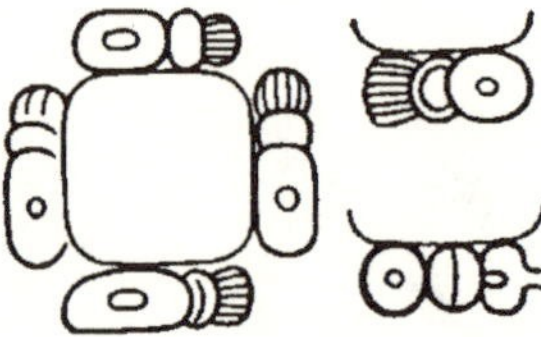

ti

tí' / ti, ta, tä

prep in, at, etc.; preposition

Yu *tí'* ti' 'preposición a, con, por instrumento, adentro' (Barrera Vásquez et al. 1980:788); tí' 'to, at, in, from, for' (V. Bricker et al. 1998:274)

Ch' *ti; ta; tä* *tä 'preposition' (Kaufman and Norman 1984:139); ta 'for, belongs to' (Knowles 1984:461); tä 'to, from, by' (Knowles 1984:463); ti 'en, a, por, de' (Warkentin and Scott 1980:98); ti 'en' (Morán 1935:26); ti' 'beside, by the side; at the edge' (Knowles 1984:465)

1. Picture: ?

1566–1915 Brasseur de Bourbourg (1869–1870, vol. 1:203): "o" 'cercle, surface, vase, collier'; Landa [1566] (Tozzer 1941:170): /ti/.

1916–1950 Thompson (1944): locative preposition; Thompson (1950:163): "ti" locative; 'to; toward'; Whorf (1942:487, fig. 2): "kan" 'snake'.

1951–1980 Barthel (1967:228): "ti" 'mouth' in Ch'olan; Kelley (1962a:290f.): /ti/; "ti" 'locativo' (segun Thompson); Kelley (1962b:41): /ti/; Kelley (1976:15, 113, 181, 191, 200, 331): "ti" 'at, in'; Knorozov (1955:70): 064 (flor?) /t(i)/; Knorozov (1958:285): /t(i)/; Knorozov (1967:82): /t(i)/; "ti" (flower); Thompson (1962:46): "ti"; Thompson (1972:49): "ti" locative 'on'.

1981–1990 V. Bricker (1986:209): /ta/, "ta" 'in, at, to' (Cholan); /ti/, "ti" 'in, at, to' (Cholan, Yucatecan); Grube (1990a:89): = T0160; Josserand et al. (1985): locative "ti"; Justeson (1984:320): J. Fox, J. Justeson, P. Mathews: general locative preposition "*ti(')" or "*ta"; /ta/; /ti/ secure only in Landa "ma-i-n-k'a-ti" for "ma' in-k'at-i"; origin in flaming torch (proto-Mayan "*tya:j"); F. Lounsbury: /ta/ or /tä/; in Yucatec /ti/; L. Schele, D. Stuart: "ti," "ta," "tä" locative preposition and /ti/; Lounsbury (1989:87): /ta/; Schele (1987d): /ta/.

1991–2008 Davoust (1995:557): "tah" 'torche'; /ti/, /ta/; Knorozov (1999, vol. 1:100): /ti/ (una flora); Macri (1991): at sites using only T0053, T0059, and T0747 as prepositions, /ti/ or /ta/.

3M3

T 0051
Z 0037
K 0064

tí' / ti, ta, tä

prep — in, at, etc.; preposition

Yu *tí'* — ti' 'preposición a, con, por instrumento, adentro' (Barrera Vásquez et al. 1980:788); tí' 'to, at, in, from, for' (V. Bricker et al. 1998:274)

Ch' *ti, ta, tä* — *tä 'preposition' (Kaufman and Norman 1984:139); ta 'for, belongs to' (Knowles 1984:461); tä 'to, from, by' (Knowles 1984:463); ti 'en, a, por, de' (Warkentin and Scott 1980:98); ti 'en' (Morán 1935:26); ti' 'beside, by the side; at the edge' (Knowles 1984:465)

1. Picture: ?

1566–1915 Brasseur de Bourbourg (1869–1870, vol. 1:203): "o" 'cercle, vase, collier'; pour "u."

1951–1980 Kelley (1976:191f., 331): (= T0053) locative (centipede, insect?); Knorozov (1955:76): 149 "lem"; Knorozov (1967:83): morphemic.

1981–1990 V. Bricker (1986:208): /ta/, "ta" 'in, at, to' (Cholan); Grube (1990a:89): = T0053; Justeson (1984:319): = 0053; J. Fox, J. Justeson, P. Mathews, L. Schele, D. Stuart: general locative preposition "*ti(')" or "*ta"; /tV/; vowel is sometimes uncertain, sometimes clearly /a/; L. Campbell, F. Lounsbury: locative preposition; B. Riese: locative preposition, possibly /ta/, /ti/; depicts torch made up of slices of pine wood tied together, cf. German "Kienspan."

1991–2008 Davoust (1995:557): "tahbachim" 'mille-pattes'; "ta" 'prép. loc."; /ta/; Grube (1994b:181): T0051 /ta/ used syllabically after 9.11.0.0.0; Knorozov (1999, vol. 1:104): "lem" (fuego ritual o relámpago); Macri (1991): at sites using only T0053, T0059, and T0747 as prepositions, /ti/ or /ta/; Vail (2000a): locative preposition; may have been read "ta" by Ch'olan speakers and "tí" by Yucatec speakers.

3M3

T 0286b
Z 0008
K 0093

tí' / ti, ta, tä

prep — in, at, etc.; preposition

2. Picture: ?

1951–1980 Knorozov (1967:86): combination of graphemes K064-050.

1991–2008 Davoust (1995:574): "ta hun" 'près du premier'; Knorozov (1999, vol. 1:85): "lem" (fuego ritual o relámpago); Ringle and Smith-Stark (1996:335–38): 0286 (retired) = 0051c; Schele and Grube (1997:170): "ta" [preposition].

3M4

T 0090
Z 0035
K 0334

tu
tu

prep		in, at, etc.; preposition with third person prefix, Set A (ergative and possessive)
Yu	*tu [ti' + u]*	tí' 'to, at, in, from, for' (V. Bricker et al. 1998:274); u(y)- 'Set A dependent pronoun, 3rd person' (Hofling with Tesucún 1997:9)
Ch'	*tu [ti; ta; tä + u]*	*tä 'preposition' (Kaufman and Norman 1984:139); ta 'for, belongs to' (Knowles 1984:461); tä 'to, from, by' (Knowles 1984:463); ti 'en, a, por, de' (Warkentin and Scott 1980:98); ti 'en' (Morán 1935:26); ti' 'beside, by the side; at the edge' (Knowles 1984:465); *u- 'ergative 3rd person' (Kaufman and Norman 1984:91)

1. Picture: ?

1566–1915 Brasseur de Bourbourg (1869–1870, vol. 1:206, 220): day Chic-chán; "chic-chán" 'chose manifestée, ou rendue visible, portée, élevée au-dessus, en avant'; '8000'; Rosny (1883:4, 24): "chicchan, chic"; Thomas (1893:248, 267): /x'/ or /ch'/.

1916–1950 Thompson (1950:58, 197): "tu."

1951–1980 Kelley (1962a:290, 293f.): clasificador numérico; /tu/; Kelley (1976:133, 181, 332): (T0089 = T0090 = T0091 = T0092?) "tu" (net frame); Knorozov (1955:71): 082 (morral) "ten"?; Knorozov (1967:101): "tem" 'altar'; Schele (1979:11): "tu" locative; Thompson (1972:41, 68): represents carrying frame made of wood and netting; read "tu" 'at his'.

1981–1990 V. Bricker (1986:209): /tu/ "t-u-" 'in the' (Ch'olan, Yucatecan); Grube (1990a:91): = T0089; Justeson (1984:322): = T0089.

1991–2008 Davoust (1995:560): "tul" 'entourer'; /tu/; Knorozov (1999, vol. 1:176): "tem," "chim" (bolsa grande que se lleva a la espalda); Ringle and Smith-Stark (1996:335–38): 0090 (retired) = 0089b.

3M4

T 0091
Z 0035
K –

tu
tu

prep — in, at, etc.; preposition with third person prefix, Set A (ergative and possessive)

2. Picture: ?

1951–1980 Kelley (1976:133, 181, 332): (T0089 = T0090 = T0091 = T0092?) "tu" (net frame); Knorozov (1967:101): "tem" 'altar'; Thompson (1972:41, 68): (carrying frame made of wood and netting) "tu" 'at his'.

1981–1990 V. Bricker (1986:209): /tu/, "t-u-" 'in the' (Cholan, Yucatecan); Grube (1990a:91): = T0089; Justeson (1984:322): = T0089.

1991–2008 Davoust (1995:560): "tul" 'entourer'; /tu/; Knorozov (1999, vol. 1:176): "tem," "chim" (bolsa grande que se lleva a la espalda); Ringle and Smith-Stark (1996:335–38): 0091 (retired) = 0089c.

3M6

T 0146
Z 0036
K 0060

si

1. Picture: ?

1566–1915 Brasseur de Bourbourg (1869–1870, vol. 1:203): "o" 'surface, vase, collier'; Thomas (1893:261): /th/?

1951–1980 Knorozov (1955:70): 065 (algodón) "pitz', petz' "; Knorozov (1967:82): /p'u/.

1981–1990 Fox and Justeson (1984:39): /si/; Grube (1990a:94): = T0057; Justeson (1984:326): J. Fox, J. Justeson, P. Mathews: /si/; J. Fox: possibly also demonstrative "-i" or clitic "-ix."

1991–2008 Davoust (1995:564): /zi/; Davoust (1997:181): "zih"; Knorozov (1999, vol. 1:103): /p'u/.

3M7

T 0068
Z —
K 0337, 0338

tz'a

1. Picture: ear flare?

1566–1915 Brasseur de Bourbourg (1869–1870, vol. 1:211): "káan káan káan" 'plusieurs fois la terre soulevée'.

1951–1980 Knorozov (1967:101): [K337, 338 in part] "hatz".

1981–1990 V. Bricker (1986:126, 209): /tu/; Grube (1990a:89): = T0339, T0356, T0366; Grube (1990b): /tz'a/; MacLeod (1989a:120): credits Grube with /tz'a/; Schele (1989c:39): when followed by /pa/, "tz'ap" 'to stick in the ground'.

1991–2008 Davoust (1995:558): /tz'a/; Schele and Grube (1997:17): /tz'a/.

3M8

T 0147
Z 0014
K 0054–56

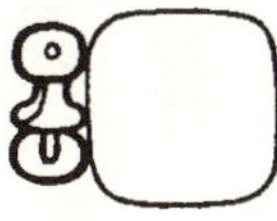

nik? / nich?

n flower; jewel?
Yu *nik* nik 'flower' (V. Bricker et al. 1998:197)
Ch' *nich* *nich 'blossom'; *nich-im 'flower' (Kaufman and Norman 1984:127)

1. Picture: jeweled flower

1951–1980 Knorozov (1955:69): 054 (pluma de quetzal?) "kuk(ul)" 'pluma' (sólo en el nombre del dios Kukulcan); Knorozov (1967:82): "k'uk' " 'feather'.

1981–1990 Justeson (1984:327): J. Fox, J. Justeson, P. Mathews: possibly = T0165.

1991–2008 Davoust (1995:564): "kuk" 'plume de quetzal'?; Knorozov (1999, vol. 1:99, 239): "tit" (adorno ritual); Stone (1995): jewel flower motif; Taube (1992:59): visual correspondence between the 'nikte' flower worn by the Classic variant and the T0147 prefix associated with God H's portrait glyph, suggesting the latter may be a flower.

3MB

T 0267
Z 0043
K 0098

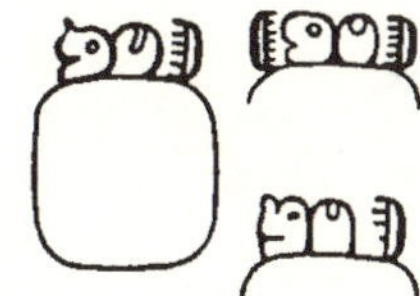

May be related to the Classic grapheme APQ.

1. Picture: bat? and ? with "ka" sign

1566–1915 Rosny (1883:24): [with T0613] nom du mazatl ('zeb'), espèce de chevreuil; 'offrande, sacrifice'.

1951–1980 Cordan (1964:34): "dzotzik"; Knorozov (1955:76): 148 "valac"; Knorozov (1967:86): composite grapheme K006-003-028; Thompson (1972:41): "lob" 'malevolence'.

1991–2008 Davoust (1995:573): "lob" 'malheur'?; Davoust (1997:101): "xul" 'fin'; Knorozov (1999, vol. 1:84): /tzo-la-ca/; combinación de 10.7.165; Schele and Grube (1997:82): "xul"? 'end of', following suggestion by W. Nahm; bat head is /xu/ and remaining elements are /lu/.

3MB

T 0030
Z —
K —

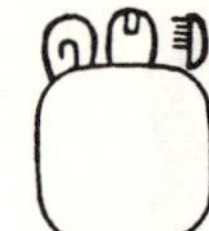

2. Picture: ? with "ka" sign

1981–1990 Grube (1990a:88): = T0031?

1991–2008 Knorozov (1999, vol. 1:84): /mu-la-ca/; combinación de 8.7.165; Ringle and Smith-Stark (1996:335–38): 0030 (retired) = 0031v; Vail (1996:314): variant of T0267.

3MB

T 0031
Z 0043a
K 0099

3. Picture: ? with "ka" sign

1951–1980 Cordan (1964:34): "kutzik"; Knorozov (1967:86): composite grapheme K084-003-028.

1981–1990 Grube (1990a:88): = T0030?

1991–2008 Davoust (1995:555): "nuc" 'grand'; Knorozov (1999, vol. 1:84): /ah-la-ca/; combinación de 109.7.165; Schele and Grube (1997:128): "xul" 'end (of)'; Vail (1996:314): variant of T0267.

3MC

T —
Z —
K —

1. Picture: ?

Appendix 1

Signs with Proposed Syllabic Values with Code and Thompson Numbers

a
BP1
0743

a
BP3
0238

a?
1G4
0012

b'(V)?
AXA

b'a
AP9
0757

b'a
AP9
0791b

b'a
XE1
0501

b'a
XE1
0558

b'a
33H
0251

b'a
33H
0252

b'e
HTF
0301

b'i, b'e
XGE
0585ab

b'u
YSB
0021

ch'a
2G2
0093a-d

ch'a?
XE7
0283

ch'a?
2G2
0634

ch'o
APB
0758a

ch'o
APB

ch'o?
HE5
0287

cha
MZ9
0668

che
1B7
0145a

chi
MR7
0671

chu
ZY9
0601v

chu
ZY9
0601

chu
ZY9
0857

chu?
ZY9
0857v

e
AA7
0542a

ha / ja
ZU1
0181

ha / ja
ZU1
0682b

he / je?
33B
0069

hi
32L
0186

hi / ji
33F
0136

ho / jo
ZUF
0589

hu / ju
1G5
0166

i
YM1
0679

k'a
MZ3
0669a

k'a?
BM1
0236

k'o?
MZP

k'u
AMC
1016c

k'u
22B
0604

k'u
22B
0149ef

k'u
22B

ka
AA1
0025

ki
1B2
0102

ko
1BA
0110

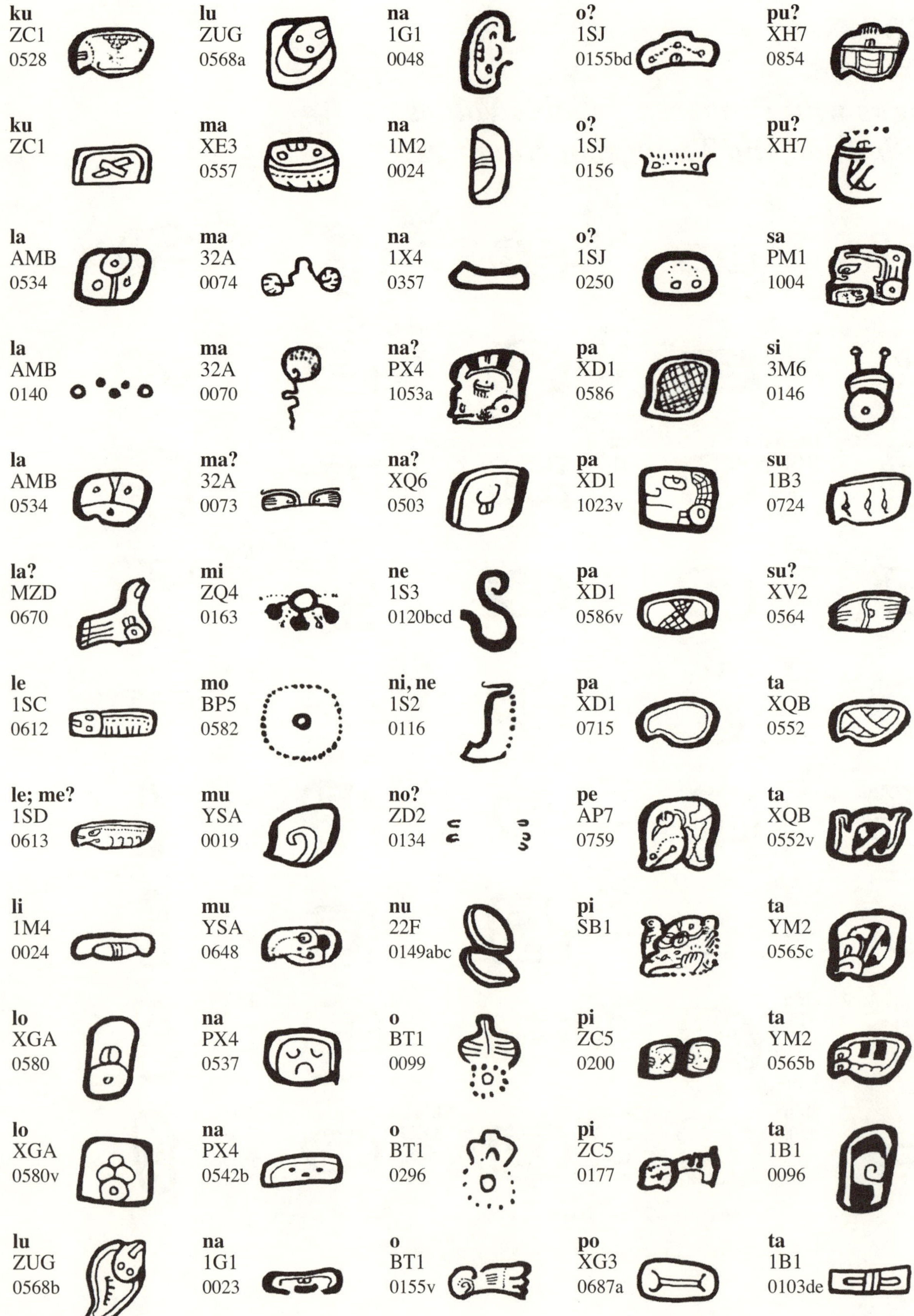

ku ZC1 0528
ku ZC1
la AMB 0534
la AMB 0140
la AMB 0534
la? MZD 0670
le 1SC 0612
le; me? 1SD 0613
li 1M4 0024
lo XGA 0580
lo XGA 0580v
lu ZUG 0568b
lu ZUG 0568a
ma XE3 0557
ma 32A 0074
ma 32A 0070
ma? 32A 0073
mi ZQ4 0163
mo BP5 0582
mu YSA 0019
mu YSA 0648
na PX4 0537
na PX4 0542b
na 1G1 0023
na 1G1 0048
na 1M2 0024
na 1X4 0357
na? PX4 1053a
na? XQ6 0503
ne 1S3 0120bcd
ni, ne 1S2 0116
no? ZD2 0134
nu 22F 0149abc
o BT1 0099
o BT1 0296
o BT1 0155v
o? 1SJ 0155bd
o? 1SJ 0156
o? 1SJ 0250
pa XD1 0586
pa XD1 1023v
pa XD1 0586v
pa XD1 0715
pe AP7 0759
pi SB1
pi ZC5 0200
pi ZC5 0177
po XG3 0687a
pu? XH7 0854
pu? XH7
sa PM1 1004
si 3M6 0146
su 1B3 0724
su? XV2 0564
ta XQB 0552
ta XQB 0552v
ta YM2 0565c
ta YM2 0565b
ta 1B1 0096
ta 1B1 0103de

ta?
XQB

ta?
XQB
0304

te
XGC

te
2G1
0087

ti
BV3
0747b

ti
3M2
0059

to
33A
0049

tu
3M4
0090

tu
3M4
0091

tz'a
XQ7
0593

tz'a
3M7
0068

tz'i
XV1
0563a

tz'u
AA3
0608

tze
PHE
1022

tze
XS3
0523

tze
XS3

tze?
PHD

tze?
PHE
1022v

tzi
XH5
0507

tzu
ZS4
0559

u
AA4
0010

u
APA

u
HE6
0001

u
HE6
0013

u
PCJ
0731

u
YG2
0516c

u
YG2
0513

u, hu
1S4
0120a

wa
2S2
0130

wa
2S2

wa
2S2
0019v

wi
1S1
0277

xa
XG4
0114

xi
SC5
1048

xo
AM6
0536

xu
APL
0791a

xu
APL
0791c

ya
32M
0126

ya
32M
0047

yi
ZUH
0017

yo
1SA
0115

yu
32D
0062

Appendix 2

Signs with Proposed Logographic Values Ordered by Yucatecan/Ch'olan Glosses

áak'ab'/ahk'äb'
night, darkness
XH9

áak/ahk
turtle
AL3

áak?/ahk?
turtle?
AL1

àal/al
child of mother
MZE

àal/al
child of mother
MZE

àal/al; yäl
child of mother; throw down
MZE

áayin/ahin?
alligator?; crocodile?
AL6

ah/aj; -ah/-aj
agentive; verbal suffix
ZU1

ah/aj; -ah/-aj
agentive; verbal suffix
ZU1

ah/aj
agentive
2S8

ah/aj
agentive
BP3

ah/aj
agentive
1G4

ah/aj
agentive
XH1

ah/aj
agentive
2S8

ah/aj
agentive
2S8

ah/aj
agentive
2S8

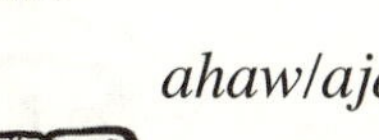
ahaw/ajaw
lord; ruler
2M1

ahaw/ajaw
lord; ruler
2M1

ahaw/ajaw
lord; ruler
2M1

ahaw/ajaw
lord; ruler; God S
PT7

b'àak/b'ak
bone; captive
HH1

b'áalam/b'ahläm; b'olon
jaguar god, God CH; nine
PT9

b'áalam/b'ahläm?; b'olay?
jaguar
AT1

b'olon
nine; many
009

ch'áah/ch'äj
droplet
2G2

ch'ak/ch'äk
cut, chop; traverse?
2M7

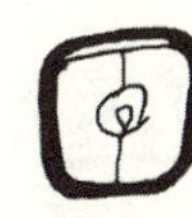
ch'é'en/ch'en?
cenote?, cave?; well?
HH2

cháak?/chak?
rain god; God B
MZ9

cháak/chahk
Chaak, God B
SS1

chak chéel; chéel
Chak Cheel
SNF

chak/chäk
red; great, large
1B9

che'?/te'; -te
tree, wood, plant
2G1

che'/te'
tree, wood, plant
XGC

èek'/ek'
star, planet; Venus
ZQD

èek'/ek'
star, planet; Venus
ZQD

éek'/ik'
black
XG8

éem/ehm
descend
HT4

ha'
water
XE2

ha'
water
XE2

há'ab'/hab'
tun; year
XH2

hix?
jaguar?
AT7

hok'/jok'; hòok'?
tie up?; leave, emerge?
ZB1

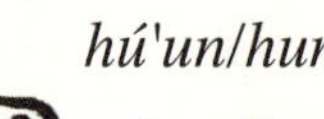

hú'un/hun
headband; paper, book
XHB

hub'?
fall?
ZQE

hub'?
fall?
ZQE

hul/jul
pierce
ZYD

hun/jun
one
001

hùuh/huj
iguana
AL9

hùuh wàah/huj waj
iguana bread
ALA

í'inah/hinaj
seed; seed maize
32H

í'inah/hinaj
seed; seed maize
32H

ib'ach?; wèech/ wech?
armadillo
APK

-il
noun suffix
1M4

Itzamna
Itzamna, God D
SSD

Itzamna
Itzamna, God D
SSD

ix kàab'/ixik kab'
lady earth; Goddess I
PCE

ix kàab'/ixik kab'
lady earth; Goddess I
PCE

ix kàab'/ixik kab'
lady earth; Goddess I
PCF

ix kàab'/ixik kab'
lady earth; Goddess I
PCE

k'àab'a'/k'ab'a'
name
ZE1

k'áak'/k'ahk
fire
2S6

k'al?
close, fasten?
MR2

k'am/ch'äm?
take; receive?
MZD

k'am/ch'äm?
take; receive
MZD

k'an/k'än
yellow, ripe
XQ1

k'at/k'ät; tan
cross; middle, center
XQB

k'at / k'ät?; tan?
middle, center
XQB

k'awil
K'awil, God K
SSF

k'awil?
K'awil, God K?
PCL

k'ìin/k'in
day, sun
XQ3

k'ìin/k'in
day, sun
XQ3

k'ìin/k'in
day, sun
AMK

k'ìin/k'in
day, sun; priest
SN4

k'ìin/k'in?
day, sun; priest?
PCK

k'ìin/k'in?
day, sun; priest?
PCK

k'uch?; ta'hol?
vulture
BV4

k'uch?; ta'hol?
vulture?
BV4

k'uch?; ta'hol?
vulture?
BV4

k'uch?; ta'hol?
vulture
BV4

k'uh(ul)/ch'uh(ul)
god; image; holy
AMC

k'uh(ul)/ch'uh(ul)
god; image; holy
AMC

k'uh(ul)/ch'uh(ul)
god; image; holy
AMC

k'uk'ulkan?
K'uk'ulkan?
SSU

k'´áak'/k'ahk
fire
2S6

k-/kä-
we; our
AA1

ká'ah/cha'
two
002

ká'an/chan
sky
XH3

ká'an/chan
sky
XH3

ká'an/chan
sky
XH3

ká'an/chan
sky
XH3

kàab'/kab'; kàab'/ chab', chäb'
earth, bee, honey, hive
YS1

kàab' ahaw/kab' ajaw
earth god; God R
PE1

kàan/chan
snake
AC6

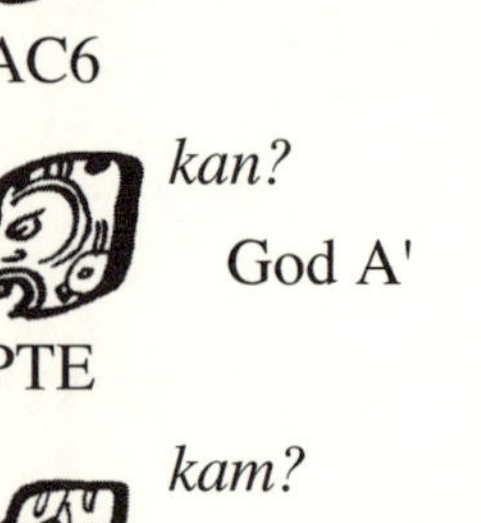

AC6 *kàan/chan*
snake

PTE *kan?*
God A'

PE7 *kam?*
death?; God A'

PE7 *kam?*
death?; God A'

004 *kan/chän; ká'an/chan*
four; sky

PTF *kan?*
offerng

AA9 *kay/chäy*
fish

MR7 *kéeh/chij*
deer

AV1 *kéeh/chij*
deer

AV1 *kéeh/chij*
deer

AV1 *kéeh/chij?*
deer?

MZB *kelem*
young male

MZB *kelem*
young male

1B2 *ki'*
tasty, delicious

SCC *kíim/chäm*
death; dead

SCC *kíim/chäm*
death; dead

PE6 *kíim/chäm?*
death; dead?

SCD *kìimil/chämal?*
death god

SCD *kìimil/chämal?*
death god

SCD *kìimil/chämal?*
death god?

PEC *kisin*
underworld god; God Q

PEC *kisin*
underworld god; God Q

BT4 *ku(y)/kuh*
owl

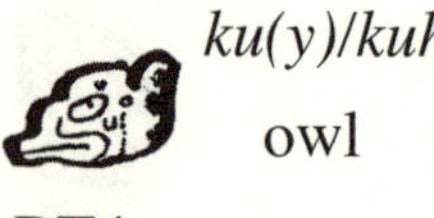

BT4 *ku(y)/kuh*
owl

HT8 *kum/chum*
seating (of haab' period)

BMA *kùutz?*
turkey

BMA *kùutz?*
turkey

BMB *kùutz? wàah*
turkey bread

010 *lahun/läjun; lah?/laj?*
ten; terminate?

SC1 *lajun/läjun*
ten

SC1 *lajun/läjun*
ten

MB2 *lòob'/lob'?*
hurt, harm, damage?

AC3 *luk'/lok'?*
leave, emerge

ma(')
no, negative
32A

màax/max
spider monkey
AME

mak wàah; mäk waj
turtle bread
ALB

mak/mäk
turtle carapace; cover
AL5

mo'
macaw
BP4

mùuk/muk?
evil omen; bury?
YSA

muwan
hawk
BT2

muyal
cloud
XGK

nah?
first?
1G1

nah
first
1G1

nah
house; dwelling
PX4

nah?
house; dwelling?
1G1

nahil/nah?
honored?; first, foremost?
1M2

nahil/nah?; nah?
honored?; first?; building
1X4

nal/näl; waxak/ waxäk
maize god; eight
PE8

nal/näl; waxak/ waxäk
maize god; eight
PE8

nal/näl
maize god
PE8

nal/näl?; xìib'/ xib'?
north; maize; man
PC4

nal/näl
maize
XQ6

nal/näl; -nal
maize; locative suffix
2S1

nal/näl; -nal
maize; locative suffix
2S1

nal/näl?; -nal?
maize; locative suffix
2S1

nal/näl; -nal
maize; locative suffix
2S1

nal/näl?; -nal?
maize; locative suffix
2S1

nal/näl?; -nal?
maize?; locative suffix?
2S1

nal/näl?; xìib'/xib?
maize god; north; man?
PC4

nal?
north
PC4

nik ahaw/nich ajaw?
wind and flower god, God H
PT3

nik ahaw/nich ajaw?
wind and flower god, God H
PT3

nik/nich
flower
AM1

nik/nich
flower
AM1

nik/nich; nikte'/ nichte'
flower; plumeria flower
XQ2

nik?/nich?
flower; jewel?
3M8

nohol?
south
ZUK

nohol?
south
ZUK

ok/och; ó'och
enter; food
ACN

ok/och; òok/ok
foot, footsteps; enter?
AP5

òoch/uch?
opossum
AP6

óox/ux
three; abundance
003

otoch/otot
house; dwelling
ZY5

otoch/otot
house; dwelling
ZY5

pàakal/päkal
shield
XQC

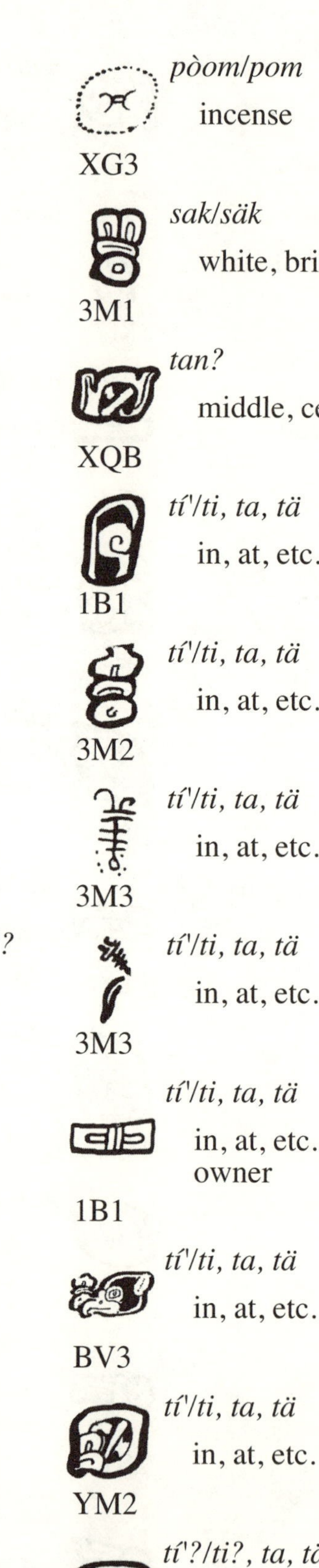

pat/pät?
make, form?
2G4

pat/pät?
make, form?
2G4

pawah
Pawah
PT4

pawah
Pawah
PT4

pawahtun
Pawahtun
PT4

pawahtun
Pawahtun
PT4

pèek'?; tzul?; tz'i'?
dog
AP1

-pih; pih
b'ak'tun; cloth
SB1

pih
b'ak'tun; cloth
ZC5

pìik/pik
skirt
XD7

pòom/pom
incense
XG3

pòom/pom
incense
XG3

sak/säk
white, bright
3M1

tan?
middle, center
XQB

tí'/ti, ta, tä
in, at, etc.
1B1

tí'/ti, ta, tä
in, at, etc.
3M2

tí'/ti, ta, tä
in, at, etc.
3M3

tí'/ti, ta, tä
in, at, etc.
3M3

tí'/ti, ta, tä
in, at, etc.; torch; owner
1B1

tí'/ti, ta, tä
in, at, etc.
BV3

tí'/ti, ta, tä
in, at, etc.
YM2

tí'?/ti?, ta, tä
in, at, etc.
YM2

tòok'/tok'
flint; bloodletter
1C1

tóolok/t'olok?
basilisk lizard?
ALC

tu
in, at, etc.
3M4

tu
in, at, etc.
3M4

tùun/tun
stone; 360-day year
ZC1

tz'áak/tz'ak
to change; succession
YS6

tz'ak?
heal; healer?
XQ7

tz'onó'ot
cenote
ZUB

tzak/tzäk
conjure
MZK

*tzúutz/*tzutz*
finish, complete
MRB

u-
he/she/it; his/her/its
HE6

u-
he/she/it; his/her/its
AA4

u-
he/she/it; his/her/its
HE6

u-
he/she/it; his/her/its
APA

uh
moon
SCE

uh?
moon?
PCJ

uh
moon
YG2

uy-/(u)y-
he/she/it; his/her/its
1SA

uy-/(u)y-
he/she/it; his/her/its
32D

uy-/(u)y-
verbal suffix; he/she/it
32M

uy-/(u)y-
verbal suffix; he/she/it
32M

wa'al/wa'
stand up
SSL

wàah/waj; óol/ol
tortilla; food; heart
XH4

wàah/waj?
tortilla; food?
XH4

wáak/wäk
six; sixteen
PH6

wáay/way
spirit companion; co-essence
AM7

wáay/way
spirit companion; co-essence
AM7

wáay/way?
spirit companion?; dream?
YS8

wí'il/we'el
food; nourishment
YG4

wíinik/winik; winal
person; winal
XS1

wíinik/winik; k'al?; uh
twenty; moon
ZU2

wíinik/winik?; winal?
person; winal
PHD

wíinik háab'/winik hab'; k'atun
k'atun
ZH1

x-?
feminine/ diminutive prefix
XG4

xìib' / xib'?; ná'ak?
man?; penis?; rise, climb?
HT2

yàan/an, ayan?
he/she/it is; there are
MZQ

yáax; yá'ax/yäx
first; green, blue
ZUJ

yáax; yá'ax/yäx
first; green, blue
ZUJ

yah?
wound?; damage?
1S5

yaxum, yaxun?
blue-green bird; cotinga?
APL

yum k'ak'?
incensario
ZVA

Appendix 3

Signs with Proposed Logographic Values Ordered by English Glosses

abundance of?
  32P -

agentive
  BP3 *ah/aj*

agentive
  XH1 *ah/aj*

agentive
  1G4 *ah/aj*

agentive
  2S8 *ah/aj*

agentive; verbal suffix
  ZU1 *ah/aj; -ah/-aj*

alligator?; crocodile?
  AL6 *áayin/ahin?*

and then
  AX7 *ii/i*

armadillo
  APK *ib'ach?; wèech/wech?*

arrive; offer maize?
  YS7 *tal?*

b'ak'tun; cloth
  SB1 *-pih; pih*

b'ak'tun; cloth
  ZC5 *pih*

basilisk lizard?
  ALC *tóolok/t'olok?*

black
  XG8 *éek'/ik'*

bone; captive
  HH1 *b'àak/b'ak*

cenote
  ZUB *tz'onó'ot*

cenote?, cave?; well?
  HH2 *ch'é'en/ch'en?*

Chaak, God B
  SS1 *cháak/chahk*

Chak Cheel
  SNF *chak chéel; chéel*

change; succession
  YS6 *tz'áak/tz'ak*

child of mother; throw down
  MZE *àal/al; yäl*

close, fasten?
  MR2 *k'al?*

cloud
  XGK *muyal*

conjure
  MZK *tzak/tzäk*

cotinga?
  APL *yaxun?*

cross; middle, center
  XQB *k'at/k'ät; tan*

cut, chop; traverse?
  2M7 *ch'ak/ch'äk*

day, sun
  AMK *k'ìin/k'in*

day, sun
  XQ3 *k'ìin/k'in*

day, sun; priest
  SN4 *k'ìin/k'in*

day, sun; priest?
  PCK *k'ìin/k'in?*

death god
  AMM -

death god
  SCD *kìimil/chämal?*

death; dead
  SCC *kíim/chäm*

death; dead?
  PE6 *kíim/chäm?*

death?; God A'
  PE7 *kam?*

deer
  AV1 *kéeh/chij*

deer
  MR7 *kéeh/chij*

deer offering
  AV6 -

descend
  HT4 *éem/ehm*

dog
  AP1 *pèek'?; tzul?; tz'i'?*

droplet
  2G2 *ch'áah/ch'äj*

earth god; God R
  PE1 *kàab' ahaw/kab' ajaw*

earth, bee, honey, hive
  YS1 *kàab'/kab'; kàab'/chab', chäb'*

eclipse
  ZQ1 -

enter; food
  ACN *ok/och; ó'och*

equinox?
  HT3 -

fall?
  ZQE *hub'?*

fan?; rattle?
  ZX8 -

feminine/diminutive prefix
  XG4 *x-?*

finish, complete
  MRB *tzúutz/*tzutz*

fire
  2S6 *k'áak'/k'ahk*

first; green, blue
  ZUJ *yáax; yá'ax/yäx*

first?
  1G1 *nah?*

fish
AA9 *kay/chäy*

flint; bloodletter
1C1 *tòok'/tok'*

flower
AM1 *nik/nich*

flower; jewel?
3M8 *nik?/nich?*

flower; plumeria flower
XQ2 *nik/nich; nikte'/nichte'*

food; nourishment
YG4 *wí'il/we'el*

foot, footsteps; enter?
AP5 *ok/och; òok/ok*

four; sky
004 *kan/chän; ká'an/chan*

God A'
PTE *kan?*

God L
SNK -

God M
ST9 -

God P; Pawahtun
PEF -

god; image; holy
AMC *k'uh(ul)/ch'uh(ul)*

hand, arm
MRG *k'ab'/k'äb'*

harvest?
ZYC -

hawk
BT2 *muwan*

he/she/it is; there are
MZQ *yàan/an, ayan?*

he/she/it; his/her/its
AA4 *u-*

he/she/it; his/her/its
APA *u-*

he/she/it; his/her/its
HE6 *u-*

he/she/it; his/her/its
1SA *uy-/(u)y-*

he/she/it; his/her/its
32D *uy-/(u)y-*

headband; paper, book
XHB *hú'un/hun*

heal; healer?
XQ7 *tz'ak?*

honored?; first, foremost?
1M2 *nahil/nah?*

honored?; first?; building
1X4 *nahil/nah?; nah?*

house; dwelling
ZY5 *otoch/otot*

hurt, harm, damage?
MB2 *lòob'/lob'?*

iguana
AL9 *hùuh/huj*

iguana bread
ALA *hùuh wàah/huj waj*

iguana?
1S4 *hùuh/huj?*

in, at, etc.
BV3 *tí'/ti, ta, tä*

in, at, etc.
YM2 *tí'/ti, ta, tä*

in, at, etc.
1B1 *tí'/ti, ta, tä*

in, at, etc.
3M2 *tí'/ti, ta, tä*

in, at, etc.
3M3 *tí'/ti, ta, tä*

in, at, etc.
3M4 *tu*

incensario
ZVA *yum k'ak'?*

incense
XG3 *pòom/pom*

Itzamna, God D
SSD *Itzamna*

jaguar
AT1 *b'áalam/b'ahläm?; b'olay?*

jaguar god, God CH; nine
PT9 *b'áalam/b'ahläm; b'olon*

jaguar?
AT7 *hix?*

k'atun
ZH1 *wíinik háab'/winik hab'; k'atun*

K'awil, God K
SSF *k'awil*

K'awil, God K?
PCL *k'awil?*

K'uk'ulkan?
SSU *k'uk'ulkan?*

lady earth; Goddess I
PCE *ix kàab'/ixik kab'*

lady earth; Goddess I
PCF *ix kàab'/ixik kab'*

leave, emerge
AC3 *luk'/lok'?*

lord; ruler
2M1 *ahaw/ajaw*

lord; ruler; God S
PT7 *ahaw/ajaw*

macaw
BP4 *mo'*

maize
XQ6 *nal/näl*

maize god; eight
PE8 *nal/näl; waxak/waxäk*

maize; locative suffix
2S1 *nal/näl; -nal*

make, form?
2G4 *pat/pät?*

man?; penis?; rise, climb?
HT2 *xìib' / xib'?; ná'ak?*

Mars
ACD -

moon
SCE *uh*

moon
YG2 *uh*

moon goddess
PC3 -

moon?
PCJ *uh?*

name
ZE1 *k'àab'a'/k'ab'a'*

night, darkness
XH9 *áak'ab'/ahk'äb'*

nine; many
009 *b'olon*

no, negative
32A *ma(')*

north; maize; man
PC4 *nal/näl?; xìib'/xib'?*

noun suffix
AMB *-al*

noun suffix
1M4 *-il*

noun suffix
1SC *-el*

offerng
PTF *kan?*

one
001 *hun/jun*

opossum
AP6 *òoch/uch?*

owl
BT4 *ku(y)/kuh*

Pawah, Pawahtun
PT4 *pawah, pawahtun*

person; winal
PHD *wíinik/winik?; winal?*

person; winal
XS1 *wíinik/winik; winal*

pierce
ZYD *hul/jul*

rain god; God B
MZ9 *cháak?/chak?*

red; great, large
1B9 *chak/chäk*

rubber
ZUQ -

seating (of haab' period)
HT8 *kum/chum*

seed; seed maize
32H *í'inah/hinaj*

shield
XQC *pàakal/päkal*

six; sixteen
PH6 *wáak/wäk*

skirt
XD7 *pìik/pik*

sky
XH3 *ká'an/chan*

snake
AC6 *kàan/chan*

south
ZUK *nohol?*

spider monkey
AME *màax/max*

spirit companion; co-essence
AM7 *wáay/way*

spirit companion?; dream?
YS8 *wáay/way?*

spirit companion?; sorcerer?
ZUD *wáay/way?*

sprout
HE5 *ch'ok?*

stand up
SSL *wa'al/wa'*

star, planet; Venus
ZQD *èek'/ek'*

stone; 360-day year
ZC1 *tùun/tun*

take; receive?
MZD *k'am/ch'äm?*

tasty, delicious
1B2 *ki'*

temple, pyramid
ZH4 -

ten
SC1 *lajun/läjun*

ten; terminate?
010 *lahun/läjun; lah?/laj?*

three; abundance
003 *óox/ux*

tie up?; leave, emerge?
ZB1 *hok'/jok'; hòok'?*

tortilla; food; heart
XH4 *wàah/waj; óol/ol*

tree, wood, plant
XGC *che'/te'*

tree, wood, plant
2G1 *che'?/te'; -te*

tun; year
XH2 *há'ab'/hab'*

turkey
BMA *kùutz?*

turtle
AL3 *áak/ahk*

turtle bread
ALB *mak wàah; mäk waj*

turtle carapace; cover
AL5 *mak/mäk*

turtle?
AL1 *áak?/ahk?*

twenty; moon
ZU2 *wíinik/winik; k'al?; uh*

two
002 *ká'ah/cha'*

underworld god; God Q
PEC *kisin*

verbal suffix
2S2 *-Vw?*

verbal suffix
33F *-hi*

verbal suffix; he/she/it
32M *uy-/(u)y-*

vulture
BV4 *k'uch?; ta'hol?*

water
XE2 *ha'*

we; our
AA1 *k-/kä-*

white, bright
3M1 *sak/säk*

wind and flower god, God H
PT3 *nik ahaw/nich ajaw?*

work?
1SD *mèen?*

wound?; damage?
1S5 *yah?*

yellow, ripe
XQ1 *k'an/k'än*

young male
MZB *kelem*

zero
XGJ -

Appendix 4

T Numbers to Three-Digit Codes

T Number	Code
0001	HE6
0002	ZQD
0010	AA4
0012	1G4
0013	HE6
0014	AMC
0015a	2S8
0015b	2S8
0015v	2S8
0017	ZUH
0017	ZUJ
0019	YSA
0019v	2S2
0020	32V
0021	YSB
0023	1G1
0024	1M2
0024	1M4
0025	AA1
0030	3MB
0031	3MB
0041	AMC
0042	1G8
0047	32M
0048	1G1
0049	33A
0051	3M3
0058	3M1
0059	3M2
0060ae	1B5
0062	32D
0063	PT4
0064	PT4
0066	32H
0068	3M7
0069	33B
0070	32A
0073	32A
0074	32A
0077v	BM2
0079	2G4
0080b	2MA
0084	2S1
0085a	22J
0085bc	2S1
0087	2G1
0090	3M4
0091	3M4
0093a–d	2G2
0095	XG8
0096	1B1
0097	2G6
0098	ZS2
0099	BT1
0102	1B2
0103de	1B1
0104	2M9
0109	1B9
0110	1BA
0112	1C1
0114	XG4
0115	1SA
0116	1S2
0120a	1S4
0120bcd	1S3
0122	2S6
0123	33C
0124	32J
0126	32M
0130	2S2
0134	ZD2
0135acd	32G
0136	33F
0137	33L
0140	AMB
0142bc	33K
0143	33G
0144abd	002
0144c	001
0145abc	1B7
0146	3M6
0147	3M8
0149abcd	22F
0149ef	22B
0152	SSD
0153	ZQ9
0155bd	1SJ
0155v	BT1
0156	1SJ
0157b	ZUD
0158	YG4
0159	APJ
0161	1GB
0162	32P
0163	ZQ4
0164	XE2
0166	1G5
0168	2M1
0171	PCE
0172	1S5
0176b	ZC6
0177	ZC5
0181	ZU1
0182	ZV1
0186	32L
0187	ZE1
0190	2M7
0192	XD9
0192ab	ZY5
0193	ZH5
0194	2M5
0200	ZC5
0207	ACN
0210	AA6
0217c	MZ1
0218abc	MRB
0221a	MZ6
0227a	HT4
0227bc	HT2
0233a	MB1
0234	MB2
0236	BM1
0238	BP3
0241	32N
0242	XHE
0243	1S7
0249	ZSJ
0250	1SJ
0251	33H
0252	33H
0256	22N
0267	3MB
0268	1C6
0270	1BB
0273	22L
0274	ZS2
0275	ZUJ
0277	1S1
0281	XQ1
0281	XQ3
0283	XE7
0285	32S
0286b	3M3
0287	HE5
0290	22K
0295	22H
0296	BT1
0298	HT8
0299	2S7
0300	2M1
0301	HTF
0304	XQB
0307	1X2
0309	1X3
0319	1SG
0326	ZQ1
0327a	AC3
0346	2G5
0357	1X4
0501	XE1
0501	XE2
0503	XQ6
0504	XH9
0506	XH4
0507	XH5
0508	XG4
0509	YS8
0510a	ZQD
0510b	ZQD
0511	XG1
0513	YG2
0516c	YG2

0518ab	2M1
0521	XS1
0523	XS3
0524	AT7
0525	XH6
0526	YS1
0527	XQ8
0528	ZC1
0533	AM1
0533v	AM1
0534	AMB
0534	AMB
0536	AM6
0537	PX4
0539	AM7
0542a	AA7
0542b	PX4
0544	XQ3
0546	ZVC
0548	XH2
0549	ZH2
0551	YSC
0552	XQB
0552v	XQB
0557	XE3
0558	XE1
0559	ZS4
0561a	XH3
0561c	XH3
0561d	XH3
0561v	XH3
0563a	XV1
0563b	XV5
0564	XV2
0565b	YM2
0565c	YM2
0567	AP5
0568a	ZUG
0568b	ZUG
0570	HH1
0572	AM7
0573	YS6
0577	ZUQ
0580	XGA
0580v	XGA
0582	BP5
0584	XH1
0585ab	XGE
0586	XD1
0586v	XD1
0588	SSL
0589	ZUF
0591	ZUB
0593	XQ7
0595	ZD3
0601	ZY9
0601v	ZY9
0604	22B
0608	AA3
0609b	XHB
0610	XE6
0611	2S1
0612	1SC
0613	1SD
0614	ZY5
0623	XQD
0624a	XQC
0626	AL3
0632	XGK
0634	2G2
0646	XQ2
0648	YSA
0652	ALA
0653v	ZYD
0662	XV3
0663	HH2
0667	MZQ
0668	MZ9
0669a	MZ3
0670	MZD
0671	MR7
0676	YS7
0679	YM1
0680	ST9
0682b	ZU1
0682b	ZU2
0684	ZB1
0685	ZH4
0686b	ZV6
0686c	ZVH
0687a	XG3
0687b	XG3
0702	HTA
0703	HT2
0712	ZYC
0713a	MRG
0714	MZK
0715	XD1
0723	2S1
0724	1B3
0725	1B4
0726	PHG
0726v	PHG
0727	XQ4
0728	ZUC
0729	ZS3
0730	XG9
0731	PCJ
0734	PCK
0735	PCK
0736ac	SCC
0736b	SCC
0737	AC6
0738b	AA9
0743	BP1
0747b	BV3
0747b	BV4
0748	BT2
0756ab	APM
0757	AP9
0758a	APB
0759	AP7
0763	AXB
0764	AC6
0765ab	AP5
0766	AX9
0774	XH4
0780	MZJ
0789	AP8
0790	ALC
0791a	APL
0791b	AP9
0791c	APL
0792a	AL7
0792b	AL7
0792v	AL6
0794	ACD
0795	AV6
0796	AV1
0797	ZUR
0798	HT7
0799	AL9
0800	AT1
0800	AT1
0801	AP1
0802	APS
0803	AX7
0803	AX7
0804	XS4
0806	ZY4
0808	XGL
0809	ZX7
0810	YGC
0812	YGD
0829	APU
0835	ZXA
0836	ZVD
0837	XGB
0839	BMA
0854	XH7
0857	ZY9
0857v	ZY9
1003c	PT9
1003v	PT7
1004	PM1
1005	PE1
1006b	PE8
1006c	PE8
1009cd	SSD
1010c	SN4
1016c	AMC
1016v	PC4
1020	SSF
1022	PHE
1022v	PHE
1023v	XD1
1024	PE7
1025b	PC3
1026	PCE
1027	PCF
1028c	MZB
1028d	PCE
1028v	MZB
1030q	SS1
1036c	APP
1037	PC4
1038a	PTE
1038b	PTF
1039	SND
1042	PE7
1047a	SCD
1047b	SCD
1048	SC5
1049	SCE
1050a	PEC
1050b	PEC
1052	PE6
1053a	PX4
1053b	AMM
1054	SNK
1055	PEE
1056	PTG
1057	SNE
1058b	ST8
1059	PT3
1059	PT3
1060b	PH6
1062	PT4
1063	PHF
1064	PCL
1065	PEJ

References

Aldana, Gerardo

2005 Agency and the "Star War" Glyph: A Historical Reassessment of Classic Maya Astrology and Warfare. *Ancient Mesoamerica* 16:305–20.

Anders, Ferdinand

1967 *Codex Tro-Cortesianus (Codex Madrid).* Graz, Austria: Akademische Druck-und Verlagsanstalt.

1968 *Codex Persesianus (Codex Paris).* Graz, Austria: Akademische Druck-und Verlagsanstalt.

Ara, Domingo de

1986 *Vocabulario de lengua tzeldal según el orden de Copanabastla.* Mexico City: Universidad Nacional Autónoma de México.

Attinasi, John J.

1973 Lak T'an: A Grammar of the Chol (Mayan) Word. Ph.D. dissertation, University of Chicago.

Aulie, H. Wilbur, and Evelyn W. de Aulie

1998 *Diccionario Ch'ol de Tumbalá, Chiapas, con variaciones dialectales de Tila y Sabanilla.* Ed. Emily Scharfe de Stairs. Serie de vocabularios y diccionarios indígenas, ed. Mariano Silva y Aceves, no. 21. Mexico City: Instituto Lingüístico de Verano.

Aveni, Anthony F., ed.

1989 *World Archaeoastronomy.* Cambridge: Cambridge University Press.

1992 *The Sky in Mayan Literature.* New York: Oxford University Press.

2001 *Skywatchers: A Revised and Updated Version of Skywatchers of Ancient Mexico.* Austin: University of Texas Press.

Aveni, Anthony F., and Gordon Brotherston, eds.

1983 *Calendars in Mesoamerica and Peru: Native American Computations of Time. Proceedings of the 44th International Congress of Americanists.* BAR International Series 174. Oxford: British Archaeological Reports.

Barrera Vásquez, Alfredo, Juan Ramón Bastarrachea Manzano, William Brito Sansores, Refugio Vermont Salas, David Dzul Góngora, and Domingo Dzul Poot

1980 *Diccionario Maya Cordemex: Maya-Español, Español-Maya.* Mérida, Mexico: Ediciones Cordemex.

Barthel, Thomas S.

1952 Der Morgensternkult in den Darstellungen der Dresdener Mayahandschrift. *Ethnos* 17:73–112.

1953 Regionen des Regengottes. *Ethnos* 18:86–105.

1954 Maya Epigraphy: Some Remarks on the Affix "al." *Proceedings of the Thirtieth International Congress of Americanists, Cambridge, 18–23 August 1952,* pp. 45–49. London: Royal Anthropological Institute.

1955 Versuch über die Inschriften von Chichen Itza viejo. *Baessler Archiv* n.s. 3:5–33. Berlin.

1963 Die Stele 31 von Tikal: Ein bedeutsamer Neufund aus der frühklassischen Mayakultur. *Tribus* 12:159–214.

1964 Commentarios a las inscripciones clásicas tardías de Chich'en Itzá. *Estudios de Cultura Maya* 4:223–44.

1965 Comentarios epigráficos marginales. *Estudios de Cultura Maya* 5:145–52.

1967 Notes on the Inscription on a Carved Bone from Yucatan. *Estudios de Cultura Maya* 6:223–41.

1968 El complejo "emblema." *Estudios de Cultura Maya* 7:159–93.

Baudez, Claude-François

2002 Venus y el *Códice Grolier*. *Arqueología Mexicana* 10(55):70–79.

Benson, Elizabeth P., ed.

1973 *Mesoamerican Writing Systems: A Conference at Dumbarton Oaks, October 30th and 31st, 1971*. Washington, D.C.: Dumbarton Oaks Research Library and Collection.

1985 *Fourth Palenque Round Table, 1980*. Palenque Round Table Series, vol. 6. Merle Greene Robertson, gen. ed. San Francisco: Pre-Columbian Art Research Institute.

Benson, Elizabeth P., and Gillett G. Griffin, eds.

1988 *Maya Iconography*. Princeton: Princeton University Press.

Berlin, Heinrich

1958 El glifo "emblema" en las inscripciones mayas. *Journal de la Société des Américanistes* (Paris) n.s. 47:111–19.

Berlin, Heinrich, and David H. Kelley

1970 The 819-Day Count and Color-Direction Symbolism among the Classic Maya. In *Archaeological Studies in Middle America,* pp. 9–20. Publication 20. New Orleans: Middle American Research Institute, Tulane University.

Beyer, Hermann

1929 The Supposed Maya Hieroglyph of the Screech Owl. *American Anthropologist* 31:34–59.

1931 Mayan Hieroglyphs: The Variable Element of the Introducing Glyphs as Month Indicator. *Anthropos* 26:99–108.

1933 A Discussion of the Gates Classification of Maya Hieroglyphs. *American Anthropologist* 35:659–94.

1937 Studies on the Inscriptions of Chichen Itza. In *Contributions to American Archaeology,* vol. 4, no. 21, pp. 29–175. Publication 483. Washington, D.C.: Carnegie Institution of Washington.

1943 The Maya Hieroglyph "Ending Day." In *Vigesimoséptimo Congreso Internacional de Americanistas: Actas de la Primera Sesion, Celebrada en la Ciudad de México en 1939,* vol. 1, pp. 344–51. Mexico City: Instituto Nacional de Antropología e Historia, Secretaria de Educación Pública.

Bill, Cassandra R., Christine L. Hernández, and Victoria R. Bricker

2000 The Relationship between Early Colonial Maya New Year's Ceremonies and Some Almanacs in the *Madrid Codex*. *Ancient Mesoamerica* 11(1):149–68.

Bollaert, William

1865–1866 *Maya Hieroglyphic Alphabet of Yucatan.* Memoirs of the Anthropological Society of London, vol. 2, pp. 46–54. London.

Boone, Elizabeth H.

2003 A Web of Understanding: Pictorial Codices and the Shared Intellectual Culture of Late Postclassic Mesoamerica. In *The Postclassic Mesoamerican World,* ed. Michael E. Smith and Frances F. Berdan, pp. 207–21. Salt Lake City: University of Utah Press.

Bowditch, Charles P.

1910 *The Numeration, Calendar Systems and Astronomical Knowledge of the Mayas.* Cambridge, Mass.: Harvard University Press.

Brasseur de Bourbourg, Charles E.

1869–1870 *Manuscrit Troano: Études sur le système graphique et la langue des Mayas.* 2 vols. Paris: Imprimerie Impériale.

Bricker, Harvey M., and Victoria R. Bricker
1983 Classic Maya Prediction of Solar Eclipses. *Current Anthropology* 24:1–18.
2007 When Was the Dresden Venus Table Efficacious? In *Skywatching in the Ancient World: New Perspectives in Cultural Astronomy,* ed. Clive Ruggles and Gary Urton, pp. 95–119. Boulder: University Press of Colorado.
n.d. *Astronomy in the Maya Codices.* Accepted for publication, American Philosophical Society, Philadelphia.

Bricker, Victoria R.
1983 Directional Glyphs in Maya Inscriptions and Codices. *American Antiquity* 48:347–53.
1985a A Morphosyntactic Interpretation of Some Accession Compounds and Other Verbs in the Mayan Hieroglyphs. In Benson 1985:67–85.
1985b Notes on Classic Maya Metrology. In Fields 1985:189–92.
1985c Noun Incorporation in the Dresden Codex. *Anthropological Linguistics* 27(4):413–23.
1986 *A Grammar of Mayan Hieroglyphs.* Publication 56. New Orleans: Middle American Research Institute, Tulane University.
1987 Landa's Second Grapheme for *u. Research Reports on Ancient Maya Writing,* no. 9. Washington, D.C.: Center for Maya Research.
1988 The Relationship between the Venus Table and an Almanac in the Dresden Codex. In *New Directions in American Archaeoastronomy: Proceedings of the 46th International Congress of Americanists, Amsterdam, Netherlands, 1988,* ed. Anthony F. Aveni, pp. 81–103. BAR International Series 454. Oxford: British Archaeological Reports.
1989 The Last Gasp of Maya Hieroglyphic Writing in the Books of Chilam Balam of Chumayel and Chan Kom. In Hanks and Rice 1989:39–50.
1991 Faunal Offerings in the Dresden Codex. In Fields 1991:285–92.
1992 A Reading for the "Penis-Manikin" Glyph and Its Variants. *Research Reports on Ancient Maya Writing,* no. 38. Washington, D.C.: Center for Maya Research.
1997a The "Calendar-Round" Almanac in the Madrid Codex. In Bricker and Vail 1997:169–80.
1997b What Constitutes Discourse in the Maya Codices? In Macri and Ford 1997:129–43.
2000 Bilingualism in the Maya Codices and the Books of Chilam Balam. *Written Language and Literacy* 3:77–115.

Bricker, Victoria R., and Harvey M. Bricker
1986 The Mars Table in the Dresden Codex. In *Research and Reflections in Archaeology and History: Essays in Honor of Doris Stone,* ed. E. Wyllys Andrews V, pp. 51–80. Publication 57. New Orleans: Middle American Research Institute, Tulane University.
1988 The Seasonal Table in the Dresden Codex and Related Almanacs. *Archaeoastronomy* 12, *Supplement to Journal for the History of Astronomy* 19:S1–S62. Cambridge: Science History Publications.
1992 A Method for Cross-Dating Almanacs with Tables in the Dresden Codex. In Aveni 1992:43–86.
2005 Astronomical References in the Water Tables on Pages 69 to 74 of the Dresden Codex. In *Painted Books and Indigenous Knowledge in Mesoamerica: Manuscript Studies in Honor of Mary Elizabeth Smith,* ed. Elizabeth H. Boone, pp. 213–29. Publication 69. New Orleans: Middle American Research Institute, Tulane University.

Bricker, Victoria R., Harvey M. Bricker, and Gabrielle Vail
2006 Astronomía en los códices mayas. In *Los Mayas de Ayer y Hoy: Memorias del Primer Congreso Internacional de Cultura Maya,* ed. Alfredo Barrera Rubio and Ruth Gubler, vol. 1, pp. 649–72. Mérida, Mexico: Universidad Autónoma de Yucatán.

Bricker, Victoria R., and Helga-Maria Miram
2002 *An Encounter of Two Worlds: The Book of Chilam Balam of Kaua.* Publication 68. New Orleans: Middle American Research Institute, Tulane University.

Bricker, Victoria R., Eleuterio Po'ot Yah, and Ofelia Dzul de Po'ot
1998 *A Dictionary of the Maya Language as Spoken in Hocabá, Yucatán.* Salt Lake City: University of Utah Press.
Bricker, Victoria R., and Gabrielle Vail
1997 *Papers on the Madrid Codex.* Publication 64. New Orleans: Middle American Research Institute, Tulane University.
Brinton, Daniel G.
1895 *A Primer of Mayan Hieroglyphics.* University of Pennsylvania Series in Philology, Literature, and Archaeology, vol. 3, no. 2. Philadelphia: University of Pennsylvania.
Bruce, Robert D.
1968 *Gramática del Lacandón.* Mexico City: Instituto Nacional de Antropología e Historia.
1979 *Lacandon Dream Symbolism: Dream Symbolism among the Lacandon Mayas of Chiapas, Mexico,* vol. 2: *Dictionary, Index and Classifications of Dream Symbols.* Mexico City: Ediciones Euroamericanas Klaus Thiele.
Campbell, Lyle
1977 *Quichean Linguistic Prehistory.* University of California Publications in Linguistics, vol. 81. Berkeley: University of California Press.
Carlson, John B.
1983 The Grolier Codex: A Preliminary Report on the Content and Authenticity of a Thirteenth-Century Maya Venus Almanac. In Aveni and Brotherston 1983:27–57.
Carrasco V., Ramón
1994 The Rings from the Ballcourt at Uxmal. In Fields 1994:49–52.
Chinchilla Mazariegos, Oswaldo
2006 A Reading for the "Earth-Star" Verb in Ancient Maya Writing. *Research Reports on Ancient Maya Writing,* no. 56. Barnardsville, N.C.: Center for Maya Research.
Chuchiak IV, John F.
2004a The Images Speak: The Survival and Production of Hieroglyphic Codices and Their Use in Post-Conquest Maya Religion (1580–1720). In *Continuity and Change: Maya Religious Practices in Temporal Perspective,* ed. Daniel Graña Behrens, Nikolai Grube, Christian M. Prager, Frauke Sachse, Stefanie Teufel, and Elisabeth Wagner, pp. 165–83. Acta Mesoamericana, vol. 14. Markt Schwaben: Verlag Anton Saurwein.
2004b Papal Bulls, Extirpators, and the Madrid Codex: The Content and Probable Provenience of the M. 56 Patch. In Vail and Aveni 2004:57–88.
Ciaramella, Mary A.
1999 The Weavers in the Codices. *Research Reports on Ancient Maya Writing,* no. 44. Washington, D.C.: Center for Maya Research.
2002 The Bee-Keepers in the Madrid Codex. *Research Reports on Ancient Maya Writing,* no. 52. Washington, D.C.: Center for Maya Research.
2004 The Idol-Makers in the Madrid Codex. *Research Reports on Ancient Maya Writing,* no. 54. Barnardsville, N.C.: Center for Maya Research.
Closs, Michael P.
1979 Venus in the Maya World: Glyphs, Gods and Associated Astronomical Phenomena. In Greene Robertson and Jeffers 1979:147–65.
1985 The Dynastic History of Naranjo: The Middle Period. In Fields 1985:65–77.
1986 Orthographic Conventions in Maya Writing: The Rule of Phonetic Complementation. *Anthropological Linguistics* 28:229–52.
1987 Bilingual Glyphs. *Research Reports on Ancient Maya Writing,* no. 12. Washington, D.C.: Center for Maya Research.

1988 The Penis-Headed Manikin Glyph. *American Antiquity* 53(4):804–11.
1989 Cognitive Aspects of Ancient Maya Eclipse Theory. In Aveni 1989:389–415.
1992 Some Parallels in the Astronomical Events Recorded in the Maya Codices and Inscriptions. In Aveni 1992:133–47.
1994 A Glyph for Venus as Evening Star. In Fields 1994:229–36.

Coe, Michael D.
1973 *The Maya Scribe and His World.* New York: Grolier Club.
1989a The Hero Twins: Myth and Image. In Kerr 1989:161–84.
1989b The Royal Fifth: Earliest Notices of Maya Writing. *Research Reports on Ancient Maya Writing,* no. 28. Washington, D.C.: Center for Maya Research.
1992 *Breaking the Maya Code.* New York: Thames and Hudson.

Coe, Michael D., and Justin Kerr
1997 *The Art of the Maya Scribe.* New York: Harry N. Abrams.

Cordan, Wolfgang
1963 *Introducción a los glifos mayas.* Serie Origo, vol. 1. Mérida, Mexico: Universidad de Yucatán.
1964 *La clave de los glifos mayas.* Serie Origo, vol. 2. Mérida, Mexico: Universidad de Yucatán.

Craine, Eugene R., and Reginald C. Reindorp
1979 *The Codex Pérez and the Book of the Chilam Balam of Maní.* Norman: University of Oklahoma Press.

Davoust, Michel
1995 *L'écriture maya et son déchiffrement.* Paris: Centre National de la Recherche Scientifique.
1997 *Un nouveau commentaire du Codex du Dresde: Codex hiéroglyphique maya du XIVe siècle.* Paris: Centre National de la Recherche Scientifique.

Deckert, Helmut, and Ferdinand Anders
1975 *Codex Dresdensis.* Graz, Austria: Akademische Druck-und Verlagsanstalt.

Dienhart, John M.
1986 The Mayan Hieroglyph for Cotton. *Mexicon* 8:52–56.

Drapkin, Julia
2002 Interpreting the Dialect of Time: A Structural Analysis and Discussion of Almanacs in the Madrid Codex. Honors thesis, Anthropology Department, Tulane University.

Dütting, Dieter
1965 Das Knoten-Graphem bei den Maya. *Zeitschrift für Ethnologie* 90:66–103.
1968 On the Decipherment of Affix T102 (T103) and the Compounds T501:102 and T630:181 of the Maya Hieroglyphic Inscriptions. *Estudios de Cultura Maya* 7:241–54.
1974 Sorcery in Maya Hieroglyphic Writing. *Zeitschrift für Ethnologie* 99:2–62.
1979 Birth, Inauguration and Death in the Inscriptions of Palenque, Chiapas, Mexico. In Greene Robertson and Jeffers 1979:183–214.
1985 On the Context-Dependent Use of Bi- and Polyvalent Graphemes in Mayan Hieroglyphic Writing. In Benson 1985:103–14.
1991 Aspects of Polyvalency in Maya Writing: Affixes T12, T229, and T110. In Fields 1991:273–84.

Eberl, Markus, and Victoria R. Bricker
2004 Unwinding the Rubber Ball: The Glyphic Expression *nahb'* as a Numeral Classifier for "Handspan." *Research Reports on Ancient Maya Writing,* no. 55. Barnardsville, N.C.: Center for Maya Research.

Edmonson, Munro S.
1965 *Quiche-English Dictionary.* Publication 30. New Orleans: Middle American Research Institute, Tulane University.
1971 *The Book of Counsel: The Popol Vuh of the Quiche Maya of Guatemala.* Publication 35. New Orleans: Middle American Research Institute, Tulane University.

Fahsen, Federico
1987 A Glyph for Self-Sacrifice in Several Maya Inscriptions. *Research Reports on Ancient Maya Writing,* no. 11. Washington, D.C.: Center for Maya Research.
1990 A Logograph in Maya Writing for the Verb "To Record." *Ancient Mesoamerica* 1:91–95.
Fields, Virginia M., ed.
1985 *Fifth Palenque Round Table, 1983.* Palenque Round Table Series, vol. 7. Merle Greene Robertson, gen. ed. San Francisco: Pre-Columbian Art Research Institute.
1991 *Sixth Palenque Round Table, 1986.* Palenque Round Table Series, vol. 8. Merle Greene Robertson, gen. ed. San Francisco: Pre-Columbian Art Research Institute.
1994 *Seventh Palenque Round Table, 1989.* Palenque Round Table Series, vol. 9. Merle Greene Robertson, gen. ed. San Francisco: Pre-Columbian Art Research Institute.
Förstemann, Ernst W.
1880 *Die Mayahandschrift der Königlichen öffentlichen Bibliothek zu Dresden.* Leipzig: A. Naumann.
1886 *Erläuterung zur Mayahandschrift der Königlichen öffentlichen Bibliothek zu Dresden.* Dresden: Warnatz and Lehmann.
1887 *Zer Entzifferung der Mayahandschriften.* Dresden: Druck von C. Heinrich.
1892 *Die Mayahandschrift der Königlichen öffentlichen Bibliothek zu Dresden.* Dresden: R. Bertling.
1893 Die Zeitperioden der Mayas. *Globus* 63:30–32.
1902 *Commentary on the Madrid Maya Manuscript (Codex Tro-Cortesianus).* Danzig: L. Saunier.
1904a [1897] Aids to the Deciphering of the Maya Manuscripts. In *Mexican and Central American Antiquities, Calendar Systems, and History,* trans. Charles P. Bowditch, pp. 393–472. Smithsonian Institution: Bureau of American Ethnology, Bulletin 28. Washington, D.C.: Government Printing Office.
1904b [1897] The Inscription on the Cross at Palenque. In *Mexican and Central American Antiquities, Calendar Systems, and History,* trans. Charles P. Bowditch, pp. 545–55. Smithsonian Institution: Bureau of American Ethnology, Bulletin 28. Washington, D.C.: Government Printing Office.
1904c [1894] The Maya Glyphs. In *Mexican and Central American Antiquities, Calendar Systems, and History,* trans. Charles P. Bowditch, pp. 499–513. Smithsonian Institution: Bureau of American Ethnology, Bulletin 28. Washington, D.C.: Government Printing Office.
1906 *Commentary on the Maya Manuscript in the Royal Public Library of Dresden.* Papers of the Peabody Museum of American Archaeology and Ethnology, vol. 4, no. 2, pp. 49–268. Cambridge, Mass.: Harvard University.
Fought, John
1965 A Phonetic and Morphological Interpretation of Zimmermann's Affix 61 in the Maya Hieroglyphic Codices. *Estudios de Cultura Maya* 5:253–80.
Fox, James A.
1997 Phoneticism, Dates, and Astronomy at Chichén Itzá. In Macri and Ford 1997:13–32.
Fox, James A., and John S. Justeson
1980 Mayan Hieroglyphs as Linguistic Evidence. In Greene Robertson 1980:204–16.
1984 Polyvalence in Mayan Hieroglyphic Writing. In Justeson and Campbell 1984:17–76.
1986 Classic Maya Dynastic Alliance and Succession. In *Supplement to the Handbook of Middle American Indians,* vol. 4: *Ethnohistory,* ed. Ronald Spores, pp. 7–34. Victoria Bricker, gen. ed. Austin: University of Texas Press.
Freidel, David A., Linda Schele, and Joy Parker
1993 *Maya Cosmos: Three Thousand Years on the Shaman's Path.* New York: William Morrow.
Furbee, Louanna, and Martha J. Macri
1985 Velar and Alveopalatal Consonants in the Maya Hieroglyphs. *International Journal of American Linguistics* 5(4)1:412–16.

Gates, William E.

1909 *Codex Perez, Maya-Tzental.* Includes reproductions of the 1864 photographs of Codex Peresianus as published by León de Rosny, 1864. Point Loma, Calif. Distributed by Karl W. Hiersemann, Leipzig.

1911 Madrid Codex. Photographed for William E. Gates, Point Loma, Calif. Unpublished photographs in the Rare Book Collection of Dumbarton Oaks Research Library and Collection, Washington, D.C.

1931 *An Outline Dictionary of Maya Glyphs: With a Concordance and Analysis of Their Relationships.* Baltimore: Johns Hopkins Press.

1932 Glyph Studies. *Maya Society Quarterly* (Baltimore) 1(4):153–82.

1933 *The Madrid Maya Codex.* Publication 21. Baltimore: Maya Society.

Genet, Jean

1934 Les glyphes symboliques dans l'écriture maya-quichée: Le glyphe symbolique de la guerre. *Revue des Etudes Mayas-Quichées* 1:23–32.

Goodman, Joseph T.

1897 The Archaic Maya Inscriptions. Appendix to *Archaeology,* vol. 6 of *Biologia Centrali-americana,* by A. P. Maudslay. London: R. H. Porter and Dulau.

1905 Maya Dates. *American Anthropologist* 7(4):642–47.

Grazioso, Liwy

2002 La guerra: Religión o política. In *Enciclopedia Iberoamericana de Religiones,* vol. 2: *Religión Maya,* ed. Mercedes de la Garza and Martha Ilia Nájera, pp. 217–49. Madrid: Editorial Trotta.

Greene Robertson, Merle, ed.

1974a *Primera Mesa Redonda de Palenque, Part I: A Conference on the Art, Iconography, and Dynastic History of Palenque, Palenque, Chiapas, Mexico, December 14–22, 1973.* Pebble Beach, Calif.: Robert Louis Stevenson School.

1974b *Primera Mesa Redonda de Palenque, Part II: A Conference on the Art, Iconography, and Dynastic History of Palenque, Palenque, Chiapas, Mexico. December 14–22, 1973.* Pebble Beach, Calif.: Robert Louis Stevenson School.

1976 *The Art, Iconography & Dynastic History of Palenque, Part III: Proceedings of the Segunda Mesa Redonda de Palenque, December 14–21, 1974, Palenque.* Pebble Beach, Calif.: Robert Louis Stevenson School.

1980 *Third Palenque Round Table, 1978, Part 2.* Palenque Round Table Series, vol. 5. San Francisco: Pre-Columbian Art Research Institute.

Greene Robertson, Merle, and Donnan Call Jeffers, eds.

1979 *Tercera Mesa Redonda de Palenque, Vol. 4: Proceedings of the Tercera Mesa Redonda de Palenque, June 11–18, 1978, Palenque. A Conference on the Art, Hieroglyphics, and Historic Approaches of the Late Classic Maya.* Monterey: Pre-Columbian Art Research Institute.

Grofe, Michael

2007 The Serpent Series: Precession in the Maya Dresden Codex. Ph.D. dissertation, Department of Native American Studies, University of California, Davis.

2008 The Early Classic Name of G1: First Dawn Lord Shines. Paper prepared for the electronic symposium "Celestial References in Mesoamerican Creation Stories," organized by Gabrielle Vail and Timothy Knowlton for the Annual Meeting of the Society for American Archaeology, Vancouver.

Grube, Nikolai

1990a *Die Entwicklung der Mayaschrift: Grundlagen zur Erforschung des Wandels der Mayaschrift von der Protoklassik bis zur spanischen Eroberung.* Berlin: Karl-Friedrich von Flemming.

1990b Die Errichtung von Stelen--Entzifferung einer Verbhieroglyphe auf Monumenten der klassischen Mayakultur. In *Circumpacifica: Festschrift für Thomas S. Barthel,* band 1: *Mittel- und Südamerika,* ed. Bruno Illius and Matthias Laubscher, pp. 189–215. Frankfurt am Main: Peter Lang.

1991 An Investigation of the Primary Standard Sequence on Classic Maya Ceramics. In Fields 1991:223–32.

1994a Hieroglyphic Sources for the History of Northwest Yucatan. In *Hidden among the Hills: Maya Archaeology of the Northwest Yucatan Peninsula, First Maler Symposium, Bonn 1989,* ed. Hanns J. Prem, pp. 316–58. Möckmühl, Germany: Verlag Von Flemming.

1994b Observations on the History of Maya Hieroglyphic Writing. In Fields 1994:177–86.

2004 The Orthographic Distinction between Velar and Glottal Spirants in Maya Hieroglyphic Writing. In Wichmann 2004:61–81.

Grube, Nikolai, and Barbara MacLeod

1990 The Wing That Doesn't Fly: Problems and Possibilities Concerning the Reading of the "Wing" Sign. In Jones and Jones 1990:167–77.

Grube, Nikolai, and Simon Martin

2000 *Notebook for the XXIVth Maya Hieroglyphic Forum at Texas.* Austin: Department of Art and Art History, College of Fine Arts, and Institute of Latin American Studies, University of Texas at Austin.

Grube, Nikolai, and Werner Nahm

1990 A Sign for the Syllable *mi. Research Reports on Ancient Maya Writing,* no. 33. Washington, D.C.: Center for Maya Research.

1994 A Census of Xibalba: A Complete Inventory of *Way* Characters on Maya Ceramics. In *The Maya Vase Book: A Corpus of Rollout Photographs of Maya Vases,* vol. 4, ed. Justin Kerr, pp. 686–715. New York City: Kerr Associates.

Grube, Nikolai, and Linda Schele

1988 A Quadrant Tree at Copan. *Copán Note* 43. Honduras: Copán Mosaics Project and Instituto Hondureño de Anthropología e Historia.

1990 Two Examples of the Glyph for "Step" from the Hieroglyphic Stairs. *Copán Note* 91. Copán, Honduras: Copán Mosaics Project and the Instituto Hondureño de Anthropología e Historia.

1994 Kuy, the Owl of Omen and War. *Mexicon* 16:10–17.

Grube, Nikolai, and David Stuart

1987 Observations on T110 as the Syllable *ko. Research Reports on Ancient Maya Writing,* no. 8. Washington, D.C.: Center for Maya Research.

Hammond, Norman

1987 The Sun Also Rises: Iconographic Syntax of the Pomona Flare. *Research Reports on Ancient Maya Writing,* no. 7. Washington, D.C.: Center for Maya Research.

Hanks, William F., and Don S. Rice, eds.

1989 *Word and Image in Maya Culture: Explorations in Language, Writing, and Representation.* Salt Lake City: University of Utah Press.

Harrison, Peter D.

1999 *The Lords of Tikal: Rulers of an Ancient Maya City.* London: Thames and Hudson.

Hernández, Christine, and Victoria R. Bricker

2004 The Inauguration of Planting in the Borgia and Madrid Codices. In Vail and Aveni 2004:277–320.

Hofling, Charles A.

1989 The Morphosyntactic Basis of Discourse Structure in Glyphic Text in the Dresden Codex. In Hanks and Rice 1989:51–71.

2000 Mayan Texts, Scribal Practices, Language Varieties, Language Contacts, and Speech Communities: Commentary on Papers by Macri, Vail, and Bricker. *Written Language and Literacy* 3:117–22.

Hofling, Charles A., with Félix Fernando Tesucún

1997 *Itzaj Maya-Spanish-English Dictionary.* Salt Lake City: University of Utah Press.

Hopkins, Nicholas A.

1991 Classic and Modern Relationship Terms and the "Child of Mother" Glyph (TI:606.23). In Fields 1991:255–65.

Houston, Stephen D.

1984 An Example of Homophony in Maya Script. *American Antiquity* 49:790–805.

1988 The Phonetic Decipherment of Mayan Glyphs. *Antiquity* 62:126–35.

1989 *Maya Glyphs.* London: Trustees of the British Museum.

1992 A Name Glyph for Classic Maya Dwarfs. In *The Maya Vase Book: A Corpus of Rollout Photographs of Maya Vases,* vol. 3, ed. Justin Kerr, pp. 526–31. New York City: Kerr Associates.

2006 An Example of Preclassic Mayan Writing? *Science* 311:1249–50.

Houston, Stephen D., ed.

1983 *Contributions to Maya Hieroglyphic Decipherment.* New Haven: Human Relations Area Files.

Houston, Stephen, Oswaldo Chinchilla Mazariegos, and David Stuart, eds.

2001 *The Decipherment of Ancient Maya Writing.* Norman: University of Oklahoma Press.

Houston, Stephen D., John Robertson, and David Stuart

1998 Disharmony in Maya Hieroglyphic Writing: Linguistic Change and Continuity in Classic Society. In *Anatomía de una civilización: Aproximaciones interdisciplinarias a la cultura maya,* ed. A. Ciudad, Y. Fernández, J. M. García, Mª J. Iglesias, A. Lacadena, and L. T. Sanz, pp. 275–96. Madrid: Sociedad Española de Estudios Mayas.

2000 The Language of Classic Maya Inscriptions. *Current Anthropology* 41(3):321–56.

2001 Quality and Quantity in Glyphic Nouns and Adjectives. *Research Reports on Ancient Maya Writing,* no. 47. Washington, D.C.: Center for Maya Research.

Houston, Stephen D., and David Stuart

1989 The *Way* Glyph: Evidence for "Co-Essences" among the Classic Maya. *Research Reports on Ancient Maya Writing,* no. 30. Washington, D.C.: Center for Maya Research.

1996 Of Gods, Glyphs, and Kings: Divinity and Rulership among the Classic Maya. *Antiquity* 70:289–312.

1998 The Ancient Maya Self: Personhood and Portraiture in the Classic Period. *RES: Anthropology and Aesthetics* 33:73–101.

Houston, Stephen D., David Stuart, and John Robertson

2004 Disharmony in Maya Hieroglyphic Writing: Linguistic Change and Continuity in Classic Society. In Wichmann 2004:83–99.

Houston, Stephen, David Stuart, and Karl Taube

2006 *The Memory of Bones: Body, Being, and Experience among the Classic Maya.* Austin: University of Texas Press.

Humboldt, Alexander von

1810 *Vues des Cordillères, et monumens des peuples indigènes de l'Amérique.* Paris: F. Schoell.

Jones, Carolyn, and Tom Jones, eds.

1997 *U Mut Maya VI.* Arcata, Calif.

Jones, Tom, and Carolyn Jones

1997 Four Weaver-Almanacs of the Madrid Codex. In Jones and Jones 1997:190–98.

Jones, Tom, and Carolyn Jones, eds.

1990 *U Mut Maya III.* Arcata, Calif.

Josserand, J. Kathryn

1991 The Narrative Structure of Hieroglyphic Texts at Palenque. In Fields 1991:12–31.

1997 Participant Tracking in Maya Hieroglyphic Texts: Who Was That Masked Man? In Macri and Ford 1997:111–27.

Josserand, J. Kathryn, Linda Schele, and Nicholas A. Hopkins

1985 Linguistic Data on Mayan Inscriptions: The *Ti* Constructions. In Benson 1985:87–102.

Justeson, John S.

1983 Mayan Hieroglyphic "Name-Tagging" on a Pair of Jade Plaques from Xcalumkin. In Houston 1983:40–43.

1984 Appendix B: Interpretations of Mayan Hieroglyphs. In Justeson and Campbell 1984:315–62.

1989 Ancient Maya Ethnoastronomy: An Overview of Hieroglyphic Sources. In Aveni 1989:76–129.

Justeson, John S., and Lyle Campbell, eds.

1984 *Phoneticism in Mayan Hieroglyphic Writing.* Publication 9. Albany: Institute for Mesoamerican Studies, State University of New York at Albany.

Justeson, John S., William M. Norman, Lyle Campbell, and Terrence Kaufman

1985 *The Foreign Impact on Lowland Mayan Language and Script.* Publication 53. New Orleans: Middle American Research Institute, Tulane University.

Justeson, John S., William M. Norman, and Norman Hammond

1988 The Pomona Flare: A Preclassic Maya Hieroglyphic Text. In Benson and Griffin 1988: 94–151.

Kaufman, Terrence S., and William M. Norman

1984 An Outline of Proto-Cholan Phonology, Morphology and Vocabulary. In Justeson and Campbell 1984:77–166.

Keller, Kathryn C., and Plácido Luciano G.

1997 *Diccionario Chontal de Tabasco.* Serie de vocabularios y diccionarios indígenas, Mariano Silva y Aceves, no. 36. Tucson: Summer Institute of Linguistics.

Kelley, David H.

1962a Fonetismo en la escritura maya. *Estudios de Cultura Maya* 2:277–317.

1962b A History of the Decipherment of Maya Script. *Anthropological Linguistics* 4:1–48.

1968a Descripción estructural interna y externa de un cartucho constante en el Codice de Dresde. *Estudios de Cultura Maya* 7:115–39.

1968b Kakupacal and the Itzas. *Estudios de Cultura Maya* 7:255–67.

1968c Mayan Fire Glyphs. *Estudios de Cultura Maya* 7:141–57.

1976 *Deciphering the Maya Script.* Austin: University of Texas Press.

1982 Notes on Puuc Inscriptions and History. In *The Puuc: New Perspectives. Papers Presented at the Puuc Symposium, Central College, May, 1977,* ed. Lawrence Mills, pp. 1–18. Scholarly Studies in the Liberal Arts, Publication 1, Supplement. Pella, Iowa: Central College.

Kerr, Justin

1989 *The Maya Vase Book: A Corpus of Rollout Photographs of Maya Vases,* vol. 1. New York: Kerr Associates.

1990 *The Maya Vase Book: A Corpus of Rollout Photographs of Maya Vases,* vol. 2. New York: Kerr Associates.

Kingsborough, Viscount Edward King

1831 *Antiquities of Mexico: Comprising Fac-similes of Ancient Mexican Paintings and Hieroglyphics.* London.

Knorozov, Yuri V.

1952 Drevnaja pis'mennost Central'noj Ameriki. *Sovietskaja Etnografija* 3:100–18. Moscow: Sovietskaja Etnografia.

1955 *La escritura de los antiguos mayas* [Spanish translation of *Sistema Pis'ma Drevnikh Maiia*]. Moscow: Editorial de la Academia de Ciencias de la URSS.

1958 The Problem of the Study of the Maya Hieroglyphic Writing. *American Antiquity* 23(3):284–91.

1963 Pis'mennost' Indeitsev Maiia. Moscow-Leningrad: Academia de Ciencias de las URSS, Instituto de Etnografia.

1967 *Selected Chapters from the Writing of the Maya Indians.* Trans. Sophie Coe, ed. Tatiana Proskouriakoff. Peabody Museum of Archaeology and Ethnology, Russian Translation Series, vol. 4. Cambridge, Mass.: Harvard University.

1982 *Maya Hieroglyphic Codices.* Publication 8. Albany: Institute for Mesoamerican Studies, State University of New York.

1999 *Compendio Xcaret de la escritura jeroglífica maya descifrada por Yuri V. Knórosov,* 3 vols., ed. Patricia Rodríguez Ochoa, Edgar Gómez Marín, and Myriam Cerda González. Mexico City: Universidad de Quintana Roo and Promotora Xcaret.

Knowles, Susan

1984 A Descriptive Grammar of Chontal Maya (San Carlos Dialect). Ph.D. dissertation, Department of Anthropology, Tulane University.

Knowlton, Timothy P.

2002 Diphrastic Kennings in Mayan Hieroglyphic Literature. *Mexicon* 24(1):9–14.

Lacadena, Alfonso

1994 Propuesta para la lectura del signo T158. *Mayab* 9:62–65.

1997a Bilingüismo en el códice de Madrid. In *Los investigadores de la cultura maya,* pp. 184–204. Publicaciones de la Universidad Autónoma de Campeche, no. 5. Campeche: Universidad Autónoma de Campeche.

1997b *Cha'/ka', Yax* and *Wi'il*: Three Examples of Adverbial Use of Adjectives in Classic Maya Inscriptions. *Texas Notes on Precolumbian Art, Writing, and Culture* 78. Austin: Center of the History and Art of Ancient American Culture, Art Department, University of Texas at Austin.

2004 On the Reading of Two Glyphic Appelatives [*sic*] of the Rain God. In *Continuity and Change: Maya Religious Practices in Temporal Perspective,* ed. Daniel Graña Behrens, Nikolai Grube, Christian M. Prager, Frauke Sachse, Stefanie Teufel, and Elisabeth Wagner, pp. 87–98. *Acta Mesoamericana,* vol. 14. Markt Schwaben: Verlag Anton Schwaben.

Lamb, Weldon

2005 Tzotzil Maya Cosmology. In *Songs from the Sky: Indigenous Astronomical and Cosmological Traditions of the World,* ed. Von Del Chamberlain, John B. Carlson, and M. Jane Young, pp. 163–72. Leicester, UK: Ocarina Books and Center for Archaeoastronomy.

Laughlin, Robert M., with John B. Haviland

1988 *The Great Tzotzil Dictionary of Santo Domingo Zinacantán with Grammatical Analysis and Historical Commentary,* vol. 2: *English-Tzotzil.* Smithsonian Contributions to Anthropology, no. 31. Washington, D.C.: Smithsonian Institution Press.

Lipp, Frank J.

1985 Mixe Ritual: An Ethnographic and Epigraphical Comparison. *Mexicon* 7:83–87.

Lounsbury, Floyd G.

1973 On the Derivation and Reading of the 'Ben Ich' Prefix. In *Mesoamerican Writing Systems: A Conference at Dumbarton Oaks, October 30th and 31st, 1971,* ed. Elizabeth P. Benson, pp. 99–143. Washington, D.C.: Dumbarton Oaks Research Library and Collection.

1974a Description of cover design. In Greene Robertson 1974a:ii.

1974b The Inscription of the Sarcophagus Lid at Palenque. In Greene Robertson 1974b:5–19.

1976 A Rationale for the Initial Date of the Temple of the Cross at Palenque. In Greene Robertson 1976:211–24.

1980 Some Problems in the Interpretation of the Mythological Portion of the Hieroglyphic Text of the Temple of the Cross at Palenque. In Greene Robertson 1980:99–115.

1982 Astronomical Knowledge and Its Uses at Bonampak, Mexico. In *Archaeoastronomy in the New World,* ed. Anthony F. Aveni, pp. 143–68. Cambridge: Cambridge University Press.

1983a The Base of the Venus Table of the Dresden Codex, and Its Significance for the Calendar-Correlation Problem. In *Calendars in Mesoamerica and Peru: Native American Computations of Time,* ed. Anthony F. Aveni and Gordon Brotherston, pp. 1–26. BAR International Series 174. Oxford: British Archaeological Reports.

1983b Glyph Values: T99, 155, 279, 280. In Houston 1983:44–49.

1984 Glyphic Substitutions: Homophonic and Synonymic. In Justeson and Campbell 1984:167–84.

1989 The Names of a King: Hieroglyphic Variants as a Key to Decipherment. In Hanks and Rice 1989:73–91.

Lounsbury, Floyd G., and Michael D. Coe

1968 Linguistic and Ethnographic Data Pertinent to the "Cage" Glyph of Dresden 36c. *Estudios de Cultura Maya* 7:269–84.

Love, Bruce

1986 Yucatec Maya Ritual: A Diachronic Perspective. Ph.D. dissertation, Department of Anthropology, University of California, Los Angeles.

1987 Glyph T93 and Maya "Hand-Scattering Events." *Research Reports on Ancient Maya Writing,* no. 5. Washington, D.C.: Center for Maya Research.

1989 Yucatec Sacred Breads through Time. In Hanks and Rice 1989:336–50.

1991 A Text from the Dresden New Year Pages. In Fields 1991:293–302.

1992 Another Glyph for *Na. Texas Notes on Precolumbian Art, Writing, and Culture* 28. Austin: Center of the History and Art of Ancient American Culture, Art Department, University of Texas at Austin.

1994 *The Paris Codex: Handbook for a Maya Priest.* Austin: University of Texas Press.

1995 A Dresden Codex Mars Table? *Latin American Antiquity* 6(4):350–61.

MacLeod, Barbara

1983 Remembrances of Cycles Past: T669b in Palenque Katun Histories. In Houston 1983:50–59.

1987 Xibal Balam Ahau. *Anthropological Linguistics* 29(4):452–61.

1988a The "Ninth Child of the Lineage": An Alternative Dynastic Reference to Moon-Jaguar on Stela 9 at Copán. *Copán Note* 50. Copán, Honduras: Copán Mosaics Project and the Instituto Hondureño de Anthropología e Historia.

1988b Renaming a Copan King: Phonetic Evidence for a More Accurate Rendering of the Name "Smoke-Imix-God K." *Copán Note* 49. Copán, Honduras: Copán Mosaics Project and the Instituto Hondureño de Anthropología e Historia.

1989a The 819-Day-Count: A Soulful Mechanism. In Hanks and Rice 1989:112–26.

1989b The Text of Altar F': Further Considerations. *Copán Note* 52. Copán, Honduras: Copán Mosaics Project and the Instituto Hondureño de Anthropología e Historia.

1990a Deciphering the Primary Standard Sequence. Ph.D. dissertation, University of Texas, Austin.

1990b The God N/Step Set in the Primary Standard Sequence. In Kerr 1990:331–47.

1991a The Classic Name for Cumku. *North Austin Hieroglyphic Hunches* 8 (February 22). [On file with author.]

1991b The DNIG, T573. *North Austin Hieroglyphic Hunches* 7 (February 10). [On file with author.]

1991c The Elusive T128. *North Austin Hieroglyphic Hunches* 4 (February 9). [On file with author.]

1991d The Flat-Hand Verb: New Evidence. *North Austin Hieroglyphic Hunches* 9 (April 17). [On file with author.]

1991e Maya Genesis: The First Steps. *North Austin Hieroglyphic Hunches* 5 (February 10). [On file with author.]

1991f Some Thoughts on a Possible *hal* Reading for T153, the "Crossed Batons" Glyph. *North Austin Hieroglyphic Hunches* 2 (February 5). [On file with author.]

1991g T128: A Reprise. *North Austin Hieroglyphic Hunches* 10 (April 18). [On file with author.]

1991h T135 (The G9 Superfix) and T108 (The "Guardian" Superfix). *North Austin Hieroglyphic Hunches* 6 (February 10). [On file with author.]

1991i The T614 "Thatch" and T79 "Anniversary Verb" Glyphs. *North Austin Hieroglyphic Hunches* 1 (January 25). [On file with author.]

1991j The T712 "Lancet" Glyph. *North Austin Hieroglyphic Hunches* 3 (February 8). [On file with author.]

1993 Musing about Rare Variants of Glyph A of the Lunar Series. *Texas Notes on Precolumbian Art, Writing, and Culture* 33. Austin: Center of the History and Art of Ancient American Culture, Art Department, University of Texas at Austin.

MacLeod, Barbara, and Brian Stross

1990 The Wing-Quincunx. *Journal of Mayan Linguistics* 7:14–32.

Macri, Martha J.

1985 Formulaic Patterns in the Maya Script. In *Proceedings of the Eleventh Annual Meeting of the Berkeley Linguistics Society,* ed. Mary Niepokuj, Mary VanClay, Vassiliki Nikiforidou, and Deborah Feder, pp. 216–25. Berkeley: Department of Linguistics, University of California.

1986 Polyadicity of Three Verbs Associated with Blood-Letting Rituals in Western Glyphic Maya. In *Proceedings of the Twelfth Annual Meeting of the Berkeley Linguistics Society,* ed. Vassiliki Nikiforidou, Mary VanClay, Mary Niepokuj, Deborah Feder, pp. 186–94. Berkeley: Department of Linguistics, University of California.

1988 A Descriptive Grammar of Palenque Maya. Ph.D. dissertation, University of California, Berkeley.

1991 Prepositions and Complementizers in the Classic Period Inscriptions. In Fields 1991:266–72.

2000a The Jog Sign as the Day Muluk. *Glyph Dwellers,* Report 10. Davis: Maya Hieroglyphic Database Project. http://nas.ucdavis.edu/NALC/R10.pdf.

2000b T536 *Xo,* from Nahuatl Xochitli 'Flower'. *Glyph Dwellers,* Report 11. Davis: Maya Hieroglyphic Database Project. http://nas.ucdavis.edu/NALC/R11.pdf.

2001 Another Example of T757 as the Day Muluk. *Glyph Dwellers,* Report 13. Davis: Maya Hieroglyphic Database Project. http://nas.ucdavis.edu/NALC/R13.pdf.

2006 Nahua Loan Words from the Early Classic Period: Words for Cacao Preparation on a Río Azul Ceramic Vessel. *Ancient Mesoamerica* 16:321–26.

2009 Scribal Interaction in Postclassic Mesoamerica. In *Astronomers, Scribes, and Priests: Intellectual Interchange between the Northern Maya Lowlands and Highland Mexico during the Late Postclassic Period,* ed. Gabrielle Vail and Christine Hernández. Washington, D.C.: Dumbarton Oaks Research Library and Collection. In press.

Macri, Martha J., and Anabel Ford, eds.

1997 *The Language of Maya Hieroglyphs.* San Francisco: Pre-Columbian Art Research Institute.

Macri, Martha J., and Matthew G. Looper

2003a *The New Catalog of Maya Hieroglyphs, Volume One: The Classic Period Inscriptions.* Norman: University of Oklahoma Press.

2003b Nahua in Ancient Mesoamerica: Evidence from Maya Inscriptions. *Ancient Mesoamerica* 14(2):285–97.

Martin, Simon, and Nikolai Grube

2000 *Chronicle of the Maya Kings and Queens: Deciphering the Dynasties of the Ancient Maya.* London: Thames and Hudson.

Martin, Simon, Marc Zender, and Nikolai Grube

2002 *Notebook for the XXVth Maya Hieroglyphic Forum at Texas.* With Introduction to Reading Maya Hieroglyphs by Linda Schele and Nikolai Grube. Austin: Maya Workshop Foundation, University of Texas at Austin.

Martínez Hernández, Juan

1926 *Paralelismo entre los calendarios maya y azteca: Su correlación con el calendario juliano.* Mérida, Mexico: Compañía Tipográfica Yucateca.

1929 *Diccionario de Motul, Maya-Español Atribuido a Fray Antonio de Ciudad Real.* Mérida, Mexico: Compañía Tipográfica Yucateca.

Martyr D'Anghera, Peter

1912 *De Orbe Novo: The Eight Decades of Peter Martyr D'Anghera,* trans. Francis Augustus MacNutt. 2 vols. New York: G. P. Putnam's Sons.

Mathews, Peter
1980 Notes on the Dynastic Sequence of Bonampak, Part 1. In Greene Robertson 1980:60–73.
1984 Appendix A: A Maya Hieroglyphic Syllabary. In Justeson and Campbell 1984:311–14.
1991 Classic Maya Emblem Glyphs. In *Classic Maya Political History: Hieroglyphic and Archaeological Evidence,* ed. T. Patrick Culbert, pp. 19–29. Cambridge: Cambridge University Press.
Mathews, Peter, and John S. Justeson
1984 Patterns of Sign Substitution in Mayan Hieroglyphic Writing: The "Affix Cluster." In Justeson and Campbell 1984:185–231.
Mathews, Peter, and Linda Schele
1974 Lords of Palenque--The Glyphic Evidence. In Greene Robertson 1974a:63–76.
Maudslay, Alfred P.
1889–1902 *Archaeology,* vols. 1–6 of *Biologia Centrali-Americana; or, Contributions to the Knowledge of the Fauna and Flora of Mexico and Central America,* ed. F. Ducane Godman and Osbert Salvin. London: R. H. Porter and Dulau.
Milbrath, Susan
1999 *Star Gods of the Maya: Astronomy in Art, Folklore, and Calendars.* Austin: University of Texas Press.
2002 New Questions Concerning the Authenticity of the Grolier Codex. *Latin American Indian Literatures Journal* 18:50–83.
Milbrath, Susan, and Carlos Peraza Lope
2003 Revisiting Mayapan: Mexico's Last Maya Capital. *Ancient Mesoamerica* 14:1–46.
Miller, Jeffrey H.
1974 Notes on a Stelae Pair Probably from Calakmul, Campeche, Mexico. In Greene Robertson 1974a:149–61.
Mora-Marín, David
2000 The Syllabic Value of Sign T77 as **k'i**. *Research Reports on Ancient Maya Writing,* no. 46. Washington, D.C.: Center for Maya Research.
Morán, Fray Francisco
1935 *Arte y Diccionario en Lengua Cholti: A Manuscript Copied from the Libro Grande of Fr. Pedro Moran of about 1625.* Publication 9. Baltimore: Maya Society.
Morley, Sylvanus Griswold
1915 *An Introduction to the Study of the Maya Hieroglyphs.* Smithsonian Institution: Bureau of American Ethnology Bulletin 57. Washington, D.C.: Government Printing Office.
1920 *The Inscriptions at Copan.* Publication 219. Washington, D.C.: Carnegie Institution of Washington.
Orejel, Jorge
1990 The "Axe/Comb" Glyph (T333) as *ch'ak*. *Research Reports on Ancient Maya Writing,* no. 31. Washington, D.C.: Center for Maya Research.
Pahl, Gary W.
1976 A Successor-Relationship Complex and Associated Signs. In Greene Robertson 1976:35–44.
Paxton, Merideth
1986 Codex Dresden: Stylistic and Iconographic Analysis of a Maya Manuscript. Ph.D. dissertation, Department of Art History, University of New Mexico.
1992 The Books of Chilam Balam: Astronomical Content and the Paris Codex. In Aveni 1992:216–46.
2001 *The Cosmos of the Yucatec Maya: Cycles and Steps from the Madrid Codex*. Albuquerque: University of New Mexico Press.
Pérez Martínez, Vitalino, Federico Garcia, Felipe Martínez, and Jeremías López
1996 *Diccionario del idioma ch'orti'*. Antigua, Guatemala: Proyecto Lingüístico Francisco Marroquín.

Pío Pérez, Juan
1866–1877 *Diccionario de la lengua maya*. Mérida, Mexico: J. F. Mólina Solis.

Porter, James B.
1988 T168 as Itsa: Maya Sorcerers and Their Succession. *Estudios de Cultura Maya* 17:65–86.

Pousse, A.
1887 Étude sur le codex Dresdensis présenté à la Société Américaine de France. *Archives de la Société Américaine de France* (Paris), 2nd series, 5:97–119, 155–70.

Prager, Christian
1997 Notes on Maya Hieroglyphic Texts in the Codices, Part 1. *Yumtzilob* (Leiden) 9:29–44.

Proskouriakoff, Tatiana
1960 Historical Implications of a Pattern of Dates at Piedras Negras. *American Antiquity* 25:454–75.
1964 Historical Data in the Inscriptions of Yaxchilán, Part 2. *Estudios de Cultura Maya* (Mexico City) 4:177–201.
1968 The Jog and Jaguar Signs in Maya Writing. *American Antiquity* 33:247–51.
1973 The Hand-Grasping Fish and Associated Glyphs on Classic Maya Monuments. In Benson 1973:165–78.

Restall, Matthew, and John F. Chuchiak IV
2002 A Reevaluation of the Authenticity of Fray Diego de Landa's *Relación de las cosas de Yucatán. Ethnohistory* 49(1):651–69.

Riese, Berthold
1982 Kriegsberichte der Klassischen Maya. *Baessler-Archiv* n.s. 30:255–321.
1984 Hel hieroglyphics. In Justeson and Campbell 1984:263–86.

Ringle, William M.
1985 Notes on Two Tablets of Unknown Provenance. In Fields 1985:151–58.
1988 Of Mice and Monkeys: The Value and Meaning of T1016, the God C Hieroglyph. *Research Reports on Ancient Maya Writing,* no. 18. Washington, D.C.: Center for Maya Research.
1990 Who Was Who in Ninth-Century Chichen Itza. *Ancient Mesoamerica* 1(2):233–43.

Ringle, William M., and Thomas C. Smith-Stark
1996 *A Concordance to the Inscriptions of Palenque, Chiapas, Mexico.* Publication 62. New Orleans: Middle American Research Institute, Tulane University.

Rosny, Léon de
1875 *L'interprétation des anciens textes mayas.* Paris: G. Bossange.
1876 Essai sur le déchiffrement de l'écriture hiératique de l'Amérique Centrale. *Revue Orientale et Américaine,* 2nd series, 1:225–61.
1878 De la formation des mots dans l'écriture hiératique du Yucatan. *Actes de la Société d'Ethnographie,* Section Américaine, 9. Paris. [Republished in *L'Amérique pré-colombienne* by Léon de Rosny, 1904.]
1882 Les documents écrits de l'antiquité américaine; Compte-rendu d'une mission scientifique en Espagne et en Portugal. *Mémoires de la Société d'Ethnographie* 1:57–100. Paris: Maisonneuve et Cie.
1883 *Codex Cortesianus, Manuscrit hiératique de anciens Indiens de l'Amérique Centrale conservé au Musée Archéologique de Madrid, photographié et publié pour la première fois avec une introduction et un vocabulaire de l'écriture hiératique yucatèque.* Paris: Maisonneuve et Cie.
1888 *Codex Peresianus: Manuscrit hiératique des anciens Indiens de l'Amérique Centrale, conservé a la Biblithèque Nationale de Paris.* 2nd ed., printed in black and white. Paris: Bureau de la Société Américane.

Saturno, William
2006 The Dawn of Maya Gods and Kings. *National Geographic Magazine* 209:68–77.

Saturno William A., David Stuart, and Boris Beltrán
2006 Early Maya Writing at San Bartolo, Guatemala. *Science* 311:1281–83.
Saturno, William A., Karl A. Taube, and David Stuart
2005 The Murals of San Bartolo, El Petén, Guatemala. Part 1: The North Wall. *Ancient America,* no. 7. Barnardsville, N.C.: Center for Ancient American Studies.
Schele, Linda
1976 Accession Iconography of Chan-Bahlum in the Group of the Cross at Palenque. In Greene Robertson 1976:9–34.
1979 *Notebook for the Maya Hieroglyphic Writing Workshop at Texas, March 24–25, 1979.* Austin: Institute of Latin American Studies, University of Texas at Austin.
1981 *Notebook for the Maya Hieroglyphic Writing Workshop at Texas, March 28–29, 1981.* Austin: Institute of Latin American Studies, University of Texas at Austin.
1982 *Notebook for the Maya Hieroglyphic Writing Workshop at Texas, February 27–28, 1982.* Austin: Institute of Latin American Studies, University of Texas at Austin.
1985a Balan-Ahau: A Possible Reading of the Tikal Emblem Glyph and a Title at Palenque. In Benson 1985:59–65.
1985b The Hauberg Stela: Bloodletting and the Mythos of Maya Rulership. In Fields 1985:135–49.
1987a Stela I and the Founding of the City of Copán. *Copán Note* 30. Copán, Honduras: Copán Mosaics Project and the Instituto Hondureño de Anthropología e Historia.
1987b The Dedication of Structure 2 and a New Form of the God N Event. *Copán Note* 35. Copán, Honduras: Copán Mosaics Project and the Instituto Hondureño de Anthropología e Historia.
1987c Two Altar Names at Copan. *Copán Note* 36. Copán, Honduras: Copán Mosaics Project and the Instituto Hondureño de Anthropología e Historia.
1987d New Data on the Paddlers from Butz'-Chan of Copán. *Copán Note* 29. Copán, Honduras: Copán Mosaics Project and the Instituto Hondureño de Anthropología e Historia.
1987e New Fits on the North Panel of the West Doorway of Temple 11. *Copán Note* 38. Copán, Honduras: Copán Mosaics Project and the Instituto Hondureño de Anthropología e Historia.
1987f *Wan,* the "Standing Up" of Stela A. *Copán Note* 28. Copán, Honduras: Copán Mosaics Project and the Instituto Hondureño de Anthropología e Historia.
1988 The Xibalba Shuffle: A Dance after Death. In Benson and Griffin 1988:294–317.
1989a A Brief Commentary on the Top of Altar Q. *Copán Note* 66. Copán, Honduras: Copán Mosaics Project and the Instituto Hondureño de Anthropología e Historia.
1989b A New Glyph for "Five" on Stela E. *Copán Note* 53. Copán, Honduras: Copán Mosaics Project and the Instituto Hondureño de Anthropología e Historia.
1989c *Notebook for the XIIIth Maya Hieroglyphic Workshop at Texas, March 11–12, 1989.* Austin: Art Department, University of Texas at Austin.
1990a *Ba* as "First" in Classic Period Titles. *Texas Notes on Precolumbian Art, Writing, and Culture* 5. Austin: Art Department, University of Texas at Austin.
1990b Preliminary Commentary on a New Altar from Structure 30. *Copán Note* 72. Copán, Honduras: Copán Mosaics Project and the Instituto Hondureño de Anthropología e Historia.
1990c The Glyph for "Hole" and the Skeletal Maw of the Underworld. *Copán Note* 71. Copán, Honduras: Copán Mosaics Project and the Instituto Hondureño de Anthropología e Historia.
1991a Some Observations on the War Expressions at Tikal. *Texas Notes on Precolumbian Art, Writing, and Culture* 16. Austin: Center of the History and Art of Ancient American Culture, Art Department, University of Texas at Austin.
1991b *Workbook for the XVth Maya Hieroglyphic Workshop at Texas, March 9–10, 1991.* Austin: Art Department, University of Texas at Austin.
1992a The Founders of Lineages at Copan and Other Maya Sites. *Ancient Mesoamerica* 3:135–44.

1992b *Notebook for the XVIth Maya Hieroglyphic Workshop at Texas, March 14–15, 1992.* Austin: Department of Art and Art History and the Institute of Latin American Studies, University of Texas at Austin.

Schele, Linda, and David Freidel

1990 *A Forest of Kings: The Untold Story of the Ancient Maya.* New York: William Morrow.

1991 The Courts of Creation: Ballcourts, Ballgames, and Portals to the Maya Otherworld. In *The Mesoamerican Ballgame,* ed. Vernon L. Scarborough and David R. Wilcox, pp. 289–315. Tucson: University of Arizona Press.

Schele, Linda, and Nikolai Grube

1988 A Future Marker on a Hand Scattering Verb at Copan. *Copán Note* 42. Copán, Honduras: Copán Mosaics Project and the Instituto Hondureño de Anthropología e Historia.

1990 A Preliminary Inventory of Place Names in the Copan Inscriptions. *Copán Note* 93. Copán, Honduras: Copán Mosaics Project and the Instituto Hondureño de Anthropología e Historia.

1992 The Founding Events at Copan. *Copán Note* 107. Copán, Honduras: Copán Mosaics Project and the Instituto Hondureño de Anthropología e Historia.

1993 *Pi* as "Bundle." *Texas Notes on Precolumbian Art, Writing, and Culture* 56. Austin: Center of the History and Art of Ancient American Culture, Art Department, University of Texas at Austin.

1994 *Notebook for the XVIIIth Maya Hieroglyphic Workshop at Texas, March 13–14, 1994.* Austin: Department of Art and Art History, the College of Fine Arts, the Center for Mexican Studies and the Institute of Latin American Studies, University of Texas at Austin.

1997 *Notebook for the XXIst Maya Hieroglyphic Forum at Texas, March 1997.* Austin: Department of Art and Art History, the College of Fine Arts, and the Institute of Latin American Studies, University of Texas at Austin.

Schele, Linda, Nikolai Grube, and Federico Fahsen

1994 The Xukpi Stone: A Newly Discovered Early Classic Inscription from the Copán Acropolis. Part II: Commentary on the Text (Version 2). *Copán Note* 114. Copán, Honduras: Copán Mosaics Project and the Instituto Hondureño de Anthropología e Historia.

Schele, Linda, Nikolai Grube, and Simon Martin

1998 *Notebook for the XXIInd Maya Hieroglyphic Forum at Texas, March, 1998.* Austin: Department of Art and Art History, the College of Fine Arts, and the Institute of Latin American Studies, University of Texas at Austin.

Schele, Linda, and Matthew Looper

1996 *Notebook for the XXth Maya Hieroglyphic Workshop at Texas, March 9–10, 1996.* Austin: Department of Art and Art History, the College of Fine Arts, and the Institute of Latin American Studies, University of Texas at Austin.

Schele, Linda, and Peter Mathews

1993 *Notebook for the XVIIth Maya Hieroglyphic Workshop at Texas, March 13–14, 1993.* Austin: Department of Art and Art History, the College of Fine Arts, the College of Liberal Arts, and the Institute of Latin American Studies, University of Texas at Austin.

1998 *The Code of Kings: The Languages of Seven Sacred Maya Temples and Tombs.* New York: Scribner.

Schele, Linda, Peter Mathews, Nikolai Grube, Floyd Lounsbury, and David Kelley

1991 New Readings of Glyphs for the Month Kumk'u and their Implications. *Texas Notes on Precolumbian Art, Writing, and Culture* 15. Austin: Center of the History and Art of Ancient American Culture, Art Department, University of Texas at Austin.

Schele, Linda, Peter Mathews, and Floyd Lounsbury

1990a The *Nal* Suffix at Palenque and Elsewhere. *Texas Notes on Precolumbian Art, Writing, and Culture* 6. Austin: Center of the History and Art of Ancient American Culture, Art Department, University of Texas at Austin.

1990b Untying the Headband. *Texas Notes on Precolumbian Art, Writing, and Culture* 4. Austin: Center of the History and Art of Ancient American Culture, Art Department, University of Texas at Austin.

Schele, Linda, and Jeffrey H. Miller

1983 *The Mirror, the Rabbit, and the Bundle: "Accession" Expressions from the Classic Maya Inscriptions.* Studies in Pre-Columbian Art and Archaeology, no. 25. Washington, D.C.: Dumbarton Oaks Research Library and Collection.

Schele, Linda, and Mary Ellen Miller

1986 *The Blood of Kings: Dynasty and Ritual in Maya Art.* Fort Worth: Kimball Art Museum.

Schele, Linda, and David Stuart

1986 Butz'-Chaan, the 11th Successor of the Yax-K'uk'-Mo' Lineage. *Copán Note* 14. Copán, Honduras: Copán Mosaics Project and the Instituto Hondureño de Anthropología e Historia.

Schellhas, Paul

1904 [1892] *Representation of Deities of the Maya Manuscripts.* Papers of the Peabody Museum of American Archaeology and Ethnology, vol. 4, no. 1. Cambridge, Mass.: Harvard University.

Seler, Eduard

1888 Der Charakter der aztekischen und der Maya-Handschriften. *Zeitschrift für Ethnologie* 20:1–10.

1892a Does There Really Exist a Phonetic Key to Maya Hieroglyphic Writing? *Science* 20 (499):121–22.

1892b A Recent Attempt to Decipher Maya Writing. *Globus* 62:59–61.

1893 Is the Maya Hieroglyphic Writing Phonetic? *Science* 21(518):6–10.

1902–1923 *Gesammelte Abhandlungen zur amerikanischen Sprach- und Alterthumskunde.* 5 vols. Berlin: A. Asher.

1976 [1915] *Observations and Studies in the Ruins of Palenque.* Pebble Beach, Calif.: Robert Louis Stevenson School.

1990 *Eduard Seler: Collected Works in Mesoamerican Linguistics and Archaeology,* vol. 1, ed. Frank E. Comparato. Culver City, Calif.: Labyrinthos.

1990–1998 *Eduard Seler: Collected Works in Mesoamerican Linguistics and Archaeology,* vols. 1–6, ed. Frank E. Comparato. Culver City, Calif.: Labyrinthos.

1993 *Eduard Seler: Collected Works in Mesoamerican Linguistics and Archaeology,* vol. 4, ed. Frank E. Comparato. Culver City, Calif.: Labyrinthos.

Siegel, Morris

1941 Religion in Western Guatemala: A Product of Acculturation. *American Anthropologist* 43(1):62–76.

Spinden, Herbert J.

1924 *The Reduction of Mayan Dates.* Papers of the Peabody Museum of American Archaeology and Ethnology, vol. 6, no. 4. Cambridge, Mass.: Harvard University.

Stephens, John L.

1841 *Incidents of Travel in Central America, Chiapas, and Yucatan.* London: John Murray.

1843 *Incidents of Travel in Yucatan.* London: John Murray.

Stone, Andrea

1990 The Two Faces of Eve: The Grandmother and the Unfaithful Wife as a Paradigm in Maya Art. Paper presented at the 89th Annual Meeting of the American Anthropological Association, New Orleans.

1995 New Light on God H in the Maya Codices. Paper presented at the 94th Annual Meeting of the American Anthropological Association, Washington, D.C.

1996 The Cleveland Plaque: Cloudy Places of the Maya Realm. In *Eighth Palenque Round Table, 1993, Palenque Round Table Series,* vol. 10, ed. Martha J. Macri and Jan McHargue, pp. 403–12. Merle Greene Robertson, gen. ed. San Francisco: Pre-Columbian Art Research Institute.

2002 Spirals, Ropes, and Feathers: The Iconography of Rubber Balls in Mesoamerican Art. *Ancient Mesoamerica* 13:21–39.

Stross, Brian

1985 Color Symbolism of a Maya Glyph: The Kan Cross. *Journal of Mayan Linguistics* 5:73–112.

1989 Olmec Vessel with a Crayfish Icon: An Early Rebus. In Hanks and Rice 1989:143–64.

1993 Man in the Maw: An Olmec *Way* in the Sky. *Texas Notes on Precolumbian Art, Writing, and Culture* 43. Austin: Center of the History and Art of Ancient American Culture, Art Department, University of Texas at Austin.

1994 Glyphs on the Classic Maya Vessels: The Introductory Formula of the Primary Standard Sequence. In Fields 1994:187–93.

Stross, Brian, and Justin Kerr

1990 Notes on the Maya Vision Quest Through Enema. In Kerr 1990:348–58.

Stuart, David

1979 Some Thoughts on Certain Occurrences of the T565 Glyph Element at Palenque. In Greene Robertson and Jeffers 1979:167–71.

1984 Royal Auto-Sacrifice among the Maya: A Study of Image and Meaning. *RES: Anthropology and Aesthetics* 7/8:6–20.

1985a The "Count of Captives" Epithet in Classic Maya Writing. In Fields 1985:97–101.

1985b A New Child-Father Relationship Glyph. *Research Reports on Ancient Maya Writing,* no. 2. Washington, D.C.: Center for Maya Research.

1985c The Yaxha Emblem Glyph as *Yax-ha. Research Reports on Ancient Maya Writing,* no. 1. Washington, D.C.: Center for Maya Research.

1987 Ten Phonetic Syllables. *Research Reports on Ancient Maya Writing,* no. 14. Washington, D.C.: Center for Maya Research.

1989a The "First Ruler" on Stela 24. *Copán Note* 7. Copán, Honduras: Copán Mosaics Project and the Instituto Hondureño de Anthropología e Historia.

1989b Hieroglyphs on Maya Vessels. In Kerr 1989:149–60.

1990 The Decipherment of "Directional Count Glyphs" in Maya Inscriptions. *Ancient Mesoamerica* 1(2):213–24.

1995 A Study of Maya Inscriptions. Ph.D. dissertation, Department of Anthropology, Vanderbilt University.

1996 Kings of Stone: A Consideration of Stelae in Ancient Maya Ritual and Representation. *RES: Anthropology and Aesthetics* 29/30:148–71.

1997 Kinship Terms in Maya Inscriptions. In Macri and Ford 1997:1–11.

1998 "The Fire Enters His House": Architecture and Ritual in Classic Maya Texts. In *Function and Meaning in Classic Maya Architecture: A Symposium at Dumbarton Oaks, 7th and 8th October 1994,* ed. Stephen D. Houston, pp. 373–425. Washington, D.C.: Dumbarton Oaks Research Library and Collection.

2000a "The Arrival of Strangers": Teotihuacan and Tollan in Classic Maya History. In *Mesoamerica's Classic Heritage: From Teotihuacan to the Aztecs,* ed. David Carrasco, Lindsay Jones, and Scott Sessions, pp. 465–513. Boulder: University Press of Colorado.

2000b Ritual and History in the Stucco Inscription from Temple XIX at Palenque. *PARI Journal* 1:13–19.

2001 A Reading of the "Completion Hand" as TZUTZ. *Research Reports on Ancient Maya Writing,* no. 49. Washington, D.C.: Center for Maya Research.

2002a Glyphs for "Right" and "Left"? mesoweb.com/stuart/notes/RightLeft.pdf (posted on Mesoweb).

2002b Spreading Wings: A Possible Origin of the **k'i** Syllable. mesoweb.com/stuart/notes/Wings.pdf (posted on Mesoweb).

2005 *The Inscriptions from Temple XIX at Palenque: A Commentary.* San Francisco: Pre-Columbian Art Research Institute.

2007 The Michol Celt. Maya Decipherment: A Weblog on the Ancient Maya Script. http://decipherment.wordpress.com/2007/04/01/the-michol-celt/ (posted April 1, 2007).

Stuart, David, Nikolai Grube, Linda Schele, and Floyd Lounsbury

1989 Stela 63, a New Monument from Copán. *Copán Note* 56. Honduras: Copán Mosaics Project and the Instituto Hondureño de Anthropología e Historia.

Stuart, David, and Stephen Houston

1994 *Classic Maya Place Names.* Studies in Pre-Columbian Art and Archaeology, no. 33. Washington, D.C.: Dumbarton Oaks Research Library and Collection.

Stuart, David, Stephen D. Houston, and John Robertson

1999 *Recovering the Past: Classic Maya Language and Classic Maya Gods. Notebook for the XXIIIrd Maya Hieroglyphic Forum at Texas.* Austin: Department of Art and Art History, the College of Fine Arts, and the Institute of Latin American Studies, University of Texas at Austin.

Stuart, David, and Linda Schele

1986 Yax-K'uk-Mo', The Founder of the Lineage of Copán. *Copán Note* 6. Copán, Honduras: Copán Mosaics Project and the Instituto Hondureño de Anthropología e Historia.

Swadesh, Morris, María C. Álvarez, and Juan R. Bastarrachea

1970 *Diccionario de elementos del maya yucateco colonial.* Centro de Estudios Mayas, Cuaderno 3. Mexico City: Universidad Nacional Autónoma de México.

Taack, George

1973 An Iconographic Study of Deer Hunting Scenes in Maya Painting: Codex Madrid and Vases from Calcehtok and Altun Ha. M.A. thesis. University of New Mexico.

Taube, Karl A.

1985 The Classic Maya Maize God: A Reappraisal. In Fields 1985:171–81.

1988 The Ancient Yucatec New Year Festival: The Liminal Period in Maya Ritual and Cosmology. Ph.D. dissertation, Department of Anthropology, Yale University.

1989a The Maize Tamale in Classic Maya Diet, Epigraphy, and Art. *American Antiquity* 54:31–51.

1989b Ritual Humor in Classic Maya Religion. In Hanks and Rice 1989:351–82.

1992 *The Major Gods of Ancient Yucatan.* Studies in Pre-Columbian Art and Archaeology, no. 32. Washington, D.C.: Dumbarton Oaks Research Library and Collection.

Taube, Karl A., and Bonnie L. Bade

1991 The Presence of Xiutecuhtli in the Dresden Venus Pages. *Research Reports on Ancient Maya Writing,* no. 35. Washington, D.C.: Center for Maya Research.

Tedlock, Barbara

1999a Continuities and Renewals in Mayan Literacy and Calendrics. In *Theorizing the Americanist Tradition,* ed. Lisa Valentine and Regna Darnell, pp. 195–208. Toronto: University of Toronto Press.

1999b Maya Astronomy: What We Know and How We Know It. *Archaeoastronomy: The Journal of Astronomy in Culture* 14(1):39–58. Austin: University of Texas Press.

Tedlock, Dennis

1992 The Popol Vuh as a Hieroglyphic Book. In *New Theories on the Ancient Maya,* ed. Elin C. Danien and Robert J. Sharer, pp. 229–40. University Museum Monograph 77. Philadelphia: University of Pennsylvania Museum.

1996 *Popol Vuh: The Maya Book of the Dawn of Life.* 2nd ed. New York: Simon and Schuster.

Tedlock, Dennis, and Barbara Tedlock

2002–2003 The Sun, Moon, and Venus among the Stars: Methods for Mapping Mayan Sidereal Space. *Archaeoastronomy: The Journal of Astronomy in Culture* 17:5–22.

2007 Moon Woman Meets the Stars: A New Reading of the Lunar Almanacs in the Dresden Codex. In *Skywatching in the Ancient World: New Perspectives in Cultural Astronomy,* ed. Clive Ruggles and Gary Urton, pp. 121–56. Boulder: University Press of Colorado.

Teeple, John E.

1931 Maya Astronomy. *Contributions to American Archaeology,* vol. 1, no. 2, pp. 29–115. Publication 403. Washington, D.C.: Carnegie Institution of Washington.

Thomas, Cyrus

1882 *A Study of the Manuscript Troano.* In Contributions to North American Ethnology, vol. 5, pp. 1–237. Washington, D.C.: U.S. Department of the Interior.

1888 Aids to the Study of the Maya Codices. In *Sixth Annual Report of the Bureau of Ethnology to the Secretary of the Smithsonian Institution 1884–1885,* pp. 253–371. Washington, D.C.: Government Printing Office.

1892a Is the Maya Hieroglyphic Writing Phonetic? *Science* 20(505):197–201.

1892b Key to the Maya Hieroglyphs. *Science* 20(494):44–46.

1893 Are the Maya Hieroglyphs Phonetic? *American Anthropologist* 6(3):241–70.

Thompson, J. Eric S.

1937 Maya Chronology: The Correlation Question. *Contributions to American Archaeology and History.* Publication 456, no. 14. Washington, D.C.: Carnegie Institution of Washington.

1939 The Moon Goddess in Middle America, with Notes on Related Deities. In *Contributions to American Archaeology and History,* vol. 5, pp. 121–74. Publication 509, no. 29. Washington, D.C.: Carnegie Institution of Washington.

1943 Maya Epigraphy: A Cycle of 819 Days. In *Notes on Middle American Archaeology and Ethnology,* vol. 1, no. 22, pp. 137–51. Washington, D.C.: Carnegie Institution of Washington.

1944 The Fish as a Maya Symbol for Counting and Further Discussion of Directional Glyphs. In *Theoretical Approaches to Problems,* no. 2. Washington, D.C.: Carnegie Institution of Washington.

1950 *Maya Hieroglyphic Writing: Introduction.* Publication 589. Washington, D.C.: Carnegie Institution of Washington.

1958 Symbols, Glyphs, and Divinatory Almanacs for Diseases in the Maya Dresden and Madrid Codices. *American Antiquity* 23(3):297–308.

1962 *A Catalog of Maya Hieroglyphs.* Norman: University of Oklahoma Press.

1970a The Bacabs: Their Portraits and Glyphs. *Monographs and Papers in Maya Archaeology,* ed. William R. Bullard, Jr., pp. 469–85. Papers of the Peabody Museum of Archaeology and Ethnology, vol. 61. Cambridge, Mass.: Harvard University.

1970b *Maya History and Religion.* Norman: University of Oklahoma Press.

1971 *Maya Hieroglyphic Writing: Introduction.* Norman: University of Oklahoma Press.

1972 *A Commentary on the Dresden Codex: A Maya Hieroglyphic Book.* American Philosophical Society, Memoirs 93. Philadelphia: American Philosophical Society.

1975 The Grolier Codex. In *Studies in Ancient Mesoamerica,* vol. 2, ed. John Graham, pp. 1–9. Contributions of the University of California Archaeological Research Facility, no. 27. Berkeley: University of California.

Tozzer, Alfred M.

1907 *A Comparative Study of the Mayas and Lacandones.* New York: Macmillan.

1921 *A Maya Grammar: With Bibliography and Appraisement of the Works Noted.* Papers of the Peabody Museum of American Archaeology and Ethnology, vol. 9. Cambridge, Mass.: Harvard University.

1941 *Landa's Relación de las Cosas de Yucatan: A Translation.* Papers of the Peabody Museum of American Archaeology and Ethnology, vol. 18. Cambridge, Mass.: Harvard University.

Tozzer, Alfred M., and Glover M. Allen

1910 *Animal Figures in the Maya Codices.* Papers of the Peabody Museum of American Archaeology and Ethnology, vol. 4, no. 3. Cambridge, Mass.: Harvard University.

Treiber, Hannelore
1987 *Studien zur Katunserie der Pariser Mayahandschrift.* Acta Mesoamericana 2. Berlin: Verlag von Fleming.

Ulrich, E. Matthew, and Rosemary Dixon de Ulrich
1976 *Diccionario bilingüe: Maya Mopán y Español, Español y Maya Mopán.* Guatemala City: Instituto Lingüístico de Verano.

Urcid Serrano, Javier
2001 *Zapotec Hieroglyphic Writing.* Studies in Pre-Columbian Art and Archaeology, no. 34. Washington, D.C.: Dumbarton Oaks Research Library and Collection.

Vail, Gabrielle
1996 The Gods in the Madrid Codex: An Iconographic and Glyphic Analysis. Ph.D. dissertation, Department of Anthropology, Tulane University, New Orleans.
1997 The Yearbearer Gods in the Madrid Codex. In *Códices y documentos sobre México. Segundo simposio,* vol. I, ed. Salvador Rueda Smithers, Constanza Vega Sosa, and Rodrigo Martínez Baracs, pp. 81–106. Mexico City: Instituto Nacional de Antropología e Historia and Dirección General de Publicaciones del Consejo Nacional para la Cultura y las Artes.
1998 Kisin and the Underworld Gods of the Maya. *Latin American Indian Literatures Journal* 14:167–87.
1999 Phonological Variation in the Maya Codices. *Glyph Dwellers,* Report 9. Davis: Maya Hieroglyphic Database Project. http://nas.ucdavis.edu/NALC/R9.pdf.
2000a Issues of Language and Ethnicity in the Postclassic Maya Codices. *Written Language and Literacy* 3:37–75.
2000b Pre-Hispanic Maya Religion: Conceptions of Divinity in the Postclassic Maya Codices. *Ancient Mesoamerica* 11(1):123–47.
2002a *Haab'* Rituals in the Maya Codices and the Structure of Maya Almanacs. *Research Reports on Ancient Maya Writing,* no. 53. Washington, D.C.: Center for Maya Research.
2002b *The Madrid Codex: A Maya Hieroglyphic Book.* A website and database available online at www.doaks.org/codex. Washington, D.C.: Dumbarton Oaks Research Library and Collection. [Superceded by Vail and Hernández 2005–2008.]
2003 *Pa'K'in*: Reflections on Eclipses and Astronomical Beings in the Texts and Iconography of the Maya Codices. Paper presented at the 102nd Annual Meeting of the American Anthropological Association, Chicago.
2005 Renewal Ceremonies in the Madrid Codex. In *Painted Books and Indigenous Knowledge in Mesoamerica: Manuscript Studies in Honor of Mary Elizabeth Smith,* ed. Elizabeth H. Boone, pp. 181–211. Publication 69. New Orleans: Middle American Research Institute, Tulane University.
2006 The Maya Codices. In *Annual Review of Anthropology,* ed. William H. Durham and Jane Hill, pp. 497–519. Palo Alto, Calif.: Annual Reviews.
2009 The Three Stones of Creation: New Evidence Concerning the "Snake [Throne] Stone" in the Maya Codices. *Glyph Dwellers,* University of California at Davis. In preparation.

Vail, Gabrielle, and Anthony Aveni, eds.
2004 *The Madrid Codex: New Approaches to Understanding an Ancient Maya Manuscript.* Boulder: University Press of Colorado.

Vail, Gabrielle, and Victoria R. Bricker
2004 *Haab* Dates in the Madrid Codex. In Vail and Aveni 2004:171–214.

Vail, Gabrielle, and Victoria R. Bricker, comps.
2003 New Perspectives on the Madrid Codex. *Current Anthropology* 44, Supplement:105–12.

Vail, Gabrielle, and Christine Hernández

2005–2008 *The Maya Hieroglyphic Codices, Version 2.0.* A website and database available online at www.mayacodices.org.

n.d. Divinatory Almanacs and Mythic Cycles in Late Postclassic Maya and Mexican Codices. Ms. in preparation.

Vail, Gabrielle, and Christine Hernández, eds.

2009 *Astronomers, Scribes, and Priests: Intellectual Interchange between the Northern Maya Lowlands and Highland Mexico during the Late Postclassic Period.* Dumbarton Oaks Research Library and Collection, Washington, D.C. In press.

Vail, Gabrielle, and Andrea Stone

2002 Representations of Women in Postclassic and Colonial Maya Literature and Art. In *Ancient Maya Women,* ed. Traci Ardren, pp. 203–28. Walnut Creek, Calif.: Alta Mira Press.

von Nagy, Christopher

1997 Some Comments on the Madrid Deer-Hunting Almanacs. In *Papers on the Madrid Codex,* ed. Victoria R. Bricker and Gabrielle Vail, pp. 27–71. Publication 64. New Orleans: Middle American Research Institute, Tulane University.

von Winning, Hasso, and Dieter Dütting

1987 Supplementary Information on the Polychrome Maya Vessel with Four Straight Walls, Illustrated on the Cover of *Mexicon* VII: 6, December 1985. *Mexicon* 9:32–34.

Wald, Robert F.

2004 The Languages of the Dresden Codex: Legacy of the Classic Maya. In Wichmann 2004:27–58.

Wanyerka, Phil, ed.

1993 *The Proceedings of the Maya Hieroglyphic Weekend.* Cleveland State University.

1997 *The Proceedings of the Maya Hieroglyphic Workshop: The Dresden Codex.* University of Texas at Austin.

1998 *The Proceedings of the Maya Hieroglyphic Workshop: Deciphering Maya Politics, March 14–15, 1998.* University of Texas at Austin.

Warkentin, Viola, and Ruby Scott

1980 *Gramatica Ch'ol.* Serie de Gramáticas de Lenguas Indígenas de México 3. Mexico City: Instituto Lingüístico de Verano.

Whittaker, Gordon

1986 The Mexican Names of Three Venus Gods in the Dresden Codex. *Mexicon* 8:56–62.

Whorf, Benjamin Lee

1933 *The Phonetic Value of Certain Characters in Maya Writing.* Papers of the Peabody Museum of American Archaeology and Ethnology, vol. 13, no. 2. Cambridge, Mass.: Harvard University.

1942 Decipherment of the Linguistic Portion of the Maya Hieroglyphs. *Annual Report of the Smithsonian Institution for 1941,* pp. 479–502. Washington, D.C.: Government Printing Office.

Wichmann, Søren

2004 *The Linguistics of Maya Writing.* Salt Lake City: University of Utah Press.

Willson, Robert W.

1924 *Astronomical Notes on the Maya Codices.* Papers of the Peabody Museum of American Archaeology and Ethnology, vol. 6, no. 3. Cambridge, Mass.: Harvard University.

Winfield Capitaine, Fernando

1988 La Estela 1 de La Mojarra, Veracruz, México. *Research Reports on Ancient Maya Writing,* no. 16. Washington, D.C.: Center for Maya Research.

Winters, Diane

1991 A Study of the Fish-in-hand Glyph, T714: Part 1. In Fields 1991:233–45.

Wisdom, Charles

1950 *Materials on the Chortí Language.* Microfilm Collection of Manuscripts on Cultural Anthropology, no. 28. Chicago: University of Chicago Library.

Ximénez, Francisco

1985 *Primera parte del tesoro de las lenguas Cakchiquel, Quiché y Zutuhil, en que las dichas lenguas se traducen a la nuestra, Española.* Guatemala City: Academia de Geografía e Historia de Guatemala.

Zender, Marc

2006 Teasing the Turtle from Its Shell: AHK and MAHK in Maya Writing. *PARI Journal* 6(3):1–14. San Francisco: Pre-Columbian Art Research Institute.

Zimmermann, Günter

1953 *Kurze Formen- und Begriffssystematik der Hieroglyphen der Mayahandschriften.* Beiträge zur mittelamerickanischen Völkerkunde, no. 1. Hamburg: Hamburgisches Museum für Völkerkunde und Vorgeschichte.

1956 *Die Hieroglyphen der Maya-Handschriften. Abhandlungen aus dem Gebiet der Auslandskunde,* Band 62–Reihe B (Völkerkunde, Kuturgeschichte und Sprachen Band 34). Hamburg: Cram, de Gruyter.

Index to the New Catalog, Volumes 1 and 2

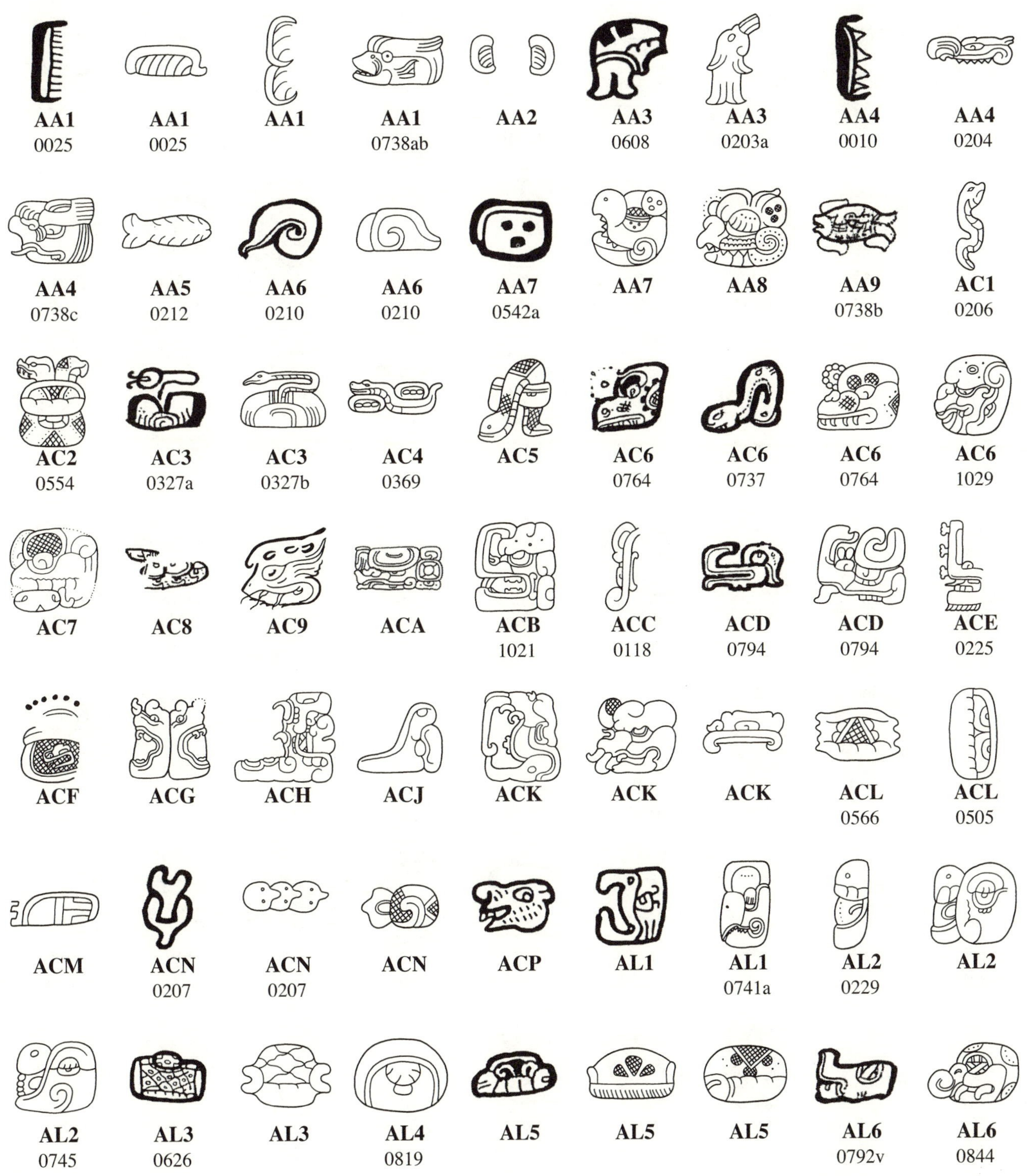

AL6
AL7 0792a
AL7 0792b
AL8 0740
AL9 0799
AL9 1068
ALA 0652
ALB
ALC 0790
AM1 0533
AM1 0533v
AM1 0533
AM1
AM2 0540
AM3
AM4 0535
AM5
AM6 0536
AM6 0536
AM7 0539
AM7 0572
AM7 0539
AM8
AM9
AMA
AMB 0534
AMB 0140
AMB 0534
AMB 0534
AMB 0178
AMB
AMC 1016c
AMC 0041
AMC 0014
AMC 1016ab
AMC 0041
AMC 0036
AMC 0043
AMD
AME
AME
AMF
AMG
AMH 0231
AMK
AMK 0755
AML
AMM 1053b
AP1 0801
AP1
AP2 0753
AP3 0752
AP4
AP5 0765ab
AP5 0567
AP5 0765ab
AP5 0845
AP6
AP7 0759
AP7 0759
AP8 0789
AP9 0757
AP9 0791b
AP9 0757
AP9 0788
APA
APB 0758a
APB
APB 0758a
APC 0758b
APD
APE

APF
APG
APH 0754
APJ 0159
APK
APL 0791a
APL 0791c
APM 0756ab
APM
APM 0756ab
APN
APP 1036c
APP 1036c
APQ
APR
APS 0802
APT
APU 0829
APV
APW
AT1 0800
AT1 0800
AT1 0751a
AT1 0751b
AT2
AT3
AT4
AT5
AT6 0832
AT7 0524
AT7 0524
AT8
AT9
AT9
ATA 0005
ATB
ATB 0834
ATC
AV1 0796
AV1
AV1
AV1
AV2
AV3 0765d
AV4
AV5 0291ab
AV5
AV6 0795
AV6 0795
AV7 0294
AX1
AX2
AX3
AX4
AX5
AX6
AX7 0803
AX7 0803
AX8
AX9 0766
AXA
AXB 0763
BM1 0236
BM1 0236
BM2 0077v
BM2 0077
BM2
BM2 0073
BM2
BM3
BM4
BM5 1067

BM6
BM7 0793a
BM8
BM9
BMA 0839
BMA
BMA
BMB
BMD
BME
BMF
BMG
BP1 0743
BP1 0743
BP1
BP1
BP2
BP3 0238
BP3 0238
BP4
BP4
BP5 0582
BP5 0582
BP5
BP6
BP7 0744a
BT1 0099
BT1 0296
BT1 0155v
BT1 0280
BT1 0279
BT1 0694
BT1 1066
BT2 0748
BT2 0748
BT2
BT3
BT4
BT4
BT4
BT5
BT6
BT6
BT7
BT8 0750
BT8 0353
BT9 0749
BV1 0747a
BV2
BV3 0747b
BV3 0747b
BV4 0747b
BV4
BV4
BV4
BV5
BV6
BV7
BV8 0237
BV9
BVA
BVB 1036b
BVC 0828
BVD
BVE 0240a
HB1 0569
HB1 0716
HB1 0778
HB1
HB2
HB3
HE1 0154

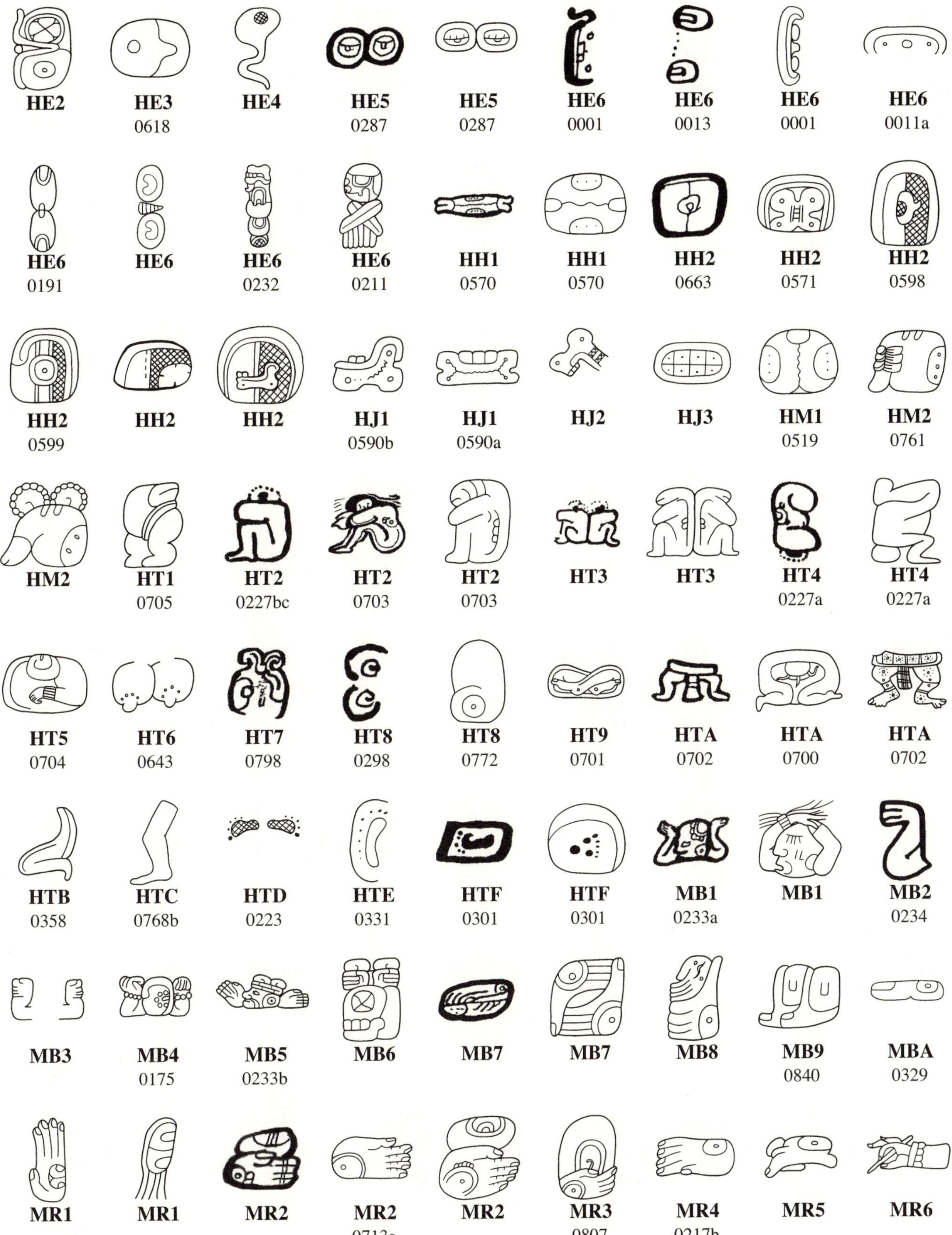
HE2
HE3 0618
HE4
HE5 0287
HE5 0287
HE6 0001
HE6 0013
HE6 0001
HE6 0011a
HE6 0191
HE6
HE6 0232
HE6 0211
HH1 0570
HH1 0570
HH2 0663
HH2 0571
HH2 0598
HH2 0599
HH2
HH2
HJ1 0590b
HJ1 0590a
HJ2
HJ3
HM1 0519
HM2 0761
HM2
HT1 0705
HT2 0227bc
HT2 0703
HT2 0703
HT3
HT3
HT4 0227a
HT4 0227a
HT5 0704
HT6 0643
HT7 0798
HT8 0298
HT8 0772
HT9 0701
HTA 0702
HTA 0700
HTA 0702
HTB 0358
HTC 0768b
HTD 0223
HTE 0331
HTF 0301
HTF 0301
MB1 0233a
MB1
MB2 0234
MB3
MB4 0175
MB5 0233b
MB6
MB7
MB7
MB8
MB9 0840
MBA 0329
MR1
MR1
MR2
MR2 0713a
MR2
MR3 0807
MR4 0217b
MR5
MR6

MR7 0671
MR7 0671
MR7
MR8
MR9
MRA 0713b
MRA
MRB 0218abc
MRB 0218abc
MRB 0218abc
MRC 0218d
MRD
MRE
MRF
MRG 0713a
MZ1 0217c
MZ1
MZ1 0217c
MZ2 0222
MZ2
MZ2
MZ3 0669a
MZ3 0669b
MZ3 0669a
MZ4 0672
MZ5
MZ6 0221a
MZ6 0221b
MZ7 0221c
MZ8 1086
MZ9 0668
MZ9 0668
MZA 0711
MZA 0220e
MZB 1028c
MZB 1028v
MZB
MZC 0673
MZD 0670
MZD
MZD 0670
MZD
MZE
MZE
MZE
MZE
MZE
MZE
MZF 0155e
MZG
MZH
MZJ 0780
MZK 0714
MZK 0714
MZL
MZM 0361
MZN
MZP
MZP
MZP
MZQ 0667
MZR 0220ab
MZS 0710
PC1 1000ab
PC2 1003b
PC3 1025b
PC4 1037
PC4
PC4 1016v
PC4 1008
PC5
PC6 0239

PC7
PC8
PC9
PCA
PCB
PCC
PCD
PCE 1026
PCE 0171
PCE 1028d
PCF 1027
PCG
PCH
PCJ 0731
PCK 0735
PCK 0734
PCL 1064
PCM
PE1 1005
PE1 1005
PE2
PE3 1078
PE4
PE5
PE5
PE5
PE6 1052
PE7 1024
PE7 1042
PE7 1044
PE8 1006b
PE8 1006c
PE8
PE8 1006a
PE8 1006a
PE9
PEA
PEB 1080
PEC 1050a
PEC 1050b
PEC 1051
PED
PEE 1055
PEF
PEG
PEH
PEJ 1065
PH1 1007
PH2
PH3 1073b
PH4 1073a
PH5
PH6 1060b
PH6 1087
PH7
PH8 1073c
PH9
PHA
PHB
PHC
PHD
PHD
PHE 1022
PHE 1022v
PHF 1063
PHG 0726
PHG 0726v
PHH
PM1 1004
PM1 1004
PM1
PM2

PM3
PM4 1070
PM4
PM5
PM5
PM6
PM7
PM8
PM9
PMA
PT1
PT2
PT3 1059
PT3 1059
PT3 1082
PT4 0064
PT4 0063
PT4 1062
PT4
PT4 1014ac
PT4 0064
PT5
PT6
PT7 1003v
PT7 1000cgi
PT8
PT9 1003c
PT9 1003a
PTA
PTB 1075
PTC
PTD
PTE 1038a
PTF 1038b
PTG 1056
PTH
PTJ
PX1
PX2
PX3
PX3
PX4 0537
PX4 0542b
PX4 1053a
PX4 0537
PX4 0542b
PX5
PX6
SB1
SB1 1033
SB2 0746
SB3
SB4 1034
SB5
SB6
SB6
SB7
SB8
SB9
SC1
SC1
SC1
SC2 1040
SC3 1042
SC4
SC4
SC5 1048
SC5 1048
SC6
SC7
SC8 1046
SC9

SCA
SCB
SCC 0736ac
SCC 0736b
SCC 0736ac
SCC 1081
SCD 1047a
SCD 1047b
SCD
SCE 1049
SCE 1049
SCF
SCF
SCG 1079
SCH 0846
SCH
SCJ
SCK
SCL
SCM 1045
SCN
SCP 0208
SN1 1011
SN2
SN3
SN3 0184
SN4 1010c
SN4 1010
SN5
SN6
SN7
SN8 1009b
SN9
SNA
SNB 1014b
SNC
SND 1039
SNE 1057
SNF
SNG
SNH
SNJ
SNK 1054
SNL
SNM
SNN 1018a
SS1 1030q
SS1 1030q
SS2 1030lmn
SS3 1030ijk
SS4 1031b
SS5 1032
SS6 1031a
SS6
SS7
SS8 1031cd
SS9
SSA
SSB
SSC 1030o
SSD 0152
SSD 1009cd
SSD 1009cd
SSD 0152
SSD
SSE 0852
SSF 1020
SSF 1030ah
SSF 1030de
SSF 1030fg
SSF
SSF 0240b

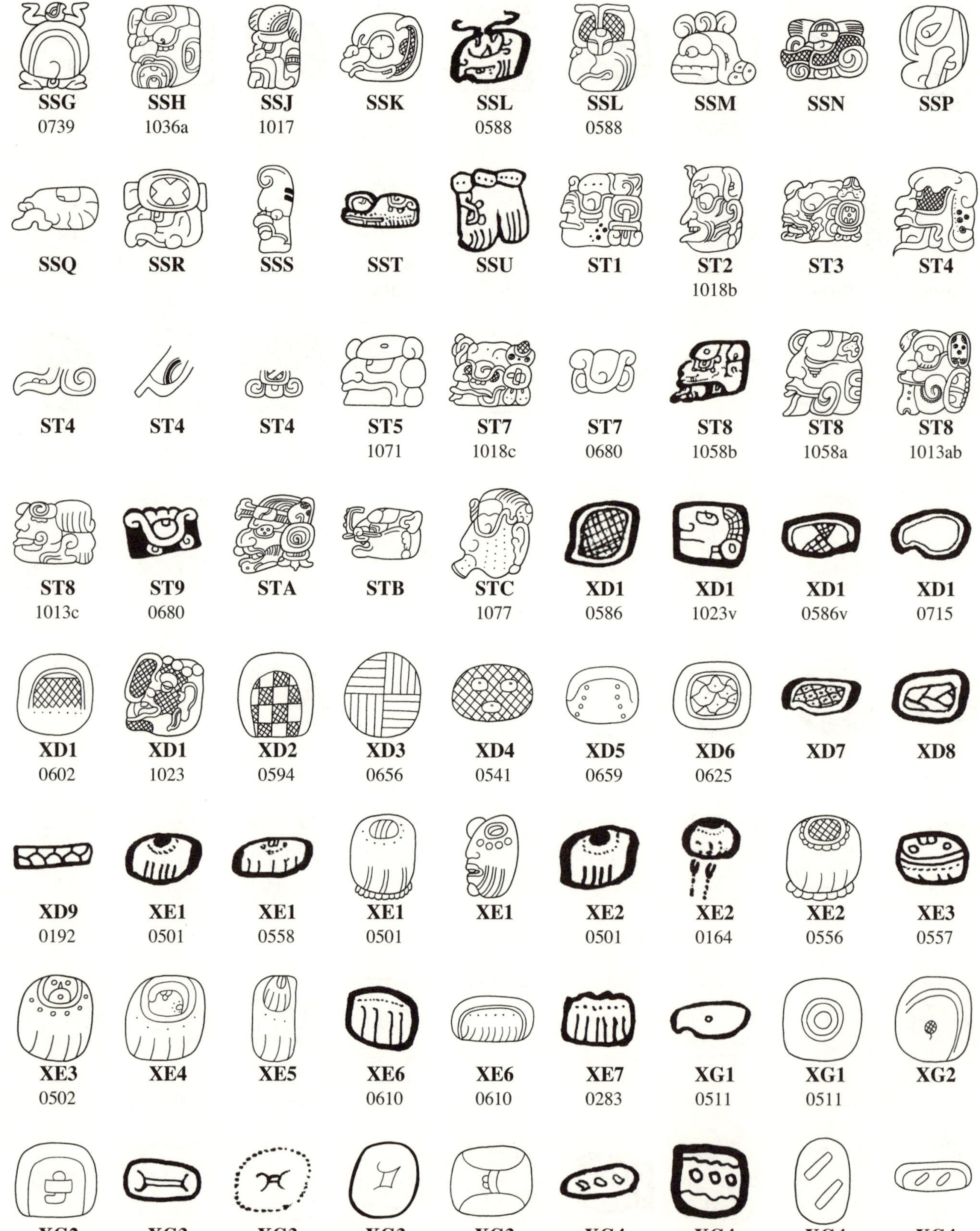
SSG 0739
SSH 1036a
SSJ 1017
SSK
SSL 0588
SSL 0588
SSM
SSN
SSP
SSQ
SSR
SSS
SST
SSU
ST1
ST2 1018b
ST3
ST4
ST4
ST4
ST4
ST5 1071
ST7 1018c
ST7 0680
ST8 1058b
ST8 1058a
ST8 1013ab
ST8 1013c
ST9 0680
STA
STB
STC 1077
XD1 0586
XD1 1023v
XD1 0586v
XD1 0715
XD1 0602
XD1 1023
XD2 0594
XD3 0656
XD4 0541
XD5 0659
XD6 0625
XD7
XD8
XD9 0192
XE1 0501
XE1 0558
XE1 0501
XE1
XE2 0501
XE2 0164
XE2 0556
XE3 0557
XE3 0502
XE4
XE5
XE6 0610
XE6 0610
XE7 0283
XG1 0511
XG1 0511
XG2
XG2
XG3 0687a
XG3 0687b
XG3 0687a
XG3 0622
XG4 0114
XG4 0508
XG4 0508
XG4 0114

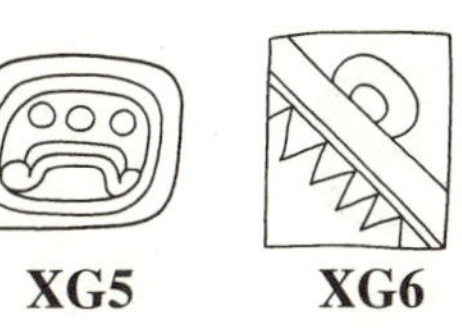
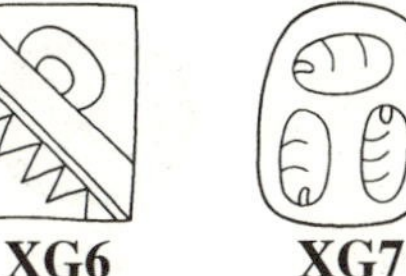

XG5	**XG6**	**XG7**	**XG8**	**XG8**	**XG9**	**XGA**	**XGA**	**XGA**
			0095	0095	0730	0580	0580v	0580

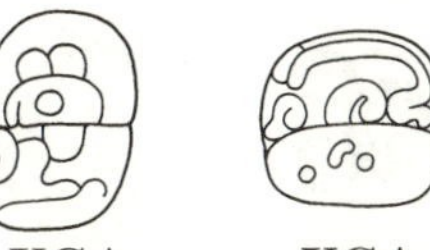

XGA	**XGA**	**XGB**	**XGC**	**XGC**	**XGD**	**XGE**	**XGE**	**XGF**
		0837				0585ab	0585ab	0627

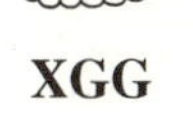

XGG	**XGG**	**XGH**	**XGJ**	**XGJ**	**XGK**	**XGK**	**XGL**	**XGM**
0583		0538			0632	0632	0808	

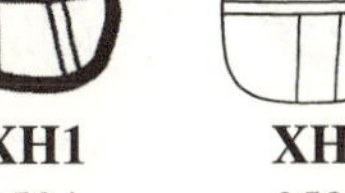

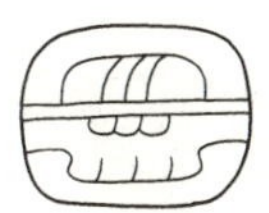

XH1	**XH1**	**XH2**	**XH2**	**XH3**	**XH3**	**XH3**	**XH3**	**XH3**
0584	0584	0548	0548	0561c	0561v	0561d	0561a	0561

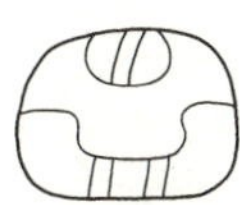
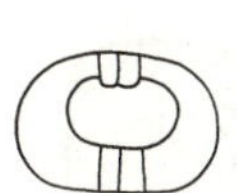

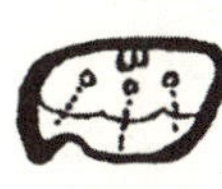

XH4	**XH4**	**XH4**	**XH4**	**XH4**	**XH5**	**XH5**	**XH5**	**XH5**
0506	0774	0506	0774		0507	0507		0779

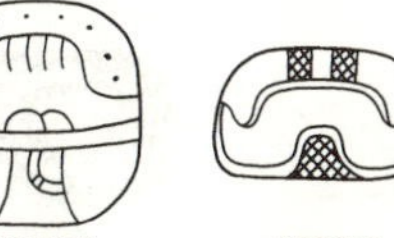

XH5	**XH6**	**XH6**	**XH7**	**XH7**	**XH7**	**XH8**	**XH9**	**XH9**
	0525	0525	0854		0854	0733	0504	0504

XH9	**XHA**	**XHB**	**XHB**	**XHC**	**XHD**	**XHE**	**XHF**	**XQ1**
1009a	0609a	0609b	0609b		0675	0242		0281

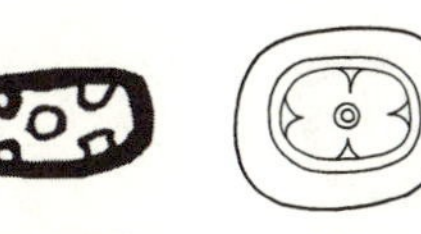

XQ1	**XQ1**	**XQ2**	**XQ2**	**XQ3**	**XQ3**	**XQ3**	**XQ3**	**XQ4**
0281		0646	0646	0544	0281	0544		0727

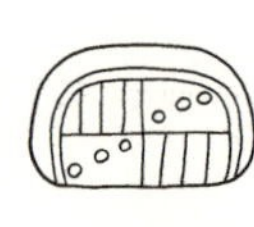

XQ5	**XQ5**	**XQ6**	**XQ6**	**XQ6**	**XQ7**	**XQ7**	**XQ8**	**XQ8**
0545		0503	0503		0593	0593	0527	0527

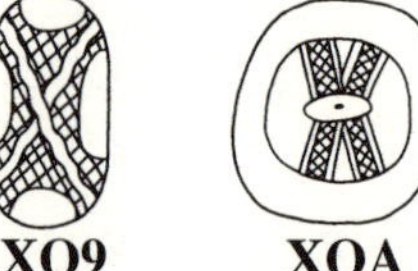

XQ9	**XQA**	**XQB**	**XQB**	**XQB**	**XQB**	**XQB**	**XQC**	**XQC**
		0552		0552v	0304	0552	0624a	0624b

XQD	**XS1**	**XS1**	**XS2**	**XS3**	**XS3**	**XS3**	**XS3**	**XS4**
0623	0521	0521	0665	0523		0520		0804

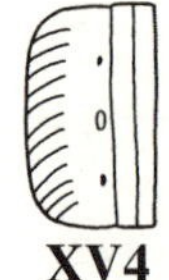

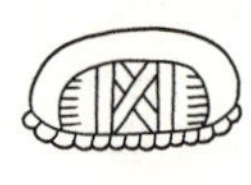

XV1	**XV1**	**XV2**	**XV2**	**XV3**	**XV4**	**XV4**	**XV5**	**XV5**
0563a	0563a	0564	0564	0662	0630	0338	0563b	

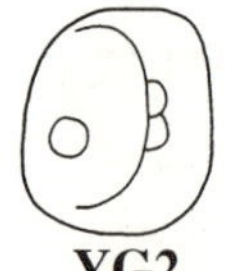

YG1	**YG2**	**YG2**	**YG2**	**YG2**	**YG2**	**YG3**	**YG4**	**YG4**
	0516c	0513	0513				0158	0158

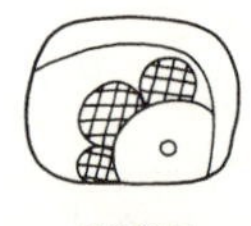

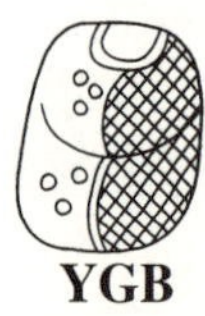

YG5	**YG6**	**YG7**	**YG8**	**YG9**	**YGA**	**YGA**	**YGA**	**YGB**
0516ab					0709			0718

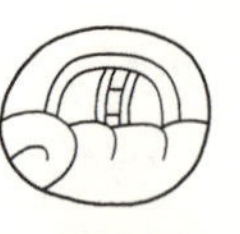

YGC	**YGD**	**YM1**	**YM1**	**YM1**	**YM2**	**YM2**	**YM2**	**YM2**
0810	0812	0679	0679		0565c	0565b	0565	

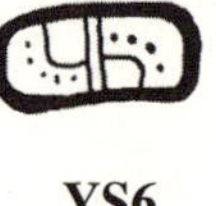

YM3	**YM4**	**YS1**	**YS1**	**YS2**	**YS3**	**YS4**	**YS5**	**YS6**
0606		0526	0526					0573

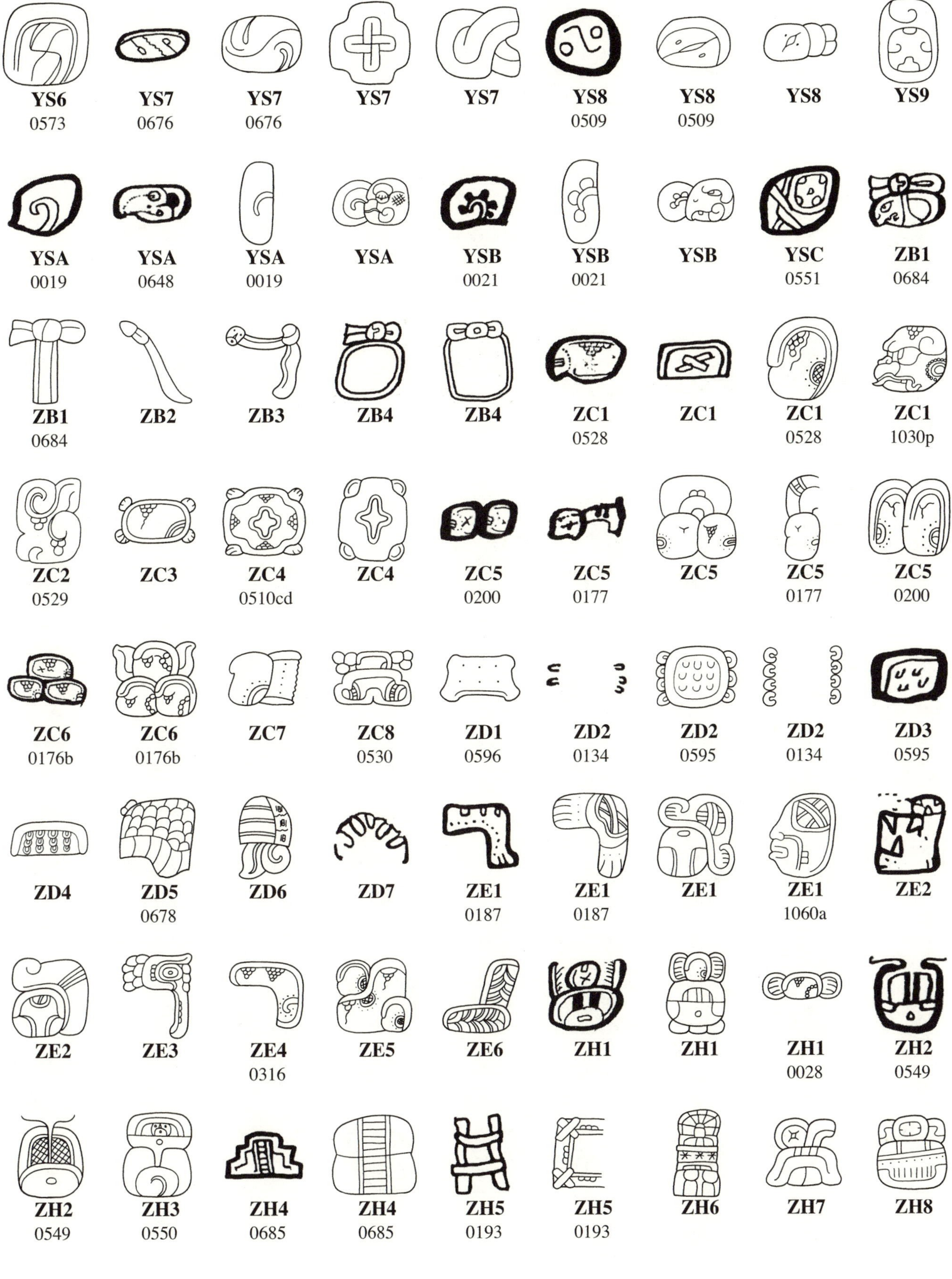
YS6 0573
YS7 0676
YS7 0676
YS7
YS7
YS8 0509
YS8 0509
YS8
YS9
YSA 0019
YSA 0648
YSA 0019
YSA
YSB 0021
YSB 0021
YSB
YSC 0551
ZB1 0684
ZB1 0684
ZB2
ZB3
ZB4
ZB4
ZC1 0528
ZC1
ZC1 0528
ZC1 1030p
ZC2 0529
ZC3
ZC4 0510cd
ZC4
ZC5 0200
ZC5 0177
ZC5
ZC5 0177
ZC5 0200
ZC6 0176b
ZC6 0176b
ZC7
ZC8 0530
ZD1 0596
ZD2 0134
ZD2 0595
ZD2 0134
ZD3 0595
ZD4
ZD5 0678
ZD6
ZD7
ZE1 0187
ZE1 0187
ZE1
ZE1 1060a
ZE2
ZE2
ZE3
ZE4 0316
ZE5
ZE6
ZH1
ZH1
ZH1 0028
ZH2 0549
ZH2 0549
ZH3 0550
ZH4 0685
ZH4 0685
ZH5 0193
ZH5 0193
ZH6
ZH7
ZH8

ZH8
ZH8
ZQ1 0326
ZQ1
ZQ2
ZQ3 0173d
ZQ3
ZQ4 0163
ZQ4 0173abc
ZQ5
ZQ6
ZQ7 0830
ZQ8 0615
ZQ8
ZQ9 0153
ZQ9 0153
ZQA
ZQB 0600
ZQC
ZQD 0510b
ZQD 0002
ZQD 0510a
ZQD 0510a
ZQD 0510b
ZQD 0002
ZQD
ZQD
ZQE
ZQE
ZQE 0325
ZQE
ZQF
ZQG
ZQH
ZQJ
ZQK
ZS1 0098
ZS1
ZS2 0274
ZS2 0098
ZS2
ZS3 0729
ZS4 0559
ZS4 0559
ZS4 0370
ZS5 0547
ZS6
ZS7
ZS7
ZS8 0767
ZS9
ZSA
ZSB 0831
ZSC 0824
ZSD
ZSE 0696
ZSF 0645
ZSG 0776
ZSH
ZSJ 0249
ZSJ 0249
ZSK
ZSL
ZU1 0181
ZU1 0682b
ZU1 0683b
ZU1 0181
ZU1 1025A
ZU2 0682b
ZU2 0683a
ZU3
ZU4

ZU5
ZU6
ZU7
ZU8 0574
ZU9
ZUA 0649
ZUB 0591
ZUB 0769
ZUC 0728
ZUD 0157b
ZUE
ZUF 0589
ZUF 0607
ZUF
ZUG 0568b
ZUG 0568a
ZUG 0568
ZUG 0597
ZUG 0083
ZUH 0017
ZUH 0017
ZUH
ZUH 0145def
ZUH
ZUJ 0017
ZUJ 0275
ZUJ 0016
ZUK
ZUK
ZUK
ZUL
ZUM 0681
ZUN 0856
ZUP 0578
ZUQ 0577
ZUQ 0576
ZUR 0797
ZUS
ZV1 0182
ZV1 0182
ZV2
ZV2
ZV3
ZV4
ZV5
ZV6 0686b
ZV7
ZV7
ZV8
ZV9 0686a
ZVA
ZVB
ZVC 0546
ZVC 0546
ZVD 0836
ZVD 0272
ZVE
ZVF
ZVG
ZVH 0686c
ZX1 0029
ZX2
ZX3
ZX4 0351
ZX5
ZX6 0355
ZX6
ZX6
ZX6
ZX6
ZX6
ZX6

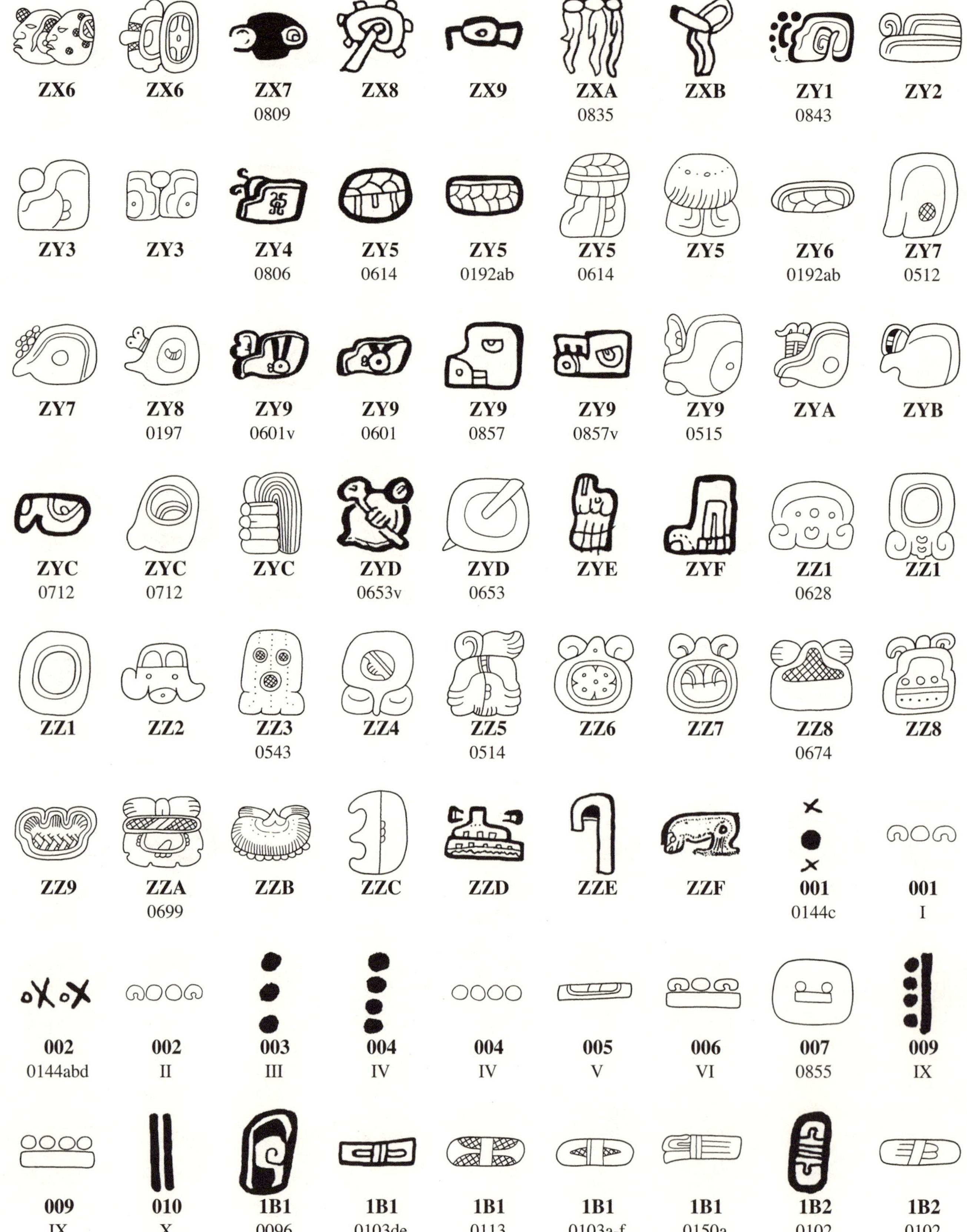
ZX6
ZX6
ZX7 0809
ZX8
ZX9
ZXA 0835
ZXB
ZY1 0843
ZY2
ZY3
ZY3
ZY4 0806
ZY5 0614
ZY5 0192ab
ZY5 0614
ZY5
ZY6 0192ab
ZY7 0512
ZY7
ZY8 0197
ZY9 0601v
ZY9 0601
ZY9 0857
ZY9 0857v
ZY9 0515
ZYA
ZYB
ZYC 0712
ZYC 0712
ZYC
ZYD 0653v
ZYD 0653
ZYE
ZYF
ZZ1 0628
ZZ1
ZZ1
ZZ2
ZZ3 0543
ZZ4
ZZ5 0514
ZZ6
ZZ7
ZZ8 0674
ZZ8
ZZ9
ZZA 0699
ZZB
ZZC
ZZD
ZZE
ZZF
001 0144c
001 I
002 0144abd
002 II
003 III
004 IV
004 IV
005 V
006 VI
007 0855
009 IX
009 IX
010 X
1B1 0096
1B1 0103de
1B1 0113
1B1 0103a-f
1B1 0150a
1B2 0102
1B2 0102

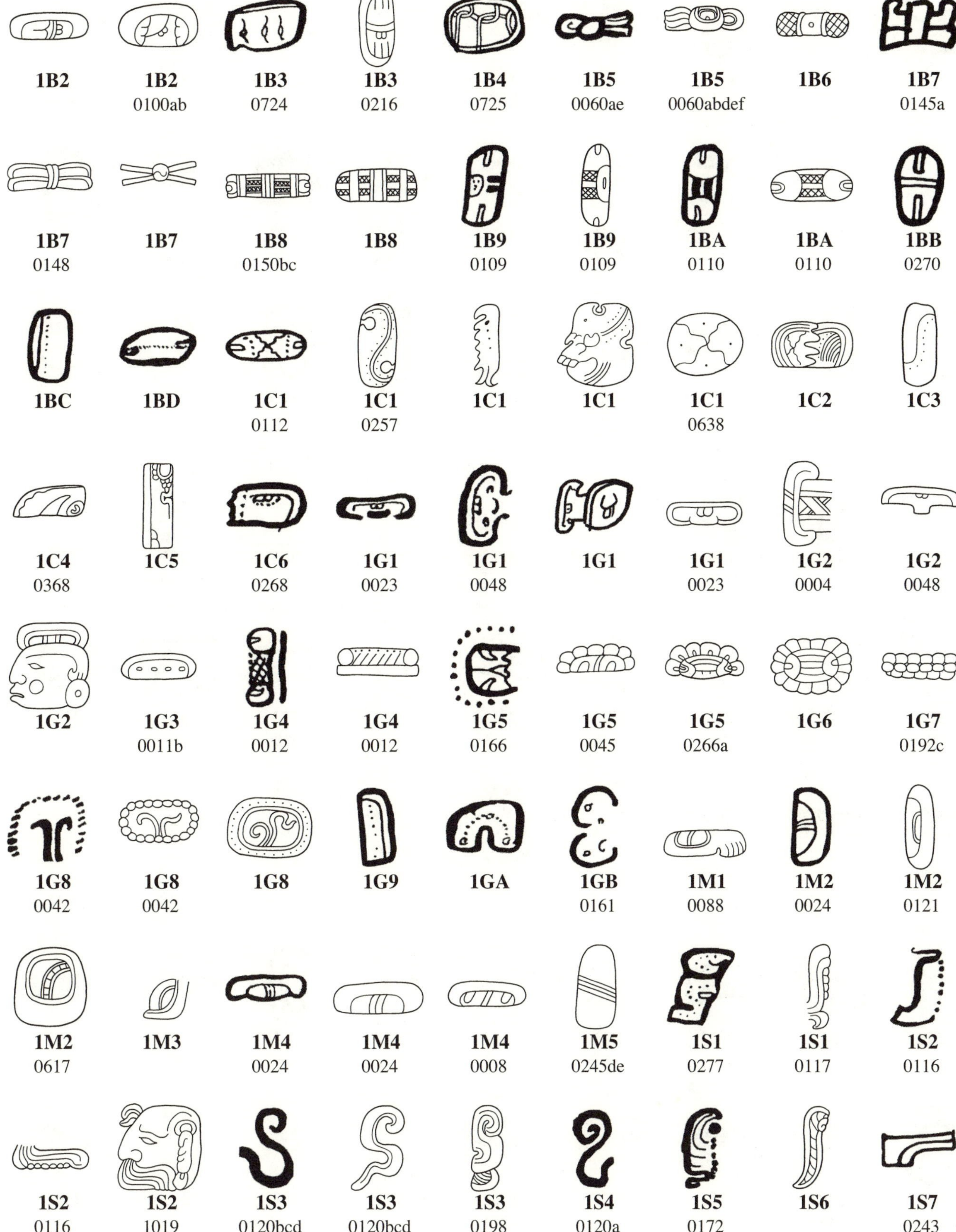
1B2
1B2 0100ab
1B3 0724
1B3 0216
1B4 0725
1B5 0060ae
1B5 0060abdef
1B6
1B7 0145a
1B7 0148
1B7
1B8 0150bc
1B8
1B9 0109
1B9 0109
1BA 0110
1BA 0110
1BB 0270
1BC
1BD
1C1 0112
1C1 0257
1C1
1C1
1C1 0638
1C2
1C3
1C4 0368
1C5
1C6 0268
1G1 0023
1G1 0048
1G1
1G1 0023
1G2 0004
1G2 0048
1G2
1G3 0011b
1G4 0012
1G4 0012
1G5 0166
1G5 0045
1G5 0266a
1G6
1G7 0192c
1G8 0042
1G8 0042
1G8
1G9
1GA
1GB 0161
1M1 0088
1M2 0024
1M2 0121
1M2 0617
1M3
1M4 0024
1M4 0024
1M4 0008
1M5 0245de
1S1 0277
1S1 0117
1S2 0116
1S2 0116
1S2 1019
1S3 0120bcd
1S3 0120bcd
1S3 0198
1S4 0120a
1S5 0172
1S6
1S7 0243

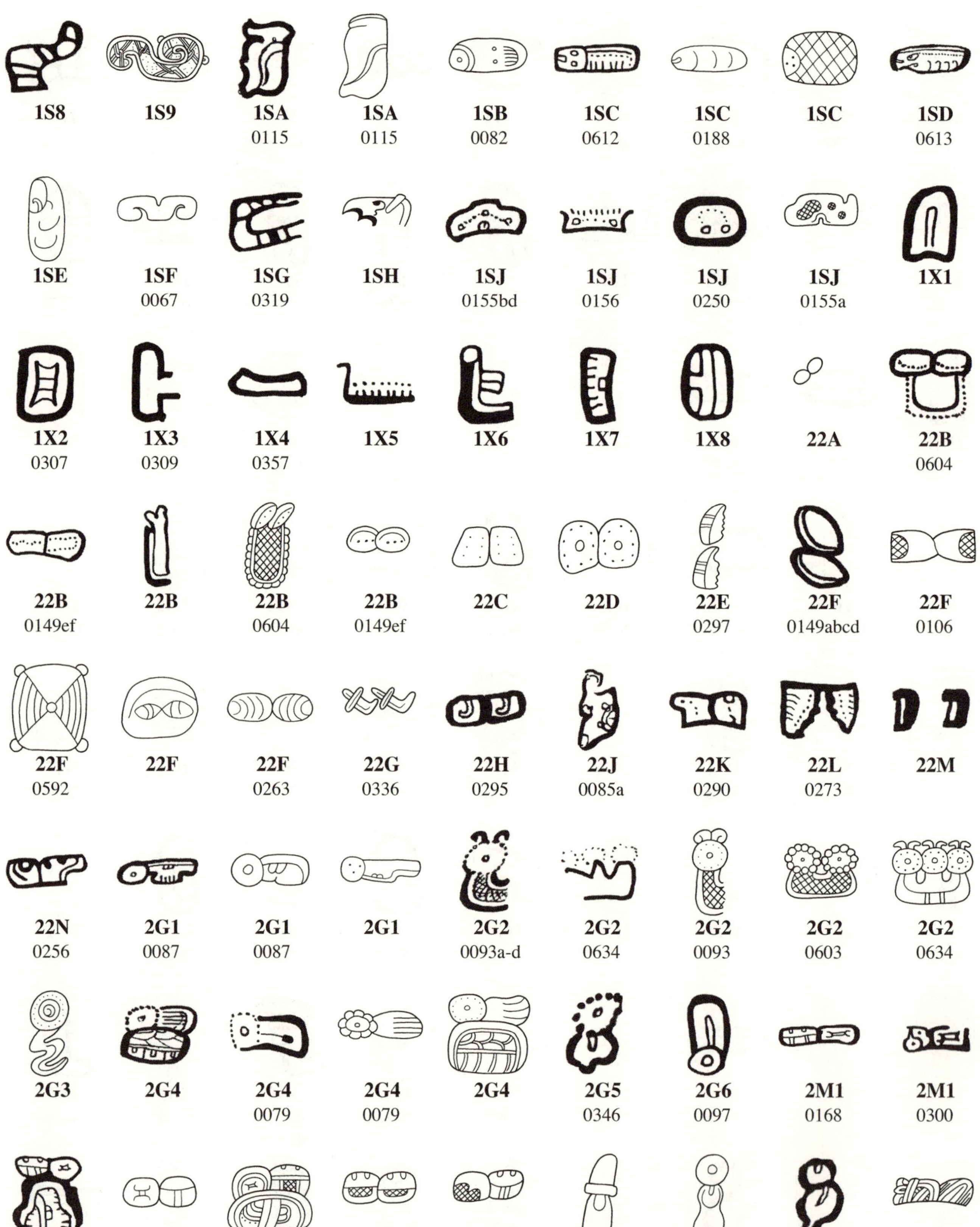
1S8
1S9
1SA 0115
1SA 0115
1SB 0082
1SC 0612
1SC 0188
1SC
1SD 0613
1SE
1SF 0067
1SG 0319
1SH
1SJ 0155bd
1SJ 0156
1SJ 0250
1SJ 0155a
1X1
1X2 0307
1X3 0309
1X4 0357
1X5
1X6
1X7
1X8
22A
22B 0604
22B 0149ef
22B
22B 0604
22B 0149ef
22C
22D
22E 0297
22F 0149abcd
22F 0106
22F 0592
22F
22F 0263
22G 0336
22H 0295
22J 0085a
22K 0290
22L 0273
22M
22N 0256
2G1 0087
2G1 0087
2G1
2G2 0093a-d
2G2 0634
2G2 0093
2G2 0603
2G2 0634
2G3
2G4
2G4 0079
2G4 0079
2G4
2G5 0346
2G6 0097
2M1 0168
2M1 0300
2M1 0518ab
2M1 0168
2M1 0518ab
2M2 0170
2M2 0284
2M3
2M4 0165abd
2M5 0194
2M6

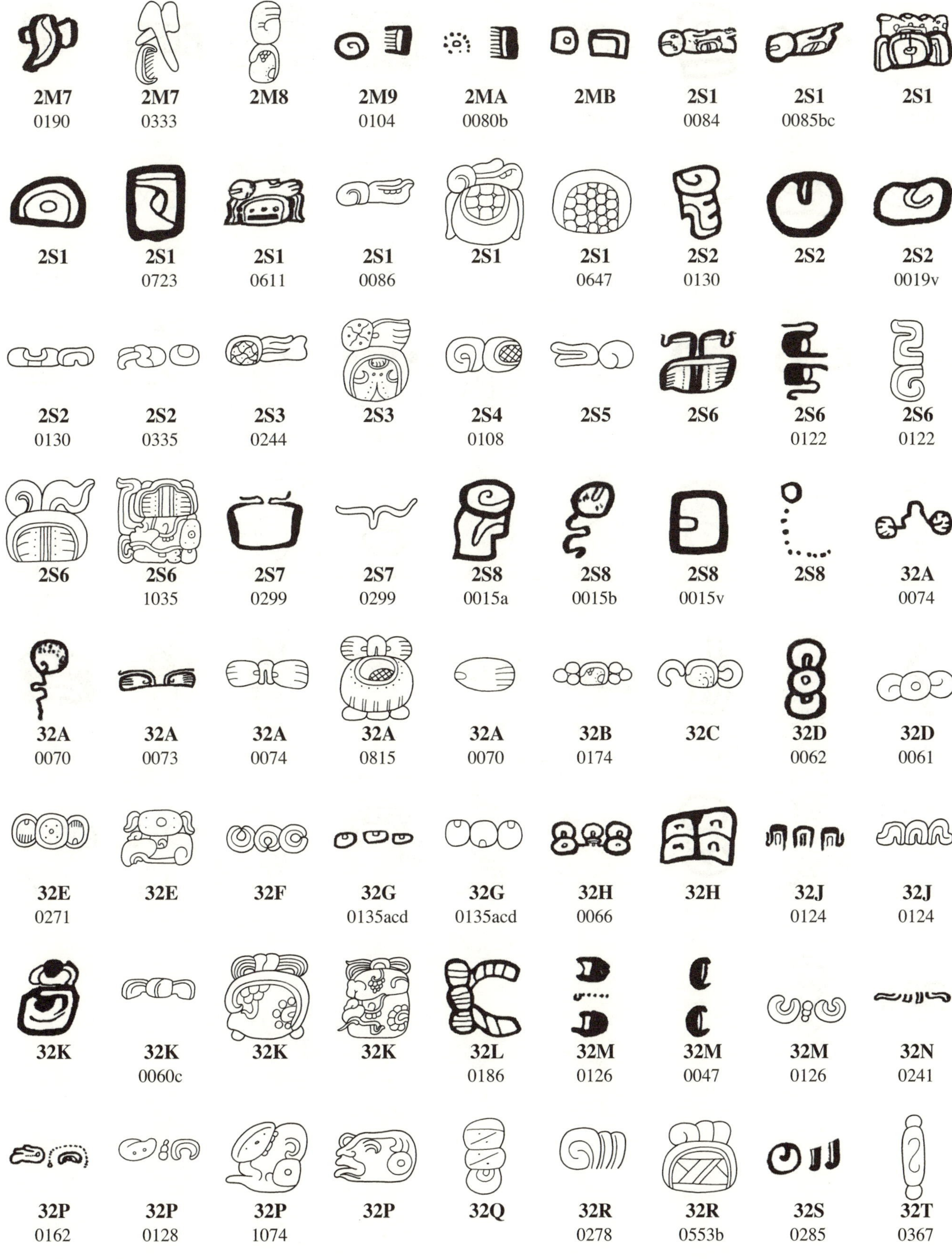
2M7
0190
2M7
0333
2M8
2M9
0104
2MA
0080b
2MB
2S1
0084
2S1
0085bc
2S1
2S1
2S1
0723
2S1
0611
2S1
0086
2S1
2S1
0647
2S2
0130
2S2
2S2
0019v
2S2
0130
2S2
0335
2S3
0244
2S3
2S4
0108
2S5
2S6
2S6
0122
2S6
0122
2S6
2S6
1035
2S7
0299
2S7
0299
2S8
0015a
2S8
0015b
2S8
0015v
2S8
32A
0074
32A
0070
32A
0073
32A
0074
32A
0815
32A
0070
32B
0174
32C
32D
0062
32D
0061
32E
0271
32E
32F
32G
0135acd
32G
0135acd
32H
0066
32H
32J
0124
32J
0124
32K
32K
0060c
32K
32K
32L
0186
32M
0126
32M
0047
32M
0126
32N
0241
32P
0162
32P
0128
32P
1074
32P
32Q
32R
0278
32R
0553b
32S
0285
32T
0367

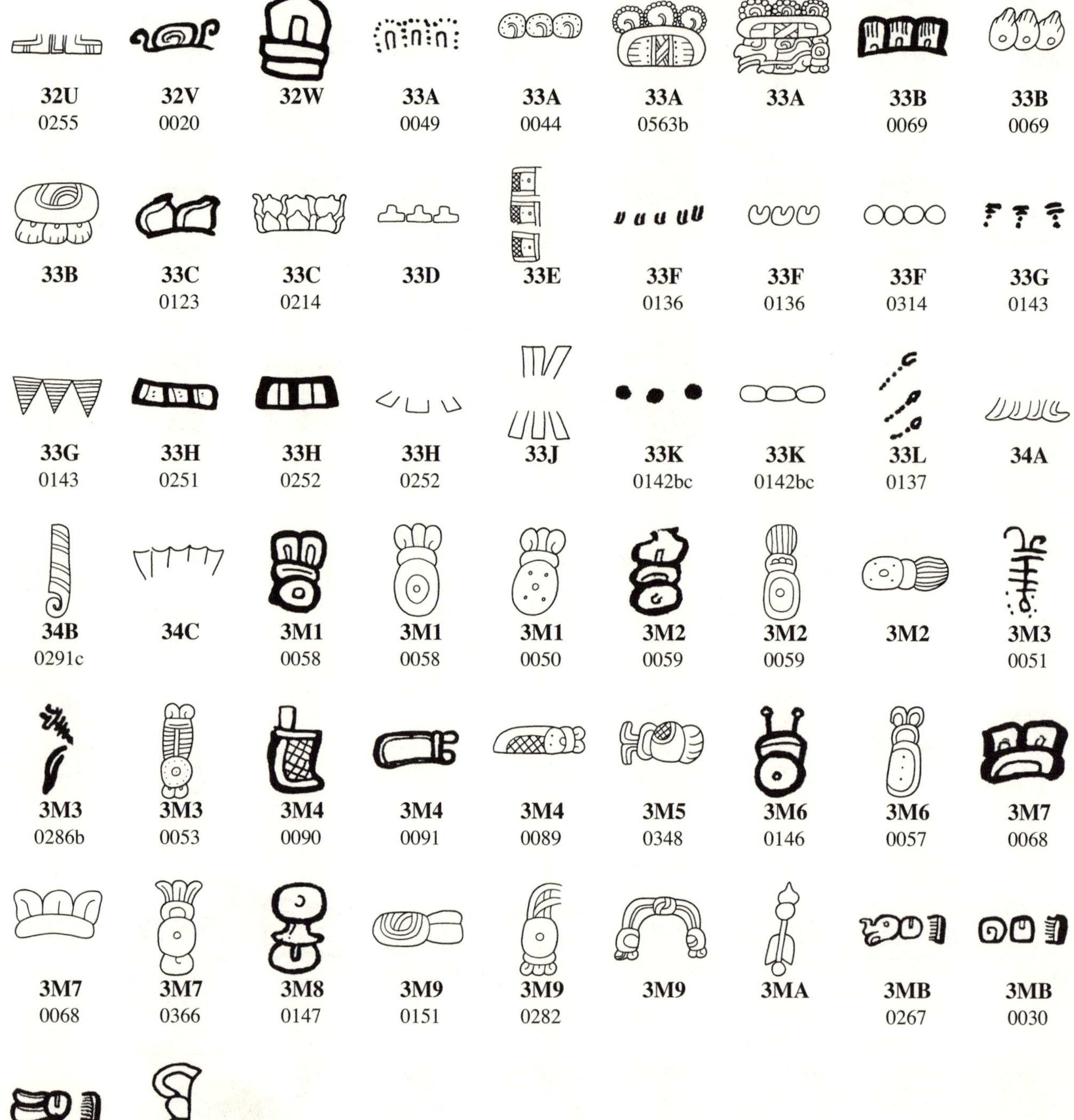
32U 0255
32V 0020
32W
33A 0049
33A 0044
33A 0563b
33A
33B 0069
33B 0069
33B
33C 0123
33C 0214
33D
33E
33F 0136
33F 0136
33F 0314
33G 0143
33G 0143
33H 0251
33H 0252
33H 0252
33J
33K 0142bc
33K 0142bc
33L 0137
34A
34B 0291c
34C
3M1 0058
3M1 0058
3M1 0050
3M2 0059
3M2 0059
3M2
3M3 0051
3M3 0286b
3M3 0053
3M4 0090
3M4 0091
3M4 0089
3M5 0348
3M6 0146
3M6 0057
3M7 0068
3M7 0068
3M7 0366
3M8 0147
3M9 0151
3M9 0282
3M9
3MA
3MB 0267
3MB 0030
3MB 0031
3MC